MW00913795

Guide to Reference Materials for School Library Media Centers

Publications Cited

Form of Citation	Publication Title
ARBA	American Reference Books Annual
BL	Booklist
BW	Book World (Washington Post)
LJ	Library Journal
RBB	Reference Books Bulletin
RRBSL	Recommended Reference Books for Small and Medium-sized Libraries
SLJ	School Library Journal
VOYA	Voice of Youth Advocates

Guide to Reference Materials for School Library Media Centers

Fifth Edition

Barbara Ripp Safford

1998
Libraries Unlimited, Inc.
Englewood, Colorado

LIBRARIES UNLIMITED, INC.
P.O. Box 6633
Englewood, CO 80155-6633
1-800-237-6124
www.lu.com

Constance Hardesty, *Project Editor*
Joan Garner, *Cover Design*
Sheryl Tongue, *Composition*

Library of Congress Cataloging-in-Publication Data

Safford, Barbara Ripp.
    Guide to reference materials for school library media centers / Barbara Ripp Safford. -- 5th ed.
    xviii, 353 p. 19x26 cm.
    Rev. ed. of: Guide to reference books for school media centers / Margaret Irby Nichols. 1992.
    Includes bibliographical references and index.
    ISBN 1-56308-545-3
    1. Children's reference books--United States--Bibliography. 2. School libraries--United States--Book lists. 3. Instructional materials centers--United States. I. Nichols, Margaret Irby. Guide to reference books for school media centers. II. Title.
Z1037.1.S34 1998
011'.02--dc21   98-29867
                                                                          CIP

Contents

Introduction

This edition of *Guide to Reference Materials for School Library Media Centers* appears at a time in which the nature of materials and collections is changing rapidly. When this publication was in its first edition, there were a limited number of reference materials produced particularly for students in K–12 schools; as the revised editions were published, more materials were available with the K–12 student as an audience. At the time of the fourth edition in 1992, we were already seeing the influence of CD-ROM and online services in transforming our notion of the reference collection from that of books on shelves to one of books, workstations, and online terminals. Today the influence of the Internet, and particularly the World Wide Web, is causing some to suggest that books are obsolete and that reference services and libraries are not far behind. Indeed, it is not possible to produce a bibliography such as this one without addressing CD-ROMs and Web sites as resources.

As an early convert to CD-ROM resources, and as a reference professor who taught Dialog™ one year, telnet the next year, Gopher the next, and the Web thereafter, I quickly became convinced that reference services would move rapidly away from book resources. About two weeks into this project, however, identifying new titles that were available in book form, I recognized that the exciting experience I was having in finding one new book source after the other, in going to the shelf to find one item and spotting three others nearby, was a vaguely familiar feeling. It eventually occurred to me that I was "surfing" the reference shelves; I couldn't wait to share my book findings with others and started referring to my reference bibliographies as "bookmarks."

Some additional comparison work in looking for specific information in depth on the Internet has convinced me that librarians still need to include book materials in their reference collections. Considering the availability of workstations, the speed of response time, or the cost of connect time, there are many bits of information that are better, cheaper, more conveniently, or only found in books. So far. Indeed, I will make a prediction that we will see the end of the CD-ROM before we see the end of the book.

Today, more and more information providers (publishers) are moving to the Web for delivery and distribution of their databases (books). These databases are being compiled from a wide array of sources and are then being packaged and repackaged in a variety of products for various markets, including K–12 students. One important factor is still to be evaluated. Accustomed as we are to free information via the Web, will schools be willing and able to pay for the kind of authenticated, organized, and accessible information we are used to via the book and the CD-ROM? One of the best transitions from book to CD-ROM was the periodical index; this is now one of the most prolific transitions from CD-ROM to the Web, and for all of the obvious reasons, including recency. On the other hand, the great and useful subject encyclopedias, the one-volume handbooks, dictionaries, glossaries, gazetteers, and the encyclopedic atlases, may be more convenient and aesthetically satisfying as books. Personally, I find myself preferring books when I am working in a library (except for periodical indexes) and happy to have the Web available when I am not in a library (except for the books I have surrounding my computer because I use them so often).

So this new edition of *Guide to Reference Materials* offers a combination of formats: most recommendations are still books, some are CD-ROMs, some are from the Web, and some are available all three ways. I suspect we will be working with all three formats for some time to come.

Scope and Purpose

This is intended to be a comprehensive list of reference materials from which librarians may select those most useful to their own collections. Materials for elementary, middle and senior high schools are included, with comments in the annotations suggesting appropriate levels. Items were selected to meet the curriculum needs of the most sophisticated schools in order to present the widest choices. Student interests are represented, even if not curricular. Parent collections are appearing in more schools for both parents of students and for students who are parents; some items are suggested for these collections. In addition, materials are included which are more likely to appear in district education libraries. Professional materials to support the activities of school libraries in areas of collection management, children's literature and curriculum planning are well represented.

The items in this work are limited to those currently available. Many materials continue to be useful, even though they are no longer in print, but they are not included in this bibliography. To find out-of-print titles, consult older editions of the book. The focus of this bibliography is the United States, although much of the material will be relevant to other English-speaking areas.

Selection

Entries have been selected from new reference titles published from 1992 through 1997. Most have been reviewed in *American Reference Books Annual*, *Recommended Reference Books for Small and Medium-sized Libraries*, *Booklist* and *Reference Books Bulletin*, *School Library Journal*, *VOYA* or other professional sources. New editions of titles from the fourth edition have been listed, as well as older titles that are still useful and whose information is still accurate.

In addition to reviews, almost all items have been personally examined. Criteria for selection include usefulness for curricular applications by elementary and secondary students and teachers, interest for students, readability, clarity of appearance and text, and accuracy and currency of information.

Many items are accessible by middle school and high school students, even if intended for adult or college level audiences. Some items appropriate for teachers rather than students have been included. Elementary and middle school teachers may also benefit from items identified for high school use.

The line between reference and circulating book is often unclear. While most reference materials are identified by type— dictionary, atlas, almanac, and so on—and are intended to answer questions, rather than to be read from cover to cover, this is not a cut-and-dried decision, especially for an editor who, as a child, read most of the *Book of Knowledge* from cover to cover. Inclusion here indicates reference use, although many annotations suggest circulating copies be purchased as well. Electronic products are no different. Many CD-ROMs are more useful in instruction than for reference; those fitting that description were not considered for inclusion.

Changes in the Fifth Edition

There are several major changes in organization from the fourth edition. The Collection Management (formerly Media Sources) chapter now lists all review journals together regardless of formats reviewed; most sources that formerly reviewed only books have now added at least the occasional nonbook item, and most sources reviewing nonbooks also review books. Distinctions seem unnecessary when school librarians are looking for the best materials regardless of format; each annotation does note what formats are included in each source. In all cases, retrospective selection bibliographies on specific subjects have been moved from the subject to Collection Management. Likewise, curriculum bibliographies have been moved from subject areas to Literature for Children and Young Adults (formerly Children's Literature—Bibliographies for Curriculum Support and Reading Guidance). The addition of a section titled Electronic Information Systems was created in the Reference chapter to list those companies with product lines moving toward the World Wide Web. Many of their products are also available in CD-ROM, magnetic tape, and even on paper. In Social Sciences, sections have been added for psychology and sociology, and in Science and Technology, the general sections for science and technology have been combined.

Notes

All items are recommended, although comments in annotations may point out some reservations. Grade level indicators are general and librarians will, of course, make local decisions; middle school refers to grades 6–8; this term has been used throughout instead of junior high school. Other than identifying platforms, the CD-ROM citations do not indicate specific system requirements because most requirements are similar and change with new versions;

librarians will need to check with producers and vendors if they have questions about equipment specifications.

Cross-references: When appropriate, cross-references to related sections are provided at the beginning of the chapter or at the beginning of the subsection.

Entries: Consecutively numbered entries include full bibliographic data, price as listed in *Books in Print Plus* or by the publisher, ISBN, ISSN, and LC card number (when available). Entries for government publications include stock number (S/N). Technological requirements are given for electronic materials. Addresses are provided for materials available from publishers not listed in standard sources.

Grade level codes: Codes, printed above the entry, indicate estimated level of usefulness for the item. "E" denotes K–5; "E+" means K–5 and up. The suggested audience levels are indicated in the annotation for other entries: middle school (grades 6–8) or high school (grades 9–12). The term *secondary level* is used in the annotation when a reviewer has used the term to indicate level.

Annotations: Most annotations describe the work's content, organization, and special features, but some include critical comments, usually indicating limitations or cautions. All works cited are recommended with the terms *recommended* and *highly recommended* denoting publications of exceptional merit.

Citations to reviews: These are listed at the end of the annotations. A list of reviewing sources and their abbreviations is given on page ii.

Index: All materials cited appear in the author/title and the subject indexes.

Acknowledgments

No project such as this could be accomplished without the help and support of many people.

Betty J. Morris at Libraries Unlimited has cheerfully answered my many questions. The faculty and staff of Rod Library, University of Northern Iowa, have provided continuous assistance; in many ways this has been a joint project among us all. In particular, Youth Collection Librarian Professor Lucille Lettow has been invaluable; her fine reference and professional collection is a model resource. My colleague Dr. Marjorie Pappas has relieved me of many responsibilities during the project, and I appreciate her commitment to this undertaking. Rodney Lyons, a graduate student in the College of Education, spent many hours checking citation details and producing worksheets. Diane Fight kept the project and me organized and on track and did all of the data input; without her there would be no fifth edition. Special thanks to Dean Glenn Hansen and Dr. James Bodensteiner of the Division of Continuing Education at UNI for making graduate assistance possible. Last, but never least, thanks to my husband, Dr. Herbert D. Safford, for his usual patience and encouragement.

Collection Management Tools

See also **Bibliographies for Curriculum Support** and **Reading Guidance in Literature for Children and Young Adults (Humanities)** and **Collection Development in Library Science (Social Science)**.

REVIEW JOURNALS

1 **ALAN Review**. Urbana, Ill.: National Council of Teachers of English, 1973– . 3 issues/yr. $15.00/yr. (1111 Kenyon Rd., Urbana, IL 61801). ISSN 0882-2840.

> **Level:** YA.
> **Focus:** YA books, authors.
> **Reviews:** Each issue, printed for filing.
> **Print:** Fiction, nonfiction, short stories, poetry.
> **Features:** Articles and interviews with YA authors and classroom applications of YA literature.

2 **Appraisal: Children's Science Books**. Boston: Children's Science Book Review Committee, Boston University School of Education and New England Round Table of Children's Librarians, 1967– . quarterly. $44.00/yr. (605 Commonwealth Ave., Boston, MA 02215). ISSN 0003-7052.

E+

> **Level:** Preschool through high school.
> **Focus:** Reviews almost all science and math books published each year that are written for children and young adults.
> **Reviews:** Some 70 trade books and series are reviewed in each quarterly issue; two signed reviews, 100–200 words each, by two reviewers, a librarian and a subject specialist; complete

bibliographic and order information and grade level; five rating codes (unacceptable to excellent).
> **Print:** Trade books in science and mathematics.
> **Features:** Articles on science books and teaching science.
> **Index:** Cumulated annually.

3 **Book Links.** Chicago: American Library Association, 1991– . 6 issues/yr. $24.95/yr. (50 E. Huron St., Chicago, IL 60611). ISSN 1055-4742.

E

> **Level:** K–8.
> **Focus:** Recommends books, media on themes.
> **Reviews:** Descriptive annotations; some retrospective items.
> **Print:** Children's books.
> **Nonprint:** Videos, Internet sites.
> **Features:** Articles about authors, awards, suggestions for matching children and books.

4 **Book Report: The Journal for Junior and Senior High School Librarians.** Worthington, Ohio: Linworth Publishing, 1982– . 5 issues/yr. $39.00/yr. (480 E. Wilson Bridge Road, Suite L, Worthington, OH 43985-2372). ISSN 0731-4388.

> **Level:** Junior high and high school, ages 12–17.
> **Focus:** Each issue is devoted to a theme (e.g., making and using audiovisuals, teaching library skills, reading motivation, public relations, microcomputers) and contains some 20 pages of feature articles; emphasis is on alternative solutions to problems.

Reviews: School librarians and teachers evaluate new titles and indicate if items are highly recommended, recommended, optional purchase or not recommended. Reviews of some 100 items, 125–275 words in length, give standard bibliographic data, ISBN, LC card number, grade level, and hardware specifications for computer software.

Print: Fiction, nonfiction, reference, professional books.

Nonprint: Videos, software, CD-ROMs.

Features: Computer applications in the library, profiles of authors who write for teenagers, trade paperbacks.

5 **Booklist: Includes Reference Books**
E+   **Bulletin**. Chicago: American Library Association, 1905– . bimonthly Sept.– June, monthly July and Aug. $65.00/yr. (50 E. Huron St., Chicago, IL 60611). ISSN 0006-7385.

Level: Preschool through high school, adults.

Focus: Print and nonprint (including software) materials suggested for school library media centers and small to medium-sized public libraries.

Booklist **reviews:** Evaluative reviews written and signed by staff members; some 12,000–13,000 reviews per year, 125–200 words in length; starred reviews indicate exceptional quality; full bibliographies/order information, DDC number, LC subject headings, and LC card number.

Reference Books Bulletin **reviews:** Evaluative reviews by members of RBB editorial board for encyclopedias, dictionaries, atlases, and other reference books; news and comments about reference materials; reviews range from 175–200 words to 800–1,000 words; general encyclopedias, atlases, dictionaries and other works which use a continuous revision policy are reviewed about every five years; reviews for the period of September through August of the following year are compiled and published in the annual *Reference Books Bulletin* [see **Retrospective Bibliographies**].

Print: Fiction and nonfiction books arranged by age level; special sections on such items as series books and easy readers.

Nonprint: Videos, CD-ROMs, software, spoken and music audios, audiobooks.

Features: Advance book reviews, news from libraries, publicity, foreign language books, small press books, lists of books on contemporary issues, high/low books, paperback reprints, magazines, occasional lists on special topics.

Index: Monthly author-title index; semi-annual cumulative indexes.

6 **Bulletin of the Center for Children's**
E+   **Books**. Champaign, Ill.: University of Illinois Press, 1945– . monthly (except Aug.). $35.00/yr. (1325 S. Oak, Champaign, IL 61820). ISSN 0008-9036.

Level: Preschool through grade 10.

Focus: Reviews books of exceptional value in writing and usefulness; warns against others that are poor in quality.

Reviews: Some 800 each year; 100–150 words in length; written by the staff; reviews describe content, characters, and theme, and indicate developmental values or curricular uses; codes, such as * (special distinction) and NR (not recommended), are used for evaluation; gives grade or age (for preschool) level.

Print: Mostly trade fiction, some nonfiction.

Features: "Bulletin Blue Ribbon Books," published each January, covers outstanding books of previous year, arranged by picture books, fiction, poetry, and nonfiction; reviews are cumulated every five years in *The Best in Children's Books*.

Index: Author-title index for each volume.

7 **Children's Software Revue**. Ypsilanti,
E+   Mich.: Active Learning Associates, 1992– . 6 issues/yr. $29.00/yr. (520 N. Adams, Ypsilanti, MI 48197). ISSN 1069-9430.

Level: Pre K–9.

Focus: Reviews and articles about computer related materials for parents, teachers, schools and libraries.

Nonprint: Software, CD-ROMs.
Features: Articles, Internet/Web sites, new releases, industry information. No advertisements.

8 **Choice.** Middleton, Conn.: Association of College and Research Libraries, 1964– . 11 issues/yr. $185.00/yr. (100 Riverview Center, Middleton, CT 06457). ISSN 0009-4978.

Level: Undergraduate.
Focus: Review of materials.
Reviews: Approximately 600 reviews/ issue.
Print: Reference, humanities, social sciences, sciences.
Nonprint: CD-ROMs, Internet/Web sites.
Features: Editorial, essays, articles.

9 **Christian Library Journal.** Grants
E+ Pass, Ore.: Christian Library Services, 1996– . 5 issues/yr. $45.00/yr. (1101 SW Rogue River Avenue, Grants Pass, OR 97526). ISSN 1097-1261.

Level: Children, YA, adults.
Focus: Reviews of secular and Christian materials from a Christian perspective.
Reviews: About 250 reviews in each issue; 5-point scale of quality and acceptability.
Print: Fiction, nonfiction, professional sources.
Nonprint: Audios, videos.
Features: Articles, columns, suggested Web sites.

10 **A Complete Guide to Young Adult Literature: Over 1,000 Critiques and Synopses from the ALAN Review.** Portsmouth, N.H.: Boynton/Cook, 1997. CD-ROM (Windows, Macintosh). $115.00. ISBN 0-86709-425-7.

This CD-ROM is a text only database of more than 1,000 *ALAN* reviews from the past twenty years. The attractive boxed reviews contain bibliographic and field information. Browse and advanced searches are simple to conduct; combination searches are available through author, grade level, theme, topic and genre fields. Items can be marked and printed as bibliographies. This product is useful for secondary librarians, teachers and students.

11 **Emergency Librarian.** Seattle, Wash.:
E+ Rockland Press, 1962– . 5 issues/yr. $49.00/yr. (P.O. Box C34069, Dept. 284, Seattle, WA 98124-1069). ISSN 0315-8888.

Level: Children and YA.
Focus: Features articles mainly on youth library services and children's literature; reviews of professional reading and books, software, and recordings.
Reviews: Sections on professional reading, outstanding new books K–12, AV materials, paperbacks for children and YA, software reviews, children's recordings and Canadian and Australian books. Reviews vary from 175–200 words in some sections to 50–100 in others.
Print: Professional reading, books K–12, paperbacks for children and YA.
Nonprint: Films, videos, sound recordings, software.
Features: Best Canadian and Australian books; best picture books, children's books, and YA novels of the year.

12 **The Horn Book Guide to Children's**
E+ **and Young Adult Books.** Boston: Horn Book, Inc., 1989– . semiannual. $35.00/yr. (11 Beacon St., Suite 1000, Boston, MA 02108). ISSN 1044-405X.

Level: Preschool through YA.
Focus: Reviews essentially all new books published in the United States for those age groups.
Reviews: Evaluative, brief; rankings are from 1 (high) to 6 (low), with top two rankings identified by symbol. Picture books and fiction arranged by age level, alphabetically by author; nonfiction by subject category.
Print: New books for children and young people by publishing season.

13 **The Horn Book Magazine.** Boston:
E+ Horn Book, Inc., 1924– . 6 issues/yr. $48.00/yr. (11 Beacon St., Suite 1000, Boston, MA 02108). ISSN 0018-5078.

Level: Preschool through YA.
Focus: This important journal reviews books that meet high standards of quality and literary merit;

directed toward parents but useful to librarians and others interested in children's literature.

Reviews: Evaluative; 150–250 words in length; 250–300 each year; starred titles judged outstanding; reviews give bibliographic/order data, size, age level (younger, age 6–8; intermediate, age 9–12; and older, 12–YA), summary of content, characterizations, themes, and comments on writing and illustrating. Categories are picture books, fiction, poetry, and nonfiction; recommended paperbacks; new editions and reissues; books in Spanish; books in the classroom.

Print: Trade books.

Features: Articles about authors and illustrators, writing and publishing; annual lists of best books; column about books in the classroom; column highlighting out-of-print books on a topic or genre that may be found in the library.

Index: By author and title in each issue; cumulated annual index.

14 **Kliatt.** Wellesley, Mass.: Kliatt, 1992– . 6 issues/yr. $36.00/yr. (33 Bay St. Rd., Wellesley, MA 02158). ISSN 1065-8602.

Level: Ages 12–19.

Focus: Selected paperback books, educational software and audiobooks recommended for libraries and classrooms serving young adults.

Reviews: Arranged by general subjects, with software and audiobook formats separate. Identified for junior high (J), senior high (S) or advanced students (A). Exceptional books are indicated with an asterisk.

Print: Paperbacks that are original and reprints or reissues of hardbacks.

Nonprint: Audiobooks, software.

Features: Annual bibliographies, e.g., of outstanding audiobooks.

Index: Title index in each issue.

15 **Library Journal.** New York: Cahners Publishing, 1876– . 20 issues/yr. $94.50. (P.O. Box 59690, Boulder, CO 80322-9690). ISSN 0360-0277.

Level: Adult, general audience.

Focus: Articles and news items on topics of professional interest to public, college, and special librarians; reviews of print and nonprint media.

Reviews: Some 250 reviews each issue; 150–175 words in length; signed reviews by practitioners, academics, or staff members; most descriptive, but some give recommendations and audience; entries, arranged by broad categories, give bibliographic/order information; starred reviews indicate outstanding quality or popular appeal; reference reviews, arranged alphabetically, introduce review section.

Print: Adult fiction and nonfiction trade books, reference books, magazines, professional reading.

Nonprint: Videos, audiobooks, software, CD-ROMs.

Features: Management and online database columns; prepublication alert; topical lists of bestsellers; "Word of Mouth," a reader's advisory column. Special spring and fall announcement issues, buyer's guide to hardware and equipment issue; best reference books of year; lists of outstanding books in science, technology and medicine.

Index: Monthly author index to book reviews, classic returns, and professional reading; six-month cumulative index in July; annual cumulative index.

16 **Library Talk: The Magazine for**
E **Elementary School Librarians**. Worthington, Ohio: Linworth Publishing, 1988– . bimonthly Sept.–May. $35.00/yr. (480 E. Wilson Bridge Road, Suite L, Worthington, OH 43085-2372). ISSN 1043-237X.

Level: Elementary school ages 6–11.

Focus: Feature articles on a special theme by librarians who work with children (e.g., library supervision, book fairs, public relations, audiovisuals, evaluation of the library and the librarian).

Reviews: Experienced librarians evaluate new books in areas of easy readers, fiction for grades 3–4, fiction for grades 5 and up, poetry, nonfiction, mysteries and fantasies, books in Spanish, traditional stories, multicultural materials, reference, videos and computer programs.

Nonprint: Videos, software, CD-ROMs.

Features: Practical ideas, paraprofessionals and part-time workers, news from publishers, free and inexpensive material, annual review of new holiday books.

17 **Media and Methods.** Philadelphia:
E+ North American Publishing, 1964– . 5 issues/yr. $29.00/yr. (1429 Walnut St., Philadelphia, PA 19102). ISSN 0025-6897.

Level: Elementary and secondary.

Focus: Practical application of instructional technology and media management; innovative projects; reviews and previews of instructional media products and equipment.

Reviews: Descriptive and evaluative, 125–200 words; signed reviews by contributing editors, including practicing school librarians; system needs and hardware requirements, price, and grade level.

Print: Books for educators, books for students.

Nonprint: Software, videos, CD-ROMs, videodiscs.

18 **Multimedia Schools: A Practical**
E+ **Journal of Multimedia, CD-ROM, Online and Internet in K–12.** Medford, N.J.: Information Today, Inc., 1994– . bimonthly September/October-May/June. $38.00/yr. (143 Old Marlton Pike, Medford, NJ 08055-8750). ISSN 1075-0479.

Level: K–12.

Focus: Electronic multimedia products for schools.

Reviews: Professional materials reviewed in a column called "Reference Shelf." Items may be in any format, but books predominate; there are 8–10 critical annotations per issue. Entries include bibliographic information and features. "Title Watch" lists new products by curriculum area. "Product Reviews in Brief" are original

reviews of CD-ROMs, videodiscs, magnetic media and Web sites written by practicing educators. Reviews are long and cover the company, price, audience, format, system requirements, a description, comments about installation, content and features, ease of use, and product support, and a final recommendation. Reviews are signed and accompanied by a "Report Card," which rates the product overall and by the four comment categories. Five stars means the product is outstanding; one star means don't consider the product.

Print: Professional materials.

Nonprint: Electronic and online multimedia formats.

Features: Articles with practical applications for and theoretical issues about technology.

19 **Online–Offline.** Bala Cynwyd, Pa.:
E+ Rock Hill, 1996– . 9 issues/yr. $63.00/yr. (14 Rock Hill Road, Bala Cynwyd, PA 19004). ISSN 1090-1930.

Level: K–8.

Focus: Media recommendations on one theme per issue.

Reviews: Descriptive annotations.

Print: Books (fiction, nonfiction, poetry), magazine articles.

Nonprint: Web sites, CD-ROMs, software, videos, audios.

Features: Extensive bibliographies.

20 **School Library Journal: The Maga-**
E+ **zine of Children's, Young Adult and School Librarians.** New York: Cahners Publishing, 1954– . 12 issues/yr. $79.50/yr. (P.O. Box 57559, Boulder, CO 80322-7559). ISSN 0362-8930.

Level: Preschool through YA.

Focus: This essential review journal also contains articles on trends, programs, books, authors, and a wide variety of other topics of interest to school and public librarians; professional news; review of youth materials.

Reviews: Some 3,000 reviews annually, with an aim toward reviewing all materials submitted; 100–250 words in length, evaluative, with recommendations; written and signed by librarians, contributing editors, and staff members; outstanding materials starred; bibliographic/order information and LC card number; reviews of professional books.

Print: Fiction and nonfiction arranged by age group, books in Spanish, reference books. Occasional sections of holiday books and books back in print.

Nonprint: CD-ROMs and software by subject discipline, videos, audios.

Features: Annual survey of school library media center expenditures; spring roundup of outstanding reference books; checklists of pamphlets, posters, free materials, and other items of interest; special buyer's guide; audiovisual software buyer's guide.

Index: Monthly index; annual author-title book review index, and audiovisual index.

21 **Science Books & Films.** Washington,
E+   D.C.: American Association for the Advancement of Science, 1965– . 9 issues/yr. $40.00/yr. (P.O. Box 3000, Dept. SBF, Denville, NJ 07834). ISSN 0098-342X.

Level: Preschool-grade 12, college, professional, general audience.

Focus: Critical evaluations by librarians and subject specialists; covers all scientific fields, mathematics, computer science, and some social sciences; some professional books; articles on topics related to use of science materials with children, young adults, and college students.

Reviews: 1,300–1,400 reviews per year, arranged by broad subject (DDC); separate sections for adults, junior high and young adults, and children's books; written and signed by librarians and scientists; bibliographies/order information; evaluative reviews include ratings—highly recommended (**), recommended (*), acceptable (AC), questionable (Q), or not recommended (NR); codes for 10 user levels; reviews are slow in appearing, sometimes long after the book is published.

Print: Trade books, some textbooks.

Nonprint: Videos, software, CD-ROMs, television series.

Features: Annual lists of notable books and films; articles on science education, science books in specific areas, and other topics of interest to teachers and parents.

Index: In each issue and annually.

22 **Tech Trends: For Leaders in Education and Training.** Washington, D.C.: Association for Educational Communications and Technology, 1985– . 6 issues/yr. $40.00/yr. (1025 Vermont Ave., NW, Suite 820, Washington, D.C. 20005). ISSN 8756-3894.

Level: K–12, college.

Focus: Computer technology applied to learning.

Reviews: 1 or 2 per issue in depth, emphasizing strengths and weaknesses with overall grade.

Print: Professional books, texts.

Nonprint: Software, CD-ROMs, Web sites.

Features: Columns and departments about technology issues, copyright, and related matters.

23 **Technology & Learning.** Dayton,
E+   Ohio: Peter Li, Inc., 1980– . 8 issues/yr. $24.00/yr. (PO Box 49727, Dayton, OH 45449-0727). ISSN 1053-6728.

Level: Elementary and secondary schools.

Focus: Articles on use of technology in schools to restructure education; the merger of the computer with video and other technologies; software reviews; new hardware, software, peripherals, and publications.

Reviews: Review sections include "Picks of the Month," which are extensive reviews, often with charts comparing products and "Quick Picks," briefer, one-product overviews. Reviewers are contributing editors, educators, or subject specialists. These critical reviews are supplemented with an extensive descriptive listing of new products.

Nonprint: Microcomputer software, multimedia.

Features: What's New describes new materials that have not yet been reviewed. There are also descriptions of updates, upgrades and new versions of software. Articles about classroom computer activities, administrative support and decision-making, controversial issues.

24 **Technology Connection: The Magazine for School Media and Technology Specialists**. Worthington, Ohio: Linworth Publishing, 1994– . 9 issues/yr. $43.00/yr. (480 E. Wilson Bridge Rd., Suite L, Worthington, OH 43085-2372). ISSN 1074-4851.

E+

Level: pre-K–12
Focus: Reviews and practical articles for media specialists and technology specialists.
Reviews: All sorts of media are reviewed by practicing media specialists, technology specialists and teachers. Items are highly recommended, recommended, optional, or not recommended. Reviews give company, date, price, platform and audience as well as critical annotations. A section called "Out for Review" lists new products which will be reviewed in later issues.
Print: Professional books.
Nonprint: Videos, multimedia, laserdiscs, online, software, CD-ROMs.
Features: Columns discuss copyright questions, general technology issues and a review of equipment.

25 **Video Librarian.** Bremerton, Wash.: Randy Pitman, 1986– . bimonthly. $47.00/yr. (P.O. Box 2725, Bremerton, WA 98310). ISSN 0887-6851.

E+

Level: Children to adult; K=Preschool-K, E=Grades 1–3, I=Grades 4–6, JrHi=Grades 7–8, HS=Grades 9–12, C=College, P=Public libraries.
Focus: Comprehensive video reviews.
Reviews: About 175 per issue arranged by subject or age level such as children, teen issues. Each signed review gives title, rating (4 stars is excellent to 1 star is poor), length, price, "Public Performance Rights" availability, date of release, annotation and audience code.
Nonprint: Videos and movie videos which cost less than $30.00.

Features: Brief articles on video issues and news, a "Final Frame" editorial comment.

26 **VOYA. Voice of Youth Advocates**. Lanham, Md.: Scarecrow Press, Dept. VOYA, 1978– . bimonthly (Apr.–Feb.). $32.50/yr. (4720A Boston Way, Lanham, MD 20706). ISSN 0160-4201.

Level: Young adults.
Focus: Youth services in public and school libraries; reviews of books for teenagers and professionals; news of interest to youth librarians.
Reviews: 250–300 each issue; descriptive with evaluative comments; written and signed by school and public librarians; arranged by format, subdivided by genre and subject; 100–200 words in length; give bibliographic/order information, grade level (M, J, S), and a coded evaluation (1Q-5Q for quality, 1P-5P for popularity).
Print: Fiction, SF/fantasy and horror, nonfiction, paperbacks and reprints, professional books, reference.
Features: Bibliographic essays on special topics; suggestions for programming; notes concerning pamphlets, booklists, and other products of interest to youth librarians.
Index: Titles and authors in each issue.

SERIALS

27 **1996 Educational Software Preview Guide.** Educational Software Preview Guide Consortium. (Distributed by ITSE, 480 Charnelton Street, Eugene, OR 97401). 131p. $15.95. ISBN 1-56484-092-1.

The aim of this guide is to suggest well-reviewed computer software for preview purposes only. All grade levels and subjects are covered. Arrangement is by curricular area and then alphabetically by program name. Information given includes hardware platforms, a brief annotation, learning/teaching mode, grade levels and price. There is a comprehensive title index and a directory of publishers. This is a useful beginning tool to use when searching for software for a particular need.

28 **Only the Best.** Alexandria, Va.:
E+　ASCD/Association for Supervision and Curriculum, 1985– . annual. $27.95 (book) $98.00 (disk). (1250 N. Pitt St., Alexandria, VA 22314-1453). ISSN 1053-4326.

The ASCD assumed publication of this source in 1994. It is intended for teachers, technology coordinators, parents, students and librarians as a selection tool for new software. Full-page reviews are arranged by subject such as arts, early childhood, foreign language and are evaluative. There is a section of titles especially recommended for special education. An interdisciplinary index and a title index conclude the volume. A CD-ROM of *Only the Best* is available ($190.00) and contains all titles reviewed since 1990. This is a convenient and trustworthy source of software reviews and is highly recommended.

29 **Reference Books Bulletin.** Chicago: American Library Association, 1984– . annual. $26.00. ISSN 8755-0962.

This compilation of reviews of reference sources found in *Reference Books Bulletin* [the journal], from September of one year through August of the following year, began in 1969. Each compilation contains unsigned reviews (a group effort of the Reference Bulletin Editorial Board), ranging from a paragraph to a page and providing detailed analysis and criticism. Omnibus articles, which have appeared in recent compilations, cover several topics and provide succinct annotations for the sources listed. Indexing provides access by subject, type of material, and title. This convenient compilation of reviews in *RBB* is an indispensable tool for developing reference collections. [R: ARBA 92]

30 **Software and CD-ROM Reviews on File.** New York: News Services, 1996– . monthly. $255.00/yr. (11 Penn Plaza, 15th Floor, New York, NY 10001). ISSN 1087-6367.

Convenient monthly summaries of reviews of applications software programs and CD-ROMs fit into an annual three-ring binder. Cumulative indexes to the year's issues are also provided monthly. Reviews are summarized from more than 100 periodicals which are listed. Software and CD-ROMs are entered separately, each section arranged by broad subject areas including education, reference, and games. Most entries are a full page of analysis of three or more reviews. Entries are composed of the title, a subject category, the version number and price. There is a thorough description and summary of reviewers' findings. Boxes highlight the hardware requirements, the producer and online assistance as well as the citations for the reviews used in the summary. A list of the reviewers' pros and cons about the product conclude the page. There are now half-page reviews of items less widely reviewed, updates of reviews from new sources for items previously included and a list of published reviews of hundreds of products not included. The cumulative index lists program titles, producers and general subject categories.

31 **University Press Books for Public and Secondary School Libraries.** New York: Association of American University Presses, 1991– . annual. free pa. ISSN 1055-4173.

Books published by cooperating university presses are reviewed for selection for this source by committees of the Public Library Association and the American Association of School Librarians. Selected books are arranged by Dewey Class or Divisions. Each title is given an indicator labeling it as outstanding, for a general audience, for special interest, or for regional general or special interest. The AASL committee also indicates if items are appropriate for junior high or high school collections. This is a useful source as many of these materials are not reviewed in the standard school review sources. Copies are free if requested on school letterhead from the Association of American University Presses, Inc., Publications Department, 584 Broadway, Suite 410, New York, NY 10012.

32 Wynar, Bohdan S., ed., Kim Dority, comp. **American Reference Books Annual.** Englewood, Colo.: Libraries Unlimited, 1970– . annual. $95.00. ISSN 0065-9959.

33 Wynar, Bohdan S., ed. **Best Reference Books, 1986–1990: Titles of Lasting Value Selected from American Reference Book Annual.** Englewood, Colo.: Libraries Unlimited, 1992. 544p. $75.00. ISBN 0-87287-936-4.

ARBA has been published since 1970 and is the most convenient and comprehensive annual review of new reference publications. It intends to cover all English language materials published in the United States and Canada, including ready reference tools, reference serials, standard reference guides on a multiplicity of topics, and electronic resources. The items are arranged by category and subject and the signed reviews list both strengths and weaknesses. School librarians need to use the source carefully as reviewers often forget school libraries and recommend tools appropriate for secondary students only for public or community college collections. Each annual volume contains both author-title and subject indexes and cumulative indexes cover five years. Selections of reference materials of continuing value are published regularly with updated information about the resources.

34 Wynar, Bohdan S., ed. **Recommended Reference Books for Small and Medium-sized Libraries and Media Centers.** Englewood, Colo.: Libraries Unlimited, 1981– . annual. $45.00. ISSN 0277-5948.

This valuable guide to reference sources addresses the needs of small and medium-sized libraries of all types. It includes reviews of 550 titles published or distributed in the United States during 1990. The reviews, written by over 200 librarians, subject specialists, and library educators, are selected from the most recent edition of *American Reference Books Annual.*

Clearly written analytical reviews that consist of several paragraphs are arranged in four major groups—general works, social sciences, humanities, and science and technology—and then by specific subject. Symbols indicate suitability for college, public, or school libraries. Indexing is by author-title and subject.

REVIEW INDEXES

35 **Book Review Digest.** Bronx, N.Y.: H. W. Wilson, 1905– . print sold on service basis; $1,095.00/yr. for CD-ROM. (950 University Avenue, Bronx, NY 10452). ISSN 0006-7326.

BRD provides excerpts from, and citations to, reviews of adult and juvenile fiction and non-fiction, trade books, and reference books. It currently covers reviews of almost 7,000 English-language publications each year that appear in 95 (26 recent additions) American, British, and Canadian periodicals in the humanities, social sciences, and general sciences, plus library review media.

Entries, arranged alphabetically by author or title (as appropriate), give author, title, paging, price, publisher and year, ISBN, a descriptive introduction to the book, age or grade level (for juvenile works), suggested *Sears* subject headings, and LC card number. Reviewing information includes citations of reviews, name of reviewers, approximate length of each review, and up to four review excerpts chosen to provide a balance of opinion.

Only works that receive a minimum number of reviews (e.g., four for adult fiction) are included, but all reviews in *Reference Books Bulletin* are indexed. This is an essential reference and selection tool for secondary schools. [R: ARBA 92]

36 **Book Review Index.** Detroit, Mich.: Gale Research, 1965– . bimonthly. $185.00/yr. (835 Penobscot Bldg., 645 Griswold St., Detroit, MI 48226). ISSN 0524-0581.

This comprehensive index cites all reviews appearing in more than 500 popular and professional periodicals. Included are adult and juvenile fiction, nonfiction, and reference books— some 132,000 review citations for about 74,000 new books each year. Arranged alphabetically by author, *BRI* gives only author, title, and the review. There is a title index. No descriptive summaries or excerpts from reviews, such as those found in *Book Review Digest*, are offered; nor is any subject access provided. *BRI* also may be accessed online through Dialog, File 137. [R: ARBA 92]

37 **Children's Book Review Index.**
E   Detroit, Mich.: Gale Research, 1975– . annual. $95.00. (215 McKay Bldg., Provo, UT 84602). ISSN 0890-5746.

Each annual cites more than 17,700 reviews of more than 10,000 children's books, preschool through grade 10. The same citations also appear in *Book Review Index*, of which this is a spin-off. Reviews cited can be found in the 470 periodicals indexed in *BRI*. It is arranged in a single alphabet by author.

38 **Media Review Digest.** Ann Arbor,
E+   Mich.: Pierian Press, 1974– . annual.
$245.00/yr. (PO Box 1808, Ann
Arbor, MI 48106). ISSN 0363-7778.

This is an index to and a digest of reviews of
films, videos, audios, CD-ROMs and miscellaneous media indexed in 130 periodicals. The
periodicals indexed range from *Booklist* and
School Library Journal to *Byte* and *PC Magazine*
to *American Anthropologist* and *Mathematics
Teacher* to *McCall's* and *Cosmopolitan*. Entries
give bibliographic information about the item
reviewed, citations of reviews, and either brief
quotations from the reviews or descriptions of
the reviews. In addition to the review digest
there is a special features section that lists film
awards and prizes, a mediagraphies section of
biographical articles, and four indexes: general
subjects, alphabetical subjects, geographical and
reviewer. This is the most comprehensive source
of nonprint review sources.

RETROSPECTIVE BIBLIOGRAPHIES

39 Awe, Susan C., ed. **ARBA Guide
to Subject Encyclopedias and Dictionaries.** 2d ed. Englewood, Colo.:
Libraries Unlimited, 1997. 482p.
$65.00. ISBN 1-56308-467-8.

Awe has selected approximately 1,000 special
subject encyclopedias and dictionaries from
American Reference Books Annual entries and
has created a useful collection management tool
for these important sources. Arranged first by
broad areas: social sciences, humanities and science and technology and then by disciplines
within the area, the entries provide bibliographic
information and annotations. Recommended for
assessing and developing high school reference
collections.

40 Barstow, Barbara, and Judith Riggle.
E   **Beyond Picture Books: A Guide to
First Readers**. 2d ed. New Provi-
dence, N.J.: Bowker, 1995. 501p.
$49.95. ISBN 0-8352-3519-X.

The second edition of *Beyond Picture Books*
includes 885 new titles among the almost 2,500
works listed. Some out-of-print titles are still
included because of their excellence. A first
reader is defined as a book with a limited amount
of print on a page, and at least one illustration a

page. Vocabulary may or may not be controlled,
but is usually limited to sight words, words with
few syllables and familiar spoken words. The
books are appropriate for primary children. The
first section is a list of 200 outstanding books,
with authors and titles only. In the main section,
books are arranged alphabetically by author and
include bibliographic information, suggested subjects, and series. In this edition, the reading level,
which is also included for each title, no longer is
based on one of the readability formulas, but
rather is rated in one of three difficulty categories: A is easiest to C more difficult. There are
separate subject, title, illustrator, readability and
series indexes. Every elementary school collection would be enhanced by this source; the subject index is an especially helpful reference tool
for librarians working with beginning readers.

41 Baskin, Barbara H., and Karen H.
E+   Harris. **Books for the Gifted Child**.
Volume 1. New Providence, N.J.:
Bowker, 1980. 263p. $34.95. ISBN 0-
8352-1161-4.

42 Hauser, Paula, and Gail A. Nelson.
Books for the Gifted Child.
Volume 2. New Providence, N.J.:
Bowker, 1988. 244p. $49.00.
ISBN 0-8352-2467-8.

Introductory chapters identify the gifted and
describe various types of literature that usually
interest them. The suggested titles were chosen
because of their potential challenge to gifted
children ages 3 to 12. Picture books, biographies,
stories, poetry, science, math, and game books
are all arranged alphabetically by author. The
authors provide lengthy annotations, complete
bibliographic information, and reading level and
evaluate the plot, characters, and style. These are
useful guides for professionals and others who
work with gifted children. It should be noted that
the books listed in volume 2 were published
between 1981 and 1987. [R: ARBA 89]

43 Berger, Pam, and Susan Kinnell.
**CD-ROM for Schools: A Directory
and Practical Handbook for Media
Specialists.** Wilton, Conn.: Eight
Bit Books, 1994. 272p. $29.95.
ISBN 0-0910965-13-7.

Important discussions about hardware and the place of CD-ROMs in the curriculum provide a framework for the collection management issues included in this work. An excellent section about specific selection criteria and a core collection bibliography of 100 titles of CD-ROMs will be welcome for those who find they need to bring some management to this new part of collections. The core titles are described and evaluated and the top ten are starred. In addition, 200 additional titles are suggested to supplement the core. The titles are further arranged by level and curricular area. A directory of producers/publishers, a glossary and a subject index conclude the volume. Although technology changes rapidly and new editions of some of the recommendations have been published, the principles that are the foundation of the book are sound and applicable to current conditions. Recommended for all levels.

44 **Books for the Teen Age.** New York: The Office of Young Adult Services of the New York Public Library, 1929– . annual. $6.00. (455 Fifth Ave., New York, NY 10016). ISSN 0068-0192.

This annual list has been published since 1929, and contains about 1,000 titles in 70 subject areas such as AIDS, horror, science fiction and fantasy and young love. The list is designed to be attractive to young people, and the brief annotations are intended to motivate readers. Its comprehensive and quality listings plus the low price make it a best buy for both middle and high school collections.

45 Calvert, Stephen J., ed. **Best Books for Young Adult Readers.** New Providence, N.J.: Bowker, 1997. 744p. $59.95. ISBN 0-8352-3832-6.

Bowker has replaced two of the "Best Book" titles, *Best Books for Junior High Readers* and *Best Books for Senior High Readers* with this new title. The purpose and scope of the new volume is to list those outstanding titles, reviewed positively elsewhere, that are appropriate for readers in grades 7–12, and thus complements *Best Books for Children*. Highly recommended for secondary schools.

46 **Children's Books of the Year.**
E+ New York: Child Study Children's Book Committee, Bank Street College, 1970– . annual. $4.00. ISSN 0684-6127.

The Child Study Children's Book Committee, composed of librarians, authors, illustrators, and professionals in education, psychology, and related fields, selects an annual list of high-quality books for children up to age 14. Children are also involved in the selection. Criteria for fiction include age suitability, realistic treatment, accuracy in portraying ethnic and religious differences, and the absence of stereotypes. Nonfiction titles are judged on clarity, accuracy, readability, and differentiation of facts from theory.

Entries provide complete bibliographic data, one-sentence annotations, and symbols noting titles of outstanding merit. Titles are divided by age group (under five, five to nine, nine and up) or by subject categories, anthologies and poetry. Indexed by author/illustrator and by title. This is a worthwhile, inexpensive annual. [R: ARBA 91]

47 Cianciolo, Patricia J. **Picture Books**
E+ **for Children.** 4th ed. Chicago: American Library Association, 1997. 213p. $38.00. ISBN 0-8389-0701-6.

The fourth edition of *Picture Books for Children* is a major revision and most titles are new. The books included were all published in hardbound editions before August 15, 1966. Cianciolo has selected books because of their excellence in both literary and artistic qualities; the introductory essay is an important explanation of her intent. The annotated entries are arranged in four broad categories: "Me and My Family," "Other People," "The World I Live In," and "The Imaginative World," with works of fiction, nonfiction and poetry in each section. Entries are arranged within each group by author and include illustrator, publisher and date and intended age group. The descriptive annotations vary from 50 to 200 words. There is a list of suggested resources, and books are indexed by author, illustrator and title. Recommended for elementary schools and for secondary schools which use picture books for literary introductions, speech contests, art classes and for child care units.

48 Denenberg, Dennis, and Lorraine
E Roscoe. **Hooray for Heroes!: Books and Activities Kids Want to Share With Their Parents and Teachers.** Lanham, Md.: Scarecrow Press, 1994. 243p. $27.50. ISBN 0-8108-2846-4.

Denenberg, a professor and former school super-intendent and Roscoe, a free-lance writer, believe that children need heroes and that reading biographies of heroes combined with activities will "enhance the impressions made on children..." The source is then, both a tool for reading guidance and an activity book. It is arranged by 4 age groups: preschool, primary, intermediate, and young people; and contains imaginative activities to be done with an adult, including such things as play, arts, crafts, food, music, drama, reading, and writing. Activities for each age group are followed by appropriate books. There is a list of collective biographies, an appendix giving a list of National Council for the Social Studies Notable Books, and three indexes: by series, description, and name. The descriptive index is uneven as the distinction between such classifications as women's rights activist and women's rights leader is not made clear, and references are to pages, not people. Many elementary and middle schools implementing values education will find this book useful. [R: ARBA 96]

49 Dwyer, Jim. **Earth Works: Recommended Fiction and Nonfiction about Nature and the Environment for Adults and Young Adults.** New York: Neal-Schuman, 1996. 507p. $39.95pa. ISBN 1-55570-194-9.

This is a bibliography to be used for both collection building and reader guidance/curriculum development. It is a guide to the best of the new and standard books about nature and the environment. Intended for both adults and young adults, some of its recommendations are for upper elementary as well. It includes popular, trade and scholarly materials appropriate for the general reader. Two-thirds of the items have been published in the 1990s. Both nonfiction and fiction are included, subdivided by subject and (for fiction) genre. Entries are numbered and include author, title, publication data, a brief description and recommended age/grade level. There are separate author, title, and subject indexes. Recommended for secondary collections. [R: ARBA 97]

50 Gallant, Jennifer Jung. **Best Videos**
E+   **for Children and Young Adults.** Santa Barbara, Calif.: ABC-CLIO, 1990. 185p. $45.00. ISBN 0-87436-561-9.

Intended as a core collection with titles published since the mid-1970s, this selection tool lists about 350 highly recommended videos for K–12 schools. Entries include audience level, suggested use, release date, description, price, credits, and a critical annotation. There are indexes by subject/title and audience/use. Though it will need to be supplemented by videos produced in the 90s, this remains a useful guide to the best of earlier videos.

51 Gillespie, John T., and Corinne J.
E   Naden, eds. **Best Books for Children: Preschool through Grade 6.** 5th ed. New Providence, N.J.: Bowker, 1994. 1411p. $65.00. ISBN 0-8352-3455-X.

This work collects titles that have been recommended by at least two standard sources, such as *Horn Book Magazine*, *Booklist*, the *Bulletin for the Center of Children's Books*, and *School Library Journal*. It lists 17,140 titles including additional recommendations given in the 15,647 complete entries; more than half of the entries were new titles published between 1989–1993. Out-of-print books were dropped from the earlier edition as were others that seemed no longer relevant. Entries are arranged by broad curricular areas and by author within each section; they are brief, giving only bibliographic information and citations to reviews. Indexing is by author, illustrator, title, and subject/grade level. Most elementary schools will want this source for collection management, for bibliographies and for reading recommendations.

52 Greenfield, Edward, Robert Layton and Ivan March. **Penguin Guide to Compact Discs and Cassettes.** rev. and updated ed. New York: Penguin USA, 1997. 1600p. $23.95. ISBN 0-14-051367-1pa.

53 **Penguin Guide to Compact Discs Yearbook.** New York: Penguin USA. annual. $15.95. ISBN 0-14-024998-2.

This is "a comprehensive survey of the finest recordings of permanent music on CD." Arranged alphabetically by composer, the evaluations range from three stars for outstanding performance, to two stars for good performance, to one star for reasonable performance. Rosettes are awarded for special items. Good prices are also pointed out. In addition to the composer listings there are special sections for concerts, recitals and collections. The *Yearbook* continues the guide; comprehensive investigation requires reference to all editions. There is no index in either work.

54 Hoffman, Andrea C., and Ann M. Glannon. **Kits, Games, and Manipulatives for the Elementary School Classroom: A Source Book.** New York: Garland, 1993. 605p. $94.00. ISBN 0-8240-5342-7.

This is a selection tool for district and school libraries. It includes items that provide hands-on student-centered learning experiences. Over 1,400 items from over 100 producers are grouped by broad subject area and then by grade levels K–3, K–6, or 4–6. Each entry gives the title, author, source, format, descriptions, price codes, and abstracts. There are separate title, descripter, and author indexes and a source directory. [R: ARBA 94]

55 Hohman, Charles, and others. **High/**
E **Scope Buyer's Guide to Children's Software**. 11th ed. Ypsilanti, Mich.: HiScope Press, 1995. 175p. $19.95. ISBN 0-929816-96-X.

Beginning with the 11th edition, this guide presents about 45 selective, in-depth reviews of computer software for children from pre-K through grade 4 rather than the shorter descriptions in the earlier editions. A useful introduction discusses criteria for buying software for this age group. The reviews range from 1 to 2 pages in length and cover concepts, skills and technical features. Accompanying sidebars present ratings, bibliographic information, age or grade levels, skills, platform requirements, price and format. Four appendices list reviews and descriptions of software recommended in previous editions, publishers, titles by content area and glossary terms. There is a title index. Highly recommended for elementary schools.

56 Hurray, Kathy Latrobe, ed. **Exploring the Great Lakes States through Literature.** Phoenix, Ariz.: Oryx Press, 1994. 149p. $24.95pa. ISBN 0-89774-731-3.

57 Hurray, Kathy Latrobe, ed. **Exploring the Mountain States through Literature.** Phoenix, Ariz.: Oryx Press, 1994. 157p. $24.95pa. ISBN 0-89774-783-6.

58 Hurray, Kathy Latrobe, ed. **Exploring the Northeast States through Literature.** Phoenix, Ariz.: Oryx Press, 1994. 260p. $24.95pa. ISBN 0-89774-779-8.

59 Hurray, Kathy Latrobe, ed. **Exploring the Pacific States through Literature.** Phoenix, Ariz.: Oryx Press, 1994. 151p. $24.95pa. ISBN 0-89774-771-2.

60 Hurray, Kathy Latrobe, ed. **Exploring the Plains States through Literature.** Phoenix, Ariz.: Oryx Press, 1994. 124p. $24.95pa. ISBN 0-89774-762-3.

61 Hurray, Kathy Latrobe, ed. **Exploring the Southeast States through Literature.** Phoenix, Ariz.: Oryx Press, 1994. 205p. $24.95pa. ISBN 0-89774-770-4.

62 Hurray, Kathy Latrobe, ed. **Exploring the Southwest States through Literature.** Phoenix, Ariz.: Oryx Press, 1994. 107p. $24.95pa. ISBN 0-89774-765-8.

These seven regional guides list print and nonprint resources for grades K–8. Arrangement within each guide is by state, and within the state listings by Dewey number for nonfiction, followed by biography, fiction and professional materials. Entries give bibliographic information, media format, interest level, a descriptive annotation, a suggested activity and subject headings. There is a directory of publishers and vendors, especially useful as many of the items are of a local nature, and separate author, title and subject indexes. These guides are useful for literature based programs, for other kinds of curriculum support and for collection development. Highly recommended to supplement bibliographies that are national in scope.

63 Katz, Bill, and Linda S. Katz, eds.
E+   **Magazines for Young People**. 2d ed.
New Providence, N.J.: Bowker,
1991. 361p. $38.00. ISBN 0-8352-
3009-0.

This is a comprehensive source of information
about periodicals for teachers and librarians in
elementary and secondary schools as well as for
public librarians and parents looking for personal
subscriptions. In addition to critical annotations
of magazines for children and young adults, there
is a section of appropriate indexes and abstracts
and a section of recommended professional journals in librarianship and education. The section
of children's magazines is divided into general,
subject and classroom categories while the young
adult section contains only subject and classroom
categories. The introductory comments to each
subject recommend first choice titles. Each entry
gives the title, the beginning date of publication,
number of issues per year, price, publisher, circulation figures, where it is indexed, its audience
and an annotation. There is an index of titles and
major subjects and an index by age groups: 1–5,
6–9, 10–12 and 13–18. Many new magazines for
young people have appeared—and disappeared—
since 1991, but this is still useful as a selection and
evaluation tool for the standard titles. Recommended for all levels.

64 Kister, Kenneth F. **Best Encyclopedias: A Guide to General and Specialized Encyclopedias.** 2d ed.
Phoenix, Ariz.: Oryx Press, 1994.
520p. $42.50. ISBN 0-89774-744-5.

This comparison of encyclopedias is useful for
both laypersons and for librarians. The in depth
analysis of 77 general encyclopedias of various
sizes and for various audiences is intended to
assist in the determination of which is the best
for any particular situation. By checking the
same standard topics in each encyclopedia and
by comparing one with another, Kister permits
the outstanding sources to emerge from the rest.
In addition to the long reviews of general encyclopedias, the work also analyzes 19 electronic,
800 subject encyclopedias, 73 out-of-print titles,
and foreign language encyclopedias in nine different languages. There is an annotated bibliography, a directory of publishers and distributors,
and a title/subject index. The readable annotations and the comparative charts and tables
make this a standard guide for every level.

65 Kuipers, Barbara J. **American Indian
Reference and Resource Books
for Children and Young Adults.**
2d ed. Englewood, Colo.: Libraries
Unlimited, 1995. 230p. $27.50pa.
ISBN 1-56308-258-6.

This source is a collection management tool for
books about Native Americans for all grade levels. It begins with discussions about selecting
such materials and the evaluative criteria that
can be used to analyze existing books in collections and for the purchase of new items. There is
also a chapter about incorporating such materials into specific curricular areas. The second part
of the book is a selective annotated bibliography
of books. Arrangement is alphabetical by author
under the major Dewey classes. Bibliographic
information is supplied, along with Fry reading
levels and suggested subject headings. Annotations are long, descriptive and evaluative. There
is an author-title index and a subject index.
Highly recommended for all grade levels.

66 Lenz, Millicent, and Mary Meacham.
**Young Adult Literature and Non-
print Materials: Resources for Selection.** Lanham, Md.: Scarecrow Press,
1994. 336p. $37.50. ISBN 0-8108-
2906-1.

All aspects of the study and use of YA materials
are covered in this comprehensive bibliography.
Bibliographies, texts, guides and handbooks,
periodicals, research sources, booktalking guides,
and a classified list of genre and special subject
bibliographies are included. The 649 entries give
complete bibliographic information and long
descriptive and evaluative annotations. There are
title, author and subject indexes and a directory
of publishers. Middle and high school librarians
will find this useful in building their own professional collections.

67 Makower, Joel, ed. **The Map Catalog:
E+   Every Kind of Map and Chart on
Earth and Even Some Above It**. 3d
ed. New York: Random House, 1992.
364p. $22.00pa. ISBN 0-679-74257-3.

This guide to selecting and purchasing maps was
revised to include changes in Eastern Europe.
The comprehensive listings of sources for all
sorts of maps and map-related materials makes
this the definitive collection development tool
for maps.

68 March, Andrew L. **Recommended Reference Books in Paperback.** 2d ed. Englewood, Colo.: Libraries Unlimited, 1992. 263p. $37.50. ISBN 1-56308-067-2.

This complete revision of the 1981 edition lists 993 recommended titles of reference books published both as alternative versions to the more expensive hardback volumes or those published only in paperback. This guide is helpful to librarians with limited budgets and for purchasing second reference or circulating copies of items they may want in hardback. It is also a useful tool for schools who may wish to purchase classroom collections or copies of sources for teachers to keep in their offices or classrooms.

69 Nicholls, Paul T. **CD-ROM Buyer's**
E+   **Guide & Handbook: The Definitive Reference for CD-ROM Users**. Wilton, Conn.: Eight Bit Books, 1993. 699p. $9.99pa. ISBN 0-910-965-08-0.

Nicholls presents a core collection of CD-ROMs by subject or application in this update of the *CD-ROM Collection Builder's Toolkit.* Each item is awarded up to four stars (one star signifies adequate; four signify excellent) in each of seven areas. The seven areas are installation, documentation, data quality, search power, ease of use, multimedia and "the bottom line," an overall rating. Other sections of the work discuss technical and hardware issues and evaluation and selection criteria. There are directories of reviews and publishers and distributors, a glossary and appendices. Although such resources quickly become dated, basic materials are listed and the thorough reviews are models for evaluating any CD-ROM product. Recommended for professional collections.

70 Patrick, Gay D. **Building the Reference Collection: A How-To-Do-It Manual For School and Public Librarians.** New York: Neal-Schuman, 1992. 187p. $32.50pa. ISBN 1-55570-105-1.

Discusses collection management of the reference collection, including analysis, selection, acquisition, weeding and replacement schedules. Part II is a core reference collection of 615 items arranged by form and subject categories, including electronic. This is a directory of publishers, a subject index and an author and title index.

71 Phelan, Carolyn. **Science Books for**
E+   **Young People**. Chicago: Booklist Publications, American Library Association, 1996. 80p. $12.50pa. ISBN 0-8389-7837-1.

The most accurate, authentic and attractive science books published in the first half of the 1990s are listed in this classified and annotated bibliography. Most have been reviewed in *Booklist.*

Divided into the basic science areas, with several sections dealing with animals, each entry gives bibliographic data, grade level recommendations and a brief summary. There are separate author and title indexes. This is an excellent source to use for collection analysis and development; teachers and parents may also find it useful in identifying high quality science books. Although some grade level recommendations extend to tenth grade, this source is primarily useful for elementary and middle school collections.

72 Phelan, Patricia, ed. with the Committee to Revise High Interest Easy Reading. **High Interest Easy Reading: An Annotated Booklist for Middle and Senior High School.** 7th ed. Urbana, Ill.: National Council of Teachers of English, 1996. 115p. $9.50. ISBN 0-8141-2097-0.

Three hundred fiction and nonfiction titles published in a two-year period are listed in subject chapters such as adventure, fantasy, mystery, sports, and supernatural. This guide is intended for students to use to identify books they might want to read; it also serves as a reference tool for teachers and librarians assisting students in finding reading materials, and as a selection tool. Entries give author, title, publishing information, an annotation and any awards the book received; there are also indicators if the book is a mulicultural title and if the subject is most appropriate for a mature reader. There is an appendix of award-winning books and a directory of publishers. Access is through separate author, title and subject indexes. Highly recommended for secondary collections.

73 Price, Anne, and Juliette Yaakov, eds. **Middle and Junior High School Library Catalog.** 7th ed. Bronx, N.Y.: H. W. Wilson, 1995. 988p. $175.00. ISBN 0-8242-0880-3.

Typical of the Wilson Standard Catalog series, this source (formerly *Junior High School Catalog*) is published on a five year cycle with annual supplements. The more than 4,000 titles were selected by a panel of librarians. Entries often include passages from reviews, and give complete bibliographic information and subject headings. Arrangement is classified and there is a combined author, title, subject and analytic index as well as a directory of publishers. Highly recommended for junior high and middle school libraries as a core collection, evaluation tool and reference source. Other resources will be needed to provide depth in important curricular areas.

74 Rees, Alan M., and Catherine Hoffman. **The Consumer Health Information Source Book.** 5th ed. Phoenix, Ariz.: Oryx Press, 1997. 240p. $59.50. ISBN 1-57356-047-2.

This list of resources for consumers is also helpful to librarians as a buying guide for health materials. It lists clearinghouses, hot lines, magazines, databases, books, professional literature and pamphlets on popular health issues. Annotations are descriptive and critical. There is a directory of publishers, and separate author, title and subject indexes. It is updated often.

75 **Reference Books for Children's**
E **Collections**. Compiled by the Children's Reference Committee, the New York Public Library. Dolores Vogliano, ed. 2d ed. New York: Office of Children's Services, The Library, 1991. 109p. $7.00pa. ISBN 0-87104-712-8.

Although recommendations in this volume are for public library collections, school librarians will find this a reasonable core list. Nine broad areas: general reference, religion, folklore and myth, social science, language, science and technology, the arts, sports and recreation and literature are further divided with appropriate sources listed in each category. Entries include bibliographic information, cost and a brief annotation and there is an author-title index.

76 Roberts, Patricia. **Alphabet: A Handbook of ABC Books and Book Extensions for the Elementary Classroom.** 2d ed. Lanham, Md.: Scarecrow

Press, 1994. 264p. $32.50. ISBN 0-8108-2823-5.

Roberts, a professor and author of *Alphabet Books as a Key to Language Patterns*, has produced a work that will be helpful to building level librarians and to their teachers. Almost 300 alphabet books are listed with citations, descriptions, and extensions with purpose, materials needed, suggested grade levels, and activities. Part 1 focuses on topic or theme books, such as city life, history, and specific places, while part 2 highlights books which are good for letter sequencing. Part 3 is an annotated bibliography. There is a list of related readings and an index. [R: ARBA 96]

77 Sader, Marion, and Amy Lewis, eds.
E+ **Encyclopedias, Atlases & Dictionaries.** New Providence, N.J.: Bowker, 1995. 495p. $89.95. ISBN 0-8352-3669-2.

This work updates and expands *Reference Books for Young Readers* (1988) and *General Reference Books for Adults* (1988). It includes items for young readers through adults in print, large print, and electronic reference works. The 200 reference items are available in the United States, in print, and cost $10.00 or more and are organized by type and intended audience. Part one is an introduction about choosing reference books and has comparative charts; parts two through six discuss encyclopedias, atlases, dictionaries, electronic sources, and large print sources. There is a preliminary list of titles reviewed. Comparative charts and individual title "facts at a glance" make the source easy to use. A bibliography, publishers' directory and index complete the work. This is an essential guide for all school libraries.

78 Sapp, Gregg. **Building a Popular Science Library Collection for High School to Adult Learners: Issues and Recommended Resources.** Westport, Conn.: Greenwood Press, 1995. 329p. $45.00. ISBN 0-313-28936-0.

Intended for public, high school, and college libraries, this source selects popular science materials (books, reference books, periodicals, videos, and CD-ROMs) that are appropriate for nonspecialists to use to improve their understanding about science and technology. Part 1 is an introductory essay about science literacy and evaluating popular materials. Part 2 is a group of bibliographies arranged by science area: biology, chemistry, mathematics, and so on. Each area has an introductory essay followed by the items in first-purchase and also-recommended categories with brief annotations including reviews cited. Of the 2,500 titles, 70% were published after 1990. An appendix keys the book review sources to their abbreviations, and there are separate author, title, and subject indexes. This is an important tool for collection building and evaluation for librarians and offers an excellent vehicle for teachers to use to integrate popular science materials into the high school science curriculum. [R: ARBA 96]

79 Schon, Isabel. **The Best of the Latino**
E+   **Heritage: A Guide to the Best Juve-**
      nile Books about Latin People and
      Cultures. Lanham, Md.: Scarecrow
      Press, 1997. 285p. $37.50. ISBN
      0-8108-3221-6.

This volume acts as a cumulation of the other Schon bibliographies, and includes new titles. Arranged by countries, it includes the United States as well as the Spanish-speaking countries of Central and South America. The brief annotations include grade level indications. There are author, title and subject indexes.

80 Schon, Isabel. **Books in Spanish for**
     Children and Young Adults: An
     Annotated Guide. Lanham, Md.:
     Scarecrow Press, 1978. 153p. $22.50.
     ISBN 0-8108-1176-6.

81 Schon, Isabel. **Books in Spanish for**
     Children and Young Adults: An
     Annotated Guide. Series II. Lan-
     ham, Md.: Scarecrow Press, 1983.
     162p. $22.50. ISBN 0-8108-1620-2.

82 Schon, Isabel. **Books in Spanish for**
     Children and Young Adults: An
     Annotated Guide. Series III. Lan-
     ham, Md.: Scarecrow Press, 1985.
     208p. $22.50. ISBN 0-8108-1807-8.

83 Schon, Isabel. **Books in Spanish for**
     Children and Young Adults: An
     Annotated Guide. Series IV. Lanham,

Md.: Scarecrow Press, 1987. 301p.
$29.50. ISBN 0-8108-2004-8.

84 Schon, Isabel. **Books in Spanish for**
     Children and Young Adults: An
     Annotated Guide. Series V. Lanham,
     Md.: Scarecrow Press, 1989. 164p.
     $20.00. ISBN 0-8108-2238-5.

85 Schon, Isabel. **Books in Spanish for**
     Children and Young Adults: An
     Annotated Guide. Series VI. Lan-
     ham, Md.: Scarecrow Press, 1993.
     291p. $40.00. ISBN 0-8108-2622-4.

This series lists books written in Spanish for both children and young adults.

86 Schon, Isabel. **A Hispanic Heritage:**
     A Guide to Juvenile Books about
     Hispanic People and Cultures. Lan-
     ham, Md.: Scarecrow Press, 1980.
     178p. $20.00. ISBN 0-8108-1290-8.

87 Schon, Isabel. **A Hispanic Heritage:**
     A Guide to Juvenile Books about
     Hispanic People and Cultures. Series
     II. Lanham, Md.: Scarecrow Press,
     1985. 164p. $20.00. ISBN 0-8108-
     1727-6.

88 Schon, Isabel. **A Hispanic Heritage:**
     A Guide to Juvenile Books about
     Hispanic People and Cultures. Series
     III. Lanham, Md.: Scarecrow Press,
     1988. 158p. $17.50. ISBN 0-8108-
     2133-8.

89 Schon, Isabel. **A Hispanic Heritage:**
     A Guide to Juvenile Books about
     Hispanic People and Cultures. Series
     IV. Lanham, Md.: Scarecrow Press,
     1991. 164p. $27.50. ISBN 0-8108-
     2462-0.

90 Schon, Isabel. **A Latino Heritage:**
     A Guide to Juvenile Books about
     Hispanic People and Cultures.
     Series V. Lanham, Md.: Scarecrow
     Press, 1995. 201p. $32.50.
     ISBN 0-8108-3057-4.

Schon has long identified juvenile books about Latin America and Spain and Latino Americans. Her series is a comprehensive listing of nonfiction and literary works with evaluative annotations. Highly recommended titles are starred. All books are written in English and grade levels are suggested. Titles are arranged alphabetically by country or region and then by author, with separate author, title, and subject indexes. This is a necessary selection tool for secondary schools.

91 Schreck, Ann L., ed. **The Elementary School Library Collection.** Williamsport, Pa.: Brodart. biennial. $142.95. ISBN 0-87272-094-2.

This collection recommends items for preschool to grade six and contains about twice the number of entries as *Children's Catalog*; it includes media and professional materials. The annotations are largely descriptive; but items are recommended for purchase in phases from one to three. Entries include bibliographic information, both reading and interest level and purchase phase recommendation. Arrangement is by Dewey Classification. Its use in collection development is improved with the CD-ROM version which permits browsing for author, title, subject, and call number as well as searching by keyword. This allows easy access to entries by several fields, and facilitates collection management. Recommended in CD-ROM format for most elementary schools.

92 Slapin, Beverly, and Doris Seale.
E+ **Through Indian Eyes: The Native Experience in Books for Children**. 3d ed. Philadelphia, Pa.: New Society Publishers, 1992. 312p. $49.95; $24.95pa. ISBN 0-86571-212-3.

First published in 1987 this has become a standard source as a guide to evaluate children's books which deal with Native American themes. Contributors in addition to the editors include Michael Dorris and Joseph Bruchac. The first part of the book includes an introduction and essays while the second part consists of book reviews that explain with examples why a book is or isn't appropriate from the perspective of the Native American. Criteria are made clearer with a section called "How to Tell the Difference" (published separately in 1992). There is a resource list, a selected bibliography and a list of American Indian authors. Contributors notes allow the reader to understand the particular

perspective of each. There is an index. Librarians can use this for selection; teachers and parents will find the essays enlightening. Recommended for all levels.

93 Smith, Brenda, and Juliette Yaakov, eds. **Senior High School Library Catalog.** 15th ed. Bronx, N.Y.: H. W. Wilson, 1997. 1467p. $42.00. ISBN 0-8242-0831-5.

The *Senior High School Catalog* has been a standard work for more than 60 years in collection development and maintenance, selection and purchasing, cataloging and classification, general reference, and readers' advisory work. The initial volume lists almost 5,000 books; the four annual supplements (1988–1991) each cite some 500 additional titles. A panel of librarians from across the United States has chosen the books cited. An effort is made to include works that reflect the interests and concerns of young adults (e.g., data processing, marriage and family, college preparation, alcoholism, teenage suicide).

The catalog is arranged by DDC, with separate sections for fiction and story collections. Entries offer bibliographic and order information (including paperback and variant editions), *Sears* subject headings, and descriptive/critical annotations. Author, title, subject and analytical (references to composite works) indexing, and a directory of publishers and distributors complete the volume, an essential holding for high school libraries.

Large high schools will want to supplement the *Senior High School Library Catalog* with two other volumes in the Wilson Standard Catalog series, the *Fiction Catalog* and its complement the *Public Library Catalog*. Many of these adult titles are appropriate for high school collections.

94 Stevens, Gregory I., ed. **Videos for Understanding Diversity: A Core Selection and Evaluative Guide.** Chicago: American Library Association, 1993. 217p. $40.00pa. ISBN 0-8389-0612-5.

This is an evaluative guide to 126 videos suggested for young adults, college students, and adults. Not all are unconditionally recommended. The reviews are in alphabetical order by title and are written by faculty from the University of Albany, SUNY. Each video is identified as having an American or global focus, and primary and secondary diversity themes are identified.

Complete information is given about date of issue, length, purchase, and rental. Long signed reviews cover content, classroom use, critical comments, and provide bibliographies. The reviews are preceded by a title and theme index and a categorical index with 15 classes with subcategories such as race, ethnicity, gender, religion, class and age. The volume has a directory of distributors. This is a valuable tool for professional collections. [R: ARBA 94]

95 Stoll, Donald R., ed. **Magazines for**
E **Kids and Teens**. rev. ed. Glassboro, N.J.: Educational Press Association of America, 1997. 118p. $15.95pa. ISBN 0-87207-243-6.

More than 200 titles are suggested for personal and school subscriptions in an easy-to-use format. Listed alphabetically, each entry gives the suggested audience, subject, subscription information, whether sample copies are available, and if readers' works are published. There is an annotated description as well. This list has a broad subject and interest scope including sports, music, foreign language, religion, animals, science and international/multicultural periodicals. While primarily intended for parents and their children, this is a useful source for school libraries as well.

96 Totten, Herman L., and Risa W.
E Brown. **Culturally Diverse Library Collections for Children**. New York: Neal-Schuman, 1994. 299p. $35.00. ISBN 1-55570-140-X.

This useful annotated bibliography lists books for elementary children about the four major minority groups in the United States: Native Americans, Asian Americans, Hispanic Americans and African Americans. Biographies, folklore, picture books, fiction, nonfiction and reference/scholarly materials for adults are listed for each group. There is a single author/illustrator/title index. Recommended for collection development and curriculum support.

97 Totten, Herman L., Carolyn Garner, and Risa W. Brown. **Culturally Diverse Library Collections for Youth**. New York: Neal-Schuman, 1996. 220p. $35.00. ISBN 1-55570-141-8.

A companion volume to *Culturally Diverse Library Collections for Children*, this volume is similar in format, but adds poetry, short stories and other literary genre and video resources to each materials list. Materials are labeled for junior high, high school or professional use. There are separate author, title and subject indexes. Recommended for collection analysis and development in middle and senior high schools.

98 VanMeter, Vandalia. **America in Historical Fiction: A Bibliographic Guide**. Englewood, Colo.: Libraries Unlimited, 1997. 280p. $38.50. ISBN 1-56308-496-1.

This new guide by the compiler of *World History for Children and Young Adults* (1992) and *American History for Children and Young Adults* (1990) focuses on fiction for secondary students and adults with settings from 1492–1995. Titles are either contemporary or classic, and were in print at the time the bibliography was published; it is intended as a selection tool as well as a guide to curriculum support. Chapters are in chronological periods from exploration and colonization and the Revolutionary period through expansion, the Civil War and the Western frontier into the 20th century, including a section on the late 20th century. Final chapters cover epic novels that move beyond one time period and books set primarily in one state. Entries contain bibliographic data for each title and an annotation; they distinguish between books for younger or more mature readers. Separate author, title and subject indexes are included. Recommended for all secondary collections.

99 Walker, Elinor, comp. **Book Bait: Detailed Notes on Adult Books Popular with Young People**. 4th ed. Chicago: American Library Association, 1988. 176p. $20.00. ISBN 0-8389-0491-2.

Fifteen teenagers in grades 7 through 9 have selected 96 works of fiction, biography, and nonfiction highlighted in this excellent guide. For each book the compiler discusses notable qualities, suggests passages for use in book talks, and briefly annotates additional genre titles. Some selections are carried over from the previous edition, but most are new recommendations. A subject index refers only to main entries, but a title index includes all books. This work is useful as a selection aid and guide to book talks for adolescents. [R: ARBA 89; BL, 1 Oct 88; VOYA, Feb 89]

100 Yaakov, Juliette, and Anne Price, eds.
E   **Children's Catalog**. 17th ed. Bronx, N.Y.: H. W. Wilson, 1996. 1373p. $100.00. ISBN 0-8242-0893-5.

This comprehensive core collection of fiction and nonfiction for preschool through grade six is published every five years with annual supplements between cycles. It includes magazines and CD-ROMs. The almost 7,000 titles are approved by an advisory committee of public and school librarians. The folklore selections have been expanded in response to the demand for new multicultural materials. Part I is the classified catalog; entries are arranged by Dewey Classification, followed by fiction and easy sections. Entries are critically annotated and include complete bibliographic information, *Sears* subject headings and grade level. Part II is a combined author, title, subject, series and analytic index. CD-ROMs are listed separately in Part III, and there is a directory of publishers. This is a selection, evaluation, bibliography, reference and cataloging tool and should be in every elementary collection.

101 YALSA and Marjorie Lewis, eds.
Outstanding Books for the College Bound: Choices for a Generation. Chicago: American Library Association, 1996. 217p. $22.00pa. ISBN 0-8389-3456-0.

Committees of the Young Adult Library Services Association of ALA have been producing genre-focused lists for the college bound since 1959. In 1984 the lists to that date were compiled by Paulin and Berlin (ALA), and this is the updated edition. The more than 1,000 books included in the lists are intended for ages 12–18 and the list itself is useful to students, teachers, parents and librarians. Both school and public librarians in YALSA serve on the selection committees. There is a table of the 36 books most cited during the 13 years in which the list has been published. Part 1 then lists by genre or subject all of the books listed from 1959–1994 in such categories as the arts, biography, fiction, nonfiction and poetry. Entries are arranged by title and include author, years on the list and a one-sentence annotation. Part 2 lists the same titles by year recommended and is then arranged by author.

An appendix lists the YALSA committee guidelines and there are author and title indexes. Recommended for high school collections.

102 Zvirin, Stephanie. **The Best Years of Their Lives: A Resource Guide for Teenagers in Crisis.** Chicago: American Library Association, 1992. 122p. $18.00pa. ISBN 0-8389-0586-2.

The author acknowledges the fine line between bibliotherapy, a practice limited to trained facilitators and medical professionals, and making available self-help books which adolescents can find on their own and which may add to their self-knowledge. This guide provides a selective annotated bibliography of factual self-help guides supplemented by related fiction and video titles. The materials are organized in nine thematic chapters, including "family matters" which deals with issues such as divorce and homelessness and "sex stuff" which includes gender identity and STD materials. About 20 titles are included in each chapter. Nonfiction items have descriptive and evaluative annotations and suggestions for use while fiction titles are limited to brief plot summaries. Most books have been published in the last decade and all were in print at the time of publication. An appendix compiled by Ellen Mandel lists 58 videos arranged under the same nine topics as the book chapters. There are separate author-title and subject indexes. This tool would be useful to librarians for selection and to counselors as a guidance tool. [R: ARBA 94]

TRADE BIBLIOGRAPHIES

103 **A-V Online.** Norwood, Mass.: Silver
E   Platter, 1991. CD-ROM (IBM PC or Macintosh). $795/yr. single user.

This cumulative list includes over 400,000 audio visual titles, including those originally released decades ago. Materials included are for all levels, preschool to graduate and professional education. The data base includes 16mm films, filmstrips, film cartridges, videotapes, transparencies, records, audiotapes, slides, CDs, CD-ROMs, and software. Each entry gives the intended audience by grade level and special interest, an abstract, and price if still available.

The data base is published for the National Information Center for Educational Media, and is often referred to as the NICEM index. The data base is also available as Dialog File 46 and partially in book form from Plexus Publishing as *Audiocassette Finder* and *Film and Video Finder*, and as a Web site www.silverplatter.com/catalog/avol.htm.

104 **Books in Print.** 9v. New Providence,
E+   N.J.: Bowker, 1948– . annual.
     $525.00/yr. ISSN 0068-0214.

105 **Books in Print Supplement.** New
     Providence, N.J.: Bowker, 1973– .
     annual. $245.00/yr. ISSN 0000-0310.

Books in Print provides bibliographic and ordering information for one and a quarter million books published and distributed in the United States. Four volumes contain entries arranged by author, four contain entries arranged by title while the ninth volume is a directory of publishers. Included are all types of books on all subjects. It does not include periodicals, books sold only to schools, and sacred texts. Entries include authors, titles, publication data, subtitles, edition information, number of pages, grade ranges, bindings, prices and publisher and standard numbers.

    Books in Print Supplement is published approximately six months after the annual edition and gives information on books not published in time for the current BIP, as well as providing updated information for titles that did appear.

106 **Books in Print Plus.** New Providence,
E+   N.J.: Bowker. CD-ROM (Macintosh,
     Windows). $1,095.00/yr.

Books in Print in combination with *Forthcoming Books* and *Subject Guide to Books in Print* is available in CD-ROM as *Books in Print Plus* which provides access to the entire database by subject headings (*Sears* and LC), by keyword, and by 19 combinable fields, such as author, publisher, ISBN and grade level. It is updated monthly.

    Books in Print Online is the most comprehensive and most current of the Books in Print database formats. It includes titles in print, forthcoming, or OP or OSI, since 1979 retrievable by multiple access points. If accessed through the Dialog (File 470), it includes book reviews from *Library Journal*, *School Library Journal*, and *Publishers Weekly*. It is also available from other online vendors. It is updated monthly.

107 **Books Out of Print.** New Providence
     N.J.: Bowker, 1983– . annual.
     $110.00/yr. ISSN 0000-0736.

Books Out of Print is available as a CD-ROM (Books Out of Print with Book Review Plus) or free on the Internet at the Bowker Web site (www.reedref.com). It includes books declared out-of-print or out-of-stock indefinitely.

108 **Children's Books in Print.** 2v. New
E+   Providence, N.J.: Bowker, 1969– .
     annual. $149.95. ISSN 0069-3480.

109 **Children's Books in Print: Subject
     Guide.** New Providence, N.J.:
     Bowker, 1989– . annual. $149.95.
     ISSN 0000-0167.

Children's Books in Print covers materials intended for children and young adults up to the age of about 18. Publishers determine which of their titles will be included in the work. In addition to author, illustrator, and title indexes, there is a section which lists the winners of some 50 children's book awards for the past ten years, and indicates if they are in or out-of-print. More than 100,000 titles are listed and include standard publication and acquisitions data.

    The *Subject Guide* indexes both fiction and nonfiction works by *Sears* subject headings, supplemented with Library of Congress subject headings and other adaptations. Titles may have multiple headings, and thus are listed more than once. Entries are arranged by author under the subject headings. Bibliographic information is supplied with each entry.

110 **Children's Reference Plus.** New
     Providence, N.J.: Bowker. CD-
     ROM (Windows). $595.00. ISSN
     0000-152X.

This CD-ROM product combines *Children's Books in Print*, *Subject Guide to Children's Books in Print*, children's titles from *Books Out of Print*, *El-Hi Textbooks* and *Serials in Print*, with children's serials, audiocassettes, and videos from other Bowker databases. It also includes full-text reviews from a variety of review journals such as *School Library Journal*, *Booklist*, and *VOYA*. Complete annotations from Bowker standard bibliographic tools (e.g.; *A to Zoo*, *Books Kids Will Sit Still For*, and *Portraying Persons with Disabilities*) are also incorporated into this product.

The database is searchable by keyword and fields or combinations of fields.

111 El-Hi Textbooks and Serials in Print.
E+   New Providence, N.J.: Bowker, 1985– . annual. $145.00/yr. ISSN 0000-0825.

This source collects textbooks and series, workbooks, tests, teaching aids, professional books, AV materials, posters and other teaching materials that are not listed in BIP. It includes materials for both elementary and high schools. About 75,000 items are listed in separate author, title, subject and series arrangements.

112 Forthcoming Books in Print.
New Providence, N.J.: Bowker, 1966– . bimonthly. $279.00/yr. ISSN 0015-8119.

Forthcoming Books is a bimonthly list of new titles and titles that are planned for publication within the next five months. It includes separate subject, author and title access.

113 Subject Guide to Books in Print. 5v.
New Providence, N.J.: Bowker. annual. $315.00/yr. ISSN 0000-0159.

Subject Guide to Books in Print indexes the nonfiction titles from BIP according to Library of Congress Subject Headings with the complete bibliographic information.

114 Scanlon, Christopher P., ed. The Video Source Book. 2v. Detroit, Mich.: Gale Research, 1979– . annual. $295.00. ISSN 0748-0881.

The Video Source Book is a guide to programs currently available in videocassette, videodisc, U-matic video tape and CD-I. It lists videos in all subject areas, entertainment and educational, arranged alphabetically by title. Entries give title, date, brief description, producer, audience, acquisition (purchase and rental) and distributor. Indexing is by alternate title, general subject, and format. A directory of distributors is also included.

115 Schwann Opus: Your Reference Guide to Classical Music. Santa Fe, N.M.: Stereophile, 1993– . 4 issues/yr. $39.95. (208 Delgado St., Santa Fe, NM 87501). ISSN 1066-2138.

116 Schwann Spectrum: Your Reference Guide to Rock, Pop, and Jazz.
Santa Fe, N.M.: Stereophile, 1992– . 4 issues/yr. $34.95. (208 Delgado St., Santa Fe, NM 87501). ISSN 1065-9161.

Beginning in 1990, the *Schwann Quarterly* split into these two publications. *Opus* lists classical music by composer and by category for collections. There is a new release section. Most titles are CDs; some laserdiscs are included. Entries contain descriptions of recordings and labels with addresses.

Spectrum also has a new release section. The popular music section includes rock, blues, folk, pop and country. Other sections include jazz, soundtracks, gospel, New Age, spoken, Christmas and children's recordings. Entries give labels and addresses. Together, these two publications serve as musical recordings in print.

117 The Software Encyclopedia: A Guide for Personal, Professional, and Business Users. 12th ed. 2v. New York: Bowker, 1997. $255.00. ISBN 0-8352-3920-9.

This item is a software-in-print source, but it does not include specifically scholastic educational software. It does include more than 20,000 titles of application, library and home educational programs that may be of interest in schools. It also includes CD-ROM products. Volume 1 is a title index with full citations and a publisher index with addresses and the titles they supply. Volume 2 arranges products by system and then by heading or application. Systems range from Atari and Apple II to Unix, and include DOS/Windows and Macintosh machines. The full citations in Volume 1 contain the title, version, release date, hardware compatibility, system requirements, publisher and cost. Recommended for large district professional collections.

118 Bowker's Complete Video Directory.
4v. New Providence, N.J.: Bowker, 1990– . annual. $249.95. ISSN 1051-290X.

119 Bowker's Video Directory of Videocassettes for Children. New Providence, N.J.: Bowker, 1998. 750p. $59.95. ISBN 0-8352-4059-2.

The first two volumes of *Bowker's Complete Video Directory* list entertainment and performance videocassettes and videodiscs, while volumes three and four list educational and special interest videos. Together there are more than 150,000 entries arranged alphabetically by title. Each entry gives complete ordering information, age and grade levels, length, a brief description, publisher, format, price and ISBN/LC or order numbers. There are numerous indexes: such as genre, series, Spanish language, close-captioned, awards, and manufacturer/distributor.

A new directory lists only videos suggested for the K–12 audience. There are 8,000 entertainment titles and 21,000 educational titles included. The format, information, and indexing are the same as in the larger directory. This less expensive tool will be useful as an elementary and middle school guide; high schools will need reference to the *Complete Video Directory.*

120 **Words on Cassette.** 1998 ed. 2v. New Providence, N.J.: Bowker, 1992– . annual. $155.00. ISBN 0-8352-3964-0.

Talking books are arranged by title with author, reader, subject and producer/distributor indexes. Entries give title, edition, author, reader, number of cassettes, time, date, price, ISBN, order number, rental availability, publisher/producer and description. More than 50,000 titles are listed on a wide array of topics such as art, biography, education, fiction, foreign language instruction, self-help subjects and religion. This is the best source for identifying non-musical cassettes.

GOVERNMENT PUBLICATIONS

121 Ekhaml, Leticia T., and Alice J. Wittig. **U.S. Government Publications for the School Library Media Center.** 2d ed. Englewood, Colo.: Libraries Unlimited, 1991. 156p. $24.50. ISBN 0-87287-822-8.

This 2d edition of a popular quick reference guide identifies 500 government publications that are potentially useful in school libraries and classrooms. Part 1 provides a brief history of government printing, explains the SuDocs Classification and depository systems, and suggests basic reference tools that provide access to government documents.

The annotated bibliography of selected publications in part 2, arranged by subject (accidents to zoos), includes books, posters, sound recordings, microfiche, pamphlets, coloring books, decals, and mobiles. Each entry includes grade level suitability and bibliographic/order information. Appendixes list GPO bookstores, agencies distributing publications not sold by GPO, suggestions for using government publications, and GPO bestsellers. Indexed by title and subject. [R: ARBA 92]

122 Kelly, Melody S. **Using Government**
E+ **Documents: A How-To-Do It Manual for School Librarians.** New York: Neal-Schuman, 1992. 160p. $29.95. ISBN 1-55570-106-X.

This guide directs the school librarian through the confusion inherent in collecting government publications. The first chapters of the work discuss sources—catalogs, information centers, agencies, clearinghouses and local depository libraries. The final chapters cover essential and recommended documents by topic and curricular area, divided by grade levels. Five appendices provide directory and other information. A title and subject index would make this source even more useful, but it is highly recommended for all libraries.

123 Maxwell, Bruce. **How to Access Federal Government Information on the Internet, 1998.** Washington, D.C.: Congressional Quarterly, 1997. $29.95pa. ISBN 1-56802-295-6.

Maxwell, who first published *How to Access the Government's Electronic Bulletin Boards* in 1995, has since produced an annual edition of the new, more comprehensive title. Included are more than 300 sites and resources available through gopher, FTP, telnet, e-mail and the WWW. The work is not intended to contain all sites, but is rather a selection of the most useful; courts and legal information is generally excluded. Arrangement is by topic, such as Business, Criminal Justice, Education, Jobs and Employment. Each source is named and described in terms of what is available with access details provided in a boxed summary. Highly recommended for libraries becoming dependent on the Internet for access to federal publications.

124 **Monthly Catalog of United States Government Publications.** Superintendent of Documents, U.S. Government Printing Office. Washington, D.C.: Government Printing Office,

1895– . monthly. $69.00/yr.
S/N 721-032-00000-1.

125 **Monthly Catalog of United States Government Publications.** Superintendent of Documents, U.S. Government Printing Office. Washington, D.C.: Government Printing Office, 1997. CD-ROM (Windows, DOS). $245.00. S/N 721-033-00000-7.

126 **www.access.gpo.gov/su_docs/dpos/ adpos400.html**

This catalog lists and indexes current publications of the major branches, departments, and bureaus of the U.S. government. The format has changed over the years, but at the present time it is arranged according to the SuDocs classification system. A Library of Congress catalog-card format uses Anglo American Cataloging Rules (AACR2) and LC subject headings, supplemented by depository and order information. Only those documents with stock numbers (S/N) are sold by SuDocs. Separate indexes in each issue, cumulated annually, give access to authors, titles, subjects, and series numbers. A serial supplement is issued each spring. Each issue also gives locations of government bookstores and over 1,400 depository libraries. *Monthly Catalog* is also available online through Dialog and BRS.

127 **Subject Bibliography Index.** Superintendent of Documents, U.S. Government Printing Office. Washington, D.C.: Government Printing Office, 1997. 20p. free. S/N 021-599-00701-2.

This free index lists more than 250 subject bibliographies (also free) that give titles of selected publications on popular topics such as smoking, drugs, and aging. The index is designed as an order form for requesting the bibliographies.

128 **United State Government Information: Publications, Periodicals and Electronic Products.** Washington, D.C.: U.S. Government Printing Office, 1994– . semiannual. free. (Request copies from Superintendent of Documents, Stop SM, Washington, DC 20401).

The brief catalog selects the most useful federal publications in a convenient form for selection

and purchasing. Arranged by topics such as health, education, history and the arts as well as a separate section about information available electronically, the guide describes the item and provides all of the bibliographic information needed to order. (Order forms are attached as are directions for obtaining materials.)

GUIDES TO FREE AND INEXPENSIVE MATERIALS

129 **Educators Grade Guide to Free Teaching Aids.** Randolph, Wis.: Educators Progress Service, 1955– . annual. $47.95. (214 Center St., Randolph, WI 53956). ISSN 0070-9387.

130 **Educators Guide to Free Films, Filmstrips and Slides.** Randolph, Wis.: Educators Progress Service, 1995– . annual. $37.95. (214 Center St., Randolph, WI 53956). ISSN 0070-9409.

131 **Educators Guide to Free Guidance Materials.** Randolph, Wis.: Educators Progress Service, 1962– . annual. $30.95. (214 Center St., Randolph, WI 53956). ISSN 0070-9417.

132 **Educators Guide to Free Health, Physical Education, and Recreation Materials.** Randolph, Wis.: Educators Progress Service, 1968– . annual. $30.95. (214 Center St., Randolph, WI 53956). ISSN 0424-6241.

133 **Educators Guide to Free Home Economics and Consumer Education Materials.** Randolph, Wis.: Educators Progress Service, 1991– . annual. $27.95. (214 Center St., Randolph, WI 53956). ISSN 0883-2811.

134 **Educators Guide to Free Science Materials.** Mary H. Saterstrom, comp. and ed. Randolph, Wis.: Educators Progress Service, 1960– . annual. $29.95. (214 Center St., Randolph, WI 53956). ISSN 0070-9425.

135 **Educators Guide to Free Social Studies Materials.** Randolph, Wis.: Educators Progress Service, 1961– . annual. $32.95. (214 Center St., Randolph, WI 53956). ISSN 0070-9433.

136 **Educators Guide to Free Videotapes.** Randolph, Wis.: Educators Progress Service, 1992– . annual. $27.95. (214 Center St., Randolph, WI 53956). ISSN 1068-9206.

137 **Educators Index of Free Materials.** Randolph, Wis.: Educators Progress Service, 1940– . annual. $49.95. (214 Center St., Randolph, WI 53956). ISSN 0537-6516.

138 **Elementary Teachers Guide to Free Curriculum Materials.** Randolph, Wis.: Educators Progress Service, 1944– . annual. (214 Center St., Randolph, WI 53956). ISSN 0070-9980.

139 **Guide to Free Computer Materials.** Randolph, Wis.: Educators Progress Service, 1983– . annual. $38.95. (214 Center St., Randolph, WI 53956). ISSN 0748-6235.

These guides include items available for free loan from a variety of companies, associations, and organizations. They are selected for authoritative and current value and each is updated annually. Arrangement is by curriculum area and indexing is by title, subject, source, and format. Recent changes in technology have occasioned combinations of former titles (the guides to free films and to free filmstrips and slides have combined to become the *Guide to Free Films, Filmstrips and Slides*, which also includes audiotapes and audiodiscs). Entries include descriptions, availability, and directions for ordering.

140 Smallwood, Carol, comp. **Free Resource Builder for Librarians and Teachers.** 2d ed. Jefferson, N.C.: McFarland, 1992. 313p. $27.50pa. ISBN 0-89950-685-2.

This source is a collection of addresses used to obtain free and inexpensive materials. Arranged by subjects, such as alcohol and drug abuse, disabilities, the environment, health and women, entries are further organized by location. Telephone numbers are included. A subject index is included. Recommended for secondary libraries maintaining a vertical file as well as for teachers building classroom material collections.

141 **Vertical File Index.** New York:
E+   Wilson, 1955– . monthly. $60.00/yr. ISSN 0042-4439.

The *Index* is a monthly service that lists current pamphlets and other free and inexpensive items such as charts, posters and maps published in the English language in both the United States and Canada. The publishers, addresses and prices are included. Each issue has a title index and a brief section that gives periodical citations for about a dozen current issues.

Talking Books and Braille

142 **Braille Book Review.** Washington, D.C.: National Library Service for the Blind and Physically Handicapped, 1932– . bimonthly. free. (1291 NW Taylor St., Washington, DC 20542). ISSN 0006-873X.

143 **Braille Books.** Washington, D.C.: National Library Service for the Blind and Physically Handicapped, 1980– . biennial. free. (1291 NW Taylor St., Washington, DC 20542). ISSN 0277-5247.

144 **Cassette Books.** Washington, D.C.: National Library Service for the Blind and Physically Handicapped, 1978– . biennial. free. (1291 NW Taylor St., Washington, DC 20542). ISSN 0360-9029.

145 **For Younger Readers: Braille and Talking Books.** Washington, D.C.: National Library Services for the Blind and Physically Handicapped, 1964– . biennial. free. (1291 NW Taylor St., Washington, DC 20542). ISSN 0093-2825.

146 **Library Resources for the Blind and Physically Handicapped.** Washington, D.C.: National Library Service for the Blind and Physically Handicapped, 197?– . annual. free. (1291 NW Taylor St., Washington, DC 20542). ISSN 0364-1236.

147 **Talking Book Topics.** Washington, D.C.: National Library Services for the Blind and Physically Handicapped, 1953– . bimonthly. free. (1291 NW Taylor St., Washington, DC 20542). ISSN 0039-9183.

These resources are all publications of the National Library Service for the Blind and Physically Handicapped. *Braille Books* lists the collection of books and magazines generally available to eligible readers, while *Braille Book Review* updates the list with new titles. *Cassette Books* lists books and magazines available to eligible readers in this audio format, and it is updated by *Talking Book Topics*. *For Younger Readers* includes both braille and cassette books for children and young adults. The sources are themselves available in a variety of formats: large print, braille, and CD-ROM.

DIRECTORIES OF PUBLISHERS AND PRODUCTS

148 **AV Market Place.** New Providence,
E+ N.J.: Bowker, 1989– . annual. $149.95. ISSN 1044-0445.

This directory lists companies, equipment products and services within a wide range of audiovisual formats: digital audio, computer systems, film, video, interactive video, multimedia, virtual reality. Companies are indexed by name under format and geographic headings.

149 **Children's Media Market Place.**
E+ 5th ed. Barbara Stein, ed. New York: Neal-Schuman, 1995. $49.95pa. ISSN 0734-8169.

Children's media market place is a directory, a collection management tool and a general reference source. It lists companies who produce books, periodicals, and nonprint materials (publishers, producers, and distributors) in more than 20 categories. The index gives directory information for each source listed in the categories. Most materials are for preschool to middle school, but some are high school level. This is a convenient directory for those who purchase materials, especially for elementary and middle schools.

150 **The Directory of Video, Multimedia & Audio-visual Products.** Overland, Kans.: Daniels Publishing Group, 1996– . annual. $85.00. (9221 Flint St., Overland Park, KS 66214). ISSN 1086-9565.

The International Communications Industries Association produces this directory which continues the *Directory of Video, Computer, and Audiovisual Products.* The 1997–98 volume is the 42d edition. It lists products and current pricing information for most pieces of media equipment and accessories a school might need. Products range from audio adapters at $1.25 to digital video recorders at $140,000. Monitors, cameras, recorders, LCD panels, scanners, switchers, screens, overheads and thousands of other products are listed by format, product and company. Sections on consultants, furniture and explanations of technical applications are also useful. A table of contents, product index and company name index precede the catalog pages, and there is a trade name index and glossary at the end of the volume as well as an ICIA Membership Directory. This edition includes a CD-ROM version of the directory. Every school system should have access to this source.

151 **Publishers, Distributors, & Wholesalers of the United States.** 2v. New Providence, N.J.: Bowker, 1981– . annual. $199.95/yr. ISSN 0000-0671.

This comprehensive directory lists more than 80,000 active publishers, distributors and wholesalers in the United States. Included are associations, small presses, museums, software producers, and manufacturers. The alphabetic name directory gives addresses, telephone and fax numbers, and imprints. There are nine indexes including geographical, ISBN prefixes, imprints, and field of activity. There is a list of inactive and out of business companies. Recommended for high school and professional collections.

Reference

GENERAL REFERENCE SERVICES
See also **Retrospective Bibliographies (Collection Management).**

152 Bopp, Richard E., and Linda C. Smith. **Reference and Information Services: An Introduction.** 2d ed. Englewood, Colo.: Libraries Unlimited, 1995. 626p. $47.50; $35.00pa. ISBN 1-56308-130-X; 1-56308-129-6pa.

This text is primarily intended for beginning reference students, but it will also be useful as a bibliography and review of reference service options. In addition to lists of the most important reference sources, the emphasis is on concepts and processes of contemporary reference services. Chapters about library instruction, professional development, and the evaluation and management of reference functions are appropriate for most secondary schools. [R: ARBA 96]

153 Katz, William A. **Introduction to Reference Work.** 7th ed. 2v. New York: McGraw-Hill, 1997. $30.25 (v1); $27.50 (v2). ISBN 0-07-034277-6 (v1); 0-07-034278-4 (v2).

This standard textbook, divided into two volumes, *Basic Information Sources and Reference Services* and *Reference Processes*, covers all aspects of reference sources and services. The seventh edition is totally updated and places a new emphasis on electronic resources (CD-ROM, online, and Internet/WWW). Katz predicts that "in a decade most reference works will be electronic format" and in this edition print is secondary.

ALMANACS AND FACT BOOKS

154 Anthony, Susan C. Facts Plus: **An Almanac of Essential Information.**
3d ed. Anchorage, Alaska: Instructional Resources Company, 1995. 250p. $15.95pa. ISBN 1-879478-10-2.

This almanac is curriculum based and arranged and designed for students in upper elementary and middle schools. Topics cover most subjects students will encounter: time and space, science and health, geography, history, language, the arts, math and numbers, and miscellaneous information for home and school. Pictures, charts and fact boxes add useful information and the large typeface is easy to read. The 1995 edition updates much of the country information after the major changes in the early 1990s. There is an index. Highly recommended for elementary collections.

155 **The Cambridge Factfinder.** 2d ed.
E+ New York: Cambridge University Press, 1997. 891p. $16.95pa. ISBN 0-521-56597-9.

This almanac was designed to supply answers to questions people really ask, based on a study of users of the *Cambridge Encyclopedia*. The information was then organized and indexed. *The Factfinder* has a European/global focus and is a useful supplement to United States almanacs in collections at all levels.

156 **Canadian Almanac and Directory.** Toronto: Canadian Almanac and Directory Publishing, 1948– . annual. $167.95. ISSN 0068-8193.

This is Canada's oldest continually published annual directory. It lists organizations and institutions, religious organizations, trade groups and unions, educational, governmental, court and legal addresses. Although the directory information is the most important part of this source there is also a quick reference section. Access is provided through a topical table of contents, alphabetical "fast finders" and a keyword index.

157 **Exegy: The Source for Current World Information.** Santa Barbara, Calif.: ABC-CLIO, 1994– . CD-ROM (Windows, Macintosh). $650.00. Item WB-6110.

Current events, country histories and statistical information, biographies, and documents comprise this convenient source that is attractive, appealing and easy to use. More than 2,000 pictures and a world atlas accompany more than 38,000 stories from the most recent five years. Updated six times a year, *Exegy* combines the advantages of CD-ROM with recency. Searching is by browse, icon clicks and hotlinks and searching with Boolean operators. Network license available. Recommended for middle and high schools. Many of these titles have been reviewed in ARBA.

158 **Facts on File News Digest CD-ROM.** New York: Facts on File News Services. annual/quarterly. (Windows, DOS or Macintosh). price varies.

The CD-ROM version of *Facts on File* is available as either an annual or with quarterly updates. Contents include the full text of the *Weekly News Service* from 1980 to the current year or quarter. Searching is possible by browse with fields to search by date, key word and topic and with Boolean capability. Articles are printable.

159 **Facts on File Weekly World News Digest.** New York: Facts on File News Services, 1941– . weekly, loose-leaf w/five-year indexes. K–12 price: $445.00/yr.

The information from this weekly news summary comes from important newspapers and magazines from throughout the world. The arrangement is by broad areas, such as world affairs, national affairs, and U.S. affairs. A miscellaneous section reports on such things as sports, people and deaths. Indexes are published twice a month and cumulated throughout the year. The newest issues are useful for current events and the material becomes an important historical resource. The earlier volumes are available and provide rich sources of data for research during the period from World War II to the present.

Related subscription services are *Editorials on File* and *Issues and Controversies on File*.

160 **The Guinness Book of Records.** Stamford, Conn.: Guinness Media, 1991– . annual. $24.95. ISSN 0300-1679.

Published since 1955, with the first American edition published in 1956, the *Guinness* is now published in 38 languages in countries all over the world. Records are listed in 12 major categories with descriptions, photographs, tips from the record holders and tips for those seeking to break the records. There is an index. All libraries will need one or more versions of this each year.

161 **Guinness Book of Records on CD-ROM.** distr. Los Angeles: Updata Publications. (Windows, Macintosh). $79.00.

Contains all of the records in the book format and is searchable with multimedia features. Suitable for all levels.

162 **Information Please Almanac.** Boston: Houghton Mifflin, 1961– . annual. $17.95. ISSN 0073-7860.

Published since the 1940s this almanac covers a broad range of factual and statistical information. Sections cover issues of current importance such as AIDS, drugs, space exploration as well as basic reference sections such as a guide to correct English. The statistical sections are similar to other almanacs. Most libraries will want to own this one.

163 Kane, Joseph Nathan. **Famous First**
E+ **Facts: A Record of First Happenings, Discoveries, and Inventions in American History.** 4th ed. Bronx, N.Y.: H. W. Wilson, 1981. 1350p. $80.00. ISBN 0-8242-0661-4.

Nine thousand first occurrences of events, discoveries, happenings, and inventions on the North American continent are recorded in this source. The first "first" is the birth of a child to European parents in 1007, and the most recent is the first front wheel drive automobile in 1980. Arrangement is alphabetical by subject with cross-references, and indexes provide access by years, day of the month, personal name, and geographic location. Students can use the first index as a chronology, the second to identify events of birthdays or school days, and the geographic index to check the "firsts" in their own states and towns. Highly recommended for all collections.

164 **Microsoft Bookshelf 98.** Redmond, Wash.: Microsoft, 1997. CD-ROM (Windows, Macintosh). $54.95. ISBN 1-57231-619-5.

There are 10 different reference works available on this disc, including the *American Heritage Dictionary of the English Language, Roget's Thesaurus, The World Almanac, The People's Chronology, The Desk Encarta* (an abridged *Encarta Encyclopedia*), *The Columbia Dictionary of Quotations, The Encarta Desk World Atlas, The National Five-Digit Zip Code and Postal Office Directory*, a Microsoft computer and Internet dictionary, and a Microsoft Internet directory. The interface with any Microsoft program has been improved and allows quick access to the dictionary, quotation book and zip code directory. Available online via the *Encarta Online Library*.

165 **New View Almanac: The First All-Visual Resource of Vital Facts and Statistics!** Woodbridge, Conn.: Blackbirch Press, 1996. 608p. $29.95. ISBN 1-56711-13-8.

More than 2,000 computer-generated graphics, some in color, illustrate statistical information in 12 areas such as health, government, drugs and crime, the environment and sports. A brief text introduction begins each area, but the highlight here is the visual presentation of the data. Not only are there charts, graphs and diagrams, but their appearance is often related to the data; for example, the consumption of take-out food is presented as a (pizza) pie chart. The graphics can be used in student presentations and the work is a good example of the kinds of interdisciplinary projects that can result from social studies and mathematics. The table of contents clearly describes the material and there is also an index. Highly recommended for middle school and high school collections.

166 **The New York Public Library Desk Reference.** 2d ed. New York: Prentice Hall, 1993. 930p. $40.00. ISBN 0-671-85014-8.

Based on real questions asked of librarians at reference desks, the information in this almanac is strongest in general information that tends not to be quickly dated: facts and dates, inventions and discoveries, symbols and signs, etiquette information and household tips, for example. It is a good one-volume ready reference tool; statistical information needs to be retrieved from other sources. Highly recommended for all libraries.

167 *New York Times* **1998 Almanac.** Toronto: Penguin Books Canada, 1997. 988p. $10.95pa. ISBN 0-14-051405-8.

E+

This almanac covers much of the same information as the *World Almanac and Book of Facts* and uses a similar organizational structure. It often adds more detail and depth of information than other almanacs and has the advantage of better layout, binding and typeface. Recommended to supplement the almanac collection at all levels.

168 **The Statesman's Year-Book.** New York: St. Martin's Press, 1864– . annual. $85.00. ISSN 0081-4601.

The definitive source of almanac information on the world's nations, *Statesman's* has been published since 1864. Introductory information has the year's chronology and comparative statistical tables. The first section lists international organizations, and the second and main section lists each country of the world alphabetically and gives for each a map showing its location, basic demographic, political, and geographical information, its key history, population, climate, constitution and government, defense, international relations, economy, energy and natural resources, industry, foreign economic relations, communications, social institutions and diplomatic representatives. There are separate place, product, and person indexes. This source should be in every secondary library collection.

169 *Time* **Magazine Multimedia Almanac.** Fremont, Calif.: The Learning Company, 1996. CD-ROM (Windows, Macintosh). $54.95. ISBN 0-763-00268-1 (Win); 0-763-04066-7 (Mac).

Full-text articles are selected from issues of *Time* from 1923 to 1996 with a decade by decade timeline. More than 24,000 articles are available as are all weekly issues from January, 1989–December, 1996. Also included are 80 video clips of major stories covered in the magazine. Many photographs, including *Time* covers, are included. Access is easy and can be done by browsing from a word list and by keyword and phrase searching. Available with site licenses and in labpacks.

170 **The Universal Almanac.** Kansas City, Mo.: Andrews & McMeel, 1991– . annual. $19.95. ISSN 1045-9820.

The newest of the general almanacs, the *Universal* duplicates much of the statistical and news sources of other almanacs, but schools will find it appealing because of its good layout, ease of use and readability, useful charts and timelines and excellent table of contents and index. Recommended for all levels.

171 Wallechinsky, David. **The People's Almanac Presents the Twentieth Century: The Definitive Compendium of Astonishing Events, Amazing People, and Strange-But-True Facts.** Boston: Little, Brown, 1995. 835p. $24.95. ISBN 0-316-92095-9.

A mandatory warning notice should go with this book: "If you pick up this book the next two hours of your day are in jeopardy." From the first section of quotations through the humanized biographies of world leaders and the chapters on disasters, crime, and war, all the way to death and strange stories, this book of 20th century facts will enlighten any reader. Wallechinsky, of *People's Almanac* and *Book of Lists* fame, knows how to make history as fascinating as possible. The reference value of this work is due to the clearly organized and detailed table of contents and the extensive index. Recommended for all secondary collections.

172 **Whitaker's Almanack.** London: J. Whitaker; distr. Detroit: Gale, 1869– . annual. $92.00. ISBN 0083-9256.

Issued annually since 1869, this British counterpart of American almanacs emphasizes Great Britain, the Commonwealth and dependent territories. Extensive information about government with statistics on such topics as housing, agriculture, employment and shipping is provided.

There are also obituaries, a directory of British royalty and peerage, literary and other prize listings and much more. There is little duplication of material contained in the American almanacs. Extensively indexed.

173 **The World Almanac and Book of Facts.** New York: Press Pub. Co., 1923– . annual. $21.45; $9.20pa. ISSN 0084-1382.

This inexpensive source continues to be one of the most useful American reference sources. It contains a chronology of the year's events, consumer information, government activities, obituaries, statistical information, state and national data, and facts and figures about sports and entertainment. An annual publication that should be in all libraries. Available on *Microsoft Bookshelf.*

174 **World Almanac for Kids, 1998.**
E   Mahwah, N.J.: World Almanac Books; distr. New York: St. Martin's Press, 1997. 320p. $16.95. ISBN 0-88687-813-6.

Facts, dates, lists, photos and banners arranged in more than 30 categories provide an interesting source for both browsing and reference. Categories include such topics as people and places in the news, countries, holidays, numbers, sports and games, and weather. Each category is divided into brief boxed fact sections, illustrated with photographs, maps and drawings. There are colored maps and world flags. Web site addresses are attached to many entries and there is an index. Highly recommended for elementary collections.

CHRONOLOGIES

175 **Day by Day: The Forties.** New York: Facts on File, 1977. 1051p. $125.00. ISBN 0-87196-375-2.

176 **Day by Day: The Fifties.** New York: Facts on File, 1979. 1015p. $125.00. ISBN 0-87196-383-3.

177 **Day by Day: The Sixties.** New York: Facts on File, 1983. 2v. $195.00/set. ISBN 0-87196-648-4.

178 **Day by Day: The Seventies.** New York: Facts on File, 1988. 2v. $195.00/set. ISBN 0-8160-1020-X.

179 **Day by Day: The Eighties.** New York: Facts on File, 1995. 2v. $195.00/set. ISBN 0-8160-1592-9.

The decade summaries are based on *Facts on File Yearbooks* and major newspapers and scholarly reference works. They try to give a sense of what it was like to live during those decades. Because the sources are contemporary, the earlier volumes do give a real sense of the differences of the times; entries in the forties volume do not reflect current interest nor opinion about the Holocaust, for example. Terminology is also contemporary with the events and "Negro" is preserved as it was used. Each volume has an introductory essay and yearly summaries by month. There are 10 categories in vertical columns (labeled A–J) in the main part of the volumes, the left page focusing on international events, the right page on U.S. issues. Day by day entries are made in each category where appropriate. Each year is preceded by a monthly summary of events not fixed to single dates and a section of photographs. An index is included in each. These volumes provide a wealth of source material for a variety of curricular areas, and for student curiosity as well. Libraries which have retained or purchased the *Facts on File Yearbooks* will need to decide if the format of the decade summaries is worth the price.

180 DeFord, Miriam, and Joan S. Jackson. **Who Was When: A Dictionary of Contemporaries.** 3d ed. Bronx, N.Y.: H. W. Wilson, 1976. 200p. $53.00. ISBN 0-8242-0532-4.

This standard source with its over-wide pages continues to be an excellent comparative guide to 10,000 individuals from 500 B.C. to the early 1970s. As the history-makers are aligned by both date and broad field of activity, it is easy for students to see who were contemporaries across a range of endeavors. Categories include government and law; military, naval, and (later) aviation; economic areas; religion; science, medicine, and technology; literature; music; and visual arts. There is an index with dates of birth and death. This resource can suggest and enhance interdisciplinary units in both elementary and secondary schools.

181 Dickson, Paul. **Timelines.** Reading, Mass.: Addison-Wesley, 1991. 357p. $10.95pa. ISBN 0-201-56753-9.

Events from 1945–1989 are arranged by month. Important events are in boxes and there are yearly sections of fads and trends, statistics, quotes or phrases, and people. A good index allows one to trace items across years. The inclusion of popular culture references gives an excellent sense of the period. Recommended for both reference and browsing.

182 **Junior Chronicle of the 20th**
E+ **Century.** New York: DK Publishing, 1997. 336p. $39.95. ISBN 0-7894-2033-3.

World events are covered with each two-page spread featuring one year. Topics include cultural and political events, wars, disasters, sports, science and inventions. The clear writing and good index make the attractive browsing book useful for reference as well. Recommended for upper elementary and middle school collections, although many high schools would find it a good addition as well.

183 Scarre, Chris, ed. **Smithsonian Timelines of the Ancient World.** New York: Dorling Kindersley, 1993. 256p. $49.95. ISBN 1-56458-305-8.

The ambitious goal of this work is to trace the human history from earliest times to 1500 A.D. from all parts of the world. Timelines show both region and areas of human achievement in grids with narrative and illustration. The grids thus show development and comparisons geographically. Topic descriptions are based upon archaeological findings and include food and environment, shelter and architecture, techology and innovation, and art and ritual. These four parts are divided into 18 chapters with maps. There is a superior use of color as a distinguishing device in both the timelines and maps. This is for both browsing and reference in secondary libraries. [R: ARBA 94]

184 Steinberg, S. H. **Historical Tables: 58 B.C.–A.D. 1985.** 12th ed. John Paxton, ed. New York: Garland Pub., 1991. 352p. $80.00. ISBN 0-8153-0259-2.

Frequently revised since its first appearance in 1939, this standard tool is more complete and complex than *Who Was When*. It covers nations rather than people chronologically and in cultural and intellectual categories. Certain eras are given specific categories, e.g., early history and the world wars. It does not include an index.

185 Wetterau, Bruce. **The New York Public Library Book of Chronologies.** New York: Prentice Hall, 1994. 640p. $16.00pa. ISBN 0-671-89265-7.

There are 250 separate chronologies arranged by subject in 14 chapters in this attractive book which serves as a source of reference information on history and culture. A history of topics collects such data as fads and crazes since 1900 and crime and criminals since 1900. Extended and related information is placed in boxed entries. An extensive index adds to the use of this tool as a reference source. Recommended for all levels.

ABBREVIATIONS AND ACRONYMS

186 De Sola, Ralph, Karen Kerchelich and Dean Stahl. **Abbreviations Dictionary.** 9th ed. Boca Raton, Fla.: CRC Press, 1995. 1347p. $79.95. ISBN 0-8493-8944-5.

This is a standard and reasonable sized list of abbreviations for a school library. It contains about 60,000 abbreviations and acronyms and in addition, 50 lists of useful information such as airline codes, nicknames, symbols, national parks and constellations. Highly recommended for all libraries.

187 Kleinedler, Steven R., and Richard A. Spears. **NTC's Dictionary of Acronyms and Abbreviations.** Lincolnwood, Ill.: National Textbook, 1995, c1993. 311p. $12.95. ISBN 0-8442-5376-6.

This work is not meant to be as comprehensive as Gale's *Acronyms, Initialisms and Abbreviations Dictionary*, and is more useful in a school library. Rather it lists the most commonly used in 2,100 entries. It gives examples and options for each entry. Highly recommended as a useful tool at all levels.

ALLUSIONS

188 Cole, Sylvia, and Abraham H. Lass. **Facts on File Dictionary of 20th Century Allusions: From Abbott and Costello to Ziegfield Girls.** New York: Facts on File, 1991. 292p. $24.95. ISBN 0-8160-1915-0.

This work focuses on modern allusions based on people (e.g., Darth Vader, John Wayne), places (e.g., Haight-Ashbury), events, phrases, and literary works. The alphabetically arranged allusions are defined and contain explanations of their backgrounds. Entry length varies but most are a paragraph or more. Cross-references and an index support the volume. [R: ARBA 92; Choice, June 91; RRB, 15 Feb 91; SLJ, May 91]

189 Webber, Elizabeth. **Grand Allusions: A Lively Guide to Those Expressions, Terms, and References You Ought to Know but Might Not.** Washington, D.C.: Farragut, 1990. 385p. $21.95; $12.95pa. ISBN 0-918535-09-3; 0-918535-03-4pa.

This is an alphabetical list of allusions, figures of speech, terms of art, foreign language phrases and jargon. Terms are both defined and illustrated by examples. Sources of allusions are literature, the Bible, politics and history. Pronunciations are given. This is an entertaining and essential source for all secondary library collections.

CULTURAL LITERACY

190 Hirsch, E. D., and others. **Dictionary of Cultural Literacy.** 2d rev. ed. Boston: Houghton Mifflin, 1993. 586p. $24.95. ISBN 0-395-65597-8.

Based on the author's book *Cultural Literacy* (1987) this dictionary contains the body of information a literate American of the late 20th century should have absorbed by the senior year of high school. The content of the list includes phrases, terms, people, events, and dates and is arranged by broad areas of knowledge, such as the Bible, mythology and folklore, proverbs, idioms, world history to 1550, and various sciences; there are brief introductions to each area. Each entry includes a definition or description and the significant cultural associations if these are not self-evident. Cross-references and an index help to locate specific pieces of information.

191 Hirsch, E. D., and others, **A First Dictionary of Cultural Literacy: What Our Children Need to Know.** 2d ed. Boston: Houghton Mifflin, 1996. 279p. $13.95pa. ISBN 0-395-82352-8.

The *First Dictionary* indicates what children should know by the end of sixth grade, according to a survey of several hundred teachers and parents. It also arranges facts and concepts into categories. An index is included.

Hirsch has also published a series of texts specifying what "should be known" by each grade level. The texts cover the categories of the *Dictionaries* and contain text, activities and suggested readings. An effort has been made to represent multicultural and nonsexist points of view. The *Core Knowledge Series* may have reference value, especially in parent collections. Beginning with *What Your Kindergartner Needs to Know: Preparing Your Child for a Lifetime of Learning* (Delta, 1997), there is a volume available for each level through grade six.

DIRECTORIES

192 Bergstrom, Joan M., and Craig Bergstrom. **All the Best Contests for Kids.** 5th ed. Berkeley, Calif.: Ten Speed Press, 1995. 288p. $8.95pa. ISBN 1-883672-29-5.

This source is for elementary and middle school children, their parents, and for school extracurricular and club advisers. There are entries for general contests and for kinds of contests (creative, educational, games, writing and drawing). For each contest entry, the directory gives an address and suggestions for participating. There is an interest chart and a month-by-month listing of deadlines. Another section contains ideas for creating contests.

193 **Directory of American Youth Organizations.** Minneapolis, Minn.: Free Spirit Pub., 1983– . (400 First Avenue North, Suite 616, Minneapolis, MN 55401). biennial. $21.95. ISSN 1044-4440.

More than 400 national American youth organizations are listed by purpose and interest, such as science, sports, religion and self-help. Each entry gives the national headquarters directory information and a brief description. School affiliated or based groups, such as SADD are included.

194 **Encyclopedia of Associations.** 2v. in 4. Detroit, Mich.: Gale Research, 1961– . annual. $435.00. ISSN 0071-0202.

195 **Encyclopedia of Associations: National Organizations of the U.S.** Detroit, Mich.: Gale Research, 1995. CD-ROM (Windows). $595.00. ISBN 0-7876-0025-3.

This comprehensive list of nonprofit national and U.S. related international organizations, including trade, business, health, sports, hobbies, religious associations, and fan clubs, are listed alphabetically by name. Volume 1 consists of three separate books labeled Volume 1, Part 1; Volume 1, Part 2; and Volume 1, Part 3. Part 1 and Part 2 contain numbered entries which give address and telephone, staff and budget, history, membership, dues, meetings, purpose, publications, and conventions or meetings. Volume 1, Part 3 is a name and keyword index to the entries in Volume 1, Parts 1 and 2. Volume 2 contains geographic and executive indexes. A supplement is published between editions with new organizations and corrected entries. Related publications include regional, state and local editions and a separate, two-part publication, *International Organizations*. Available on magnetic tape, online as DIALOG File 114 and Nexis File ENASSC, as a SilverPlatter CD-ROM and via GaleNet.

196 **PhoneDisc USA Residential.** 2d ed. Bethesda, Md.: Digital Directory Assistance, 1998. CD-ROM (Windows). annual subscription with quarterly updates. $129.00.

One of several CD-ROM products from Digital Directory, this consists of two discs that cover about 75,000,000 residential phone numbers and addresses. Searching is by name with limits by address, city and state. Such databases can never be up-to-date, but quarterly updates, comprehensiveness of coverage and search ease make them attractive, nonetheless. Other products cover a range of areas, businesses and combinations.

ELECTRONIC INFORMATION SYSTEMS

197 **EBSCO*host.*/EBSCO Publishing Databases.** Ipswich, Mass.: EBSCO, 1989– . (10 Estes St., Ipswich, MA 01938). 800-653-2726. www.epnet.com. Internet (WWW), CD-ROM, tapeloads. Pricing varies by format, site licensing, updates.

MAS FullTEXT databases index and abstract more than 400 titles and provide full text in three versions: Premier containing full text for 210 titles, Elite for 140 titles and Select for 70 titles. All three include coverage of *The New York Times.* Available from EBSCO*host,* CD-ROM and tape. Also available as *Magazine Article Summaries* which are citations and abstracts only, no full text.

Middle Search Plus is designed for middle and high schools and covers 170 titles, with 51 searchable full-text periodicals. It includes *Collier's Encyclopedia. Primary Search* is appropriate for elementary schools and covers 115 periodicals with 31 full-text magazines as well as two almanacs and an encyclopedia. All of the school-based *Search Plus* databases are available from EBSCO*host,* and as CD-ROM and tape; all are available with a Spanish interface.

EBSCO has a variety of other proprietary and licensed databases which may be of use to schools, such as *Newspaper Source, TOPICsearch* and *Vocational Search.*

198 **The Electric Library.** Wayne, Pa.: Infonautics, 1994– . (900 W. Valley Rd., Ste. 1000, Wayne, PA 19087-1830). Internet (WWW). Price varies.

This online, full-text research collection is especially intended to support K–12 curricular needs. It includes hundreds of newspapers and magazines and several wire services as well as reference books, photographs and maps. While many of the sources might be considered of secondary quality, the search capabilities are among the finest available. Natural language searching, simple screens and useful limiting make this service easy enough for elementary students. Searches and documents may be saved to disk and printed.

Available only through the Internet, *Electric Library* offers selected resources and a fast search engine that does not go beyond its holdings.

Users must have an Internet Service Provider for access.

199 **FirstSearch.** Dublin, Ohio: OCLC, 1991– . (6565 Frantz Road, Dublin, OH 43017-3395). 800-848-5800. www.oclc.org. Internet (WWW). K–12 pricing available.

FirstSearch is an online, indexing and reference service especially designed with a simple, menu-driven interface that permits easy user access. Beginning with TELNET access, the Web version started in 1995, and continues to develop more searching and other functions. Comprising 70 databases, the system provides a range of citations, abstracts and full text from books, journals and other materials. Document delivery methods vary. This powerful information system is appropriate for high schools.

200 **NewsBank InfoWeb.** New Canaan, Conn.: NewsBank, 1997– . 800-762-8182. www.newsbank.com. Internet (WWW), CD-ROM, microfiche. School library pricing available.

NewsBank, producers of full-text newspaper articles in microform and CD-ROM, is loading sections of its database onto its Internet delivery system, *InfoWeb.* It is also broadening its traditional newspaper database to include full-text magazine articles and documents, particularly early American documents previously available in microform. Current *InfoWeb* resources include, among others, *NewsFile* and *Global NewsBank,* both also available as CD-ROM databases. Other product lines will make the transition to *InfoWeb.*

The CD-ROM databases from NewsBank include a wide range of resources such as *NewsSource* which contains thousands of full-text articles from more than 100 newspapers and wire services and full-text articles from 30 periodicals as well as citations for 100 periodicals. Fifty-two individual newspapers from 27 states and the District of Columbia are available as individual CD-ROMs with simple searching structures as are two "national" newspapers, *The Christian Science Monitor* and *USA Today.* State and regional databases are a relatively new product line. Texas and Ohio databases are the first two available.

NewsBank's *CDjr.* is a collection of newspaper and magazine information sources specifically designed for middle and junior high students. It contains both full-text and citations *Popular Periodicals* is available in either Basic or Standard collections which cover different numbers of titles. The *ScienceSource Collection* includes 25,000 article summaries from natural, physical and applied science journals and magazines and is updated nine times a year.

201 **ProQuest Direct.** Ann Arbor, Mich.: UMI, 1998– . (300 N. Zeeb Rd., Ann Arbor, MI 48106). 800-521-0600. www.umi.com. Internet (WWW), CD-ROM. Pricing varies by format, product, update cycles, site access points and document delivery alternatives.

The UMI database collection is available through a Web interface, *ProQuest Direct*; version 1.6 is specifically designed for K–12 students. Topics included in the graphical search sequence are health, sports/entertainment, people, plants and animals, the arts, earth science, social studies, critical issues, technology and news. Searches can be accomplished by a hierarchical system or by entering search terms.

Individual databases are also available as CD-ROMs, online, and on magnetic tape. *Newspaper Abstracts* covers leading national newspapers from 1989 forward. Backfiles from 1985–1988 are available. *Magazine Express* cites 150 periodicals with full-text for 100 of the publications; this database also includes two newspapers. *General Periodicals* indexes 1,600 titles with many of them in full text. *Resource/One* is a database that combines types of sources for current coverage. *PowerPages* combines with other products for document delivery.

202 **SearchBank.** Foster City, Calif.: Information Access, 1996– . (362 Lakeside Drive, Foster City, CA 94404). 800-227-8431. www.library.iacnet.com. Internet (WWW), CD-ROM (Macintosh, DOS and Windows 95). Price varies by coverage.

SuperTOM includes 230 indexed periodicals with 185 in full-text as well as reference books and newspaper articles. (The CD-ROM version includes 180 periodicals, 136 in full text.) Updates are daily on the Web and monthly on CD-ROM. *SuperTOM Jr.* includes 60 periodicals, 50 with full text.

PrimaryTom is designed for elementary students; all thirty magazines indexed are in full text and there are four reference books and newspaper articles included. It is available only in CD-ROM. *TOM Health and Science* indexes 71 periodicals, with 62 in full text as well as 80 pamphlets, and two related reference sources.

203 **SIRS Researcher.** Boca Raton, Fla.: SIRS, 1988– . (P.O. Box 2348, Boca Raton, FL 33427-2348). 800-232-7477. www.sirs.com. Internet (WWW), CD-ROM (Macintosh, Windows, DOS), print. Pricing varies by format, updates, access source, and site access points.

The *Researcher* is the central SIRS product and is a general database with full-text articles about topics such as social issues, science, health, history and politics. Articles are selected from more than 1,000 American and international newspapers, magazines, journals and government publications. Coverage is from 1988 to the present. Available via the WWW and in CD-ROM versions. More than 30 of the original paper looseleaf subject supplement series are available on an annual subscription basis.

SIRS Discoverer is appropriate for the younger student; it divides articles into 15 categories such as animals, fiction, just for fun, science, history and government and sports. There are readability-coded, full-text articles selected from more than 450 magazines and newspapers with photograph features and fact sections on countries, states and provinces. Search choices are hierarchical, keyword and subject. The database also includes an almanac, dictionary and thesaurus. Available via the WWW and in CD-ROM versions.

SIRS Renaissance provides articles selected from more than 5,000 magazines and newspapers about architecture, culture, film and television, literature, music, the performing and visual arts and philosophy and religion. CD-ROM (DOS and Windows).

Government Reporter contains seven distinct databases: full-text federal government documents, Supreme Court cases, directories of Supreme Court justices (historical), Congress (current), and federal agencies, lists of Congressional committees and a selection of historic documents. CD-ROM (DOS, Windows and Macintosh).

204 **WilsonWeb.** Bronx, N.Y.: H. W. Wilson, 1996– . (950 University Avenue, Bronx, NY 10452-4224). 800-367-6770. www.hwwilson.com. Internet (WWW), CD-ROM, print. Subscription rates.

Web access to the H. W. Wilson databases permits point and click searching of the indexes to which each library subscribes, including simultaneous searches of multiple indexes. Search refinements include field searches, proximity and truncation. Local customizing of screens and displays is possible. Wilson indexes and print database formats vary from citations to abstracts to full text.

Wilson periodical indexes include the *Readers' Guide, Readers' Guide for Young People, General Science, Humanities, Social Science* and others. *Current Biography* and the *World Authors* series are available in full text. The most economical way of searching Wilson indexes remains the *Wilsonline Online Retrieval System*, which permits searching fees based on actual access times. *WilsonDisc* makes each index available on a separate CD-ROM which can be used on a stand-alone station or networked. Print versions of the indexes remain available as well. Document delivery is also available via *WilsonDoc* service.

ENCYCLOPEDIAS—ONE VOLUME

See also specific disciplines and subject areas.

205 Chernow, Barbara A., and George A. Vallasi, eds. **The Columbia Encyclopedia.** 5th ed. New York: Columbia University Press, 1993. 3048p. $125.00. ISBN 0-395-62438-X.

Revised only about every 15 years, this one-volume encyclopedia contains about 50,000 articles, some 60% reflecting revisions since the 1975 edition. Entries average about 200 words although some are much longer. The articles are clear, accurate and objective and suitable for high school students. Some 500 black and white illustrations add to the narrative. The encyclopedia is international in scope, but written for American readers. Coverage includes biographies (including contemporary entries), places, events, natural science and technology and religions. There are excellent bibliographies as sources to supplement the quick facts within the encyclopedia. This is a reliable source whose only weakness is its lack of index. Highly recommended as a first purchase single volume encyclopedia.

There is a *Concise Columbia* (3d edition, 1994) which is also available as part of the *Microsoft Bookshelf* CD-ROM and online through *FirstSearch*.

206 Crystal, David, ed. **The Cambridge Encyclopedia.** New York: Cambridge University Press, 1994. 1528p. $49.95. ISBN 0-521-44429-2.

This is an excellent single-volume encyclopedia, updated every two or three years. There are about 30,000 concise articles with an average length of 125 words. The articles are divided into a main alphabetical list of about 25,000 articles and a supplementary section with more than 5,000 ready reference, almanac-like entries. Coverage is best in science, biography, geography, humanities and social science; there are not many entries about popular culture. Illustrations are excellent and include maps and drawings. Although the scope is international, there is a distinct British and European emphasis. Useful at all levels as a quick reference tool.

207 **Random House Children's Encyclopedia.** New York: Random House, 1991. 644p. $50.00. ISBN 0-679-85093-7.

This set has no content relationship to the *Random House Encyclopedia* [208] but is the American edition of the Dorling Kindersley *Children's Illustrated Encyclopedia*. The first American edition was published in 1991 and was revised in 1993 to reflect political changes. There are only 425 main articles, arranged alphabetically, each with one or two pages of text and illustrations (photographs, drawings, cutaways, maps) with cross-references in "Find Out More" boxes. Information about science and technology predominate, with humanities receiving the least coverage. As usual with Dorling Kindersley products, the wonderful illustrations cover up the lack of text information. While there are separate articles on major European and Asian countries, there are none for countries in Africa or South America. This is a beautiful browsable volume, but there is more information in the *First Connections* CD-ROM encyclopedia.

208 Mitchell, James, ed. **Random House Encyclopedia: New Revised Third Edition.** New York: Random House, 1990. 2912p. $125.95. ISBN 0-394-58450-3.

Although badly outdated because of the political changes of the early 1990s, this attractive encyclopedia remains viable because of its thematic illustrated essays on the trends of history, science, and culture. It is divided into a Colorpedia which includes about 11,000 color illustrations. There are seven sections, each introduced by an expert in the subject, with subsections displayed in two-page spreads; cross-references allow links to related topics and to chronological continuity. There is an extensive timeline, and a 25,000 entry Alphapedia which gives broad but shallow information and acts as an index to the Colorpedia. This is followed by an atlas of 80 Rand McNally maps. This one-volume encyclopedia is for both browsing and reference.

ENCYCLOPEDIA SETS

See also specific disciplines and subjects.

209 **Academic American Encyclopedia.** 21v. Danbury, Conn.: Grolier, 1996. $842.00/set. ISBN 0-7172-2060-5.

210 **Grolier Multimedia Encyclopedia.** Danbury, Conn.: Grolier, 1998. CD-ROM (Windows, Macintosh). 1 disc, Standard Edition, $40.00; 2 disc, Deluxe Edition, $60.00.

211 **Grolier Multimedia Encyclopedia Online.** Multi-user site license based on size of school. http://gi.grolier.com.

The newest of the major high school and adult encyclopedias, the *Academic American Encyclopedia* has been described as the *"USA Today* approach to encyclopedias." The entries are short (500 words or less) and written informally, and the almost 30,000 articles are accompanied by 18,000 illustrations and maps. The set is beautifully designed and coverage is based on American curriculum. Articles are clear, accurate and objective. Emphasis is on the arts and humanities and science and technology and about 35% of the articles are biographical. There are good bibliographies and an outstanding index. Grolier

has remained committed to keeping the set contemporary and up to date.

Available in CD-ROM as the *Grolier Multimedia Encyclopedia*, the first of the electronic works has added text, video clips, sound, browse and advanced search capabilities, and special features such as timelines, guided tours, interactives, and a knowledge explorer. Included is an atlas with 1,200 maps, 31 guided tours, and the complete *American Heritage Dictionary*. One can mark, save, copy and print text and illustrations. There is a good help system. The Deluxe Edition permits the user to switch from the Grolier article to related online articles in the *Encyclopedia Americana* for more detailed information or to related online articles in the *Book of Knowledge* for similar explanations.

The set is also available online as the *Grolier Multimedia Encyclopedia Online*. The entries include some not found in the print edition, and it is updated on an ongoing basis with new and updated articles every month. The text is browsable alphabetically by article title and is searchable in full-text. Cross-references are hyperlinked. Included is an 850 map atlas accessible directly or through articles. More than 5,000 pictures as well as sounds are available. Many articles are linked through the Grolier Internet Index to selected Web sites.

All versions of the *Academic American Encyclopedia* are highly recommended for middle schools and high schools. This is a reliable, current, easy to search attractive encyclopedia.

212 **Childcraft: The How and Why Library.** 15v. Chicago: World Book, 1996. $218.00/set. ISBN 0-7166-0196-6.

The 15 volumes of *Childcraft* include literary works, information and activities. Science materials are particularly strong. While not an encyclopedia, the set is useful for those who work with preschool and primary children and should be available in elementary school libraries.

213 **Children's Britannica.** 20v. Chicago: Encyclopedia Britannica, 1994. $250.00/set. ISBN 0-85229-2399-2.

Since a serious revision in 1988 which edited the set for an American market, the *Children's Britannica* has earned a place as an extra encyclopedia in upper elementary and secondary collections. Its British origins give slightly different perspectives on certain events; the coverage of the Revolution is excellent. As it does not follow American curriculum, it also includes some information not typically found in the sets that are closely tied to what American schools teach. More than 4,000 articles, a clear typeface and more color pictures each printing add to the usefulness and appearance of the set.

214 **Children's Encyclopedia.** New York:
E+   Dorling Kindersley, 1997. CD-ROM (Windows, Macintosh). 1 disc, $39.95. ISBN 0-7894-2233-6 Windows; 0-7894-2236-0 Macintosh.

This colorful product draws on one of the original traditions of the encyclopedia as a browsing tool for learning. The CD-ROM contains text (can be read to the user), illustration, animation, video and directed motion which engage the child learner and makes information exciting. The user can search by subject, key word and hierarchical devices; there are icons for more in-depth information and cross-references for related items. Web connection is optional. Quizzes and the kind of jokes youngsters find hilarious are additional features.

There are, however, some features which will prevent the encyclopedia from being a useful reference source. Each user must log on before allowed to proceed to the encyclopedia; this feature even allows tracking of items searched. The information is shallow; several actual assigned topics were not included at all. The control panel is extremely complex, and the noises that accompany changes in windows/screens is immediately irritating and grows more so with every minute. The encyclopedia is more for the child who wants to read his/her way through the set than for reference and reports. Intended for the 7–12 year-old and recommended only as an additional purchase.

215 **Collier's Encyclopedia.** New York: Collier, 1997. 24v. $1,499.00/set. ISBN 1-57161-093-6.

216 **Collier's Encyclopedia.** Bellevue, Wash.: Sierra Online, 1998. CD-ROM. 3 discs. (Windows 95). $80.00.

The print version of *Collier's* has gained a reputation as one of the finest of the large adult sets. Kister has even given it the designation as the "Best of the Big Sets." The combination of broad

entries with longer articles and a good revision policy along with its readability make it an excellent choice for secondary schools. The design has been improved and more color illustrations and maps are added each year.

The 1998 edition of the CD-ROM is produced by a software vendor rather than Collier itself.

217 **Compton's Encyclopedia & Fact-Index.** 26v. Chicago: Compton's Learning Co., 1993. $569.00/set. ISBN 0-85229-554-5.

218 **Compton's Interactive Encyclopedia.** Cambridge, Mass.: Softkey Multimedia, 1998. CD-ROM (Windows). 1 disc, Standard Edition, $49.95; 2 disc, Deluxe Edition, $69.95.

Compton's underwent a major revision in 1992 and is a more up-to-date and attractive set since then. There are more than 6,000 main articles with another 30,000 short articles in the "Fact Index." The short articles tend to be more current than the main articles. Entries are relatively short and clear and are written in order to be interesting. Subject strengths are contemporary individuals, biology and the environment and geography. It has begun to deal with controversy and has added more illustrations. *Compton's* audience is much the same as *World Book*, and it cannot compare to its rival; it is, however, a reliable second purchase for all elementary and secondary collections.

The *Compton's Interactive Encyclopedia* on CD-ROM has become a sophisticated and exciting product. It began with animation, video and sound clips in 1989 and has added to both its multimedia enhancements and its search and retrieval capabilities since then. It is also full of features that make it an elegant tool. A spell-check in the search modes offers suggestions rather than just reporting no hits, the "newsroom" uses the computer's internal clock to present today's date in history, and the timeline is interactive with articles, so returning to it doesn't take the user back to the beginning. A variety of search possibilities, a virtual sky map, an atlas, a topic tree, an interactive explore-by-pictures entertainment feature, and a built-in editor for producing multimedia reports make this a resource with more potential than any other CD-ROM encyclopedia. The Internet connection feature allows the user to download monthly updates to information and to connect to a Web launcher such as AOL, Netscape or Microsoft Explorer. This is the one CD-ROM encyclopedia that takes advantage of all of the possibilities of the medium. Highly recommended for all levels.

219 **Encarta 98.** Seattle, Wash.: Microsoft, 1998. CD-ROM (Windows 95). 2 disc, Standard Edition, $55.00; 3 disc, Deluxe Edition, $80.00.

Based on the *Funk and Wagnalls Encyclopedia* but with additional information, *Encarta*'s content strength is that it includes much non-curricular material; its weakness is that little is covered in much depth. Online updates help keep the information current. The third disc is a report-making feature. The searching and multimedia make it one of the easiest to search and the most entertaining.

Encarta is available online as part of the *Encarta Online Library* (www.encarta.cognito.com) which also includes *Microsoft Bookshelf* and a database of 900,000 reference works and periodical articles developed in conjunction with Information Access Company.

220 **Encyclopedia Americana.** 30v. Danbury, Conn.: Grolier's, 1997. $1,600.00/set. ISBN 0-7172-0129-5.

221 **Encyclopedia Americana.** Danbury, Conn.: Grolier's, 1997. CD-ROM (Windows, Macintosh). $495.00.

222 **Encyclopedia Americana Online.** Danbury, Conn.: Grolier's, 1998. Subscription fees based on school size/stand alone $495.00/yr.

This is the oldest of the American encyclopedias; although published for an American audience, the scope is international. It is a comprehensive source in which many of the 52,000 articles address the topic in depth. Articles range in length from ready reference definitions to book-long entries with tables of contents and glossaries. Many of the signed entries contain bibliographies. The set is arranged alphabetically with one of the most extensive indexes found in any set. Its weaknesses are that the basic articles have not

been kept up to date and that it is drab in appearance with few pictures and a rather staid layout.

The *Americana* CD-ROM attempts to search the vastness of the database quickly; the compromise is a fairly complex though powerful search engine. There are almost no illustrations (except for tables and diagrams) on the disc. Articles on the CD-ROM are in some cases, more updated than in the print copy. It includes the *Merriam-Webster Collegiate Dictionary,* the *Academic Press Dictionary of Science and Technology,* and *Helicon's Chronology of World History.*

Americana Online originated in late 1966 and is an ever-improving product. One advantage over the CD-ROM or paper versions is that article updates are added continuously. More than half of all entries are linked to related Web sites. Browse, subject, hierarchical and Boolean searches are allowed.

223 **First Connections: The Golden Book Encyclopedia.** San Diego, Calif.: Jostens Learning Corp., 1992. CD-ROM (Macintosh). $149.95.

Based on the *Golden Book Encyclopedia*, *First Connections* is for primary children and would be useful for older students learning English as a second language. There are about 1,500 articles, and about 3,000 illustrations, 100 animations and about 60 minutes of audio. The searching is simply designed with an alphabetical browse supplemented with a category path, a question-answer path, and a multimedia path. Students can choose to have a robot-like voice read articles or parts of articles to them, but the pronunciation is often awkward and incorrect. The data on the CD-ROM has not been updated since 1988, so the geopolitical information, especially about eastern Europe is out of date. As with the print *Golden Book Encyclopedia*, the only advantage of this product is as an introduction for the youngest students to the encyclopedia as a source of information and as a way to have a successful first reference experience. If the teacher and librarian carefully select the topics to be studied by the student, this tool helps children achieve that success. A User's Guide and a Teacher's Guide come with the CD-ROM, and will help design those first projects. With these caveats, *First Connections* is highly recommended for primary schools.

224 **Infopedia.** Version 2.0. Fremont, Calif.: The Learning Company, 1996. CD-ROM (Windows, Macintosh). $59.99. ISBN 0-763-00227-5 Windows; 0-763-00228-3 Macintosh.

Funk and Wagnalls New Encyclopedia is the base of this source which also includes the *World Almanac, Merriam-Webster's Collegiate Dictionary, Dictionary of English Usage, New Biographical Dictionary, Roget's 21st Century Thesaurus,* and the *Hammond World Atlas.* Searching is clear, easy and flexible. There is a browse index as well as a keyword search function with Boolean operators. It is also possible to limit searches to specific titles of the reference sources and to media: photographs, maps, videos, animations, audio and there is even a page browsing function. Although the audio and video features are acceptable, the animations are the weakest part of the source. Hyperlinks permit connections between articles and sources. Full editing, viewing, marking and print features are included. A project folder creates custom timelines and formats research papers. Updated annually. Highly recommended for upper elementary and all secondary levels.

225 **New Book of Knowledge.** 21v. Danbury, Conn.: Grolier, 1996. $695.00/set. ISBN 0-7172-0527-4.

The 1997 edition continues a major revision of this outstanding set of encyclopedias for grades 3–8. It is based on the American elementary school curriculum but also has articles of general interest to its audience. It has both broad and direct articles, and often includes literary excerpts. It is strong in science and technology and has many entries that explain how to do experiments and other projects. The articles are clearly written and some use of controlled vocabulary is made. The articles are divided with headings and a good typeface and the many illustrations give it an attractive look. The articles are signed and carefully updated. Many cross-references and a good index provide easy access to information. Highly recommended for all elementary and middle school collections.

226 **The New Encyclopaedia Britannica.** 15th ed. 32v. Chicago: Encyclopedia Britannica, 1994. $1,599.00/set. ISBN 0-85229-571-5.

227 **Britannica CD 98.** Chicago: Encyclopaedia Britannica, 1998. CD-ROM (Windows 95). 3 discs, $125.00.

228 **Britannica Online.** Chicago: Encyclopaedia Britannica. (www.britannica.com). Price varies based on size of school.

Britannica (or *Britannica 3*, as it is sometimes called), the largest and most famous English-language encyclopedia, began in Scotland in 1768 but moved to this country in 1901. In 1974, the work appeared in a unique three-part arrangement that has evoked criticism from those who think the new organization makes the encyclopedia more difficult to use. Critics generally agree, however, that it is an authoritative set, providing more depth of coverage on more subjects than any other encyclopedia in English.

The Micropaedia contains short articles for ready reference that range in length from a few sentences to 3,000 words. Some give cross-references to the definitive articles in the Macropaedia volumes. The essays in the Macropaedia range from two to the length of a book. Two extensive index volumes and the Propaedia (a study guide that relates ideas, people and events treated in the other two parts) provide access to the entire encyclopedia. There has been a concerted effort to bring the set up to date and to add illustrations but one still finds inconsistencies in currency between the articles in the Micropaedia and the Propaedia. Nonetheless this is the most comprehensive of the English-language encyclopedias and it should be in most high schools.

One of the major advantages of the *Britannica* on CD-ROM is that it solves the issue of the complexity of searching that is inherent in the print version. It uses natural language searching, which allows the user to key in a question as it would normally be asked, and also provides for Boolean searching. Added in the new version are 8,500 images, 1,200 maps, 15,000 Internet links and a beginning file of animations and video clips. The CD-ROM also includes *Merriam-Webster's 10th Collegiate Dictionary.* The '98 interface replaces Netscape with Microsoft's Internet Explorer. Unlike the 1998 version, the 1997 version of the *Britannica CD* can be used with Windows or Macintosh platforms.

Britannica Online is the Web version and is in many ways, except price, the ideal way to access the set. The comprehensiveness of the print is combined with the ease of searching of the CD-ROM (and now includes an alphabetical browse feature) with regular updates and links to relevant World Wide Web sites. The menu bar for each major article permits one to view the article index, Internet links and related articles within the encyclopedia. At first available only to universities and individuals, *Britannica Online* is now available to schools at a price based on enrollment.

229 **The World Book Encyclopedia.**
1997 ed. 22v. Chicago: World Book, Inc., 1995. $559.00/set. ISBN 0-7166-0095-1.

230 **Information Finder: A CD-ROM Reference Based on the World Book Encyclopedia.** Chicago: World Book, Inc., 1993. DOS, 1997. $65.00.

231 **The World Book Multimedia Encyclopedia: The Authoritative CD-ROM Encyclopedia.** Chicago: World Book, Inc., 1997. CD-ROM (Windows). 1 disc, Standard Edition, $40.00; 2 disc, Deluxe Edition, $70.00.

Published first in 1917, *World Book* remains the first purchase for upper elementary, middle and high school libraries. It earns its reputation based on its curriculum relevance, its short and specific-entry approach, its readability and its accuracy and currency. The index and multitude of cross-references make it easily accessible. More color illustrations have been added each edition, and the design of the set remains outstanding.

The conservative *World Book* first CD-ROM version, *Information Finder*, the DOS, text-only version, is still available. It includes the *World Book Dictionary*. The searching patterns and information are outstanding, and it is a good choice for those who do not require multimedia enhancements. The lack of such "enhancements" results in faster information retrieval.

World Book Multimedia is now produced in cooperation with IBM and includes illustrations, animation, maps, audio clips and video clips. While the search features are the easiest of all the CD-ROM encyclopedias, the amount of multimedia is still limited, although the new

edition offers 100 virtual reality tours, the free searches are carried out in boring text typeface. The Windows version is a hybrid product with pre-selected Internet sites to extend the information on the disc. It also allows downloads of updates. The Report Wizard feature helps students compile information.

GRANT RESOURCES

232 **Foundation Directory.** New York: Foundation Center; dist. by Columbia University Press, 1960– . annual. $435.00. ISSN 0071-8092.

Part 1 lists private or community foundations with assets of $2,000,000.00 or more and grants of $200,000.00 or more in a year. Entries are by state and then alphabetical by the name of the foundation and give information such as address, financial data, purpose, fields of interest, types of support, a selected list of recently funded grants, limitations, and application information. Among the several indexes, the most useful are geographic (by city as well as state), types of support, subject and foundation name. Part 2 lists foundations with assets between one and two million dollars and grants between $50,000.00 and $200,000.00. Also available as CD-ROM. Most districts will want access to this source.

233 **National Guide to Funding for Children, Youth and Families.** New York: Foundation Center, 1990– . biennial. $145.00pa. ISSN 0190-7476.

This is a directory to grant funding from foundations, corporations and other charitable organizations for projects which support children, young people and families. The 1997 edition included 3,635 entries from more than 3,000 groups. Information included is based on statements of interest or actual grants of $10,000.00 or more reported to the Foundation Center. General areas of concern are child-development, welfare, family services, at-risk youth, and child abuse/violence prevention; these general categories include many projects directly related to schools and school libraries. The descriptive entries are arranged alphabetically by state and foundation name. There are 34 data elements included where appropriate such as directory information, and organization information about the purpose and activities they support. Applicant information is included and there may be lists of recent grants awarded. The six indexes (names, geographic, types of support, foundation and corporate programs, subject and foundations and corporations) refer to the entry number. Highly recommended for school system professional collections. [R: ARBA 97]

INDEXES
See also **Electronic Information Systems**

234 Appel, Marsha C. **Illustration Index.** 4th ed. Lanham, Md.: Scarecrow Press, 1980. 458p. $34.00. ISBN 0-8108-1273-8.

235 Appel, Marsha C. **Illustration Index V, 1977–1981.** Lanham, Md.: Scarecrow Press, 1984. 411p. $34.00. ISBN 0-8108-1656-3.

236 Appel, Marsha C. **Illustration Index VI, 1982–1986.** Lanham, Md.: Scarecrow Press, 1988. 531p. $47.50. ISBN 0-8108-2146-X.

237 Appel, Marsha C. **Illustration Index VII, 1987–1991.** Lanham, Md.: Scarecrow Press, 1993. 492p. $59.50. ISBN 0-8108-2659-3.

Each edition of the Index identifies pictures from about 10 popular magazines that libraries are likely to hold: *American Heritage*, *National Geographic*, and *Sports Illustrated*, for example. All illustrations within these magazines are indexed, with the exception of advertisements. The most recent edition covers the years 1987–1991 and includes 28,000 entries arranged by subject headings; entries vary from broad (accidents) to specific (sand dollars) and include individuals. Entry citations include the magazine title, volume, page, and details about the illustration. This source is a convenient way for students to identify illustrations for reports, especially for scanning into computer-generated presentations. Copyright information is included in the introductory section of the volume.

238 **Children's Magazine Guide.** New Providence, N.J.: Bowker, 1981– . 9 issues/yr. $59.00/yr. (P.O. Box 7247-8598, Philadelphia, PA). ISSN 0743-9873.

This is an easy-to-use periodical index that covers more than 50 children's magazines. It clearly indicates the simple bibliographic information children need to access the subjects they search, and there is even a place to check off which magazines are held in a library. This is an essential purchase for all elementary schools. An award-winning video is available as an instruction tool.

RULES OF PROCEDURE

239 Riddick, Floyd M., and Miriam H. Butcher. **Riddick's Rules of Procedure: A Modern Guide to Faster and More Efficient Meetings.** New York: Scribner's, 1985. 224p. $14.95pa. ISBN 0-8191-8064-5.

Since most people find *Robert's Rules of Order* difficult to use, this simplified guide to parliamentary procedure is recommended. It discusses various processes alphabetically, making it easier to locate a specific rule. The reader can search under such entries as "Amendments and the Amending Process," "Main Motions," and "Debate." The table of contents and index also assist the user in finding appropriate headings. The work is authoritative; Riddick is a former parliamentarian of the U.S. Senate, and Butcher is a former president of the American Institute of Parliamentarians. [R: BL, 15 May 86; WLB, Mar 86]

240 Robert, Sarah Corbin, and others. **The Scott, Foresman Robert's Rules of Order Newly Revised.** 9th ed. Glenview, Ill.: Scott, Foresman, 1991. 706p. $27.50; $15.00pa. ISBN 0-06-275002-X; 0-06-276051-3pa.

This version of *Robert's Rules of Order* is a good choice for school libraries. This edition represents a major revision with new content based on contemporary need. In addition to the text with meeting rules there is a center guide with charts, tables and lists which help clarify meaning. A copy of this should be in every library.

Anthropology

See also **Native Americans (Ethnic Minorities).**

241 Levinson, David and Melvin Ember, eds. **Encyclopedia of Cultural Anthropology.** 4v. New York: Holt, 1996. $395.00/set. ISBN 0-8050-2877-3.

The subjects covered in this set will be familiar to every high school librarian as a list of topics students research year after year. Such things as crime, death and dying, dreams, gangs, genocide, homelessness, poverty and prisons are included, as are birth, cannibalism, humor, Marxism, and taboo. Written with high school students as one of the intended audiences, the 340 articles in the encyclopedia will be useful in sociology, psychology, human biology, geography, family life, women and ethnic studies, global issues and multidisciplinary units involving many parts of the curriculum. The work is based on cultural anthropology but draws as well on biological and applied anthropology, archaeology and linguistics. Entries vary from long survey articles to about two pages, but essays have subtopics to help with understanding. Entries are signed and have references. Some entries are theoretical and conceptual. Articles are arranged alphabetically throughout the set with cross-references. This is a resource that will be used widely and it is highly recommended for high schools. [R: ARBA 97]

242 Mason, Paul, ed. **Atlas of Threat-**
E+   **ened Cultures.** Austin, Tex.: Raintree/Steck-Vaughn, 1997. 96p. $32.83. ISBN 0-8172-4755-6.

The threatened cultures described in this book have been affected by environmental change, social problems, outside influences and loss of language and other cultural identifiers. The format, with photographs, sidebars and explanations, is suitable for elementary students, while the text is occasionally technical. Much attention is paid to the lifestyles of the indigenous peoples who are the focus of the book. Most middle schools and some elementary schools will find this both useful and thought provoking.

Biography

See also specific subject areas, such as **Ethnic Minorities, Literature** and **Women's Studies** for other biographical sources.

BIBLIOGRAPHIES AND INDEXES

243 **Biography Index.** New York: Wilson, 1946– . quarterly. $135.00/yr. ISSN 0006-3053.

Published since 1946 in four quarterly updates and a bound cumulation, this is a guide to material appearing in the more than 2,800 periodicals indexed in Wilson publications, other biographical periodicals, approximately 2,000 current books of individual and collective biography and as incidental biographical material in other books. It covers biographies and autobiographies, fiction, obituaries, collections of letters, diaries, memoirs, juvenile literature and book reviews. It is international in scope and covers all subject areas. Arranged alphabetically by biographee with cross-references, there is also an index to professions and occupations. Keys to periodicals and a checklist of books analyzed allow transition from the citations and serve as a selection tool for general biographical collections.

Biography Index is also available in several electronic formats with coverage beginning from July 1987 and including a quarter of a million records. Access is via Wilsonline, as a CD-ROM (Wilsondisc), and on the WilsonWeb. Electronic access permits both controlled vocabulary and keyword searching.

244 Breen, Karen. **Index to Collective**
E+ **Biographies for Young Readers**. 4th ed. New Providence, N.J.: R. R. Bowker, 1988. 494p. $48.00. ISBN 0-8352-2348-5.

This is a buying guide, an evaluation tool, and a reference index. It is an alphabetical listing of individuals whose biographies have appeared in collective biographies primarily written for elementary and junior high school students, with some high school and adult titles as well. More than 12,000 people from 1,200 books are identified and indexed by book. The work is inclusive rather than selective; the list of titles is gathered from the holdings of libraries, from the *Elementary School Library Catalog*, from *Books in Print*, and from queries to publishers. Individuals are listed alphabetically with subject identifier and a key to the collective biography. There is a list of subject headings used, as well as a classified list of biographies. There is an index by title, and a guide to the keys used for the books.

245 **Research Guide to American Historical Biography**. 5v. Washington, D.C.: Beacham Pub., 1991. $189.00. ISBN 0-933833-09-1.

246 **Research Guide to Biography and Criticism**. 2v. Washington, D.C.: Research Pub., 1992. $139.00. ISBN 0-933833-27-X.

247 **Research Guide to European Historical Biography, 1450–Present**. 8v. Vols. 1–4, Washington, D.C.: Beacham Pub., 1992. $299.00. ISBN 0-933833-28-8, Vols. 5–8, Washington, D.C.: Beacham Pub., 1993. $299.00. ISBN 0-933833-30-X.

The first three volumes of *Research Guide to American Historical Biography* cover more than 275 men and women who made significant contributions to society whether in government, business, labor, education, or other areas. For each signed entry there is a chronology, and an indication of the individual's historical significance. An overview of sources and an evaluation of the principal sources indicates "A" if an academic source, "G" if for general audiences, and "Y" for young people. In addition to typical biographical sources (including children's biographies), fiction books, films, plays and places (museums and landmarks) are listed. Volumes 4 and 5 focus on another 170 people, with an emphasis on women, minorities, Native Americans, explorers, artists, and entertainers. Each volume has a cumulative index. The Appendices in each volume group the entries by era and have state listings of the museums and landmarks. Two other bibliographies by the same publisher and following the same format are *Research Guide to Biography and Criticism*, which covers literary figures and *Research Guide to European Historical Biography, 1450–Present* which covers 400 men and women influential in the development of Europe. Recommended for high schools especially for the non-traditional listings.

DICTIONARIES AND ENCYCLOPEDIAS

248 **Biography Today: Profiles of People**
E **of Interest to Young Readers**. Detroit, Mich.: Omnigraphics, 1992– . quarterly. $52.00. ISSN 0933-5315.

This source follows the same publishing pattern as *Newsmakers* with three paperbound issues and one cumulative hardbound volume. The individuals profiled include the kinds of celebrity figures students from 4th to 8th grade would recognize from sports and television and music. Also included are child celebrities such as winners of spelling bees and other national contests. Information provided focuses on the individual's childhood, youth, education and early memories as well as more typical biographical material. Photographs and suggestions for further reading accompany each entry. The reading level is appropriate for the audience.

The annual cumulation has name, place of birth, birthday and general (occupations, ethnic origin, etc.) indexes. This is a reasonable choice for current biographical information in an elementary school library, and some middle schools may prefer this to *Newsmakers* or *Contemporary Biography*.

249 Concise Dictionary of American Biography. 4th ed. New York: Scribner's, 1990. 1536p. $155.00. ISBN 0-684-19188-1.

All individuals from the *Dictionary of American Biography* and its supplements are integrated into one alphabetical list in this volume. The abridged entries include only dates, ancestry, education and accomplishments and range in length from minimal (2–14 lines) to medium (15 lines to a full column with some specifics such as titles, battles, significance) to extended (multipage with details). Errors have been corrected and new data included. Most middle and high school libraries will prefer the original and longer set, but cost may dictate the condensed version.

250 Crystal, David, ed. **Cambridge Biographical Dictionary**. New York: Cambidge University Press, 1996. 495p. $16.95pa. ISBN 0-521-56780-7.

Published in the U.K. as *Chambers Biographical Dictionary*, this standard tool is international in scope and includes both living and deceased figures. This edition emphasized the addition of women and individuals from the twentieth century. Criteria for inclusion are achievement and recognition, and entries reflect an assessment of the significance of an individual's contribution. This is an outstanding comprehensive biographical source, and is recommended for secondary schools.

251 **Current Biography Yearbook**. New
E+ York: Wilson, 1955– . annual. $78.00. ISSN 0084-9499.

252 **Current Biography**. New York: Wilson, 1940– . annual. $72.00. ISSN 0011-3344.

Published monthly except December as a periodical and annually as a yearbook, *Current Biography* lists approximately 20 people in each monthly edition and about 200 in each annual. The contents are alphabetical, but there is a list of contents by occupation/area of achievement. Indexes cumulate through each decade, and a separate cumulative index covering 1940–1990 is

available. The profiles are objective, accurate, and updated in new volumes when appropriate. Most are reviewed by the biographee before they are printed in the yearbook. Entries include name and pronunciation, birth and other basic information, and an address where the individual may be reached. Long articles emphasize achievement, each is accompanied by a photograph and a list of further reading. All volumes contain obituaries.

253 **Current Biography 1940–Present**. Bronx, N.Y.: H. W. Wilson, 1996. CD-ROM (Macintosh, Windows, and WilsonWeb). $499.00 (1–4 users). renewal $149.00.

254 **Current Biography 1983–Present**. Bronx, N.Y.: H. W. Wilson, 1996. CD-ROM (Macintosh, Windows). $239.00 (1–4 users).

All 13,500 biographies and 8,500 obituaries published in *Current Biography* since it began in 1940 now appear on one CD-ROM. The data base is searchable by name, profession, place of origin, gender, race/ethnicity, date of birth, and keyword. A smaller data base, *Current Biography 1983–Present* is also available.

255 **Dictionary of American Biography**. 10v. and 10 suppl. New York: Scribner's, 1928– . $1599.99. ISBN 0-68419-075-3.

256 **Dictionary of American Biography, Comprehensive Index**. New York: Scribner's, 1996. 1091p. $110.00. ISBN 0-68480-482-4.

Modeled after the *British Dictionary of National Biography*, the *DAB* is the definitive source of historical biography. Individuals are not included until several years after their death, so as to insure some objective measure of their lasting significance. It now includes almost 20,000 names and efforts have been made in recent years to include more women and minorities. The 10th supplement brings the set to individuals who died before 1980. Essays are written by scholars and are interesting and easy enough for most middle school students to understand. Highly recommended for all secondary schools.

257 Byers, Paula Kay and Suzanne Michele Bourgoin, eds, **Encyclopedia of World Biography**. 2d ed. Detroit, Mich.: Gale Research, 1998. 17v. $975.00. ISBN 0-7876-2221-4.

First published by McGraw-Hill in 1973 with supplements through 1995, this new edition by Gale Research combines the 7,000 entries from the first edition and the supplements in one set with updated and revised information. Five hundred additional entries for women and multicultural individuals have been added. Coverage includes historical and contemporary figures from all parts of the world. Portraits and photographs as well as brief introductions about the significance of each entry add interest and understanding to the signed articles of about 800 words; each entry contains a bibliography. The extensive index in volume 17 includes places and events as well as names. Category and subcategory topics bring together names of relevant individuals; for example, under the heading "Stamp Act" there are lists of its defenders and opponents. Entries relate to every curricular area, and are written in an appropriate manner for secondary students. The set is highly recommended for middle and high schools.

258 Magill, Frank N., ed. **Great Lives**
E+   **from History: American Series**. 5v. Pasadena, Calif.: Salem Press, 1989. $365.00. ISBN 0-89356-551-2.

259 Magill, Frank N., ed. **Great Lives from History: Ancient and Medieval Series**. 5v. Pasadena, Calif.: Salem Press, 1988. $365.00. ISBN 0-89356-545-8.

260 Magill, Frank N., ed. **Great Lives from History: British and Commonwealth Series**. 5v. Pasadena, Calif.: Salem Press, 1987. $365.00. ISBN 0-89356-535-0.

261 Magill, Frank N., ed. **Great Lives from History: Renaissance to 1900 Series**. 5v. Pasadena, Calif.: Salem Press, 1989. $365.00. ISBN 0-89356-551-2.

262 Magill, Frank N., ed. **Great Lives from History: Twentieth Century Series**. 5v. Pasadena, Calif.: Salem Press, 1990. $365.00. ISBN 0-89356-565-2.

These multi-volume sets each contain more than 450 biographies. Individuals were selected from all phases of life including politics, the arts, science, and in the volumes covering more contemporary history, entertainment and sports. Each signed entry is about 2,000 words and covers areas of achievement and an evaluation of the person's contribution. Basic biographical information is also covered, such as early life and career. Each entry has a bibliography. There are indexes of names with cross-references, of areas of achievement, and of places with which the individuals were associated. Although the articles are written by scholars, the information is easily understood and the sources are recommended for middle and high schools.

263 McGuire, William and Leslie Wheeler, eds. **American Social Leaders**. Santa Barbara, Calif.: ABC-CLIO, 1993. 500p. $65.00. ISBN 0-87436-633-X.

The subjects in this biographical encyclopedia are social reformers from colonial times to the present. The individuals were selected because they led movements that affected government, human rights, justice, education, values, equality, peace, physical fitness, the environment, and consumer protection. Included are figures such as Jimmy Hoffa and Abbie Hoffman, both Andrew and Dale Carnegie, Carry Nation and Ralph Nader, and both Martin Luther and Coretta Scott King. Each 1–2 page entry has an assessment of the contributions based on the individual's total career, and a bibliography. Listings are alphabetical with cross-references and the source has good type face, some photographs, and entries are easy to read. Recommended for secondary school collections as a supplement to other biographical sources. [R: ARBA 94]

264 **Merriam-Webster's Biographical**
E+   **Dictionary**. Springfield, Mass.: Merriam-Webster, 1995. 1184p. $27.95. ISBN 0-87779-743-9.

This standard source was completely revised in 1988 and is updated and reprinted often. It lists more than 30,000 historical figures from all times and from all countries, but with an American and British emphasis. Pronunciations, variant spellings of names and pseudonyms are given with brief identification annotations. This useful source should be in all collections.

265 **Newsmakers**. Detroit, Mich.: Gale Research, 1988– . quarterly. $93.00/yr. ISSN 0899-0417.

Published three times a year as a magazine and once as an annual cumulated hard copy, *Newsmakers* highlights living Americans of current interest. About 200 profiles appear in the annual volumes. A table of contents identifies individuals included and for each entry there is a picture, and clear headings divide the article into career, sidelights, and quote boxes. There is a bibliography with each entry. Annual volumes have nationality, occupation, and subject indexes for the year and a total cumulative index for the series since its beginning as *Contemporary Newsmakers* in 1985. There is not a great deal of duplication with *Current Biography*, and secondary schools will want to consider both titles.

266 **Nobel Prize Winners: An H. W. Wilson Biographical Dictionary**. Bronx, N.Y.: H. W. Wilson, 1987. 1165p. $90.00. ISBN 0-8242-0756-4.

267 **Nobel Prize Winners: Supplement 1987–1991**. Bronx, N.Y.: H. W. Wilson, 1992. 143p. $35.00. ISBN 0-8242-0834-X.

268 **Nobel Prize Winners: 1992–1996 Supplement**. Bronx, N.Y.: H. W. Wilson, 1997. 160p. $35.00. ISBN 0-8242-0906-0.

Winners of the Nobel Prize from 1901 to 1986, including 566 men, women and institutions are arranged in alphabetical order. There are introductions to Alfred Nobel and to the award, and a list by type of award and year. Entries are from 5 to 6 columns and emphasize the work for which the individual won the award, as well as standard biographical information. Each entry includes a photograph of the winner and a bibliography of both book and periodical information about the individual and books by the individual. The first supplement includes a list of all the winners from 1901 to 1991 and biographies of the winners from 1987 to 1991. The second updates the series by including winners from 1992 to 1996. This series is recommended especially because of the emphasis on the winner's body of work that resulted in the awarding of the prize, and because it is useful to many curricular areas.

269 Schlessinger, Bernard S. and June
E+ H. Schlessinger, eds. **The Who's Who of Nobel Prize Winners, 1901–1995**. 3d ed. Phoenix, Ariz.: Oryx Press, 1996. 251p. $49.95. ISBN 0-89774-899-9.

The arrangement of this source, by kind of award (literature, chemistry, peace, and so on) and date adds an element of historical development to the primary purpose of providing biographical information about the winners. Each signed entry gives the name of the winner and the prize as well as birth and death dates, information about parents, spouse(s) and children. There is a list of selected publications by the individual and a list of sources for more information. A brief commentary is also included. There is an introduction explaining the awards, and indexes by name, educational institution, nationality and religion refer the user to the entry number. This source would be an appropriate reference for any school library.

270 **Who's Who in America**. Chicago: A. N. Marquis, 1899– . biennial. $450.00. ISSN 0083-9396.

This remains the standard source of identification of living Americans with positions of responsibility and levels of significant achievement from federal, state, and local government, the military, business, institutions, the professions, and entertainment. Each entry supplies basic biographical information, including occupation, family education, awards, religion, and address; the most significant information concerns career development: activities, writing, and work. Volume 3 provides geographic, profession, and retiree indexes and a necrology.

Who Was Who in America (Chicago, Marquis) contains entries removed from *Who's Who in America* at the death of the biographee and includes, as a historical record, individuals from 1607. Regional editions of *Who's Who* are also available, such as *Who's Who in the Midwest*.

NICKNAMES AND PSEUDONYMS

271 Mossman, Jennifer, ed. **Pseudonyms and Nicknames Dictionary**. 3d ed. 2v. Detroit, Mich.: Gale Research, 1986. $239.00. ISBN 0-8103-0541-0.

First published in 1980 with only contemporary figures, and expanded in a second edition to include historical figures as well, the third edition contains 80,000 pseudonyms and nicknames used by over 55,000 individuals. The scope is international and from all time periods. Authors, entertainers, athletes, fashion designers, guerilla leaders, gunfighters, and cult leaders are all included. Entries are cross-referenced and give real names and basic biographical information. Citations to sources for the information are given.

272 Room, Adrian. **A Dictionary of Pseudonyms and Their Origins: With Stories of Name Changes**. Jefferson, N.C.: McFarland, 1989. $45.00. ISBN 0-89950-450-7.

After seven interesting chapters on names, why people change their names (and a chapter on people who kept their original names), the main part of this resource lists about 4,000 pseudonymous names. Entries were selected because the people are familiar, but some were chosen just because of their interesting stories. The story behind each name change is the unique quality of this source which also gives original name, years of birth and death, nationality and occupation. Arrangement is alphabetical by pseudonym with multiple pseudonyms linked. Included are popes, actresses, musicians, authors, politicians, and historical figures. There is a bibliography. This is the kind of source one goes to for a quick answer and then spends 20 minutes more, just browsing. High school libraries will find it useful.

273 Sharp, Harold S., comp. **Handbook of Pseudonyms and Personal Nicknames**. 2v. Lanham, Md.: Scarecrow Press, 1972. $59.50/set. ISBN 0-8108-0460-3.

274 Sharp, Harold S., comp. **Handbook of Pseudonyms and Personal Nicknames: First Supplement**. 2v. Lanham, Md.: Scarecrow Press, 1975. $82.50. ISBN 0-8108-0807-2.

275 Sharp, Harold S., comp. **Handbook of Pseudonyms and Personal Nicknames: Second Supplement**. Lanham, Md.: Scarecrow Press, 1982. 289p. $35.00. ISBN 0-8108-1539-7.

Together these volumes list about 37,000 people who have been known by pseudonyms or nicknames. Individuals are listed in alphabetical order by their original names with cross-references from nicknames and/or pseudonyms. Each entry gives the "real" name, birth and death dates, identification, nationality, and occupation. Coverage is worldwide and both historical and contemporary. This is a comprehensive source for secondary schools.

276 Urdang, Laurence, ed. **Twentieth Century American Nicknames**. Bronx, N.Y.: H. W. Wilson, 1979. 398p. $42.00. ISBN 0-8242-0642-8.

Twentieth Century American Nicknames updates and complements Shankle's *American Nicknames* (2d ed., Wilson, 1955). These sources not only include well-known people such as politicians, military figures, socialites, entertainers and gangsters, but also American cities and towns, states, and professional and college sports teams, horses, places, restaurants, companies, and government agencies. Each original name is listed and described with cross-references from nicknames. Highly recommended for middle and high schools for general reference and for American studies classes.

Business and Economics

See also **Consumer Education (Consumer Information)**.

ALMANACS AND HANDBOOKS

277 Argenti, Paul A., ed. **The Portable MBA Desk Reference: An Essential Business Companion**. New York: Wiley, 1994. 688p. $29.95. ISBN 0-471-57681-6.

This is for the business generalist, the student and anyone who needs information about business terms. It covers the disciplines of accounting, marketing, managing, economics, finance, international business, manufacturing and business strategy. Entries were reviewed by a board of experts and are particularly noteworthy for being written in non-technical language. Part 1 is an alphabetical listing of phrases, rules, principles, theories, laws, and trends. Articles begin with a concise definition and then include descriptions, discussions, and/or examples. Part 2 is a bibliography of sources of business information arranged in 48 headings. Citations are annotated. Seventeen useful appendices contain top 100 company lists, directories of federal agencies and statistical information. Page edges are labeled for quick access to the proper section. This is an excellent source to support business, government and current events assignments. Highly recommended for all high school collections. [R: ARBA 95]

278 DeVries, Mary A. **The Complete Secretary's Handbook**. 7th ed. Englewood Cliffs, N.J.: Prentice-Hall, 1993. 664p. $19.95. ISBN 0-13-159666-7.

This is a book for everyone as word processing and other computer applications tend to make each person his/her own secretary. It is as much about organizational skills as about office practice skills. It includes model letters and compares and integrates computer information with traditional topics. Details of management such as keeping records, files, and calendars are included. A glossary and an excellent index make this a tool to fill many information requests. [R: ARBA 94]

279 Downes, John and Jordan Elliot Goodman. **Finance and Investment Handbook**. 4th ed. Woodbury, N.Y.: Barron's, 1995. 1392p. $35.00. ISBN 0-8120-6465-8.

Now in a 4th edition, this is a combination handbook, dictionary, and guide to general investment finance. One section describes 30 key investment alternatives and variations with minimum purchase amounts, risks, and tax implications. Other chapters show how to read and analyze corporate reports and financial pages. There is a 50,000 key term dictionary and a ready reference section that is largely a directory of sources of information, major financial institutions, mutual funds, and public trading companies located in the U.S. and Canada. Appendices include a chart of the currencies of the world. There is a general index. Recommended for both general information and as support for economics and business curricula in high school libraries.

280 **Hoover's Handbook of American Business: Profiles of Major U.S. Companies**. Austin, Tex.: Reference Press, Inc., 1992– . annual. $79.95/set. ISSN 1055-7202.

281 **Hoover's Handbook of World Business**. Austin, Tex.: Reference Press, Inc., 1992– . annual. $39.95; $29.95pa. ISSN 1055-7199.

Hoover's Handbooks have quickly become indispensable tools for tracking businesses world wide. Beginning as a one-volume list of 500 public and private companies, the current format separates businesses into more manageable volumes. Each title provides company profiles that give trading information, an overview of the company, its history, its executives, and location(s). Summaries of what the company does, its key competitors, and its financial performance complete the profiles. Emphasis is on the largest and most influential companies. *American Business* has more than 750 profiles in 2 volumes; *World Business* has more than 225 global "giants" from Europe, South America, and Asia who do business in the United States. The handbooks have lists of biggest, best, top paying, and other superlatives. Information pages are well designed and easy to interpret. High schools will find these guides essential for any curriculum area that covers business and industry.

Hoover's makes information available in a variety of formats in addition to the handbooks. There are smaller paperback editions, a CD-ROM (*Hoover's Company and Industry DataBase on CD-ROM*), a fax service (*Company Profiles on Demand*) for individual company profiles available 24 hours a day, 7 days a week for a small fee, and a Web site (www.hoovers.com—also available as a service on AOL, and Lexis-Nexis).

282 **The Irwin Business and Investment Almanac.** Chicago: Irwin Professional Pub., 1996. annual. $75.00. ISSN 1072-6136.

The standard almanac in business and investment, this source uses summaries, graphs and statistics to describe current business indicators. There is a review of the business year (October–September), industry surveys, and sections on U.S. trade, regional and international data, largest companies, and other issues relating to economic matters. A list of financial terms, a state information guide, and a business information directory are also included. The detailed table of contents and index help locate data. This source is appropriate for high schools.

BIOGRAPHY

283 Ingham, John N. and Lynne B. Feldman. **Contemporary American Business Leaders: A Biographical Dictionary.** Westport, Conn.: Greenwood Press, 1990. 788p. $105.00. ISBN 0-313-25743-4.

This is an extension of the four-volume *Biographical Dictionary of American Business Leaders* (1983) and a companion to *African American Business Leaders* (1994). The dictionary adds 150 individuals who have been important and influential in business since the end of World War II. Students will recognize such names as Bill Gates, Steve Jobs, Donald Trump, Anne Klein, and Frank Perdue; other entries are under company names and include multiple biographies about several executives. There are also some joint entries, such as Christie and Hugh Hefner. Each entry gives a biography with emphasis on the

business career and includes a bibliography of works both by and about the individual. An appendix lists subjects by industry, company, geographical location, and birthplace. There are 7 African Americans and 12 women in the dictionary. A good index includes personal names, company names, and product names. Recommended for schools that need biographical information that provides depth on business careers, and for American culture and economics classes.

DICTIONARIES AND ENCYCLOPEDIAS

284 **Encyclopedia of American Business History and Biography: The Airline Industry.** New York: Facts on File, 1992. 531p. $85.00. ISBN 0-8160-2675-0.

285 **Encyclopedia of American Business History and Biography: The Automobile Industry, 1896–1920.** New York: Facts on File, 1990. 485p. $85.00. ISBN 0-8160-2084-1.

286 **Encyclopedia of American Business History and Biography: The Automobile Industry, 1920–1980.** New York: Facts on File, 1989. 520p. $85.00. ISBN 0-8160-2083-3.

287 **Encyclopedia of American Business History and Biography: Banking and Finance to 1913.** New York: Facts on File, 1990. 528p. $85.00. ISBN 0-8160-2193-7.

288 **Encyclopedia of American Business History and Biography: Banking and Finance, 1913–1989.** New York: Facts on File, 1990. 505p. $85.00. ISBN 0-8160-2194-5.

289 **Encyclopedia of American Business History and Biography: Iron and Steel in the Nineteenth Century.** New York: Facts on File, 1989. 381p. $85.00. ISBN 0-8160-1890-1.

290 **Encyclopedia of American Business History and Biography: Iron and**

Steel in the Twentieth Century. New York: Facts on File, 1994. 512p. $85.00. ISBN 0-8160-2195-3.

291 **Encyclopedia of American Business History and Biography: Railroads in the Nineteenth Century**. New York: Facts on File, 1988. 491p. $85.00. ISBN 0-8160-2012-4.

292 **Encyclopedia of American Business History and Biography: Railroads in the Age of Regulation, 1900–1980**. New York: Facts on File, 1988. 518p. $85.00. ISBN 0-8160-1371-3.

Volumes of the *Encyclopedia of American Business History and Biography* are published separately, and have been classified separately, but if the complete encyclopedia is purchased, may be more useful in a school library when kept as a set. Each business or industry is generally covered in two volumes, separated chronologically. Alphabetically arranged entries are on business or industrial figures and the businesses. The intent of the series is to present the history of the impact of business on American life. Standard entries are from 3,000 to 5,000 words although entries for major figures such as Henry Ford and Howard Hughes may be 10,000 words. Each biography entry includes basic data, a picture, references, and emphasizes the individual's career. Articles about business and industry matters include such things as history, relevant legislation, conferences, and labor issues. Individual titles and the entire encyclopedia are recommended for high schools, depending on need; they are useful for economics, American studies, and industrial arts curricula.

293 Friedman, Jack P. **Dictionary of Business Terms**. 2d ed. New York: Barron's, 1994. 700p. $11.95pa. ISBN 0-8120-1833-8.

Business students and everyone else in a school will find this dictionary useful. Clear concise vocabulary that defines, explains, and gives examples, and more than 7,000 entries about accounting, advertising, business law, marketing, real estate, and other topics make this a good choice to support many aspects of curriculum. Arranged in alphabetical order with cross-references, this dictionary is recommended for high school libraries.

294 **How Products Are Made: An Illustrated Guide to Product Manufacturing**. Detroit, Mich.: Gale Research, 1994– . biennial. $75.00. ISSN 1072-5091.

Planned to produce a new volume with approximately 100 products every two years, this series describes the background, history, raw materials, design, manufacturing process, quality control, by-products, and future for manufactured products such as food, clothing, appliances, tools, sports equipment, and furniture. Products included are as varied as condoms and cat litter. The manufacturing process is illustrated with black and white photographs or drawings. Entries are arranged alphabetically and are multiple pages. There is a separate index for each volume. This source answers hard to find reference questions about many manufacturing processes, and is suitable for middle school as well as high school. [R: ARBA 95]

295 Jorgensen, Janice, ed. **Encyclopedia of Consumer Brands**. 3v. Detroit, Mich.: St. James Press, 1994. $260.00/set. ISBN 1-55862-335-3.

The three volumes are divided by type of product. Volume 1 includes consumable products: food, pet food, beverages and tobacco. There are over 200 multiple page entries about the brand, its history, marketing, advertising, and the product itself. There is an at-a-glance fact box, and a list for further reading attached to each signed entry. Volume 2 follows the same pattern for personal products: clothes, cosmetics, health, cleaning, non-prescription drugs, and office supplies. Volume 3 includes durable goods: appliances, cars, electronics, furniture, cameras, sporting goods, and toys. There is an index to names, to companies and persons and to brand categories. This set has many uses, the obvious curricular relationships are to any aspect of business, consumer science, economics, commercial art, current events, industrial arts, and sociology, and as a focus for planning interdisciplinary units among these subjects. [R: ARBA 95]

296 Pearce, David W., ed. **The MIT Dictionary of Modern Economics**. 4th ed. Cambridge, Mass.: MIT Press, 1992. 474p. $40.00; $15.95pa. ISBN 0-262-16132-X; 0-262-66078-4pa.

This authoritative and regularly updated dictionary is appropriate for high school teachers and advanced students. It contains almost 3,000 entries, including words, phrases, concepts, and institutions, as well as biographical entries for winners of the Nobel Award for Economics; and has broadened its scope from pure economics by adding business terms. Its listings are international, but with a British and American emphasis. Entries generally vary from one paragraph to a column (although the Keynes biography is four columns). There are some mathematical formulae and models. [R: ARBA 93]

297 Rosenberg, Jerry Martin. **Dictionary of Business and Management**. New York: Wiley, 1993. 374p. $39.95; $14.95pa. ISBN 0-471-57812-6; 0-471-54536-8pa.

The author, a graduate professor at Rutgers University and the author of similar works on banking and investment, has updated this dictionary to include over 7,500 entries from accounting to advertising to business law to economics to government to the stock market. Alphabetical definitions with synonyms and separate meanings for each discipline are clear, concise, and understandable for both the expert and students. Appendices include useful statistical tables. This is a good business dictionary for high school collections. [R: ARBA 95]

298 Siegel, Joel G., Jae K. Shim and Stephen Hartman. **Dictionary of Personal Finance**. New York: Macmillan, 1992. 391p. $70.00. ISBN 0-02897393-3.

Despite the authors' absurd attitude that "personal finance and financial planning are the most important areas affecting individuals..." this dictionary will be useful in secondary school collections. It includes terms found in the popular financial press which deal with all aspects of money management and consumer concerns. It covers accounting, taxes, debt management, finance, investments, banking, housing, insurance, business law, career planning, retirement and estate planning, and claims to cover "any other related fields" although one might note, for example the omission of any entry for "tithing." Arrangement is alphabetical with cross-references, and the good

typeface, clear explanations, wide applications, minimal mathematics, and seven useful appendices make it especially helpful. [R: ARBA 93]

299 Taylor, Paul F. **The ABC-CLIO Companion to the American Labor Movement**. Santa Barbara, Calif.: ABC-CLIO, 1993. 237p. $55.00. ISBN 0-87436-687-9.

Intended for both the general reader and the scholar, this encyclopedia covers the years 1828–1981. The language is easy to understand and the explanations are clear and concise. Illustrations add to the narrative. Included are labor leaders, major unions, court decisions, legislation, and opposition to the labor movement. Entries are in alphabetical order with cross-references and there is a chronology beginning in 1828. There is a bibliography and an index. This is an excellent source and is highly recommended for high school collections. [R: ARBA 95]

300 Terry, John V. **Dictionary for Business & Finance**. 3d ed. Fayetteville, Ark.: University of Arkansas Press, 1995. 405p. $18.00pa. ISBN 1-55728-344-3.

Now in its third edition, this dictionary has quickly become a standard source of business definitions for students. Coverage includes such fields as banking, investing, insurance, real estate, economics, statistics, and legal and tax terms associated with these subjects. This edition adds 200 terms to ensure currentcy. Arrangement is alphabetical, and entries are encyclopedic in nature. High schools with business programs will need this dictionary. [R: ARBA 96]

DIRECTORIES

301 **Editor and Publisher Market Guide**. New York: Editor and Publisher, 1943– . annual. $50.00. ISBN 0-9646564-3-3.

Intended as a marketing guide for print advertising, this annual statistical guide forecasts retail sales for the United States and Canada by state or province and cities with one or more daily newspapers. Tables include population, disposable and total household incomes, total retail sales in a number of areas, e.g. food, apparel, and gasoline. City information includes names of stores, banks, industries, and military and educational institutions. There are also state and province summaries. This kind of information is useful not only for marketing classes, but also for general information about states and cities not usually so easily available in traditional sources. Possibilities for math and social studies integrated units are abundant.

302 Gelbert, Doug. **Company Museums, Industry Museums and Industrial Tours: A Guidebook of Sites in the United States That Are Open to the Public.** Jefferson, N.C.: McFarland, 1994. 314p. $45.00. ISBN 0-89950-916-9.

More than 500 museums and tours of American industry are listed alphabetically by state. Entries give location, phone number, admission fees, hours, directions and a narrative of highlights. Sites related to both whole industries (agriculture, business, communication, energy, fishing, food and beverage, forest products, health services, manufacturing, mining, public services and transportation) and individual companies are listed. Only those sites with regularly scheduled public tours are included. An appendix lists sites by industry and there is a site (name) index. There are some obvious omissions and some misleading and missing cross-referencing, but this remains a useful tool for planning school field trips and family vacations, as well as a source for addresses for informational materials in studies of American industry. Appropriate for secondary collections. [R: ARBA 95]

SMALL BUSINESS

303 Lonier, Terri. **Working Solo Sourcebook: Essential Resources for Independent Entrepeneurs.** New York: Portico Press, 1995. 315p. $24.95; $14.95pa. ISBN 1-883282-50-0; 1-883282-60-8pa.

This is both a directory and a bibliography of resources for entrepreneurs. Over 1,000 sources of supplies, equipment, seminars and workshops are listed with sidebars of tips and techniques. Organized by 40 topics from advertising to customers to office supplies and equipment to taxes, there is a separate chapter on youthful entrepreneurs. Within each chapter is an annotated bibliography of books, magazines, and documents and an annotated directory. Cross-references lead across chapters and there is an index. This source can be used as a selection tool, as a general reference, and to support business education programs. [R: RBSL 96]

304 **The Source Book of Franchise Opportunities.** Burr Ridge, Ill.: Irwin Professional Pub, 1987– . annual. $35.00pa. ISSN 1056-8654.

An introduction to franchise operations is followed by descriptions of more than 3,000 franchise opportunities. Directory information is supplied for about 2,000 others. Franchises are listed by product or service type. Some of the entries are from the *U.S. Department of Commerce Franchise Opportunities Handbook*, but others are unique to this source.

Careers

See also **Guides to Free and Inexpensive Materials (Collection Management).**

BIBLIOGRAPHIES

305 LeCompte, Michelle, ed. **Job Hunter's Sourcebook: Where to Find Employment Leads and Other Job Search Resources**. 3d ed. Detroit, Mich.: Gale Research, 1996. 1106p. $70.00. ISBN 0-8103-9075-2.

This is a guide to finding a job as opposed to planning a career, and it is comprehensive and useful for anyone in the job market. Part 1 lists high-interest professional and vocational occupations in alphabetical order and lists sources of help-wanted ads, placement and referral services, and other resources including joblines and electronic lists. There is a master list of hundreds of alternate or related job titles with links to the main listing. Part 2 consists of essays with bibliographies on job-related issues; e.g., interviewing skills, working at home, part-time work, summer jobs, and internships. Recommended for high schools for vocational guidance units and for helping students looking for jobs.

DICTIONARIES, ENCYCLOPEDIAS, AND HANDBOOKS

306 **Career Discovery Encyclopedia**.
E+   6v. Chicago: J. G. Gerguson Publishing, 1997. $129.95/set. ISBN 0-89434-184-7.

The entries for occupations in this set are two pages in length and describe the work, preparation, current salaries and demand. There is a picture of a person engaged in the occupation and a list of addresses to write to for more information. There is a general index and an index to skill requirements. The information is presented clearly and is appropriate for upper elementary and middle school students.

307 **Dictionary of Occupational Titles**.
     4th ed. 2v. U.S. Employment Service. Washington, D.C.: Government Printing Office, 1995. $40.00. S/N 029-013-00079-9.

The Department of Labor has produced a standard list of jobs and their titles since the first edition of the *DOT* in 1939. The purpose of this standardization is to support employment and job search services. Each occupation is assigned a code (librarians in schools are 100.167-030), a job title, industry designations and alternate titles, related jobs, and statements that describe and define jobs as well as a definition trailer that suggests suitable ability, educational level, and strength, among other categories. An occupational group arrangement, an alphabetical index of titles and an index by industry designation make the document easier to use. High schools should have copies of this for reference collections and counselors' desks.

308 Hopke, William E., ed. **The Encyclopedia of Careers and Vocational Guidance**. 10th ed. 4v. Chicago, Ill.: Ferguson Publishing, 1996. $149.95. ISBN 0-8239-2532-3.

309 Hopke, William E., ed. **Encyclopedia of Careers & Vocational Guidance**. Chicago, Ill.: Ferguson Publishing, 1993. CD-ROM (Macintosh, Windows). $199.95. ISBN 0-89434-172-3; 0-89434-173-1.

This set has been updated about every three years since its first publication in 1967. It is the most comprehensive guide to occupations that most schools will need. Volume 1 consists of industry profiles arranged alphabetically with general information about each industry, business, or service occupation. Each profile discusses career opportunities, educational requirements and the outlook for the occupation. There are sources of additional information, and a comprehensive index. Volumes 2–4 list occupations, with their DOT numbers, alphabetically with comprehensive indexes in each volume. The set covers professional, technical, and general occupations and provides detailed information about aspects of the work, qualifications and preparation required, working conditions, earnings and career paths. The encyclopedia is highly recommended for middle school career units and for high school reference and guidance collections.

310 Krantz, Les. **National Business Employment Weekly Jobs Rated Almanac**. 3d ed. New York: J. Wiley, 1995. 340p. $16.95pa. ISBN 0-471-05495-X.

This source has undergone several title and publisher changes in its several editions, but *Jobs Rated Almanac* survives as part of the title. It rates 250 jobs by more than 12 factors, such as income, physical demands, security, stress, perks, and travel opportunities if applicable. Each category is introduced by a comments section. There are also overall rankings of each category, and a final inclusive ranking. This remains an inexpensive work and will be of interest to secondary students.

311 **Occupational Outlook Handbook**. Compiled by U.S. Department of Labor, Bureau of Labor Statistics. Washington, D.C.: Government Printing Office, 1959– . biennial. $38.00pa. S/N 029-001-03021-5.

The Department of Labor has published this handbook biennially since 1959 and it remains the first-purchased career source for any library. The 1996/97 (22d) edition lists 250 occupations that cover about 87% of all jobs held in the

United States. There is also a data section for occupations not completely described which covers another 5% of jobs held. There are some special features including sections on future jobs, career information sources, and suggestions on finding a job, but the most important information concerns the jobs themselves. For each of the 250 occupations, the source lists the DOT number, the nature of the work and working conditions, training and advancement possibilities, the job outlook, earnings and related occupations. There is a list of sources of additional information for each job. Occupations are listed within 12 categories, which seem to be in a hierarchy from executive, administrative and management, to professional to service to construction trades to handlers, helpers and laborers. There is also a section on the armed forces. It is necessary to use the contents or index for quick access to the occupations. The handbook is updated by the *Occupational Outlook Quarterly*. The Web edition of the handbook is found at http://stats.bls.gov:80/ocohome.htm.

DIRECTORIES

312 **Peterson's Hidden Job Market**. Princeton, N.J.: Peterson's Guides, 1995– . annual. $17.95. ISSN 1081-9800.

The title of this annual has changed, but it remains a guide to jobs in smaller fast-growing high-technology companies that are adding employees rapidly. This is a directory of such companies arranged alphabetically by state and company name. Each entry gives directory information, number of employees, company growth record, and a contact name. An industry index, a company index, and a metropolitan area index aid in locating opportunities. [R: ARBA 95]

313 **Peterson's Internships**. Princeton, N.J.: Peterson's Guides, 1995– . annual. $29.95. ISSN 1082-2577.

A few of these internships are open to high school students, and many schools will want access to the volume. Areas offering internships that are covered are business and technology (including hotels and motels), publishing, creative and performing arts, fine arts, museums and theaters, environment and parks, human services, law, criminal justice, and research; there are also international listings. Each internship listing gives an address, general information, availability, benefits, eligibility and a person to contact. A section offers suggestions on referral and placement. Indexes are by fields of interest, geography, and employer. [R: ARBA 95]

Consumer Information

314 Berliant, Adam. **Used Car Reliability and Safety Guide**. 2d ed. Cincinnati, Ohio: Betterway Books, 1997. 384p. $14.99pa. ISSN 1075-6248.

More than 840 makes and models of cars and trucks from 1983 to about 1993 are covered in this guide to the safest and most reliable purchases. The author is a specialist in analyzing government data and the information in this source comes from owners reports filed with the National Highway Traffic and Safety Administration. Problems are listed only if there are 50 or more complaints in general, or fewer complaints about specific problems. It does not include problems with tires. The main part of the book is a troubleshooter's guide listed by manufacturer and then model. For each entry there is a buyer's

summary, accident ratings, theft alert, recall alert, hotspots, controversy, and what specifically to test. Final sections include charts of safety comparisons and a recall index. There is also a glossary. Recommended for high school collections. [R: ARBA 96]

315 **Consumer Buying Guide**. Lincolnwood, Ill.: Publications International, 1978– . annual. $6.99pa. ISBN 0-451-19242-7 (1997 ed.)

Published by *Consumer Guide Magazine*, this source reviews such items as televisions, camcorders, other electronic products, appliances, power tools and fitness equipment. A good table of contents leads to products; there is no index. An excellent chapter introduction describes features and expectations of each type of product and the reviews follow. Comments about products are supplemented with various ratings such as "Budget Buy," "Best Buy," or simply "Recommended." This is a helpful guide.

316   Consumer Reports. **Buying Guide**. Yonkers, N.Y.: Consumers Union, 1947– . annual. 13th subscription issue.

Published in December of each year as part of the annual subscription to *Consumer Reports*, this guide covers appliances, home electronics and both new and used automobiles. It also lists product recalls from the past year and charts repair records for items such as television sets, ranges and vacuum cleaners. Articles cite the last issue of *Consumer Reports* to review the products and the index cites eight years of original reports.

317   Consumer Reports. **Cars: The Essential Guide for Buyers and Owners**. Yonkers, N.Y.: Consumers Union, 1997. CD-ROM (Windows). $17.95.

This CD-ROM includes information from the research of Consumers Union about cars, minivans, pickups and sport-utility vehicles from 1989–1998. Ratings and reliability records are reported and it is possible to match a vehicle to specific needs. A video sequence shows how to negotiate with a dealer. Leasing and maintenance are also covered. Recommended for high schools.

318   **Edmund's New Cars Prices & Reviews**. Beverly Hills, Calif.: Edmund Publications, 1996– . semiannual. $8.99pa. ISSN 1086-5470.

319   **Edmund's New Trucks Prices & Reviews**. Beverly Hills, Calif.: Edmund Publications, 1996– . semiannual. $8.99pa. ISSN 1089-8735.

Formerly *Edmund's New Cars Prices Buyer's Guide*, this source has been published for many years. It includes both American and imported cars and has begun to standardize the vocabulary used in describing the models. In addition to new car descriptions and ratings which report on new features, safety data, standard and optional equipment, base prices and accessories, there are useful essays about car shopping. A glossary of car buying, a 10-step guide to buying a new car, editor's picks, charts of specs and EPA mileage ratings, crash test data and many other useful sections make this an indispensable tool for new car buying.

New Trucks follows the same format to discuss pickups, vans, and sport utility vehicles, and will also be used in high school collections.

320   **Edmund's Used Cars Prices & Ratings**. Beverly Hills, Calif.: Edmund Publications, 1995– . semiannual, $7.99pa. ISSN 1086-8035.

Formerly *Edmund's Used Cars Prices*, and published for more than 30 years, this guide describes models from the past ten years, both American and imported. It includes cars, trucks, vans and SUVs. Brief descriptions rate used cars in terms of safety, reliability, performance, comfort and value, with an overall rating as well. Trade-in, market values and a value-adjustment table provide information to the consumer. Both reference and circulating copies should be purchased for high school collections.

321   Gillis, Jack and Mary Ellen R. Fise. **The Childwise Catalog: A Consumer Guide to Buying the Safest and Best Products for Your Children, Newborns through Age Five**. 3d ed. New York: HarperCollins, 1993. 472p. $14.00pa. ISBN 0-06-273182-3.

This source is published under the auspices of the Consumer Federation of America. Using narrative, checklists, tables, and charts the safety of children is covered through chapters on child care, health matters, food and diet, travel, making the child's environment safe inside and outside, and protection from abuse and kidnapping. A long section lists products within three age categories: newborn to six months, . . . to two years, and . . . through five years. There is a directory of products and services and an index. Recommended to support curricula in health, family living and sociology classes, and for schools with parenting collections. [R: ARBA 94]

Current Social Issues

See also **Psychology, Sociology** and **Health and Family (Science)**.

322 Adamec, Christine A. and William L. Pierce. **The Encyclopedia of Adoption**. New York: Facts on File, 1991. 382p. $50.00. ISBN 0-8160-2108-2.

The encyclopedia brings together information on adoption from a variety of disciplines and is intended to be a source for both experts and general readers. Entries are not technical, for the most part, and are easy to understand. Articles vary in length, but tend to be multi-page with subcategories and references. Since the source is multidisciplinary, it has information that can supplement sociology, psychology, family living, health and even history curricula (there is a good entry on the Orphan Train). Nine appendices are included: some are tabular, some directory, and there is a list of periodicals and newsletters. A bibliography and index complete the volume. [R: ARBA 93]

323 Costa, Marie. **Abortion: A Reference Handbook**. 2d ed. Santa Barbara, Calif.: ABC-CLIO, 1996. 339p. $39.50. ISBN 0-87436-827-8.

This is a balanced resource and guide to further information. The author has made an effort to cover the wide range of opinion about the subject and this is reflected in the language used and the information included in every section of the work. Information is presented and resources recommended about social, psychological, legal, medical, political, and moral aspects of the issues. The first chapter discusses the historical context of abortion and contains a chronology. The biographical section is balanced between those who defend and oppose abortion. Another section covers statistical information and reviews legal issues. There is a directory of organizations (again reflecting the myriad points of view) and annotated bibliographies of both print and nonprint materials. A glossary and an index complete the work. The second edition updates much of the material, and those owning the first edition should replace it. Highly recommended. [R: ARBA 97]

324 **The CQ Researcher**. Washington, D.C.: Congressional Quarterly, 1991– . annual. $309.00. ISSN 1056-2036.

Reports on topics of current interest in politics, science, and the arts, of about 12,000 words are issued four times a month with quarterly paperback and annual cumulations with cumulative indexes. Each report includes an annotated table of contents, and covers an overview of the issue, background, chronology, current situation, opposite viewpoints, and an outlook. There are illustrations, charts, graphs and sidebars with bibliographies and additional information sources. Topics are all of current interest such as cloning, sports gender equity, and alcohol advertising. The reports provide enough basic data for anyone to become informed on these issues. Also available via the Internet. Highly recommended for high school libraries.

325 Flanders, Carl N. **Abortion**. New York: Facts on File, 1991. 256p. $24.95. ISBN 0-8160-1908-8.

326 Flanders, Stephen A. **Capital Punishment**. New York: Facts on File, 1991. 208p. $24.95. ISBN 0-8160-1912-6.

Each of the volumes in the Library in a Book series is designed as a "one-step source of information," giving background information in part 1 and a guide to sources in part 2. The first section includes a historical survey; statistics; attitudes and trends; a chronology (1965 through 1989 for *Abortion* and 1924 through 1989 for *Capital Punishment*); significant court cases, with background, legal issues, decisions, and impact; and biographical data for persons who have played leading roles in the controversy.

The bibliographic section offers a generic library search (e.g., using the library catalog, indexes), a bibliographic essay on basic sources; and an annotated bibliography that cites books, articles, government documents, brochures and pamphlets, audiovisual materials, and more. Other features include lists of organizations (pro/anti abortion and anti-death penalty groups) and acronyms. *Abortion* offers a state-by-state survey of public funding of abortion and consent/notification laws. *Capital Punishment* provides state-by-state lists of laws on the subject and the annual number of executions since 1977. Indexed.

The approach of these controversial topics is balanced and impartial. Volumes in the series include *Suicide* and *Eating Disorders*. For high school level. [R: BL, 1 Mar 90]

327   Magel, Charles R. **Keyguide to Information Sources in Animal Rights**. Jefferson, N.C.: McFarland, 1989. 267p. $42.50pa. ISBN 0-89950-405-1.

This is a selective bibliography to materials available about most aspects of animal rights that have been published in the United States, the United Kingdom, Canada, Australia, and New Zealand. It omits items about the use of animals for recreation or labor and literary works about animals. Part one is an overview by discipline: science, education, law, vegetarianism, with entries chronological within each category. Part two lists items in one chronological order and includes anti-animal rights materials. Part three is a directory of 182 national and international animal rights organizations. Among the five appendices is a selection of documents about the rights of animals. There is a good general index.

328   McCue, Margi Laird. **Domestic Violence: A Reference Handbook**. Santa Barbara, Calif.: ABC-CLIO, 1995. 273p. $39.50. ISBN 0-87436-762-X.

The author, a consultant on domestic violence, has written a useful volume in the Contemporary World Issues series. As with most of the series, the work deals with the United States, the series title notwithstanding. The book covers issues such as the causes of domestic violence, its extent, services to the victims and possible solutions from historical, social, psychological and legal perspectives. Beginning with an introductory essay on the definition and background of domestic violence, there is a chronology, a list of biographical sketches, facts, statistics, and legal issues, a directory of organizations, and an annotated bibliography of print and nonprint resources. There is an index. This will serve as an introduction to the topic and its sources for high school sociology and family life classes. [R: ARBA 97]

329   **Opposing Viewpoints Series**. San Diego, Calif.: Greenhaven Press, 1980– . $15.95/volume. ISBNs vary by title.

330   **Opposing Viewpoints, Jr. Series**. San
E+   Diego, Calif.: Greenhaven Press, 1990– . $12.95/vol. ISBNs vary by title.

Opposing Viewpoints books present a balanced debate, in pro/con format, of important current issues. Each volume covers one topic, with chapters divided into key questions; opposing viewpoints are presented for each. Recent issues include such topics as censorship, chemical dependency, the death penalty, and welfare. Each volume also includes critical thinking activities and excellent bibliographies of sources easily available to students. Highly recommended for high school collections, for reference and circulating collections.

The Opposing Viewpoints, Jr. Series (intended for upper elementary and middle school students) presents issues as well, but the emphasis at this level is on critical thinking skills such as separating fact from opinion. Also recommended; this set could be useful at all levels.

331   **The Reference Shelf**. Bronx, N.Y.: H. W. Wilson, 1948– . 6 issues/yr. $15.00/title; $65.00/yr. ISSN 0197-6923.

Five volumes per year provide current opinions and information on social issues and trends; the sixth volume is a collection of important speeches from the previous year on a diverse range of subjects and an index to the entire year's issues. Each of the other five issues focuses on one topic and provides articles, excerpts from books and speeches about the topic from various points of view. Beginning in 1997, the set has shifted to a more attractive and accessible design. Recent topics have included the right to privacy, crime, free trade and gambling. Some back issues are available at $15.00/issue. This tool conveniently assembles important source material on the selected topics. Recommended for all high schools.

332   Weilant, Edward, and Chris John Miko, eds. **Opinions '90: Issues.** Detroit, Mich.: Gale Research, 1991. $129.00. ISSN 1050-0383.

Opinions compiles the results of public opinion polls conducted by pollsters, market researchers, statisticians, and others. Each of the quarterly issues (including the cumulation) contain information, arranged by subject, on about 150 to 200 polls and surveys, Details for each are provided—scope, purpose, methodology, groups surveyed, and sample questions. Tables, charts, and graphs present the results. Indexed by poll name, group surveyed, and subject. The appendix lists the organizations, firms, and centers that conducted the surveys. For high school level. [R: BL, 15 Jan 91]

Education

See also **Collection Management** for sources of instructional materials.

BIBLIOGRAPHIES

333 Freed, Melvyn N, and others. **The Educator's Desk Reference: A Sourcebook of Educational Information and Research (EDR)**. New York: Macmillan, 1989. 536p. $49.95. ISBN 0-02-910740-7.

Despite the absence of any reference to school libraries, and the minor and outdated computer section, this is an excellent source of research tools, sources, publications, associations, and texts. It covers the research process (methodologies, statistics, and sampling) and has both bibliography and index. This belongs in every system professional collection, and would be useful in building professional collections as well.

334 Friedes, Harriet. **The Preschool Resource Guide: Educating and Entertaining Children Aged Two through Five**. New York: Plenum Press, 1993. 247p. $27.50; $17.50pa. ISBN 0-306-44464-X; 0-306-44473-9pa.

Parents, teachers, caregivers, librarians, and students in child development and child care classes will find the resources and suggestions in this work useful. Books, magazines, toys, software, audios, and videos are recommended for children from 2–5. There is also a section of resources for adults such as books, journals, and professional associations. There are charts of growth and development and characteristics of books and reading activities that are appropriate for specific ages. Final sections discuss skills for kindergarten readiness and toy safety. There is an index. [R: ARBA 94]

335 Totten, Samuel, and others. **Cooperative Learning: A Guide to Research**. New York: Garland, 1991. 390p. $48.00. ISBN 0-8240-7222-7.

This work covers key research on cooperative learning (as opposed to competitive learning) that has appeared in articles, essays, monographs, reports, dissertations, papers, and book reviews since the late 1960s. After an introduction the bibliography is arranged by strategies, subject areas, general topics, research, book reviews, film and video, games, newsletters, and organizations. The work is comprehensive and inclusive and annotations note if weaknesses occur in the sources. Most entries are from the United States, Canada, England and Israel. There is an author and title index. This source should be in professional collections and used as a selection tool. [R: ARBA 92]

336 Totten, Samuel, and others. **Middle Level Education: An Annotated Bibliography**. Westport, Conn.: Greenwood Press, 1996. 428p. $79.50. ISBN 0-313-29002-4.

This comprehensive, up-to-date reference tool for teachers, administrators, researchers, and parents emphasizes the practical aspects of middle level education as well as the research related to educational practice and to adolescents. The annotations are evaluative and the source covers a wide variety of sources: essays, articles, reports, newsletters, books, dissertations, videotapes, and textbooks. Topics discussed are philosophy, early adolescent development, middle level programs, facilities, teaming, and flexible/block scheduling.

There is a directory of organizations involved in middle education. This is a first purchase for professional system collections and for middle school holdings. [R: ARBA 97]

BIOGRAPHY

337 Ohles, John F., ed. **Biographical Dictionary of American Educators**. 3v. Westport, Conn.: Greenwood Press, 1978. $195.00. ISBN 0-8371-9893-3.

The 1,665 entries in this 3 volume set present an historical record from colonial times to the American bicentennial. It identifies and depicts educational leaders in states, in the nation and within subject fields. Individuals had to be near retirement or deceased to be included; they were nominated by various institutions and organizations. Each signed entry contains basic biographical information and extended annotations describing education, employment, and contributions. Lists of publications by the individual are included, as are references used in the preparation of the annotation. Efforts were made to include women and minorities. Appendices give such classifications as field of work and chronology of birth dates. There is also a chronology of important dates in American education. There is an index. This set would be of use both in professional libraries and as a resource for students in American studies classes.

DICTIONARIES AND ENCYCLOPEDIAS

See also Encyclopedia of English Studies and Language Arts in Language (Humanities).

338 Alkin, Marvin C., ed. **Encyclopedia of Educational Research**. 6th ed. 4v. New York: Free Press/Macmillan, 1992. $360.00. ISBN 0-02-900431-4.

The title should be "results of educational research." Articles are based on all types of contributions to knowledge, with extensive bibliographies. Sixteen broad topics cover current information about education, with alphabetical entries within these categories. Some subjects are not covered because there has been no reliable research. Extensive bibliographies complete the entries. While written by experts, the language is suitable for students, educational practitioners, and lay persons. The charts, tables, and index

facilitate its use. This is a valuable title to supplement the *International Encyclopedia of Education* and for those collections which cannot afford the larger set.

339 Anderson, Lorin W., ed. **International Encyclopedia of Teaching and Teacher Education**. 2d ed. New York: Pergamon, 1995. 684p. $150.00. ISBN 0-08-042304-3.

The second edition of the encyclopedia reflects changes because of the shift in editorship from an Australian to an American and because of new practices in teaching. It retains the original intent of providing a structure for the examination of key concepts about teaching. Contributors are international, but 54 percent are North American. The work provides overviews of specific areas that are of use and interest to individual elementary and secondary teachers as a guide to practice, and to teacher committees working on school and curricular reform. The new edition is current in reflecting theoretical changes in education and includes a new emphasis on multidisciplinary approaches and assessment alternatives. The work is divided into two parts: teaching and teacher education. Teaching is organized into eight topical sections such as instructional programs and strategies and students and teaching/learning. There is an index. Two areas in which treatment is disappointing are school libraries and computer technology. Nonetheless the encyclopedia is recommended for every professional collection. [R: ARBA 97]

340 Chambliss, J. J., ed. **Philosophy of Education**. New York: Garland Pub., 1996. 720p. $95.00. ISBN 0-8153-1177-X.

This single volume encyclopedia has a place in professional collections. The 228 signed articles by 184 authors, most from the United States but also from other countries, cover educational philosophy from ancient Greece to the present. Included are articles on people, and topics from politics, religion, rhetoric, and the social sciences as well as from education. Theory is emphasized rather than practice; the discussion on literacy as "a notion that denigrates the oppressed" is a good illustration of the focus. Most articles range in length from 600–5,000 words, but only 14 have more than 3,000 words. There is a bibliography and a name and subject index. [R: ARBA 97]

341 Husen, Torsten and T. Neville
Postlethwaite, eds. **The International Encyclopedia of Education**. 2d ed. 12v. New York: Pergamon; New York: Elsevier Science, 1994. $2,995.00. ISBN 0-08-041046-6.

The first edition of the encyclopedia was published in 1985 and 2 supplements were added in 1989 and 1990. This new edition includes new articles and old articles have been updated. There are 1,266 entries (all in English) from 95 countries; a list of entries is in volume 1. The long signed articles provide comprehensive coverage of all aspects of education and there are bibliographic references. A good index is in volume 12. While the cost of the set will be prohibitive to many, large professional collections should hold this as the definitive source of background information in all matters educational.

342 Lewy, Arieh, ed. **International Encyclopedia of Curriculum**. New York: Pergamon Press, 1991. 1064p. $95.00. ISBN 0-08-041379-X.

Topics in this work were selected by analysis of ERIC entries, curriculum textbook surveys and by the editor. Entries are of two kinds, curriculum in general (theories, principles and generalizations) and curriculum related to specific study areas. Signed essays from one to five pages present basic information and bibliographies. It is possible to follow developments, movements and eras of reform. Contributors are primarily from Europe, English-speaking countries and Israel. There are separate contributors, name, and subject indexes. The encyclopedia is recommended for every district or agency professional library to support teachers taking courses and for committees working on curricular revision. [R: ARBA 93]

343 Lindsay, Mary P. **Dictionary of Mental Handicap**. New York: Routledge, 1989. 345p. $55.00. ISBN 0-415-02810-8.

Intended for laypeople as well as professionals who work with the mentally handicapped, this dictionary brings together words and terms from the multiple disciplines involved: sociology, medicine, education, psychology, and psychiatry. Thus it includes diagnosis, treatment, training, and education. The perspective is British, but it covers both British and American terminology. Arrangement is alphabetical with cross-references, and it has bibliographic references. This is a useful work for professional collections.

344 Reynolds, Cecil R. and Lester Mann, eds. **Encyclopedia of Special Education: A Reference for the Education of the Handicapped and Other Exceptional Children and Adults**. 3v. New York: Wiley, 1987. $375.00/set. ISBN 0-471-828580.

This set contains over 2,000 signed articles arranged alphabetically with cross-references. The articles, which vary in length, each have bibliographies and provide concise summaries of information on all aspects of special education, rehabilitation, and childhood exceptionality, such as testing, legal issues, and educational programs. The essays include historical background and discuss changes in perspectives about exceptional people, their treatment and education. The encyclopedia is highly recommended for professional libraries.

345 Unger, Harlow G. **Encyclopedia of American Education**. 3v. New York: Facts on File, 1996. $175.00/set. ISBN 0-8160-2994-6.

The brief and sometimes shallow entries make this source more suitable for students, parents, and board members than for educators. The 2,500 entries are comprehensive in scope and cover public and private education from preschool through college and university. Topics include people, terms, concepts, court cases, and administrative and pedagogical issues. Entries are alphabetical, vary in length from one paragraph to four pages and have bibliographic references. One concern is that the editor and consultants are geographically parochial and this may account for omissions and inaccuracies in coverage of other parts of the country. Although many educational associations are included, there is no article on the American Association of School Librarians. Coverage does not include recent practices in K–12 schools; there are no general entries on such topics as assessment or constructivism. This is not an alternative to the *International Encyclopedia of Education* despite the similarity of titles and the tempting price. [R: ARBA 97]

346 Williams, Leslie R. and Doris Pronin Fromberg, eds. **Encyclopedia of Early Childhood Education**. New York: Garland Pub., 1992. 518p. $95.00. ISBN 0-8240-4626-9.

This is a comprehensive reference work that reflects a wide range of scholarship within the group of contributors and the editorial board. Coverage is the education and care of children from birth to eight years. It also discusses policy issues, training of child care providers, and resources. Articles are signed with references and are arranged within chapters by topic. Each chapter has an outline of its contents, and there is an index. Six chapters include such topics as history and background, sociocultural contexts, children and development, and curriculum. This source has a wide audience, and should be available in professional collections, parenting collections, and in high school collections to support the child care and development curriculum. [R: ARBA 93]

DIRECTORIES
See also **College and Vocational School Guides (Education)**.

347 **The College Board Guide to High Schools**. 2d ed. New York: College Entrance Examination Board, 1994. 1779p. $125.00. ISBN 0-87447-4663.

This directory attempts to list information about all U.S. schools that contain a 12th grade, including those in Puerto Rico and the U.S. Virgin Islands and Department of Defense schools whether public, private, or parochial. The information is furnished by the schools and some entries are incomplete. Listings are by state and then alphabetically by name of school. Data categories are directory information, school code used by SAT/ACT, type of school, general information, enrollment, program offerings, test scores, student post graduate plans, and neighboring schools. The latter category is to make it easier to compare schools in an area. Indexes include specialized schools, alternative schools, single-sex schools, and vocational or technical schools. There is also a general index. The guide can be used as a directory, and by parents, students and educators as one source to provide school comparisons.

348 **The Directory for Exceptional**
E+ **Children**. Boston: Porter Sargent, 1954– . annual. $60.00. ISSN 0070-5012.

This is a comprehensive directory to those educational and training facilities that offer services to exceptional children. Approximately 3,000 facilities and organizations are classified by type of disability and then listed alphabetically by state and town. Facilities include state, public and private schools and clinics. Programs are listed for children identified as learning disabled, autistic, emotionally disturbed, orthopedic and neurological disabled, blind or partially sighted, deaf and hearing impaired, and speech and language impaired. Residential schools and day programs are included. For each facility, there is a description, directory information, size, ages served, programs offered and staff. Associations and agencies (federal and state), societies and foundations are also listed. The index refers to item numbers. This source should be available to counselors, teachers, and parents.

349 **Guide to Summer Camps and Summer Schools**. 27th ed. Boston: Porter Sargent, 1995. 560p. $35.00; $25.00pa. ISBN 0-87558-133-1; 0-87558-134-Xpa.

Issued since 1977/78, this reliable comprehensive source of summer academic and tutorial programs, travel programs, specialized study programs, and recreational camps lists about 1,300 such programs in the U.S. and Canada. An extensive table of contents and an index make it possible to access all of this information. The principal section gives directory information, brief descriptions of purpose and activities and fees for each program or camp; entries are grouped according to emphasis. Academic programs are listed first, followed by programs with special features— from bicycle tours to circus skills and camps for preschoolers. A classified section lists programs by feature, age level, and gender. This guide should be in district and parent collections, and available for counselors and students.

350 **The Handbook of Private Schools**. Boston: Porter Sargent, 1952– . annual. $80.00. ISSN 0072-9884.

Sargent's *Handbook*, published annually for almost 80 years, is a standard guide to independent schools in the United States and Canada. It organizes the data by region, state, and city. Over 1,600 schools (both day and boarding) are profiled with information about size, grades included, faculty, enrollment and admissions data, costs, and name of admissions director. The entries also give information about the last graduating class and their post graduate plans, including six of the colleges they chose to attend. Curriculum information and extracurricular programs are described, as well as the school and its history. Certain features are classified for easier identification: military programs, ungraded schools, small and large boarding schools, elementary level boarding schools, single-sex schools, learning difference programs, and international and/or bilingual schools. Schools that pay for entries (about 250) have larger displays. A separate section lists firms and agencies dealing with private schools. There is a general index. Independent schools will want this, Bunting and Lyon and Patterson's; while public schools and professional collections can select the one that best fits their needs.

351 Hawks, John. **Youth Exchanges: The Complete Guide to the Homestay Experience Abroad**. New York: Facts on File, 1994. 234p. $22.95. ISBN 0-8160-2922-9.

The purposes of this guide are to provide information for those involved in international youth exchanges and to encourage high school students to try the experience. The author, a former exchange student and involved in programs as an adult, gives a multiple-perspective explanation of what students might expect from an exchange. Part 1 has narrative chapters that discuss preparations for an exchange and what to expect, including problems and what it is like to come home again. Part 2 is a directory of 50 exchange programs. There are seven appendices including passport information, customs procedures and an index to exchange programs by country. A classified bibliography and general index conclude the volume. Recommended for high school collections. [R: ARBA 96]

352 Hubbs, Don. **Home Education Resource Guide: A Comprehensive Guide for the Parent-Educator to Curriculums, Correspondence Schools**. 3d ed. Tempe, Ariz.: Blue Bird Pub., 1994. 144p. $11.95pa. ISBN 0-933025-25-4.

This self published guide will be useful in collections which assist home schooling parents. It provides a directory of correspondence courses, textbooks and supplements, magazines, how-to home school books, newsletters, support groups and national organizations. [R: ARBA 96]

353 **The Independent Study Catalog: NUCEA's Guide to Independent Study Through Correspondence.** Princeton, N.J.: Peterson's Guides. biennial $16.95pa. ISBN 1-56079-460-7.

This biennial guide lists more than 10,000 courses from over 100 accredited colleges and universities. Credit courses offered range from preschool to graduate level, and can be applied to diploma or degree programs. Non-credit courses are also listed. After introductory essays that supply useful information about correspondence education, the colleges, universities or other institutions are listed giving the courses by level and area. Indexes include geographical area, major areas of study, and subject areas.

354 Levin, Shirley. **Summer on Campus: College Experiences for High School Students**. 2d ed. New York: College Entrance Board, 1995. 321p. $15.00pa. ISBN 0-87447-526-0.

High school students searching for summer college programs will find more than 400 listed in this guide. Both commuting and residential programs are included. Introductory sections explain why the summer exposure to college experiences can benefit high school students at all grade levels, and describe opportunities and discuss finances. Programs are arranged alphabetically by state and college and provide program descriptions, directory information, setting, admission requirements and procedures, course offerings, housing, and cost. There are many indexes tailored to every need: commuter only programs, free tuition programs, credits available, program length, programs for junior high students, course offerings, and so on.

355 Lipkin, Marjorie B. **The Schoolsearch Guide to Private Schools for Students with Learning Disabilities**. 2d ed. Belmont, Mass.: Schoolsearch, 1992. 334p. $34.95. ISBN 0-96-20326-4-6.

More than 400 private (including parochial) schools in the country are identified by this source as providing some sort of services to the learning disabled. Some are LD programs within regular schools, while some are separate schools specifically for LD students. Also included are schools which accommodate students with minimal learning disabilities. Information is presented in chart form and includes admission, general information, student body profiles, programs, unique features, extracurricular activities, summer programs, and expenses. There are comparison charts and state maps which are useful for identifying a radius of support available. Introductory essays are good discussions of diagnosis and options. There is an index of schools by name. School systems will want this guide to share with parents.

356 Modoc Press, Inc., comp and ed.
     **The Macmillan Guide to Correspon-
     dence Study**. 6th ed. New York:
     Macmillan, 1996. 782p. $100.00.
     ISBN 0-02-860266-8.

This comprehensive guide to correspondence study, supplemented by audio, video, and computer distance learning opportunities, gives the detailed information needed for approaching this kind of education. It used data supplied from the included accredited schools to describe programs, courses and course descriptions, admission requirements and procedures, and tuition requirements. Sections are divided according to the type of institution: colleges and universities; privately owned schools that offer vocational, high school, college and professional studies; and private foundations, non-profit organizations, government and military programs. There is a comprehensive subject index. This source is more complete than the *Independent Study Catalog* for those collections that can afford the price difference.

357 **NCEA/Ganley's Catholic Schools in
     America**. 24th ed. Montrose, Colo.:
     Fisher Pub Co., 1996. $42.50pa.
     ISBN 9-9962-05-738.

Both statistical data and directory information are given in this source, whose title has varied from edition to edition. The main section of the volume is based on reports from the archdiocesan and diocesan offices of education. Listed by state, ecclesiastical body, and city, it lists directory information for each school and gives enrollment and name of the principal. Other sections show enrollment trends, staffing data, extended care programs and historical statistics.

358 **Patterson's American Education**.
     rev. ed. Mount Prospect, Ill.: Educa-
     tional Directories, 1954– . annual.
     $83.00. ISSN 0079-0230.

This vast directory, published since 1904, covers most secondary schools in the United States. It includes almost 12,000 public school districts, and over 30,000 public schools, private and Catholic schools, Bureau of Indian Affairs schools, Defense Department schools, and 6,000 post secondary programs. The first part lists secondary schools by state (with state department of education information), city/county. The second section lists schools classified by 60 or so categories. Schools are located by mailing address, not the school system; system offices are included by city. Each school entry gives enrollment, grade range, principal's name, and school directory information. Some institutions of higher education are also listed. There is an index by name of school.

359 **Patterson's Elementary Education**.
     Mount Prospect, Ill.: Educational
     Directories, 1989– . annual. $81.00.
     ISSN 1044-1417.

This annual, published since 1989, complements *Patterson's American Education* with information about elementary schools in the United States. All types of schools are included, as are all combinations of grade levels, including kindergarten, middle, and K–12 schools. Arrangement and information are the same as the secondary school volume.

360 **Peterson's Private Secondary
     Schools**. Princeton, N.J.: Peterson's
     Guides, 1993– . annual. $23.95. ISSN
     1066-5366.

Formerly titled *Peterson's Guide to Independent Secondary Schools* and *Peterson's Guide to Private Secondary Schools*, this comprehensive guide lists 1,500 schools alphabetically by name of school, and includes independent day and boarding schools and parochial schools. An introductory section discusses the reasons for choosing a private education and the planning, testing, and finances involved. There are separate sections for 400 paid full descriptions with illustrations, for special needs schools and junior boarding schools. Directories classify schools in 23 different ways, including by their feeder schools. There is a quick reference chart by state and a general index. Independent schools will want Sargent, Bunting and Lyon and Peterson's, but public school systems will find Peterson's most useful. [R: ARBA 95]

361 **Peterson's Summer Opportunities**
E+ **for Kids and Teenagers**. 14th ed. Princeton, N.J.: Peterson's Guides, 1997. 1,207p. $26.95pa. ISBN 1-56079-587-5.

Intended as a guide students themselves can use to find "the right summer program," this list of 1,600 summer camps, academic options and travel adventures begins with suggestions for planning a summer program, including questions to ask before signing anything. There is a chart which gives quick, brief information about enrollment, residence, age, sex, activities, jobs available. The chart also gives a page reference to the full profile. The profile section is arranged geographically and gives directory and general information, program focus, sports, and fees. A final section has 231 in-depth descriptions. Specialized directories cover arts, sports, special needs, and religious programs, among others. An index refers to all sections of the guide. This guide can be of use for students looking for summer programs to attend, or for students looking for summer work experiences.

362 **Peterson's Summer Study Abroad: A Guide to Summer Academic and Language Programs**. Princeton, N.J.: Peterson's Guides, 1995. annual. $18.95. ISSN 1069-6504.

This guide complements *Peterson's Study Abroad* and includes 900 summer programs ranging from 1 week to a full summer. Most programs offer academic credit and many are open to pre-college students with a usual minimum age of 16. All programs listed are open to all students, not restricted to students enrolled at or attending the sponsoring institution. Multi-country programs are listed first, followed by listings arranged by single country and city. Program descriptions include host, academic focus, schedule, eligibility requirements, living arrangements, costs, and

person to contact. Indexes are by field of study, program sponsor, host institution, and internship opportunities. The advertisements are difficult to distinguish from the listings, but a careful search provides accurate information. [R: ARBA 96]

363 **Private Independent Schools**. Wallingford, Conn.: Bunting and Lyon, 1943– . annual. $99.00. ISSN 0079-5399.

Bunting and Lyon's "Blue Book" is another standard independent school handbook intended for parents, students, teaching candidates and counselors. There is an introduction to the process of selecting a private school based on the company's consulting service. Schools are arranged by state and country. Descriptions may be full or brief; all are by subscription, and are interfiled. Yellow pages list summer programs, and blue pages are a geographic grid showing 14 selected characteristics of the schools.

HANDBOOKS, ALMANACS, AND YEARBOOKS

364 Colangelo, Nicholas, and Gary A. David, eds. **Handbook of Gifted Education**. 2d ed. Boston: Allyn and Bacon, 1997. 582p. $64.00. ISBN 0-205-26085-3.

This excellent handbook is intended for both scholars and practitioners. It has 44 chapters with extensive references arranged in six main sections, such as program models and teaching practices and creativity and thinking skills. There are separate name and subject indexes. This source should be in every collection serving professionals who work with gifted children.

365 National Center for Educational Statistics. **The Condition of Education**. Washington, D.C.: Government Printing Office. annual. $25.00. S/N 065-000-0097-8.

366 National Center for Educational Statistics. **Digest of Education Statistics**. Washington, D.C.: Government Printing Office. annual. $44.00. S/N 65-000-00904-8.

367 National Center for Educational Statistics. **Education Indicators**. Washington, D.C.: Government Printing Office. annual. $15.00. S/N 065-000-00387-2.

368 National Center for Educational Statistics. **Mini-Digest of Education Statistics**. Washington, D.C.: Government Printing Office. annual. Free. ISSN 0502-4102.

369 National Center for Educational Statistics. **Projections of Educational Statistics to 2006: An Update**. Washington, D.C.: Government Printing Office. annual. $14.00. S/N 065-000-00853-0.

370 National Center for Educational Statistics. **Projections of Education Statistics to 2006. Pocket Projections**. Washington, D.C.: Government Printing Office. annual. $25.00. S/N 065-000-00871-8.

371 National Center for Educational Statistics. **Youth Indicators**. Washington, D.C.: Government Printing Office. annual. $12.00. S/N 065-000-00898-0.

Condition of Education contains 60 indicators that help interpret the current situation of American education. An executive summary is followed by indicators such as access, achievement, economic outcomes, growth, diversity, and human and financial resources. All information is general with no comparative data by state of institution.

The *Digest* has been published annually (with a few exceptions) and compiles useful statistical information about K–12 and higher education. Included are numbers of schools and colleges, numbers of teachers, enrollments and graduates. Other issues such as funding and employment and some social concerns such as drug use and school violence are covered. All information is statistical and presented in tables.

The data in *Education Indicators* were collected in order to compare such categories as "time spent on homework," "books at home," "use of calculators in school," and reading literacy and other evidence of student achievement among the United States and other industrialized economies. Such comparisons are deemed important if the U.S. is to compete in foreign markets. There are 45 indicators in 6 categories, each with tables and two-toned blue graphs to illustrate the findings. The appendices include matrices of comparative data on educational systems, supplemental notes and tables, a list of sources and a glossary. While this information could be useful in world culture classes, it would be even more useful in a professional collection.

The Mini-Digest is a pocket-sized compilation of statistics from material found in the *Digest*, the *Condition of Education*, and *Youth Indicators*. Statistics are published in English, Spanish and French.

Projections uses charts and tables to predict seven year state and national predictions for elementary and secondary enrollments, graduates, classroom teachers and expenditures. It also includes national predictions for higher education. Demographic and economic assumptions are indicated as is methodology and data sources.

Pocket Projections compiles statistics selected from material in *Projections*.

Youth Indicators reports investigations about factors outside of school which influence learning. There are statistical compilations of data about such things as family structure, economic factors, sports participation, spending patterns, drug use, and crimes reported with graphs, tables and charts. Listings are under broad categories: home, school, health, citizenship and values, and the future. There is an index.

All of these items will be useful in professional collections; the pocket versions would be useful in school board handbooks, and many are available on the Web from www.ed.gov.

372 **Requirements for Certification of**
E+ **Teachers, Counselors, Librarians, Administrators for Elementary and Secondary Schools**. Chicago: University of Chicago Press, 1989– . annual. $37.00. ISSN 1047-7071.

Published since 1935, this annual gives the state requirements for regular, temporary and emergency certification as well as regional accrediting association recommendations for certification. States are listed alphabetically, and requirements for certification include those for elementary and secondary classroom and subject area teachers, specialists (such as counselors and librarians) and administrators. Reciprocal arrangements are described. It also gives addresses of state offices of certification.

373 Williams, Phillip. **The Special Education Handbook: An Introductory Reference**. Philadelphia, Pa.: Open University Press, 1991. 434p. $138.00. ISBN 0-335-09314-0.

This is intended as a desk reference for those with responsibilities in special education. The dictionary includes more than 1,000 terms related to learning difficulties, testing, emotional behavior, neurological, sensory and mental handicaps, medicine, psychology, social work, and legislation. There are brief definitions and discussions of significance arranged alphabetically with cross-references; many entries have references, and there are some tables which add clarification. This is a useful tool for collections in districts moving toward inclusion of special education students, as a reference for teachers not trained in special education. [R: ARBA 93]

INDEXES

See also **Electronic Information Systems (Reference)**.

374 **ERIC**. Bethesda, Md.: United States Educational Resources Information Center, 1966– . dist. via many vendors in CD-ROM and online, e.g. SilverPlatter annual CD-ROM. $650.00.

Originally published in print as two separate indexes, *Resources in Education* which indexed unpublished reports and *Current Index to Journals in Education*, the electronic versions are combined. As it is a government publication it is not copyright protected so many vendors can offer it. This is the most comprehensive index of educational materials in the world and should be available to district students, teachers and administrators.

375 **Exceptional Child Education Resources**. Reston, Va.: Council for Exceptional Children, 1977– . quarterly. $85.00. ISSN 0160-4309.

376 **Exceptional Child Education Resources**. Reston, Va.: Council for Exceptional Children, distr. by SilverPlatter Information, Inc. 1995– . CD-ROM (Windows, Macintosh). $795.00.

This indexing and abstracting source is published quarterly as a journal with volume 4 indexing the year. It includes documents, journal articles, books, dissertations and nonprint media. Citations and abstracts are listed in acquisition order and by type with indexes. Although the Council acts as a clearinghouse for ERIC, the resources are not all included in the ERIC database, thus the importance of this resource. It is available as ECER on SilverPlatter CD-ROM and via the Internet at http://www.cec.sped.org/home.htm.

COLLEGE AND VOCATIONAL SCHOOL GUIDES

377 Barnett, Lynn, ed. **Directory of Disability Support Services in Community Colleges, 1992**. Washington, D.C.: American Association of Community Colleges, 1992. 180p. $10.00. ISBN 0-87117-249-6.

This is a alphabetical listing of institutions by state, including Puerto Rico, the trust territories, and Canada, which offer support services and accommodations for disabled students. For each college, the source lists directory information, total enrollment of disabled students and their graduation statistics, as well as the type of disabilities for which services and facilities are available. There is a summarizing chart showing support services and accommodations available. Miscellaneous appendices include the text of PL 101-336. There are both a special features index and an institutional index. This important source should be in professional collections and high school counseling reference collections.

378 Bear, John. **College Degrees by Mail: 100 Good Schools That Offer Bachelor's, Master's, Doctorates, and Law Degrees by Home Study**. Berkeley, Calif.: Ten Speed Press, 1995. 216p. $12.95pa. ISBN 0-89815-760-9.

The author, a long-time expert in nontraditional college experiences, has a relaxed attitude about a college education, but this is a serious investigation of legitimate ways of earning credit or degrees from good programs in good institutions. The guide includes correspondence, cable, videotape, computer, and independent study program options. One page descriptions of the 100 accredited schools from the U.S., Canada, England, and Israel complete the work. There are clear warnings to stay away from non-legitimate schools. Recommended for both professional and guidance reference collections. [R: ARBA 96]

379 Bruce-Young, Doris Marie, and William C. Young. **The Higher Education Moneybook for Women & Minorities**. Washington, D.C.: Young Enterprises International, 1996. 413p. $25.00pa. ISBN 0-9639490-1-2.

Many of the grants and loans described in this work are available to anyone, some give preference to women and/or minorities, and some are available only to women and/or minorities. The table of contents does not give the titles for some chapters and is thus confusing to the user, but the arrangement is by level of college: general undergraduate programs then undergraduate programs by major. The same pattern is followed for graduate programs and postdoctoral programs. There is also a chapter that discusses federal and state funding. Each program description gives the sponsor's name and address, a description with the purpose of the award highlighted, amount offered, deadline dates, and a phone number. Indexes are alphabetical by sponsor, by state, and by keyword. This is a convenient source that brings together information that is found scattered among other sources; it is recommended for high schools. [R: ARBA 92]

380 **Chronicle Two-Year College Databook**. Moravia, N.Y.: Chronicle Guidance Publications, 1979– . annual. $22.46. ISSN 0191-3662.

This directory of 750 two-year programs available in both two-year and four-year institutions is useful for students wanting associate degrees and employment in specific areas and for students wanting to transfer to four-year colleges to complete the B.A. degree. Part 1 lists two-year majors alphabetically by major, then by state and institution. Part 2 contains tabular data about institutions listed alphabetically by state then college. Data include name and directory information,

calendar, location, enrollment, admissions requirements, cost and availability of financial aid. One appendix has narrative paragraphs about the institutions, one lists accrediting associations, and one lists recent college name changes or closings. There is an index to charts.

Chronicle also produces the *Vocational School Manual*, the *Four-Year College Databook* and the *Financial Aid Guide*. CD-ROM products include the *CD-ROM C-Lect College Module* which contains both the two-year and four-year databooks ($200.00 including site license), the *CD-ROM C-Lect Vocational School Module*, the *Financial Aid Module* and other titles and combinations.

381 Custard, Ed, and Dan Saraceno. **The Complete Book of Catholic Colleges**. New York: Princeton Review/Random House, 1997. 268p. $21.00pa. ISBN 0-679-77889-6.

This guide lists 193 Catholic colleges and universities in the United States and Puerto Rico. The entries for each college give typical information about the setting, majors, sports, admissions and cost. Indexes and supplements list the institutions by selectivity, state, size, and settings. Most high schools will want this in their college guide collections.

382 **Education for the Earth: The College Guide for Careers in the Environment**. 2d ed. Princeton, N.J.: Peterson's Guides, 1995. 319p. $14.95pa. ISBN 1-56079-407-0.

More than 200 institutions currently offering undergraduate environmental programs are included in this guide. The schools were selected from the Peterson database and from recommendation by five national environmental groups. Section one describes careers in six types of environmental occupations with profiles of individuals actually working in that area. Section two lists prebaccalaureate programs for technical positions listed alphabetically by state and institution, while section three lists B.A. programs and profiles alphabetically by name of institutions. Brief facts are given about each institution; schools may have more than one program. Descriptions of each program include basic facts, special features, recommended career paths, and a person to contact. There is a geographic index and a subject index classified by major area. This is a valuable source for high school guidance reference collections. [R: ARBA 96]

383 Hutcheson, Polly, and the National Commission for Cooperative Education, eds. **Directory of College Cooperative Education Programs**. Phoenix, Ariz.: Oryx Press, 1996. 219p. $49.95. ISBN 0-89774-998-7.

A helpful introduction explains that cooperative programs are those that integrate classroom experience with related paid work experiences. This source lists 460 colleges with such programs, including community and technical colleges, liberal arts colleges, universities and graduate schools alphabetically by state. Entries give directory information and descriptions of both the institution and the program. Information includes the number of students per year, the types of programs, and other details. There is an institution name index and a programs and degrees index. This kind of education appeals to many students, and this is a convenient source to begin looking for an appropriate program. Recommended for high school collections. [R: ARBA 97]

384 Meltzer, Tom. **The Princeton Review Student Access Guide to the Best 306 Colleges**. New York: Villard Books, 1994. 701p. $18.00. ISBN 0-679-76146-2.

Princeton Review produces materials to prepare students to take the various standardized tests colleges and universities require for admission. This guide is intended to assist students in making choices about the colleges and universities they want to attend. The selections are based on the comments of more than 50 independent college counselors and the responses of students already attending the schools. Most of the school profiles are drawn from at least 100 students from the respective campuses who completed a questionnaire. Schools are ranked in 61 categories with the top 20 listed. Categories include rankings of professors and academics, but much of the focus is on the quality of life on campus and in the geographical area. The second part of the work has two page campus profiles with sidebars that contain the ratings of the school by the students and some directory and statistical information as well as deadlines for applications. The center layout features summaries of student comments, financial aid information and a section from the school's admissions staff. Schools are arranged alphabetically by key word. There is a list of the consulted independent counselors by state, a list of schools with programs for the learning disabled, and an index of the schools. This work supplements the more traditional college guides.

385 **Peterson's Choose a Christian College: A Guide to Academically Challenging Colleges Committed to a Christ-Centered Campus Life**. Christian College Coalition. 5th ed. Princeton, N.J.: Petersons's Guides, 1996. 150p. $14.95pa. ISBN 1-56079-670-7.

This source lists only the 83 members of the Christian College Coalition which are among the 600 or so colleges and universities with denominational or religious traditions. The institutions are in the United States and Canada and after an introduction about the advantages of choosing a Christian college there are one-page profiles of the schools from Peterson's database. Listed alphabetically by name of institution, the entries give typical Peterson information plus a special note about the atmosphere of the school. There is also a section of special programs available to Coalition members. A table of contents lists the institutions by state, and there are indexes by major, athletics, study abroad, and graduate majors.

386 **Peterson's College Money Handbook**. Princeton, N.J.: Peterson's Guides, 1996– . annual. $24.95. ISSN 1070-616X.

This is both a quick resource and an in-depth reference to college costs and financial aid opportunities. Charts, tables, and lists help organize the information given. The source describes federal aid, state aid (alphabetically by state), and private aid (listing the top 40 sources). The main part of the work profiles financial aid at 1,545 colleges; the emphasis is freshman costs. Indexes guide the user to non-need scholarships, athletic grants, co-op programs, ROTC programs, tuition waivers and tuition payment alternatives such as deferred, installment, and prepayment and guaranteed rates. This is more useful for information and planning than for locating the advertised $35 billion in financial aid. [R: ARBA 95]

387 **Peterson's Competitive Colleges**.
Princeton, N.J.: Peterson's Guides,
1984– . annual. $16.95pa. ISSN 0887-
0152.

This guide to selective institutions list the schools
in one-page "briefs" which feature such data as
academic standards, computers, and admissions.
Statistical information about applications and
admissions, return rate, and typical career patterns is also provided. Costs are included. There
are indexes to both majors and geographical
location. Both libraries and counseling collections will need this source.

388 **Peterson's Distance Learning**. 2d ed.
Princeton, N.J.: Peterson's Guides,
1997. 486p. $24.95pa. ISBN 1-56079-
664-2.

This directory offers information about colleges
and universities in the United States and Canada
which offer courses to students off site. Course
delivery methods included may be cable, satellite, video or audio tape, fax, computer, confer-
encing, or some combination; independent study
and correspondence courses are not covered. An
introduction discusses the pros and cons of this
kind of education and there is a section on
assignment of credits and applicability of credits
to degree programs and a section on finances.
The programs are listed alphabetically by institution with brief profiles including courses available, delivery method, student services,
application, and cost. Some programs have more
complete full descriptions of two or more pages
in a separate part. Interspersed are profiles of
real students taking coursework in this way.
There are both course and geographic indexes.
The directory will be useful in high school collections. [R: ARBA 97]

389 **Peterson's Guide to Two-Year Col-
leges**. Princeton, N.J., Peterson's
Guides, 1989– . annual. $21.95pa.
ISSN 0894-9328.

More than 1,500 profiles of two-year colleges are
included in this standard Peterson reference
source. The introductory sections describe the
advantages of a two-year college as well as information about choosing and applying to such
institutions. The comprehensive index allows
ready access to the schools. High school collections may need several copies of this tool.

390 **Peterson's Sports Scholarships and
College Athletic Programs**. Princeton, N.J.: Peterson's Guides, 1994– .
biennial. $21.95. ISSN 1069-1383.

After introductory articles suggesting how to go
about gathering and using the information provided, this source lists more than 1,700 colleges
and universities with athletic program profiles.
Not all of the 1,350 4-year institutions listed offer
sports scholarships, but all of the 350 2-year institutions do. Profiles are arranged alphabetically
by college with 4-year programs listed first. Each
institutional entry describes the sports programs,
facilities, records, coaches, scholarships and
other aid packages. There are separate men's
and women's sports indexes and a geographic
index that lists the state and then the college
name. High school college reference collections
will find this a useful, though not exhaustive
source. [R: ARBA 95]

391 **Peterson's Vocational and Technical
Schools: Accredited Institutions
Offering Career Training Programs**.
2v. (East and West). Princeton, N.J.:
Peterson's Guides, 1994– . biennial.
$34.95/volume. East: ISSN 1069-
1367. West: ISSN 1069-1375.

Each volume offers institutions with postsecond-
ary awards, certificates, or diplomas requiring
less than two years of study. Programs vary from
12 weeks to 2 years and cover careers in business,
health, personal services, technology, such as
banking, cosmetology, piloting, medical technology, real estate, travel, and taxidermy. There is a
state-by-state listing of profiles of institutions,
the programs they offer, the length, fees, and
placement rates. The east/west division is the
Mississippi River. There is an index to career
training programs in each volume, a list of
accrediting bodies, and an alphabetical list of
institutions. Recommended for high school vocational reference collections. [R: ARBA 95]

392 Phifer, Paul. **College Majors and
Careers: A Resource Guide for Effec-
tive Life Planning**. 3d ed. Chicago:
Ferguson, 1997. 188p. $14.95. ISBN
0-89434-179-0.

This source is intended to assist students in
choosing a career and in learning about the education necessary to pursue it. Each of the 61

majors contains an overview and related occupations with required degrees or other education.
The kind of related vocational and leisure activities, skills, values and personal characteristics of
individuals in the field are listed. There are
sources for further exploration including professional organizations. A self-assessment survey
asks realistic questions. There is a glossary and
indexes by both major and occupation. This is an
extremely useful source for both career exploration units and for pre-college selection. Highly
recommended for all secondary collections.

393 Straughn II, Charles T., ed. **Lovejoy's College Guide for the Learning Disabled**. 3d ed. New York: Macmillan, 1993. 177p. $22.00. ISBN 0-671-84771-6.

Good introductory essays discuss the special concerns the learning disabled have in deciding to go
to college, in coping with change and in finding
careers. Rather lengthy descriptions of colleges
with special programs are listed alphabetically by
state and then by institution. Special services are
identified in boxes and basic information about
the college or university with general descriptions of the environment and programs. There is
a sports index, an index by college name, and a
list of sources of information.

394 Thomas, Carol H. and James L. Thomas, eds. **Directory of College Facilities and Services for People With Disabilities**. Modoc Press, comp. 4th ed. Phoenix, Ariz.: Oryx Press, 1996. 423p. $125.00. ISBN 0-89774-894-8.

Now in its 4th edition, the directory includes
more than 1,500 colleges, universities and technical schools in the United States and Canada
that have facilities and services that make it possible for students with disabilities to obtain edu-
cations there. Entry information is provided
from questionnaires returned from postsecond-
ary educational institutions. Listings are alphabetical by state and province, and then
alphabetically by institution. Profiles include
directory information, degrees offered, numbers
of disabled students attending by category of
disability, and information about facilities, such
as dormitories and services such as adaptive
physical education. Indexes are by disabilities
and by name of institution.

395 Whiting, Ernestine, ed. **The Black Student's Guide to Scholarships: 500+ Money Sources for Black & Minority Students**. 4th ed. Lanham, Md.: Madison Books, 1996. 224p. $14.95. ISBN 1-56833-079-0.

More than 650 sources of scholarships are listed
in this introductory guide for Black students (and
others, as many of the grants are for all minority
groups). Information about financial aid from
government sources and a glossary precede the
guide's list of scholarships which are arranged
alphabetically by title. This access is supplemented by three indexes: institiution, discipline
and state. Each entry lists eligibility and deadlines, amounts and the person or office to contact with address and phone number. This is not
a comprehensive list, but is presented in a non-
threatening and supportive manner. There are
samples of language to use when sending post-
cards requesting information, and an overall
tone of encouragement. This should be a first
purchase for high school reference and guidance
collections. [R: ARBA 95]

INSTRUCTIONAL TECHNOLOGY
See also **Collection Management** and **Library Science**.

396 **Educational Media and Technology Yearbook**. Englewood, Colo.: Libraries Unlimited, 1985– . annual. $60.00. ISSN 8755-2094.

This annual publication serves as a summary of
the year's activities and achievements in media
and technology. Sections on trends and issues,
current developments, and the year in review
identifies major activities in the field; while lists
of organizations, associations and graduate programs provide directory assistance. There is a list
of state media standards or guidelines. A
mediography includes important print and nonprint materials published during the previous
year.

397 Schroeder, Don and Gary Lare. **Audiovisual Equipment and Materials: A Basic Repair and Maintenance Guide**. 2v. Lanham, Md.: Scarecrow Press, 1979–1989. Vol. I: $18.50pa. ISBN 0-8108-1206-1. Vol. II: $20.00. ISBN 0-8108-2265-2.

This repair guide will be useful to those who find themselves involved in the maintenance and use of both old and new audiovisual equipment. Volume II deals with TV receivers, VCRs, CD players and videodisc players and describes tools, cleaning supplies, simple maintenance procedures and cabling. Instructions are non-technical and are complemented by black and white photographs.

Volume I (1979) is still available and will continue to be helpful to those who are maintaining film projectors, overhead and opaque projectors, screens, and cassette recorders.

Tests

398   Murphy, Linda L., Jane Close Conoley, and James C. Impara, eds. **Tests in Print IV: An Index to Tests, Test**

Reviews, and the Literature on Specific Tests. 2v. Lincoln, Neb.: Buros Institute of Mental Measurements, University of Nebraska-Lincoln, 1994. $325.00/set. ISBN 0-910674-53-1.

Intended for people who develop, study or buy testing products, the source gives descriptive lists and references to commercially published tests. For each test, the entry gives title, purpose, population, publishing date, scores, administration, price data, time required, author, publisher, comments, levels, test references, and a cross-reference to its citation in the *Mental Measurements Yearbook*. There is a title index, and index of acronyms, a classified subject index, a publishers directory and index, an index of names, and an index of scores. Most district professional libraries will want this set. [R: ARBA 95]

Ethnic Minorities

See also **Retrospective Bibliographies (Collection Management), United States History** and **Women's Studies (Social Sciences), Language** and **Literature (Humanities)**.

ATLASES

399   Allen, James P. and Eugene J.
E+   Turner. **We the People: An Atlas of America's Ethnic Diversity**. New York: Macmillan, 1988. 315p. $175.00. ISBN 0-02-901420-1.

This unique atlas uses historical geographic data to examine various ethnic populations as they are distributed among 3,100 counties and major towns and cities in the United States. The information is based on 1980 census figures. It is possible to use the text and maps not only to locate ethnic groups, but to trace their migration. Included are Native Americans, Western, Northern, Eastern, and Southern Europeans, and groups from the Middle East, Africa, Middle and South America, and Asia and the Pacific Islands. Attractive maps, narrative, charts and bibliographies provide facts in separate sections for each

group. A final chapter discusses the demonstrated patterns in diversity among ethnic groups in this country. This outstanding reference source should be available in every secondary school, and should be available to teachers in elementary schools.

BIBLIOGRAPHIES AND RESOURCES

400   **Guide to Multicultural Resources 1997/1998**. Fort Atkinson, Wis.: Highsmith Press, 1997. $49.00pa. ISBN 0-917846-83-4. ISSN 1050-4249.

This directory of organizations, colleges, agencies, libraries and museums provides important sources of information on African American, Asian Pacific, Hispanic American, and Native American groups. Another section deals with minorities in general. Entries give names, addresses and e-mail or Web addresses. Good indexes include organization, geography, subject, publication and video. This convenient source combines information found in other sources and would be useful in many secondary or professional collections.

401 Weinberg, Meyer, comp. **Racism in Contemporary America**. Westport, Conn.: Greenwood Press, 1996. 838p. $125.00. ISBN 0-313-27390-1.

This is the third volume in a series that began with *Racism in the United States* (1990) and *World Racism and Related Inhumanities* (1992). Together with this volume, the set includes about 36,650 entries. This volume alone contains 14,671 citations. Included are books, dissertations, legislative hearings, journal articles and investigative accounts under 87 subject headings such as affirmative action, discrimination, elementary and secondary education, health, law, multiculturalism, slavery, humor, anti-Semitism, concentration camps, and sexism. Numbered entries are arranged alphabetically by author within these topics. There are author and subject indexes. This bibliography will be useful for collection management in high schools, and as a reference source for further information for students and teachers.

ENCYCLOPEDIAS

402 Auerbach, Susan, ed. **Encyclopedia of Multiculturalism**. 6v. New York: Marshall Cavendish, 1994. $449.95/set. ISBN 1-85435-670-4.

This ambitious encyclopedia attempts to examine many aspects of American history and contemporary society from the point of view of diverse groups of Americans, emphasizing those who are in the minority. Intergroup relations and multicultural implications of events, history, arts, entertainment, media, civil rights, discrimination, people, places, concepts, laws, and organizations are all areas included in the work. Entries are alphabetical throughout the volumes and vary in length from brief definitions to essays of 5,000 words, with average entries of from 500–2,000 words. Graphs, tables, photographs and maps enhance the text, although there are no color illustrations. Each volume has a list of all contents, and volume six is an index and a classified list of topics, as well as containing a timeline, a list of selected resources, an organization and agency directory, a filmography, and a classified bibliography. Because this is not in itself an encyclopedia of minority groups, it complements the approach of *Gale Encyclopedia of Multicultural America*. Recommended for secondary school collections. [R: ARBA 95]

403 Galens, Judy, Anna Sheets, and Robyn V. Young, eds. **Gale Encyclopedia of Multicultural America**. 2v. Detroit, Mich.: Gale Research, 1995. $125.00/set. ISBN 0-8103-9163-5.

This comprehensive reference tool lists ethnic and ethno religious groups (such as the Amish and the Mormons) alphabetically with 100 original essays. Groups are included because of their research value despite small populations in some cases. Twelve representative Native American groups are included; Nigerian Americans are included while other African groups are clustered in the African American entry. Entries are signed and were written and reviewed by scholars. Each entry includes the country or region of origin, the major immigration waves, and the experience in the United States. Such topics as acculturation, language, religion, employment and contributions are discussed. There is a directory of media for each culture and a list of sources for further study. Many photographs add meaning to the text. There are some errors or omissions in the set: the Czech and Slovak Museum and Library is listed in the Czech article, but not in the Slovak article and while the term Cajun is used extensively in the article on Acadia there is no such entry in the subject index. The encyclopedia fills an important need for this kind of information and is recommended for secondary collections. [R: ARBA 96]

404 Kennett, Frances, with Caroline MacDonald-Haig. **Ethnic Dress**. New York: Facts on File, 1995. 192p. $40.00. ISBN 0-8160-3136-3.

This is a coffee table book with some reference application. It has about 500 illustrations with narratives spotlighting people from cultures that have not accommodated to western fashion, but rather have preserved their clothing as a cultural document. Such clothing helps retain a sense of identity and the book includes examples of folk dress, national dress, traditional costume, everyday dress, festival and holiday dress, and some examples of religious dress. The volume is arranged by continent/region with maps at the end of each section. There is a glossary, a brief bibliography and an index. This is not intended to be a definitive work, but merely illustrative of some non-western clothing. Suggested for high school collections where clothing is an important aspect of world culture curriculum. [R: ARBA 96]

405 Levinson, David, ed. **Encyclopedia of World Cultures**. 10v. Boston, Mass.: G. K. Hall, 1991–1996. $1100.00/set. ISBN 0-8161-1840-X.

This is an expensive set, but will become a standard in the discipline. The work began as a project in 1987 and publication proceeded from 1991–1996. The set is arranged by region which allowed the editors to reflect the political changes of the early 1990s in the appropriate volumes. Almost 1,000 scholars, experts, and members of the cultures contributed articles to the encyclopedia. The first nine volumes include the regions: North America and Greenland, Oceania, South Asia, Europe and the Mideast (including North Africa), East and Southeast Asia, Russia and Eurasia (including China), South America, Middle America and the Caribbean. Each volume has an introductory essay by its volume editor, and within each volume, entries are alphabetical with cross-references within and among volumes. The signed entries vary in length from a few lines to several pages, but all have bibliographies. Articles tend to broad definitions of cultures, noting differences within the essays. There are about 1,500 cultural summaries with maps and glossaries in the nine volumes. The entries are of cultures and include culture names, ethnonyms, orientation (identification, location, demography, linguistic affiliation), history, economy, kinship, marriage and family, sociopolitical organization, and religion. Attempts to use proper names acceptable to the culture may prove frustrating to the user; more references from common names (i.e. Eskimo) to preferred names would have been helpful. Volume 10 includes a list of cultures by country, an ethnonym index, and a subject index. Highly recommended for high school collections. [R: ARBA 94]

406 Thernstrom, Stephan, ed. **Harvard Encyclopedia of American Ethnic Groups**. Cambridge, Mass.: Belknap Press, 1980. 1076p. $115.00. ISBN 0-674-37512-2.

This is a comprehensive guide to more than 100 American groups with ethnic, religious, cultural, or regional identities. In addition there are almost 30 essays on related issues. For each signed group entry, the entire range of experience is discussed from the group's origins, migration, arrival and settlement, to its economic, social, cultural, religious life, and its experiences with education and politics. Maps and tables are included. This is a standard source, though now somewhat limited, especially for Asian peoples. Recommended for high school collections.

AFRICAN AMERICANS

407 **The African American Almanac**. 7th ed. Detroit, Mich.: Gale Research Inc., 1996. 1450p. $165.00. ISBN 0-8103-7867-1.

Previously published as *The Negro Almanac*, this has become the standard source of general information about the African American experience since its first publication in 1967. The 1989 edition was the first revision by Gale Research. There are 33 chapters with comprehensive information about history, civil rights, legal issues, social issues, labor and other economic issues, and the current status of Blacks in the United States. Statistics, illustrations, biographies, documents, and an extensive chronology extend the narrative descriptions. An index makes the source useful for ready reference and reports. Despite the wealth of new information sources, this remains an essential holding for secondary school collections.

408 **African American Biography**. 4v.
E+ Detroit, Mich.: U*X*L, 1994. $112.00/set. ISBN 0-8103-9234-8.

This is one of the tools Gale Research has developed from information in its databases and printed under the UXL imprint for upper elementary and middle school audiences. This set lists 300 African Americans living and deceased with an emphasis on contemporary figures. Volume 1 has a list of all included. One finds Harriet Tubman and the Harlem Globetrotters, but no Crispus Attucks or Sally Hemmings. Individuals were selected from sports, entertainment, politics, literature, religion, and science areas as well as from history. For each person there is a picture, a quote, a summary significance, a life history which emphasizes their career. Controversy is not ignored; it is noted that some find Kathleen Battle difficult to work with, and there is a reference to the molestation charge against Michael Jackson. A classified index to all volumes is in each volume. This is an attractive and useful set and is highly recommended. [R: ARBA 95]

409 Altman, Susan. **The Encyclopedia of African-American Heritage**. New York: Facts on File, 1997. 308p. $37.95. ISBN 0-8160-3289-0.

This volume provides upper elementary and secondary students with readable, comprehensive historical information about African American culture. It covers people, places, culture and politics in the United States as well as information about Africa and the black nations in the Caribbean. Alphabetical entries vary from a paragraph to several pages with photographs and a few maps to supplement the text. Highly recommended for elementary and middle schools and to complement the *African American Almanac* in high school collections.

410 Altman, Susan R. **Extraordinary**
E+   **Black Americans from Colonial to Contemporary Times**. Chicago: Childrens Press, 1993. 224p. $15.95pa. ISBN 0-516-40581-0.

More than 80 short biographies of Black Americans are arranged in chronological order. The individuals were selected because of their contributions, because they were involved in critical historical events or because they shed light on little known aspects of culture. Entries average about two pages. Drawings and other illustrations accompany the articles. Individuals are those likely to appear in textbooks—Crispus Attucks, James Armistead, Nat Turner and Harriet Tubman, for example. Some entries are not biographical, but are about events or occurrences such as "Slave Uprisings," and "The Emancipation Proclimation." Both the table of contents and the index provide access. The entries are clear and while the biographical information is sometimes shallow, the book will be useful to upper elementary and middle school students.

411 **Black Americans Information Directory**. Detroit, Mich.: Gale Research, 1990– . biennial. ISSN 1045-8050.

This is a comprehensive directory of more than 5,000 organizations, agencies, programs, and publications including library collections, museums, Black colleges and universities and Black studies programs, broadcast media, publications and videos arranged in topical chapters. There is a list of the top 100 Black businesses. A new section gives information on scholarships, fellowships and loans. Some information comes from other Gale publications; some from federal sources; some is original for this source. The directory is indexed by organization name and key word.

412 **The Black Resource Guide**. Washington, D.C.: Black Resource Guide, Inc., 1981– . annual. $69.95. ISSN 0767-8282.

This source is a complement to the *Information Directory* as it lists several kinds of organizations not appearing in the other source. Included are adoption agencies, church organizations, embassies and consulates, and fraternal organizations. It does include the "Black Pages" of local Black business directories, book publishers and other media sources. It also includes directory information to key people: public administrators, politicians, and members of the judiciary. There is an appendix with statistical census data.

413 Brockman, Norbert. **An African Biographical Dictionary**. Santa Barbara, Calif.: ABC-CLIO, 1994. 440p. $60.00. ISBN 0-87436-748-4.

Leaders of modern Africa are profiled in easily read and candid entries. Arranged alphabetically with an index, the articles range from about half a page to two pages; some entries have photographs. Appendices have real reference value such as a list of sub-Saharan states with colonial names, nations and their leaders. Individuals are classified by both nation and by field of accomplishment. This is an essential source for any kind of study of modern Africa. [R: SLJ May 1995]

414 Cantor, George. **Historic Land-**
E+   **marks of Black America**. Detroit, Mich.: Gale Research, 1991. 372p. $29.95. ISBN 0-8103-7809-4.

Since sites and monuments related to minority cultures are often omitted from typical travel guides, the necessity to produce individual guides to specific cultures has resulted in the publication of a number of such tools. This one is intended to provide both information for students and to be used as an itinerary for trip planning. There is a foreword with a brief history of Black America and then the sites are listed by region: Midwest, Northeast, South Central, Southeast, and the West. Within each region, listings are alphabetically by state; there is a separate chapter on Ontario. A timeline, list of further reading, and an index complete the work. Schools may find this source useful both as a general reference and in planning field trips. [R: ARBA 93]

415 Chase, Henry. **In Their Footsteps: The American Visions Guide to African-American Heritage Sites**. New York: Holt, 1994. 584p. $35.00; $16.95pa. ISBN 0-8050-3246-0; 0-8050-2089-6pa.

Black historic sites in the lower 48 states and Canada are highlighted in this directory. Included are historical markers, statues, houses, Underground Railroad stations, art museums, historical museums, cemetaries and churches. Useful introductory information includes a survey of the history of African Americans with a timeline from 1539 to 1993. Arrangement is by five regions: South, North, Midwest, West and Canada. Maps are included for each region and each is introduced by a well-known author who has lived in the region; within each region, towns with sites are listed alphabetically. Each site entry includes the name, address or location, hours, admission charges and a narrative description. There is a brief list of books for further reading and there is an index. Recommended as a history supplement and for actual or virtual field trips. [R: ARBA 95]

416 Cowan, Tom and Jack Maguire. **Timelines of African-American History: 500 Years of Black Achievement**. New York: Perigee Books, 1994. 386p. $15.00pa. ISBN 0-399-52127-5.

More than 1,500 entries give the dates of major events in African American history from 1492 to 1993. A good introduction leads to time divisions (1492–1599, the 17th and 18th centuries and each 50 year period thereafter) which are further divided by year and topic. Coverage includes history, politics, civil rights, business, religion, education, literature, arts and sports. Basic facts, descriptions and explanations are given for each event. Side boxes highlight special topics and a footer lists other events or people contemporary with the events from African American history

discussed on that page in order to present a chronological relationship. A continuing theme from 1882 to 1946 is the number of lynchings each year. An index provides further access for ready reference. Recommended for secondary libraries. [R: ARBA 95]

417 King, Anita, comp. **Contemporary**
E+   **Quotations in Black**. Westport, Conn.: Greenwood Press, 1997. 298p. $39.95. ISBN 0-313-29122-5.

This work records quotations from 236 contemporary African Americans and black Africans and supplements the author's *Quotations in Black* (1981) which emphasized quotations from historical figures. More than 1,000 quotations reflect universal ideas from blacks of all occupations; women are well represented. Arrangement is alphabetical by person quoted with a subject/ keyword index. Some portraits are included. Recommended for all libraries.

418 Salzman, Jack, David Lionel Smith, and Cornel West. **Encyclopedia of African-American Culture and History**. 5v. New York: Macmillan Library Reference, 1996. $425.00/ set. ISBN 0-02-897345-3.

This ambitious set goes far toward accomplishing its goal of covering all aspects of the African American experience. It has 2,200 entries, 1.8 million words, and 1,000 illustrations, and covers African Americans from the beginning of the 17th century through the 20th. About two-thirds of the entries are biographical, covering only African Americans—no other races and no Africans are included despite their influence. Musicians, writers, slaves, poets, sports figures, politicians, inventors, diplomats are all included. The remaining entries cover events, eras, legal cases, music, art, the professions, and all 50 states as well as cities of significance. Broad topics such as literature, religion, the effects of the Civil War and intellectual life cover 20 or more pages, while more specific entries vary from a paragraph to two pages. A list of articles precedes the alphabetical listings. Most articles are informative, do not avoid controversy, and are balanced. Volume five includes extensive tables and statistics in appendices listing such things as awards, businesses, population, religions, sports. There is a list of biographies by profession and an index. This is an outstanding set and is highly recommended for all secondary collections. [R: ARBA 97]

419 Smith, Jessie Carney, ed. **Images of Blacks in American Culture: A Reference Guide to Information Sources**. Westport, Conn.: Greenwood Press, 1988. 390p. $65.00. ISBN 0-313-24844-3.

More than just a listing of resources, this guide is composed of bibliographic essays addressing the stereotypical ways in which African Americans have been portrayed in American culture. There are separate chapters on Blacks in art, in film and television, music and song, in literature (including children's books) and even in toys and games. Other chapters address specifically the images of Black women and Black men. A final chapter describes special collections on the topic. The 10 essay chapters include bibliographies, media lists, and directory information where appropriate. This guide would add depth and interest to a high school Black history/sociology collection.

420 **Who's Who Among African Americans**. Detroit, Mich.: Gale Research, 1996– . biennial. $140.00. ISSN 1081-1400.

Previously titled *Who's Who Among Black Americans*, this source lists 20,000 biographies in alphabetical order. Entries are chosen from figures in business, government, the professions, and performers who are seen as significant contributors to American culture. Typically, information comes directly from the biographees via questionnaires with some information from secondary sources. Information includes name, occupation, personal information, education, career information, honors, special achievement, military service and directory data. A list of obituaries, a geographic index (by state and city), and an occupation index are useful. The foreword is worth reading. Any library holding *Who's Who in America* should also have this.

421 Williams, Michael W., ed. **The Afri-**
E+ **can American Encyclopedia**. 6v. North Bellmore, N.Y.: Marshall Cavendish, 1993. $449.90/set. ISBN 1-85435-545-7.

This is a comprehensive source for both historical and contemporary accounts of all aspects of

African American life. The set covers people, organizations, landmarks, professions, entertainment and sports, family life, religion, politics, law and government and culture. Entries on African countries and tribes add historical background, while specific entries on such things as books, films, and athletes add detail. Articles vary from one paragraph to several pages in length; short articles provide definitions, longer articles are summaries, and a broad overview of about 20 major topics are 5,000 words and have bibliographies attached. Useful appendices list research centers and libraries, colleges and universities, and newspapers, magazines and radio and television stations. There is an extensive classified bibliography. A list of people by profession and a thorough index complete the set. Recommended for upper elementary through high school. [R: ARBA 94]

ASIAN AMERICANS

422 Li, Marjorie H., and Peter Li, comps.
E+ and eds. **Understanding Asian Americans: A Curriculum Resource Guide**. New York: Neal-Schuman, 1990. 186p. $29.95pa. ISBN 1-55570-047-0.

The audience for this book includes teachers, principals, librarians, students, parents and anyone who works with Asian Americans. It contains essays, survey results about perceptions of Asian Americans, classroom activities to promote understanding of cultural diversity and an annotated bibliography of almost 400 titles of factual, cultural, and literary works about Asians and Asian Americans. Approximately half the titles are for K-12, while the remainder are for the general reader; the latter are listed under specific ethnic groups: Chinese, Indian, Japanese, and Other. The appendices include a chronology of Asians in America from 1761–1988, and legislation that has effected the group. This source is for selection, evaluation, and curricular support, and would be most useful in a middle school collection.

423 Ng, Franklin, ed. **Asian American Encyclopedia**. 6v. New York: Marshall Cavendish, 1995. $449.95/set. ISBN 1-85435-677-1.

All of the editors and contributing editors of this source are of Asian descent, and they have ensured the articles from many contibutors are accurate and balanced. All Asian American groups are covered and their commonalities and differences are discussed. The 2,000 alphabetical entries and 1,100 illustrations, charts, tables, graphs, and 50 maps combine to present a wealth of information about Asian Americans. Included are biographies of individuals in the arts, education, government, science and sports as well as those non-Asians who have been influential in Asian causes. Other articles deal with history, immigrant policy, law, court cases, cultural practices and organziations. There are major articles on the countries of origin of the six largest groups, Chinese, Filipino, Japanese, Indian, Korean and Vietnamese, and shorter treatment of other groups, such as the Hmong. Articles tend to be of broad entry with subdivisions and vary in length from brief definitions to 4,000 word essays. Volume one has a useful introduction, and volume six includes several features such as a timeline, an organization directory, lists of media sources and an extensive bibliography. There is a classified index and a general index; the latter does not include subject subdivisions for major topics such as music, but merely lists many page numbers. This reference set is highly recommended for secondary collections. [R: ARBA 96]

424 Zia, Helen and Susan B. Gall, eds. **Notable Asian Americans**. New York: Gale Research, 1995. 468p. $65.00. ISBN 0-8103-9623-8.

Fifteen different Asian ethnic cultures are represented in the 250 sketches in this work. Individuals may be living or dead and include actors and astronauts, authors and illustrators of children's books, business leaders, athletes, scientists and members of Congress and others from a wide variety of fields. There is a list of entries and both occupation and ethnicity indexes before the alphabetical entries. Each signed article gives a name and ethnic reference, an informal biography with subheadings for clarity, and a list of references. Many have photographs. The subject index includes people, places, organizations, and terms. This source is highly recommended for all secondary collections.

HISPANIC AMERICANS

425 **Hispanic Resource Directory**. Juneau, Ala.: Denali Press, 1991– . triennial. $47.50. ISSN 2517-4724.

Over 6,000 groups in the United States are arranged in 16 chapters. Included are national, regional, and state associations, libraries and museums, secondary and post secondary institutions with significant Hispanic enrollments, bilingual education, Hispanic study programs, media, diplomatic offices, and many other kinds of groups. Entries give typical directory information. There is a statistical appendix and organization, geographic, and contact person indexes. This source is recommended for system professional collections, as well as high schools.

426 Kanellos, Nicolas and Claudio Esteva-Fabregat, eds. **Handbook of Hispanic Cultures in the United States**. 4v. Houston, Tex.: Arte Publico Press, 1993. $60.00/volume. ISBNs: Anthropology, 1-55885-102-X; History, 1-55885-100-3; Sociolgy, 1-55885-101-1; Literature & Art, 1-55885-074-0.

This attractive and useful set was produced with financial backing from both Spanish and American sources. The volumes are divided by subject and can be purchased separately. Volume 1 deals with literature and art and includes a section on adolescence that highlights Hispanic young adult authors and titles, as well as children's songs and games and folklore. There are also separate sections on Puerto Rico, Cuba, Chicano, Latina women writers, Latino art, theater, music and film. The art section has color plates. The subject of volume 2 is anthropology and includes information on such cultural matters as religion, ethnicity, social problems, and food, while volume 3 is historical and volume 4 is sociological and deals with immigration, political involvement, labor, education, feminism, and portrayals of Hispanics in media. Each volume includes bibliographic citations and an index. Highly recommended for high school collections. [R: ARBA 95]

427 Kanellos, Nicolas, ed. **The Hispanic-American Almanac: A Reference Work on Hispanics in the United States**. Detroit, Mich.: Gale Research, 1993. 780p. $99.50. ISBN 0-8103-7944-9.

This comprehensive source defines Hispanics by social class, ethnicity, linguistic and cultural background, while recognizing the wide areas of diversity within the group. It is intended for students and laypeople and is arranged in 25 subject chapters which are signed and have relevant subject bibliographies. A chronology precedes the chapters which include such topics as a long historical overview, significant documents, the family (subdivided by area of origin), language, literature, art, theater, film, music, and prominent Hispanics. There is a glossary of Spanish terms, a general bibliography and an index. More than 400 photographs, drawings, maps and tables add to the value of this source which would be useful in secondary collections. [R: ARBA 94]

428 Kanellos, Nicholas. **Hispanic Firsts: 500 Years of Extraordinary Achievement**. Detroit, Mich.: Gale Research, 1997. 372p. $44.95. ISBN 0-7876-0517-4.

A long foldout chronology of important Hispanic events from the sixteenth century to 1997 serves as the structure of this yearly chronology of the contributions of Hispanics to the United States. Subject areas covered are art, business, education, film, government, labor, literature, media, military, performing arts, religions, science/technology, sports and theater. Entries are brief and there are many illustrations; sources are included. An excellent bibliography; and both general and chronological indexes add to the value of the work as a reference source. Recommended for secondary collections.

429 Meier, Matt S. **Mexican American Biographies: A Historical Dictionary, 1836–1987**. Westport, Conn.: Greenwood Press, 1988. 270p. $55.00. ISBN 0-313-24521-5.

This is a narrative biography volume, not merely a who's who. Selected for significant achievement in professional life or civic affairs, 270 entries are arranged in alphabetical order. While coverage is from the 1830s to 1988, 200 of the listings are of contemporary figures. Appendices list the individuals by professional field and by state, and there is an index. Recommended for secondary school libraries.

430 Meier, Matt S., and Feliciano Rivera. **Dictionary of Mexican American History**. Westport, Conn.: Greenwood Press, 1981. 498p. $59.95. ISBN 0-313-21203-1.

This is a good source of historical information, covering events, places and people from 1519, with some references to even older cultures. The main body of information covers 1835–1980. The 1,000 entries are usually brief but there are some longer signed articles with reference lists. Arrangement is alphabetical with cross-references to related entries. There are eight useful appendices, including a chronology, a glossary, and a list of journals. An index is included. This source is an important complement for regular American history resources as well as a source in ethnic studies.

431 Sinnott, Susan. **Extraordinary Hispanic Americans**. Chicago: Childrens Press, 1995. 240p. $15.95. ISBN 0-516-40582-9.

From Spanish explorers to Hispanics whose contributions will spill over to the next century, the individuals selected for this work represent the wide scope of what it means to be Hispanic American. Conquistadors, priests, musicians, artists, politicians, union leaders and sports figures representing all of the backgrounds that share a Spanish-speaking heritage are listed chronologically. Entries range from three to five pages and are illustrated. There is a brief bibliography and an index. For upper elementary and middle school students.

432 Tardiff, Joseph C. and L. Mpho Mabunda, eds. **Dictionary of Hispanic Biography**. New York: Gale Research, 1996. 1011p. $120.00. ISBN 0-8103-8302-0.

Activists, artists, sports figures, scientists, journalists, politicians, and businessmen and women from Spanish-speaking countries and the United States are among the 470 notable people in this dictionary. Covering the period from the 15th century to the present, about 70% of the individuals are contemporary people who reviewed their own entries for accuracy. A foreword addresses the issues of inclusion. There is a table of contents that defines the historical period for each person. The narrative signed essays are from one to three pages in length and include a list of references and if appropriate, a list of published works by the individual. About 200 of the entries are accompanied by a photograph. There is an occupation index, a nationality/ethnicity index, and a subject index. A clear layout and a good typeface make this source appropriate for middle and high school students. Highly recommended. [R: ARBA 97]

433 Tenenbaum, Barbara A., and others, eds. **Encyclopedia of Latin American History and Culture**. 5v. New York: Scribner's, 1996. $449.00/set. ISBN 0-684-19253-5.

Scholarship about Latin America has increased greatly in the last decade and this set collects both old and new research and makes it accessible for students, teachers, and general readers. There are 5,287 entries written by 832 contributors representing all aspects of history and culture. This set does include Brazil and the Portuguese empire, and all of the historic Spanish empire. It covers countries and other places, events, institutions and practices, treaties and laws, organizations, wars, religions, literature, art, race and ethnicity, politics, economics, music, science and medicine, sports and entertainment, education, and the military. There are 3,000 biographical sketches. Entries are 100 words or more and are in alphabetical order with cross-references. Articles are signed and have references; many photographs add to the narrative. Maps are on the endpapers. Volume five contains an appendix that classifies biographies by occupation, including royalty and outlaws. There is also a list of contributors and an index. This is a good set for language, history, and culture classes and is recommended for high school collections. [R: ARBA 97]

434 **Who's Who Among Hispanic Americans**. Detroit, Mich.: Gale Research, 1991– . biennial. $100.00. ISSN 1052-7354.

Updated biennially, this source lists more than 10,000 contemporary individuals who trace their ancestry to Spain or to Spanish speaking countries in the Western hemisphere. Included are significant people in all the professions, government, civil rights, and entertainment. There are indexes by current geographic location, occupation, and by nation of ethnic/cultural heritage. This should be part of a secondary library's who's who collections.

JEWS

435 Alpher, Joseph, ed. **Encyclopedia of Jewish History: Events and Eras of the Jewish People**. New York: Facts on File, 1986. 287p. $40.00. ISBN 0-8160-1220-2.

More than 100 historical entries arranged chronologically and 12 appendices on culture and ethnography provide a comprehensive panorama of events, eras, and key figures from ancient to modern times. Entries are signed and are about 800 words with many illustrations, maps, photographs, and diagrams. Key illustrations are on the upper right of each double page article and cross-references lead to related articles. There is an important introductory essay, a timeline of Jewish and world history, a glossary and an index. Recommended for high school collections needing depth in this area.

436 American Jewish Committee. **American Jewish Year Book**. New York: American Jewish Committee, 1899– . annual. $30.00. ISSN 0065-8987.

This is a basic annual publication that contains essays on aspects of Jewish life in America and in other countries in addition to standard yearbook information. There is a directory of Jewish organizations, foundations, and community councils and a list of Jewish periodicals. Also included are important statistical data and the Jewish calendar for several years. Obituaries of important Jewish Americans who died the previous year are listed, as well as an index to obituaries in previous editions. There is also a selected list of essays that appeared earlier. An index completes each volume.

437 DeLange, Nicholas. **Atlas of the Jewish World**. New York: Facts on File, 1984. 240p. $45.00. ISBN 0-87196-043-5.

The text and illustrations provide commentary to the maps in this useful work which covers the historical and cultural backgrounds of the Jewish people and how they have achieved their status near the end of the 20th century. While there are fewer than 50 maps, there are over 300 black and white and color photographs. A chronology, a glossary, a gazetteer and a bibliography are included; there is an index. This attractive and useful source is highly recommended for secondary collections.

438 Friesel, Evyatar. **Atlas of Modern Jewish History**. rev. ed. New York: Oxford University Press, 1990. 159p. $60.00. ISBN 0-19-505393-1.

This is a revised and updated translation of the Hebrew edition and covers the 17th to the 20th centuries, to the mid 1980s. The atlas is not well organized, mixing statistical, geographic, thematic, and cultural arrangement. The information is excellent and the maps, diagrams, and text provide comprehensive coverage of the time period. A general index and a geographic name index help with access. The source would be useful for both world culture and ethnic studies.

439 Shamir, Ilana, gen. ed. and Shlomo
E+ Shavit, ed. **The Young Reader's Encyclopedia of Jewish History**. 1st American ed. New York: Viking Kestred, 1987. 125p. $17.95pa. ISBN 0-670-81738-4.

This attractive topical encyclopedia is arranged chronologically from nomadic tribes of about 500 B.C. to the kibbutz today. There are 28 such topics illustrated with photographs, reprints of art works, maps, drawings and diagrams. A timeline shows how Jewish history relates to world history. A glossary and an index complete the volume. This is an attractive source for elementary and middle schools.

440 Wigodor, Geoffrey, ed. **The New Standard Jewish Encyclopedia**. 7th ed. New York: Facts on File, 1992. 1001p. $59.95. ISBN 0-8160-2690-4.

The first edition of this work was published in 1958 and the most recent in 1977. This 7th edition is labeled the "new revised edition." It is a comprehensive one-volume encyclopedia that covers Jewish history, religion and culture. Included are people, places, ethical issues, events, education, scholarship and groups. It is arranged alphabetically with cross-references but no index. The articles vary from brief identifications to longer articles for geographic regions and major subject disciplines. The longest article is on Israel. Many photographs and drawings accompany the text. This is an excellent basic source for ready reference information and is recommended for secondary collections. [R: ARBA 93]

NATIVE AMERICANS

441 Avery, Susan, and Linda Skinner.
E **Extraordinary American Indians**. Chicago: Childrens Press, 1995. 288p. $15.95. ISBN 0-516-40583-7.

The biographies of individuals selected for their accomplishments are arranged chronologically and include names often referred to in upper elementary and middle school curricula. Over fifty Native Americans, including several families with members who share an entry, are described in articles that average about four pages. Each entry has a portrait and other illustrations. The individuals were carefully selected and the writing is clear. Some entries are of events rather than people. There is an excellent bibliography and an index. Recommended for upper elementary and middle school students.

442 Cantor, George. **North American Indian Landmarks: A Traveler's Guide**. Detroit, Mich.: Gale Research, 1993. 409p. $34.95. ISBN 0-8103-8916-9.

This source is for students and travelers and includes sketches of 340 sites related to Native American history from the earliest times to the present. It includes such things as monuments, plaques, parks, museums, reservations, battlefields, birthplaces and grave sites from 45 states and 6 provinces. Entries are arranged by region (Northeast, Southeast, Great Lakes, Great Plains/North, Great Plains/South, Southwest and Great Basin, and Pacific Coast and Arctic). Listings are then alphabetical by state or province. Each entry is descriptive with a box at the end with practical information for visitors such as location, hours, admission information, and a telephone number. There are more than 70 photographs and maps. An outline of history and of current issues, a timeline, an alphabetical listing of tribes, a glossary, a bibliography for further reading and an index add to the reference value of the work. This is an accurate source and highly recommended for secondary collections. It complements *Discover Indian Reservations*. [R: ARBA 94]

443 Champagne, Duane, ed. **Native**
E+   **America: Portrait of the Peoples**.
Detroit, Mich.: Visible Ink Press,
1994. 786p. $18.95. ISBN 0-8103-
9452-9.

This is an abridged version of the 1994 edition of
Gale's *Native North American Almanac*. The
author is of Chippewa descent and is a university
scholar; advisors and contributors include Native
Americans and non-Native Americans, and the
work is framed with a foreword and an afterword
written by Native American activists. The focus of
the work is both Canada and the United States
and both historical and contemporary. Chapters
are written by experts engaged in Native life and
issues and represent diverse points of view. Ten
chapters cover the tribes in the United States and
Canada by cultural region with sections on languages, religion, health, arts, literature, media,
and activism. Most chapters include biographies.
Maps and over 200 illustrations and photographs
add to the text. There is an abundance of valuable
information in this work although the format does
not lend itself to ease of use. Reference to the
index is essential and at times the index is not as
complete as it should be. It is highly recommended, however, for reference collections in elementary schools where it will be used by teachers,
and for student collections in middle and high
schools. [R: ARBA 95]

444 Ciment, James. **Scholastic Encyclo-**
E+   **pedia of the North American Indian**.
New York: Scholastic Reference,
1996. 224p. $17.95. ISBN 0-590-
22790-4.

Native American tribes and groups, geographic
regions, and special topics are integrated into
one alphabetical arrangement with cross-
references in red. More than 140 groups and 11
regions (Plains, e.g.) are covered; special topics
include such items as the Native American in
the movies, languages, missions, and Red
Power. The regional entries summarize the
tribes of the area and their way of life and the
effects of the European settlement. Tribal
entries average one page and include a map
showing the group's original location, the language family, lifeways, current location and variant tribal names. The essays have subheadings
and there are related boxed entries with portraits and other illustrations. The book also has
a timeline, four maps, places to visit, a resource

guide with fiction, nonfiction, and video titles, a
glossary and an index. This is a nicely organized
and useful volume for elementary and middle
school collections. [R: SLJ Nov 96]

445 Davis, Mary B, and others, eds.
     Native America in the Twentieth
     Century: An Encyclopedia. New
     York: Garland Pub., 1994. 787p.
     $95.00. ISBN 0-8240-4846-6.

This source will help to establish that Native
Americans are not just mysterious historical figures. It emphasizes important aspects of Native
American life in the United States during the
20th century. Broad overview articles discuss art,
education, health, and law, and are followed by
alphabetically arranged articles on specific
aspects of these broad subjects and articles about
the 20th century status of nations, tribes, and
peoples. Articles are signed; contributors are
both non-Native American and Native American, with tribal affiliation included for Native
American contributors. A complete list of articles is included as a contents list, and a detailed
subject index completes the access aids. This is
an accurate and authoritative work and is highly
recommended for all high school collections. [R:
ARBA 95]

446 **Encyclopedia of American Indian**
     Civil Rights. Westport, Conn.:
     Greenwood Press, 1997. 417p.
     $65.00. ISBN 0-313-29338-4.

This source lists events, individuals, court cases,
laws, treaties, incidents and issues that are
related to the civil rights of Native Americans.
Arranged alphabetically after a useful introduction, the 600 signed entries also have suggested
readings. The index, photographs and general
bibliography add to the reference applications of
the source which supplements both cultural and
political science curricula in high schools.

447 **The Encyclopedia of North American**
     Indians. Tarrytown, N.Y.: Marshall
     Cavendish, 1997. 11v. $459.95. ISBN
     0-7614-0227-6.

The 1,700 entries are arranged alphabetically by
topic throughout 10 volumes with a general
index in volume 11 along with a topical guide,
lists of nations and tribes, suggestions for further
reading and addresses of museums and centers.

Both historical and contemporary people, places, events, beliefs and nations are listed. The geographical scope includes not only the United States, but Canada, Mexico, Greenland, the Caribbean, Central and South America. Entries vary in length from a few paragraphs to several pages and there are many illustrations.

The contributors are recognized authorities; about two-thirds are Native people. Highly recommended for all secondary collections.

448 Gill, Sam D. and Irene F. Sullivan. **Dictionary of Native American Mythology**. Santa Barbara, Calif.: ABC-CLIO, 1992. 425p. $65.00. ISBN 0-87436-621-6.

Mythology here includes religion, ritual, entertainment, and myth. The source lists references to stories from these elements which describe Native American culture. The entries are to the stories and include their characters, themes, events, gods, spirits, rituals, and practices. Arrangement is alphabetical, often by Native American language with cross-references. Entries include title, tribe, culture area, description, and bibliographic references. There is an extensive general bibliography and an index by tribe. [R: ARBA 94]

449 Griffin-Pierce, Trudy. **The Encyclo-**
E   **pedia of Native America**. New York: Viking, 1995. 192p. $25.00. ISBN 0-670-85104-3.

The author, of Catawban ancestry, has written a text that is arranged by seven regions of the United States, including the Northeast, Southeast, Great Plains, Great Basin, Northwest, California, and the Southwest. There is also an introduction about the earliest peoples and an epilogue about Native Americans today. Each chapter has a quotation, a language map, and introduction about the peoples in the region, and the results of European contact. Rather than comprehensive coverage of tribes, the author has chosen one or more prototypes from each region and describes that group. Boxed facts and illustrations add to the interesting text. There is an index. This encyclopedia does not provide the breadth of information as other sources, but serves as a good introduction. Recommended for elementary collections.

450 Hirschfelder, Arlene D. and Paulette Molin. **The Encyclopedia of Native American Religions**. New York: Facts on File, 1992. 367p. $40.00. ISBN 0-8160-2017-5.

This volume includes comprehensive coverage of the known scholarship about the spiritual traditions of native people in both the United States and Canada before contact with Europeans, as affected by contact with Europeans, and as practiced by contemporary Native Americans. Information is limited by the amount of research available, and by sensitivity to privacy associated with many traditions and practices. Within this framework, the source provides information on religions, ceremonies, native healing, religious protection laws, identified sacred sites, people (Catholic and Protestant missionaries, native practitioners who do not mind being identified), and general religious matters. It does not include stories or texts of religious content. There is an extensive list for further reading and a subject/ classified list that refers to topics rather than to pages. Highly recommended for secondary collections. [R: ARBA 93]

451 Johansen, Bruce E. and Donald A. Grinde. **The Encyclopedia of Native American Biography: Six Hundred Life Stories of Important People**. New York: Holt, 1997. 463p. $50.00. ISBN 0-8050-3270-3.

Both historical and contemporary Native Americans are included in this volume. Some 600 artists, athletes, politicians, leaders and writers are covered. The entries often contain quotations, suggestions for further reading and photographs. There is an excellent general index. Highly recommended for secondary schools.

452 Johnson, Michael. **The Native Tribes of North America: A Concise Encyclopedia**. New York: Macmillan, 1994. 210p. $85.00. ISBN 0-02-897189-2.

This encyclopedia was written from a British point of view to correct the image of the Native American typically held by the British public, but it is also useful to an American audience because of the depth of information presented. It covers 400 native groups with an emphasis on lifeways in the 19th century, while also providing information on original location and current locations and conditions. The arrangement is regional and matches curricular approaches; it includes Canadian, subarctic and Arctic peoples. Tribes are not alphabetical within the geographic sections, so the index and table of contents are important. There are 18 sketch maps and many illustrations; color and monochrome plates are inserted. In all cases, including the front and back jacket covers, all items in illustrations are carefully labeled and distinguished. The captions to all illustrations are filled with additional information. Coverage is sensitive and in depth; the groups commonly referred to as Sioux are divided and properly named, even minor treaties often omitted from other sources are included as are details about current locations of tribes that have been separated. This is not a graphically arresting source, but it has a vast amount of information. Highly recommended for secondary collections. [R: SLJ Nov 94]

453 Klein, Barry T. ed. **Reference Encyclopedia of the American Indian**. 8th ed. West Nyack, N.Y.: Todd Publications, 1997. 883p. $125.00; $95.00pa. ISBN 0-915344-75-0; 0-915344-74-2pa.

There are four main sections to this combination directory, bibliography, and biographical dictionary which covers both the United States and Canada. Section 1 is a directory arranged alphabetically by state of all kinds of organizations that affect the Native American including reservations, communities, government agencies, schools, colleges, sources of financial aid, museums, monuments, parks, and more. New to this edition are listings for Native American education programs in public schools, casino and gambling establishments and major Native American events. Section 2 is a directory of similar Canadian organizations. Section 3 is a bibliography of 4,500 print books arranged alphabetically with both a subject index and publisher index. Section 4 contains 2,500 biographical sketches with a separate index/list. The scope of this source makes it useful for secondary school collections.

454 Langer, Howard J., comp. and ed. **American Indian Quotations**. Westport, Conn.: Greenwood Press, 1996. 260p. $49.95. ISBN 0-313-29121-7.

This entry into the new group of quotation books representing those omitted from the standard sources is complicated by the questionable authority of some of the earliest quotations which are necessarily translations recorded by others. In addition, some of the 800 entries are not really quotations, but merely refer to the names of things which may be attributable to Native Americans, such as Talking Leaves, the Chisholm Trail, and Love Medicine. Nonetheless, this is a useful source that will fill the existing gap as intended. The quotations are arranged in chronological order by author; each author is identified by dates and tribal affiliation and a brief informational note. There are portraits of 22 of the authors. Entries are numbered and the source and date are given for each. A second section gives unattributal quotations. There are separate author, subject/key word and tribal indexes, each of which enhance the use of the book. Most secondary schools will want to add this to their quotation collections. [R: ARBA 97]

455 Malinowski, Sharon, ed. **Notable Native Americans**. New York: Gale Research, 1995. 492p. $65.00. ISBN 0-8103-9638-6.

This excellent biographical tool covers 265 Native Americans throughout history and from many fields. About one third of the entries are historical; the rest are of 20th century and contemporary figures. The consulting editor, George H. J. Abrams, and all of the advisory board members are of Native heritage. Abrams's introduction is an excellent overview of current thinking about the historical and current issues of importance in Native American culture. Entries are listed by tribe/nation and by occupation or tribal role; 88 different tribes are represented. Entries are alphabetical and give name, tribal affiliation and occupation. Most articles are from one to three pages with subheadings to provide clarity; many have photographs. Attached to the articles are bibliographies, and when appropriate, lists of works by the individual. There is a subject index. Highly recommended for secondary libraries.

456 Nies, Judith. **Native American His-**
E+ **tory: A Chronology of the Vast Achievement of a Culture and Their Links to World Events**. New York: Ballantine Books, 1996. 420p. $13.95. ISBN 0-345-39350-3.

This chronology is unique because it matches Native American history and culture to the context of world cultures. Coverage is from 28,000 B.C. with the most detailed entries beginning in 1400 A.D. after which the sections are by century. Native American peoples from Mexico and the United States are included. The entries are presented in two columns, one for world history and one for Native American history so that date comparisons can be easily made. The juxtaposition of events is truly enlightening; e.g., Galileo was arrested at about the same time that the Zunis were in revolt against the Spanish. Another strength of the work is the illustrations, boxes and maps; the photographs not only add to meaning, but are given full explanations. There is a selected bibliography and an index. The book would have been strengthened by the inclusion of tribes from Canada and the Arctic regions. Nonetheless, this is an excellent source for integrating Native American history into any curriculum area and is highly recommended for teachers and students at all levels. [R: SLJ May 97]

457 Porter, Frank W., III, gen. ed. **The**
E+   **Chelsea House Series on Indians of North America**. 63v. New York: Chelsea House, 1989–1997. $1256.85/set. ISBN 1-55546-685-0.

Published as individual volumes, a library may wish to circulate one set and keep another together in the reference collection. Each volume follows the same format; narrative chapters discuss where the group originated and what life was like before and after the arrival of European explorers and settlers. The series is notable for recognizing the contemporary life of the group and for identifying its leaders. A quick fact section gives a good summary about the group. There are many illustrations: drawings, maps, photographs, color photographs of artifacts. More than 70 volumes are available, including some topical volumes on literature and women's roles in Native societies. Each volume is authored by an expert on the group. Upper elementary students could use the set; it is especially recommended for middle and high school collections.

458 Prucha, Francis Paul. **Atlas of American Indian Affairs**. Lincoln: University of Nebraska Press, 1990. 191p. $50.00. ISBN 0-8032-3689-1.

The maps in this atlas are intended to be a graphic representation of statistical data about the experience of the Native American. There are ten sections with 109 black and white maps with narrative introductions. They show cultural and tribal areas, census figures from 1890–1980, land cessions, reservations from 1880–1987, agencies, schools, and hospitals. Separate sections are included for Oklahoma and Alaska. Other historical chapters show army and Native American frontiers and there is a portfolio of event maps. These clear maps are arranged in chronological order within the sections, and provide wonderful source material for problem solving and critical thinking assignments. Recommended for middle and high school collections.

459 Tiller, Veronica E., ed. **Discover Indian Reservations USA: A Visitors' Welcome Guide**. Denver, Colo.: Council Publications, 1992. 402p. $19.95. ISBN 0-9632580-0-1.

This travel guide and reference tool is intended to promote visits to reservations and to provide accurate, updated information about modern day tribes and communities. The guide includes reservations throughout the United States except Alaska (because of its extensive sites that are beyond the possibilities of this volume). A list of federal and state reservations and a fold-out map make a useful introduction. Reservations are listed from west to east, with the locations alphabetical within each state. For each reservation, there is a tribal profile, a description of the reservation, the specific tribes and bands now living there, their businesses and industries. Directory information is given as well as descriptions of cultural institutions, historical sites, special events, recreational opportunities, accommodations, and any restrictions. Photographs, maps and portraits enhance the narrative. There are cross-references to satellite areas of tribes within and between state boundaries. One appendix lists all tribes and communities under large tribal names with state and reservation names, while a second appendix is a Pow Wow directory arranged by state and month. The volume has a general index. [R: ARBA 93]

460 Waldman, Carl. **Atlas of the North**
E+   **American Indian**. New York: Facts on File, 1985. 276p. $35.00; $17.95pa. ISBN 0-87196-850-9; 0-8160-2136-8pa.

This narrative history of the Native American is accompanied by 96 maps and many photographs. Seven chronologically arranged sections begin with ancient people and civilizations and moves to chapters concerned with the effects of the European settlement of North America on its Native peoples. A final section deals with the contemporary Native American. Appendices contain a chronology, a list of tribes of both the U.S. and Canada with both historical and contemporary locations, a list of major Native American place names, and a directory of museums, societies, and reconstructed villages. A bibliography and an index complete the volume. Highly recommended for all levels.

461 Waldman, Carl. **Encyclopedia of**
E+ **Native American Tribes**. New York:
Facts on File, 1988. 293p. $45.00.
ISBN 0-8160-1421-3.

Two or three page descriptions of more than 150 Native American tribes in the United States, Canada, and Mexico are presented in alphabetical order by tribal name. Entries are also under names of cultural groups, civilizations and language families. Cross-referencing and indexing are good, but not complete; the entry for Fox lists Mesquakie as a part of the group, but neither cross-reference nor index leads from Mesquakie to the Fox entry. For each group there is historical and cultural information, major conflicts, and very brief notes about the group today. There are color illustrations, maps, and a glossary. This remains a useful source for basic information and could be used by both upper elementary and secondary students.

462 Waldman, Carl. **Who Was Who in**
E+ **Native American History: Indians**
and Non-Indians from Early Con-
tacts Through 1900. New York: Facts
on File, 1990. 410p. $50.00. ISBN
0-8160-1797-2.

This volume complements both of Waldman's other sources. It is a historical who's who of Native Americans, and others who played a role in their history prior to the 20th century. More than 1,000 entries of tribal leaders, important warriors, explorers, soldiers, traders, govern-

ment officials, and reformers are arranged in alphabetical order with cross-references. Appendices list the individuals by tribe and the non-Native Americans by categories of contribution. Each entry gives the name, any tribal name, birth and death dates if known, brief descriptions of significance, and family connections. There are a few black and white illustrations. Recommended for collections holding Waldman's other two volumes.

463 Waldman, Carl. **Word Dance: The**
E+ **Language of Native American Cul-**
ture. New York: Facts on File, 1994.
290p. $25.95. ISBN 0-8160-2834-6.

Waldman has contributed several useful volumes to the study of the Native American and this is an excellent companion to his other works. This is a glossary/dictionary/encyclopedia with short-entry definitions of terms and their relationships to broader concepts. It emphasizes Native American (both U.S. and Canada) culture and history. Entries are alphabetical with cross-references and consist of a heading, alternative spellings, synonyms, and the definitions. Pen and ink drawings add visual appeal and help with understanding. There is a classified appendix with references to articles with such headings as animals, anthropology, arts and crafts, and a bibliography. Recommended for reference collections at all levels. [R: ARBA 95]

464 Wolfson, Evelyn. **From Abenaki to**
E+ **Zuni: A Dictionary of Native Ameri-**
can Tribes. New York: Walker, 1988.
215p. $18.95; $9.95pa. ISBN 0-8027-
66789-3; 0-8027-7445-8pa.

Brief entries of 68 tribes are listed alphabetically. A phonetic spelling and meaning are given for each. The information is primarily cultural, but there is a historical review and brief information about the contemporary situation of the group as well. Each tribe is described in 2-4 pages, and there are many photographs. A map shows cultural areas and there is a list of major tribes by regions. A glossary and index complete the volume. Recommended for elementary and middle schools.

Etiquette

465 Brainard, Beth. **Soup Should Be**
E   **Seen, Not Heard! The Kids' Eti-**
     quette Book: A Complete Manners
     Book for Children. New York: Dell
     Pub., 1990. 151p. $12.95pa. ISBN 0-
     440-50333-7.

This is a spiral bound, appropriately illustrated
etiquette guide for children. The text has 10 sections with such topics as how to make introductions and telephone manners. The text is easy to
read and understand. Elementary and middle
schools should have one copy in the reference
collection and at least one circulating copy.

466 Dresser, Norine. **Multicultural Man-**
    ners: New Rules of Etiquette for a
    Changing Society. New York: Wiley,
    1996. 285p. $15.95pa. ISBN 0-471-
    11819-2.

This guide addresses both personal and business
issues that arise in a cross-cultural environment.
Real situation descriptions illustrate the kinds of
misunderstandings that arise when cultural differences in spatial territories, body language, word
choice and perspective come into play. Appropriate behavior is suggested and described. Recommended for high school collections.

467 Post, Emily. **Emily Post's Etiquette**.
    16th ed. New York: HarperCollins,
    1997. 845p. $28.00. ISBN 0-06-
    270078-2.

One of the standard etiquette books through its
multiple editions since 1922, this tends to be
more formal than other sources, despite its
updating for contemporary mores. Separate sections deal with personal life, professional life,
communications, travel and tipping, entertaining, celebrations and ceremonies, gifts, and wed-
dings. An index leads easily to specific concerns.
For middle and high school, and professional
collections.

468 Post, Elizabeth L., and Joan M.
E+   Coles. **Emily Post's Teen Etiquette**.
     HarperCollins, 1995. 192p.
     $11.50pa. ISBN 0-06-273337-0.

This guide for teenagers covers traditional points
of etiquette such as use of the proper fork and
thank-you notes, but also includes topics of particular interest to today's teenager. Appearance,
dating, parties and family relationships, including divorce and step family matters. New communication technologies and strategies (beepers
and call waiting) are addressed. Recommended
for upper elementary and secondary schools.

Genealogy and Personal Names

FLAGS

469 Shearer, Benjamin F. and Barbara S.
E+   Shearer. **State Names, Seals, Flags,**
     and Symbols: A Historical Guide.
     Westport, Conn.: Greenwood Press,
     1994. 438p. $49.95. ISBN 0-313-
     28862-3.

This is an authenticated source of state official
symbols and the origins of state names. First
published in 1987, this edition expands coverage
to U.S. districts and territories. Arrangement is
by topical chapter, with state information alphabetically within chapters. Beginning with names
and nicknames, there are about two paragraphs
explaining the origin of each state's name. Mottoes are given with origins, followed by descriptions of seals, flags, capitols, flowers, trees, birds,
and songs; and new in this edition, legal holidays
and observations, license plates, and commemorative postage stamps. A final chapter includes
the miscellaneous "officials" most states have:
insects, rocks, animals, fish, colors, sports,
dances, poems, beverages and the like. Center
color plates show flowers, birds, flags, and seals.

All of this information is carefully annotated with citation notes. There is a selected bibliography of state histories and an index. Highly recommended for all libraries. [R: ARBA 95]

470 **Ultimate Pocket: Flags of the World**.
E+   New York: DK Publishing, 1997. 240p. $12.95. ISBN 0-7894-2085-6.

This small guide contains more than 300 flags of countries, provinces, states and territories. Entries are organized by continent and contain, in addition to a color illustration of the national flag, a brief note about its history and origin. Location maps show the country in context of its neighbors and other national emblems are also shown. Flags of political units within the nation are clustered several to a page. The table of contents and index are necessary to locate a specific country as the countries are not alphabetical within the continent arrangement. All collections will find this current flag book useful.

GENEALOGY

471 Cerny, Johni, and Arlene Eakle, eds. **The Source: A Guidebook of American Genealogy**. Salt Lake City, Utah: Ancestry Publishing Co., 1984. 786p. $49.95. ISBN 0-916489-00-0.

472 Cerny, Johni, John Cerny, Arlene Eakle. **Ancestry's Guide to Research: Case Studies in American Genealogy**. Salt Lake City, Utah: Ancestry Publishing Co., 1985. 364p. $19.95pa. ISBN 0-916489-01-9.

Titling this "the" source is appropriate for this comprehensive guide to genealogical research which intends to "identify, locate, and interpret" every basic form of relevant published record covering the period from the first European colonization to 1910. Divided into three major sections with an introduction, appendices, glossary and indexes, the guide covers major record sources, published genealogical sources, and special resources that include ethnic groups other than Europeans. Each of the three sections is further divided into categories. A companion guide is *Ancestry's Guide to Research* which uses diagrams, reproductions, state-by-state guides, problems likely to be encountered and writing for records. This how-to guide helps the researcher access the records in *The Source.*

473 Lawson, Sandra M., comp. **Generations Past: A Selected List of Sources for Afro-American Genealogical Research**. Library of Congress. Washington, D.C.: Government Printing Office, 1988. 101p. $25.00. ISBN 0-84-4406-04-X.

This is a selected list of 361 sources from the Library of Congress collection of use to researchers looking for their Afro American ancestry. The emphasis is on such things as family histories from the 19th century or earlier, and Afro American business and city directories from that period up to 1959. In addition there are guidebooks, collective biographies, U.S. local histories, genealogic periodicals and organizations. Items have LC numbers and there is complete bibliographic information. There is an author-title index. The source is a complement to James Rose and Alice Eichholz *Black Genesis* (Gale, 1978), the beginning guide to African American genealogy.

474 United States National Archives and Records Service. **Guide to Genealogical Research in the National Archives**. Washington, D.C.: National Archives and Record Service, 1985. 304p. $35.00. Archives #W100001.

This guide lists and describes the basic sources available in the National Archives for genealogical researchers. Sources include population, immigration, and military records and there are sections about specific groups such as Native Americans and African Americans. Appendices, illustrations, tables, and cross-references complement the narrative descriptions.

PERSONAL NAMES

475 Dunkling, Leslie and William
E+   Gosling. **The Facts on File Dictionary of First Names**. New York: Facts on File, 1984. 305p. $24.95. ISBN 0-87196-274-8.

American and British names are the focus of this guide which attempts to cover first names in general use since the 17th century, and lists some 4,500 with their variations. For each name there is a paragraph entry which tells the background of the name including its language of origin and meaning, how it was introduced, its earliest recorded use, any surnames from which it was derived and statistical evidence of the extent it has been used and by whom. Names are listed in alphabetical order; interesting appendices list the top 50 names for boys and girls in selected years 1925–1983, including names used by both whites and non-whites. Recommended for upper elementary through high school collections.

476 Hanks, Patrick. **A Dictionary of First**
E+   **Names**. New York: Oxford University Press, 1990. 443p. $39.95. ISBN 0-19-211651-7.

This source is international in scope and has a good introduction about cultural and ethnic naming. Names are listed alphabetically and entries give language source and meaning, famous people with the name, cognates in other languages, and short or pet forms. There are

supplements included in the volume with common Arab and Asian-Indian names. This is a good complement to volumes limited to European names.

477 Hanks, Patrick and Flavia Hodges. **A Dictionary of Surnames**. New York: Oxford University Press, 1988. 826p. $85.00. ISBN 0-19-211592-8.

Limited to common surnames, primarily British with European cognates. Names were taken from telephone directories and historical, cultural and national surveys. A bibliography of sources used is included. Names are alphabetical and give name, languages, derivation, popularity, cognates, and other variations. This is a scholarly source, but appropriate for high schools. Schools with large populations of students with non-European surnames will find this source disappointing; even common European names are omitted.

Geography and World Studies

ATLASES

See also **Atlases** in specific subject areas such as **History**.

478 **Atlas of the World**. 5th ed. New York:
E+   Oxford University Press, 1997. 328p. $75.00. ISBN 0-19-521368-8.

The quality and color of the maps and the 75,000 entry index make this atlas a good choice for schools. An introduction to world geography with both narrative and maps covers the earth, people, production and quality of life. There is a section of 66 city maps with its own index, followed by the world maps arranged by continent and country. Grid indexes on the endpapers complement the fine index. Recommended for all levels. [R: ARBA 94]

479 Brawer, Moshe. **Atlas of Russia and the Independent Republics**. New York: Simon & Schuster, 1994. 144p. $75.00. ISBN 0-13-051996-0.

Russia and the 14 new states that emerged at the break up of the Soviet Union are the focus of this

atlas which describes the physical and human characteristics of the newly independent nations. An introductory survey frames the work with sections about natural features, history, and population and is followed by sections on the independent republics. Each republic is treated with narratives, maps, and city maps; and the coverage includes regions, climate, population, economy, history, government and the capital. The red tones of the maps and graphs sometimes make the illustrations unclear, but the atlas is a useful one, nonetheless. There is an annotated bibliography classified by country and an index of place names which lists variant forms and spellings. [R: ARBA 96]

480 Brawer, Moshe, ed. **Atlas of the Middle East**. New York: Prentice Hall, 1988. 140p. $75.00. ISBN 0-02-905271-8.

Nineteen countries are covered in this atlas, including Egypt and Libya. There is an introduction to the region and its physical features and political history. There is a chart showing military balance. The countries are treated with encyclopedic entries, including maps, charts, fact boxes. There is a bibliography and a list for further reading and an index. The brown-toned graphics do not make this an attractive volume, but it is accurate and provides thorough coverage of this important area.

481   Castello-Cortes, Ian, ed. **The Dorling**
E+   **Kindersley World Reference Atlas**.
       2d American ed. New York: Dorling
       Kindersley, 1996. 731p. $49.95. ISBN
       0-7894-1085-0.

The second American edition of this attractive atlas updates the political changes of the early 1990s. More than 5,000 illustrations, 600 maps, and 25,000 facts and statistics are included in this work. Computer-generated graphics including icons, charts, and chronology boxes are visually exciting. Divided into four sections, the atlas presents geographic and historical backgrounds of the world as it is today, almanac data and maps on the 192 countries defined by the United Nations, narrative on 8 major global issues, and an index/gazetteer with international organizations, geographic place names, and a glossary of geographic terms. The visual appeal is marred by the colors used but not explained and some small insert maps that are so small the details are impossible to read. Nonetheless, the atlas is highly recommended for every elementary and middle school library. [R: ARBA 95]

482   **Concise Atlas of the World**. 3d ed.
E+   New York: Oxford University Press,
       1996. 176p. $39.95. ISBN 0-19-
       521265-7.

This attractive atlas is especially suitable for students. The design, illustrations and text make it easy to use and the map quality is excellent. Arrangement includes a general introductory section, a U.S. map section, and a comprehensive world map section. The index includes more than 40,000 place names. A final section highlights areas that are currently newsworthy such as Bosnia and the West Bank/Gaza Strip. Recommended for all collections.

483   Espenshade, Edward B. Jr., ed.
E+   **Goode's World Atlas**. 19th ed. Chi-
       cago: Rand McNally, 1995. 371p.
       $24.95. ISBN 0-528-83130-5.

Goode's Atlas has been the standard school atlas for most of the 20th century. It is especially

designed to meet the curricular needs of American students, and includes introductory materials about reading and interpreting maps and atlases. Seven sections cover the world and the continents, and include the ocean floor; there are also many city maps. Thematic maps cover topics from natural resources to economics to culture. The index lists all places on the maps in the atlas and provides a pronunciation guide. *Goode's* is the first-purchase atlas for collections at every grade level, and a library might choose to maintain a circulating classroom set as well.

484   **Europe Today: An Atlas of Reproduc-**
       ible Pages. Wellesley, Mass.: World
       Eagle, 1993. 156p. $49.95. ISBN
       0-930141-35-0.

More than simply outline maps, the pages in this set are full of interesting perspectives, silhouettes, graphs, and lists. Sections cover the land, people, governments and organizations, economy, energy, and education. In addition, there are 33 country maps. This is a useful supplement to *Maps on File*, and adds depth to the coverage of Europe. Recommended for secondary collections where students and teachers will find the pages useful for scanning into individual presentations.

485   **The Eyewitness Atlas of the World**.
E+   New York: Dorling Kindersley; distr.,
       Boston: Houghton Mifflin, 1994.
       160p. $24.95. ISBN 1-56458-297-3.

High quality maps, beautiful images, and an informative text combine to make an attractive atlas appropriate for all grade levels. Maps are created with digital technology and there are over 1,000 diagrams, photographs, and other artworks. The atlas begins with an overview of Earth, its position in space, its structure and the continuous restructuring of its landscape. The world is then arranged by continent with a regional approach within each continental area. There are so many illustrations, that the pages occasionally become overly cluttered resulting in visual fatigue. Nonetheless this atlas will be useful for reference and browsing in both elementary and secondary schools. [R: ARBA 96]

486   **Geography on File**. 1v. New York:
E+   Facts on File, 1995. $155.00 looseleaf
       w/binder. ISBN 0-8160-3172-X.

The 1995 edition of this standard teaching and reference tool updates changes in the former Soviet Union and other political changes in Europe and elsewhere. More than 250 maps, charts and graphs are arranged in two parts: climate, topography, people, economy and resources are in part 1, while part 2 shows major geographic regions, boundaries, and major cities. The maps are clear and easy to read and are copyright free in loose-leaf bindings. The set is updated annually with cumulative indexes and are intended to supplement established units of study. This set is a complement to *Maps on File*. [R: ARBA 96]

487 Graham, Alma and Robert Thomas.
E+   **Basic Map Skills**. Maplewood, N.J.: Hammond, 1995. 80p. $8.33pa. ISBN 0-8437-7403-7.

The title of the cover of this volume is *Discovering Maps: A Children's World Atlas*. While not as attractive as the *DK World Reference Atlas*, this is an excellent source for students who are learning to use an atlas; indeed this could be used as a class text. There are examples of types of maps—physical, political, relief, and road maps, and a discussion about how to use them; there are also activities and exercises to practice. The remaining half of the work is a set of maps of the world's continents. There are "where in the world" charts that compare such things as hottest and coldest, highest and lowest, and rivers, lakes, waterfalls, volcanoes, animals, trees, gems, cities, landmarks, marvels, buildings, food, crops, and sports. The work ends with a map index and the answers to the activity questions. [R: ARBA 95]

488 **Latin America Today: An Atlas of Reproducible Pages**. Wellesley, Mass.: World Eagle, 1992. 151p. $49.95. ISBN 0-930141-45-8.

Similar to the other titles in this series, this work has a variety of maps, charts, and tables about the land, peoples, countries, cities, and governments of Latin America. There is also information about the economy and education, and 20 individual country maps (including Haiti, but not Puerto Rico). A front index as well as a table of contents makes the pages accessible for reference.

489 **Maps on File**. New York: Facts on
E+   File, 1981– . annual. $165.00. ISSN 0275-8083.

About 500 copyright-free, reproducible black and white maps are contained in two loose-leaf ring binders. Maps included are world and regional, continents, U.S. states. There are more than 100 separate topical maps for demographics, resources, political, cultural and historical features. Cities, borders, and geographic features are shown. A 5,000 entry index leads to the appropriate map(s), and annual updates keep the source current. Highly recommended for all levels.

490 Mattson, Catherine M., and Mark T.
E+   Mattson. **Contemporary Atlas of the United States**. New York: Macmillan, 1990. 118p. $100.00. ISBN 0-02-897281-3.

Computer generated graphics with good color and use of symbols, additional illustrations and well-organized narrative make this attractive atlas a good choice for all levels. It was published using projected statistics for the 1990s. Sections with subtopics deal with geographic features, history, culture (an especially useful section with multiple categories from demographic to health to crime, and so on), economy, transportation, government and environment. There is an annotated bibliography and a good subject index.

491 Mattson, Mark T. **Macmillan Color
E+   Atlas of the States**. New York: Macmillan, 1996. 377p. $100.00. ISBN 0-02-864659-2.

This is more of an oversized, abundantly illustrated fact book about the states with some maps, than an atlas. Indeed, the maps are the most annoying part of the work, as the problem of trying to fit too many locations into maps that are smaller than a page is poorly solved. This leads to locations placed where there is room, rather than placing important locations; this is especially noticeable in densely populated states. Universities are indicated on most maps, but none on the Maryland map, and only two on the Pennsylvania map. Students in Piqua, Ohio, will be startled to find the spelling of their town as Pique. The rest of the "atlas" is convenient, attractive, and accurate. States are listed alphabetically and are given extensive coverage which includes the origins of the name, colored pictures and descriptions of the seal and flag, state festivals and special events, and a small map showing the state's location within its region (which often does not include all the surrounding states). Information is provided about history, climate, weather, environment, plants and animals, topology, lakes and rivers, population and economy in narrative, charts, tables, and maps. Population distribution and density of Native Americans, African Americans, Hispanic Americans and Asian Americans in each state is clearly shown, and may be the most useful feature not easily found elsewhere. Each state's ranking among the states in several categories is included. There is a fast facts section after the state pages with statistical information in tables, including cities with populations of more than 25,000. Recommended for all levels as long as there is a good road atlas also available. [R: ARBA 97]

492 **National Geographic Atlas of the**
E+ **World**. rev. 6th ed. Washington, D.C.: National Geographic Society, 1995. 136p. $85.00; $65.00pa. ISBN 0-7922-3040-X; 0-7922-3036-1pa.

Every school should have this oversize atlas. In addition to the narrative essays, the plates, maps, graphics, satellite photographs, fold-out maps, inset charts, and comprehensive index make this beautiful resource useful for reference or browsing. In addition to sections on the land areas of the world, there are maps of the ocean floors. The maps are of exceptional quality and clarity. Highly recommended.

493 **PC Globe Maps 'n' Facts: The**
E+ **Comprehensive World Atlas for the Entire Family**. school ed. Novato, Calif.: Broderbund, 1993. CD-ROM (Windows, Macintosh). $34.95.

A CD-ROM atlas with almanac type information, the core of the data base is 227 country maps: political, physical, statistical, time zones. Maps are arranged hierarchically from the world to regions to subregions to country, with each level giving more detail. One can zoom into maps and link to relevant information about countries, and cities with statistical charts, flags, and anthems. The user can create a special atlas with just those features needed. All maps and information can be printed or copied into other programs. Sophisticated, yet easy to use switching and defaults make this a friendly program without a high learning curve. Recommended for all levels.

494 **Planet Earth: Macmillan World**
E+ **Atlas**. New York: Macmillan, 1997. 415p. $34.95. ISBN 0-02-861266-3.

The many satellite images symbolize the perspective of the title in this beautiful and unique atlas. In addition to information typically provided in contemporary atlases, such as ecological zones and topographic maps, transportation and time zones, almost all of the maps (excluding Antarctica and small islands) are shown in the same scale. This feature alone makes this a first purchase for schools; students will find this enables them to make comparisons that are impossible in other sources. The comprehensive index includes symbols of geographic features. Highly recommended for all collections.

495 **Rand McNally Road Atlas & Trip**
E+ **Planner: United States, Canada, Mexico**. Skokie, Ill.: Rand McNally, 1991– . annual. $4.95. ISSN 1075-1688.

Updated annually, this work's claim that it is "American's most up-to-date, useful road atlas" appears to be justified. Detailed maps of the 50 states, Canadian provinces, and Mexico identify principal highways (e.g., free or toll-limited access, four-lane, double-lane), paved and unpaved roads, and scenic rouges. Mileage and driving times between major cities, rest areas, campgrounds, airports, dams, national parks and forests, points of interest, mountain peaks, major colleges and universities, and ferries are all indicated. A new edition is published every October.

496 Royal Geographical Society. **Atlas of Exploration**. New York: Oxford University Press, 1997. 248p. $40.00. ISBN 0-19-521353-X.

More than 300 color illustrations (photographs, paintings and engravings), and 100 especially drawn maps complement a narrative that traces the discoveries about our world from first civilizations to today. Space exploration is not included. The first chapter covers early explorations, and then chapters are arranged by continent with final chapters on exploration of the oceans and other underexplored areas and environmental research. Each two-page entry within chapters contains maps, narrative, and illustrations. After the entries there is a section of brief biographies of explorers, geographers, and cartographers as well as a time chart. An index provides access. This is a beautiful volume useful to middle and high school history classes.

497 **State Maps on File**. 7v. New York:
E+   Facts on File, 1994. $550.00/set. ISBN 0-8160-0116-2.

498 v. 1: **New England**. 146p. $99.00. ISBN 0-8160-0117-0.

499 v. 2: **Mid-Atlantic**. 142p. $99.00. ISBN 0-8160-0118-9.

500 v. 3: **Southeast**. 242p. $99.00. ISBN 0-8160-0119-7.

501 v. 4: **Midwest**. 182p. $99.00. ISBN 0-8160-0120-0.

502 v. 5: **Mountain & Prairie**. 180p. $99.00. ISBN 0-8160-0121-9.

503 v. 6: **Southwest**. 160p. $99.00. ISBN 0-8160-0122-7.

504 v.7: **West**. 160p. $99.00. ISBN 0-8160-0123-5.

Seven volumes, arranged by region make up the complete set, but regional volumes can be purchased separately. Reproducible outline, political, historical, geographic, environmental, cultural, economic, and natural resource maps are included. Maps are designed to complement curricula, and use 1990 census figures. Each volume has an index of place names. Schools should purchase at least the volume which includes their state, and many schools will want the whole set.

505 Ulack, Richard, and Gyula Pauer. **Atlas of Southeast Asia**. New York: Prentice Hall, 1988. 171p. $100.00. ISBN 0-02-933200-1.

The atlas gives detailed maps and information about 10 countries in Southeast Asia: Indonesia, the Philippines, Malaysia, Singapore, Bruni, Thailand, Burma, Vietnam, Kampuchea, and Laos. Each country receives encyclopedic coverage with narrative, maps, pictures, and diagrams. There is a regional overview that covers physical, historical, political, cultural, and demographic topics. There is a selective bibliography and an index. Highly recommended for high school collections.

ENCYCLOPEDIAS, DICTIONARIES, AND HANDBOOKS

506 Biger, Gideon, with the International Boundaries Research Unit. **The Encyclopedia of International Boundaries**. New York: Facts on File, 1995. 543p. $125.00. ISBN 0-8160-3233-5.

Contemporary land boundaries defined by official agreement or accepted by the adjacent countries are the focus of this unusual political science source. Listings are alphabetical by the first country sharing a boundary with cross-referencing. Each country entry describes the country, its area, population, political structure, all boundaries and has some historical narrative about both the country and the boundary as well as a summary of the boundary's present situation. Cross-references lead to any other boundaries. Maps of boundaries and crossings were created especially for this encyclopedia, but there are not enough of them and they are often misplaced. The map accompanying the United States article shows only its Mexican border and the Mexican-American border article has no map. The complexities of Chinese borders require many more maps than those supplied. There is a glossary, a list of boundaries, and a select bibliography by country. The subject index includes references to boundaries created by rivers, mountain peaks and treaties. This interesting work provides an additional dimension to geography, world culture and political science reference material. Recommended for high schools with strong social science programs. [R: ARBA 96]

507 Cal, Timothy L., ed. **Worldmark**
E+   **Encyclopedia of the States**. 4th ed. New York: Gale Research, 1997. 690p. $135.00. ISBN 0-471-83213-8.

Now published by Gale Research, the 4th edition of the one-volume *Worldmark Encyclopedia of the States* continues to be a convenient source for extensive information about the states in an arrangement that facilitates comparisons. Each section of data is numbered in the same way for each of the states; there is a historical background and then statistically based demographic, political, economic, and social information. States are arranged in alphabetical order, each with a black and white map, tables, and a short bibliography. Following the states are entries for the District of Columbia, Puerto Rico and the

Caribbean and Pacific dependencies. Data are more extensive than in *Facts About the States*, but the two sources are complementary. Libraries holding the second edition may not need to update to the third as changes were minimal.

508 **Exploring Your World: The Adven-**
E+   **ture of Geography**. rev. ed. Washington, D.C.: National Geographic Society, 1993. 608p. $31.95. ISBN
0-87044-762-9.

This encyclopedia of geography begins with an introductory essay about the nature of geography, its relation to the earth and the physical processes that effect it, the relationship of places to other places and between people and the environment. The essay is followed by 334 articles of varying length arranged alphabetically with cross-references and an index. Many color illustrations, diagrams, and charts add to the effectiveness of the volume. Articles deal with both physical and cultural geography; the cultural articles tend to be more extensive, sometimes covering many pages. Recommended for elementary and middle schools.

509 Gall, Timothy and Susan Gall, eds.
E+   **Junior Worldmark Encyclopedia**
of the Nations. 9v. New York:
U*X*L, 1996. $225.00/set. ISBN
0-7876-0741-X.

510 **Jr. Worldmark CD-ROM**. New York:
U*X*L, 1996. CD-ROM (Macin-
tosh). $325.00. ISBN 0-7876-1099-2.

Gale Research has produced a second version of the *Worldmark Encyclopedia*, and published it under its new imprint of materials especially intended for upper elementary and middle school collections. One improvement for this level is that the 193 countries are presented in alphabetical order in 9 volumes rather than by continent as in the original set. Each volume has the same glossary repeated and each volume indexes the whole set. The typeface is clear and crisp and there are maps, charts, graphs, and photographs especially selected which often show pictures of children. The 35 headings for each country are numbered and defined to make comparisons among countries easier. The headings are listed and repeated

as a table in each volume. Bibliographic citations are included. The CD-ROM version allows searching by field. Not only does this retrieve information quickly, it encourages comparison of data. This set is highly recommended for elementary and middle schools and some high school collections would find it appropriate as well.

511 Guy, Arnold. **The Third World**
Handbook. 2d ed. Chicago: Fitzroy
Dearborn, 1994. 213 p. $45.00. ISBN
1-884964-12-5.

This source treats the emergence of the third world since 1945 and focuses on the countries from Africa, the Middle East, Eastern Asia and Latin America and their memberships in United Nations and regional collaboration projects. The second edition includes some of the successor states of the former Soviet Union. Chapters are organized by the problems faced by the countries, especially those which deal with economies, population, resources, and exploitation. There are a few biographical notes and there is a country gazetteer with limited political information. An index completes the work. This is a more complex source than the *Encyclopedia of the Third World*, and should be an added purchase when more depth is needed. [R: ARBA 95]

512 Kane, Joseph N., Janet Podell, and
E+   Steven Anzovin, eds. **Facts About**
the States. 2d ed. Bronx, N.Y.:
H. W. Wilson, 1994. 624p. $60.00.
ISBN 0-8242-0849-8.

A single-volume quick reference source listing all states, the District of Columbia, and Puerto Rico. Each entry begins with its seal, a U.S. map highlighting and describing the location of the state. Brief factual information includes the Post Office abbreviation, the name given to inhabitants, date admitted to the union, capital, state nicknames, mottos, songs, and symbols. A narrative discusses the typical encyclopedic information such as geography and climate, history, and so on. There is a section on unusual facts, the state in literature, and a guide to resources. The appendix provides comparative tables and rankings by population, climate, literacy, and many other areas. This convenient source should be in collections at all levels.

513 Kurian, George Thomas. **Encyclope-
dia of the First World**. 2v. New York:
Facts on File, 1990. $145.00/set.
ISBN 0-8160-1233-4.

This set has a full range of social and economic
information on the noncommunist countries that
make up the industrial and postindustrial world.
Included are the countries in Western Europe
and North America, as well as Australia, New
Zealand, and Japan. Using the same format as
Encyclopedia of the Third World, each chapter
contains data for one country (classified under
more than 30 subheadings) that ranges from historical background, geographical features, climate, and weather to foreign policy, defense,
and international commerce. Other topics covered are the political structure and government,
legal system, law enforcement, economy, agriculture, manufacturing, labor, and education. The
same publisher also produces the Facts on File
National Profiles series, which contains identical
material on clusters of countries at $35.00 per
volume. Works in the series include Australia
and New Zealand, the Benelux Countries, the
British Isles, Japan, North America, and Scandi-
navia. [R: ARBA 91; BL, 1 Sept 90; LJ Aug 90]

514 Kurian, George Thomas. **Encyclopedia of the Third World**. 4th ed. 3v.
New York: Facts on File, 1992.
$225.00/set. ISBN 0-8160-2261-5.

This source gives an extensive treatment to the
poorest, least industrialized, economically developing countries of the world. It gives balanced
descriptions of the political, economic, and social
systems of each country. After a section of international and regional organizations associated with
these countries, the countries are listed alphabetically and each is described according to a standard
structure which permits easy comparisons among
nations. Such data as weather, ethnic composition
of the population, freedom and human rights,
local governments, law enforcement and health
supplement more expected categories such as historical background, government, economy, and
foreign policy. Volume three contains 16 comparative and summary appendices, glossary, a chronology, a classified bibliography and an index.
Recommended for high school collections.

515 **Lands and Peoples**. 6v. Danbury,
Conn.: Grolier, 1997. $259.00/set.
ISBN 0-7172-8020-9.

516 **Lands and Peoples Special Edition:
The Changing Face of Europe**. Danbury, Conn.: Grolier, 1996. 130p. free
with set. ISBN 0-7172-8019-5.

Volumes in this set are organized by continent,
with Europe having two volumes. Each country
in the continent is profiled with text, maps, flags,
fact and figure boxes and many illustrations.
Major headings for each country are land, people, economy and history. There is an index in
volume 6 which is also published as a separate
paperback. In its many revisions, the set continues to be based on fact, and to avoid bias or ste-
reotype. This edition features the complete
revision of the treatment of the Central and
South America volume. This is a standard source
for upper elementary and middle school collections, and many high schools will want it as well.

Grolier continues the practice of including
a special edition as one way of updating the
information in the basic set. *The Changing Face
of Europe* volume traces the developments, especially in central Europe, which followed the
breakup of the Soviet Union. These special edition supplements are intended to be used in conjunction with the rest of the volumes in the set.

517 Small, R. J., and Michael Witherick.
A Modern Dictionary of Geography.
3d ed. New York: Halsted Press,
1995. 265p. $24.95pa. ISBN 0-470-
24986-2.

The British focus of this dictionary does not
restrict its use by American students. Published
since 1986 and revised regularly, the 3d edition
has 200 new entries and new maps and diagrams.
There are 140 illustrations. The entries are about
both physical and human geography and present
clear definitions. Arranged alphabetically with
cross-referencing, the topics range from acid rain
to caste to dairy farming to food chain to sink-
hole to zero population growth. The dictionary
will be useful for many curriculum areas in addition to geography and is recommended for secondary schools.

518 **The World Factbook**. Washington,
D.C.: Central Intelligence Agency,
1997. 572p. $32.95. ISBN 1-57488-
100-0.

The CIA *World Factbook* gives up-to-date basic
information about the countries of the world

including geography, people, government, economy, transportation, communications, and defense forces. Information is presented in tables and there is a small map accompanying each entry. The countries are listed alphabetically, followed by Taiwan, and there is an entry for "world." Reference maps in color show regions, standard time zones, and other comparative or summary information. The factbook is available in print, microfiche, computer disc, and on the Internet at www.odci.gov. The Web version is published first, in July of every year.

519 **World Facts & Maps**. Skokie, Ill.: Rand McNally, 1997. 216p. $10.95pa. ISBN 0-528-83695-1.

The first section of this guide gives an overview of the current areas of conflict in the world, with backgrounds, chronologies, and issues. The following section lists every country in the world with brief facts, locator maps, and data about the people, languages, government, economics and history. Maps are in gray tones rather than in color, but are sufficient for their purpose in this volume. A copy of this should be in every secondary reference collection, and the price suggests its use in circulating classroom sets.

520 **Worldmark Encyclopedia of the Nations**. 9th ed. 5v. New York: Gale Research, 1997. $345.00/set. ISBN 0-7876-0074-1.

Gale Research has purchased and republished an updated and improved version of the original *Worldmark Encyclopedia*. Still arranged in 5 volumes: United Nations, Africa, the Americas, Asia & Oceania, and Europe, the set emphasizes change in "political freedom, economic development, social progress, and the practice of international cooperation." The ninth edition has 25 new country articles (there are 202 countries listed) and all country entries have been modified to reflect changes; all maps have been redrawn. Volume 1 includes tables of world data and a calendar of religious holidays. There is a glossary and index in each volume and a guide to the country information headings in volumes 2–5. Complete encyclopedic information is given for each country, including many aspects of economic life, the status of the press, its international role, and famous persons. Bibliographies are included for each country. High schools and some middle schools will find this source indispensable.

GAZETTEERS

521 Hobson, Archie, ed. **The Cambridge**
E+ **Gazetteer of the United States and Canada: A Dictionary of Places**. New York: Cambridge University Press, 1995. 743p. $49.95. ISBN 0-521-41579-9.

This is a comprehensive guide to both geographic glossary terms and place names which are interfiled in alphabetical order. Included are such expected entries as states, provinces, territories, capitals, and municipalities (over 10,000 population for U.S. cities; over 8,000 population for Canadian cities). Also included are places in the news, of historical or cultural interest, likely travel destinations, generic or metaphorical places, neighborhoods, extinct cities and towns, regional names, military installations, industrial locations, national forests, and legendary places. For place name entries, definition, size and location are given while for the glossary entries, definition and physical or historical significance is explained. About half of the 20 maps at the end of the work are historical, about half contemporary. This is a comprehensive work with few errors or omissions and is highly recommended for libraries at all levels. [R: ARBA 97]

522 **Merriam-Webster's Geographical**
E+ **Dictionary**. 3d ed. Springfield, Mass.: Merriam-Webster, 1997. 1361p. $29.95. ISBN 0-87779-546-0.

This standard dictionary, issued regularly since 1972, is a comprehensive listing of place names. There are about 50,000 entries which describe, locate, and give pronunciation of cities, towns, counties, countries, and geographical features. Over 250 maps help identification. Each entry has population, area, and brief facts about the economy and history where appropriate. While the emphasis is on the United States and Canada, students will find most of the place names they need from throughout the world. Cross-references of alternative names lead to the main entries. This is a first-purchase for collections at all levels.

EXPLORATION

523 Baker, Daniel B. **Explorers and Discoverers of the World**. Detroit, Mich.: Gale Research, 1993. 637p. $59.95. ISBN 0-8103-5421-7.

More than 320 world explorers from ancient Greece to space exploration including women and non-Europeans are listed alphabetically in this source. Entries are a page or more with selected bibliography and include name and dates with accomplishments and a bibliography for further research. Illustrations accompany many articles. There is a chronology of exploration by area, area maps with names of explorers and a list of explorers by area. There is an index. This edition is for older users than the UXL edition. [R: ARBA 94]

524 Goetzmann, William H., and Glyndwr Williams. **The Atlas of North American Exploration: From the Norse Voyages to the Race to the Pole.** New York: Prentice Hall, 1992. 224p. $40.00. ISBN 0-13-297128-3.

The perspectives of this atlas are both European exploration and the Native American response. The importance of the native population's influence on the Europeans, either as friends, guides and mapmakers or as enemies is emphasized. After an introduction, there are five chronologically arranged sections which are further divided into two-page narratives and maps. Contemporary illustrations and quotations accompany the narratives, while the colored maps show routes and symbols clearly. The work covers earliest explorations (with a section on the fantasy/legendary explorations), the opening of the continent, expanding frontiers, expansion from ocean to ocean, and exploration of the far north, within the time periods 1497 to 1909. There is a bibliography and an index. This is an outstanding historical atlas and is highly recommended for secondary collections. [R: ARBA 94]

525 Saari, Peggy and Daniel B. Baker.
E+ **Explorers and Discoverers: From Alexander the Great to Sally Ride.** 4v. New York: U*X*L, 1995. $76.00/ set. ISBN 0-8103-9787-8.

This set, an edition of *Explorers & Discoverers* intended for upper elementary and middle school collections, includes biographies of 171 men, women and machines (e.g., the Apollo spacecraft) which have explored the world and now the universe. There was an attempt to include women and non-European explorers who may have been overlooked in previous works on the subject.

There are 160 actual entries with 176 illustrations and maps including the same 16 regional maps in each volume. Entries are alphabetical and consist of four to five pages with some longer entries for major figures. The drawings, portraits, photographs and maps combined with the text layout with sidebars, subdivisions, and boxed insets make the information easily accessible for the audience. Each volume contains an index to all volumes as well as a chronology of exploration and a listing of explorers by country of birth. This nicely designed set is recommended for both elementary and middle school collections, and some high schools will also find it useful. [R: ARBA 96]

526 Stefoff, Rebecca. **The Young Oxford Companion to Maps and Mapmaking.** New York: Oxford University Press, 1995. 303p. $40.00. ISBN 0-19-508042-4.

This is an encyclopedia of the development of mapmaking and inherently of exploration and world history. It includes biographies of map makers, geographers and explorers, and there are entries for important maps, expeditions, organizations, terms, techniques of map making, types of maps and regions of the world and how they were explored and mapped. Articles such as Native American map makers, the National Geographic Society, triangulation, and road maps provide information not easily found elsewhere. Entries include text, wonderful illustrations, including beautiful old map reproductions and sources for further reading. After the alphabetical entries, the source has a chronology of mapmaking, a directory of publishers, collections and exhibitions of maps, a classified bibliography and an index. Highly recommended for middle school collections as a source for interdisciplinary units incorporating geography, history, mathematics and art. [R: SLJ, May 95]

TRAVEL

See also guides to historical and cultural sites in **Ethnic Minorities**.

527 Smallwood, Carol. **Educational Guide to the National Park System.** Lanham, Md.: Scarecrow Press, 1989. 387p. $39.50. ISBN 0-8108-2137-0.

More than 300 facilities operated by the national park system are arranged by 47 subject categories depending on the major emphasis of the facility. Some examples of categories are architecture, Blacks, fossils, Native American culture, presidents, and western expansion. The description of each facility includes its address, purpose, free or rental materials available, curriculum applications, and *Sears* subject headings. This is a multipurpose tool: it is a reference to the parks, a selection guide to materials, a cataloging aid, a directory, and a curriculum guide for cross-discipline units. Indexing is by state and name. Recommended especially for middle schools, although other levels would also find it useful.

528 Stevens, Joseph E. **America's National Battlefield Parks: A Guide**. Norman, Okla.: University of Oklahoma Press, 1990. 337p. $37.50; $21.95pa. ISBN 0-8061-2268-4; 0-8061-2319-2pa.

The military history of the U.S., both tactical and human, is reflected in *America's National Battlefield Parks*. This is a guide to the 38 national parks and monuments; the sites are arranged geographically by 5 regions (east to west) and then alphabetically by name within the region. Maps and illustrations accompany the text. For each site there is a brief description, an explanation of its significance, and directory information. Tourist information, such as directions for reaching the site, facilities, activities and whether or not the site is handicapped accessible is included. There is a long historical narrative and tour suggestions for each site. An index allows the book to be used for reference as well as a tourist guide. Useful for supplementary history material.

AFRICAN STUDIES

529 Diagram Group. **Peoples of Africa**. 6v. New York: Facts on File, 1997. $119.00. ISBN 0-8160-3482-6.

The first five volumes treat the cultures in the environmental regions of the continent: Central, East, North and West, while the sixth volume profiles the 52 countries and 400 important African individuals. The regional volumes are organized by tribes and groups within each area. History, culture, language, religions, art and life-styles of nearly 20 contemporary groups are covered. Maps, timelines, lists and illustrations supplement the text. Volumes can be purchased separately. Recommended for all secondary collections.

ASIAN STUDIES

530 Hook, Brian, ed. **The Cambridge Encyclopedia of China**. 2d ed. New York: Cambridge University Press, 1991. 502p. $49.50. ISBN 0-521-35594-X.

This is a major revision of the 1976 first edition, with additions, changes of old entries and reflecting new scholarship. Illustrations are new as well. Divided into seven main sections, the volume addresses land and resources, people, society, history, culture, art and architecture and science and technology with historical perspectives. Each of these sections is further broken into topics. There are good illustrations and over 40 maps. Eight appendices include transliterations tables. There is a bibliography of further reading, a glossary, and an index. The good format and typeface enhance use. Recommended for secondary collections. [R: ARBA 93]

531 **Japan: An Illustrated Encyclopedia**. 2v. Tokyo: Kodansha, 1993. $250.00/ set. ISBN 4-06-931098-3.

This beautiful encyclopedia is a compact, selected and condensed revised version of the ninth volume *Kodansha Encyclopedia of Japan*. It was compiled with scholars from Japan and from around the world. In addition to its 11,000 entries, there are more than 100 in-depth featured articles and pictorial essays. Articles range from 50–4,000 words, and there are over 4,000 illustrations (photographs, charts, graphs, and tables). The purpose of the work is to explain how 20th century Japan came to be and focuses on politics, government, economics, art, music, and history. It is arranged alphabetically with cross-references and a topical guide. Other features include an atlas of Japan, an illustrated chronology, a classified list of sources for further reading, and a bilingual index of titles. Highly recommended for high schools with world culture, and particularly Asian studies curricula. [R: ARBA 94]

532 Johnson, Grodon. **Cultural Atlas of India**. New York: Facts on File, 1996. 240p. $50.00. ISBN 0-8160-3013-8.

This introduction to India and the Indian subcontinent provides text, maps and illustrations about the history, religion, art, literature, science and social institutions of this diverse region. The first two sections deal with India, while the third section covers Bangladesh, Bhutan, Nepal, Pakistan and Sri Lanka. Supplementary material includes a chronology, a glossary, a bibliography and an index. Highly recommended for secondary collections, in particular to support high school world culture courses.

533 **Kodansha Encyclopedia of Japan**. 9v. New York: Kodansha, 1983. $780.00/set. ISBN 0-87011-620-7.

This is the most comprehensive encyclopedia of one culture ever published in a language foreign to that culture. Over 20 years in planning, writing and publishing, the work contains 9,417 entries. Most entries are from 50 to 500 words in length; some general articles are more extensive, and there are 26 long survey articles. More than 1,000 photographs, maps and charts enhance the text. Arrangement is alphabetical with cross-references and an index in volume 9. There are many signed articles and many bibliographies. The abridged version will be preferred by all but those who need the depth of coverage this standard source provides.

534 Robinson, Francis. **The Cambridge Encyclopedia of India, Pakistan, Bangladesh, Sri Lanka, Nepal, Bhutan, and the Maldives**. New York: Cambridge University Press, 1989. 520p. $69.95. ISBN 0-521-33451-9.

This authoritative source covers in depth a part of the world sometimes neglected by other material. For each country categories included are land, people, history, politics, foreign relations, economies, religions, societies, and culture and where appropriate the categories are further divided. Emphasis is on each country's post-colonial situation. Good graphics add to the narrative and include tables, charts, figures and maps. There is an extensive index. The information is intended for both the general reader and as a basis for the specialist. Recommended to support world culture and government classes in high schools.

EUROPEAN AND RUSSIAN STUDIES

535 Brown, Archie, Michael Kaser and Gerald S. Smith, eds. **The Cambridge Encyclopedia of Russia and the Former Soviet Union**. 2d ed. New York: Cambridge University Press, 1994. 604p. $49.95. ISBN 0-521-35593-1.

First published in 1982 as the *Cambridge Encyclopedia of Russia and the Soviet Union*, this edition has been revised to reflect recent political change. It includes Russia and other cultural groups from both the Empire and the Union. Encyclopedic signed articles treat aspects of the physical environment, the people, religion, history, art and architecture, language and literature, cultural life, science, politics, the economy, society, the military, and international relations. Illustrations include photographs, charts, and maps while good use of typography indicates transitions between subdivisions and highlighted information. A glossary, a list of further reading, and an index are included. This source is essential to support Russian language programs and any serious world culture program. [R: ARBA 95]

LATIN AMERICAN STUDIES

536 Collier, Simon, Harold Blakemore, and Thomas E. Skidmore, eds. **The Cambridge Encyclopedia of Latin America and the Caribbean**. 2d ed. New York: Cambridge University Press, 1992. 479p. $69.95. ISBN 0-521-41322-2.

Coverage in this revised work is topical rather than geographical. There are good regional explanations of the areas covered: Latin America, South America, Central America, Mesoamerica, the Caribbean and the West Indies, but the approach emphasizes a broad subject arrangement. Included are physical environment, the economy, the people, history, politics and society, and culture. These topics are further subdivided: for example, culture includes language, literature, music, the visual arts, theater and cinema, media, and science. Because of the broad coverage, this source would be useful for cross-discipline studies of Latin America for middle and senior high school students. There are photographs, maps, and charts, some in color. The index can provide access to specific country information. [R: ARBA 94]

537 Moss, Joyce, and George Wilson. **Peoples of the World: Latin Americans: The Culture, Geographical Setting, and Historical Background**.

Detroit, Mich.: Gale Research, 1989. 323p. $39.95. ISBN 0-8103-7445-5.

The volume surveys the history, geographical setting, and culture of 45 indigenous and national people of Latin America. The old cultures (Aztec, Incan, and Mayan) and contemporary populations of 24 nations are each covered in 3 to 11 pages. Special features include line drawings, photographs, and maps; a glossary of foreign and unusual terms; a selective bibliography; and a subject index. Despite a few misspellings that resulted primarily from confusion about the use of Portuguese and Spanish words, this work is recommended for junior high and high school levels. [R: ARBA 90; LJ, 15 Oct 89]

MIDDLE EASTERN STUDIES

538 Hiro, Dilip. **Dictionary of the Middle East**. New York: St. Martin's Press, 1996. 367p. $30.00. ISBN 0-312-12554-2.

The author has written several books on India and the Middle East and brings a global, rather than American perspective to the subject. He focuses on the "core" countries: Bahrain, Egypt, Iran, Iraq, Israel, Jordan, Kuwait, Lebanon, Oman, Qatar, Saudi Arabia, Syria, the U.A.E., and the Palestinian territories. The scope of the work includes political and military history, religion, country profiles, ethnic groups, government and

politics, language and literature, issues related to oil and gas production and markets, ideologies, places, and 20th century biographies and treaty information. There is an index to supplement the dictionary arrangement. The ten maps, eight sharing only two pages are insufficient, but the strengths of the book greatly outweigh this shortcoming. Highly recommended for high school collections. [R: ARBA 97]

539 **The Middle East and North Africa**. London: Europa Publications, 1964–. annual. $325.00. ISSN 0076-8502.

This annual publication adds new essays and updates information each year. There are general survey essays about such topics as religions, terrorism, resources, and calendars; there is a selected bibliography. The second section is a list of regional organizations, and the main section surveys 21 Middle Eastern countries alphabetically from Algeria to Yeman. Items covered for each country include the constitution and government, legislative and judicial systems, religion, finance, trade and industry, defense, education, and tourism. Directories of press, publishers, and media are included. Narratives about history, current issues, and economics complete the data. There are a few maps and tables. High schools with need for comprehensive information on the area will find this a useful and accurate reference. [R: ARBA 96]

Handicapped

See also **Education** for **College and Vocational School Guides**.

HANDBOOKS AND GUIDES

540 Abrams, A. Jay and Margaret A. Abrams. **The First Whole Rehab Catalog: A Comprehensive Guide to Products and Services for the Physically Disadvantaged**. White Hall, Va.: Betterway Publications, 1990. 240p. $16.95pa. ISBN 1-55870-131-1.

This directory of information about and sources of devices and services that can help the disabled live independently is arranged by sections. In the

chapter on home management, there are subsections on clothes, sleeping, and furniture. Other major sections include personal care, access, communication, mobility, transportation, health and fitness, recreation, and education and vocation. Each listing has a product description, the name of the company that distributes it, and the address and phone number. Many product listings are accompanied by illustrations. In addition there is a list of catalogs, books with bibliographic descriptions and organizations with descriptions and addresses. An appendix lists other groups, such as government, advocacy, and support agencies. There is an index. Recommended for reference, parent, counseling, and professional collections.

541 **The Complete Directory for People with Disabilities**. Lakeville, Conn.: Grey House Pub., 1992– . annual. $125.00. ISSN 1063-0023.

First published in 1991 this source has grown to include 8,000 entries of publishers, associations, and manufacturers of products, all intended as resources for both physically and mentally disabled individuals. The institutions and products are listed in 27 topical chapters, each with directory information and purpose statement. There is a disability/need index, a publisher index, and a title/entry name index. Highly recommended for professional and parent collections. [R: ARBA 93]

542 Cremona, Candida H. **Access Travel U.S.A: A Directory for People With Disabilities**. Fort Lauderdale, Fla.: Creative Hospitality Concepts, 1994. 170p. $19.95pa. ISBN 0-9642279-0-8.

This is a directory of hotels, cruise ships, ski areas, and means of transportation with facilities and services for the disabled. Tables describe accessibility with categories appropriate to each type of facility, such as sizes of rooms or cabins, width of doors, availability of ramps or elevators. The table of 27 ski resorts shows which types of disabilities have been provided for at each area. The transportation section covers airlines, busses, trains and car and van rentals. A separate part of the work has a list of accessible hotels listed by state. This section is disappointing, because it often lists only one or two hotels for the entire state. There is a list of information resources, a TTY directory, and an index. This edition is more useful for holiday travel than for business or school-related travel; a second edition should concentrate on expanding the latter. Nonetheless, this is a good addition to the collection for meeting the needs of disabled students and teachers or those responsible for a disabled family member. Recommended for high schools.

543 Paciorek, Michael J. and Jeffery A. Jones. **Sports and Recreation for the Disabled: A Resource Handbook**. 2d ed. Carmel, Ind.: Cooper Pub. Group, 1994. $20.00pa. ISBN 1-88412-504-2.

This guide is intended for physical educators, special educators, and others who work with the disabled. After a good introduction on the impact of competitions including the Special Olympics, the book describes more than 50 sports and recreation activities arranged alphabetically from all-terrain vehicles to floor hockey to martial arts to wrestling. There are sports for individuals, pairs and teams. For each sport or activity entries give the name and address of the National Governing Body, the disability National Governing Body, and the primary disability for which the sport is appropriate or intended. The section includes an overview of the sport, adaptive equipment needed and suppliers or manufacturers of the equipment, other resources, and references. There are drawings and illustrations to accompany the descriptions. Appendices list such things as Special Olympics chapters and directors. Highly recommended.

544 Shrout, Robert Neil. **Resource Directory for the Disabled**. New York: Facts on File, 1991. 392p. $45.00. ISBN 0-8160-2216-X.

Organizations, devices and publications are divided into four categories of disabilities: general resources, and resources for the mobility impaired, the visually impaired and the hearing impaired. Under each category, directory information is given about travel aids, recreation and social opportunities, organizations, employment opportunities, educational opportunities, appliances, computer accessories, sports equipment, and video tapes. Some entries are annotated. There is an index. Highly recommended for professional, parent, and high school collections. [R: ARBA 93]

HEARING IMPAIRED

545 Bornstein, Harry, Karen L. Saulnier, and Lillian B. Hamilton, eds. **The Comprehensive Signed English Dictionary**. Washington, D.C.: Gallaudet College Press, 1983. 456p. $29.95. ISBN 0-913580-81-3.

This dictionary is based on Signed English. An introductory essay about learning Signed English is followed by 3,100 words and 14 markers representing English usage. The words are arranged in alphabetical order with illustrations and descriptions. This is only a partial dictionary and is part of a series of texts used in teaching Signed English.

546 Butterworth, Rod R. and Mickey Flodin. **The Perigee Visual Dictionary of Signing: An A-to-Z Guide to Over 1,250 Signs of American Sign Language**. rev. and expanded ed. New York: Perigee Books, 1991. 480p. $13.00pa. ISBN 0-399-51695-6.

This dictionary is based on the American Sign Language. There are 1,250 signs arranged alphabetically and clearly laid out three to a page. Each entry illustrates the sign, prints the word, gives a memory aid, and an example. Introductory material gives the history of the language, suggestions for how to use it, sample illustrations of hand shapes and a quick chart of the alphabet and numbers. Supplements at the end of the dictionary show inflections, articles, and new signs. There is an index.

547 Gustason, Gerilee. **Signing Exact English**. Los Alamitos, Calif.: Modern Signs Press, 1993. 431p. $40.00; $21.95pa. ISBN 0-916708-22-5; 0-916708-26-8pa.

This dictionary is based on Signing Exact English (SEE). There have been several versions of SEE, and this dictionary has been published in editions reflecting the various alternatives. This has a foreword to SEE 2 and lists its principles and suggestions for use. There are charts of the alphabet, numbers, contractions, and affixes, followed by signs for words from A to Z. Entries show the word, a description, and picture, with motion shown in blue. Other products using SEE are available from this publisher.

548 Lang, Harry G. and Bonnie Meath-Lang. **Deaf Persons in the Arts and Sciences: A Biographical Dictionary**. Westport, Conn.: Greenwood Press, 1995. 424p. $69.50. ISBN 0-313-29170-5.

Multicultural sources dealing with ethnicity abound, but there are not so many materials about the deaf culture. This absorbing work accomplishes the goals of other such sources in that it serves as reassurance and encouragement for members of the culture and as enlightenment for those outside the group. This biographical dictionary includes about 150 individuals who were deaf from birth or who were deaf because

of accident or illness later in life but for whom deafness was a major factor. The source is international (western) and dates of figures range from the 1500s to the present.

The biographies are engaging and stress accomplishments and ways in which the individuals challenged attitudes and barriers. Included are musicians and dancers, scientists, educators, politicians, inventors, actors, writers and artists. Alphabetically arranged entries are two or more pages with references, and there are a few illustrations. An appendix gives brief information about an additional 121 individuals while a second appendix lists main entries by field. There is a selected bibliography and an index. Highly recommended for secondary collections.

549 Sternberg, Martin L. A. **American Sign Language: A Comprehensive Dictionary**. New York: Harper & Row, 1981. 1132p. $43.95. ISBN 0-06-014097-6.

This 1981 edition is the most comprehensive of the American Sign Language dictionaries. The first edition was in 1962 and it has been published in abridged (1987) and concise (1990) editions. A revised and abridged edition was published in 1994. It is a true dictionary with pronunciation, parts of speech, rationale and description of over 5,000 entries arranged alphabetically with cross-references. There is an introduction describing the history, development and theory of the American Sign Language. There is a bibliography, and foreign language indexes for Japanese, Russian, French, German, Spanish, Italian, and Portuguese.

550 Sternberg, Martin L. A. **The American Sign Language Dictionary on CD-ROM**. version 2.0. New York: HarperCollins, 1996. CD-ROM (Windows, Macintosh). $79.95. ISBN 0-06-279039-0.

The CD-ROM is based on Sternberg's 1994 revised and abridged edition of the *American Sign Language Dictionary*. It has over 2,000 signs in 5 languages (English, Spanish, French, German, and Italian) with new signs downloadable monthly from the HarperCollins Web site (www.harpercollins.com). This is a product that uses the capacity of CD-ROM interactivity to its ultimate. There are video clips showing the signs, and the user may change the speed and/or size of the clip for clarity. In addition to the dictionary itself there are games, practices, and tests so that one can use this as a learning device. The dictionary itself can be approached alphabetically or by browsing hierarchically by category such as animals, sports, or verbs. There are quick options for review, go-tos and cross-references. Buttons and bars and help areas make getting around this sophisticated data base very easy. There is a guided tour of the product and an ASL overview which gives its history, helpful hints for learning, discusses it as a modern foreign language, has Frequently Asked Questions, and lists resources including an extended bibliography, services and devices. Although there have been some reports of difficulty in loading and operating the CD-ROM, there is an 800 technical support line. The disc does include sound for hearing users to assist in learning the language. Highly recommended for secondary collections.

VISUALLY IMPAIRED

See also **Talking Books and Braille (Collection Management)**.

551 Sardegna, Jill and T. Otis Paul. **The Encyclopedia of Blindness and Vision Impairment**. New York: Facts on File, 1991. 340p. $50.00. ISBN 0-8160-2153-8.

A useful collection of alphabetical entries about blindness, issues, and topics intended for both professionals and laypersons. Subjects include health, medications, surgery, social issues, myths and misconceptions, economic issues, education, adaptive aids and organizations. Entries vary from a few sentences to several pages. There are 13 useful appendices including dog guide schools, federal agencies and periodicals. There are 5 tables of statistics, an extensive bibliography and an index. This source would be useful in both student and professional collections. [R: ARBA 92]

History

See also **Chronologies (Reference)**.

ATLASES

552 **Atlas of World History**. Skokie, Ill.: Rand McNally, 1995. 192p. $45.00; $24.95pa. ISBN 0-528-83780-X; 0-528-83779-6pa.

First published in 1981, this atlas is a standard source. The maps are intended to form a general view of human history accompanied by textual essays on issues and themes related to the adjacent simple, colorful maps. Beginning with a section on the Ancient World and continuing through a section on the Emergence of the Modern World, the atlas emphasizes major forces and trends in both political and social history. Rand McNally adds to this British publication a section of United States historical maps and tables. There is a timeline, bibliographies and an index.

553 Barraclough, Geoffrey, ed. **The Times Atlas of World History**. 4th ed. Maplewood, N.J.: Hammond, 1993. 360p. $95.00. ISBN 0-7230-0534-6.

This standard atlas was first published in 1978. This edition updates the work to the early 1990s. It is comprehensive in scope, attempting to include all peoples in all parts of the world from all ages. It does not merely list national histories, but looks at history from a focus on world events and world trends. There are about 130 color plates, as well as maps and other illustrations. There is a world chronology and a geographical background to world history followed by the atlas in seven chronologically ordered sections, each with multiple subdivisions. The sections combine text, illustration and maps to describe the topic. There is a glossary and index. Most secondary schools will want this historical atlas.

554 Gilbert, Martin. **Atlas of World War I**. 2d ed. New York: Oxford University Press, 1994. 1 atlas. $19.95; $12.95pa. ISBN 0-19521075-1; 0-19-521077-8pa.

This introductory guide to various aspects of World War I is from a British perspective and thus complements the *Facts on File Historical Atlas of World War I*. The author is the official biographer of Churchill and author of other World War II books and atlases. Largely a military history, it also deals with some technical, economic, and diplomatic issues. The work deals with overall campaigns and does not provide detailed battle maps. Arranged chronologically the 164 clear black and white maps illustrate the development of the war in chapters that deal with the prelude to the war, and then yearly sections interspersed with chapters about the war in the air and at sea, and the effect of the war outside of Europe and its aftermath. The only text is provided within boxes on the maps. The bibliography is selective and annotated and the index provides interrelationships and continuity. Recommended for high school collections. [R: ARBA 96]

555 **Historical Maps on File**. New York: Facts on File, 1985. 345p. $155.00 loose-leaf w/binder. ISBN 0-87196-708-1.

More than 330 outline maps emphasizing political, military, and economic history are arranged in chronological order in categories from Ancient Civilizations to Europe (1500–Present) and in geographical sections for the United States, the Western Hemisphere, Africa and the Middle East, Asia, and Australia. Emphasis is on Western Civilization with just over 50 maps on Africa and Asia. The black-and-white maps, loose-leaf format, and copyright permission make this a useful set for both teachers and students.

556 Livesey, Anthony. **The Historical Atlas of World War I**. New York: Holt, 1994. 192p. $45.00. ISBN 0-8050-2651-5.

This atlas is a military history of campaigns and battles of the war. After an introduction, the maps are arranged in a five-part chronology by year, from 1914–1918. Entries are two-page essays accompanied by several maps and other illustrations and quotation boxes. There is an epilogue, a brief bibliography and both general and place name indexes. This is an excellent source and is highly recommended for high school collections. [R: ARBA 95]

557 Pimlott, John. **The Historical Atlas of World War II**. New York: Holt, 1995. 224p. $45.00. ISBN 0-8050-3929-5.

Following the same format as the *Historical Atlas of World War I* this source covers the military history of the Second World War in five parts: 1919–1939, 1939–1942, June, 1942–July, 1943, July, 1943–December, 1944, and December, 1944–September, 1945. There are general and place name indexes. This atlas should be a standard item in high school collections. [R: ARBA 95]

558 Rossi, Renzo. **The Atlas of Human**
E+   **History**. 6v. New York: Macmillan, 1996. $175.00/set. ISBN 0-02-864505-7.

This source combines abundant maps and illustrations with text that complements the attractive pictures with substantial information. The six volumes are arranged both chronologically and geographically with the first three volumes covering primates and early *Homo sapiens*, Stone Age peoples, and the rise of civilizations in Egypt and the Middle East. The final three volumes cover early civilizations in Europe, Asia, and the Americas. Each volume is divided into chapters that deal with individual cultures, with two pages of color maps, charts, artifacts, and other illustrations followed by two pages of text with black and white illustrations, some repeating the color drawings. Topics discussed for each group include migration patterns, settlement, daily life, culture and technological innovations. With new archeological evidence appearing almost daily, the source would have appeared more authoritative and maintained a better effect of recency had it accompanied some of its "facts" about such issues as the date of the original peopling of the Americas with a comment that such information is debated among the experts. Each volume has its own introduction, glossary and index. Intended for upper elementary and middle school students, many high schools will also find it useful. [R: ARBA 97]

559 Talbert, Richard J. A., ed. **Atlas of Classical History**. New York: Routledge, 1989. 224p. $18.50pa. ISBN 0-415-03463-9pa.

This comprehensive and scholarly coverage of classical Mediterranean history to the time of Constantine has clear maps and text easily understood by high school students in either classics programs or in general world history and culture classes. The maps and narrative include information on city plans, nation states, military campaigns, and trade routes. It is arranged chronologically from the Aegean in the Bronze Age to the Roman Empire in A.D. 314, and includes a chart of the reigns of the Roman Emperors plus a classified list of items for further reading.

DICTIONARIES AND ENCYCLOPEDIAS

560 Commire, Anne, and Deborah Klezmer, eds. **Historic World Leaders**. 5v. Detroit, Mich.: Gale Research, 1994. $225.00/set. ISBN 0-8103-8408-6.

Biographies of 620 important political figures fill the five volumes in this set. Volumes are by area, with volume one containing 155 names from Africa, the Middle East, Asia, and the Pacific. Volumes two and three cover Europe, while volumes four and five cover North and South America. Individuals and groups included are no longer active in leadership positions and were selected because they "stormed barricades" and made rules for others to follow, or broke rules established by others. Special efforts were made to include women and minorities. The signed sketches are from four to ten pages and include a photograph or drawing, an indication of why the individual is notable, quotations by or about the person, vital statistics, a chronology and suggestions for further reading. There are some sidebars of related figures. Contents of all volumes are in each volume; there is a cumulative index in volume 5. Appendices include a table of political and royal leader chronologies and maps. Recommended for secondary collections. [R: ARBA 95]

561 **History of the World: The Essential**
E+ **Multimedia Reference Guide to World History**. New York: Dorling Kindersley, 1995. CD-ROM (Windows). $79.95. ISBN 0-7894-0267-X.

This CD-ROM demonstrates the strengths and weaknesses of the CD-ROM as reference tool. It provides multiple approaches to the history of the world: by time period, biography, regional overview, historical themes, and historical objects, as well as combinations of these. Navigating is sophisticated, but becomes easy after a bit of experimenting and there is a help feature that gives good directions and suggestions. Enough sound, pop-up windows, video clips, the inevitable game and other features are present to occupy any reluctant student. A browse index and cross-referencing make it possible to find specific information. There are copying and printing options. The weakness of the program is its shallow information which not only results in lots of time spent learning little (although enjoying it a lot), but also results in such things as cross-references so broad as to be incomprehensible except as events in the same time period, video clips used appropriately for one subject and less appropriately for another, and text so simple as to be misleading. There are so few quiz questions that repetition becomes quickly boring; indeed an hour spent with the program elicits about all of its information. Recommended for elementary schools as a reference source, and for middle schools as a self-teaching tool.

562 **Hutchinson Dictionary of World**
E+ **History**. Santa Barbara, Calif.: ABC-CLIO, 1993. 699p. $49.50. ISBN 0-87436-765-4.

This is a convenient one-volume dictionary covering global events from earliest recorded history to the present. About 5,000 entries cover major civilizations, events, leaders, and nations of historical significance. There are few entries concerned with science or the arts. Arranged alphabetically, the entries range in length from a sentence to a paragraph with entries for nations somewhat longer. Maps, chronologies for special articles, and boxed quotations add to the definitions. Eight useful appendices list political and royal leaders, global and regional organizations, political thinkers and economists, significant political upheavals, natural and man-made disasters, assassinations, and historical urban population rankings. There is a world chronology that includes prehistory. This is an excellent dictionary of its kind and would be useful in collections at all levels. [R: ARBA 95]

563 Kohn, George C. **Dictionary of Historic Documents**. New York: Facts on File, 1991. 400p. $45.00. ISBN 0-8160-1978-9.

This is a dictionary of more than 2,200 significant documents from ancient times to the present, from Hamurrabi's Code to the Strategic Arms Limitation Treaty, arranged alphabetically with cross-reference. It is a source of information about the documents, not the items themselves. Each entry is brief (the U.S. Constitution is only 21 lines), but is intended to show why the item is significant. Entries also contain information about names of persons and places involved. Included are treaties, charters, laws, judicial decisions, decrees, proclamations, papal bulls, speeches, letters, and essays. The emphasis is Western history. There is a selective, classified bibliography and an index.

564 Langer, William L., comp. and ed. **An Encyclopedia of World History: Ancient, Medieval, and Modern, Chronologically Arranged**. 5th ed. Boston: Houghton Mifflin, 1973. 1569p. $45.00. ISBN 0-395-13592-3.

This one-volume handbook of world history has the same format as the publisher's *Encyclopedia of American History*. Entries are chronological from prehistory through 1970. There is coverage of political, cultural, and geographic history. Maps and tables of heads of state, and an extensive index are included. This source is for ready reference, research ideas, and tracing historic events and trends.

565 **Larousse Dictionary of World History**. New York: Larousse, 1994. 996p. $40.00. ISBN 0-7523-5001-3.

This is a comprehensive survey of international political, military and diplomatic history. Although it has a U.K. perspective, the editors have tried to provide geographic, racial, and gender balance and to include as much American as British information. A special attempt was made to include information about Eastern Europe. The 7,500 articles are arranged alphabetically with cross-references. There are some tables, but their location is sometimes problematic and there is no index to them. A comparison with the *Hutchinson Dictionary of World History* shows a similar pattern of entries. Some libraries may want both; either is a good purchase. [R: ARBA 95]

566 Lentz, Harris M., III. **Assassinations and Executions: An Encyclopedia of Political Violence, 1865–1986**. Jefferson, N.C.: McFarland, 1988. 275p. $45.00. ISBN 0-89950-312-8.

Coverage in this work is of world leaders (heads of state and other major world figures) who have been assassinated, executed, or whose lives have been threatened by attempted assassination. The years covered are from 1865–1986 although earlier figures are discussed in a prologue. Entries are in chronological order and vary from one sentence paragraphs to one page. There is a bibliography and an index.

567 Palmowski, Jan. **A Dictionary of Twentieth-Century World History**. New York: Oxford University Press, 1997. 693p. $15.95pa. ISBN 0-10-280016-7.

This dictionary is current to October, 1996 and includes 2,500 individuals and events with global importance. Arrangement is alphabetical with cross-references, and entries deal with political, military, religious and cultural affairs. Articles are brief so that total coverage is comprehensive. Some maps and tables are included. This is a good ready reference source for secondary collections.

568 Sifakis, Carl. **Encyclopedia of Assassinations**. New York: Facts on File, 1991. 228p. $35.00. ISBN 0-8160-1935-5.

Over 300 assassinations or attempted assassinations from about 400 B.C. to the 1980s are presented in this dictionary. Coverage is world wide. Entries vary from a paragraph to five pages; some entries are illustrated with photographs and some have recommendations for further reading. There is an appendix with the entries arranged by country, a selected bibliography and an index.

569 Somerset Fry, Plantagenet. **The Dorling Kindersley History of the World**. New York: Dorling Kindersley, 1994. 384p. $39.95. ISBN 1-56458-244-2.

This ambitious and colorful volume covers the history of the world from the beginnings of life on earth to the 1990s in 384 pages of mostly pictures. The 20 chapters are arranged chronologically with catchy titles such as "Conquest and Plague" to go along with the dates included in the chapter heading. At the beginning of each chapter is a double-page world map with pictures illustrating some of the major developments during that particular era. A brief narrative introduces the chapter and a timeline runs across the bottom of the two pages. Then a larger timeline, divided into regions—Oceania, Americas, Europe, Asia and Africa—covers the next two pages. The timeline is illustrated with pictures of models or artifacts. Then a series of pages is devoted to narrative and illustration of some of the events of that chapter's era in each of the regions. Insert maps, photographs, biographical sketches, and drawings are prominent. There are supplementary reference pages which have more timelines featuring architecture, population, inventions, and the modern world, and some United States fact tables. There is a two-page glossary. The index is neither complete nor well-organized; the listing for Czechoslovakia, for example, has a hard-to-find reference on a timeline, but does not mention more information on another page, no doubt because the heading there is a reference to the "Prague Spring" and is listed in the index only under Prague. The issues discussed on these pages are never resolved by any reference in the index, or the text, for that matter, to the Velvet Revolution or to the division of the country. Students will be left thinking the intellectuals of "Czechoslovakia" are still debating communism. The difficulties of sustaining continuity in this sort of work are obvious. The reference use of this history will be limited to browsing for a topic to research elsewhere. Nonetheless, the volume will be visually appealing to many students in elementary and middle schools. [R: ARBA 95]

570 Stearns, Peter N. **Encyclopedia of Social History**. New York: Garland, 1994. 856p. $95.00. ISBN 0-8153-0342-4.

The study of social history which has become a major discipline since the 1960s is reflected in this comprehensive one-volume work which investigates individuals and groups such as the working classes, women, children, minorities and their daily and family life. It covers the world from classical to modern societies and describes arts, consumerism, crime, illness beliefs, education, leisure, rural and urban life and social structures. An introduction is followed by a topical list of contents and a list of contributors. Alphabetically arranged signed articles with references range from one to five pages and are written clearly and entertainingly. Recommended as an excellent reference for all social science areas in high schools. [R: ARBA 95]

571 Urwin, Derek W. **A Dictionary of European History and Politics, 1945–1995**. New York: Longman, 1996. 423p. $18.95pa. ISBN 0-582-25874-X.

This work presents clear, balanced and concise summaries of the most significant events, issues, territorial changes, organizations, and people in Europe since the end of World War II. It intends to show the social and political changes during the second half of the 20th century. Entries are alphabetical with cross-references. The coverage of changes through the early 1990s is thorough and the volume presents a useful source of information about time and place for schools that need coverage about Europe. Highly recommended. [R: ARBA 97]

572 Wetterau, Bruce. **World History: A Dictionary of Important People, Places and Events From Ancient Times to the Present**. New York: Holt, 1994. 1173p. $60.00. ISBN 0-8050-2350-X.

E+

This is a revision of the *Macmillan Concise Dictionary of World History* (1983). It includes 100,000 new words, some entries have been updated and enlarged and new entries have been added, especially about social history. Entries about myth, legend, and most cities were removed. Coverage is international but emphasis is on the United States and Europe. The 10,000 articles and 135 chronological outlines are arranged together in alphabetical order. The articles deal with people, events, nations and empires, and are very brief with one or two sentences of identification and significance. The chronological outlines which cover countries and events are longer: the outline for the Napoleonic Wars is slightly more than two pages while the United States chronology is 29 pages. The clear typeface and quick definitions make this a good choice for all levels. [R: ARBA 95]

ANCIENT

573 Adkins, Lesley, and Roy A. Adkins. **Handbook to Life in Ancient Rome**. New York: Facts on File, 1994. 404p. $40.00. ISBN 0-8160-2755-2.

Both archaelogical and historical evidence are represented in this thematically arranged guide to the history of Rome from its beginnings in the 8th century B.C. to the 5th century A.D. The first chapter, "Republic and Empire," gives a chronological overview as well as biographies, a list of the emperors, and basic information about government and law. This framework is followed by chapters on the military, daily life, travel and trade, religion, and the economy as well as geography, and language and literature. The articles are summaries with references for further exploration. About 150 black and white illustrations and 4 tables add meaning to the text. The useful and readable information will answer questions for both world history and Latin students, and for readers of novels set in the era. Highly recommended for high school collections. [R: ARBA 96]

574 Baker, Rosalie F., and Charles F. Baker. **Ancient Greeks: Creating the Classical Tradition**. New York: Oxford University Press, 1997. 245p. $35.00. ISBN 0-19-509940-0.

This biographical source introduces 37 philosophers, poets, dramatists, political figures and scientists. Entries are arranged by period and each contains from three to eight pages of text, illustration and a summary sidebar. Introductions to each period include background and maps. Less well known individuals are summarized in a chapter at the end of each period. Concluding the volume is a timeline, a glossary, and both general and occupational indexes. Recommended for secondary collections.

575 Manley, Bill. **The Penguin Historical Atlas of Ancient Egypt**. New York: Penguin Books, 1996. 144p. $16.95pa. ISBN 0-14-51331-0.

This attractive volume presents a comprehensive introduction to the history and culture of ancient Egypt. Many color illustrations supplement the text and there are lists, timelines and a useful index. Coverage is from about 5000 B.C. to 305 B.C. Recommended for secondary collections.

576 Sacks, David. **Encyclopedia of the Ancient Greek World**. New York: Facts on File, 1995. 306p. $40.00. ISBN 0-8160-2323-9.

The author, who holds an M.A. in Greek and Roman history from Oxford University, intends this work to provide the most essential information about ancient Greece. It is intended for those, including high school students, who know little or nothing about the Greeks, and who want access to only the most important data about a wide range of subjects within the broad range of material on ancient Greece. The encyclopedia covers political history, social conditions, wars, religion, myth and legend, places, science, culture and daily life. There is complete coverage of Athenian democracy and there are biographies of leaders, thinkers and artists. Black and white photographs and maps accompany some articles. Although the work covers 2100 B.C. to 146 B.C., the emphasis is the classical era of the 400s and 300s B.C. An introduction explaining who the ancient Greeks were and where they came from precedes entries arranged alphabetically with linking cross-references. Articles range from 100 to 3,000 words, with longer articles about major events, such as the Peloponesian War. There is a good extensive index. Highly recommended for secondary schools with classical curricula and/or world history courses. [R: ARBA 97]

577 **The Visual Dictionary of Ancient Civilizations**. New York: Dorling Kindersley, 1994. 64p. $15.95. ISBN 1-56458-701-0.

This is a beautifully illustrated and carefully labeled historical and archeological guide to 14 early civilizations. Each culture/theme is highlighted in facing pages with an introductory paragraph. Color photographs of artifacts or models are labeled to illustrate the theme and narrative. Egypt, Greece, and Rome receive three sets of double pages, each explaining a different aspect of the culture. Mesopotamia, India, and China each receive two sets, while the remainder have only one set of facing pages. There are two timelines, illustrated and organized geographically. One is from 3500 B.C. to 500 B.C. and the other from 500 B.C. to A.D. 1600. In an attempt to be comprehensive geographically, the work extends the traditional meaning of ancient, in order to include the Mayas and Aztecs. There is an index. It is obvious that a work that depends on large illustrations and has only 64 pages will inevitably be superficial in its treatment of the subject; the danger is that oversimplification leads to misunderstanding. This is clearly an introduction to its subject and should be so considered; it is to be regretted that there is no list for further reading. For elementary collections. [R: ARBA 95]

MIDDLE AGES AND RENAISSANCE

578   Loyn, H. R., ed. **The Middle Ages: A Concise Encyclopedia**. New York: Thames and Hudson, 1991. 352p. $24.95pa. ISBN 0-500-27645-5.

This useful source contains selected articles which present a summary of current thoughts on key people, events and themes, battles and treaties of Europe from about 400 to 1500. It is arranged in alphabetical order with cross-references, including to related topics of interest. Entries vary from one paragraph to a page and have citations. The volume is illustrated with maps and genealogical tables. The encyclopedia is a source for reference and as a guide for curriculum.

MODERN HISTORY

579   Cook, Chris and John Stevenson. **The Longman Handbook of Modern European History 1763–1985**. Reading, Mass.: Addison-Wesley, 1992. 435p. $57.50. ISBN 0-582-07291-3.

This is a useful handbook of chronological, statistical and tabular information about European history since 1763. It focuses on political and diplomatic events and social and economic history. There is a section of biographies as well. The table of contents and index provide access to the data. There is a glossary and a classified bibliography. A few maps are included.

WORLD CONFLICTS

580   Brune, Lester H., ed. **The Korean War: Handbook of the Literature and Research**. Westport, Conn.: Greenwood Press, 1996. 460p. $79.50. ISBN 0-313-28969-7.

This resource supplements older books about the war because it includes new sources of information, new interpretations of old information and benefits from newly de-classified information

from several places. There are bibliographic essays on topics about the war with references at the end of each chapter. Essays discuss major works and ways in which recent research has modified former interpretations or raised issues. There are 23 chapters under such headings as International Aspects, Military Aspects, and the U.S. Homefront during the war; this latter section includes McCarthyism, women and minorities, and cinema and television. There is an author index and a subject index. Recommended for high school collections. [R: ARBA 97]

581   Chandler, David G. **Battles and Battlescenes of World War Two**. New York: Macmillan, 1989. 160p. $19.95. ISBN 0-02-897175-2.

Entries from two to four pages are provided for 52 major battles or battlescenes from World War II. Each entry includes a chart of basic information: dates, locations, objective, combatants (generals and armies), numbers of men and equipment, casualty data, results, and suggested readings. A narrative explains the significance of the battle, and each entry is accompanied by a map and photographs. A chronology at the end of the book lists the battles in sequence. There is an index. This is a reference book that supplies information about the military history of the war in a useful format.

582   Dear, I. C. B., ed. **The Oxford Companion to World War II**. New York: Oxford University Press, 1995. 1343p. $60.00. ISBN 0-19-866225-4.

Contributors to this one-volume encyclopedia are all historians who provide a balanced and non-sensational approach to the war years. The work emphasizes military and political history, but there is extensive coverage of social issues as well; there are excellent articles on the effects of the war on children and on women's roles in the war. Articles vary in length; some are as brief as a paragraph. There are long articles on the countries involved in the war; the entry for Germany is more than 30 pages. Entries are signed or written by the editor and some articles have references. Coverage is generally for the time period from September 1, 1939 to September 2, 1945. More than 100 black and white maps as well as illustrations, charts and tables add clarity to the text. A section of nine color maps follow the alphabetical listings and there is a chronology.

Most middle schools and high schools will want this source for its full coverage of the war and its impact. [R: ARBA 97]

583 Grossman, Mark. **Encyclopedia of the Persian Gulf War**. Santa Barbara, Calif.: ABC-CLIO, 1995. 522p. $65.00. ISBN 0-87436-684-4.

This is the first comprehensive reference source about the war, and it attempts to provide balanced coverage, recognizing that the event is still very close, that controversy exists in interpretation and that many materials are still classified and unavailable to the researcher. The coverage is thus limited to information which was available four years after the event. The scope includes the basis of the conflict, and people, places, and countries involved. Much space is given to describing weapons systems used by the United States, the Coalition, and Iraq. There are photographs and 15 maps. Entries are alphabetical and range from a half page to about four pages, with references. Perhaps the most useful information is contained in the appended material. There are tables, a glossary of military slang used during the war, a glossary of Arabic words and about 80 related documents. An extensive narrative chronology begins with 636 A.D. and provides detailed coverage beginning in 1990. There is a bibliography and an index. Recommended for all secondary collections. [R: ARBA 92]

584 Gutman, Israel, ed. **Encyclopedia of the Holocaust**. 4v. New York: Macmillan, 1990. $360.00/set. ISBN 0-02-896090-4.

The encyclopedia, a four volume work, contains approximately 1,000 entries covering aspects of the Holocaust defined as the Nazi plan to physically destroy the Jews of Europe. Entries are generally one or two page signed articles with photographs, maps, and bibliographies. There are longer articles about events in specific countries. The set includes geographical, social, legal and biographical information, as well as articles about literature, trials, and museums. There are entries as well on other groups, such as gypsies, who were Nazi targets. Volume 4 has a glossary, a chronology, an appendix of charts, and a thorough index. This set should be in every high school that has a unit on the Holocaust.

585 Keegan, John, ed. **The Times Atlas of the Second World War**. New York: HarperCollins, 1989. 254p. $29.99. ISBN 0-06-0161778-7.

One of the best features of this outstanding atlas is its world perspective of World War II. There are 87 geographic/chronological essays with 450 full-color maps, photographs, charts and tables. The key to map symbols is reproduced from one page on a card insert. One section of the book shows both military and civilian casualties by country. There is a bibliography, a glossary, and an index. This attractive atlas will be used for both assignments and interest browsing.

586 Kutler, Stanley I., ed. **Encyclopedia of the Vietnam War**. New York: Scribner's, 1996. 711p. $90.00. ISBN 0-13-276932-8.

The encyclopedia begins with an extensive chronology from the 7th century B.C. to 1995, divided into three sections: Southeast Asia, the United States, and the war. Following is an alphabetically arranged series of signed articles ranging in length from 1 paragraph to 12 pages. Longer articles are overviews. Other entries are about military affairs: strategy and tactics, weapons and weapon systems, battles and actions, the air war, and the armed forces of all combatants. There are also entries about society and politics, diplomacy, cultures and peoples, protests and selected biographies. Photographs and 14 maps add to the text. Each entry has a bibliography and there is a classified bibliographic guide. Documents include the Gulf of Tonkin Resolution and the Paris Peace Accords. There is a list of Medal of Honor recipients. A synoptic outline and an index provide access to details. All secondary collections will want this comprehensive work. [R: ARBA 92]

587 Olsen, James, ed. **Dictionary of the Vietnam War**. Westport, Conn.: Greenwood Press, 1988. 585p. $79.50. ISBN 0-313-24943-1.

Brief descriptive reference essays provide a good source of information about the Vietnam War era for students and teachers. Focusing on the period between 1945 and 1975 the signed or source-referenced entries are about the people, military operations and equipment, controversies and legislation associated with the war. Entries are in alphabetical order with cross-references. Five appendices include a glossary of acronyms and slang expressions, a selected classified bibliography, a chronology of the war, and maps. There is an index.

588 Polmar, Norman and Thomas B. Allen. **World War II: America at War, 1941–1945**. New York: Random House, 1991. 940p. $35.00. ISBN 0-394-58530-5.

The stated purpose of this work is to describe how the war touched and shaped the American way of life and the American character, but despite this the coverage is predominately the military aspects of the war. The history proceeds from the sinking of the Panay in 1937 to an Epilogue which discusses effects of the war from 1946–1990. There is a war chronology followed by the main part of the work, an alphabetical listing of topics. Entries vary from a brief identification sentence to several pages. Appendices include military rank comparisons, army and air force battle streams and navy battle stars. There is a personality index and a code and project names index. The emphasis on the work is the American viewpoint, thus coverage of the Holocaust, for example, is limited to one paragraph. [R: ARBA 93]

589 Pope, Stephen and Elizabeth-Anne Wheal. **The Dictionary of the First World War**. New York: St. Martin's Press, 1995. 561p. $40.00. ISBN 0-312-12931-9.

An excellent introduction gives an overview of the war which is followed by alphabetical listings of 1,200 entries. Cross-references provide both access and interconnections. Entries vary from one-line definitions to eight or more columns. Longer essays cover fronts, theaters, and generic terms, while articles also include major offensives, political movements, tactics, forces, and weapons systems. The mostly military focus extends to people, spies, and propaganda. There is a select chronology by month and 25 maps located at the end of the text. Recommended for secondary collections. The authors also wrote *A Dictionary of the Second World War* (Bedrick Books, 1990). [R: ARBA 97]

590 Sandler, Stanley, ed. **The Korean War: An Encyclopedia**. Hamden, Conn.: Garland, 1995. 416p. $75.00. ISBN 0-8240-4445-2.

An introduction, a chronology, and a section of maps precede the alphabetically arranged articles in this one-volume encyclopedia. Emphasis is on the military aspects of the war but entries include places, people, civilian reactions, negotiations, medical services, and the involvement of individual countries as well as campaigns and battles, commands, equipment and weapons. The articles are one page or longer, are signed and have bibliographies. A section of illustrations is inserted in the text. There is a good classified bibliography and an index. Highly recommended for high school collections.

591 Summers, Harry G. **Korean War Almanac**. New York: Facts on File, 1990. 352p. $29.95; $14.95pa. ISBN 0-8160-1737-9; 0-8160-2463-4pa.

592 Summers, Harry G. **Vietnam War Almanac**. New York: Facts on File, 1987. 414p. $27.95; $14.95pa. ISBN 0-8160-1017-X; 0-8160-1813-8pa.

These two handbooks provide thorough and balanced approaches to the two wars. The author, a veteran of both wars and a military analyst, uses the same arrangement for both books. Part 1 provides setting in terms of geography, history, and politics. Part 2 is a chronology and Part 3 is an alphabetical listing of the places, people, events, battles, weapons, and military companies. The entries vary from one paragraph to one page and are supplemented with photographs and maps. Longer entries have suggestions for further reading. There is a selected bibliography and an index in each book. The almanacs are excellent tools for secondary teachers and students.

593 Summers, Harry G., Jr. **Historical Atlas of the Vietnam War**. New York: Houghton Mifflin, 1995. 224p. $39.95. ISBN 0-395-72223-3.

Designed to correct the limited access to adequate maps covering the Vietnam War, this volume presents 100 clear, excellent color maps showing location, events, battles, and developments. There are inset maps to show location details and over 150 photographs. Each section has a two-page narrative and map; relevant quotations are interspersed with the narrative. Sections include geographic setting, background history of the area from 500 B.C. through the Indochina Wars to the Americanization of the war. There is a bibliography and two indexes, one of places and one of names. Although confined to the military history of the Vietnam War this atlas is highly recommended in order to complement materials already held on the war in high school collections. [R: ARBA 97]

594 Tucker, Spencer C., ed. **The European Powers in the First World War: An Encyclopedia**. New York: Garland, 1996. 783p. $95.00. ISBN 0-8153-0399-8.

More than 600 entries written for both students and scholars are in this comprehensive encyclopedia. Coverage includes causes, battles and campaigns, weapons systems and terms of peace. Non-military subjects are also included: medicine, art, literature, music, nations and diplomacy; there are 350 biographies. Clear maps are grouped together in the front of the volume. Articles are alphabetical with cross-references and have references for additional reading. Most entries are brief, approximately one column in length; the longest are about eight columns. There is a subject index. A companion volume is *The United States in the First World War* by Venzon (1995). Recommended for support of world history curriculum in secondary schools. [R: ARBA 92]

595 Van Creveld, Martin, ed. **The Encyclopedia of Revolutions and Revolutionaries: From Anarchism to Zhou Enlai**. New York: Facts on File, 1996. 494p. $75.00. ISBN 0-8160-3236-X.

People, groups and ideologies are the focus of this work which includes the most important revolutions in history. Almost 1,300 entries from one paragraph to four pages cover every continent (except Australia which hasn't had any revolutions) from antiquity to the present. Entries are alphabetical with cross-references and have boxed quotations interspersed. Articles cover all aspects of revolution and entries range from Washington to the Weathermen, from the Red Brigade to the Velvet Revolution, and include contemporaries such as Havel and Walesa. There is a classified bibliography and an index of see references as well as a chronological index. This is a useful source which provides a unique perspective to information found elsewhere. Recommended for high school collections; it may be appropriate for some middle schools as well. [R: ARBA 97]

596 **The World at Arms: The Reader's Digest Illustrated History of World War II**. Pleasantville, N.Y.: Reader's Digest Association; distr., New York: Random House, 1989. 480p. $29.95. ISBN 0-89577-333-3.

This popular rather than scholarly history of World War II is recommended for both middle and high school collections. The six sections with titles such as "The Reich Rampant" and "The Japanese Juggernaut" have readable narrative essays with inserted features. There are 50 color maps and 800 illustrations. A special reference section provides a chronology of the war, a casualty count, a glossary and an index. A library might wish to purchase both reference and circulating copies.

ASIA

597 Embree, Ainslie T., ed. **The Encyclopedia of Asian History**. 4v. New York: Scribner's, 1988. $380.00/set. ISBN 0-684-18619-5.

The encyclopedia is a major information source for schools with a strong curriculum in Asian studies. About 2,700 signed articles ranging in length from a few paragraphs to several pages were written by authorities for a general audience. There are accompanying photographs and maps. Coverage is geographically comprehensive: central, eastern and southeastern Asia. Emphasis is on political, social, intellectual and economic history with less attention paid to cultural history. Articles are arranged through the four volumes alphabetically with cross-references and there is an index in volume 4 which also has a list of entries, a list of contributors, and a list of maps. A synoptic outline shows the relationship of articles.

CHINA

598 O'Neill, Hugh B. **Companion to Chinese History**. New York: Facts on File, 1987. 397p. $27.50. ISBN 0-87196-841-X.

Those requiring concise information on Chinese history and culture from the earliest times to 1985 will welcome this volume, which contains nearly 1,000 entries that range from a sentence to several pages. Articles focus on important historical events, movements, philosophies, religions, and notables (e.g. explorers, emperors, military leaders). Special features include copious cross-references, 14 pages of maps, a chronology from 1506 to 1985, and tables that list dynasties from 2205 B.C. to A.D. 1911. This is an excellent ready-reference source for secondary schools. [R: ARBA 88]

ITALY

599 Coppa, Frank J., ed. **Dictionary of Modern Italian History**. Westport, Conn.: Greenwood Press, 1985. 496p. $105.00. ISBN 0-313-22983-X.

Covering the eighteenth century to the present, the dictionary provides a survey of events, people, institutions, systems, and problems of Italy in political, economic, social, cultural and religious aspects. The signed entries are mostly short and readable; they vary from 100 to 900 words. There are longer entries (Mazzini, for example) with bibliographies; many sources are in Italian. Arrangement is alphabetical with cross-referencing and an index affords additional access. Appendices include a chronology of events, lists of heads of state, and a list of popes. This is a useful source for high schools with strong European history or Italian language programs.

LATIN AMERICA

600 **The Cambridge History of Latin America**. 11v. New York: Cambridge University Press, 1985–1995. price varies. Separate ISBNs.

The major source of Latin American history, this set covers the Spanish- and Portuguese-speaking countries of America south of the United States and the Spanish-speaking Caribbean island nations, Cuba, Puerto Rico, the Dominican Republic, and by convention, Haiti.

Volumes 1–5 cover the period from the first contacts between Native Americans and Europeans in the late fifteenth century to 1930. Volumes 6–10 cover the history of Latin America since 1930 by topic and by area. Volume 11 contains bibliographic essays. Entries are long essays with maps. A planned three-volume related set will cover the history of the Native peoples of the Americas: North, Middle, and South. Volumes can be purchased separately.

SPAIN

601 Kern, Robert W. and Meredith D. Dodge, eds. **Historical Dictionary of Modern Spain, 1700–1988**. Westport, Conn.: Greenwood Press, 1990. 697p. $95.00. ISBN 0-313-25971-2.

This dictionary contains basic material about modern Spain for European history and Spanish language students and teachers. It provides quick introductory information on a broad range of subjects. Arrangement is alphabetical with cross-references and an index. Entries generally range from one to three pages with longer entries for more important topics (Franco gets 8½ pages.) Articles include people, places, events, writers, artists, and composers; there are a few surprising omissions; there is no separate article for the Prado, for example, although there are index references. There are some maps, but no other illustrations. A chronology and selected and classified bibliography are appended.

UNITED KINGDOM AND THE REPUBLIC OF IRELAND

602 Englefield, Dermot J. T., Janet Seaton, and Isobel White. **Facts About the British Prime Ministers: A Compilation of Biographical and Historical Information**. Bronx, N.Y.: H. W. Wilson, 1995. 439p. $55.00. ISBN 0-8242-0863-3.

This work parallels the standard *Facts About the Presidents* and provides biographical information about all of the people who have held the office from 1721–1995, Walpole to Major. An introduction about the role of the prime minister is followed by a chronological record of the individuals which combine historical, political and personal information. Each is accompanied by a portrait or photograph, with brief biographical data, the reigning monarchs during their tenure, and their political affiliation. Brief lists of careers and significance, background, and publications are included. The final part of the work contains 80 lists and tables which permit comparative analysis. Compiled by a former Librarian of the House of Commons and two staff members, this source may be of use in high school collections. [R: ARBA 96]

603 Haigh, Christopher, ed. **The Cambridge Historical Encyclopedia of Great Britain and Ireland**. reprint ed. New York: Cambridge University Press, 1990. 392p. $29.95pa. ISBN 0-521-39552-6.

This comprehensive work surveys British and Irish history from 100 B.C. to A.D. 1975. Some 60 scholars compiled the 7 chronological chapters with thematic subsections on England, Scotland, Wales, and Ireland. Marginal notes serve as fact guides, which are useful for ready-reference. A who's who section provides essential data on notables. Numerous excellent illustrations make this an attractive volume. Recommended for high schools. [R: BL, 15 Apr 86; SLJ, May 86]

604 Mitchell, Sally, ed. **Victorian Britain: An Encyclopedia**. New York: Garland Pub., 1988. 986p. $125.00; $32.50pa. ISBN 0-8240-1513-4; 0-8153-0803-5pa.

The encyclopedia is a comprehensive overview of the complex, interdisciplinary field of Victorian studies. It covers persons, events, topics, groups, and artifacts of Great Britain from 1837–1901. Emphasis is on social, economic, political and cultural matters. Brief signed entries are arranged in alphabetical order with cross-references and an extensive index. Recommended for high schools with strong English literature or world culture programs.

UNITED STATES
Biography

605 Gould, Lewis L., ed. **American First Ladies: Their Lives and Their Legacies**. New York: Garland, 1996. 686p. $95.00. ISBN 0-8153-1479-5.

Separate scholars wrote the essays for each of the entries from Martha Washington to Hilary Clinton. Information provided consists of families, interests and contributions but focuses on the role of the woman as first lady. Read sequentially, one gains a sense of the changing role and public access to the president's wife. Controversy is described, but the essays are more descriptive than critical. Each essay is accompanied by a portrait and each has a bibliography. A good index allows for further developmental and comparative approaches. This source is appropriate for both middle and senior high school students. [R: ARBA 97]

606 Rubel, David. **Scholastic Encyclope-**
E+ **dia of the Presidents and Their Times**. New York: Scholastic Reference, 1997. 232p. $16.95. ISBN 0-590-49366-3.

Published in 1994 and updated in 1997 this is not just another biography of presidents, but puts the presidential terms into context with the history of the period. Graphically complex, yet easy to read and navigate, the information is both interesting and easily understood. The presidents serve as the basis of each entry with dates, a portrait, brief facts and some kind of "first." Text describes the presidency in columns while newspaper-like inserts with headlines and articles spotlight important political and social history from the times and center bars highlight people (often the first lady), inventions, events, and more information about the president's life with illustrations and captions. Political campaigns and elections are described. Article length varies according to the length and importance of each presidency. Cross-references in the text and main article references in the index are printed in red. Highly recommended for elementary and middle schools because the approach adds a dimension not found in other sources. [R: SLJ, Nov 94]

607 Thrapp, Dan L. **Encyclopedia of Frontier Biography: In Three Volumes**. 3v. Glendale, Calif.: Arthur H. Clark, Co., 1988. $195.00/set. ISBN 0-87062-191-2.

608 Thrapp, Dan L. **Encyclopedia of Frontier Biography: Supplemental Volume**. Spokane, Wash.: A. H. Clark, Co., 1994. 610p. $65.00. ISBN 0-87062-222-6.

This biographical dictionary lists 4,500 famous and ordinary citizens of the American frontier. It lists only people no longer living, of either sex and any race who are of significance because of what they did, bad or good, or because they are interesting figures. Included are explorers, fur traders, cattlemen, travelers, military men, renegades, desperados, artists, writers, scientists, missionaries and pioneers, and many Native Americans. If one looks carefully, one might even find a horse or two. Entries are alphabetical by last name, Native American names by first element. For each entry a narrative gives the name, aliases, occupation, dates, a summary of the career, circumstances of the death, an assessment of the life and a bibliography. There is an index.

The supplement adds 1,030 entries, with emphasis on areas not fully covered in the original set. Russian pioneers from Alaska and California, as well as Spanish and Mexican names have been added. Coverage has been extended for South Carolina, Georgia, and Florida from the period 1782–1846, and of the Old Northwest. The format follows the earlier pattern, and there is an index. This set can be used to identify pioneers, but also to learn about the kind of people who moved into the frontier. Recommended for high school collections. [R: ARBA 95]

609 Wakelyn, John L. **Biographical Dictionary of the Confederacy**. Westport, Conn.: Greenwood Press, 1977. 601p. $85.00. ISBN 0-8371-6124-X.

Introductory essays and biographical entries of 651 Confederate wartime leaders, (business and intellectual as well as political and military), may be appropriate for collections where this depth of information is needed. There is a chronology and five appendices with charts and tables showing, for example, the geographic and occupational affiliations of the biographees. There are also a bibliography and an index.

Atlases

610 Adams, James T., ed. **Atlas of American History**. 2d rev. ed. New York: Scribner's, 1985. 320p. $75.00. ISBN 0-684-18411-7.

The standard atlas of American history which complements the Scribner reference set of *The Dictionary of American History*, *The Album of American History* and *The Dictionary of American Biography* is still useful despite its age. The atlas

is arranged chronologically in 11 chapters; the second revised edition added a current (1978–1984) issues chapter. The editors also revised old maps by adding new information and new statistics. The 200 maps are black and white and easy to read and understand. There is an extensive index which extends access to the maps and allows the user to trace developments from one era to another. This is one of the first purchases for any secondary reference collection.

611 Beck, Warren A., and Ynez D. Haase. **Historical Atlas of the American West**. Norman, Okla.: University of Oklahoma Press, 1992. $21.95pa. ISBN 0-8061-2456-3.

The 78 maps in this atlas add significant information to the study of the development of the American West, defined for this resource as those 17 continental states west of the Missouri River. The maps range in chronology from explorations in the sixteenth century to the location of World War II prisoner of war and Japanese internment camps. The atlas includes maps of geographic, flora and fauna data. Maps are on the left pages and narratives about the maps are on the facing pages. Maps are black and white, clear and easily read. An appendix shows Spanish-Mexican land grants, and there is an index. This is an excellent atlas for both middle and high schools.

612 Ferrell, Robert H., and Richard Natkiel. **Atlas of American History**. rev. ed. New York: Facts on File, 1995. 192p. $29.95. ISBN 0-8160-3441-9.

Each section of this atlas has a narrative introduction followed by pages of small maps and illustrations. Maps are shown in several tones to illustrate migration or other trends and developments. There are 250 maps and 116 other illustrations, some in color. The maps are arranged in six chronological sections, from the colonial era through the present; the atlas emphasizes military history and is especially good for recent history. There is an index.

613 **Historical Atlas of the United States**. rev. ed. Washington, D.C.: National Geographic Society, 1994. 288p. $100.00. ISBN 0-87044-970-2.

The arrangement of this beautiful atlas is thematic with chronologic sections within the sections: The Land, People, Boundaries, Economy, Networks, and Communities. The narratives and maps and illustrations and graphics are interspersed with timelines. There is a bibliography and an index. This oversize atlas is for both browsing and reference.

614 McEvedy, Colin. **The Penguin Atlas of North American History to 1870**. New York: Viking Penguin, 1988. 112p. $11.95pa. ISBN 0-14-051128-8.

North American history from 20,000 B.C. to A.D. 1870 is the focus of this small atlas. The continental United States is emphasized, but some coverage for Mexico and the Caribbean is provided. The 48 full-page maps, in blue, black, white, and gray, and 9 inset maps are clear and uncluttered. The text, printed on the lefthand page, explains boundary changes shown in the map on the right. The maps are not indexed, but the text is. This work does not replace more extensive atlases, but it does provide the basic information high school students require for the time period covered. [R: ARBA 89; BL, 1 Feb 89]

615 McPherson, James M., ed. **The Atlas of the Civil War**. New York: Macmillan, 1994. 223p. $40.00. ISBN 0-02-579050-1.

McPherson is the Pulitzer Prize winning author of *Battle Cry of Freedom* and holds the endowed chair as professor of American History at Princeton; he was assisted in the preparation of this atlas by other distinguished historians. The viewpoint of the work is northern, and the editor makes clear in his introduction the perspective that determines the direction of the essays. The war is divided by year, each with an essay. There are overview maps with markers for battles. Then the battles and campaigns are arranged chronologically with narrative, battle maps, photographs, contemporary quotations and a timeline. An epilogue completes the work. A good table of contents, and both general and place name indexes assure access to specific information. This is an attractive and definitive military and political historical atlas of the Civil War and every secondary library should own it. [R: ARBA 96]

Chronologies

616 Carruth, Gordon. **The Encyclopedia of American Facts and Dates**. 10th ed. New York: HarperCollins, 1997. 1056p. $45.00. ISBN 0-06-270192-4.

617 Carruth, Gordon. **What Happened When: A Chronology of Life and Events in America**. New York: NAL-Dutton, 1991. 1408p. $8.99pa. ISBN 0-451-16902-6.

The encyclopedia is a chronology of important events in American history from 986 to the 1990s. It is organized within time periods before 1800, and by year thereafter. Items are placed in one of four columns devoted to political events, the arts, popular culture, and a miscellany of business, education, religion, and science. The book is useful for both a sense of an era and for an awareness of chronology. There is an extensive index which also makes it useful for ready reference. *What Happened When* is an abridged edition with similar information in a similar order, but with a less useful format. Most libraries will prefer the full version.

618 **Chronicle of America**. rev. ed. New
E+ York: DK Publishing, 1997. 1016p. $59.95. ISBN 0-7894-2091-0.

Beginning with events leading up to 1492, the chronology traces the history of the United States with illustrations and sidebars of major events. After the entry for 1997 there is an information section about each of the states, the presidents and the structure of the federal government. The excellent index makes the attractive book truly useful with entries for persons, places, events and social and scientific topics. Recommended for all levels.

619 Rubel, David. **The United States in**
E+ **the 19th Century**. New York: Scholastic, 1996. 192p. $18.95. ISBN 0-590-72564-5.

This timeline covers the major events in the United States from the Federalist period through the "Gay Nineties." Among the other sections are the Civil War era and the "Gilded Age." Each chapter presents an introduction to the period and organizes the material into four categories: science and technology, arts and entertainment, social trends and politics. People, events and issues are highlighted with boxed features. Many illustrations accompany the text. There is a glossary and an excellent index. Suitable to support all areas of the curriculum, and to suggest interdisciplinary units. Also available is *The United States in the 20th Century* (1995).

Dictionaries and Encyclopedias

620 Adams, James T., ed. **Album of American History**. 6v. in 3. New York: Scribner's, 1981. $295.00/set. ISBN 0-684-16848-0.

621 **Album of American History**. Supplement I. New York: Scribner's, 1985. 280p. $75.00. ISBN 0-684-17440-5.

Until the Library of Congress American Memory Project, the *Album* was the major source of illustration for American history projects. Originally published in 1944 as a companion to the *Dictionary of American History*, it provides photographs of artifacts, reproductions of art works, and portraits in chronological order. Its strength is in social history, with an array of objects from colonial mousetraps to a portrayal of Miss Piggy as librarian. Accompanying text identifies each item. Now published with its original six volumes in three, including an excellent index, and a supplement covering 1968–1982, it remains a useful and easily accessible source of visual information.

622 Cayton, Mary Kupiec, Elliott J. Gorn and Peter W. Williams, eds. **Encyclopedia of American Social History**. 3v. New York: Scribner's, 1993. $350.00/set. ISBN 0-684-19246-2.

Treatment of major issues involving social groups and everyday life is the focus of this work. Multipage, signed and referenced essays deal with such topics as social identity, ethnic and racial subcultures, patterns of everyday life, family, education and literacy. The 180 essays are arranged in 14 sections within the three volumes. Articles are scholarly, but accessible to high school students; an extensive index increases the reference value of the set. This is an important complement to sources emphasizing political and military history. [R: ARBA 94]

623 Cooke, Jacob Ernest and others, eds. **Encyclopedia of the North American Colonies**. 3v. New York: Scribner's, 1993. $320.00/set. ISBN 0-684-19269-1.

This is a significant publication; it expands any coverage of the history of North America that previously existed. Coverage is from Erik the Red in the 10th century to the 1820s in New Mexico and the 1860s in Alaska. The encyclopedia goes beyond the English colonies (although they are well covered, and in new ways) to include the colonies of the Netherlands, France, and Spain, and the Russian settlements in the Pacific Northwest. In addition, it explores more than political history and thus includes information on medicine and disease, ranching and farming, missions, slave resistance, interracial societies, science, the arts, religion, family, childhood, and the roles of women. As it discusses distinct cultures of the colonial period, it covers Native Americans and African Americans. Entries are arranged topically throughout the three volumes. Volume one covers geography, politics and economics; volume two covers social history; and volume three covers culture. Each topic may be divided by colonies and by other subtopics. The 274 articles are from 1,000 to 15,000 words and are not only descriptive but interpretive. They are signed and have bibliographies. The detailed table of contents and the index make it possible to find exact information. Highly recommended for high school collections and for middle schools with good American history programs.

624 Current, Richard N. ed., **Encyclopedia of the Confederacy**. 4v. New York: Simon & Schuster, 1993. $355.00/set. ISBN 0-13-275991-8.

This comprehensive resource provides a social, political, and cultural overview of the South during the Confederacy. Approximately 1,400 topics by more than 300 contributors cover a broad scope including the war, campaigns and battles, features of the government and politics, the economic system, religion and culture, the roles of ethnic minorities and women, and the history and origins of the Confederacy. The signed articles are arranged alphabetically throughout the set with a synoptic outline and an index in volume 4. Nine appendices include the Constitution of the Confederate States of America. Articles vary from one column to several pages and are easy to comprehend. Recommended for both middle and high school collections.

625　**Dictionary of American History**. rev. ed. 8v. New York: Scribner's, 1976–1978. $800.00/set. ISBN 0-684-13856-5.

626　**Dictionary of American History. Supplement**. 2v. New York: Scribner's, 1996. $200.00/set. ISBN 0-684-19579-8.

627　**Concise Dictionary of American History**. New York: Scribner's, 1983. 1140p. $100.00. ISBN 0-684-17321-2.

This set, first copyrighted in 1940, remains a standard and authoritative source of information about American history. Political and military history are well covered, and the set has always included entries such as barbed wire, barn raising, and bathtubs. The 1976–1978 edition addresses inadequacies in social history, science, and culture with its 7,200 articles. Native Americans and African Americans are also better represented in this edition. The 1996 supplement extends coverage from 1976 to 1995 and adds 757 entries with 469 new topics such as acid rain, computer viruses and fiber optics. Attention to Native Americans and African Americans is extended, and there is more information about Hispanics, Asian Americans and women. Both the set and the supplementary volumes are arranged alphabetically with cross-references; the supplement's cross-references are to the complete set. Indexing is thorough. *The Concise Dictionary* is a true abridgment of all of the articles in the original. When price is an issue, libraries may want to consider this version.

Since biographies are not included in the *Dictionary of American History*, reference must be made to the *Dictionary of American Biography*. Illustrations are in the *Album of American History* and maps are in the *Atlas of American History*. Middle school and high school students and their teachers will find all of these sources easily accessible.

628　Faragher, John M., ed. **The Encyclopedia of Colonial and Revolutionary America**. reprint ed. New York: DaCapo, 1996. 494p. $24.50pa. ISBN 0-306-80687-8.

Entries about people, places, events, ideas, and developments of early America are designed for quick reference in this encyclopedia. Arrangement is alphabetical with cross-references; topic guides and an index provide other access. The entries are short, and a few are signed and have bibliographies. Over 150 black and white illustrations accompany the text. While the information included goes beyond other sources, there are interesting omissions, with no mention of Virginia's Harrison family, or participation of French assistance/participation in the Revolution. Recommended for middle and high school collections.

629　Foner, Eric and John A. Garraty, eds. **The Reader's Companion to American History**. Boston: Houghton Mifflin, 1991. 1226p. $35.00. ISBN 0-395-51372-3.

Three types of articles make up this source: short encyclopedic articles, interpretive essays and biographies. The entries are arranged in alphabetical order with many cross-references and an elaborate index; it is notable because the articles are not only readable, but interesting and even amusing. The approach is history as literature, rather than as a listing of dry and unrelated facts. Coverage encompasses all sorts of history— social as well as political, family life, art, music, religion, and the diversity of the population. It is an authoritative source with the longer articles signed and with bibliographies. About 20 maps and tables help with interpretation. Highly recommended for secondary students and teachers.

630　Fritze, Ronald. **Legend and Lore of the Americas Before 1492: An Encyclopedia of Visitors, Explorers, and Immigrants**. Santa Barbara, Calif.: ABC-CLIO, 1993. 319p. $65.00. ISBN 0-87436-664-X.

Fritze discusses the theories about African, Asian, and European discoverers who supposedly found America before Columbus. While he balks at including extraterrestrial explorers, he covers all of the stories from the earliest times to 1492. Among the 216 entries are individuals such as St. Brendon and Prince Madoc, groups such as the Hebrew Lost Tribes and the Norse, and believers such as Thor Heyerdahl and the Mormons. Related topics include evidence used in support of one or more theories such as the transmission of the sweet potato. Arrangement is alphabetical and there is a good index. Articles vary from 50 to several thousand words and consist of narratives explaining associated persons, authors who have written about the theory, places, concepts, and organizations. Maps, drawings, photographs, and bibliographies accompany the narratives. The presentations try to show multiple viewpoints, but the accumulated depiction is that valid evidence for pre-Columbian discovery is scarce indeed. This is a wonderful book that would support the discovery unit of American history classes in grades 7–12. Highly recommended. [R: ARBA 94]

631 Gallay, Alan, ed. **Colonial Wars of North America, 1512–1763: An Encyclopedia**. New York: Garland, 1996. 856p. $95.00. ISBN 0-8240-7208-1.

This is one title in the group of new American historical reference works filling the need for special materials on typically ignored periods. And like the others, it gives comprehensive geographical and political coverage by including the Spanish southwest, Russian Alaska, Canada and the West Indies with the traditional treatment of the western European east coast colonies and by including all involved groups: Europeans, Africans, and Native Americans. The work covers the chronological period between the Spanish conquistadors and Pontiac's War. Topics range from groups, colonies, biographies, and intercultural relationships to locales, forts and various aspects of war such as weapons, technology, supplies and medical services. Most of the alphabetically arranged articles are one page, but some are as long as five; longer articles have bibliographies and all are signed. The 700 essays are preceded by a good overview introduction and a chronology from 1512 to 1763. There are a few illustrations. This is an outstanding source that will supplement more traditional sources that treat this period only briefly. Recommended for both middle school and high school history reference collections. [R: ARBA 97]

632 Garraty, John A., ed. **The Young**
E+ **Reader's Companion to American History**. New York: Houghton Mifflin, 1994. 964p. $39.95. ISBN 0-395-66920-0.

This outstanding encyclopedia of American history for students and teachers from upper elementary to high school should be in every collection. Its organization is alphabetical with cross-references and an excellent index; and the signed articles, written by distinguished contributors, are interestingly written on interesting topics: political, cultural, military, and social life are all covered. There was a special attempt to include information about women and minorities, and controversial topics are not omitted. Most articles are brief, intended to be clear and concise explanations and to encourage further research. The article on the Civil War, for example, is only six pages. Photographs, other illustrations, charts, portraits and color plates, as well as a crisp typeface, make this an attractive volume. It is based on the adult *Reader's Companion to American History*. Highly recommended as first purchase by all school libraries. [R: ARBA 96]

633 Graham, Otis L., Jr. and Meghan R. Wander, eds. **Franklin D. Roosevelt: His Life and Times: An Encyclopedic View**. reprint ed. New York: DaCapo, 1990. 512p. $22.50pa. ISBN 0-306-80410-7.

This volume in the Presidential Encyclopedia series is far more than a biographical work, since its focus is on the historical period between 1933 and 1945. The 321 readable entries cover notables, events, and concepts of the period. Each is supported by a bibliography, often annotated, and illustrations. There are several in-depth articles on complex topics, such as the elections in which Roosevelt was a candidate. The work, suggested for high school level, is an excellent reference tool for the years of the Roosevelt presidency. [R: ARBA 86]

634 Kirkendall, Richard S., ed. **The Harry S. Truman Encyclopedia**. New York: Macmillan, 1990. 368p. $65.00. ISBN 0-8161-8915-3.

Virtually every event, issue, and notable person from the Truman presidency is included in this volume. Well-written, factual entries that vary from 200 words to several pages are followed by short bibliographies of important works on the topic. Cross-references, an extensive index, and a list of articles inside the front and back covers are also included. This attractive work is suggested for high schools. [R: ARBA 91; BL, 15 Feb 90; VOYA, July 90; WLB, Apr 90]

635 Klingaman, William K. **Encyclopedia of the McCarthy Era**. New York: Facts on File, 1996. 502p. $50.00. ISBN 0-8160-3097-9.

This is a unique source that covers a brief but important era in modern American history. Emphasizing the period from McCarthy's famous "I hold in my hand..." speech in February of 1950 to the Senate's censure of McCarthy in the Summer of 1954, the encyclopedia also covers events in the post-war period that led up to the atmosphere that encouraged McCarthyism. The 250 entries are arranged alphabetically with cross-references; most articles are from two to three pages, but some are longer; the entry for McCarthy is eight pages. One hundred well-selected photographs complement the text. Topics covered are people, education, religion, sports, entertainment, law, as well as domestic and foreign politics. Other entries include organizations, journals, books, plays, television programs, and films. A chronology from 1919 to 1960 follows the articles; there is a select bibliography and an index. Highly recommended for high school collections. [R: ARBA 97]

636 Kutler, Stanley I., and others, ed. **Encyclopedia of the United States in the Twentieth Century**. 5v. New York: Scribner's, 1996. $385.00/set. ISBN 0-13-210535-7.

The purpose of this set is to provide both narrative description and analysis of the major topics and themes of the United States during the century. Six parts are arranged in four volumes: the American people; politics; global America; science, technology, and medicine; the economy; and culture. An introduction and an extensive chronology classified by the major topics are in volume one. The articles are long and signed with cross-references and bibliographic essays. Topics are broadly covered, geographically where appropriate, and with attention to developing notions of gender and ethnicity. Maps and tables are included, and there is an index in volume four that is repeated in a separate paperback. This set is recommended for high school collections where it will support all social studies areas. [R: ARBA 97]

637 Levy, Leonard W. and Louis Fisher, eds. **Encyclopedia of the American Presidency**. 4v. New York: Simon & Schuster, 1994. $355.00/set. ISBN 0-13-275983-7.

This comprehensive reference work treats the subject of the presidency from a multidisciplinary approach. Intended for historians, lawyers, political scientists, politicians, economists, journalists and students, the set provides a balanced view of the executive branch. More than a thousand articles by 335 contributors are arranged alphabetically. Coverage includes people (presidents, vice-presidents, first ladies, also-rans, and executive branch officials), presidential powers, constitutional and party roles, the White House, relationships with the Congress and Judiciary, public policy, and contemporary and historical events. There are bibliographies and tables; volume 4 has a synoptic outline, and both a case index and a general index. This encyclopedia is the definitive source of information on the presidency and is recommended for high school collections. [R: ARBA 95]

638 Levy, Peter B. **Encyclopedia of the Reagan-Bush Years**. Westport, Conn.: Greenwood Press, 1996. 442p. $49.95. ISBN 0-313-29018-0.

The encyclopedia has 250 entries that emphasize the presidencies with additional articles on general trends. Broad entries cover foreign affairs, issues, events, trends, laws, people, and quotations and vary from 100 to 1,000 words. Topics are both political and popular. Included are such subjects as "Broccoli," "Just Say No," "Air Traffic Controllers Strike," "Panama Invasion," "Persian Gulf War," "Teflon Presidency," and "Thousand Points of Light." Articles have suggested readings and cross-references to related entries. There are photographs and tables and an appendix with a statistical profile. An index lends access. One may argue that such a recent time period is difficult to treat objectively or even that the choice of relevant entries is speculative. Nonetheless, this source is surprisingly useful for the contemporary researcher and it is recommended to support history, government and sociology curricula in high school collections. [R: ARBA 97]

639 Miller, Randall M. and John David Smith, eds. **The Dictionary of Afro-American Slavery**. Westport, Conn.: Greenwood Press, 1988. 866p. $99.50. ISBN 0-313-23814-6.

Three hundred signed articles covering slavery in North America (mostly the United States) are arranged in alphabetical order with cross-references. The entries are multi-page with bibliographic references, but are written for non-specialists and are easily understood. Coverage is from the first English settlement to the Reconstruction era and include laws, events, people, regions, states, and social, intellectual, institutional, and political aspects of slavery. The articles are supplemented with charts, tables, and maps. There is a chronology and a subject index. This source is highly recommended for middle and high school history and sociology classes.

640 Neely, Mark E., Jr. **The Abraham Lincoln Encyclopedia**. New York: DaCapo, 1984. 356p. $18.95pa. ISBN 0-306-80209-0.

This illustrated encyclopedia of the president provides authoritative information about the people, places, events, groups, politics, and ideas associated with Lincoln and his times. Signed articles are arranged alphabetically with cross-references and vary in length from one column to two pages, and have lists of sources. Accompanying chronologies complement the arrangement and there is an index. This is a good source for high school students, and expands the biographical information by focusing equally on the time period.

641 Newton, Michael and Judy Ann Newton. **The Ku Klux Klan: An Encyclopedia**. New York: Garland, 1991. 639p. $75.00. ISBN 0-8240-2038-3.

This work describes how the Klan developed rapidly from a social club founded by six Confederate veterans in 1866 into a terrorist organization. A preface presents a good summary history followed by a classified list of entries. Included are organizations, places, events, related, affiliated and front groups, legislation, general terms, and individuals. The biographical entries include members, allies, opponents, victims and targets. Entries are brief with citations to mostly secondary sources listed in the bibliography. There is a central insert of 40 photographs. This is an accessible source for secondary school students. [R: ARBA 92]

642 Olson, James S. **Historical Dictionary of the 1920s: From World War I to the New Deal, 1919–1933**.

Westport, Conn.: Greenwood Press, 1988. 420p. $65.00. ISBN 0-313-25683-7.

The brief essays on individuals from politicians to movie stars, social movements, organizations, legislation, treaties, political events, sports, fads and ideas prominent in the United States during the 1920s provide useful information for high school students in history, literature, and sociology classes. The entries are arranged in alphabetical order with cross-references and have suggestions for further reading. There is a detailed chronology, a selected and classified bibliography and an index. While most of the entries are biographical, the source as a whole gives a good overview of the decade.

643 Phillips, Charles and Alan Axelrod,
E+   eds. **Encyclopedia of the American West**. 4v. New York: Macmillan Library Reference/Simon & Schuster Macmillan, 1996. $375.00/set. ISBN 0-02-897495-6.

For the purposes of this set, "the West" means all of the states west of the Mississippi River except Louisiana, but including Hawaii and Alaska as well as some parts of Canada and Mexico. The intent is to provide a study of the American West by today's standards of scholarship, and so it pays attention to women, minorities, native peoples, social history and cultures. It covers the early Spanish period to the early twentieth century. There are 1,700 entries, many are long, all are signed and have suggested readings. Articles are about such specific topics as art and architecture, barbed wire, the Dust Bowl, and Roy Rogers and Dale Evans. People included are bankers, cattle ranchers, actors, detectives, educators, gunfighters, outlaws, prostitutes, missionaries and other religious leaders, and pioneer figures. Writing is informal and should appeal to secondary school students. Arrangement is alphabetical and pages are numbered consecutively throughout the set. There are 42 maps and an index. There is also a classified list of biographical entries. Minor errors abound as others have noted, and the informal writing leads to questionable interpretations. It was interesting to read in the Iowa article that "some Iowans live in cities," when according to the 1990 Census, about 60% do. Cedar Falls is given credit for producing farm implements, which will irritate its sister city of Waterloo which does. Indeed the entire article begs for a good editor; unfortunately the editor wrote the Iowa article; in fact, the editors wrote 290 of the 1,700 articles. Librarians may wish to review other coverage in this work (which seems so promising for both middle and high school collections) before purchasing. [R: ARBA 97]

644 Richter, William L. **The ABC-CLIO Companion to American Reconstruction, 1862–1877**. Santa Barbara, Calif.: ABC-CLIO, 1996. 505p. $60.00. ISBN 0-87436-851-0.

This source begins with a preface and introduction that give an excellent overview of the subject, better than most comprehensive texts and encyclopedias contain. Then the alphabetically arranged articles give more specific information about the 11 secessionist states and how the Reconstruction era affected them. Articles are generally long with cross-references to related articles and bibliographies. There is an informal quality to the writing that will appeal to students. Coverage is from 1865 to 1877 and includes people (both carpetbaggers and scalawags), events, organizations and agencies, education, experiments and laws. The accompanying illustrations are all from the Library of Congress collections. A chronology, an extensive bibliography and an index complete the work. Highly recommended for middle and high schools. [R: ARBA 97]

645 Rutland, Robert A., ed. **James Madison and the American Nation, 1751–1836: An Encyclopedia**. New York: Simon & Schuster, 1994. 509p. $95.00. ISBN 0-13-508425-3.

Although the focus of the book is Madison and his point of view, the work is at least as important for the time span it covers as for the viewpoint of the president. The post-revolutionary period to Madison's death in 1836, is often especially difficult to research. The 400 signed articles from 88 expert contributors (professors, curators, museum directors, and editors) are arranged in alphabetical order with cross-references and include a variety of events, people, and places that were important in Madison's era. The range of articles includes agriculture, Baltimore, Jean Lafitte, Napoleon, and the War of 1812. Using the life of Madison as a framework for the entries lends a sense of historical continuity to the entire work. A synoptic outline further organizes the work by Madison's thought, Madison's

America, politics and foreign affairs in the age of Madison, and lists of his contemporaries, both American and foreign. Documents, illustrations and a chronology all enhance the value of this item. Students will find the information helpful, while teachers may be inspired to pay more attention to this era in American history. Highly recommended for secondary collections. [R: ARBA 96]

646 Slatta, Richard W. **The Cowboy Encyclopedia**. Santa Barbara, Calif.: ABC-CLIO, 1994. 474p. $54.00. ISBN 0-87436-738-7.

The focus of this encyclopedia is the cowboy, not the West in general. A bull icon and typeface for headings emphasizes the nature of the work. It includes information about both Canadian and Latin American cowboys, but the emphasis is on the cowboy in the western United States. Coverage is comprehensive and includes history and culture and myth and legend. Articles are arranged alphabetically in broad entries with subheadings and give the historical context and cultural significance of each topic. Entries include such things as equipment, dress, work, women, places, and images conveyed by movies, fiction and music. Photographs and drawings illustrate the text. Sources are listed and there is an extensive bibliography. In addition appendices list film and video sources, museums, periodicals, and cultural happenings in celebration of the cowboy. Highly recommended as an American history and culture class resource for both middle and high school collections. [R: ARBA 96]

647 Venzon, Anne Cipriano, ed. **The United States in the First World War: An Encyclopedia**. New York: Garland, 1995. 830p. $95.00. ISBN 0-8240-7055-0.

A work in the Garland Military History of the United States series, this encyclopedia covers individuals, campaigns and battles, weapons and other equipment, laws, events, peace conferences and treaties, army divisions, foreign relations, the involvement of women and minorities and domestic issues. The long (1–14 pages) and scholarly articles are signed and have see also references to related articles. Arrangement is alphabetical and there is also an index. Maps accompany the text. Recommended for high school collections. [R: ARBA 96]

648 Whisenhunt, Donald W, **Encyclopedia USA: The Encyclopedia of the United States of America Past & Present**. 24v.– (in progress). Gulf Breeze, Fla.: Academic International Press, 1983– . $40.00/volume. ISBN 0-87569-076-9.

This astonishing work in progress is an attempt to produce comprehensive coverage of American history—political, religious, military, social and biographical. The first volume (volumes are about 250 pages each) was published in 1983 and by 1997, 24 volumes were completed, the most recent covering Dulles–Earthquakes in America. Meanwhile, 1997 also brought the publication of the first supplement (Abb–Ale). Volumes may be purchased separately, or on a subscription basis. There is an index volume covering volumes 1–10. Articles most often are signed and begin with a defining sentence and are readable and clear. Most have bibliographies. Topics range from the traditional to the unexpected and there are many that will not be easily found elsewhere. Highly recommended for those willing to commit to the future. [R: ARBA 94]

649 Wilson, Charles R. and William Ferris, eds. **Encyclopedia of Southern Culture**. Chapel Hill, N.C.: University of North Carolina Press, 1989. 1634p. $69.95. ISBN 0-8078-1823-2.

This comprehensive source covers the 11 states of the former Confederacy as well as Delaware, Kentucky, Maryland, Missouri, West Virginia, Oklahoma, and the District of Columbia. Southern Ohio, Indiana, Illinois and pockets of Southern sympathies in other areas are also included. The encyclopedia uses findings of contemporary scholarship to present basic data and bibliographies about southern culture and how the patterns developed. An interdisciplinary approach is taken so that the source can be used as a basis for cross-discipline curriculum courses on the American South. In addition to these purposes, the source remains a reference tool. There are 24 major sections from Agriculture to Women's Life, including such things as Black life, literature and violence. Each section has three divisions: an overview, alphabetical thematic articles and alphabetical topics and biographies. The biographies profile living and deceased persons from Davy Crockett to Willie Nelson. There are many black and white photographs and some maps. There are cross-references and an extensive general index. Highly recommended for high school collections.

Source Material

650 The Associated Press. **Twentieth-Century America: A Primary Source Collection from The Associated Press**. 10v. Danbury, Conn.: Grolier, 1995. $349.00. ISBN 0-7172-7494-2.

This set provides a sense of history with the immediacy and details from the events themselves. The 10 volumes consist of news stories reprinted just as originally transmitted by the Associated Press to member newspapers where they were most often printed as sent, so they represent what Americans were reading in their newspapers at the time. The work is chronologically arranged both as a set and within each volume. Each volume has chapters dedicated to major events or issues with good chapter outlines. Each issue is introduced with background notes and then the stories appear as filed with dates added for clarity. Many AP photos accompany the articles and other photo essays act as a running timeline. Volume two, for example, covers the Depression years from 1929–1939 and include chapters on both the political and economic recovery efforts of the New Deal and on other events of the era such as crime and the movies. Volume ten covers the period from 1988 with chapters on the end of the Cold War, the Gulf War, violence, and the early part of the Clinton administration. There is also a general index. This is an important set which provides a supplement to history, government and other social science reference material. Highly recommended for middle and high schools. [R: ARBA 96]

651 **Everything Civil War: The Ultimate Guide to Civil War Products, Services, Places of Interest, Organizations, Archives, and Accommodations**. Silverdale, Wash.: Willow Creek Press, 1996. 304p. $19.95pa. ISBN 0-9657183-1-6.

Products, services, organizations, accommodations, places and archives are listed in this unique resource. Material is listed alphabetically within the categories with entries giving addresses, electronic addresses, telephone numbers and brief annotations. Sources cover clothing, books, touring and other Civil War paraphenalia. This work is useful for re-enactors as well as teachers and students.

652 Yanak, Ted and Pam Cornelison. **The Great American History Fact-Finder**. Boston: Houghton Mifflin, 1993. 496p. $24.95; $14.95pa. ISBN 0-395-65992-2; 0-395-61715-4pa.

E+

With approximately 2,000 concise summaries of people, events, organizations, and cultural references, this is a comprehensive ready reference guide to a variety of information about historical and contemporary America. Entries include a variety of individuals from presidents to baseball players. Arranged alphabetically with cross-references (occasionally the cross-references intrude on the information; see, e.g. John Quincy Adams) the entries are brief introductions to the topic. There are maps, tables, political cartoons, photographs and portraits to add visual appeal. The appendices include maps, tables, and documents, including the Articles of Confederation. There is a good index. This is recommended for all level collections. [R: ARBA 94]

Hobbies and Games

AMUSEMENTS

653 Loeffelbein, Robert L. **The Recreation Handbook: 342 Games and Other Activities for Teams and Individuals**. Jefferson, N.C.: McFarland, 1992. 237p. $24.95pa. ISBN 0-89950-744-1.

E+

These made-up sports and games or recreational activities are for children and teenagers to play during informal or loosely structured leisure time. The requirements are that rules be few and simple, equipment cheap and easy to obtain, that different numbers of players of all ages can participate and any size playing space available will work; changes within any of these categories are possible. The 342 games are arranged by type: some examples are aquatic, basketball, bat and ball, bowling, football/soccer, combative, table games, word-play and story telling, activities for rainy days, carnivals and parties, and crafts and game construction. For each activity there is a brief description, players, equipment, and space requirements, directions and variations. This source will be useful to teachers, parents, librarians, and teenagers working as recreation leaders. Recommended for both reference and circulating collections at all levels. [R: ARBA 94]

654 Munson, Robert S. **Favorite Hobbies and Pastimes: A Sourcebook of Leisure Pursuits**. Chicago: American Library Association, 1994. 366p. $55.00pa. ISBN 0-8389-0638-9.

This source presents essays on a variety of spare-time activities supplemented with sources of additional information. It includes hobbies, animals, computers, arts, sports, science, travel, continuing education and volunteerism. There are 84 specific examples from antiques to writing, ceramics to ice hockey, computers to snowmobiles. For each activity there are four to six pages of background and history, equipment and techniques, with a list of related reference books, periodicals and associations. Both Dewey Decimal and Library of Congress classification numbers are attached to the activities so the user may begin browsing the regular library collection for more information. There is a subject index. Suggested for middle and high school collections. [R: ARBA 95]

655 Thompson, William N. **Legalized Gambling: A Reference Handbook**. Santa Barbara, Calif.: ABC-CLIO, 1994. 209p. $39.50. ISBN 0-87436-729-8.

The author is at the University of Las Vegas and has many years experience in dealing with the issues of legalized gambling. The work discusses political, economic, social and religious issues associated with the topic and provides a historical overview of gambling in North America. There is a chronology and a section of biographies. Legislation, statistics, and organizations form other sections and there is a section specifically dealing with pros and cons of gambling which is not a balanced view. The discussion of economic issues ignores the impact on surrounding businesses. There is a good list of print and non-print resources, a glossary and an index. [R: ARBA 95]

656 Throgmorton, Todd H. **Roller Coasters: An Illustrated Guide to the Rides in the United States and Canada, With a History.** Jefferson, N.C.: McFarland, 1993. 154p. $25.95. ISBN 0-89950-805-7.

The history of roller coasters is followed by a location guide to parks and coasters in the East, Midwest, South, West and Canada. For each coaster, the entry gives its name, the date it was built, description, builder and statistics about heights, drops, and length of ride. Photographs of the coasters are included, but are often separated from the descriptions. There is an appendix of coasters operating listed alphabetically by state and a list dividing coasters into wooden or steel construction with references to the regional listing. [R: ARBA 94]

CARD GAMES AND BOARD GAMES

657 Frey, Richard L., Geoffrey Mott-
E+ Smith, and Alfred H. Morehead. **The New Complete Hoyle: The Authoritative Guide to the Official Rules of All Popular Games of Skill and Chance**. rev. ed. New York: Doubleday, 1991. 692p. $25.95. ISBN 0-385-24962-4.

This *Hoyle* traces its lineage to the original book of rules by Edmund Hoyle in 1746. The revised edition gives rules for adult and children's card games, board games, and tile games. It also includes dice games and casino gambling games as well as some parlor games. For each game, there is an introduction and history, its standard rules, variations, and comments on strategy. Charts and other illustrations are included when necessary. There is an alphabetical table of contents, a glossary, and appendices about general processes such as cutting, shuffling, and dealing. This is a standard and authoritative source of game rules and has a place in any public school library.

658 Keene, Raymond. **The Simon & Schuster Pocket Book of Chess**. New York: Simon & Schuster, 1989. 192p. $12.95; $7.95pa. ISBN 0-671-67923-6; 0-671-67924-4pa.

Keene, a British chess champion and international grand master since 1976, has written widely on the game. This work emphasizes chess strategy and tactics and covers rules, algebraic notation, popular openings, the middle game, and the end game. Also included are profiles of world champions and grand masters, a commentary on computer chess, and tournament tips. Some 200 full-color diagrams illustrate the text, and review quizzes conclude each chapter. Highly recommended for beginners and those who wish to review their knowledge of the game. [R; BR, 1 June 89; BR, Nov/Dec 89; Kliatt, Sept 89]

COLLECTING

659 Breen, Walter. **Walter Breen's Com-
E+ plete Encyclopedia of U.S. and Colonial Coins**. New York: Doubleday, 1987. 768p. $100.00. ISBN 0-385-14207-2.

Every major variety of U.S. coin, both current and obsolete are included in this comprehensive handbook. The collector will not only find coins from the English colonies, but from the kingdom of Hawaii as well. The guide is arranged in two parts; the first, on early coins has 16 chapters. The second part deals with coins minted by the federal government, commemorative, private, frontier, and territorial issues. Each major section has an overview. Narratives describe the historical significance of each issue and its physical characteristics. Complete information is given about the designer/engraver and the mint and quantity minted. There are over 4,000 illustrations showing details of coins, front and reverse. Some auction prices are given as indications of market value; the encyclopedia's major purpose, however, is description, not pricing. There is a bibliography and a list of coin conventions, a glossary and both name and subject indexes. This is an exhaustive record and will not only be of use to collectors; history teachers should find a wealth of supplemental information in this encyclopedia.

660 Krause, Chester L. **Standard Catalog of United States Paper Money**. 16th ed. Iola, Wis.: Krause Publications, 1997. 248p. $24.95. ISBN 0-87341-5361.

Limited to only the United States, this catalog lists and illustrates paper money in the same format as the multiple Krause coin catalogs.

661 Krause, Chester L. and Clifford Mischler. **Standard Catalog of World Coins 1601–1700**. Iola, Wis.: Krause Publications, 1996. 2288p. $65.00pa. ISBN 0-87341-2710.

662 Krause, Chester L. and Clifford Mischler. **Standard Catalog of World Coins: Eighteenth Century, 1701–1800**. 2d ed. Iola, Wis.: Krause Publications, 1997. 1304p. $65.00pa. ISBN 0-87341-5264.

663 Krause, Chester L. and others. **Standard Catalog of World Coins 1801–1900**. Iola, Wis.: Krause Publications, 1996. 1622p. $45.00pa. ISBN 0-87341-4276.

664 Krause, Chester L. and others. **Standard Catalog of World Coins**. 25th ed. Iola, Wis: Krause Publications. 1997. 1712p. $47.95pa. ISBN 0-87341-4977.

These publications have varied in number of volumes and coverage (the twenty-fifth edition lists coins from 1801), but taken together they list and illustrate coins from all over the world, and include date and grade. Listings are by country. There are numerous indexes and features.

665 **Scott Standard Postage Stamp Catalogue**. Sidney, Ohio: Scott Publishing, 1867– . annual. $32.00. ISSN 0737-0741.

Published annually, the *Scott Catalogue* attempts to list all authentic (declared legal for postage by the issuing country) postage stamps in the world. There are about 400,000 of them in this edition. Volume 1 includes stamps from English speaking countries, and stamps from other countries are listed alphabetically throughout the next four volumes. For each stamp there is a Scott identification number, and information about the paper and ink colors, styles, denomination, year and retail values. Supplemental information on condition, grade, values, terminology is appended. A topical listing index leads one to stamps with pictures of mushrooms, space, drums, rabbits, and so forth. This is the standard stamp guide. Volumes are issued and available separately.

666 Sugar, Bert Randolph, comp. and ed. **The Sports Collector's Bible**. 4th ed. Indianapolis, Ind.: Bobbs-Merrill, 1983. 578p. $12.95pa. ISBN 0-672-52605-0.

Most of this book focuses on baseball trading cards, but sections also cover other baseball collectibles (e.g., programs and scorecards, autographs, books and yearbooks, pins, pennants). The work is valuable only as a checklist of collector's items. Indexed. [R: ARBA 85]

667 Yeoman, R. S. **A Guide Book of United States Coins**. Racine, Wis.: Western Publishing, 1947– . annual. $11.95. ISSN 0072-8829.

For fifty years Yeoman's "Red Book" of coins has been a standard guide to U.S. coins and their values. This is not a price list, but reflects retail prices averaged from data supplied by contributing dealers several months before publication. For some coins these data are unavailable, and thus their values are unknown. There is a coin conditions chart and an introductory essay about the history of coins. The guide is arranged chronologically and geographically; and by original value (dimes, quarters, and so on). Commemoratives are included. Detailed illustrations of authentic coins help in identification. In addition to an index, there is a list of numismatic magazines.

Holidays and Special Days

668 **Chase's Calendar of Events**. Lincolnwood, Ill.: Contemporary Books, 1995– . annual. $59.95pa. ISSN 0740-5286.

E+

Since 1958, Chase has provided a chronology of events for the year. Now with over 12,000 entries, the standard chronological calendar is supplemented with spotlights of major events in history, education, and religion, world wide. Each calendar entry supplies the date and day, where the day is in the yearly cycle, and an alphabetic listing of births, anniversaries, events, special weeks and other notables. A special entry of birthdays today completes the day's listing. There is also an almanac-like section of information that is likely to be useful, and a good alphabetical index. No school library of any size should be without this source.

The 1998 *Chase's Calendar* includes a CD-ROM (Windows) version. The disc contains all of the data from the print version with multiple search and link capabilities. The interface is clear and simple to use. Items can be downloaded to disc or printed.

669 **Chase's Sports Calendar of Events**.
E+ Lincolnwood, Ill.: Contemporary Books, 1996– . annual. $29.95pa. ISSN 1091-2959.

Following the pattern of the general *Chase's Calendar*, this guide lists almost 6,000 entries for sponsored sports and recreational events, anniversaries, birthdays and holidays. Stock car racing, sled-dog racing, winter festivals and pancake races join football, baseball, and basketball entries. Addresses and Web sites of teams are included as are lists of members of halls of fame. Indexing is by name, keyword, and location. Libraries at all levels will find this useful.

670 Gregory, Ruth W. **Anniversaries and**
E+ **Holidays**. 4th ed. Chicago: American Library Association, 1983. 262p. $40.00. ISBN 0-8389-0389-4.

This standard source, while not so attractive nor so updated as Chase's, is a good supplement and is especially good because of its international scope. Over 180 countries are covered although the emphasis is the United States. It provides quick identification of notable anniversaries, holy days, holidays and special event days and good coverage of Christian, Jewish, and Islamic fixed and moveable days. An extended bibliography and an index are included.

671 Hatch, Jane M., comp. and ed. **Amer-**
E+ **ican Book of Days**. 3d ed. Bronx, N.Y.: H. W. Wilson, 1978. 1214p. $87.00. ISBN 0-8242-0593-6.

This source complements other calendar sources by giving more in-depth information about fewer events. It gives the names of most legal and public holidays, both federal and state, with extended narratives about major political, religious, scientific and social events as well as birthdays and anniversaries. There are notes about moveable holidays and an extensive topical index which permits tracing developments; e.g., all possible dates of significance for a study of the American Revolution. Despite its copyright date, this 3d edition is still a standard source.

672 Henderson, Helene, and Sue Ellen
E+ Thompson, eds. **Holidays, Festivals, and Celebrations of the World Dictionary Detailing More than 2,000 Observances from All 50 States and More than 100 Nations**. 2d ed. Detroit, Mich.: Omnigraphics, 1997. 822p. $84.00. ISBN 0-7808-0074-5.

This comprehensive guide lists more than 2,000 holidays, festivals, celebrations, holy days and feast days from all 50 states and more than 100 countries. It does not include the birth or death dates of famous people. The useful introduction discusses calendar systems with an overview of the end of the second millennium. The work is arranged alphabetically by the name of the holiday; this volume adds a directory listing of contact sources. Many indexes provide access to the holidays: chronological, religious, subject, legal and ethnic. Appendices give brief information about state admission dates, presidents and tourist information. There is a bibliography and a list of Web sites. This volume is a companion to the publisher's *Holiday Symbols*. Useful at all levels.

673 Limburg, Peter R. **Weird! The Complete Book of Halloween Words**. New York: Bradbury Press/Macmillan, 1989. 122p. $12.95. ISBN 0-02-759050-X.

Written in a conversational style, this slim volume presents etymologies of terms and words related to Halloween and traces them to their present day use within the context of the holiday. "Do You Know," which addresses several related words, follows several of the definitions. A table of contents and an index give structure to the randomly arranged entries. The book is profusely and humorously illustrated with pen-and-ink drawings. A worthwhile addition to the holiday collection. [R: ARBA 91; BL, 1 Sept 89; SLJ, Sept 89]

Law

DICTIONARIES AND ENCYCLOPEDIAS

674 Axelrod, Alan, and others. **Cops, Crooks, and Criminologists: An International Biographical Dictionary of Law Enforcement**. New York: Facts on File, 1996. 321p. $45.00. ISBN 0-8160-3016-2.

Over 600 major and significant figures, both living and deceased make up this biographical dictionary. Those selected for inclusion are those concerned with laws, the nature of crime, criminals, and those involved in solving crime. The work is international in scope, but emphasizes American and British figures. Police, lawyers, judges, private detectives, and some criminals are included. After a worthwhile introduction, entries are alphabetical. They include name, dates, identification and from one to four columns of information with references. Many portraits are included and there is an index. Recommended to supplement historical collections and for schools where law and criminal justice are studied. [R: ARBA 97]

675 Black, Henry C. and others. **Black's Law Dictionary: Definitions of the Terms and Phrases of American and English Jurisprudence, Ancient and Modern, with Guide to Pronunciation**. 6th ed. St. Paul, Minn.: West Pub. Co., 1993. 1657p. $29.50. ISBN 0-314-76271-X.

First published in 1891, *Black's* is now in a 6th edition that reflects changes in tax, finance, commerce, health care, environmental and criminal law. Terms are listed alphabetically with cross-references, and entries give basic legal definitions, word usages, citations, and pronunciation. Entries range in length from one sentence to multiple-pages with subdivisions. Appendices include a copy of the Constitution, a time chart of Supreme Court membership, and an organizational chart of the federal government. This is not only a standard reference tool for law, but an important supplement to all high school social studies courses. Also available in a 1992 abridged edition.

676 Bosmajian, Haig, ed. **Academic Freedom**. New York: Neal-Schuman, 1989. 161p. $35.00. ISBN 1-55570-004-7.

677 Bosmajian, Haig, ed. **The Freedom of Expression**. New York: Neal-Schuman, 1988. 117p. $35.00. ISBN 1-55570-003-9.

678 Bosmajian, Haig, ed. **Freedom of Religion**. New York: Neal-Schuman, 1987. 163p. $35.00. ISBN 1-55570-002-0.

679 Bosmajian, Haig, ed. **The Freedom to Publish**. New York: Neal-Schuman, 1989. 230p. $35.00. ISBN 1-55570-005-5.

680 Bosmajian, Haig, ed. **The Freedom to Read**. New York: Neal-Schuman, 1987. 205p. $35.00. ISBN 1-55570-001-2.

These five books represent the 1st Amendment in the Classroom series, and provide introductory background and framework for each amendment. These are followed by 20 or more case histories, arranged chronologically, which demonstrate the interpretation of the amendments in court decisions from the past 30 years. Each volume lists the text of the applicable amendments and a diagram of the judicial circuits/court system. This set is for both professional collections and for high school government reference.

681 DiCanio, Margaret. **The Encyclopedia of Violence: Origins, Attitudes, Consequences**. New York: Facts on File, 1993. 404p. $45.00. ISBN 0-8160-2332-8.

The focus of the encyclopedia is the United States and Canada and the taxonomy, issues and organizations that relate to violence in North America. Entries are alphabetical with cross-references and vary in length from one paragraph to multiple pages; the article on anger, for example, is four pages. The assumptions upon which the encyclopedia is based are that violence is "male, political, and personal." Some omissions can be noted: there is an entry on Asian gangs in New York, but not anywhere else in the country; an article appears on wife abuse, but not spouse abuse. The information in the article on multiple personality as related to child abuse has since been questioned by new research. There are appendices about organized crime, limitations of studying violence, and a classified list of resources. A bibliography and index complete the volume. [R: ARBA 94]

682 Fay, John J. **The Police Dictionary and Encyclopedia**. Springfield, Ill.: Charles C. Thomas, 1988. 370p. $32.75. ISBN 0-398-05494-0.

Some 5,000 terms, phrases, and concepts from law enforcement, police slang, and street slang are clearly defined. Important Supreme Court cases that affect law enforcement are summarized. The appendixes include definitions of felony and capital offenses, sentences for various types of crimes, methods of execution, and other useful information. This work is designed for law enforcement professionals, but its subject matter and clear language make it useful for a broad audience.

683 Gifis, Steven H. **Law Dictionary**. 4th ed. Woodbury, N.Y.: Barron's Educational Series, 1996. 640p. $16.95. ISBN 0-8120-3096-6.

Intended for law students, this clear and concise dictionary contains entries in understandable language. Arranged alphabetically with cross-references, each entry gives a definition supported by a statement of significance in a legal context, and an indication of the area of law to which the term is useful. This is a good choice for a law dictionary for high school libraries.

684 **The Guide to American Law: Everyone's Legal Encyclopedia**. 12v. St. Paul, Minn.: West Pub. Co., 1985. $540.00/set; $139.95 for supplements. ISBN 0-314-73224-1. ISSN for annuals 0895-0989.

This comprehensive encyclopedia of American law is written in plain, non-technical language and provides information on a broad scope of legal information. It describes, explains, and provides insight and analysis of legal principles and concepts, historical movements and events and international law as it relates to Americans. It contains entries on landmark documents, legal organizations, federal regulatory departments and agencies, important legislation and accounts of famous trials. It also has biographies and even quotations. Boxed definitions, tables, charts and color plates add to clarity of the signed entries. The first 12 volumes of the encyclopedia were published in 1985; volumes 1–10 are arranged alphabetically with cross-references and each contains tables of cases cited, legislative acts and the table of contents of volume 11 which is an appendix of useful supplementary forms and document texts. Volume 12 contains the indexes, including an extensive subject index. A yearbook which updated and added articles was published in 1987; and there have been annual supplements since 1990. Gale Research plans a new second edition, in 12 volumes, renamed *West's Encyclopedia of American Law*. This is an expensive set which would stand alone as a legal reference, but is also useful for reports in all high school social studies classes.

685 Hill, Gerald N. and Kathleen Thompson Hill. **Real Life Dictionary of the Law: Taking the Mystery Out of Legal Language**. Los Angeles: General Publishing Group, 1995. 479p. $19.95. ISBN 1-881649-74-1.

An attorney and his wife have compiled a dictionary of law that is clear and concise and intended to make the terms understandable by anyone. Definitions are explained as well as defined with verbal illustrations from real-life situations. Approximately 3,000 terms are listed alphabetically with cross-references, and definitions range in length from one paragraph to two columns. Boxed quotes lend interest and clarity and pronunciation of foreign language terms is given. Appendices include a copy of the Constitution, a description of the court system, a list of major Supreme Court decisions, a directory of state bar associations, a chart showing which states have capital punishment, a brief section of legal trivia and the top 30 popular films with legal themes or settings. Designed to make the law seem less threatening to the lay person, this dictionary is recommended for all secondary school and professional collections. [R: ARBA 96]

686 Knappman, Edward W., ed. **Great American Trials**. Detroit, Mich.: Visible Ink Press, 1994. 872p. $44.95; $17.95pa. ISBN 0-8103-8875-8; 0-8103-9134-1pa.

Brief summaries of 200 important American trials from the 1600s to the early 1990s are the focus of this work. The trials were selected for inclusion if they had historical or legal significance, if they dealt with political controversy or showed legal ingenuity, if they captured public attention or created literary fame. Three tables of contents list the trials chronologically, alphabetically and by category. There are more trials for murder, manslaughter and homicide included than any other single category. There is minimal coverage of Supreme Court decisions as these are found in other sources. There is a good introduction to law, the court system, court procedures, rules of evidence and the appeals process. Trial summaries are then arranged chronologically. There are seven trials from the 1600s, eleven from the 1700s, and many from the 1800s. From 1900 on, the trials are listed by decade. Each trial has a fact box that tells the defendant's name, the crime charged, the defense and prosecuting attorneys, the judge, place, dates and verdict. There is also a sentence explaining the significance of the trial. Then the trial description and summary covers fewer than five pages. Entries are signed and have suggestions for further reading. An attempt has been made to turn legalese into plain English, and there is a glossary. A comprehensive index makes this a quick reference tool as well. Highly recommended for middle and high school collections to support history and government research. [R: ARBA 95]

687 Lieberman, Jethro K. **The Evolving Constitution: How the Supreme Court Has Ruled on Issues from Abortion to Zoning**. New York: Random House, 1992. 751p. $26.00. ISBN 0-679-40530-5.

This encyclopedia summarizes the relationship of the Supreme Court and the Constitution with introductory essays on the Constitution, its interpretation, and how the Court works. Then an alphabetically arranged listing by topic gives clear discussions of issues based on the Constitution and cases with references to a case list. Supplements include time charts, biographies of the justices and tables of cases. This is a detailed work that makes clear the ways that the Court works in the United States. Highly recommended for high school collections. [R: ARBA 94]

688 Walker, David M. **The Oxford Companion to Law**. Oxford: Clarendon Press, 1980. 1366p. $65.00. ISBN 1-9-866110-X.

A concise guide to legal ideas and concepts, doctrines and principles from a British perspective. American law is well-covered, and there is also information about other English speaking countries, Western Europe, and some coverage of non-Western law. This source is for both lawyers and laypeople and combines brief entries with definitions of multiple facets of terms. Articles about national legal systems are longer. Arrangement is alphabetical with cross-references. References are attached to articles and classified in an appendix.

HANDBOOKS

689 Durham, Jennifer L. **Crime in America: A Reference Handbook**. Santa Barbara, Calif.: ABC-CLIO, 1996. 318p. $39.50. ISBN 0-87436-841-3.

This work is an introduction to crime problems in the United States during the 20th century. It is broad in scope and covers white collar crime, organized crime and gangs, as well as general criminal activity. It follows the format of the other volumes in the Contemporary World Issues series with a long introductory survey, a chronology, a few biographies, a section of facts, statistics and documents with tables and graphs, a directory of related organizations and lists of both print and nonprint resources. This nonprint bibliography does include Web sites and computer data bases. A glossary and an index conclude the volume. This is useful in secondary schools where it will often be used as more than just an introduction. [R: ARBA 97]

690 Edmonds, Beverly C. and William R. Fernekes. **Children's Rights: A Reference Handbook**. Santa Barbara, Calif.: ABC-CLIO, 1996. 364p. $39.50. ISBN 0-87436-764-6.

This guide contains information about the current condition of children's status throughout the world. The introduction gives a comprehensive overview of children's rights and there are also sections on international declarations, guidelines and charters designed to protect children. United States policy recommendations and relevant Supreme Court decisions are also covered. A chronology, biographical section, statistics, a directory of organizations, a bibliography of print and nonprint materials including CD-ROMs, computer software and Web sites, a glossary and an index complete the volume. This is one of the better volumes in the Contemporary World Issues series and is recommended for high school collections. [R: ARBA 97]

691   Fishman, Stephen. **The Copyright Handbook: How to Protect and Use Written Works**. Berkeley, Calif.: Nolo Press, 1992. $24.95pa. ISBN 0-87337-241-7.

This guide to copyright includes both obtaining copyright protection and aspects of the copyright law. It is intended for writers, librarians, teachers, and their students. Its focus is on copyright protection for a written work and thus does not discuss music, art, photography, or software. The first part is an overview of the copyright law and how to go about copyrighting material. Part 2 discusses aspects of the law and has a good description of "fair use." The new edition adds a chapter on electronic publishing, as another form of writing. The work includes sample forms for registering copyright and there is an index. [R: ARBA 96]

692   Hall, Kermit and others, ed. **The Oxford Companion to the Supreme Court of the United States**. New York: Oxford University Press, 1992. 1032p. $45.00. ISBN 0-19-505835-6.

This handbook was designed to present the Court as an institution that has had to deal with both external pressure and internal conflict, and it reveals a wide base of information about the court including its processes, practices, procedures, and decisions. Other topics are conceptual, historical and social. Vocabulary terms and biographical references are also included. Entries are signed and some are referenced. Appendices include a list of nominations to the court and trivia and traditions. There is both a case index and a topical index. Highly recommended for high school collections. [R: ARBA 94]

693   Hempelman, Kathleen A. **Teen Legal Rights: A Guide for the '90s**. Westport, Conn.: Greenwood Press, 1994. 236p. $39.95. ISBN 0-313-28760-0.

Almost a decade has gone by since the last easily available source for teenagers about their rights and responsibilities. This volume updates information for the 90s and is intended for teens, their parents, teachers, and others who work with them. The book also covers laws that affect teens indirectly. Information is presented in a question-answer format with tables, photographs, further reading about each issue, a glossary, and an index. The 18 chapters include such titles as "Behind the Wheel," "At School," "If Your Parents Divorce," "Your Sexual Life," "Gay and Lesbian Teens," and "How to Find the Law." Circulating and reference copies should be in every secondary school collection as well as professional collections and on administrators' desks. [R: ARBA 96]

694   Kinnear, Karen L. **Gangs: A Reference Handbook**. Santa Barbara, Calif.: ABC-CLIO, 1996. 237p. $39.50. ISBN 0-87436-821-9.

This survey of the available literature and other resources is both a narrative that provides some background about the causes, treatment, and prevention of gang issues, and also serves as a tool leading to further research. An opening chapter discusses context of gangs, including why people join gangs, racial and ethnic gangs, and females and gangs. There is also an essay on the increased violence in gang activities. This is followed by sections typical of this series (Contemporary World Issues): a chronology, biography, facts section, print and nonprint resources. The latter is especially good as it includes videos, online and Internet sources. There is an index. [R: ARBA 97]

695   Kinnear, Karen L. **Violent Children: A Reference Handbook**. Santa Barbara, Calif.: ABC-CLIO, 1995. 251p. $39.50. ISBN 0-87436-786-7.

The focus of this survey of literature and ready reference guide is children who commit violent acts. As usual with this series (Contemporary World Issues) the topic mentions such violence in other countries, but is most concerned with a United States perspective. There is no real definition here of child, and the term is used interchangeably with juveniles and youth. Following the structure of other volumes in the series there are introductory essays on causes, treatment and prevention, followed by ready reference material. A bibliography and directory conclude the volume. [R: ARBA 96]

696 Kruschke, Earl R. **Gun Control: A Reference Handbook**. Santa Barbara, Calif.: ABC-CLIO, 1995. 408p. $39.50. ISBN 0-87436-695-X.

The author of this survey has a law degree and is a professor of political science with a long interest in the issues involved in gun control. This source is intended as an advanced introduction to the issues and resources involved, rather than as a comprehensive survey and focuses on scholarly issues rather than on any emotional debate. Essays about context and issues are followed by ready reference sections of dates, facts, biographies, and legislative and statistical data. This is a good choice for high school collections. [R: ARBA 97]

697 Simpson, Carol Mann. **Copyright for**
E+ **Schools: A Practical Guide**. 2d ed. Worthington, Ohio: Linworth Publishing, 1994. 116p. $29.95. ISBN 0-938865-57-9.

This edition of Simpson's excellent copyright book is filled with situations and questions with which librarians are often confronted. After introductory chapters of copyright background information, chapters discuss print, nonprint, software, and Internet resources specifically as well as a chapter on library functions that involve copyright issues such as interlibrary loan, document delivery and reserves. Eight useful appendices give sample policies, notices, release forms and so on. This practical guide should be in every library.

698 **The Supreme Court at Work**. Washington, D.C.: Congressional Quarterly, 1990. 351p. $25.95pa. ISBN 0-87187-540-3.

An abridged version of *Guide to the U.S. Supreme Court*, this includes information from 4 of the 8 sections: Origins and Development of the Court, The Court at Work, Members of the Court, and Major Decisions. There are documents and texts appended, including the Rules

of the Supreme Court, and an appendix lists nominations to the Court, a glossary of legal terms and a list of Acts of Congress held unconstitutional. Both subject and case indexes are included.

699 Witt, Elder. **Congressional Quarterly's Guide to the U.S. Supreme Court**. 3d ed. 2v. Washington, D.C.: Congressional Quarterly, 1996. $289.00. ISBN 1-56802-130-5.

First published in 1979, and updated in 1990, libraries which found the earlier editions useful will want the new two-volume edition. Information is presented in eight parts which cover all aspects of the history and work of the court. All members of the court and all major decisions are covered. Documents and texts are in an appendix and there are both subject and case indexes.

CRIME

700 Bailey, William G., ed. **The Encyclopedia of Police Science**. 2d ed. New York: Garland Pub., 1995. 865p. $95.00. ISBN 0-8153-1331-4.

Despite the tone of the introduction which contains a harangue on the Rodney King case, this 2d edition of the encyclopedia is useful for high schools. Coverage includes police administration, types of crimes, social issues, investigative procedures, and biographical and historical information. The new edition of more than 200 entries added an international perspective. Articles are long, from 2–6 pages each, and are signed with bibliographies. Tables add to the text. There are both a general index and an index of legal cases.

701 Hall, Rob. **Rape in America: A Reference Handbook**. Santa Barbara, Calif.: ABC-CLIO, 1995. 202p. $39.50. ISBN 0-87436-730-1.

This is a balanced overview of both the historical treatment and contemporary attitudes toward rape in a social context. It also presents the development of legal procedures in both law enforcement and the judicial system. As a volume in the Contemporary World Issues series, the work follows the standard organization of the series: An introduction is followed by a chronology, a few biographies, a fact and data section, an organization directory, and lists of both print and nonprint resources. Recommended for high school collections. [R: ARBA 96]

702 Kadish, Sanford H., ed. **Encyclopedia of Crime and Justice**. 4v. New York: Free Press, 1983. $105.00/per volume. ISBN separate for each volume.

Written for the educated lay person, this set deals with fundamental issues in American law. Backgrounds from English law are naturally included and there is some coverage of European and other national legal systems. Articles are grouped in broad topics and then treated from multiple perspectives: there is one long entry on drugs and crime which has sections on behavioral aspects, legal aspects, and treatment and rehabilitation. The broad topics are in alphabetical order with cross-references, and volume 4 has both a legal index and a general index, as well as a glossary. Longer articles (of as many as 10,000 words) are signed and have bibliographies. This source is not as comprehensive as *Guide to American Law,* but provides a less expensive alternative for high schools.

703 Ryan, Patrick J. **Organized Crime: A Reference Handbook**. Santa Barbara, Calif.: ABC-CLIO, 1995. 297p. $39.50. ISBN 0-87436-746-8.

The author is an associate professor of criminal justice and has produced a good ready reference tool to be used as a starting place for research. There is an introduction that provides context of the role of organized crime in this country, discussing the Mafia and the kinds of activities associated with organized crime. There is a historical section tracing the first gangs to modern groups, including new kinds of gangs. Another major section involves the issues in controlling organized crime. There is a chronology, a biography, a quick reference section, a directory, a glossary and a bibliography of both print and nonprint materials. Recommended for high school history and sociology collections. [R: ARBA 96]

HUMAN RIGHTS

704 **Amnesty International Report**. [Title varies]. London: Amnesty International Publications, 1976– . annual. $28.95; $18.95pa. ISSN 0309-068X.

This annual report assesses the status of human rights in countries around the world. Introductory chapters highlight issues and areas of concern. Arranged alphabetically by country with an overview and a narrative of 2–3 pages. Appendices include the Articles of Amnesty International and Human Rights Treaties. Useful for high school current events, world culture, government, and sociology classes.

705 Brownlie, Ian, comp. and ed. **Basic Documents on Human Rights**. 3d ed. Oxford: Oxford University Press, 1992. 631p. $39.95pa. ISBN 0-19-825712-0.

This handbook provides representative documentary sources of human rights. The collection is arranged in chapters of document origin, such as the United Nations, the International Labor Organization, and regions of the world.

Library Science

See also **Instructional Technology** in **Education, Collection Management, Children's Literature (Humanities)**.

BIBLIOGRAPHIES

706 Burroughs, Lea. **Introducing Chil-**
E+ **dren to the Arts: A Practical Guide**
for Children's Librarians and Educators. Boston: G. K. Hall, 1988. 306p. $38.50. ISBN 0-8161-8818-1.

This volume covers seven fields of the arts: architecture, art, dance, music, poetry, story and theater. For each there is a survey of its history, a description of its internal structure and suggested program ideas that offer children an opportunity to experience and understand the form. A filmography and a bibliography are provided for every field; the bibliography includes older works considered to be classic. This excellent guide is especially useful for classroom teachers and for librarians.

707　Rudin, Claire. **The School Librarian's Sourcebook**. New York: R. R. Bowker, 1990. 504p. $38.00. ISBN 0-8352-2711-1.

Although dated, this bibliography is still available, and provides a basic list of items useful for background in all areas of school librarianship: administration, collections, services, instruction, and technology. Sections are divided into more specific topics. Entries have long annotations which cover purpose, contents, potential use, and author's background. Other items are included at the end of the sections. There is a list of professional periodicals in the appendix, and there are author, title, and subject indexes.

DICTIONARIES, ENCYCLOPEDIAS, AND YEARBOOKS

708　**The Bowker Annual Library and Book Trade Almanac 1996**. [Annual title varies]. New York: R. R. Bowker, 1996– . annual. $169.95. ISSN 0068-0540.

This standard source is published annually and should be available to all librarians. Most useful are statistics on book prices in several categories, and other publishing information. Special feature articles are about current library and publishing issues and vary each year.

709　Prytherch, Ray, comp. **Harrod's Librarians' Glossary: 9,000 Terms Used in Information Management, Library Science, Publishing, the Book Trades, and Archive Management**. 8th ed. Brookfield, Vt.: Ashgate Pub. Co., 1995. 692p. $99.95. ISBN 0-566-07533-4.

This excellent dictionary, first published in 1938, includes 9,000 terms, 1,400 new in this edition. It defines and explains terms and concepts from the library and publishing professions and related fields. The new terms are

from archival, conservation and preservation, and records management areas. Also new are vocabulary terms from computer technology and networking. It is international in scope, and gives a good description of Z39 standards, and a list of specifics. The clear summaries, broad scope and alphabetical arrangement makes this work preferable to *Keenan's Concise Dictionary of Library and Information Science* (Bowker-Sauer, 1996). All librarians will want access to this glossary. [R: ARBA 97]

710　Soper, Mary Ellen, and others. **The Librarian's Thesaurus**. Chicago, Ill.: American Library Association, 1990. 164p. $25.00pa. ISBN 0-8389-0530-7.

The terms in this source cover librarianship in general and will be of use to school librarians. Areas covered are concepts, procedures and processes, and technology; these areas are divided into subsections. Explanations are thorough and cross-references help relate terms to one another. There is an excellent subject index.

CATALOGING

711　Byrne, Deborah J. **MARC Manual: Understanding and Using MARC Records**. Englewood, Colo.: Libraries Unlimited, 1991. 260p. $29.50pa. ISBN 0-87287-813-9.

Intended for anyone unfamiliar with MARC records, this is an excellent introduction to the background, structure, terminology and application of the data base. Librarians can use this for their own professional development, as well as a guide for training assistants and volunteers. In addition to the basic use of MARC, there is a chapter on the MARC authority format.

712　**C. A. Cutter's Three-Figure Author Table**. Swanson-Swift revision. distr., Englewood, Colo.: Libraries Unlimited, 1969. 29p. $17.00. ISBN 0-87287-209-2.

713　**C. A. Cutter's Two-Figure Author Table**. Swanson-Swift revision. distr., Englewood, Colo.: Libraries Unlimited, 1969. 4p. $11.00. ISBN 0-87287-208-4.

714 Cutter, Charles A. **Explanation of the Cutter-Sanborn Author-Marks (three-figure tables)**. 4th ed. Northampton, Mass.: Forbes Library, n.d. 8p.

715 **Cutter-Sanborn Three-Figure Author Table**. Swanson-Swift revision. distr., Englewood, Colo.: Libraries Unlimited, 1969. 34p. $18.00. ISBN 0-87287-210-6.

The two-figure table is used by small libraries; larger libraries use one of the three-figure forms. The Cutter-Sanborn table has a different number-figure pattern and is not compatible with the other two tables.

716 Chan, Lois Mai. **Immroth's Guide to the Library of Congress Classification**. 4th ed. Englewood, Colo.: Libraries Unlimited, 1990. 436p. $42.50; $32.50pa. ISBN 0-87287-604-7; 0-87287-763-9pa.

This is an easily understandable introduction to Library of Congress Classification. The 4th edition includes changes in schedules and policies as well as new schedules. The guide explains current practices in both classification and book numbering. There are many clear examples throughout the text as well as appendices with tables of general applications and schedules. A thorough index aids in use.

717 **Dewey for Windows**. New York: OCLC Forest Press, 1996. CD-ROM (Windows). $400.00/single workstation license; $500.00/multiple workstation license; 150.00/year annual replacement disc.

The 21st edition of the DDC is also available in a CD-ROM version. One of the real advantages of the electronic edition is the ability to view the index, schedules, tables, and manual on one screen. A variety of search indexes facilitates identification of the proper classification. There are suggested LC Subject Headings most often identified with an assigned number.

718 Dewey, Melvil. **Dewey Decimal Classification and Relative Index**. 21st rev. ed. 4v. John P. Comaromi, and others, eds. Albany, N.Y.: Forest Press, 1996. $325.00/set. ISBN 0-910608-50-4.

719 Dewey, Melvil. **Abridged Dewey Decimal Classification and Relative Index**. 13th ed. Joan S. Mitchell, and others, eds. Albany, N.Y.: Forest Press, 1997. 1023p. $88.00. ISBN 0-910608-59-8.

The twenty-first edition of the DDC continues major reclassifications begun in the twentieth edition and intends to continue through multiple editions. Changes not only reflect political and social change with added subjects and extended numbers, but also involve complete revisions in which the old schedules are completely replaced with new classifications. In this edition, one thus sees changes in the geographic table reflecting the breakup of the Soviet Union, expanded and revised coverage of Judaism and Islam, and total revision of 351–354 (public administration), of 370 (education) and of 560–590 (life sciences). Tables of relocations, reductions, and comparative and equivalence tables for major revisions are in volume 1. The manual and internal notes have been clarified and expanded and are extremely useful. All libraries using an earlier edition will need to have this new edition. Smaller libraries using the abridged edition in 1 volume will find the same changes reflected. This new edition returns to the concept of a true abridgement; i.e., numbers are shortened, not adapted.

720 Fountain, Joanna F. **Subject Headings for School and Public Libraries: an LCSH/Sears Companion**. 2d ed. Englewood, Colo.: Libraries Unlimited, 1996. 250p. $48.00. ISBN 1-56308-360-4.

This publication, originally based on actual headings used by a Texas school district and now extended to headings used by other libraries and bibliographic utilities, is intended to be useful for libraries switching from *Sears* Subject Headings to Library of Congress Subject Headings. This list uses standard thesaurus formats: BT, NT, RT, and so on. Headings indicate whether they are identical to *Sears*, identical to LC, identical in both, or a modified LC heading. The list includes names from the LC name authority file to make local authority work less burdensome. There is a list of free-floating subdivisions and instructions for their use. Explanations are clear and concise. This list could be used by any library trying to integrate different subject authority lists.

721 Intner, Sheila S., and Jean Weihs. **Standard Cataloging for School and Public Libraries**. 2d ed. Englewood, Colo.: Libraries Unlimited, 1996. 278p. $32.50. ISBN 1-56308-349-3.

Intended as a text for students in library science programs, this source is equally of use to practitioners who wish to update themselves of all the many recent changes in cataloging and classification. Coverage of AACR2R, *Sears* Subject Headings, Library of Congress Subject Headings, and Dewey and LC classification is followed by applications in bibliographic utilities and local systems. Appropriate examples are given throughout. Excellent discussions of cataloging policy, decision making, and management are included. One wishes for more than 8 pages on MARC formats, but the rest of the text is clear and reliable. A glossary and selected bibliography are helpful. There are indexes to topics, to names, and to the figures and examples.

722 **MARC Bibliographic Format Guide**.
E+ rev. ed. McHenry, Ill.: Follett, 1996. $59.95. ISBN 0-695-62022-3.

The design of this guide is a flip chart which enables it to be easily used by a cataloger working at a computer; it is also useful to anyone who is using MARC. There is a useful introduction which explains MARC elements, and then explanations of fields, subfields, and indicators with examples for each area of MARC. An appendix contains sample records for a variety of formats. This edition of the guide, which is updated periodically, contains format integration changes. Follett also publishes a companion authority format guide. Highly recommended for all collections.

723 Maxwell, Margaret F. **Handbook for AACR2, 1988 Revision: Explaining and Illustrating the Anglo-American Cataloging Rules**. Chicago, Ill.: American Library Association, 1989. 436p. $42.00pa. ISBN 0-8389-0505-6.

The handbook is designed to assist catalogers in the application of the most common rules for

descriptions, choices of access points, and forms of headings. It is especially useful for librarians doing original cataloging and undertaking automation projects. It will assist in the understanding of the rules governing MARC descriptions.

724 Miller, Joseph, ed. **Sears List of Subject Headings**. 16th ed. Bronx, N.Y.: H. W. Wilson, 1997. 786p. $54.00. ISBN 0-8242-0920-6.

The two most recent editions of *Sears*, used by many small and medium sized school and public libraries, have resulted in a major revision. Inverted headings are canceled and replaced with uninverted forms, new headings have been added to reflect both new knowledge and international political changes. While principles of cross-referencing remain the same, the terminology has been made to conform to NISO standards and uses BT, NT, RT, SA, and UF to be consistent with the thesauri format. A welcome new feature is the list of canceled or replaced headings. All libraries using *Sears* headings need this new edition.

725 Olson, Nancy B. **Cataloging Computer Files**. Lake Crystal, Minn.: Soldier Creek Press, 1992. 123p. $25.00pa. ISBN 0-936996-47-1.

First published in 1983 and revised in 1988, this third edition follows the major revisions of *AACR2R* (1988). The work discusses each area of descriptive cataloging as well as main and added entries, subject headings, classification, and MARC tagging. There are 40 examples, many are CD-ROM titles. Recommended for collections that produce, edit, or interpret computer file records for catalogs. [R: ARBA 94]

726 RTSD Filing Committee. **ALA Filing Rules**. Chicago, Ill.: American Library Association, 1980. 50p. $15.00pa. ISBN 0-8389-3255-X.

727 Seely, Pauline A. **ALA Rules for Filing Catalog Cards**. 2d abridged ed. Chicago, Ill.: American Library Association, 1968. 260p. $14.00pa. ISBN 0-8389-0001-1.

For libraries with card catalogs, this remains the standard guide for filing. The 1980 edition brought card filing in line with online filing; e.g., numbers are filed before alphabetical headings. For those libraries whose card catalogs retain the traditional filing, the ALA rules for filing catalog cards, 2d edition, abridged (1968) is the standard filing guide.

728 Subject Cataloging Division, Processing Department. **Library of Congress Subject Headings**. Washington, D.C.: Library of Congress, 1992– . annual. $150.00. ISSN 1048-9711.

This is an annual publication updating the subject authority records that have evolved from the first headings used in 1898. Since some 6,000–8,000 new headings are added each year, there are several additional formats to keep current. Weekly updates are available via computer tape and the Internet. [gopher://marvel.loc.gov] Quarterly microfiche editions of the *LCSH* are available as are quarterly CD-ROM editions, *CDMARC SUBJECTS*. Updates are also in the *Cataloging Service Bulletin*.

729 Winkler, Lois, ed. **Subject Headings for Children**. 2d ed. 2v. Albany, N.Y.: Forest Press, 1997. $80.00pa. ISBN 0-9106808-58-X.

The source for Library of Congress juvenile subject headings. Since 1965 the Library of Congress has used regular subject headings for children's materials but has also assigned some unique headings and used different applications of regular headings. This list brings these subject headings together with the LC name authority file of persons who are subjects of children's biographies. Each heading provides a likely Dewey number since most children's libraries use the DDC. Volume 1 is a list of headings and classification numbers; Volume 2 is a key word index intended for use by both librarians and patrons. There are no standard thesaurus terms used.

730 Wynar, Bohdan S. and Arlene G. Taylor. **Introduction to Cataloging and Classification**. 8th ed. Englewood, Colo.: Libraries Unlimited, 1992. 633p. $47.50; $37.50pa. ISBN 0-87287-811-2; 0-87287-967-4pa.

The eighth edition of this standard introductory textbook for cataloging and classification has changes in almost all areas of bibliographic control. *AACR2R* has been implemented; new

editions and supplements of *LCSH*, LC classification, DDC, and *Sears* are now in use. Networking and online catalogs are part of a librarian's way of life. Many chapters are entirely new or have been fully revised to show the continuity in development of cataloging rules. This edition has resulted in a state-of-the-art professional text. Cataloging professionals will certainly appreciate this latest edition.

731 Zuiderveid, Sharon, ed. **Cataloging Correctly for Kids: An Introduction to the Tools**. rev. ed. Chicago: American Library Association, 1991. 78p. $16.00pa. ISBN 0-8389-3395-5.

This guide is a collected series of related articles intended to help those who catalog children's collections understand the current cataloging tools used in this country. The first article discusses the guidelines for standardized cataloging of children's materials. Other articles discuss the Annotated Card program at the Library of Congress, *AACR2R*, Dewey, *Sears*, Filing Rules, and MARC. Cataloging vendors, special problems of cataloging nonbook materials, automation and MicroLIF are also discussed. While this is not, despite its title, a how-to-catalog manual, the articles explain why contemporary cataloging for children is the way it is. This booklet is useful because it contains important information about a variety of cataloging issues in one convenient source.

CENSORSHIP

732 Foerstel, Herbert N. **Banned in the U.S.A.: A Reference Guide to Book Censorship in Schools and Public Libraries**. Westport, Conn.: Greenwood Press, 1994. 231p. $45.00. ISBN 0-313-28517-9.

The tension between attempts to suppress or restrict written speech and the protection of the First Amendment has seldom been so worrisome as in the last part of this century. Following an excellent overview introduction Foerstel describes eight major book challenges, beginning with Kanawha County in 1973. A second chapter covers the legal issues and cases and the disturbing nature of *Hazelwood*. The views of five of the most-censored American children's and young adult authors are expressed in another section. A final section lists and discusses the cases surrounding the 50 most-often banned books in schools and libraries in the United States in the 1990s. Some of the "most challenged" lists produced by the People for the American Way are in appendices and there is an excellent bibliography on intellectual freedom issues. Highly recommended for all library collections.

733 **Hit List: Frequently Challenged**
E   **Books for Children**. Chicago: American Library Association, 1996. 61p. $22.00. ISBN 0-8389-3458-7.

734 **Hit List: Frequently Challenged Books for Young Adults**. Chicago: American Library Association, 1996. 92p. $22.00. ISBN 0-8389-3459-5.

The books identified in these two publications are among those most often targeted in censorship attempts. The children's *Hit List* includes 23 titles, while the YA list includes 26, 10 of which were also in the first (1989) edition. Entries are alphabetical by author in the children's guide and alphabetical by title in the YA guide, otherwise the entry formats are identical. A summary of the book is followed by a list of challenges, review sources, lists of background articles, awards won by the title, and bibliographies which include the title in recommended lists. Both books contain appendices which explain how A.L.A. can help librarians in censorship cases. These are useful titles for librarians and for students to use in intellectual freedom units.

735 Hoffmann, Frank W. **Intellectual Freedom and Censorship: An Annotated Bibliography**. Lanham, Md.: Scarecrow Press, 1989. 244p. $27.50. ISBN 0-8108-2145-1.

This annotated bibliography, which includes books, articles, and legal material, is divided into five parts: theoretical foundations of intellectual freedom and censorship, key court cases, professional concerns, procensorship/anticensorship stances of individuals and groups, and cases in the mass media. Critical annotations and a subject index conclude the volume. The average high school collection is likely to contain many of the items cited here. [R: ARBA 90; BL, Aug 89]

736 Office for Intellectual Freedom and Intellectual Freedom Committee,

comp. **Intellectual Freedom Manual**. 5th ed. Chicago: American Library Association, 1996. 393p. $35.00pa. ISBN 0-8389-0677-X.

Including both background information and practical advice for dealing with censorship issues, the manual covers all types of libraries, all formats of information sources, and all kinds of users. The first part reprints the Library Bill of Rights and the various statements of its interpretation in relation to such issues as the rights of minors and electronic information sources. The second part deals with the freedom to read, and the third with preparedness, including writing a selection policy. The fourth part contains separate statements about intellectual freedom in various types of libraries, while part five discusses court cases. The final section identifies ways in which the American Library Association and state organizations can assist librarians facing censorship attacks as well as discussing lobbying efforts. There is a selected bibliography and an index. The manual is a useful source for government classes and librarians' units on intellectual freedom. In addition, it should be in the professional collection and on every librarian's desk in elementary, middle, and senior high schools.

737 Reichman, Henry. **Censorship and Selection: Issues and Answers for Schools**. rev. ed. Chicago: American Library Association, 1993. 172p. $18.00pa. ISBN 0-8389-0620-6.

This joint publication of the American Library Association and the American Association of School Administrators provides all educators with information about selection policy development, suggested procedures to follow in challenges, and guidance in combatting censorship attempts.

738 West, Mark I. **Trust Your Children: Voices Against Censorship in Children's Literature**. New York: Neal-Schuman, 1988. 176p. $24.95pa. ISBN 1-55570-021-7.

Eighteen author interviews discuss the reasons why would-be censors have objected to certain books for children and adolescents. The authors explain how they felt when their books were targeted, and some relate instances in which they were forced to make changes in their writings in order to appease editors. This practical volume contains information useful for high school reports and research papers on censorship. [R: BR, Sept/Oct 89; LJ, 1 Nov 88; WLB, Mar 89]

COLLECTION DEVELOPMENT POLICIES AND PROCEDURES

739 Anderson, Joanne S., ed. **Guide for**
E+ **Written Collection Policy State-ments**. 2d ed. Chicago: American Library Association, 1996. 40p. $15.00pa. ISBN 0-8389-3455-2.

The trend toward having an overall collection policy (part of which is a selection policy) began in academic libraries, but this edition of the written policy guide includes generic advice, collection levels, and language codes applicable to or adaptable by any library regardless of size or type. There is an introductory guide and a list of all the elements that should be included in such a policy statement. The appendices include sample worksheets for preparing data for a policy statement. There is also a glossary.

740 Doll, Carol A., and Pamela Petrick
E+ Barron. **Collection Analysis in the School Library Media Center: A Practical Approach**. Chicago: American Library Association, 1990. 73p. $15.00pa. ISBN 0-8389-3390-4.

This small guide offers forms and step-by-step directions for various methods of evaluating collections. Quantitative data collecting includes methods based on circulation and copyright date information; qualitative methods are based on checking against standard bibliographic tools. Sampling techniques are also suggested. Other important topics discussed are weeding and ways to estimate updating costs. This is an extremely useful source, particularly when supplemented with local curricular need measurements suggested by other authors.

741 Latrobe, Kathy Howard and Mildred Knight Laughlin, comps. **Multicultural Aspects of Library Media Programs**. Englewood, Colo.: Libraries Unlimited, 1992. 217p. $27.50. ISBN 0-87287-879-1.

This is a compilation of background information, bibliographic references and curricular activities designed to increase awareness among librarians about various minority cultures. The author of each section is a member of the culture or has experience in working with people from the culture. Formats of each section are not identical because the individual authors were encouraged to develop their sections independently and appropriately for the specific culture. The final part of the work addresses issues in collection development. There is a glossary and an index. Most librarians will want access to this work. [R: ARBA 93]

742 Lenz, Millicent and Mary Meacham. **Young Adult Literature and Nonprint Materials: Resources for Selection**. Lanham, Md.: Scarecrow Press, 1994. 336p. $37.50. ISBN 0-8108-2906-1.

This is a comprehensive bibliography of materials to use in collection building for young adults, defined in this work as ages 10 to 18. The scope of items reflect those that deal with curriculum materials, recreational reading, listening, and viewing, and personal interest materials. The selection tools date from around 1988 to 1993, in addition to continuing serial sources.

Sources are arranged in categories such as comprehensive sources, periodicals, resources for research, and specific genres and subjects. A separate section covers selection tools for A-V materials. For each entry there are lengthy descriptive annotations. There are separate indexes for titles, authors, and subjects, and there is a directory of publishers. Professional collections and large secondary libraries will find this source useful. [R: ARBA 95]

743 Sitter, Clara L. **The Vertical File and Its Alternatives: A Handbook**. Englewood, Colo.: Libraries Unlimited, 1992. 256p. $32.50. ISBN 0-87287-910-0.

The vertical file remains a legitimate source of information in school libraries, especially when subjects are integrated into the catalog, and despite the increasing use of Internet resources. This handbook gives suggestions for all aspects of handling the peculiar nature of vertical file materials, including selection, organization, processing, circulating, and weeding. This is the tool to guide librarians, aides, and volunteers in maintaining this part of the collection.

744   Slote, Stanley J. **Weeding Library Collections: Library Weeding Methods**. 4th ed. Englewood, Colo.: Libraries Unlimited, 1997. 284p. $42.00. ISBN 0-87287-633-0.

Slote's work, a classic that focuses on an essential, if unpopular, professional activity, is recommended for all types of libraries. He discusses traditional approaches to weeding as well as newer concepts, such as computer applications to the task. Examples of the approach used by over 40 libraries of all kinds are especially useful. He also provides a complete analysis of the literature. Highly recommended. [R: BL, 1 Apr 90; LJ, 1 May 90; SLJ, Apr 90]

745   Van Orden, Phyllis J. **The Collection**
E+   **Program in Schools: Concepts, Practices, and Information Sources**. 2d ed. Englewood, Colo.: Libraries Unlimited, 1995. 376p. $42.50; $32.50pa. ISBN 1-56308-120-2; 1-56308-334-5pa.

This is a comprehensive text about all aspects of collection management in school libraries and has practical information as well as background and theory. The 2d edition contains a new emphasis on intellectual freedom, issues of protecting intellectual property, the effect of multicultural studies on collections, and preservation of materials. Most importantly there is an expansion of collection development to include sources outside the library, whether accessed because of resource sharing or through telecommunications technology. This has now become a standard source for all school library programs.

AUTOMATION AND NETWORKING

746   Cibbarelli, Pamela R., comp. and ed. **Directory of Library Automation Software, Systems, and Services**. Medford, N.J.: Information Today, 1996. 457p. $79.00. ISBN 0-938734-65-2.

Cibbarelli, who's consulting business has been involved with library automation since 1983, has compiled an essential survey of library automation software, systems and services. Criteria for inclusion are that the items be targeted to the library marketplace, have installations in North America, and be commercially available. Automation

software is the principle focus of the work and is listed alphabetically by product name. Directory information, including e-mail address, is given followed by completed data categories such as hardware and systems requirements, components, features, Z39.50 compatability, MARC and barcode formats, price and supplier's comments. Enough information is given that buyers can make preliminary comparisons. Several smaller, but useful sections include directories of retrovenders and products, consultants, database hosts and CD-ROM database distributors. There is a list of discontinued products and name changes, a selected bibliography, Internet resources, and an index. All schools and school systems implementing or updating automation systems need this work. [R: ARBA 94]

747   Pappas, Marjorie L., and others.
E+   **Searching Electronic Resources**. Worthington, Ohio: Linworth Publishing, 1996. 117p. $24.95. ISBN 0-938865-52-8.

The introduction to this work places electronic searching skills within a general framework of information finding and processing. Other chapters use specific catalog, encyclopedia, periodical index, and instructional resources to describe the information seeking strategies involved. Search strategy forms showing the kinds of searching permitted by each resource and the procedures to follow in beginning searching are presented so they can be displayed by workstations and used by students. This source is both an analysis and learning tool for librarians and a guide for students. A second edition is in process. Recommended for all levels.

MANAGEMENT

748   **Information Power: Building Partnerships for Learning**. Chicago: American Library Association, 1998. 205p. $31.50. ISBN 0-8389-3470-6.

This joint publication of the Association of School Librarians and the Association for Educational Communication and Technology is the newest approach in the series of national standards and guidelines that began with the 1920 "Certain" report. The document provides a foundation for professional practice built on information literacy standards. Subsequent chapters deal with techniques and practices that support program development which enhances learning and teaching. Appendices include policy statements and a discussion of student performance assessment. While the document is intended to focus on student learning as the major goal of 21st century school library programs, it also acts as an informative guide for contemporary practices in school libraries. This should be in every library and in every administrator's office.

749 Loertscher, David V. **Taxonomies of the School Library Media Program**. Englewood, Colo.: Libraries Unlimited, 1988. 336p. $26.50pa. ISBN 0-82787-662-4.

The author suggests models for building exemplary library media programs. The three basic components, according to Loertscher, are warehousing (the facility, equipment, materials), direct services to students and teachers, and resource-based teaching (use of multiple resources in a variety of formats to achieve curricular objectives). Vertical program features are added according to interests, talents, and school needs, and may include such things as library skills, reading motivation, and cultural literacy.

Two specific models are analyzed: "Services of School Resource Centers" by Haycock, and *Helping Teachers Teach* by Turner. The work concludes with a chapter on evaluation of programs and services. The appendixes critique and reproduce several evaluative instruments, including the Purdue Self-Evaluation System (PSES). A bibliography concludes the volume. Recommended. [R: BL, July 88; SLJ, Oct 88; VOYA, Oct 88]

750 Morris, Betty J., with John T.
E+   Gillespie and Diana L. Spirt. **Administering the School Library Media Center**. 3d ed. New Providence, N.J.: Bowker, 1992. 567p. $45.00. ISBN 0-8352-3092-9.

This worthwhile work begins with a brief history of media centers; the authors then address program development, instructional objectives for media skills, and administrative responsibilities. The revised edition covers AASL's *Information Power* and updates all sections.

751 **School Library Management Note-**
E+   **book**. 3d ed. Worthington, Ohio: Linworth Publishing, 1994. ringbound. $36.95. ISBN 0938865-29-3.

This work is a combination bibliography and procedure manual. It discusses the major management functions of school libraries: planning, organization, collection management, circulation, personnel, budgeting and technology. Each section contains relevant articles from *Book Report* and *Library Talk* and sample forms. The format encourages individual librarians to insert specific routines and forms from their own centers, thus completing a personal procedure manual. An extensive operational bibliography is appended. Recommended as a structural tool for all levels.

752 Velleman, Ruth **A. Meeting the Needs of People With Disabilities: A Guide for Librarians, Educators, and Other Service Professionals**. Phoenix, Ariz.: Oryz Press, 1990. 288p. $37.95. ISBN 0-89774-521-3.

This revision of the author's *Serving Physically Disabled People* (1979) will help those seeking information and services for people with handicaps. The text covers civil rights of disabled persons, new technologies, rehabilitation, barrier-free environments (which include libraries), and more. Each chapter ends with a suggested reading list, and there is an extensive bibliography of books and periodicals. A directory of agencies and services conclude the volume. [R: LJ, 15 June 90]

INFORMATION SKILLS

753 Borne, Barbara Wood. **100 Research Topic Guides for Students**. Westport, Conn.: Greenwood Press, 1996. 234p. $39.95. ISBN 0-313-29552-2.

Borne uses the pathfinder approach to suggest resources in various formats for typical high school research topics. The pathfinders are intended to assist public and school librarians in working with students, but are also useful for students working independently. The 100 topics are divided in broad subject areas; there are 17 topics such as acid rain, quarks, and UFOs listed in the section on science and technology. Sixteen topics such as the Holocaust and the Underground Railroad are included under social studies, and there are biographical entries for V. C. Andrews, Bill Gates, John Lennon and 18 others. Almost half the pathfinders (46) are for social issues that will be familiar to all librarians such as child abuse, gun control, and prison reform. Each pathfinder includes a background scope statement, Dewey numbers for browsing, reference sources in books or on CD-ROM (with a heavy dependence on the *CQ Researcher*). Some topics include videos and fiction books. The least useful sections are periodical indexes which are the same for all topics and online services which only name the same services (America Online, the now merged CompuServe, Prodigy, Knight-Ridder Information, and Internet) on each pathfinder. It is understandable that online sources may be more complex and ephemeral than book sources, but simply listing them is about as helpful as recommending "reference books." The pathfinders conclude with national organization addresses and suggestions for narrowing the topic and of related topics. Appendices include directions for note taking and searching databases and a discussion of bibliographic citations and plagiarism. There is also a template for pathfinders, including as do all the 100, the note at the end to ask a librarian for help. A bibliography and index complete the work. Despite its limitations, most middle and high schools will want this in their collections. [R: ARBA 97]

754   Martin, Fenton S. and Robert U. Goehlert. **How to Research the Congress**. Washington, D.C.: Congressional Quarterly, 1996. 107p. $29.95; $19.95pa. ISBN 0-87187-870-4; 0-87187-869-0pa.

755   Martin, Fenton S. and Robert U. Goehlert. **How to Research the Presidency**. Washington, D.C.: Congressional Quarterly, 1996. 134p. $29.95; $19.95pa. ISBN 1-56802-029-5; 1-56802-028-7pa.

These two research guides follow the same format to explain in a clear and logical progression the best ways to find information about the two branches of government. Beginning with introductions that discuss types of resources and research strategy, they go on to list selected sources and describe them briefly. Beginning with secondary sources, there are sections listing specific subject resources such as almanacs or factbooks, atlases, biographical dictionaries, dictionaries, handbooks, encyclopedias, bibliographies, indexes, CD-ROMs, databases, journals, newspapers and statistical sources. Primary sources follow a similar pattern, with the Congressional volume listing items related to finding and interpreting laws and statutes while the Presidential volume has a section for each president. Each has relevant appendices, a selected bibliography of major books, a glossary, and author and title indexes. These guides are useful for topic selection as well as for source location. Recommended for high school collections. [R: ARBA 97]

756   Smallwood, Carol. **Library Puzzles and Word Games for Grades 7–12**. Jefferson, N.C.: McFarland, 1990. 220p. $24.95pa. ISBN 0-89950-536-8.

The puzzles and games in this work are designed to introduce middle and high school students to reference tools "in a way that is memorable and fun." The problems presented require students to consult standard reference sources, such as dictionaries, encyclopedias, and almanacs, and to explore maps and the library catalog.

The four sections—crossword puzzles, word searches, multiple choice, and matchups—each contain 20 activities arranged in order of difficulty. The puzzles cover world history, geography, foreign languages, and other curricular areas. Answers are provided at the end of the book. Careful editing to correct typographical errors would have improved this work, which is appropriate for grades 7 and up.

757   Whiteley, Sandy, ed. **The American Library Association Guide to Information Access: A Complete Research Handbook and Directory**. New York: Random House, 1994. 533p. $35.00; $19.00pa. ISBN 0-679-43060-1; 0-679-75075-4pa.

This handbook is intended for high school and college students, and independent researchers. It consists of more than 3,000 reference sources, both book and electronic, as well as suggestions for identifying and approaching them. The first part of the handbook has advice essays for each of the three audiences and a chapter on style manuals. Some students will find the tone of the essays patronizing. Parts two and three discuss electronic reference sources in general and five types of locations where information can be found: libraries, archives, newspapers, government agencies, and depository collections. The final part of the work lists 36 often-researched broad subjects such as education and gardening and discusses for each the relevant general sources, and such subject specific resources as periodical indexes, electronic sources, periodicals, government publications, government agencies, libraries, associations, LC subject headings and any special approaches related to the topics. There is an index. The source is recommended both for independent use by high school students and as a tool for teachers and librarians to use in instruction. [R: ARBA 95]

PLANNING FACILITIES

758 Fraley, Ruth A., and Carol L. Anderson. **Library Space Planning: A How-To-Do-It Manual for Assessing, Allocating and Reorganizing Collections, Resources and Facilities**. 2d ed. New York: Neal-Schuman, 1990. 194p. $39.95pa. ISBN 1-55570-040-3.

Designed for managers in all types of libraries this update of a 1985 publication offers practical suggestions for the use of library space. Step-by-step instructions are given for planning, measuring the collection, assessing facilities, budgeting, and maintaining the library during the moving process. Special features include diagrams and charts, floor plans, sample bid specifications, and other helpful information. A bibliography and index conclude the volume. [R: LJ, 15 Apr 90]

759 Hart, Thomas L. **Creative Ideas for Library Media Center Facilities**. Englewood, Colo.: Libraries Unlimited, 1990. 75p. $18.50. ISBN 0-87287-736-1.

This small work describes 27 media center projects designed to help create an imaginative learning environment. Some ideas deal with the physical facility, such as theme-based decorations, while others suggest programs and activities. Colorful illustrations support the descriptions. A bibliography on the psychological impact on learning of light, color, and other environmental features complete the volume. [R: SLMQ, Spr 91]

Military Science

760 Chant, Christopher. **The Military**
E+   **History of the United States**. 16v. New York: Marshall Cavendish, 1992. $449.95/set. ISBN 1-85435-361-9.

This set surveys the wars in which the United States has been involved from the Revolution to the Gulf War. Because the volumes are roughly chronological, it is also possible to use the set to study the evolution of the military and its influence. Most wars are covered in one volume, with information about the Civil War, World War II, and the Vietnam War each encompassing two volumes. Minor wars are treated together in several volumes. Each war is discussed in terms of its causes, the battles and campaigns, and related events. The illustrations of weapons and uniforms are outstanding; 1,500 illustrations, many in color, and many contemporary with the events

described, are incorporated throughout the volumes. Boxed summaries, quotations, and diary and journal articles extend the narratives. Each volume has a table of contents, separate index, glossary, and annotated bibliography. Volume 16 is a set index and contains a glossary and bibliography. This set is recommended for collections in upper elementary, middle and high schools. [R: ARBA 93]

761 Diagram Group. **Weapons, an**
E+   **International Encyclopedia from 5000 B.C. to 2000 A.D.** New York: St. Martin's Press, 1991. 336p. $29.95; $18.95pa. ISBN 0-312-03951-4; 0-312-03950-6pa.

Weapons in this source are limited to those used specifically for combat, rather than for hunting or sport shooting. This is a representative collection of all types from all ages and all cultures arranged by function (e.g., hand weapons) and from simple to complex. There are tables which show development and many illustrations to show comparisons. Three regional and 13 historical indexes, a list of related names and a general index make this both a reference and browsing source. The 1990 edition includes new chapters about weapons developed during the 1980s and projected for the 1990s. Recommended for all levels.

762   Dupuy, R. Ernest and Trevor N. Dupuy. **The Harper Encyclopedia of Military History from 3500 B.C. to the Present**. 4th ed. New York: Harper & Row, 1993. 1654p. $65.00. ISBN 0-06-270056-1.

War and military affairs from the beginnings of recorded history are covered chronologically and geographically in this comprehensive guide. It is intended as both a survey and as a ready reference tool for scholars and students. It has an exhaustive general index. Recommended for secondary libraries.

763   Flintham, Victor. **Air Wars and Aircraft: A Detailed Record of Air Combat, 1945 to the Present**. New York: Facts on File, 1990. 415p. $40.00. ISBN 0-8160-2356-5.

This work recounts modern aviation history around the world and documents every operational use of aircraft in warfare from 1945 to the present, including civil wars, international police actions, and the abortive attempt to rescue American hostages in Iran in 1980. Arranged geographically and subdivided chronologically, the volume discusses all significant conflicts in which aircraft were involved. A table of units, listing numbers and types of aircraft that participated, bases from which they operated, roles they played (e.g., liaison, night fighter) and dates, supports the entry for each conflict. Over 200 black-and-white photographs and 100 maps illustrate the book.

Appendixes contain military aircraft designations (e.g., British, American, Soviet), a glossary, and a bibliography. A comprehensive index concludes the work. [R:ARBA 91; LJ, Jan 90; RBB, 1 May 90]

764   Sherrow, Victoria. **Women and the Military: An Encyclopedia**. Santa Barbara, Calif.: ABC-CLIO, 1996. 381p. $60.00. ISBN 0-87436-812-X.

There are 400 entries in this encyclopedia which covers the roles women have assumed in American military history from Deborah Samson fighting as a man in the American Revolution to spies, nurses, support services in the military to equality with men in the contemporary branches of the armed forces. Scandals, successes, and criticisms of women in the military are all included. Articles are alphabetical with see also entries and references. There is an extensive bibliography as well as an index. There is an occasional contradiction e.g., women from both the Revolution and the Civil War are given credit for receiving the first official military pension, but the book fills a need for information missing from typical collections. This is a good supplement for American history as well as women's studies. Recommended for high schools. [R: ARBA 97]

765   Taylor, Michael. **Encyclopedia of the World's Air Forces**. New York: Facts on File, 1989. 224p. $35.00. ISBN 0-8160-2004-3.

From Comoros's single Cessna 402 to the flying power of the United States, the greatest in history, this comprehensive work covers the military air power of 147 nations. Entries, arranged alphabetically by country, vary from one-third of a page to six pages and include the following information: population, number of air force personnel, official air force name in the local language, location of headquarters, number of major air bases, number of airplanes (fixed-wing combat, fixed-wing noncombat, combat helicopters, and noncombat helicopters), aircraft by model, a narrative description, and one or more photographs of aircraft (most in color). Indexed. [R: BL, Apr 89; BR, Sept/Oct 89; LJ, Apr 89]

766   Tomajczyk, Stephen F. **Dictionary of the Modern United States Military: Over 15,000 Weapons, Agencies, Acronyms, Slang, Installations, Medical Terms, and Other Lexical Units of Warfare**. Jefferson, N.C.: McFarland, 1996. 785p. $125.00. ISBN 0-7864-0127-3.

This is a broad look at contemporary military language. Coverage of such topics as weapons systems, equipment, strategies, and military installations is complemented with information about psychological and social issues such as drugs, stresses on families, domestic violence, sexual harassment, and rape. Related government and private agencies and organizations are also included and there are biographical entries as well. Some slang terms are vulgar, and discussions of sexual issues are frank. Arrangement is alphabetical, and there are cross-references. Most entries are brief, some are as long as a column. There are three appendices dealing with chemical agents, military designations, and military ranks. There is an extensive bibliography and a topical index. Recommended for high schools both for its use in career collections and for general reference. [R: ARBA 97]

767 U.S. Department of Defense, comp. **America's Top Military Careers: The Official Guide to Occupations in the Armed Forces**. Indianapolis, Ind.: JIST Works, 1993. 473p. $19.95pa. ISBN 1-56370-124-3.

This is a reprint of the Department of Defense's military career guide. It contains complete description of almost 200 careers for both enlisted personnel and officers. For each career described, information is given on training and education, working conditions, physical demands, projected openings, advancement opportunities, civilian counterpart careers, duty locations, and pay and benefits. The first section lists occupations by categories such as human services or media and public affairs. Section 2 describes typical career paths. There are section introductions about each service branch. There is an appendix on career mapping, a glossary and indexes by DOT number, occupation, and title. This is a first purchase for high school guidance reference collections. [R: ARBA 94]

768 Windrow, Martin and Francis K. Mason. **A Concise Dictionary of Military Biography: The Careers and Campaigns of 200 of the Most Important Military Leaders**. New York: Wiley, 1991. 337p. $24.95; $15.95pa. ISBN 0-471-53441-2; 0-471-55181-3pa.

Previously published by Osprey Publishing (1975) with the subtitle: "Two hundred of the most significant names in land warfare, 10–20th century", this dictionary lists 200 leaders from all cultures, whether successful or not. Strategists and theorists are included as well as field commanders. This is a useful supplement for history units. [R: ARBA 93]

769 Wintle, Justin, comp. **Dictionary of War Quotations**. New York: Free Press, 1989. 506p. $35.00. ISBN 0-02-935411-0.

This well-designed, well-organized volume contains quotations on war from ancient to modern times. The 4,000 quotations are divided into three sections: general quotations on the nature of warfare; those about specific battles and wars, arranged chronologically; and those about military commanders, arranged alphabetically by name. Entries range from brief statements to paragraphs to entire poems. Indexed by subject and author. This attractive work is recommended for high schools. [R: ARBA 91; LJ, 1 Mar 90]

The Occult and Unexplained Phenomena

770 Angelo, Joseph A., Jr. **The Extraterrestrial Encyclopedia: Our Search for Life in Outer Space**. rev. ed. New York: Facts on File, 1991. 240p. $40.00. ISBN 0-8160-2276-3.

Written by a space scientist, this work focuses on the search for extraterrestrial life and reviews space exploration and scientific approaches. Some will be disappointed there is not even a mention of Rosewell, but there is a thoughtful article on UFOs. Emphasis is on astronomy, astrophysics, and the space program. Entries are alphabetical with cross-references and vary in length from a sentence to several columns. This updates the 1985 edition. Recommended for high school collections. [R: ARBA 93]

771   Clark, Jerome. **The UFO Encyclopedia**. 3v. Detroit, Mich.: Apogee Books, 1990–1996. $228.00/set. ISBN 0-614-12897-8.

This serious and comprehensive exploration of UFOs began as a supplement to *Sach's UFO Encyclopedia* (1980) and *Strong's Encyclopedia of UFOs* (1980). The first volume has 84 entries on UFOs in the 1980s, including seven major topics such as abduction phenomena, crashes of UFOs, and government cover-ups of UFO data. The other two volumes, which are illustrated, cover earlier periods from earliest reports to 1959 in 113 entries (including one on hoaxes) in Volume II and from 1960–1980 in Volume III. Each volume is alphabetical and has a separate index.

772   **Encyclopedia of Occultism & Parapsychology**. 4th ed. 2v. Detroit, Mich.: Gale Research, 1996. $299.00/set. ISBN 0-8103-5487-X.

First published in 1978 as an integrated merger of two early twentieth century standard sources, each edition of the encyclopedia has added updates, revisions, and new information. Coverage includes the occult sciences, magic, demonology, superstitions, spiritualism, mysticism, metaphysics, physical science, and people. Arranged alphabetically, articles vary in length from a paragraph to several pages; some articles have recommended readings. There is a general index and eight categorical indexes with about 60 topics.

773   Guiley, Rosemary. **Atlas of the Mysterious in North America**. New York: Facts on File, 1995. 178p. $35.00. ISBN 0-8160-2876-1.

This source is a survey of places associated with mysterious occurrences in the United States and Canada. It is selective so as to be geographically balanced, and includes sites of mythology, legend, folklore and sacred sites of pre-Columbian peoples. There are eight chapters in three sections:

"places as power" which include earthworks, mounds, stoneworks; "the supernatural," including haunted places, ghost lights and phantom ships; and "beings" including water monsters and mysterious creatures. Each section contains a map with numbers keyed to the sites which are arranged alphabetically by state and province. Each chapter has a narrative explanation before the state listings. Entries are very brief with identification and description; many photographs add to the descriptions. There is a list of organizations and publications dealing with the mysterious and both bibliography and classified suggested reading list. A general index completes the volume. [R: ARBA 95]

774   Guiley, Rosemary. **The Encyclopedia of Witches and Witchcraft**. New York: Facts on File, 1989. 421p. $45.00; $22.95pa. ISBN 0-8160-1793-X; 0-8160-2268-2pa.

The comprehensive coverage of the encyclopedia includes the history of witchcraft in Western civilization from about 1450 to 1700, the modern religion of witchcraft, and topics related to witchcraft, such as folk magic, sorcery, divination, ceremonial magic, occultism and shamanism. Also included are biographies of famous witches and witch hunters and articles on witchcraft in particular countries. Entries are alphabetical with cross-references and are generally one column or longer. There is a bibliography and an index. Guiley is also the author of the *Encyclopedia of Ghosts and Spirits* (Facts on File, 1992) and the *Encyclopedia of Angels* (Facts on File, 1996).

775   Opie, Iona and Moira Tatem, eds. **A Dictionary of Superstitions**. New York: Oxford University Press, 1989. 494p. $39.95; $15.95pa. ISBN 0-19-211597-9; 0-19-282916-5pa.

Divination, spells, cures, charms, signs and omens, rituals and taboos are listed alphabetically by the central idea of the superstition. An analytic index with thematic entries grouped by concept or linked by cross-reference furthers access. Content emphasis is based on the traditions of Great Britain and Ireland. Chronologically arranged quotations are included to illustrate the history and development of ideas. There is a select bibliography.

Political Science

See also **History, Law, Military Science**.

WORLD GOVERNMENT
Biography

776 Abrams, Irwin. **The Nobel Peace Prize and the Laureates: An Illustrated Biographical History, 1901–1987**. Boston: G. K. Hall, 1988. 269p. $45.00. ISBN 0-8161-8609-X.

Complete and accurate information on the Nobel Peace Prize including the mechanics of the selection process is included in the first part of this work. The remainder consists of biographies of the winners, arranged in four chronological periods with historical introductions to each period and a biography for each recipient. Each essay is about three pages and has a black and white portrait and a bibliography divided by primary and secondary sources. Appendices include tables listing prize winners by country and occupation, Nobel's will and a chronological list of winners. There is also an index.

777 Bicentenary of the U.S. House of Representatives. **Women in Congress, 1917–1990**. Washington, D.C.: U.S. Government Printing Office, 1991. 266p. $20.00pa. ISBN 0-160-27160-6.

One or two page biographies with black and white photographs describe the 129 women who served in the United States Congress from 1917–1990. The biographies focus on the women's political life and careers and do not avoid controversy. Entries are alphabetical. The source is useful for reference for the individual biographies and taken as a whole the work is an enlightening political and social document.

778 Blumbert, Arnold, ed. **Great Leaders, Great Tyrants?: Contemporary Views of World Rulers Who Made History**. Westport, Conn.: Greenwood Press, 1995. 354p. $49.95. ISBN 0-313-28751-1.

The premise of these evaluative sketches is that the 52 individuals were selected because while they may have achieved much their methods were often tyrannical; indeed some of the men and women may be classified as either primarily great or primarily tyrannical. Given the total of all the biographical discussions, the questions arise as to the possibility of leadership without tyranny and the tendency of tyranny to destroy itself. The group investigated range from ancient Greece, Rome and China to 20th century figures such as Castro, Indira Gandhi, Mao Zedong, and Tito. Obvious tyrants, Hitler and Mussolini, for example, are excluded. Each essay is by a different author and provides background biographical information, an introduction for historical context and a pro/con discussion about tyranny and leadership. The essays vary in quality and since each author deals with both points of view about an individual there does not seem to be much passion in the debates. This biographical source presents alternative contemporary accounts of famous and infamous historical figures and is appropriate for high school collections. [R: ARBA 96]

779 **Current Leaders of Nations**. Lansdale, Pa.: Current Leaders, 1990. $119.00. $35.00/yearly update. ISBN 0-9624900-0-8.

This service provides a three-ring binder that contains reproducible profiles of leaders throughout the world. "Leaders" are defined as those who wield power, rather than heads of state, such as monarchs. When leadership changes, subscribers to the yearly update receive a new profile within one month. Entries, arranged by the name of the country, include leader's name (with pronunciation), title, and portrait; basic data about the nation, with its location pinpointed on a small map; political background of the country; and information about the leader. Signed profiles give personal background, trace the leader's rise to power, describe leadership style and domestic/foreign policy, and give a mailing address and current bibliography. There is no index. This convenient compilation is recommended for grades 8 through 12. [R: ARBA 92; BR, Mar/Apr 91; LJ, Jan 91; RBB, 15 Jan 91; WLB, Jan 91]

780 Lipset, Seymour Martin, ed. **Who's Who in Democracy**. Washington, D.C.: Congressional Quarterly, 1997. 247p. $85.00. ISBN 1-56802-121-6.

This relatively brief list of 156 biographical sketches is of interest because it is global in scope and includes both historical and contemporary individuals. Each man or woman has contributed some way in the development of democracy; thus entries are as diverse as John Locke, John Adams, Elizabeth Cady Stanton, Nelson Mandela and Boris Yeltsin. This gives users a broad range of the nature of democracy and the contributions of those selected for inclusion. Recommended for high school collections.

781 O'Brien, Steven G. **American Political Leaders: From Colonial Times to the Present**. Santa Barbara, Calif.: ABC-CLIO, 1991. 473p. $65.00. ISBN 0-87436-570-8.

More than 400 profiles of American men and women elected, nominated, or appointed to national office are included in this convenient work. Each profile gives the name, dates, offices held, and offers anecdotes, quotations, and interpretations in addition to typical biographical information. Entries are one or two pages and have bibliographies for further reading. There are about 100 black and white portraits. There is a contents list of all entries which are arranged in alphabetical order with cross-references. There is a timeline of all individuals included. Recommended for middle and high school collections.

782 Ragsdale, Bruce A. and Joel D. Treese. **Black Americans in Congress, 1870–1989**. Washington, D.C.: U.S. Government Printing Office, 1996. $16.00. S/N 052-071-00891-8.

This is a convenient source of biographical information about the African Americans who have served in Congress since 1870. Arranged in alphabetical order by last name, each entry is about two pages, has a photograph, and a list of sources for further reading.

783 **Who's Who in American Politics**. New York: Bowker, 1968– . biennial. $225.00. ISSN 0000-0205.

Almost 30,000 politically influential men and women are listed in this directory. Members of the executive branch, including appointed officials, members of Congress, including their assistants, and members of the judiciary are listed as are governors and state elected officials and state supreme court justices. Mayors of cities with populations of more than 50,000 are listed. National and state party chairs and officers and national political party committee members are included. Also listed are some who hold influence rather than office. There are photographs of national executive and legislative leaders and governors. For each individual the entry gives party affiliation, personal and professional data, telephone, FAX and Internet addresses. Separate sections have lists of Congress by state, Congressional committee chairmen, U.S. Court of Appeals by district, and lists of governors. The index lists names and persons of national scope by state of residence. This source is listed online through NEXIS and Dialog.

Dictionaries and Encyclopedias

784 **Congressional Quarterly's Encyclopedia of American Government**. 2d ed. 3v. Washington, D.C.: Congressional Quarterly, 1994. $159.95/set. ISBN 1-56802-057-2.

The *Congress A to Z*, The *Presidency A to Z*, and the *Supreme Court A to Z*, form a single encyclopedia set that covers the federal government in an attractive and clear manner appropriate for both middle school and high school students. Information comes from the huge and reliable database of Congressional Quarterly's government and political resources. Each volume is arranged alphabetically with cross-references. There is a contents list of articles as well as an index, reference list and selected bibliography in each. Brief articles are written in simple, clear language, and cover topics, terms, people, laws, events, cases, policies and procedures. Highly recommended. Volumes are available separately. [R: ARBA 94]

785 Derbyshire, J. Denis, and Ian Derbyshire. **Political Systems of the World**. New York: St. Martin's Press, 1996. 684p. $95.00. ISBN 0-312-16172-2.

The purpose of this guide is both comparative and descriptive. The first part of the volume compares constitutions, ideologies, forms of government and political processes. The second part lists information about nations alphabetically by continent and country. Brief information about each country and its social and economic status is followed by an extended history of its politics and government. Part three extends this treatment to colonies and dependencies and lists global and regional organizations. Seventy-eight tables and 9 regional maps are included. There is an index. While much of the information in this source can be found elsewhere, the focus of the work on the political systems and ideologies of 192 nations and 42 dependent states may be useful to advanced high school classes. [R: ARBA 97]

786 Evans, Graham and Jeffrey Newnham. **The Dictionary of World Politics: A Reference Guide to Concepts, Ideas, and Institutions**. New York: Simon & Schuster, 1991. $60.00. ISBN 0-13-210527-6.

Definitions are included of more than 600 terms relating to ideas, concepts, institutions and events associated with political issues around the world. The only references to people are those which are associated with theories or practices such as Marxism or the Marshall Plan. Articles vary in length from a paragraph to two pages and are arranged alphabetically. There is an extensive selected bibliography. Recommended for secondary school collections.

787 Kurian, Geroge Thomas, ed. **The Encyclopedia of the Republican Party; The Encyclopedia of the Democratic Party**. 4v. Armonk, N.Y.: Sharpe Reference, 1997. $399.00/set. ISBN 1-56324-729-1.

As one might expect from the title alone, organization is not the strength of this set. Volumes one and two are devoted to the Republican Party and volumes three and four are about the Democratic Party. The first part of volumes one and three consist of long histories of each party with subheadings, cross-references and a bibliography. Also in volumes one and three are alphabetical sections with signed articles about issues and ideology. Entries vary from one to ten pages, longer articles having subheadings, cross-references and bibliographies. Still, in volumes one and three, biographies of presidents arranged alphabetically are followed by biographies of vice-presidents who never became president followed by losing

presidential candidates followed by Speakers of the House followed by other notable party members past and present followed by lists of all members of Congress from the respective parties and similar lists of governors. Volumes two and four describe party conventions, give complete party platforms and contain appendices with more lists of individuals. Volumes two and four also contain a series of vital indexes for just the respective party volumes: there are general indexes, biographical indexes, geographical indexes, and indexes of minorities and women. It should be noted that the issue entries are parallel for each party with additional entries that relate only to one party; indeed some of the issue entries are identical in both volumes. All of this makes the *Britannica* seem simple to use; nonetheless, much of the information is useful and not easily found elsewhere. In particular, the issues sections and the text of party platforms are valuable resources. One hopes the next edition by this new reference publisher will benefit from the wisdom of more experienced publishers and simplify the arrangement so that it no longer resembles a badly designed Web site. High school teachers and students can use the information in this source if they can find it. [R: SLJ, May 1997]

788 Lipset, Seymour Martin, ed. **The Encyclopedia of Democracy**. 4v. Washington, D.C.: Congressional Quarterly, 1995. $395.00/set. ISBN 0-87187-675-2.

The distinguished editor, editorial board, and international contributors have compiled a work that attempts to place democracy in an international framework in order to investigate its common characteristics. Articles include biographies, country studies, regional overviews and topical analysis, and discuss economic and historical issues, governing, international relations and types of democracies. The time frame is from 431 B.C. to 1995. An important introduction precedes lists of the 417 articles arranged alphabetically and by subject. Entries include such topics as African transitions to democracy, censorship, federalism, Hobbes, and Margaret Thatcher. The articles range from 300 to 8,500 words and the longer articles have bibliographies. An appendix lists 20 primary source documents from throughout history and there is an index. Recommended for high schools with programs in political thought or international politics. [R: ARBA 97]

789 Patrick, John J. **The Young Oxford Companion to the Supreme Court of the United States**. New York: Oxford University Press, 1994. 368p. $40.00. ISBN 0-19-507877-2.

This book focuses on the role played by the Supreme Court in maintaining the relationship between law and liberty. Articles discuss the history and development of the Court, cases, issues, operating procedures, organizations, justices and the Constitution and its amendments. Entries for cases and individuals begin with brief facts. Biographies and many other articles are illustrated. Cross-references and bibliographies accompany most articles. One appendix lists the justices by presidential appointment; a second is about visiting the Supreme Court building. The 1997 printing includes a third appendix, a 1996 supplement. A general bibliography and an index conclude the volume. Highly recommended for elementary and middle school. This volume, with *The Young Oxford Companion to the Presidency of the United States* and *The Young Oxford Companion to the Congress of the United States*, provide complete coverage of the branches of the federal government.

790 Pious, Richard M. **The Young Oxford Companion to the Presidency of the United States**. New York: Oxford University Press, 1994. 304p. $35.00. ISBN 0-19-507799-7.

This attractive and accurate encyclopedia of the presidency lists alphabetically entries about many aspects of the executive branch of government. Included are people (presidents, vice-presidents, and selected first ladies), constitutional powers, election and succession, advisors (staff, cabinet and unofficial), decisions, policies, perks, and theories. Entries are clearly defined and give basic information with photographs, cross-references, and further reading. Most articles are from one half column to two columns, but major figures such as Lincoln receive up to eight columns. Narratives are honest evaluations rather than sanitized for young readers. Appendices include tables about presidential election results, terms, dates, and historic sites and libraries. There is a classified further reading list with some items appropriate for students. An index ties themes together as well as locates specific information. Highly recommended for elementary and middle schools; some high

schools will want it as well. This volume, with *The Young Oxford Companion to the Congress of the United States* and *The Young Oxford Companion to the Supreme Court of the United States* provide complete coverage of the branches of the federal government. [R: ARBA 95]

791 Plano, Jack C. and Milton Greenberg. **The American Political Dictionary**. 10th ed. Orlando, Fla.: Harcourt Brace, 1996. 606p. $27.93pa. ISBN 0-03-0173170-5.

This work has been published since 1962 with many editions keeping it current. It is both a dictionary and a study guide and covers political ideas, liberties, parties, the legislative process, executive offices, public administration, the judiciary, finance and taxation, business and labor, foreign policy, and state and local government. Arrangement is in topical chapters with related terms alphabetically within chapters. Definitions are easy to understand and give examples and significance. There is an index. This should be a standard work in any secondary reference collection.

792 Ritchie, Donald A. **The Young Oxford Companion to the Congress of the United States**. New York: Oxford University Press, 1993. 239p. $40.00. ISBN 0-19-507777-6.

More than 200 entries examine Congress objectively and critically. Included are events, procedures, terms, powers, traditions, and the Capitol. There are 62 articles about leaders of Congress, past and present, and groups of members (e.g., women, minorities). Articles are arranged alphabetically and vary from a paragraph to a column to a page; many have suggestions for further readings and black and white photographs or drawings. Boxed lists add to the narrative. Appendices offer a chronological table of majority and minority members, advice for visiting Congress and for doing research about Congress. There is an index. Highly recommended for elementary and middle schools; high schools may want it as well. This volume, combined with *The Young Oxford Companion to the Presidency of the United States* and *The Young Oxford Companion to the Supreme Court of the United States* give a library good coverage of the federal government in an attractive series.

793 Shafritz, Jay M., Phil Williams and Ronald S. Calinger. **The Dictionary of 20th-Century World Politics**. New York: Holt, 1993. 756p. $60.00. ISBN 0-8050-1976-6.

This is a dictionary of concise and clear definitions and explanations of history, people, theories, ideas, events, doctrines, terms, treaties and agreements. It is international in scope and has about 4,000 entries arranged chronologically with cross-references. Entries are brief (World War II is covered in only four pages). Photographs and boxes of details and explanations enhance the narratives. An appendix lists key concepts organized by subject. This useful dictionary is recommended for high school collections. [R: ARBA 94]

794 Shafritz, Jay M. **The HarperCollins Dictionary of American Government and Politics**. New York: Harper Perennial, 1992. 656p. $50.00. ISBN 0-06-270031-6.

Based on the former *Dorsey Dictionary*, this source has about 5,500 entries of concepts, terms, phrases, and processes about American national, state, and local government and politics. Articles are included on Supreme Court cases, laws, people, associations, journals, 100 government agencies, and over 150 terms of political slang. There is some related coverage of terms from economics, law, and sociology. All items are in one alphabetical arrangement, and are mostly brief paragraphs. One of the appendices arranges 14 key concepts with references to the alphabetical listings. There are photographs and prints as well as boxed lists and explanations which make the dictionary even more useful. Recommended for secondary collections. [R: ARBA 93]

795 Taylor, Peter J., ed. **World Government**. rev. ed. New York: Oxford University Press, 1995. 256p. $45.00. ISBN 0-19-521096-4.

This work looks in detail at individual governments within regions of the world. It discusses boundaries, constitutions, and actual forms of governments. Boxes, photographs, maps, charts, tables, and diagrams complement the narrative. The introduction includes definitions of states, powers, and relationships among states. There is

a glossary, and an index. The handbook is an excellent source for comparative political and governmental information and is recommended for secondary schools.

796 Vile, John R. **Encyclopedia of Constitutional Amendments, Proposed Amendments, and Amending Issues, 1789–1995**. Santa Barbara, Calif.: ABC-CLIO, 1996. 427p. $75.00. ISBN 0-87436-783-2.

Almost 11,000 amendments to the U.S. Constitution have been proposed since 1789. This encyclopedia updates two old sources, Ames (1896) and Musmanno (1929), to provide 400 entries that cover the 27 ratified amendments, the subjects addressed in the other 10,900 proposed amendments, reform proposals to rewrite the Constitution, organizations, Supreme Court decisions, issues and about 50 brief biographies of Constitutional reformers. Entries are alphabetical with cross-references and often have recommendations for further reading. There are four appendices, an extensive bibliography, a list of cases and an index. This is a well-designed reference source and is highly recommended for high schools. [R: ARBA 97]

797 Wellek, Alex, ed. **The Encyclopedic Dictionary of American Government**. 4th ed. Guilford, Conn.: Dushkin Pub. Group, 1991. 338p. $12.95. ISBN 0-87967-883-6.

The 1,500 entries in this easy to use dictionary include the major terms, concepts and offices of the U.S. government. Some brief definitions are interspersed with longer articles which are signed. Illustrations such as maps, diagrams, photographs and charts extend clarity. There is a separate listing of major Supreme Court decisions, a list of important laws, a list of the presidents, and topic guides. Recommended for secondary collections. [R: ARBA 93]

Handbooks and Almanacs

798 **The Almanac of American Politics**. Boston: Gambit, 1972– . biennial. $65.95. ISSN 0362-076X.

Useful information about elected officials is gathered in this handbook. Arranged alphabetically by state, as well as Puerto Rico, the Virgin

Islands, Guam, and American Samoa, the work lists governors, senators, and representatives. Each individual's entry lists current biographical and political information. There are descriptions of Congressional districts, and committee assignments, ratings by interest groups and journals, key votes and election results. Also included in the work is a list of Senate and House committees, subcommittees, and joint committees, campaign finance charts and demographic information. There is an index. Each biennial issue has special features about current issues. Highly recommended for high school collections.

799 Baker, Daniel B., ed. **Political Quotations: A Collection of Notable Sayings on Politics from Antiquity through 1989**. Detroit, Mich.: Gale Research, 1990. 509p. $39.95. ISBN 0-8103-4920-5.

Political quotations from Homer to George Bush and Margaret Thatcher can be found in this volume. The 4,000 numbered quotations, arranged chronologically within topical sections, are cited by speaker, source, and date. The topical arrangement is further enhanced by author/speaker and keyword indexes. This book, a valuable supplement to general works such as *Bartlett's Familiar Quotations*, is recommended for high school libraries. [R: ARBA 91; WLB, Dec 90]

800 Button, John. **The Radicalism Handbook: Radical Activists, Groups and Movements of the Twentieth Century**. Santa Barbara, Calif.: ABC-CLIO, 1995. 460p. $49.50. ISBN 0-87436-838-3.

Previously published as *The Cassell Handbook of Radicalism*, this source lists 360 individuals and 84 groups who work to try to bring about change and ensure peace, justice, and a safe environment. Only liberal radicals are included, and the source is international in scope, with only 90 Americans included. An attempt has been made at gender balance. After an introduction to radicalism in the 20th century there is an alphabetical listing of the people and groups, movements, events, and campaigns selected from fields such as civil and human rights, gay and lesbian rights, labor movements, liberation theology, radical economics, and women's rights. Entries are generally about one page with bibliographies. Appendices classify the entries by country and by

area topic; there is a list of 80 worthy Americans who were not included because of the attempt to balance the source internationally. Recommended for high school political science collections. [R: ARBA 96]

801 **Congressional Quarterly's Politics in America**. Washington, D.C.: Congressional Quarterly, 1990– . annual. $89.95. ISSN 1064-6809.

Similar to *The Almanac of American Politics*, this work gives assessments of senators and representatives by their key votes, and interest group ratings. Election data is also supplied. Arranged alphabetically by state, governors and lieutenant governors, senators, and representatives are listed. There are state maps with districts labeled and boxes with legislative data. Appendices include committee assignments, seniority lists, House districts with close races and other information about current issues. There is an index. This information is available online, and via subscription Web access where information is updated continuously.

802 Cook, Chris, comp. **The Facts on File World Political Almanac**. 3d ed. New York: Facts on File, 1995. 536p. $45.00. ISBN 0-8160-2838-9.

Now in a third edition that reflects the political changes of the early 1990s, this work provides facts and figures about the world after 1945. Narrative and chronological tables give easily accessible information about international political organizations and movements, heads of state and government, legislatures and constitutions, political parties, elections, treaties, population and urbanization. A section on world violence discusses international conflicts, civil strife, terrorism, and UN peacekeeping efforts. Another section is on the nuclear age and arms control. There is a dictionary of political terms, events, and actions, a biographical dictionary and an index. The source is useful because it collects information available elsewhere in one convenient volume. Recommended for high school collections.

803 Diller, Daniel C. **The Middle East**. 8th ed. Washington, D.C.: Congressional Quarterly, 1994. 432p. $42.95; $29.95pa. ISBN 1-56802-038-4; 0-87187-999-9pa.

This handbook provides useful and clear political and economic information as well as historical background about the political situation in the countries that make up the Middle East. There is an overview of the area and sections on current issues: the Arab-Israeli conflict, U.S. policy in the area, the Persian Gulf, Mideast oil, and the role of Islam. These articles are followed by 12 country profiles. Appendices include sketches of leaders, major events from 1900–1994, and important documents; and there is an extensive bibliography and an index. The text is supported by 19 maps, fact boxes and tables. The reader will look in vain for information about human rights and there are perhaps two sentences on the status of women. Nonetheless, the information provided will support world history, current events, and world culture curricula. [R: ARBA 96]

804 Wetterau, Bruce. **Congressional Quarterly's Desk Reference on American Government**. Washington, D.C.: Congressional Quarterly, 1995. 349p. $49.95. ISBN 0-87187-956-5.

Despite the question and answer format, the good table of contents, cross-references, and extensive index give this some ready-reference use. Designed in this format because of frequently asked questions at the Congressional Quarterly reference library, the handbook poses and answers some 600 questions about how government works. Divided into sections on the government in general (including the Constitution, wars and scandals) the Presidency, Congress, Campaigns and Elections and the Supreme Court, the resource covers only federal government from 1789–1994. Charts, tables, and lists clarify information. The index refers to question rather than page number. Suggested for secondary school collections. [R: ARBA 96]

805 **The World Almanac of U.S. Politics**. Mahwah, N.J.: Pharos Books, 1997. $29.95pa. ISBN 0-88687-811-X.

This convenient source brings together most of the information students and teachers need in government classes. Election information, budget and legislative processes, political parties, how and where to write or call to ask for information or state a position, voter registration, and political parties are all covered. There is a directory and biographies of important members of all branches of federal government, and information as well about state and local government. One feature is "a typical day for a..." that describes what an elected official might accomplish in a day. An index leads to precise information. Highly recommended for both middle and high school collections. [R: ARBA 95]

806 **The World Almanac of U.S. Politics**. New York: World Almanac. biennial. price varies. ISSN 1043-1535.

This is both a handbook of government information and a directory of officials. Background information is given about elections, the legislative and budgetary processes, political parties and campaign financing. Suggestions are made for how to write to Congressional representatives and directions given about where to write and call. Directory information is given for officials in all three branches of the federal government, for state government and for the 50 largest city governments. Indexes are by subject and name. Most secondary and professional collections will want this source.

INTERNATIONAL RELATIONS

See also **World Conflicts** in **History**.

807 **Everyone's United Nations**. 10th ed. New York: United Nations, 1986. 484p. $9.95pa. ISBN 92-1-100274-5.

Published since 1948, this guide describes the structure and work of the United Nations in narrative chapters with some tables and charts. The efforts included are peacemaking and peace keeping, disarmament, economic and social development, human rights, decolonization, and international law. An appendix includes the U.N. Charter. There is an index. This is a basic guide to the United Nations.

808 Institute for Defense and Disarmament Studies. **Peace Resource Book**. Cambridge, Mass.: Ballinger Pub. Co. biennial. ISSN 0740-9885.

Formerly titled the *American Peace Directory*, this is both a directory and a handbook. It gives the addresses and telephone numbers of more than 7,000 peace groups in the United States. It also is a guide to the literature with over 1,000 items of peace literature listed. There is a section discussing issues and strategies, information on world military spending, and a list of colleges with peace programs. There is an author index.

809 Jentleson, Bruce W., and Thomas G. Paterson, eds. **Encyclopedia of U.S. Foreign Relations**. 4v. New York: Oxford University Press, 1997. $450.00/set. ISBN 0-19-511055-2.

More than 1,000 articles discuss how Americans and their government have interacted with the rest of the world. Entries reflect political, economic, military, cultural, ideological and environmental issues as well as people, countries, regions, wars, treaties and conferences. Topics range from "Alien and Sedition Acts" to "Amistad Affair" to "Gulf War." Most of the signed articles are under 1,000 words, but there is longer treatment of major topics such as the American Revolution, the world wars, and immigration. Charts, tables, maps and bibliographies accompany many articles. A list of entries and a comprehensive index make it easy to find information. Highly recommended for high school government, history and world culture collections.

810 O'Toole, G. J. A. **The Encyclopedia of American Intelligence and Espionage: From the Revolutionary War to the Present**. New York: Facts on File, 1988. 539p. $50.00. ISBN 0-8160-1011-0.

A unique source that covers a wide range of American intelligence organizations, operations, events, terms, and agents. It covers the role of intelligence in nine wars. More than 700 entries are arranged alphabetically and vary in length from 1 column to more than 10 pages. Some photographs enhance the text, and there is an extensive bibliography. An index supports the reference value of the work. Recommended for secondary libraries.

811 Plano, Jack C. and Roy Olton. **The International Relations Dictionary**. 4th ed. Santa Barbara, Calif.: ABC-CLIO, 1988. 446p. $56.50; $24.75pa. ISBN 0-87436-477-9; 0-87436-478-7pa.

This work is arranged to complement standard textbooks in international politics and this makes it somewhat awkward to use as a reference tool.

Entries cover concepts, terms, events, and facts and are grouped into subject matter chapters with terms listed within the chapters. Definitions are supplemented with a paragraph of significance which includes the historical background and contemporary importance of the term. Entries are numbered and there is an index. There is a guide to major concepts. Recommended for high school collections.

812 Thackrah, John Richard. **Encyclopedia of Terrorism and Political Violence**. New York: Routledge, 1987. 308p. $37.50. ISBN 0-7102-0659-3.

Coverage in this work includes the ideas, theories, terms, people, countries, and incidents of international terrorism with a Western orientation and emphasis on the second half of the 20th century. Arranged alphabetically with cross-references, the entries range in length from two paragraphs to two pages. Articles are clear and readable. There are references, a select bibliography and an index. Suitable for high school collections.

813 Watson, Bruce W., Susan M. Watson, and Gerald W. Hopple. **United States Intelligence: An Encyclopedia**. New York: Garland, 1990. 792p. $110.00. ISBN 0-8240-3713-8.

The scope of this work is post World War II to 1990, and the people, events, terms, rules, laws and groups dealing with American intelligence work. Prefatory materials include an extensive list of acronyms and a description of major weapons systems. Entries are alphabetical with definitions and explanations of the terms; they vary in length from one paragraph to several pages. The many appendices include information about the federal laws and executive orders under which intelligence forces operate. Suitable for high school collections.

814 **Yearbook of the United Nations**. Lake Success, N.Y.: Dept. of Public Information, United Nations, 1946– . annual. price varies. ISSN 0082-8521.

This annual publication provides comprehensive and up-to-date coverage of the activities of the United Nations. It includes major reports, descriptions of operational activities, views of member states, and describes the activities of related organizations. Divided into major sections such as political questions, regional issues, economic, social and legal issues, and operation of the U.N. as an organization, the source offers the best description of the institution. Appendices include a roster of member states, the Charter, the structure of the organization, and a list of information centers and services. There is a subject index and an index of resolutions and decisions. The 1995 50th Anniversary edition contained extra historical information. This is a more complete source than *Everyone's United Nations*.

UNITED STATES GOVERNMENT
Biography

815 Brownson, Anna L., ed. **Biographical Directory of the American Congress (1774-1997)**. 10th ed. Washington, D.C.: Congressional Quarterly, 1995. 2115p. $79.00. ISBN 0-87289-124-0.

This is a list of all members of Congress, arranged chronologically by Congress (by state) beginning with the Continental Congress of 1774 to the present Congress. There are also lists of members of the Presidents' Cabinets from 1789–present. Biographies of the more than 12,000 men and women who have served in Congress include dates, education, occupation, party affiliation, length of service, contributions made while in Congress, and subsequent careers. The biographies are useful for state history classes as well as for general government and American history curricula.

816 Diller, Daniel C. and Stephen L.
E+   Robertson. **The Presidents, First Ladies, and Vice Presidents: White House Biographies, 1789–1997**. Washington, D.C.: Congressional Quarterly, 1997. 180p. $24.95pa. ISBN 1-56802-311-1.

This convenient source gathers together biographical information about the presidents, their wives or sisters, daughters and nieces who acted as White House hostesses, and all of the vice-presidents who were never elected president. One or two page entries include pictures. An introductory section describes the president's daily schedule. Useful in all collections.

817 Freidel, Frank and Hugh Sidey. **The**
E+   **Presidents of the United States of America**. 14th ed. Washington, D.C.: White House Historical Association, 1996. 96p. $12.95; $9.95pa. ISBN 0-912308-57-5; 0-912308-56-7pa.

This small volume is useful because it contains all of the official portraits of the presidents. Each portrait is accompanied by a page summary of the administration of the president. The table of contents lists the artists. Entries are chronological and there is an index. Recommended for all levels.

818 Klapthor, Margaret Brown. **The**
E+   **First Ladies**. 8th ed. Washington, D.C.: White House Historical Association, 1996. 90p. $12.95; $9.95pa. ISBN 0-912308-59-1; 0-912308-58-3pa.

Similar to its companion volume, *The Presidents of the United States*, this work is a joint project of the White House Historical Association and the National Geographic Society. Each entry consists of a two-page spread and a full-page portrait, usually in color, of the first lady. The text provides a readable account of her private and political life. Women who served as official hostesses but were not wives of presidents receive a brief profile and a small portrait. Suggested for upper elementary through high school levels. [R: ARBA 91]

Handbooks and Almanacs

819 **The Book of the States**. Lexington, Ky.: Council of State Governments, 1935– . biennial. $85.75. ISSN 0068-0125.

This biennial publication provides comparative information about the 50 states and the District of Columbia, as well as some data on Puerto Rico, the Virgin Islands, American Samoa, and Guam. Each entry gives the constitution, the branches of government, elections, finances, management, and programs and issues. There are state pages with historical and other information. Data are presented in narratives, charts, and tables. Essays in each edition highlight particular current issues. There is an index. *State Elective Officials and the Legislatures* is published by the council on the alternate years. A CD-ROM combining *The Book of the States* with other directory services of the council is in preparation.

820 Elliot, Jeffrey M., and Sheikh R. Ali. **The State and Local Government Political Dictionary**. Santa Bernadino, Calif.: Borgo Press, 1995. 325p. $39.00; $29.00pa. ISBN 0-8095-0703-X; 0-8095-1703-5pa.

Arranged alphabetically within subject matter chapters, approximately 300 terms related to the organization and function of state and local government are defined. Entries also include a statement of significance. Items are numbered and there is an index.

821 **The Municipal Year Book**. Chicago: International City Manager's Association, 1934– . annual. $77.95. ISSN 0077-2186.

Essays discuss management trends and issues; and comparative and descriptive statistical data are provided about such things as staffing, salaries, per capita income, tax structure, and bond ratings for all incorporated communities in the U.S. and Canada with populations over 25,000. The directories of municipal officials include 70,000 names and phone numbers. There is a good bibliography of reference sources. An index is cumulative for the most recent years.

822 **The United States Government Manual**. Washington, D.C.: Office of the Federal Register, National Archives and Records Administration. Government Printing Office, 1935– . annual. $30.00pa. ISBN 0-16-049122-3 (1997/1998).

This is an overall guide to the organization of the federal government. Charts and diagrams illustrate the relationships of one part of the government to another as well as the relationships within departments, agencies and bureaus. All three branches of government are included with names, addresses and telephone numbers of individual office holders. There is a useful subject index. This is an essential holding for any level at which government is studied. Available on the Internet via the NARA homepage, www.access.gpo.gov/nara.

Congress

823 Bacon, Donald C., Roger H. Davidson, and Morton Keller, eds. **The Encyclopedia of the United States Congress**. 4v. New York: Simon & Schuster, 1995. $355.00/set ISBN 0-13-276361-3.

Supported by Congress, the Lyndon Baines Johnson Library and Foundation, and the University of Texas, this comprehensive source provides to a wide audience a balanced, easy to use work about Congress, its history and the way it works. The editors are a journalist, a political science professor, and a history professor, and 550 authorities contributed more than 1,000 entries. Several hundred illustrations, tables, and charts augment the text. Articles are arranged alphabetically and there is a list of all entries in volume one and both synoptic contents and index in volume four. In addition to comprehensive essays on major topics and eight essays on the historical development of the Congress, there are articles about policymaking; landmark laws; the relationships of the states to the Congress; procedures; links between Congress and the other branches of government; elections; perceptions of Congress in literature, movies, and humor; the Capitol; Congressional culture; and even cuisine. Articles are signed and have small bibliographies. Middle school students would be able to use this source, and it is highly recommended for high school collections. [R: ARBA 96]

824 Christianson, Stephen G. **Facts About the Congress**. Bronx, N.Y.: H. W. Wilson, 1996. 635p. $55.00. ISBN 0-8242-0883-8.

This is a concise and useful source which shows major developments and achievements in the U.S. Congress from 1798 to the present by describing every Congress in chronological order from the 1st (1787–1791) to the 104th (1993–1995). Each Congress is divided into clear sections that tell when the Congress met and give such data as a background summary of contemporary events, major legislation passed as well as proposed legislation that failed, the relationship between that Congress and the sitting President, and scandals (if any). A chronology and a table of key votes accompanies the chapter for each Congress. Entries are from five to seven pages and have a list of books for further reading. Not only is this source useful for ready reference, but it provides the information that enables the student to follow changes in the Congress for any time period. A bibliography, eight appendices including a table of pay rates and a list of Congressional buildings, a glossary, and an index make the work even more useful. Any social studies area can draw from this source. Highly recommended for secondary school collections. [R: ARBA 97]

825 Dole, Robert J. **Historical Almanac of the United States Senate: A Series of "Bicentennial Minutes" Presented to the Senate during the One Hundredth Congress**. Washington, D.C.: U.S. Government Printing Office, 1989. $28.00. S/N 052-071-00857-8.

Senator Robert Dole's historical vignettes, presented as "Bicentennial Minutes" during the 100th Congress, are arranged chronologically in nine chapters that cover the entire history of the Senate from 1787–1989. The volume is nicely illustrated and has a chronology and an index. It is a lovely little book with interesting tidbits of history ready to enliven any teacher's lectures, and to serve as a sample of the kind of presentation any history class could create.

826 **How Congress Works**. 2d ed. Washington, D.C.: Congressional Quarterly, 1991. 157p. $26.95. ISBN 0-87187-598-5.

This is one of the best sources about the practical working procedures and processes of the U.S. Congress. It explains in essays with illustrations and notes about party leadership, the legislative process, the committee system, the Congressional staff, and lobbying and political interest group pressures. The appendix includes the requisite "How a Bill Becomes a Law," a list of the leadership, votes, overrides, and a list of the longest sessions. There is a good index. Recommended for secondary school collections.

827 Michael, W. H. **Official Congressional Directory**. Washington, D.C.: U.S. Government Printing Office, 1887– . biennial. $30.00. ISSN 0160-9890.

This standard official source has both directory and biographical information about each member of Congress arranged alphabetically by state. It includes photographs. The work also includes directory information for other government agencies, press information, statistical data, and maps of Congressional districts. There is a name index. A convenient source recommended for libraries at all levels. Much of this information is also available on the WWW at www.access.gpo.gov/congress/cong016.html.

828 United States, Bureau of the Census. **Congressional District Atlas**. Washington, D.C.: U.S. Department of Commerce, Bureau of the Census, 1964– . biennial. $42.00. ISSN 0090-8061.

This atlas of the 50 states, the District of Columbia, American Samoa, Guam, Puerto Rico, and the American Virgin Islands contains maps for each political entity showing its congressional districts with lists of place names, counties, and county subdivisions with a congressional district. There are also reverse lists of districts with the names of place names included. Native American reservations and their districts are also indicated. The atlas issued in 1993 will be valid through at least the 108th Congress.

The Presidency

829 Blassingame, Wyatt. **The Look-it-up**
E+ **Book of Presidents**. rev. ed. New York: Random House, 1996. 154p. $14.99; $8.99pa. ISBN 0-679-90353-4; 0-679-80358-0pa.

Brief biographies of the presidents are arranged chronologically in this easy-to-read source. Entries are from two to six pages and are accompanied by cleverly selected portraits, photographs, maps, cartoons, and other illustrations. There is an achievement chart also arranged chronologically. Recommended for elementary and middle school collections.

830 DeGregorio, William A. and Connie
E+ Jo Dickerson. **The Complete Book of U.S. Presidents**. 5th ed. New York: Random House, 1997. 769p. $15.99. ISBN 0-517-18353-6.

Basic information on all presidents is arranged with a chapter for each president, chronologically (Cleveland gets two chapters). Information provided includes typical biographical information and physical description, personality, ancestors, early romance(s) and extramarital affairs, and bibliographies of books about and books by each president. The appendices include the political composition of Congress from 1789 on, curiosities about the presidents and the presidency, and a ranking of the presidents according to accomplishments. There is an index. Recommended for middle school and high school.

831　Graff, Henry F., ed. **The Presidents: A Reference History**. 2d ed. New York: Macmillan, 1996. 811p. $105.00; $39.95pa. ISBN 0-684-80471-9; 0-684-80551-0pa.

The extensive essays on each of the presidential administrations focus on the president's career and on the events and accomplishments of his presidency. Each author is a specialist on his president, and the summaries of the administration are not necessarily sympathetic. The articles are in chronological order and include bibliographic essays about the time period as well as the presidents. The new edition adds three presidencies and an article on the demands on the First Ladies from Martha Washington to Hilary Clinton. The essays are scholarly but easily approachable by high school and some middle school students. Highly recommended because it provides material not found in standard biographical articles in other reference sources. [R: ARBA 97]

832　**Inaugural Addresses of the Presidents of the United States from George Washington 1789 to George Bush 1989**. Washington, D.C.: U.S. Government Printing Office, 1989. 350p. $16.00. s/n 052-071-00879-9.

The full address of each president is accompanied by a portrait, the event date, and a description of other events of inauguration day. Information is also provided about the five presidents never inaugurated (the five vice-presidents who succeeded to office on the death of the president who were never elected on their own). This is a convenient source of these documents.

833　Kane, Joseph Nathan. **Facts about**
E+　　**the Presidents: A Compilation of Biographical and Historical**

Information. 6th ed. Bronx, N.Y.: H. W. Wilson, 1993. 432p. $55.00. ISBN 0-8242-0845-5.

This standard source provides data about the lives of the presidents, their backgrounds, terms in office and therefore, about the office itself, in a useful one-volume reference. The first part of the work is a chapter about each president in chronological order giving genealogic and family history, information about elections, cabinets, appointments, and the vice president, highlights about his life and administration. Data is given in tables and listings rather than in narrative. There are portraits and other illustrations. The second part of the book gives collective data in comparative form and thus compiles a summary and statistical record of the presidency as a whole. There is an index. Recommended for all levels.

834　Nelson, Michael, ed. **Congressional Quarterly's Guide to the Presidency**. 2d ed. Washington, D.C.: Congressional Quarterly, 1996. 1800p. $289.00. ISBN 1-56802-018-X.

This is a comprehensive guide to the nature of the presidency and how it has been shaped. Arranged in topical sections with essays, boxed fact inserts, charts and tables, information includes the historical development of the office, its powers, its relationship with citizens and the rest of the government, how the White House operates, and elections and impeachment. There are also biographies of all of the men who have held the office and of the vice presidents. The extensive and detailed table of contents and the good index make it possible to use this for ready reference as well as for extended research. This should be in every high school collection, and middle schools with government in the curriculum will need it as well.

835　Podell, Janet and Steven Anzovin. **Speeches of the American Presidents**. Bronx, N.Y.: H. W. Wilson, 1988. 820p. $65.00. ISBN 0-8242-0761-0.

This collection of 180 speeches from 40 presidents (Washington through Reagan) is a way to study the presidency by studying the texts of their most important official speeches. The number of speeches vary from one to 13 (for FDR). Most speeches are given in full; few are from before or after the presidency. A black and white portrait or photograph accompanies each president's section. Each speech has a brief narrative providing the setting of the occasion. Arrangement is chronological by president and there is an index.

836 Waldrup, Carole Chandler. **The Vice Presidents: Biographies of the 45 Men Who Have Held the Second Highest Office in the United States**. Jefferson, N.C.: McFarland, 1996. 271p. $35.00. ISBN 0-7864-0179-6.

The author points out that 30% of the vice presidents have succeeded to the presidency in some manner, and that the roles of the vice presidents have varied greatly in scope and influence. The chronological entries from John Adams to Albert Gore each feature a portrait and a description of the life and achievements that include birth and family, education and habits and political career. The essays average six pages and have bibliographies. The Gore bibliography consists of an article from *Parade Magazine* and one from the *Saturday Evening Post*, but bibliographies of the others are more respectable. The book is spoiled by a pedantic writing style, but

many of the individuals will not be covered to this extent in most other sources. Appropriate for middle and senior high school collections. [R: ARBA 97]

Supreme Court

837 Paddock, Lisa. **Facts about the Supreme Court**. Bronx, N.Y.: H. W. Wilson, 1996. 569p. $55.00. ISBN 0-8242-0896-X.

Arrangement of this guide to the Court is chronological by the term of the Chief Justice, beginning with the Jay Court and concluding with the current Rehnquist Court. Each Court section lists the members of the Court with terms served, gives a background of national events for perspective, has biographies of the Chief Justice and the Associate Justices, and evaluates significant cases by discussing facts, issues, the opinion and its significance. Additional features of the work include excellent introductory and historical information, a glossary, photographs and charts and both case and general indexes. Highly recommended for secondary collections.

Psychology

838 Biggs, Donald A., and Gerald Porter. **Dictionary of Counseling**. Westport, Conn.: Greenwood Press, 1994. 229p. $59.95. ISBN 0-313-28367-2.

This is a non-technical dictionary whose best audience will be teachers and parents who work with counselors as well as those taking classes in counseling. Professional counselors will find it more useful for the references attached to the definitions, which are basic, if not superficial. Definitions include a brief defining sentence and a narrative explaining or giving examples. Entries include people, organizations, professional journals, and terms in alphabetical order with related cross-references and there is an index. Recommended for parent and professional collections. [R: ARBA 95]

839 Colman, Andrew M., ed. **Companion Encyclopedia of Psychology**. 2v. New York: Routledge, 1994. $199.95/set. ISBN 0-415-06446-5.

While intended for teachers, students, and the general public, this work is more theoretical than the *Encyclopedia of Psychology* and is more useful for educators in district professional collections. Articles are divided into 13 sections that contain several essays. Topics included are such things as biological aspects of behavior, cognition, learning and skills, emotion and motivation, individual differences, developmental psychology, and abnormal psychology. Articles are signed, illustrated, and have bibliographies. [R: ARBA 95]

840 Corsini, Raymond J., ed. **Encyclopedia of Psychology**. 2d ed. 4v. New York: Wiley, 1994. $475.00/set. ISBN 0-471-55819-2.

841 Corsini, Raymond J. and Alan J. Auerbach, eds. **Concise Encyclopedia of Psychology**. 2d ed. New York: Wiley, 1996. 1035p. $175.00. ISBN 0-471-13159-8.

This authoritative work contains approximately 2,500 entries about all aspects of psychology, including such topics as cults, education, mental disease, child development, aging, crime, parapsychology, and child abuse. The signed entries are from about two to six columns in length and have suggestions for further reading. Volume 4 contains brief biographical references and a huge bibliography of about 15,000 entries. There are name and subject indexes. This source is for advanced high school psychology programs, and would also find use in professional collections.

The one-volume edition of the encyclopedia condenses about 2,000 articles from the set. It contains 95 percent of the entries and includes diagrams and tables. A biographical section of 1,000 important psychologists with brief identifying sentences follows the articles. There is a name and subject index. The size of the work makes it difficult to handle, but its information may be sufficient for many high school collections. [R: ARBA 95, 97]

842 Doctor, Ronald M., and Ada P. Kahn. **The Encyclopedia of Phobias, Fears and Anxieties**. New York: Facts on File, 1989. 487p. $50.00. ISBN 0-8160-1789-0.

High school teachers and students will find this source beneficial in health classes or any course that studies psychology. Alphabetically arranged entries describe over 2,000 fears, anxieties, and phobias; suggest ways to treat each; and provide brief biographies of noted professionals in the field. Specific phobias are listed under their common and medical names, with the most complete information under the common name. A bibliography of over 2,500 entries and a brief index conclude the volume. [R: ARBA 90; BL, 15 Oct 89; BR, May/June 90]

843 Lewis, James R. **The Dream Encyclopedia**. New York: Gale Research,

1995. 416p. $14.95. ISBN 0-7876-0155-1.

Nearly 250 topics are discussed in this comprehensive guide to psychological, physiological, and mythological studies of dreams and their interpretation. The work consists of two sections; the first part is the alphabetically arranged topical encyclopedia which includes short articles on people, research, sleep-related issues, ethnic groups, historical periods, and even dreams in movies. Articles have lists of reference sources. The second part is an alphabetical list of 700 dream symbols with brief explanations or interpretations of the dream elements. There is a directory of organizations dealing with all aspects of dreams. This source would be useful for high school psychology classes as well as for general interest. [R: ARBA 96]

844 Pettijohn, Terry F., ed. **The Encyclopedic Dictionary of Psychology**. 4th ed. Guilford, Conn.: Dushkin Pub. Group, 1991. 298p. $12.95. ISBN 0-87967-885-2.

This single-volume work provides easy access to the language, institutions, and practices involved in the study of psychology. Twelve hundred articles and briefer entries are prepared by authorities in the field; longer articles are signed. Arrangement is alphabetical with cross-references and the entries are written in clear articles illustrated with maps, diagrams, photographs, charts and tables. Preliminary information includes a list of the biographies included and topic guides with boxed relational cross-references and subject maps, a boxed hierarchical guide. This is an excellent source for high school collections. [R: ARBA 93]

845 Ramachandran, V. S., ed. **Encyclopedia of Human Behavior**. 4v. San Diego, Calif.: Academic Press, 1994. $595.00/set. ISBN 0-12-0226920-9.

This comprehensive source attempts to cover all major disciplines in the study of human behavior that are of concern and interest to the public. It is intended for both professionals and students. There is a complete table of contents in the first volume and volumes 2–4 have volume contents. There is an index in volume 4. Arrangement is alphabetical by broad topic. The essay articles are long, generally from four to ten pages, and most under 15 pages. Each signed article is clearly organized with an outline, a glossary, cross-references, and guides to further reading. Entries include such topics as AIDS and sexual behavior, anxiety and fear, dreaming, family systems, logic, cybernetics, brainwashing, phobias, semantics, and reading. Students and teachers from almost every curricular area from biology to health to family living to sociology, government, psychology, mathematics and language arts will find relevant information in this useful encyclopedia. Highly recommended for high school collections. [R: ARBA 95]

846 Statt, David A. **The Concise Dictionary of Psychology**. 3d ed. New York: Routledge, 1998. 136p. $14.95. ISBN 0-415-179-408.

More than 1,400 entries of from 10 to 120 words are included in this dictionary. The standard arrangement is supplemented with many cross-references, but there is no pronunciation. Terms, people, tests, and behaviors are defined clearly and simply with informal language. Drawings, charts and diagrams add to the text. The third edition is scheduled for publication. Highly recommended for high school collections.

847 Stratton, Peter, and Nicky Hayes. **A Student's Dictionary of Psychology**. 2d ed. New York: Routledge, 1993. 223p. $49.50. ISBN 0-340-56926-3.

Although British in origin, with the resulting confusions of differing spellings, this dictionary is comprehensive and concise. The definitions range from one to five sentences and are clearly written at an introductory level, offering both meanings of words and phrases and explanations of how the terms are used in psychology. Drawings and charts also help with understanding. The second edition includes new entries, expanded cross-references, updating and new definitions. There are no biographical entries. This is a good dictionary to support high school psychology classes.

Sociology

848 Barker, Robert L. **The Social Work Dictionary**. 3d ed. Washington, D.C.: National Association of Social Workers, NASW Press, 1995. 447p. $34.95. ISBN 0-87101-253-7.

This dictionary is for social work professionals and for the people who work with them. Terms come from administration, research, policy development, government programs, health and mental health issues, clinical practice, ethics and history. Included are organizations, trends and people. Listed alphabetically the terms are in bold typeface and are defined clearly, with multiple meanings when necessary. Appendices include a chronology of social work, the NASW Code of Ethics, and directories for State Boards and NASW chapter offices. Recommended for parent reference shelves and professional collections. [R: RBSL 96]

849 Borgatta, Edward F. and Marie L. Borgatta, eds. **Encyclopedia of Sociology**. 4v. New York: Macmillan, 1992. $340.00/set. ISBN 0-02-897051-9.

This new source was preceded by a series of handbooks on special topics in sociology which were published in the 1960s and 1970s and together formed a sort of encyclopedia. The 370 entries in the current set involve social issues, problems, concepts and interests, and include such topics as families, race, gender, crime, and health. The long signed articles are alphabetical throughout the 4 volumes with cross-references and there is an index in volume 4. Emphasis is on the United States, but there are articles on other nations and cultures. Recommended for high schools with strong psychology, sociology, family life, and world culture programs. [R: ARBA 93]

850 Dynes, Wayne R., and others. **Encyclopedia of Homosexuality**. 2v. New York: Garland, 1990. $150.00. ISBN 0-8240-6544-1.

This first comprehensive work on homosexuality remains one of the best sources on the topic. The 770 biographical, topical and thematic articles, arranged alphabetically by topic, cover historical medical, psychological, sociological and transcultural information. A subject cross-reference guide in the front of volume one and a detailed subject index in volume two provide access. The focus of the set is Western, but African, Eastern, and other groups receive coverage. Articles deal with contrasting viewpoints and include bibliographies. This encyclopedia is appropriate for high school collections.

851 Fantasia, Rick and Maurice Isserman. **Homelessness: A Sourcebook**. New York: Facts on File, 1994. 356p. $45.00. ISBN 0-8160-2571-1.

The authors, professors of history and sociology respectively, have compiled a comprehensive resource that covers many aspects of the issue of homelessness and includes definitions, organizations, discussions of issues, places, people, special groups of homeless populations, and history and background. An introductory essay about the homeless in American society is followed by alphabetical entries which range in length from one to two pages. Appendices list resource groups for the homeless, estimated counts of the homeless by state, and a copy of the U.S. Conference of Mayors 1993 States report on the homeless in 26 major cities. There is a bibliography of books and articles and an index. This basic tool is highly recommended for high school sociology and contemporary issues programs. [R: ARBA 95]

852 **The Gay Almanac**. New York: Berkley, 1996. 525p. $16.95pa. ISBN 0-425-15300-2.

853 **The Lesbian Almanac**. New York: Berkley, 1996. 534p. $16.95pa. ISBN 0-425-15301-0.

These two almanacs are identical in structure with some content in common. Each adds information and illustrations appropriate to the relevant perspective. Both were compiled by staff from the National Museum and Archive of Lesbian and Gay History. Coverage includes health and legal issues, history, trivia, and a directory of community centers. Structure is in 9 sections such as history with a chronology from the 16th century to the present, notable North Americans who are gay/lesbian, quotations by and about gays/lesbians, a glossary, statistics and gay/lesbian roles in activism, art, families, literature, religion and sports. Travel suggestions, an AIDS primer, and a directory of organizations and resources

are also included. Various lists of suggested reading are spread throughout. Each volume has an index. These are valuable resources and are recommended for high school collections. [R: ARBA 97]

854 Hombs, Mary Ellen. **American Homelessness: A Reference Handbook**. 2d ed. Santa Barbara, Calif.: ABC-CLIO, 1994. 272p. $39.50. ISBN 0-87436-725-5.

This source complements *Homelessness: A Sourcebook* and would be a good second purchase. After an overview of research on the topic, subject chapters review the problems, events, individuals and give factual material. There are definitions, a chronology, and biographies. Print and nonprint resources are listed and there are both a glossary and an index. [R: ARBA 95]

855 Lerner, Richard, Anne C. Petersen, Jeanne Brooks-Gunn. **Encyclopedia of Adolescence**. 2v. New York: Garland, 1991. $150.00. ISBN 0-8240-4378-2.

Recent research is reflected in this outstanding set, which covers all aspects of adolescence and ranges across disciplines from education and psychology to history and medicine. More than 200 entries cover such topics as eating disorders, drug dependency, cystic fibrosis, phobias, teenagers as parents, academic achievement, and important figures in theory development (e.g. Freud). All are contributed by scholars and other subject specialists. Charts frequently illustrate the text, and bibliographies support all entries. Cross-references and a subject index provide access. Highly recommended for secondary schools. [R: ARBA 92; LJ, 15 May 91; WLB, May 91]

856 Levinson, David, ed. **Encyclopedia of Marriage and the Family**. 2v. New York: Macmillan, 1995. $175.00/set. ISBN 0-02-897235-X.

This excellent encyclopedia is based on a broad and inclusive, interdisciplinary definition of the terms and the 169 articles are from broad viewpoints with subdivisions that deal with related issues. For example the article on divorce has sections about the legal, social, economic, and emotional issues and the effects of divorce on children. Coverage includes such topics as marriage and family types, sexual beliefs and behaviors, family law, communes, ethnicity, gangs, reproduction, and values and religion. Volume 1 contains a list of the signed articles and a list of contributors, and there is an index in volume 2. The articles are arranged in alphabetical order with cross-references; longer articles are signed and have bibliographies. Recommended for high school collections to support family life, health, and sociology curricula. [R: ARBA 96]

857 Maddox, George L., ed. **The Encyclopedia of Aging: A Comprehensive Resource in Gerontology and Geriatrics**. 2d ed. New York: Springer Pub. Co., 1995. 1216p. $159.00. ISBN 0-8261-4841-7.

First published in 1986, the field of aging has changed so rapidly that only 20% of the material is unchanged. This source is multidisciplinary in its approach and is for the non-expert, although some medical information is technical. There is a preliminary list of entries which are then arranged in alphabetical order with cross-references which help to trace issues. Articles are from one to two columns, occasionally longer and are signed. They include many aspects of aging including medical, social, legal, and economic. There is a subject index and an extensive bibliography. Recommended for high school sociology and family life collections. [R: ARBA 96]

858 Manheimer, Ronald J., ed. with North Carolina Center for Creative Retirement, University of North Carolina at Asheville. **Older Americans Almanac: A Reference Work on Seniors in the United States**. Detroit, Mich.: Gale Research, 1994. 881p. $99.50. ISBN 0-8103-8348-9.

Thirty eight chapters cover experiences of and attitudes toward aging from colonial times to the early 1990s. The source is comprehensive in scope, covering history, demographics, diversity, mental, physical, and social processes, government, politics, law, employment and retirement, health care, and lifestyles. Each topic is covered

with facts and narrative that are both informative and explanatory. The entries try to balance advantages and disadvantages to choices the older American faces. Interspersed are sketches and portrait boxes of real people experiencing aging issues. Other charts and tables add to the text. Each section has references for additional reading. A table of contents and index assist in locating specific information and there is an extensive general bibliography. This is an excellent source to support sociology and family life programs in high schools, and would also be useful in social history reference work. [R: ARBA 95]

859 Russell, Paul Elliott. **The Gay 100: A Ranking of the Most Influential Gay Men and Lesbians, Past and Present**. New York: Carol Pub. Group, 1994. 386p. $24.95. ISBN 0-8065-1591-0.

These essays complement the standard biographies of these important men and women because their sexuality is often not mentioned in the standard biographies. These 60 men, 38 women, and two groups that include both men and women were selected and ranked based on their influence on 20th century American and European gay and lesbian identity. Individuals are from ancient times to the present and some are included for whom there is no clear evidence to confirm their homosexuality. After a long introductory essay, the 100 figures are listed in order of influence. Recommended for high school collections. [R: ARBA 96]

860 Stewart, William. **Cassell's Queer Companion: A Dictionary of Lesbian and Gay Life and Culture**. New York: Cassell, 1995. 278p. $18.95pa. ISBN 0-304-34301-3.

The 2,500 terms in this dictionary represent the diversity of perspectives within the gay and lesbian community. The entries are brief and arranged alphabetically with cross-references. The scope of the work is broad as it touches on politics, history, film, literature, popular culture, style, and people. The entries include slang terms, some of which are explicit. The emphasis is the U.K. and the U.S., but coverage is worldwide. [R: RSBL 97]

Sports

BIOGRAPHY

861   Condon, Robert J. **Great Women**
E+   **Athletes of the 20th Century**. Jefferson, N.C.: McFarland, 1991. 180p.
$25.95. ISBN 0-89950-555-4.

This is a selection of 50 historically important
women athletes born in the late 19th and 20th
centuries, with an emphasis on achievement during the 20th century. Each woman is discussed
with a two-page biography which includes essential dates and a photograph. The book is
arranged in a sort of ranked order: the top five,
pioneers, and 35 more. The appendix identifies
the author's pick of the greatest woman athlete
of all time. There is an index. This is a title that
will have both browsing and reference appeal
and can be useful from upper elementary
through high school. [R: ARBA 93]

862   **The Lincoln Library of Sports**
E+   **Champions**. 6th ed. 14v. Columbus,
Ohio: Frontier Press, 1993. $399.00/
set. ISBN 0-912168-14-5.

First published in 1974, the current edition has
fewer individuals than earlier editions. The 297
figures from 25 sports are listed alphabetically
with a capsule summary followed by a four to ten
page sketch which emphasizes the individual's
career. Each entry is accompanied by a portrait
photograph, and there are 2,400 pictures
throughout the volumes, many are full-page and
in color. The emphasis is on North American
athletes, and only about 70 of the entries are
women. The first volume has a table of contents,
and there is an index in the final volume. This set
is appropriate for elementary and middle school
collections. [R: ARBA 95]

863   Sullivan, George. **Great Lives:**
E+   **Sports**. New York: Scribner's/Mac-
millan, 1988. 273p. $22.95. ISBN 0-
684-18510-5.

Students in grades 5 through 8 who require
report material about outstanding athletes will
find this a useful source. The alphabetically
arranged biographies of 24 men and 5 women,
representing 12 sports, highlight personal and

athletic achievements. Photographs and short
bibliographies are included. A table of athletes,
arranged by time period, concludes the volume.
[R: BL, 1 Jan 89; BR, May/June 89; SLJ, Jan 89]

864   Woolum, Janet. **Outstanding Women**
Athletes: Who They Are and How
They Influenced Sports in America.
Phoenix, Ariz.: Oryx Press, 1992.
279p. $39.95. ISBN 0-89774-713-5.

Sixty women athletes from 19 different sports
from the late nineteenth century to 1991 are
included in this source which highlights women's
sporting experiences in America. A few of the
women are not American, but fall into the category of "influencing" American sports. The work
is in three sections. Part 1 is a history of women's
sports; the second part contains the biographies,
arranged alphabetically. Each entry is about 2
pages with a photograph, some with performances charted, and all with suggestions for further reading. The final part of the book has a
bibliography and a list of organizations. The
appendices list Olympic women medallists by
sport, awards and championships, and arranges
the athletes in the book by sport. Coverage over-
laps but does not duplicate Condon's *Great
Women Athletes*. Recommended for middle and
senior high schools. [R: ARBA 93]

CHRONOLOGIES

865   Jarrett, William S. **Timetables of**
E+   **Sports History: Basketball**. New
York: Facts on File,1990. 77p. $17.95.
ISBN 0-8160-1920-7.

866   Jarrett, William S. **Timetables of**
Sports History: Football. New York:
Facts on File,1989. 96p. $17.95. ISBN
0-8160-1919-3.

These year-by-year chronologies, designed for
young readers aged 10 and up, cover regular and
postseason games, All-Star games, players,
teams, stars, awards, honors, Halls of Fame, and
much more. Each year is covered on a separate
page, with columns for different aspects of the
game (e.g., college, professional, postseason

play). Basketball spans the history of the organized sport from 1891 through the 1989 season, covering college and professional games. Football narrates 100 years of professional and college football history. [R: ARBA 90; ARBA 91; BL, Aug 89; BL, Dec 89; VOYA, Feb 90]

DICTIONARIES AND HANDBOOKS

867 Anshel, Mark H., ed. **Dictionary of the Sport and Exercise Sciences**. Champaign, Ill.: Human Kinetics Books, 1991. 163p. $25.00. ISBN 0-87322-305-5.

There are more than 3,000 terms used by sports scientists in this dictionary which has clear and up-to-date definitions of the terms used in adaptive physical education, exercise physiology, and sport pedagogy, psychology, and sociology. Terms related to biomechanics, motor control, development, and learning are included. The volume does not cover sports medicine, physical education, dance or other specific sports. High school library and professional collections will find this a useful reference source. [R: ARBA 93]

868 Cook, Charles. **The Essential Guide to Hiking in the United States**. New York: M. Kesend Pub., 1992. 228p. $18.95pa. ISBN 0-935576-41-X.

This is a guide to major trails and hiking areas in the 50 states, arranged alphabetically by state, each with a map, a resource guide and directory. In addition to the trails highlighted there are references to smaller, local trails. Other sections discuss the basics of hiking such as gear and clothing. The focus here is on day hiking. [R: ARBA 93]

869 Crisfield, Deborah. **Pick-up Games: The Rules, the Players, the Equipment**. New York: Facts on File, 1993. 192p. $27.95. ISBN 0-8160-2700-5.

The games that are included in this guide are based on regular sports such as badminton, baseball, croquet, frisbee, golf, lacrosse, soccer, tennis or volleyball. Each entry gives the established rules and playing areas, then shows informal variations. Each variation is described by number of players, equipment, area, ages, and rules. Other games such as tag and jump rope are also included. There is an appendix of games by

number of players, a glossary, a list of suggested reading and an index. This source has a wide audience of parents, teachers, and students. [R: ARBA 94]

870 The Diagram Group. **Rules of the Game**. rev. ed. New York: St. Martin's Press, 1990. 320p. $24.95. ISBN 0-312-04574-3.

Despite its British origin, the revised edition of *Rules of the Game* is a useful reference work that covers more than 150 sports. Each article, arranged under one of 13 headings (e.g., water, court, team), contains detailed coverage of objectives, playing area, equipment, rules, timing, scoring, participants, and officials. Color illustrations are numerous. A chart lists national and international governing bodies in the United States, Canada, and the United Kingdom for the sports included. General and sports indexes conclude the volume. A number of sports have been added to the revision (e.g., jujitsu, windsurfing, hang gliding), and articles that appeared in the earlier edition have been revised and updated. For high school libraries. [R: BL, 1 Jan 90]

871 **The Guinness Book of Sports**
E+ **Records**. New York: Facts on File, 1991– . annual. $21.95. ISSN 1054-4178.

Information pulled from the Guinness database lists records in 77 sports listed alphabetically from aerobatics to frisbee to tug-of-war, including bungy jumping and inline skating as well as more traditional sports. Entries include a brief history of the sport and then list world, U.S. and (if applicable) Olympic records. Boxed lists and charts, photographs, quotations, interview profiles and trivia questions enliven the routine lists. There are name and subject indexes. All levels will want this annual source.

872 Hickok, Ralph. **Encyclopedia of North American Sports History**. New York: Facts on File, 1992. 516p. $50.00. ISBN 0-8160-2096-5.

This history of sports does not emphasize individuals and teams, but rather the evolution of sport and its administration, legal, financial, issues, and scandals. Entries are about sports, even those which are now obsolete, general topics, (such as Blacks in sports, and television and sports), historical biography, major awards, stadiums, fields and arenas, and sports organizations. Entries are alphabetical and vary from two paragraphs to a page or more. Longer articles have references; there are illustrations. A classified bibliography and an index complete the work. For secondary collections. [R: ARBA 93]

873 **The Information Please Sports**
E+   **Almanac**. Boston: Houghton Mifflin, 1990– . annual. $11.95. ISSN 1045-4980.

This comprehensive annual look at the sporting year covers winners and losers year by year and sport by sport. There is a good table of contents but no index. It includes separate coverage of college and professional sports, and other professional sports from golf and bowling to horse and auto racing. For each sport there is an essay describing the year in review with the last year's statistics, standings, leaders, teams, playoff, awards, and a brief history. Separate sections cover halls of fame and awards, who's who in sports, ballparks and arenas, directories of sports business and the media, Olympic Games and international sports. Other features include an obituary section, rankings of top teams, coaches, players, and key games. Recommended for all collections.

874 **Racing on the Tour de France: And**
E+   **Other Stories of Sports**. Columbus, Ohio: Saner-Bloser, 1989. 63p. $19.95pa. ISBN 0-88309-546-7.

The 18 articles in this book, drawn from the last 20 years of *Highlights for Children* magazine, cover children's activities and sports, even fencing and skydiving. Each of the three-page essays includes a history of the sport and the rules, equipment, and skills required to play it. Sidebars list facts, organizations, books about the sport, and further activities. Recommended for upper elementary and middle school levels. [R: SLJ, Mar 90]

875   Rooney, John F. and Richard Pillsbury. **Atlas of American Sport**. New York: Macmillan, 1992. 198p. $80.00. ISBN 0-02-897351-8.

This book is a delight to the eye and the intellect from the first map (showing *Sports Illustrated* subscriptions per capita throughout the United States) to maps showing the distribution of types of equestrian events and the distribution of birthplaces of heavyweight champions. The work explores the geographical elements of sports in the United States by mapping such distributions as facilities, players, and activities. Sports were chosen for inclusion if data were available to make these kinds of representations. Introductory chapters discuss sport and society, sports and regions, and the world of American sport. With narrative, tables, photographs, charts and the maps, individual sports then are presented alphabetically and include such varied events as baseball, fox hunting, golf, lacrosse, the rodeo, tennis, wrestling and many others. Some women's sports are represented. There is also a sports gazetteer and both general and geographical indexes. In addition to its basic reference applications and its browsing interest, this source is an inspiration for interdisciplinary units involving math, sociology, physical education, geography, language arts and computer skills. [R: ARBA 94]

876   Sherrow, Victoria. **Encyclopedia of Women and Sports**. Santa Barbara, Calif.: ABC-CLIO, 1996. 382p. $60.00. ISBN 0-87436-826-X.

The valuable introduction to this work traces the history of women and sports as a parallel to the struggle for women's rights. The scope of the encyclopedia includes biographies of women, sports, sporting events, associations, issues such as eating disorders and steroids, dress and equipment, and awards. Emphasis of the entries is primarily the last half of the 20th century and American.

Entries are alphabetical with both see and see also cross-references. More than 50 photographs are included, but they are not balanced among the entries and many are repetitive. A timeline covers the topic from 776 B.C. (when women were forbidden to even watch the Olympics) to 1996. There is a good bibliography and an index. Highly recommended for secondary schools as a supplement to history classes, and for women studies and sports. [R: ARBA 97]

877 **Sports Illustrated for Kids: The Everything You Want to Know about Sports Encyclopedia**. Portland, Oreg.: Creative Multimedia, 1994. CD-ROM (Windows). $30.00.

This exciting multimedia encyclopedia requires a sound card (and earphones). The content is broad and includes the major team and individual sports as well as such sports as curling and bullfighting. Searching is well explained and simple to follow with object clicks to individual sport tables of contents. Included are video clips (shown on a TV screen), slide shows (in framed slides), and brief text. Interviews with kids who participate in the sport add a good dimension. There are addresses to write for more information on most sports. One of the games has not only questions about specific sports, but explanations and background about the right answers, and becomes an important learning device. Highly recommended for all levels. Find a dedicated workstation.

878 White, Jess R., ed. **Sports Rules Encyclopedia**. 2d ed. Champaign, Ill.: Human Kinetics Pub., 1990. 732p. $19.95pa. ISBN 0-87322-457-4.

This is a compilation of the official rules of 52 sports, most reprinted from the national associations' rule books. The table of contents lists all sports covered which are arranged alphabetically and include such sports as archery, croquet, cricket, trampolining and wrestling as well as more typical sports. Each set of rules gives safety, diagrams of fields or courts, equipment, the name of the governing organization, and magazines and journals which cover the sport. An appendix lists organizations concerned with sports for the disabled, and another lists 22 associations and their addresses with rules not included in this source. This source will be useful to students and to teachers and other adults with responsibilities for organized sports programs.

BASEBALL

879 **The Baseball Encyclopedia: The Complete and Definitive Record of Major League Baseball**. 10th ed. New York: Macmillan, 1996. 3000p. $59.95. ISBN 0-02-860815-1.

This is the statistical guide to the sport that will settle arguments. After a brief history of the game, lists and tables and names and numbers deal with teams and players, and home versus road performance, trades, world series, playoffs, and all-star games. Sections include the Negro Leagues and the All-American girls professional

baseball league. Appendices list sources, decisions of the Records Committee and major changes in playing and scoring rules. Middle and high school collections will want this.

880 Dickson, Paul. **The Dickson Baseball Dictionary**. New York: Facts on File, 1989. 438p. $14.95pa. ISBN 0-380-71335-7.

E+

This dictionary is for lovers of baseball and words. It includes 5,000 words, terms, and phrases related to and coined from the sport, and as in a regular dictionary lists terms from A to Z and gives part of speech, definition, synonyms, usage notes, origin, etymology and use of the term outside of baseball. It does not include biographical entries, but does include terms coined from players; e.g. "Ruthian." It is illustrated with photographs and is both a reference and browsing source. There is a good bibliography. Recommended for all collections.

881 Filichia, Peter. **Professional Baseball Franchises: From the Abbeville Athletics to the Zanesville Indians**. New York: Facts on File, 1993. 290p. $25.95. ISBN 0-8160-2647-5.

This unique sports reference lists every city in which established major or minor league baseball has been played professionally since 1869. It includes the Negro leagues. Arranged alphabetically by city name, teams are listed by name, nickname, and dates with notes about other cities where the franchise moved. There is a list of teams without cities in their names with reference to the city where they played. There is an appendix of leagues, a bibliography, and a team nickname index. A state index would also have been helpful. This is a history and social reference work as well as a ready-reference fact finder, and it has browsing interest as well. Recommended for secondary collections. [R: ARBA 94]

882 Johnson, Lloyd, Miles Wolff and Steve McDonald, eds. **The Encyclopedia of Minor League Baseball: The Official Record of Minor League Baseball**. 2d ed. Durham, N.C.: Baseball America, 1997. 666p. $48.95. ISBN 0-9637189-8-3.

This work is the most comprehensive guide to minor league baseball. Information about teams, leagues and players and managers is presented in a variety of sections. There is a chronology titled "This Date in Minor League History" which covers 1883–1996. Recommended for secondary collections, especially in areas with minor league teams.

883 LaBlanc, Michael L., ed. **Baseball**.
E+   Detroit, Mich.: Gale Research, 1994. 572p. $39.95. ISBN 0-8103-8858-8.

This history, a volume in the Professional Sports Team Histories series, traces the development of American professional baseball, emphasizing the 20th century. After an introductory summary chapter of baseball as a whole, separate chapters show the development of current major league franchises, arranged by league and division as they were organized in the early 1990s. Team histories are told in the order that major players and coaches brought fame to the team's performance. There are charts, photographs and player profiles. A final essay briefly describes the Negro Leagues. Bibliographies are included with each chapter and there is a personal name index. This is a useful volume for baseball history and is appropriate for upper elementary through high school. [R: ARBA 95]

884 Light, Jonathan Fraser. **The Cultural Encyclopedia of Baseball**. Jefferson, N.C.: McFarland, 1997. 888p. $75.00. ISBN 0-7864-0311-X.

This source complements all of the statistical guides with historical and anecdotal information. Arranged alphabetically, the entries cover parks, teams, players, plays and all sorts of other delightful facts. Some illustrations and a great many quotations add to the fun. This is a source that will be used to satisfy reference inquiries (what uniform numbers have been retired from each team) and for browsing pleasure. Despite the expense, this is recommended for all secondary collections.

885 Lowry, Philip J. **Green Cathedrals:**
E+   **The Ultimate Celebration of All 273 Major League and Negro League Ballparks**. 2d ed. Reading, Mass.: Addison-Wesley, 1992. 275p. $15.95pa. ISBN 0-201-62229-7.

The purpose of this source is to list every ballpark ever used for a professional game in the Major and Negro Leagues from 1871 to the present. Such games include regular season, playoff, league championships, old era and modern World Series, and all-star. It does not include pre-season or exhibition games, nor minor leagues. In addition to the anecdotes, stories, and statistics given for each ballpark, the book shows how parks have changed and gives a basis for comparing players from different time periods. The foreword and introduction are worth reading. There is a list of all leagues included. The first part of the book lists current major league ballparks arranged alphabetically by city, and part two describes former parks. Each entry gives alternate names or nicknames of the parks, the teams who play or played there, capacity, largest crowd, surface, dimensions, fences, former and current uses; and a section labeled "phenomena" tells historical data, special features, changes and other interesting details in a personal style: "the best crab cakes in baseball were served [at old Memorial Stadium in Baltimore]." This wonderful book belongs in every sports collection at all grade levels. [R: ARBA 94]

886 Neft, David and Richard M. Cohen.
E+   **Sports Encyclopedia: Baseball**. 17th ed. New York: St. Martin's Press, 1997. 720p. $19.99pa. ISBN 0-312-15213-2.

This is a standard work, which contains accurate and complete information through the season previous to publication. The print is small and there is no index, but the records cover year-by-year rosters with players' statistics for teams in each league and statistics for batters and pitchers by period since 1901. Fans will appreciate this volume in reference collections from upper elementary through high school. [R: ARBA 95]

887 **Official Baseball Register**. St. Louis, Mo.: Sporting News, 1973– . annual. $12.95pa. ISSN 0162-542X.

A comprehensive and authoritative work, the *Register* contains batting, baserunning, pitching, and fielding records for players, clubs, and leagues. Also included are the records of managers, umpires, All-Star games, the Championship series, and the World Series. The *Register* gives lifetime personal and statistical data for every active player and manager in the major leagues.

888 **Total Baseball: The Official Encyclopedia of Major League Baseball**. 5th ed. New York: Viking/Penguin, 1997. 2458p. $64.95. ISBN 0-670-87511-2.

Both statistics and narrative are offered in this guide. The player position sections make up the bulk of the book, with brief biographical and playing data. The arrangement is clear and the information accessible. The narrative essays add a dimension to the work that is absent from the other statistical guides and cover such things as movies about baseball and the sport in other countries. This is a usable and useful guide for secondary collections.

BASKETBALL

889 LaBlanc, Michael L., ed. **Basketball**.
E+ Detroit, Mich.: Gale Research, 1994. 420p. $39.95. ISBN 0-8103-8860-X.

After an extensive history of professional basketball in the United States (the NBA), the development of each team is described in chapters that chronologically follow the careers of leading players or coaches who characterize an era in the team's history. Photographs and charts accompany the text and there is a bibliography of books, articles and other publications at the end of each team's chapter. There is an index of personal names. As in the other books in the Professional Sports Team Histories, the text readability and interest levels range from upper elementary through high school.

890 **NBA Register**. St. Louis, Mo.: Sporting News, 1983– . annual. $12.95pa. ISSN 0739-3067.

The *Register* provides personal data and career statistics of every active professional player and rookie, plus a section of records and statistics for active coaches.

891 **The Sporting News Official NBA**
E+ **Guide**. St. Louis, Mo.: Sporting News, 1994– . annual. $15.95. ISSN 0078-3862.

This annual is the guide to the history and current activities of the National Basketball Association. It contains directories of the teams and all players, histories of the game, team photographs, court diagrams, the past year in review, official rules, and lists of names and statistics. There is an index. Recommended for all collections.

FISHING

892 **The Dorling Kindersley Encyclopedia of Fishing**. New York: Dorling Kindersley, 1994. 288p. $39.95. ISBN 1-56458-492-5.

This lavishly illustrated visual encyclopedia gives narrative descriptions and explanations with charts, boxes, tables, and color photographs of equipment and clothing, fishing techniques, and species of game fish. Divided into sections on tackle, bait, flies, fish, techniques, and water, the encyclopedia deals with both freshwater and saltwater fishing. The table of contents, and both general and scientific name indexes provide good access to the information. This is both a browsing and reference item.

FOOTBALL

893 LaBlanc, Michael L., ed. **Football**.
E+ Detroit, Mich.: Gale Research, 1994. 535p. $39.95. ISBN 0-8103-8861-8.

Although there is a brief discussion of the development of football and how it developed from rugby into a college sport in America, the focus of this book, as in the other titles in the Professional Sports Team Histories series is on the history of the National Football League and its team franchises. Each team is described in a separate section; arrangement is by conference and division as they were organized in the early 1990s. Given the sometimes bizarre shifts in ownership and city affiliations, these histories can be complex, e.g. most of the "history" of the Indianapolis Colts occurred in Baltimore. A personal name index does not help much with these distinctions. Appropriate for upper elementary through high school.

894 Neft, David, and Richard M. Cohen.
E+ **The Sports Encyclopedia. Pro Football, the Modern Era, 1972–1996**. 15th ed. New York: St. Martin's Press, 1997. 768p. $19.99pa. ISBN 0-312-15662-6.

This inexpensive and comprehensive statistical record book of professional football gives statistics chronologically and by conference and division. Annual rankings, game scores, players' performances and win-loss records are all included. A narrative gives highlights of the preceding year. There are no indexes and chapter titles are more clever than helpful, but most school libraries will want this in the reference collection. [R: ARBA 95]

895 **Pro Football Register**. St. Louis, Mo.: The Sporting News, 1991– . annual. $15.95. ISSN 0071-7258.

The *Register* focuses on players and coaches. Each player's entry gives age, weight, birthplace, education, awards, honors, records, and year-by-year performance statistics for his professional career. Information for each coach includes biographical data and a career summary. The annual's arrangement is alphabetical in each section.

896 **Total Football: The Official Encyclopedia of the National Football League**. New York: HarperCollins, 1997. 1652p. $55.00. ISBN 0-06-270170-3.

This guide provides comprehensive coverage of every player in the league since its beginning in 1920. It also gives college draft results and chooses the 300 greatest players and 25 greatest games. Some history of football and the league is included. Most high school collections will find this useful.

HOCKEY

897 **Hockey Guide**. St. Louis, Mo.: Sporting News, 1985– . annual. $10.95pa. ISSN 0278-4955.

898 **Hockey Register**. St. Louis, Mo.: Sporting News, 1969– . annual. $14.95pa. ISSN 0090-2292.

These annual publications thoroughly cover the National Hockey League. The *Guide* reviews the previous season and playoffs, and gives the current season's schedule and entry draft; complete team directories, including managers, team rosters, and records; and team and player statistics for every North American hockey league and American college team.

The *Register* provides career information for all players during the previous season, with names listed alphabetically in separate sections for forwards, defenders and goaltenders. Each entry gives vital statistics, injuries, shooting side, and career statistics.

899 Hollander, Zander, ed. **Inside Sports Magazine Hockey**. Detroit, Mich.: Visible Ink Press, 1997. 725p. $19.95. ISBN 0-7876-0876-9.

Visible Ink Press, Gale Research's popular press imprint, adds the former *Complete Encyclopedia of Hockey* to its list of titles. This hockey guide includes not only statistical information, but also a history of the National Hockey League, brief biographies of Hall of Fame players, records and rules. Good full-page photographs and good typeface add to the text. There is an index. Recommended for secondary collections.

900 LaBlanc, Michael L., ed. **Hockey**.
E+ Detroit, Mich.: Gale Research, 1994. 472p. $39.95. ISBN 0-8103-8862-6.

Hockey has one of the most interesting histories of any sport, and this volume from the Professional Sports Team Histories series traces hockey's development from its beginnings in ancient Britain to its organized professional status today. After this introductory chapter, separate sections trace the history and development of every NHL team, arranged by division. Each team chapter includes charts, photographs and player profiles, as well as a season-by-season summary of the team's performance. A final essay about the Stanley Cup concludes the text. There is an index of personal names. This book is appropriate for both reference and circulating collections and is easy enough for upper elementary fans and comprehensive enough for high school students. Recommended for all levels.

OLYMPIC GAMES

901 Wallechinsky, David. **The Complete Book of the Olympics**. New York: Viking Press, 1992. 763p. $29.95; $14.95pa. ISBN 0-316-92054-1; 0-316-92053-3pa.

This provides a comprehensive listing of every event in every modern (since 1896) Olympic game with a brief narrative, date, place, number of competitors, and nations represented. When appropriate, note is made of the world record in the event and the top finishers, countries and times. Introductory material includes a list of the games, places, and dates, medal totals arranged by country and a brief history of the Olympics and some of the issues surrounding the games. Organization of the volume is by event, then chronological. It includes discontinued events. There is no index. This is a source of information not easily found elsewhere. [R: ARBA 93]

SOCCER

902 LaBlanc, Michael L. and Richard Henshaw. **The World Encyclopedia of Soccer**. Detroit, Mich.: Visible Ink Press, 1994. 430p. $39.95; $14.95pa. ISBN 0-8103-8995-9; 0-8103-9442-1pa.

This is a comprehensive guide to the international sport of soccer. Entries cover history, rules, and tactics. About 80 players are profiled as are teams from major nations. Special sections cover disasters and tragedies, the international ruling body, FIFA (the Federation Internationale de Football Association), soccer in the United States, women's soccer and Olympic soccer. Seven appendices include a timeline, glossary, early rules, cup competitions, stadiums, witchcraft, and pre-Columbian games. Recommended for secondary collections. [R: ARBA 95]

903 Rollin, Jack. **The World Cup, 1930–1990: Sixty Glorious Years of Soccer's Premier Event**. New York: Facts on File, 1990. 191p. $24.95. ISBN 0-8160-2523-1.

The first section of this work, which surveys the competition, covers each of the 14 previous tournaments (starting in 1930), reports events on and off the field, provides basic statistics for each game, and provides several black-and-white photographs. Two-page biographies of 21 famous players comprise the second section; a third covers all teams that made the 1990 finals.

Appendixes include World Cup records, World Cup trivia, FIFA-affiliated countries, and "Looking Ahead: USA 1994." Indexed by personal name. This handbook is useful at all levels. [R: ARBA 92]

WRESTLING

904 Chapman, Mike. **Encyclopedia of American Wrestling**. Champaign, Ill.: Human Kinetics, 1991. 533p. $25.95pa. ISBN 0-88011-342-1.

This is a book of wrestling records with some historical information. Fourteen chapters, each with a narrative introduction, list tournament and award winners year by year and weight class by weight class. It covers the Olympics, world tournaments, the AAU National Freestyle Championships, the U.S. Freestyle Senior Open, the Greco-Roman Nationals, the collegiate Nationals, the Midland Championships, the Junior nationals , and the Junior World Tournaments. Lists of hall of fame members and a discussion of professional wrestling are included. An appendix has biographies of members of the National Wrestling Hall of Fame. This is a useful compilation of the facts and records of wrestling.

Statistics

□ ──────────────────────────────── □

THE WORLD

905 O'Donnell, Timothy S., and others, eds. **World Economic Data**. 3d ed. Santa Barbara, Calif.: ABC-CLIO, 1991. 261p. $35.00. ISBN 0-87436-658-5.

This fact book contains reliable data about the world's economy. Part 1 gives information on 171 nations, including budgets, international liquidity, imports/exports, trading partners, tourism, natural resources, and natural gas production. U.S. economic indicators, covered in part 2, include business cycles, gross national production, employment, energy, inflation, banking, gold, stocks, and bonds. World currency rates and data on U.S. foreign trade by region and nation also appear. Highly recommended for high schools. [R: ARBA 93]

906 Showers, Victor. **World Facts and Figures**. 3d ed. New York: Wiley, 1989. 721p. $109.95. ISBN 0-471-85775-0.

With tabular data for 218 countries, and 2,664 cities based on 19 subjects, this source provides a means of identifying and comparing countries and cities in the same way states, cities, and small towns in the United States are popularly ranked. Each country's profile includes data about such categories as area, population, birth and death rates, life expectancy, energy production, GNP, and rates of illiteracy. Rankings allow comparisons within a variety of areas from educational institutions to engineering projects. One can find the 100 largest libraries and the 561 highest, biggest, and longest man-made objects. There are also demographic and geographic rankings. Tables are clear and easy to read. There is a selected classified bibliography and an extensive index. Highly recommended for high school collections.

UNITED STATES

907 Bureau of Statistics, Treasury Department. **Statistical Abstracts of the United States**. Washington, D.C.: Government Printing Office, 1878– . annual. $37.85. ISSN 0081-4741.

Since 1878 this has been the standard summary of statistics on the social, political, and economic organization of the United States. The emphasis is on national data such as population, vital statistics and many other aspects of the country, from changes in population and area 1790–1990 to recent trends in sporting and athletic goods. Hundreds of tables are grouped in broad subject areas with sources identified. There is an extensive index. The data is available on the Internet at http://www.census.gov/prod/www/abs/cc97stab.htm but most libraries will continue to want the book version as well.

908 Crampton, Norman. **The 100 Best Small Towns in America**. New York: Prentice Hall, 1993. 392p. $12.00pa. ISBN 0-671-84671-X.

The criteria for selection in this version of "best" books were a population between 5,000 and 15,000 and growing, and an independent economic base not dependent on a large metropolitan area. The eligible towns were then evaluated on per capita income, population diversity, percent of population in the 25–34 year age group, percent of college graduates, number of physicians, numbers of serious crimes, and amount of local funding for education. The authors also wanted to balance the town locations across the

country and almost all states are represented; comparisons were thus made within states rather than within the country as a whole. Final decisions were based on the advantages of being a county seat town, having a local newspaper, having a college, scenery, proximity to a metropolitan area and telephone interviews with people who actually live in the towns. The results are presented on a map of the U.S. and then by alphabetical listings by town presenting all of the data found and excerpts from the interviews. A set of tables showing rankings by the various criteria concludes the book. Useful as a source for state reports as well as a formula to follow for interdisciplinary projects. [R: ARBA 94]

909 Savageau, David and Geoffrey Loftus. **Places Rated Almanac: Your Guide to Finding the Best Places to Live in North America**. 5th ed. New York: Macmillan, 1997. 421p. $21.95. ISBN 0-02-861233-7.

Published since 1981 this source ranks areas in the United States and Canada on the basis of such categories as living costs, job outlook, housing, transportation, education, health care, crime, the arts, recreation and climate and gives an almanac-like collection of interesting, odd, and useful information about the metropolitan areas where most people live. There are separate chapters on each of the 10 rankings and profiles of the areas ranked. Charts, tables, maps and diagrams add to the listings.

An appendix gives a list of complexities and components of the choices and a list of the areas ranked by state and province. The CD-ROM version contains all the data for the rankings and allows one to choose and weight components that go into the rankings so that the user determines what is most important in order to create personalized rankings. The almanac is useful for a variety of curricular areas and can be the foundation for interdisciplinary math and social studies units.

910 **State Rankings**. Lawrence, Ks.: Morgan Quitno Corp., 1990– . annual. $43.95. ISSN 1065-1403.

This is an easy to read and useful source to compare states in all sorts of categories. All categories are ranked by state and listed alphabetically for each state. The sources of the 546 tables are federal agencies and commercial business data sources, and health organizations. Sources are all indicated. Tables include rankings by categories such as agriculture, crime, education (including number of public libraries and books in libraries per capita), health, and so on. Tables are easy to read because they give data in whole numbers and are shaded for quick access. A good index leads to specific information. Individual state profiles are also available and the source is available as a computer file.

911 **Statistical Record of Children**. Detroit, Mich.: Gale Research, 1994– . biennial. $99.00. ISSN 1075-5063.

Statistics from the U.S. Census Bureau and other sources are arranged with commentary in a way that will be useful for making national and international comparisons. Data presented in 900 tables deal with such topics as adoption, health, educational proficiency and standards, economic well-being, child care, and crime. The statistics are about children up to the age of 14 except for some categories where data cover a broader age range, such as from ages 12–17. Tables are arranged alphabetically by broad subject category and are numbered sequentially. There is an excellent keyword index that makes it simple to trace data by state. This is an important source for any professional collection in district libraries where it will provide reliable statistical data to be used to support curricular and general educational reform. [R: ARBA 95]

912 Thomas, G. Scott. **The Rating Guide to Life in America's Small Cities**. Buffalo, N.Y.: Prometheus Books, 1990. 538p. $41.95; $20.95pa. ISBN 0-87975-599-7; 0-87975-600-4pa.

This complements other rating guides which look only at larger metropolitan areas by listing "micropolitan" areas. The criteria for inclusion is an area with a central city of at least 15,000 residents, in a county of 40,000 residents which is not part of a designated metropolitan area. This includes about 6.5% of the population. After an introduction there is a list of the areas by state. Based on such categories as climate, diversions, education, sophistication, health care, housing, public safety, transportation and urban proximity, the areas are ranked by state. There are also

top ten summaries by region and a national ranking. There is a list of tables and an index. This can be a source to support geography and sociology classes, to inspire interdisciplinary units, and for browsing. Highly recommended for secondary collections.

913 United States. Bureau of the Census. **Historical Statistics of the United States, Colonial Times to 1970**. 2v. Washington, D.C.: Department of Commerce, Bureau of the Census, 1975. $68.00. S/N 003-024-00120-9.

The standard source for historical data, this covers a variety of topical information with statistics. Part one covers such things as population, migration, crime, crops, earnings, and prices, while part two focuses on manufacturing, transportation, energy, and government. Both volumes have time period and subject indexes. The statistics provide a survey of American history from a perspective that is supplemental to that provided in textbooks. Highly recommended for middle and high school collections.

914 **USA Counties**. Washington, D.C.: U.S. Department of Commerce, Bureau of the Census, 1992. CD-ROM (Windows, Macintosh). $150.00.

This CD-ROM includes all data published in the *City and County Data Book* (1983, 1988, and 1994) and the *State and Metropolitan Area Data Book* (1982, 1986, and 1991) with revisions not found in the originals. Data are from the Bureau of the Census and other federal agencies. Demographic, economic, and governmental data from 3,475 variables are available for single county profiles or multi-county comparisons. Information is based on the 1990 census and later estimates with a variety of data about states, counties, cities and places in the United States. Data tables and area rankings help give meaning to the statistics. For example, one table ranks the top 25 U.S. counties by total population, growth, people per square mile, highest percentage of population under 18. There are tables by state, by county, by cities with populations of more than 25,000 and places with populations of 2,500 or more. Subjects included in rankings include agriculture, banking, crime, health, housing, personal income, vehicles available, and many others.

Data are more easily retrieved in the CD-ROM version, but ease of comparison may still suggest the purchase of print versions as well. Some of the information is available on the Internet at www.census.gov. In whatever format, the data remain useful for applications of statistical data in social studies classes.

Women's Studies

See also other subjects and disciplines such as **Biography, Political Science, Sports** and **Literature (Humanities)**.

ATLASES

915 Fast, Timothy and Cathy Carroll Fast. **The Women's Atlas of the United States**. rev. ed. New York: Facts on File, 1995. 246p. $75.00. ISBN 0-8160-2970-9.

First published in 1985, the revised edition of *The Women's Atlas* examines new issues and the ways in which former issues changed in a decade. Thematic mapping of data with new computer generated maps and the use of symbols and charts make the atlas graphically interesting. Chapters include education, employment, family, health, crime and politics and use narrative and maps to discuss these issues within 11 geographic regions. An appendix, bibliography of sources consulted for map data, and an index complete the volume. A list of only seven books for further reading might well have been omitted, and there are some minor errors; e.g., Louisa Adams is referred to as Louise in both index and text. [R: ARBA 96]

BIOGRAPHY

916 Bataille, Gretchen M., ed. **Native American Women: A Biographical Dictionary**. New York: Garland, 1993. 333p. $40.00. ISBN 0-8240-5267-6.

A dictionary of more than 200 women, the majority of whom lived in the twentieth century. The women are listed alphabetically with other names by which they are known. There are brief signed entries about their lives and contributions with references for further reading and information. Appendices list the women by primary area of specialization, by decade of birth, place of birth and by tribal affiliation. There is also an index. [R: ARBA 94]

917 James, Edward T., ed. **Notable American Women, 1607–1950: A Biographical Dictionary**. 3v. Cambridge, Mass.: Belknap Press, 1973. $45.00. ISBN 0-674-62734-2.

918 Sicherman, Barbara, and Carol H. Green, ed. **Notable American Women, The Modern Period: A Biographical Dictionary**. Cambridge, Mass.: Belknap Press, 1983. 773p. $32.00pa. ISBN 0-674-62733-4.

Modeled on the *Dictionary of American Biography*, this set stands alone but is a good complement to that set which contained only 700 women of 15,000 entries. The preparation of the first set of *Notable American Women* was supported by Radcliffe College. It includes women from 1607 to those who died before the end of 1950; only 5 women included were born after 1900. Arranged throughout the volumes alphabetically, entries are from 400 to 7,000 words and have bibliographies. There is a good introductory essay and a classified list of entries in volume three.

The supplemental volume includes 442 women who died between January 1, 1951 and December 31, 1975. There was a major effort to include minority women, and foreign-born women are included as well. Criteria for selection include an influence on time or field, a pioneering or innovative quality, the significance of achievement, or a relevance of the career in the history of women. The volume follows the pattern of the main set with an excellent introduction, full entries with bibliographies and a classified list of entries. This set should be in middle and high school collections.

919 Opfell, Olga S. **Queens, Empresses, Grand Duchesses and Regents: Women Rulers of Europe, A.D. 1328–1989**. Jefferson, N.C.: McFarland, 1989. 282p. $37.50. ISBN 0-89950-385-3.

This volume includes lively biographical sketches of 40 women who have served as reigning monarchs or ruling regents in Europe. Consorts are excluded. Four- to eight-page essays on each ruler, arranged alphabetically, include a portrait of the subject and a selective bibliography. Indexed. Recommended for secondary schools. [R: ARBA 90]

920 Salem, Dorothy C., ed. **African American Women: A Biographical Dictionary**. New York: Garland, 1993. 622p. $75.00. ISBN 0-8240-8782-3.

The group of women selected for inclusion in this dictionary includes those chosen for both historical reasons and for contemporary accomplishment. Nearly 300 women from Lucy Terry (b. 1730) to Gail Devers (b. 1966) are listed alphabetically with cross-references from alternative names and related articles. The entries are both summaries and analytical descriptions of their work and contributions. Each entry is about one page, is signed, and has a brief bibliographic essay. There are photographic inserts. An appendix classifies the individuals by career, and there is an index. Coverage and content sometimes duplicate information in *Black Women in America*. [R: ARBA 94]

921 Talgen, Diane and Jim Kamp, eds. **Notable Hispanic American Women**. Detroit, Mich.: Gale Research, 1993. 448p. $59.95. ISBN 0-8103-7578-8.

Nearly 300 women of Hispanic heritage are included in this dictionary, almost all of whom lived in the 20th century and many of whom are contemporary figures with whom personal interviews were conducted. There is a contents list of entries with an occupation index and an ethnicity index preceding the alphabetically arranged signed articles. The biographical sketches vary from 500 to 2,500 words and many

are accompanied by photographs. Information includes personal, family and career details; the writing is informal, and details often seem irrelevant. A subject index completes the work. [R: ARBA 94]

922 Tinling, Marion. **Women Remembered: A Guide to Landmarks of Women's History in the United States**. Westport, Conn.: Greenwood Press, 1986. 796p. $85.00. ISBN 0-313-23984-3.

This guide provides access to monuments, memorials, and buildings associated with feminist history in America. It does not include items associated with women who were living at the time of publication, nor women famous only because of their associations with men, nor generic landmarks associated with groups of women. All of the sites included are public and include statues, markers, homes, bridges, trails, parks, public artwork, and institutions. Arranged by five geographic regions, the entries are then arranged by state, by city, and by name. Cross-references and an index help locate entries. There is a bibliography for each state. An appendix has a classified list of women by region; another has a list of significant dates. This is a useful guide for fieldtrips and for supplemental women's history projects.

923 **Who's Who of American Women**. Chicago: Marquis Who's Who, Inc., 1971– . biennial. $225.00. ISSN 0083-9841.

Published since 1958 this version of *Who's Who* follows the format of the companion volume. The 20th edition lists 29,000 notable living women, based on accomplishment, position, or achievement.

ENCYCLOPEDIAS AND HANDBOOKS

924 Bernikow, Louise. **The American Women's Almanac: An Inspiring and Irreverent Women's History**. New York: Berkeley, 1997. 388p. $16.95pa. ISBN 0-425-15616-8.

A reference search in this work may get lost in the sheer fun of finding a new quotation, photograph or poster. Coverage includes politics, the female body, the female body in motion, the female mind, writers and artists, entertainers, media, domestic life and work. Each section begins with an essay and includes brief entries about related people and events. The index allows some access for reference, but the volume will be most useful for identifying topics for reports. It will also be used for browsing and the illustrations may be useful for student reports. Recommended for high school collections.

925 Clark, Judith Freeman. **Almanac of American Women in the 20th Century**. New York: Prentice Hall, 1987. 274p. $15.95pa. ISBN 0-13-022658-0.

This is a chronology of facts and details of American women's lives from 1900 to the mid 1980s. It combines almanac entries, biographies and topic essays arranged by decade. Entries include events, issues, popular culture, education, labor, politics, science, art, and culture—all from women's perspectives. Illustrations add to the narrative. There is a name index.

926 Cullen-DuPont, Kathryn. **The Encyclopedia of Women's History in America**. New York: Facts on File, 1996. 339p. $45.00. ISBN 0-8160-2625-4.

Alphabetical entries cover laws and court cases, speeches, books, organizations, terms and phrases, documents and individual women. The women included were selected based on such criteria as those who affected American history, those important in the debate about equal rights, barrier breaking women, and those who made contributions to cultural and intellectual life. Thus there are writers, artists, politicians, and activists from all parts of the political spectrum. Entries vary in length and have suggestions for further information. An appendix lists 34 full-text documents, there is an extensive bibliography and an index. Recommended for both middle and high schools. [R: ARBA 97]

927 Franck, Irene M. and David Brownstone. **The Women's Desk Reference**. New York: Viking, 1993. 840p. $29.95. ISBN 0-670-84513-2.

The authors, who are experienced in reference compilations rather than women's studies, have collected basic reference material on key issues to all women of all ages, from traditionalist to feminist perspectives. Arranged alphabetically with cross-references, but without an index, the entries represent a wide array of concerns, issues, people, organizations, events, and include medical and anatomical terms. Tables and fact boxes accompany the text and some entries list additional resources or suggestions for further reading. Entries vary from a quarter of a page to eight pages or more. Each entry presents a balanced overview, an indication of controversy, and a description of the significance of the topic to women. A special information section includes documents, bibliographies and statistics. This is a useful, basic, and balanced approach to the subject and is highly recommended for high school collections. [R: ARBA 95]

928 Franck, Irene, and David Brownstone. **Women's World: A Timeline of Women in History**. New York: Harper Perennial, 1995. 654p. $22.50. ISBN 0-06-273336-2.

This chronology presents the woman's side of history from 35,000 B.C. to 1993. Running heads and an index provide easy access to the data which is arranged in various chunks of time. From A.D. 1500 on, the entries are divided into categories of politics/law/war, religion/education/ everyday life, science/technology/medicine, and arts/literature. After 1830, the entries become year by year. Illustrations, quotations, documents and sidebars add interest as well as information. Useful as a history supplement and for women's studies in high schools. [R: ARBA 96]

929 Hine, Darlene Clark, ed. **Black Women in America: An Historical Encyclopedia**. 2v. Brooklyn, N.Y.: Carlson Pub., 1993. $195.00/set. ISBN 0-926019-61-9.

This is a comprehensive guide to the lives of 641 individual Black women most of whom are significant on a national level. There are also entries to more than 150 general topics and organizations involving Black women. Listed alphabetically, the signed entries have bibliographies and many have photographs. The length of the articles vary from one or two columns to multiple pages, especially for the topical entries. Entries are balanced and easily comprehensible. The appendices include a chronology, a classified bibliography, including a directory of research centers, and the biographies classified by occupations. There is an extensive index. Recommended as a first purchase among the new biographical sources about Black women for high school libraries. [R: ARBA 94]

930 Maggio, Rosalie, comp. **The Beacon Book of Quotations by Women**. Boston: Beacon Press, 1992. 390p. $25.00. ISBN 0-8070-6764-4.

This is a good supplement to standard quotations books. It is arranged by topic, from absence to youth, with cross-references. Quotes appear in the original language, even if that might seem to be sexist today. Quotes included vary from short to long, and identify source of quotation by name, place, and date; the women quoted are from all times and locations. There is a name index with biographical identifier and a broad subject index. [R: ARBA 94]

931 McElroy, Lorie Jenkins, ed. **Women's Voices: A Documentary History of Women in America**. 2v. Detroit, Mich.: U*X*L, 1997. $55.00. ISBN 0-7876-0663-4.

Primary source materials covering historical events that have affected women are arranged by subjects such as education, suffrage and reproductive rights. Included are diaries, speeches, memoirs, poetry and documents. Each entry includes biographical sketches of the author and a historical overview that places the entry in context. Many photographs, a glossary, a timeline and an index add to the use of the set. Recommended for secondary libraries.

932 McFadden, Margaret, ed. **Women's Issues**. 3v. Pasadena, Calif.: Salem Press, 1997. $270.00/set. ISBN 0-89356-765-5.

Almost 700 entries cover the nature of women's lives in the United States and Canada. Contemporary and historical photographs, charts, tables, maps and chronologies complement the text. There is an alphabetical list of all articles in the front of each volume as well as both name and comprehensive indexes. Entries cover a range of issues, terms, people, organizations, events, court cases, legislation, education, employment, feminist theory, women's health, politics, race, ethnicity, religion and sports. Articles begin with

a statement of significance and relevance and end with cross-references. Articles vary in length from 100 to 4,000 words; long articles are signed and have bibliographies. Individual articles are broad in scope and are not definitive; students will have to look at other sources for complete information. [R: RBB, June 97]

933 Olsen, Kirstin. **Chronology of Women's History**. Westport, Conn.: Greenwood Press, 1994. 506p. $39.95. ISBN 0-313-28803-8.

This is an inclusive but not exhaustive chronology of women's experience throughout the world from 20,000 B.C. to 1993. Before 1900, the chronology is in time periods that vary, prehistory to 3000 B.C., 1501–1600, 1626–1650, and 1806–1810, for example. After 1900, the entries are annual. Within the chronology, events and names from categories such as daily life, government, literature, performing arts, athletics, activism, science, and religion are presented. Many women are identified by name, dates, and accomplishments within the framework of the chronology. There is no easy access to any time period except for the guide dates across the tops of the right pages. There is a thorough index. This is a good supplement to other chronologies that have focused on male accomplishments. [R: ARBA 95]

934 Parry, Melanie, ed. **Larousse Dictionary of Women**. New York: Larousse Kingfisher Chambers, 1996. 741p. $40.00. ISBN 0-7523-0015-6.

Three thousand individuals, both living and historical and representing a global scope, are included in this alphabetically arranged source. While the emphasis is on nineteenth and twentieth century women, the coverage is broader than in other sources. Each entry gives the full name, dates, nationality and an identifier. Some entries include photographs. There are supplementary sections including a chronology of women's achievements from Eve to 1996, a group of quotations about women by women and about women by men. There are no special indexes for nationality or occupation, but the source will be useful in high schools.

935 Partnow, Elaine, comp. and ed. **The New Quotable Woman: From Eve to the Present**. rev. ed. New York: Facts

on File, 1992. 736p. $40.00. ISBN 0-8160-2134-1.

Combining *Quotable Woman from Eve to 1799* and *Quotable Woman, 1800-1975* and updating to include new quotations, this is an excellent supplement to traditional quotation books.

936 Read, Phyllis J. and Bernard L. Witlieb. **The Book of Women's Firsts: Breakthrough Achievements of Almost 1,000 American Women**. New York: Random House, 1992. 511p. $24.00; $16.00pa. ISBN 0-679-40975-0; 0-679-74280-8pa.

This work can be seen as a complement to the standard *Famous First Facts* with a limited scope and extended purpose. It covers women's firsts in the United States and its territories from pre-Revolutionary colonial days to the present. The inclusion criterion was that the woman had to have done what "no woman before was known to have done in the U.S." Occasional entries do include "one of the first..." Some groups also are listed. The achievements vary from the serious to the frivolous, outrageous and funny, and one can expect to find senators, scientists, artists, astronauts, counterfeiters, murderers, and spies. One listing is the "first woman to have survival gear named after her," and it is gratifying, but not surprising to know that the "first woman to give birth to her own grandchildren" is a school library media specialist. Entries are alphabetical by last name, with the "first" highlighted and then a brief explanation which includes a statement if the activity had been done somewhere else in the world before the American accomplishment. Recommended for reference and browsing. [R: ARBA 94]

937 Taeuber, Cynthia M., comp. and ed. **Statistical Handbook on Women in America**. 2d ed. Phoenix, Ariz.: Oryx Press, 1996. 354p. $54.50. ISBN 1-57356-005-7.

This work brings together statistical data from a variety of government sources. It includes historical information, primarily from World War II, current information, and projected data to show the economic, health, and social lives of American women. Divided into topical sections with introductory essays, the tables and charts cover such categories as education, crime, and employment. Some data are sorted by age, race, and

marital status. There is a glossary and an index. This is a unique source and should be in high school collections.

938 Tierney, Helen, ed. **Women's Studies Encyclopedia**. 3v. Westport, Conn.: Greenwood Press, 1989. $184.90/set. ISBN 0-313-24646-7.

This reference work is designed to contain information from a variety of disciplines that clarify and illuminate women's role in history. Articles range in length from 700 to 1,500 words, are contributed and signed or written by the editor, and incorporate a wide variety of feminist approaches. The separation of the volumes into sciences, literature, arts, learning, history, philosophy, and religion create some problems of locating information (e.g., librarianship and legal terms are both in the sciences volume which covers natural, behavioral and social sciences!). Articles are arranged alphabetically within these volumes and there are separate indexes. This is a basic source for high schools with serious women's studies programs.

939 Zophy, Angela Howard, ed. **Handbook of American Women's History**. New York: Garland, 1990. 763p. $95.00. ISBN 0-8240-8744-5.

Summary definitions of historical significance are paired with focused bibliographies. Emphasis is on concepts, events, organizations and historical persons from the 19th and 20th centuries. Signed entries are from one to two columns. Arrangement is alphabetical with both cross-references and an index. This is a useful source for high school collections.

INDEXES

940 Ireland, Norma Olin. **Index to Women of the World From Ancient to Modern Times: Biographies and Portraits**. Lanham, Md.: Scarecrow Press, 1970. 573p. $32.50. ISBN 0-8108-2012-9.

941 Ireland, Norma Olin. **Index to Women of the World From Ancient to Modern Times: A Supplement**. Lanham, Md.: Scarecrow Press, 1988. 774p. $79.50. ISBN 0-8108-2092-7.

These two volumes provide an index to biographies of women contained in collective biographies, other reference sources and some periodicals. Coverage is of more than 13,000 women, international in scope from Biblical days to the present. It includes books for younger readers in its indexing. Arrangement in each volume is alphabetical by name, and entries give identifying dates, field of activity and the references.

942 Manning, Beverly. **We Shall Be Heard: An Index to Speeches by American Women, 1978 to 1985**.

Lanham, Md.: Scarecrow Press, 1988. 620p. $62.50. ISBN 0-8108-2122-2.

This work continues *Index to American Women Speakers*, which covers 1828–1978 and includes material published from 1978–1985, including older speeches from new collections. The index locates speeches printed in books and periodicals by 2,500 women including activists, political figures, feminists and historical figures. Full citations are by author; there are subject and title indexes.

Literature for Children and Young Adults

GENERAL WORKS

943 Cullinan, Bernice E., and Lee
E+ Galda. **Literature and the Child**. 4th
ed. Fort Worth, Tex.: Harcourt
Brace College Publishers, 1997.
608p. $57.25. ISBN 0-15-503956-3.

This text of children's literature focuses on the selection, criticism and introduction of books from pre-school through grade nine. The first section provides a structure for the literature, primarily via a genre approach, and a portrait of the history of the development of literature for children. There is also a chapter about the reading act and the responses it provokes. The second section discusses each genre, with sample critiques of specific works within each genre. Finally, the third section looks closely at multicultural literature and using children's literature in the classroom. Author and illustrator profiles, bibliographies and teaching ideas appear throughout the text. Appendices list award winners, resources, publishers and other useful items. Recommended for professional collections.

944 Donelson, Kenneth L., and Alleen
Pace Nilsen. **Literature for Today's
Young Adults**. 5th ed. New York:
Longman, 1997. 486p. $55.89. ISBN
0-673-99737-5.

The newest edition of this standard text about young adult literature puts more emphasis on multicultural materials. The work begins with an introductory section about the young adult and young adult books and then discusses the body of work by genre. A final section discusses evaluating and promoting books, censorship and the history of young adult literature from 1800 to the present. Features such as author profiles and comments and boxed bibliographies add interest to the text. Appendices list selection tools and resources. A subject index and a combined author-title index conclude the volume. Middle and high school collections will find this source essential.

945 Hearne, Betsy, and Roger Sutton,
eds. **Evaluating Children's Books: A
Critical Look; Aesthetic, Social and
Political Aspects of Analyzing and
Using Children's Books**. Urbana-
Champaign, Ill.: University of
Illinois, Graduate School of
Library and Information Science,
1993. 161p. $18.50pa. ISBN 0-87845-
092-0.

This is a collection of papers and a transcript of a panel discussion presented at an Allerton Park Institute. Reviewers, editors, academics and librarians discuss current issues in children's book publishing such as nonfiction, illustration, censorship and multiculturalism. The essays are informed, sometimes blunt, and thoughtful. References are included with the articles, and a good index allows access to particular points.

946 Huck, Charlotte S., and others.
E+ **Children's Literature in the Elementary School**. 6th ed. Madison,
Wis.: Brown & Benchmark, 1997.
783p. $67.55. ISBN 0-697-27960-X.

This classic children's literature text retains its attractive look, useful teaching suggestions, and expectations for high standards of quality in books for children, preschool through middle school. A new chapter on biography has been added. The authors continue to integrate multicultural materials within all chapters, rather than to separate them in one section. The book focuses on the book, the reader and teaching.

Useful appendices include awards, selection aids and publishers. Name and subject indexes are provided. This is a first purchase for elementary professional collections, and most middle schools will want it as well.

947 Lukens, Rebecca J. A **Critical Hand-**
E **book of Children's Literature**. 5th ed. New York: HarperCollins, 1995. 352p. $26.95. ISBN 0-673-46937-9.

948 Lukens, Rebecca J., and Ruth K. J. Cline. **A Critical Handbook of Young Adult Literature**. New York: Harper-Collins, 1995. 210p. $22.50. ISBN 0-06-501108-2.

Librarians and teachers will find these texts useful in working with students and books in literary discussions. The intent of the authors is to teach students to go beyond the "I like it" stage of criticism to understand why a particular book is meaningful. Each handbook discusses the literary elements with examples from literature for young people. The young adult volume includes a chapter on poetry, while the children's volume has chapters on poetry, picture books and nonfiction. Each volume is indexed. Highly recommended as a background literary handbook for those who work with students.

949 Lynch-Brown, Carol, and Carl M.
E+ Tomlinson. **Essentials of Children's Literature**. 2d ed. Boston: Allyn & Bacon, 1995. 386p. $34.00. ISBN 0-205-16751-9.

This concise text can act as a resource for librarians and teachers. It discusses children and children's literature, literary and visual elements of books and then has chapters devoted to genres, each with recommended authors and titles. The final chapters concern planning a literature curriculum and teaching strategies for experiencing and responding to literature. Appendices list awards and professional resources. There are author-title and subject indexes. While not as detailed or attractive as the standard texts, this is a convenient and satisfactory desk reference.

950 Norton, Diane E., with Saundra E.
E+ Norton. **Through the Eyes of a Child**. 4th ed. Englewood Cliffs, N.J.: Merrill, 1995. 713p. $64.00. ISBN 0-02-388313-8.

The strength of this children's literature text is the combination of critical analysis and strategies for leading children to books. A new section emphasizes artists, illustration and children's response to art. There are introductory chapters about children, literature and evaluating literature for children. The remainder of the work discusses literature and involvement by genre, including separate chapters on multicultural literature and informational books. The book is accompanied by a computer database with 2,600 titles which allows the user to search by name, title and topic and to compile bibliographies for printing. Users can also add titles and annotations to the database. Recommended for elementary professional and parent collections.

951 Sloan, Glenna Davis. **The Child as**
E+ **Critic: Teaching Literature in Elementary and Middle Schools**. 3d ed. New York: Teachers College Press, 1991. 209p. $38.00; $18.95pa. ISBN 0-8077-3156-0; 0-8077-3110-2pa.

This guide to working with books and children is based on the literary theories of Northrop Frye. Sloan briefly describes how these theories can be used to create meaningful literary discussion with both elementary and middle school children. She illustrates the kinds of questions that can elicit thoughtful responses from children and suggests titles of books and poetry to use. Highly recommended for both teachers and librarians who lead book discussions with students.

952 Smith, Lillian H. **The Unreluctant**
E+ **Years: A Critical Approach to Children's Literature**. Chicago: American Library Association, 1991. 183p. $25.00. ISBN 0-8389-0557-9.

This reprint of a children's literary classic that appeared in 1953 is as timely today as it was four decades ago. (This volume has a new introduction by Kay E. Vandergrift.) Smith considered children's books as literature and applied critical standards and the interests of children in identifying quality. Librarians responsible for selecting and using books for children will want to read and reread this slim, perceptive work.

953 Sutherland, Zena. **Children &**
E+ **Books**. 9th ed. New York: Longman, 1997. 720p. $55.95. ISBN 0-673-99733-2.

First published 50 years ago and long known for its former editor, May Hill Arbuthnot, this children's literature textbook emphasizes the best books and authors. The introductory sections about children and books in general are followed by genre overviews which emphasize the major authors in each category. A third section discusses ways to bring children and books together, while a final section covers issues such as censorship. Lavish color illustrations, viewpoint boxes, extensive bibliographies and useful appendices make this an attractive and stimulating work that parents, teachers and librarians will find helpful. Highly recommended for elementary and middle schools.

954 Vandergrift, Kay E. **Children's Liter-**
E+ **ature: Theory, Research, and Teaching**. Englewood, Colo.: Libraries Unlimited, 1990. 277p. $32.50. ISBN 0-87287-749-3.

While this work treats the study of children's literature as an academic discipline, it is useful to practitioners who select and use literature with children. The first three chapters survey literary theory, research, and teaching the field. Succeeding chapters provide course syllabi with numerous examples, worksheets that can be used in evaluating books or instructional media, and ideas for continuing education activities relevant to children's literature (e.g., in-service workshops, institutes). An extensive bibliography includes works about literary theory, research, and teaching children's literature. A detailed general index includes all titles mentioned in the text. Recommended.

AWARDS
See also **Booktalking**.

955 **Children's Books: Awards and**
E+ **Prizes**. New York: Children's Book Council, Inc., 1969– . annual. ISSN 0069-3472.

Published since 1969, this comprehensive list of awards earned by both children's and young adult books lists awards selected by adults and awards selected by children in the United States as well as the U.K. and some international awards. Included are the many state children's choice awards. Winners are listed for all years. There is an alphabetical list of awards in the front of the volume and title and persons indexes. This convenient source is highly recommended for all schools.

956 **The Newbery and Caldecott Awards:**
E+ **A Guide to the Medal and Honor Books**. Chicago: Association for Library Service to Children, 1988– . annual. ISSN 1070-4493.

This annual publication describes the awards and the award process and lists every year's award and honor winners in reverse chronological order. The current year's listing features the award winner with a photograph of the most recent winning author/illustrator and an illustration of the book jacket. Annotations are given for both winning and honor books. One of the most useful sections of the book is the list of media used in the production of Caldecott books. Highly recommended.

957 Smith, Henrietta M., ed. **The Coretta**
E+ **Scott King Awards Book: From Vision to Reality**. Chicago: American Library Association, 1994. 115p. $28.00pa. ISBN 0-8389-3441-2.

This book was published on the 25th anniversary of the Coretta Scott King Award. It describes the history of the Award and then lists the Author and Illustrator Award winners and honor books in reverse chronology. Each title is annotated. A 19 plate color insert shows illustrations from some of the Illustrator Awards. A final section has biographies of selected winning authors and illustrators. There is a general index. Highly recommended for elementary and middle schools.

BIBLIOGRAPHIES

958 Brown, Muriel, and Rita Schoch
E+ Foudray. **Newbery and Caldecott Medalists and Honor Book Winners: Bibliographies and Resource Material through 1991**. 2d ed. New York: Neal-Schuman, 1992. 511p. $59.95. ISBN 1-55570-118-3.

First published in 1982 and revised ten years later, this is a bibliographic resource for finding information about authors and illustrators whose books won the awards or were honor books. The 327 individuals are listed in alphabetical order and each entry contains the awards received, a bibliography of books published by the individual, and background reading from books and journals about the individual. If an author or illustrator has designated a special collection to contain original manuscripts and other papers, that is given as well. Appendices list the annual

Newbery and Caldecott award and honor winners chronologically and there is an author/illustrator/title index. This is a convenient source for building curriculum resources for these awards.

959 Hendrickson, Linnea. **Children's**
E+ **Literature: A Guide to the Criticism**. Boston: G. K. Hall, 1987. 696p. $39.50. ISBN 0-8161-8670-7.

A critical guide to children's literature, this bibliography identifies books, articles, unpublished dissertations, and ERIC documents that have appeared since 1960. Citations, grouped under authors and their works or subjects, themes, and genres, are indexed by author, title, subject, and critic. A brief annotation describes each item but does not evaluate it. Students of children's literature, teachers, and librarians will find this bibliography useful. [R: BL, 15 June 87]

960 Marantz, Sylvia S., and Kenneth A.
E Marantz. **The Art of Children's Picture Books**. 2d ed. New York: Garland Pub., 1995. 293p. $43.00. ISBN 0-8153-0937-6.

This annotated bibliography includes citations of books and journals about all aspects of picture books from their history and production to their "use" with and by children. School librarians will find citations about suggestions for approaching the picture book and about individual illustrators especially relevant. Art teachers will also find this information useful.

961 Subramanian, Jane M. **Laura**
E+ **Ingalls Wilder: An Annotated Bibliography of Critical, Biographical, and Teaching Studies**. Westport, Conn.: Greenwood Press, 1997. 115p. $55.00. ISBN 0-313-29999-4.

This extensive bibliography about Wilder and her family includes critical studies, biographies for adults and children, teaching ideas and materials, a list of Wilder-related newsletters and review citations for each of the *Little House* books and related titles. Teachers and librarians will find this useful for preparing Wilder units.

BIBLIOGRAPHIES FOR CURRICULUM SUPPORT & READING GUIDANCE
See also **Retrospective Bibliographies (Collection Management)**.

962 Adamson, Lynda G. **Recreating the Past: A Guide to American and World Historical Fiction for Children and Young Adults**. Westport, Conn.: Greenwood Press, 1994. 494p. $55.00. ISBN 0-313-29008-3.

Much of the material in this version of Adamson's work appeared in the 1987 title *A Reference Guide to Historical Fiction for Children and Young Adults*. This version is a bibliography of fiction which conveys historical ideas in a meaningful way. There is a good introduction addressing the reason for including historical fiction in instruction. The 970 titles with complete bibliographic information and brief annotations are arranged in 29 chronological sections from prehistory and the ancient world to 1961 and after, including some Vietnam era literature. Within sections, titles are listed alphabetically by author. Each annotation includes date and setting, characteristics of the protagonist, theme, reading and interest levels. Awards are noted, but it is not a critical guide. Many titles published originally for adults are included for young adult readers. The seven appendices make the book useful as both a selection tool and as a bibliographic guide; included are grade and interest levels, subject lists of minority and famous people, and sequels and series. There is an author, title and illustrator index.

963 Anderson, Vicki. **Fiction Sequels for**
E+ **Readers 10 to 16: An Annotated Bibliography of Books in Succession**. 2d ed. Jefferson, N.C.: McFarland, 1998. 192p. $29.95pa. ISBN 0-77864-0185-0.

Anderson defines sequels as books that have the same characters and similar themes but that can stand alone. This bibliography lists 2,500 such titles appropriate for children over 10; most are recent titles, but some are older classics. Sequels were selected for their type, suitability for the age level, and availability, not for their literary quality. Entries are arranged alphabetically by author and include title, each book's numerical position in the sequence, publisher, date and a brief annotation. A title list gives each work's author.

964 Anderson, Vicki. **Native Americans**
E+ **in Fiction: A Guide to 765 Books for Librarians and Teachers, K-9**. Jefferson, N.C.: McFarland, 1994. 166p. $31.50. ISBN 0-89950-907-X.

The author has identified almost 800 titles published since 1960 about Native Americans. This index lists the books by tribe, then alphabetically by author. Titles were selected from actual collections and are appropriate for elementary to middle school. Each entry gives author, title, publisher, date, and indication of appropriate grade level, a description and subject indicators. An appendix lists tribe and sub-tribe names with their associated region; a second appendix lists books by grade level and tribe. Author, title and subject indexes complete the access features. Because many older titles are out of print, this source is intended as a key to existing collections rather than as a buying guide.

965 Apseloff, Marilyn Fain, comp. **They**
E **Wrote for Children Too: An Annotated Bibliography of Children's Literature by Famous Writers for Adults**. Westport, Conn.: Greenwood Press, 1989. 202p. $59.95. ISBN 0-313-25981-X.

This bibliography lists picture books, stories, poetry, drama and nonfiction for children by famous authors usually associated with adult literature. Works that have been ably adapted for children are also included. Entries, arranged chronologically from ancient times (e.g., the *Aeneid*) to the twentieth century, usually include author, title, illustrator, publisher, date, type of work, paging, age level, country of author's origin (most are American or English), and an annotation. Adapter or reteller and awards are cited when applicable. This is a useful, though not an essential, purchase for elementary school libraries. [R: ARBA 90; RBB, 1 Nov 89]

966 Austin, Mary C. **Literature for**
E+ **Children and Young Adults about Oceania: Analysis and Annotated Bibliography with Additional Readings for Adults**. Westport, Conn.: Greenwood Press, 1996. 326p. $69.50. ISBN 0-313-26643-3.

This bibliography of fiction and informational books as well as folktales, poetry and drama is arranged by region/country. All books are written in English or have been translated. Long annotations are both descriptive and analytic. This is a comprehensive bibliography and lists all items found; many are out of print but may be in collections. The book includes a list of distributors, and separate author, title and subject indexes. Other books in the series include *The Indian Subcontinent in Literature for Children and Young Adults* (1991) and *Africa in Literature for Children and Young Adults* (1994).

967 Barrera, Rosalinda B., and others,
E+ eds. **Kaleidoscope: A Multicultural Booklist for Grades K–8**. 2d ed. Urbana, Ill.: National Council of Teachers of English, 1997. 215p. $14.95. ISBN 0-8141-2541-7.

This selective bibliography updates the first edition (1994) and includes 600 titles for K-8 published from 1993–1995. The scope of multicultural groups includes African Americans, Asian Americans, Hispanic Americans and Native Americans. Books are listed about these cultures within the United States as well as within their native lands and other places where they may reside are listed. Books are arranged in a variety of genre and subject chapters such as "People and Places," "Poetry, Verse, and Song," "Fiction for Intermediate Readers," and "Folktales, Myths, and Legends." Entries give bibliographic information, recommended grade level and a descriptive annotation. There is a list of award-winning books, a list of resources and a list of author, subject and title indexes. Recommended for elementary and middle schools.

968 Berman, Matt. **What Else Should I**
E+ **Read?: Guiding Kids to Good Books**. 2v. Englewood, Colo.: Libraries Unlimited, 1995–1996. $24.50/volume. ISBN: 1-56308-241-1 (v.1); 1-56308-419-8 (v.2).

Each of the two volumes in this set contain 30 book webs, reproducible for bulletin boards and bookmarks. (Permission is granted to one library or one classroom per set of books.) The 60 main titles are analyzed by several elements in the book that might be of special interest to students, and three to eight other related titles are identified. These extra titles are briefly annotated on the bookmark templates. Suggestions are made for display and dissemination of the bookmarks. An introductory chapter repeated in each volume discusses ways of implementing reading programs and book discussion groups. Recommended for intermediate and middle grades.

969 Carter, Betty. **Best Books for Young Adults: The Selections, the History, the Romance**. Chicago: American Library Association, 1994. 214p. $28.00pa. ISBN 0-8389-3439-0.

The first half of this work is a history of the Best Books for Young Adults selection committee of the Young Adult Services Division of ALA. The discussions inherently involve the development of books for young adults in the last quarter of this century, and the issue of such lists selected by adults for young adults. The second part of the book lists all those books selected from 1966–1993, arranged first by author and then by year. There is also a list of the "best of the best." An index provides quick access to authors and titles discussed or listed. Recommended for middle and high school collections.

970 Christenbury, Leila, ed. **Books for You: An Annotated Booklist for Senior High Students**. 11th ed. Urbana, Ill.: The National Council of Teachers of English, 1995. 432p. $21.95pa. ISBN 0-8141-0367-7.

More than 1,000 books published from 1990–1994 are arranged in 36 categories such as dating and sexual awareness, the Holocaust, mysteries, spies and crime, romance, and war and war stories. Titles related to multicultural themes are collected and repeated in a special section. Each entry gives author, title, publisher, number of pages and indicates if the item is fiction or nonfiction. An annotation is intended to motivate readers, as this source is intended for students; teachers and librarians will find it useful as well, for reader advisory work and for selection. There is a directory of publishers and an appendix of award-winning books. Separate author, title, and subject indexes provide access. Recommended for all secondary collections as most titles are perfectly appropriate for middle school students.

971 Clyde, Laurel and Marjorie Lobban. **Out of the Closet and into the Classroom: Homosexuality in Books for Young People**. Port Melbourne, Vic., Australia: ALIA Press, 1992. 150p. $35.00pa. ISBN 1-875589-02-3.

This bibliography lists 128 books published in English in the U.K., the U.S. and Australia, intended for children and young adults with clearly identified homosexual characters or incidents. It omits books with adolescent homosexual characters if the work was written for an adult audience. Most entries are fiction, but a few are autobiographical. Most date from 1970–1988, but some date from as early as 1962. Four categories of books are identified, those with homosexual main characters, those with supporting homosexual characters, those with background homosexual characters, and those titles which mention homosexuality. Entries are arranged alphabetically by author and annotations are about one page. Appendices analyze the titles by character and date of publication. There is a title index. [R: ARBA 94]

972 Dreyer, Sharon Spredemann. **The**
E+ **Bookfinder 4: When Kids Need Books: Annotations of Books Published 1983 through 1986**. Circle Pines, Minn.: American Guidance Service, 1989. 642p. $89.95; $44.95pa. ISBN 0-913476-50-1; 0-913476-51-Xpa.

Counselors, psychologists, teachers, librarians and other professionals seeking books that can help children ages 2–15 cope with problems will find this an indispensable series. The first *Bookfinder* (1977) covered 1,031 books published through 1974; *Bookfinder 2* (1981) listed 723 books from 1975 to 1978; and *Bookfinder 3* (1985) presented 725 books published from 1979 to 1982. This latest addition to the series has 731 titles published from 1983 to 1986.

Titles, arranged alphabetically by author under main and secondary subject headings, deal with some 450 psychological, behavioral and developmental themes. The detailed annotation that follows each entry provides a synopsis; a commentary on the book's strengths, weaknesses, literary merit and illustrations; qualifications of the author; sequels; approximate age level; and other formats (e.g., film, cassettes, Braille, large print). [R: BL, 1 Mar 90]

973 Estes, Sally, ed. **Genre Favorites for Young Adults: A Collection of Booklist Columns**. Chicago: Booklist Publications, American Library Association, 1993. 64p. $7.95pa. ISBN 0-8389-5755-2.

974 Estes, Sally, ed. **Growing Up Is Hard to Do: A Collection of Booklist Columns**. Chicago: Booklist

Publications, American Library Association, 1994. 64p. $7.95pa. ISBN 0-8389-7726-X.

Each of these booklets contain the useful bibliographies that appear in *Booklist*. They have been updated and edited for these publications. *Genre Favorites* is arranged in 10 categories such as love stories, whodunits, sports fiction, and diaries. *Growing Up* has 12 lists such as "Growing Up an Outsider," and "Growing Up Gay Aware." Each title has complete bibliographic information, grade level recommendations and short annotations. These lists are filled with relevant titles and are essential for librarians working with middle and high school students.

975 Fakih, Kimberly Olson. **The Litera-**
E+ **ture of Delight: A Critical Guide to Humorous Books for Children**. New Providence, N.J.: Bowker, 1993. 269p. $40.00. ISBN 0-8352-3027-9.

Humorous books of all types and for all ages are listed in this reference source. Almost 800 titles are listed in 17 categories from physical humor to jokes and riddles to parody and irony and crude humor. Entries include bibliographic citations, format designations, grade levels and brief descriptive annotations. Five indexes, including subject and character, provide access to the individual titles. Recommended for all levels.

976 Friedberg, Joan Brest, and others.
E+ **Portraying Persons with Disabilities: An Annotated Bibliography of Nonfiction for Children and Teenagers**. 2d ed. New Providence, N.J.: Bowker, 1992. 385p. $39.95. ISBN 0-8352-3022-8.

This work updates the authors' older book, *Accept Me As I Am* (Bowker, 1985), and is a companion to the fiction bibliography by Robertson (1001). Most titles have been published since 1984, but outstanding older and out-of-print titles are included, since they may be in existing collections. Introductory chapters discuss criteria for selecting books on this topic and patterns of writing and publishing about disabilities. Four chapters list books in the broad categories of physical problems, sensory problems, cognitive and behavior problems and multiple and severe disabilities. Each broad category is further divided into specific disability-type sections. Entries give

the bibliographic citation, a reading level and an indicator of the disability. Annotations give thorough summaries and a critical analysis. Separate author, title and subject indexes provide further access. Highly recommended for all collections.

977 Gerhardstein, Virginia Brokaw. **Dickinson's American Historical Fiction**. 5th ed. Lanham, Md.: Scarecrow Press, 1986. 352p. $35.00. ISBN 0-8108-1867-1.

Dickinson's bibliography is for teachers and librarians needing a list of adult American historical novels published from 1917–1984. There are 3,048 novels arranged in chronological order by setting. Brief annotations are descriptive of the historical context rather than being critical of accuracy or literary merit. The frontier section is further divided geographically. There are separate author-title and subject indexes.

978 Gordon, Lee, and Cheryl Tanaka. **World Historical Fiction Guide for Young Adults**. Fort Atkinson, Wis.: Highsmith Press, 1995. 301p. $30.00. ISBN 0-917846-41-9.

The authors note the difficulty of identifying fiction books for middle and high school students studying world history or world culture, and provide this selective list as a resource for that purpose. The introduction includes a discussion of a variety of reporting methods as alternatives for the dreaded written book report. Titles are listed by continent and country. There are no listings for American history; main characters must include non-Americans. Some contemporary settings are included for those areas in which limited historical fiction is available. Entries give bibliographic information, a descriptive annotation, citations for reviews, reading level, subject areas and time period. There is a box in the entry for indicating a library's holdings. Title, author, subject and chronological indexes provide access to the list. This is primarily a curricular aid, but it can also be used for collection development. Recommended for middle and high school collections.

979 Grindler, Martha C., Beverly D.
E Stratton, and Michael C. McKenna. **The Right Book, The Right Time: Helping Children Cope**. Boston: Allyn & Bacon, 1997. 200p. $25.95pa. ISBN 0-205-17272-5.

This is a guide to books that might be used for bibliotherapy for children in grades K–6. Introductory chapters explain that bibliotherapy is not the same as direct counseling and frames the ways in which librarians and teachers can suggest and display a wide variety of books from which children may choose. The books selected are arranged by broad subjects such as adoption, divorce, sharing and friendship. Each entry gives the title, author and publisher, the length, age appropriateness, gender and race of main character, other topics the book covers and a brief overview. There are no indexes, rather the book is accompanied by both DOS and Macintosh computer disks that contain the data base and allow searching by fields and field combinations.

980 Hall, Susan. **Using Picture Story-**
E+   **books to Teach Literary Devices:**
      Recommended Books for Children
      and Young Adults. 2v. Phoenix, Ariz.:
      Oryx Press, 1990–1994. $29.95/volume. ISBN 0-89774-582-5 (v.1);
      0-89774-849-2 (v.2).

These two volumes list picture storybooks by the literary devices they demonstrate. Such devices include alliteration, metaphor, tone, understatement and many others. Volume 1 includes five chapters about using picture storybooks in literature classes at all levels. Librarians will also find these suggestions useful for exploring literature with students. Entries give bibliographic citations, brief story annotations, examples of a literary device used in the book, other devices used, a description of the art style and a suggestion for curricular applications. Recommended for all grade levels.

981 Harms, Jeanne McLain, and Lucille
E   Lettow. **Picture Books to Enhance**
      the Curriculum. Bronx, N.Y.: H. W.
      Wilson, 1996. 521p. $38.00. ISBN 0-
      8242-0867-6.

The authors, both experienced in working with the integration of children's literature across the curriculum, have identified picture books which can be used in a thematic approach. The themes most often used by teachers are listed with relevant picture book titles. Approximately 1,500 current titles are included. A picture book index lists all titles by author, and gives bibliographic information, a brief annotation and an analysis

of themes. There is also a title index. This source is indispensable for planning units and can also act as a buying guide. Highly recommended for elementary collections.

982 Hartman, Donald K., and Gregg
      Sapp. **Historical Figures in Fiction**.
      Phoenix, Ariz.: Oryx Press, 1994.
      352p. $45.00. ISBN 0-89774-718-6.

This bibliography is intended to identify biographical novels and to suggest ways of using them with students. More than 4,000 novels about 1,500 historical figures are included. The items listed were published between 1940 and 1992. Individuals are listed alphabetically and entries give the person's name and dates, a character description, and a list of titles about the person with reading levels, notes and review citations. There are author, title and occupational indexes; a chronological index would also have been useful. Recommended for all levels.

983 Herald, Diana Tixier. **Teen Genre-**
      flecting. Englewood, Colo.: Libraries
      Unlimited, 1997. 134p. $23.50. ISBN
      1-56308-287-X.

Teenagers who read tend to read specific genres and this book helps identify the titles within the genres that teens like to read. Arranged by categories such as historical novels, fantasy, contemporary and romance, each chapter has an introduction and titles listed with brief annotations under subcategories. Only authors and titles are given. Additional lists are included, including YALSA lists which have bibliographic information. The author's enthusiasm is infectious; these are popular books and this source will help any teacher or librarian with unfamiliar genres or titles. Highly recommended for middle and high school reading guidance.

984 Holsinger, M. Paul. **The Ways of**
      War: The Era of World War II in
      Children's and Young Adult Fiction:
      An Annotated Bibliography. Lanham, Md.: Scarecrow Press, 1995.
      487p. $57.50. ISBN 0-8108-2925-8.

Full annotations accompany citations for 750 novels about World War II and 266 other titles published in Great Britain that were never published in the United States. The entries include recommended grade levels and a quality indicator that ranges from "best of the best" to mediocre. Arrangement is alphabetical by author with a title index; a geographic/thematic index is useful. This bibliography includes books for all grade levels, but most of the titles are for middle school readers.

985 Howard, Elizabeth F. **America as Story: Historical Fiction for Secondary Schools**. Chicago: American Library Association, 1988. 137p. $23.00pa. ISBN 0-8389-0492-0.

A bibliography of recommended historical fiction consists of titles published for a younger audience than Dickinson's, most were recommended by standard sources such as *School Library Journal* and *Horn Book Magazine*. The titles are listed in seven chronological chapters from the colonial period to the present. Entries are about a page in length and provide bibliographical data with a summary of the book and possible activities to use with it. Grade levels are suggested. Librarians, language arts and social studies teachers will find this bibliography useful.

986 Immell, Myra, and Marion Sader. **The Young Adult Reader's Adviser**. 2v. New Providence, N.J.: Bowker, 1992. $79.95/set. ISBN 0-8352-3068-6.

The classic *Bowker Reader's Adviser* has been published for more than 80 years, and this is a new version especially designed for young adults. It is a group of bibliographies arranged by broad disciplines: literature/language arts, math and computers in volume 1, social sciences, history, science and health in volume 2. Each discipline area includes a narrative introduction. Some 17,000 entries of books for middle and high school students (middle school materials are marked with an asterisk while advanced materials are marked with a square bullet). Special author profiles give biographical/critical information and list works by and about the author; similar profiles of specific subjects give background information in addition to bibliographies. Profile indexes, author indexes and title indexes are in each volume. This is a selection tool, a reading guidance tool, and a guide for students to use in planning their own reading agendas. This is an essential work for secondary schools.

987 Jensen, Julie M. and Nancy L.
E   Roser, eds. **Adventuring with Books: A Booklist for Pre-K–Grade 6**. 10th ed. Urbana, Ill.: National Council of Teachers of English, 1993. 603p. $19.95. ISBN 0-8141-0079-1.

Intermediate children can use this source themselves to identify books they might want to read which are listed in 13 major categories. Teachers and librarians will use the selective list for guidance in working with preschool, primary and intermediate students. Some of the categories are genres, some are subject; they include such topics as biography, celebrations, classics, historical fiction, poetry and science and math. About 2,000 books are listed. Entries include interest level rather than age or grade levels. There is a section of books that have won prizes and have been included on special lists, a directory of publishers and an author index, illustrator index, subject index and title index. This is both a reading advisory tool and a selection tool, and every elementary school collections should have at least one copy.

988 Kennedy, DayAnn M., Stella S.
E   Spangler, and Mary Ann Vanderwerf. **Science & Technology in Fact and Fiction: A Guide to Children's Books**. New York: Bowker, 1990. 319p. $38.00. ISBN 0-8352-2708-1.

989 Kennedy, DayAnn M., Stella S. Spangler, and Mary Ann Vanderwerf. **Science & Technology in Fact and Fiction: A Guide to Young Adult Books**. New York: Bowker, 1990. 363p. $38.00. ISBN 0-8352-2710-3.

These guides provide selection information about fiction and nonfiction books for children and young adults on space, aeronautics, computers, robots, and a wide range of other scientific and technical topics. *Children's Books* focuses on recommended books for preschool through age 12; *Young Adult Books* recommends titles for grades 7 through 12. The authors, in consultation with teachers and librarians, chose titles from resources reviewed in standard review media, such as *Appraisal*, *Children's Literature Association Quarterly*, and *School Library Journal*. Choices are based on literary quality, scientific accuracy, clarity in writing style, appropriateness of topic and illustrations, coordination of text and illustrations, and scope of material.

For each recommended work, the entry gives a summary, evaluation, reading level, and order information. These volumes offer sound advice in selecting books on scientific topics for young people. [R: ARBA 91; RBB, 1 Apr 90; RBB, 15 Oct 90; WLB, June 90]

990 Kennemer, Phyllis K. **Using Literature to Teach Middle Grades About War**. Phoenix, Ariz.: Oryx Press, 1993. 209p. $29.95. ISBN 0-89774-778-X.

Intended as a guide for teachers and school librarians planning resource based teaching and learning thematic units, this book focuses on major wars typically studied in U.S. history classes. It provides plans for six units based upon the Revolution, the Civil War, World War I, World War II, the Vietnam War and the Gulf War. Other conflicts, including the Korean War were omitted because there were insufficient resources. Each unit plan includes a chronology, recommended books in four categories—picture, factual, biographies and fiction, sample lesson plans, suggested questions and activities, glossaries, and evaluations. Appendix A offers planning guides while Appendix B has sample reporting recording and evaluation forms. There is an author-title index of recommended books. The work is intended for grades 6–8, but the concept and format could be easily translated to lower and upper grades and other subject disciplines. [R: ARBA 94]

991 Kobrin, Beverly. **Eyeopeners II!** New
E+   York: Scholastic, 1995. 305p. $6.95. ISBN 0-590-48402-8.

The original *Eyeopeners* was published by Viking in 1988 and this edition adds 800 more titles to the collection of nonfiction books that are appropriate for integrating into instruction. Kobrin gives age ranges, annotations, and many suggestions and ideas for using the books. While *Eyeopeners II!* includes materials for preschool through high school, most of the titles are for elementary and middle school grades. The introductory chapters about nonfiction and children and criteria for selection are valuable. Highly recommended, especially for elementary schools.

992 Lima, Carolyn W., and John A. Lima.
E   **A to Zoo: Subject Access to Children's Picture Books**. 4th ed. New Providence, N.J.: Bowker, 1993. 1158p. $55.00. ISBN 0-8352-3201-8.

Both in-print and out-of-print titles are included in this guide to subject access to 14,000 picture books. Almost 800 subject headings are used to suggest appropriate books. A separate section gives bibliographic information about the titles and the subject headings assigned to each, but there are no annotations. The bibliographic guide also acts as an author index. Separate title and illustrator indexes provide other access points.

993 Lynn, Ruth Nadelman. **Fantasy**
E+   **Literature for Children and Young Adults: An Annotated Bibliography**. 4th ed. New Providence, N.J.: Bowker, 1995. 1092p. $55.00. ISBN 0-8352-3456-8.

This is the definitive work on fantasy for young people. It is comprised of both a bibliography of 3,148 entries covering almost 5,000 fantasy titles and a research list of over 10,000 books, articles and dissertations about fantasy and authors of fantasy. The bibliography is arranged by type of the genre, especially useful with students who prefer only high fantasy or time travel or one of the other subgenres. The introduction is an excellent overview of the genre and the list of outstanding titles in each subgenre should be used as a standard buying and reading guide. This work is for teachers, librarians and students who like fantasy, and especially for teachers and librarians who don't like fantasy so they can provide some assistance to their readers. Highly recommended for all levels as the work covers books for grades 3–12.

994 Marantz, Sylvia S., and Kenneth
E   Marantz. **Multicultural Picture Books: Art for Understanding Others**. 2v. Worthington, Ohio: Linworth Publishing, 1994, 1997. $25.95 (v.1); $34.95 (v.2). ISBN 0-938869-22-6 (v.1); 0-938865-63-3 (v.2).

This source identifies and describes the text and illustrations of picture books about world cultures and the experience of members of those cultures who have emigrated to America, Asian and Middle Eastern cultures are divided by country, while Africa and Latin America are treated as continents. Volume I has an abbreviated section on European cultures dealing with the former Soviet Union and historical books relating the immigrant experiences. One section describes aboriginal cultures of North America, and a final chapter lists multicultural or cross-cultural books. Each category includes folk tales and contemporary stories. Volume II follows the same pattern and reviews recently published picture books and nonfiction. Discussion of art elements and the many cover reproductions distinguish these titles. Recommended for elementary collections.

995 Miles, Susan Goodrich. **Adoption Literature for Children and Young Adults: An Annotated Bibliography**. New York: Greenwood Press, 1991. 201p. $39.95. ISBN 0-313-27606-4.

This annotated bibliography of more than 500 books about the adoption experience covers both fiction and nonfiction from preschool to young adult reading levels. It includes items published since 1900, but emphasizes current issues such as transracial and transnational adoption, special needs, surrogacy, open adoption, and searching for birth parents. The source can be a selection tool for librarians, and a resource tool for parents, adopted children, and others working with them. The tool is arranged by four age-groups and within the group, alphabetically by author. One of the appendices is a directory of adoption-related organizations, and there are separate author, title, and subject indexes. Recommended for all levels. [R: ARBA 93]

996 **More Kids' Favorite Books: A**
E+ **Compilation of Children's Choices, 1992–1994**. New York: Children's Book Council, 1995. 126p. $9.95pa. ISBN 0-87207-130-8.

This title updates *Kids' Favorite Books* (Children's Book Council and I. R. A., 1992). Selected by about 2,000 students in five test sites from around the United States, the 300 titles in this book were the most popular of 1,500 titles the children read and evaluated over a three-year period. Arranged by age group, including a section for all ages, the books are for beginning readers up to about eighth grade. Both fiction and informational books are listed. Brief annotations accompany

the bibliographic citations and the book is illustrated with pictures and covers from some of the books listed. Useful for teachers, parents and librarians, this is recommended for elementary and middle schools.

997 **More Teachers' Favorite Books for**
E+ **Kids: Teachers' Choices, 1994–1996**. Newark, Del.: International Reading Association, 1997. 20p. $8.00. ISBN 0-87207-179-0.

Approximately 90 titles from *The Reading Teacher's* annual lists of outstanding books tested by teachers, librarians and students are included in this update of *Teachers' Favorite Books for Kids* (I. R. A., 1994). Arranged by primary, intermediate and middle levels, each entry has both a summary and a critical analysis that often includes instructional ideas. There are author/illustrator and title indexes. This edition also contains four supplementary articles about using books in the classroom. Recommended for elementary and middle schools.

998 **More Teens' Favorite Books: Young Adults' Choices, 1993–1995**. Newark, Del.: International Reading Association, 1996. 52p. $9.95pa. ISBN 0-87207-149-9.

Teenagers themselves vote on books in the annual project carried out by book publishers and the International Reading Association. This guide lists the most popular choices from three years of voting. It updates *Teens' Favorite Books* (I. R. A., 1992). Listed by topic/genre, each entry gives bibliographic information and a brief descriptive annotation. There is also a section for adults with suggestions for motivating young adults to read. There are author and title indexes. Recommended for teachers, students and librarians in middle and high schools.

999 Roberts, Patricia L. **Alphabet Books**
E **as a Key to Language Patterns: An Annotated Action Bibliography**. Hamden, Conn.: Library Professional Publications/Shoe String Press, 1987. 263p. $36.00. ISBN 0-208-02151-5.

Roberts' introduction, a comprehensive essay on language patterns and their relationship to children's language and learning styles, explains her approach to alphabet books. For each of almost 500 titles, including some in which the alphabet is used to organize a topic (e.g., *Ancient Egypt from A to Z*), she describes the book's approach, provides response activities, and gives the specific language pattern used. Some titles are recommended. Indexed by author and title. This bibliography also has use as a selection aid. [R: ARBA 89; BL, 1 Oct 87]

1000 Roberts, Patricia L. **Counting Books Are More Than Numbers: An Annotated Action Bibliography**. Hamden, Conn.: Library Professional Publications, 1990. 270p. $36.00. ISBN 0-208-02216-3.

This bibliography focuses on picture books that introduce children, preschool through second grade, to the concepts and skills of mathematics. The 350 annotated titles each contain bibliographic information; grade level; and a section called "Features," which identifies specific skills and concepts taught or reinforced by the book.

The volume is divided into four chapters: ABC and 1-2-3 books; rhyme (e.g., counting, singing); collections of related objects and stories, arranged by subject; and collections of unrelated objects, arranged by number of items counted. The appendix lists some of the titles by the skill taught (e.g., the concepts of infinity, ordinals). Teachers will find this a useful bibliography. [R: ARBA 91; BL, 15 Mar 90]

1001 Robertson, Debra. **Portraying**
E+ **Persons with Disabilities: An Annotated Bibliography of Fiction for Children and Teenagers**. 3d ed. New Providence, N.J.: Bowker, 1992. 482p. $39.95. ISBN 0-8352-3023-6.

This title replaces the *Different Drummer* bibliographies (Bowker, 1977, 1984) and complements the new nonfiction volume by Friedberg and others. The introductory matter includes discussions about the writing and publication of fiction about the disabled. The bibliographic chapters parallel those in the nonfiction title, with major categories being physical problems, sensory problems, cognitive and behavior problems and multiple/severe disabilities. Citations include reading levels and name of disabling condition, and the long annotations include an analysis. There is a professional bibliography in addition to the three standard indexes. Highly recommended for all collections.

1002 Rochman, Hazel. **Against Borders: Promoting Books for a Multicultural World**. Chicago: American Library Association, 1993. 288p. $25.00pa. ISBN 0-8389-0601-X.

This excellent work addresses the issues and controversies surrounding multicultural literature. Rochman, who lived under apartheid in South Africa and who is assistant editor for *Booklist's* youth section, believes that books make a difference. Her introduction attempts to put multiculturalism in perspective. The first half of the book consists of thematic essays about literature and culture with examples drawn from a variety of literary works. The second half is an annotated bibliography of fiction, nonfiction and videos about the Holocaust, apartheid, ethnic groups in the United States and issues from other regions around the world. There is a thematic index to the books mentioned in the essays, and a general author-title index. Highly recommended for all secondary schools, for selection, reading guidance and unit planning.

1003 Rosow, La Vergne. **Light 'n Lively**
E+ **Reads for ESL, Adult, and Teen Readers**. Englewood, Colo.: Libraries Unlimited, 1996. 343p. $40.00pa. ISBN 1-56308-365-5.

This bibliography is arranged by themes such as arts, sports and science. Within each theme, recommended books are listed in order of difficulty with easier titles first. Each entry includes a thoughtful and motivating annotation. The author encourages reading aloud as a technique for creating readers. An author, illustrator, title and subject index adds further access. Recommended for all levels to support reading guidance.

1004 Rudman, Masha Kabakow, Kath-
E+ leen Dunne Cagne, and Joanne E. Bernstein. **Books to Help Children Cope with Separation and Loss: An Annotated Bibliography**. 4th ed. New Providence, N.J.: Bowker, 1993. 514p. $55.00. ISBN 0-8352-3412-6.

The 4th edition contains more than 760 titles, including some of the outstanding titles from the 1989 publication as well as new titles. In addition to the annotated bibliographic entries, there are essays about separation and loss and their affect on young people, and a chapter on the practice of bibliotherapy. An extended bibliography of material about these topics is included for adult readers. An appendix lists organizations of assistance for these situations, and separate author, title, subject and interest level indexes provide ample access to the children's literature bibliography. Recommended for all levels for professional and counseling collections.

1005 Samuels, Barbara G., and G. Kylene Beers, eds., with the Committee on the Middle School and Junior High Booklist. **Your Reading: An Annotated Booklist for Middle School and Junior High**. 10th ed. Urbana, Ill.: National Council of Teachers of English, 1996. 381p. biennial. $21.95. ISSN 1051-4740.

About 1,200 books selected from two years of new fiction and nonfiction books and reissues are arranged in seven sections with 24 chapters to make access easy for students looking for good books to read. Section and chapter titles lead students to such topics as growing up, problems and challenges, shudder and shake, and science all around. There is an appendix of 100 books from 25 years of young adult books, a list of award-winning books, a directory of publishers and indexes by author, title, and subject. Highly recommended for middle and junior high school collections.

1006 Storey, Dee. **Twins in Children's and**
E+ **Adolescent Literature: An Annotated Bibliography**. Lanham, Md.: Scarecrow Press, 1993. 399p. $42.50. ISBN 0-8108-2641-0.

More than 350 twin stories are included in this annotated bibliography which lists both in print and out-of-print titles published from 1904 to 1992. This is an inclusive rather than selective list, and contains everything from *Sweet Valley High* and the *Bobbsey Twins* to *Jacob Have I Loved*. Entries include bibliographic citations and genre indications, grade levels, summaries, descriptions of the twins, comments from the author and a topic classification. Titles are indexed according to character importance: main, secondary or minor, and according to the nature of the twins: fraternal or identical. There are also separate author/illustrator, title and subject indexes. This is a reading guidance tool for all twins and twin wannabes.

1007 Stott, Jon C. **Native Americans in**
E+ **Children's Literature**. Phoenix, Ariz.: Oryx Press, 1995. 239p. $26.50pa. ISBN 0-89774-782-8.

As Joseph Bruchac says in the introduction, this book belongs in all school libraries. Stott combines critical narrative with bibliographies to describe why some books are true to the Native American experience and why others are not. Chapters deal with stereotypes and misrepresentations, picture books and traditional stories, trickster and hero tales and cultural conflict. An appendix suggests ways of incorporating Native stories in the language arts [or library literary] program. Indexes include author/illustrator/title, and subject. Highly recommended.

1008 Thiessen, Diane and Margaret
E Matthias, eds. **The Wonderful World of Mathematics: A Critically Annotated List of Children's Books in Mathematics**. Reston, Va.: National Council of Teachers of Mathematics, 1992. 241p. $17.00pa. ISBN 0-87353-353-4.

The editors of this bibliography have evaluated children's books which have mathematics themes as a major emphasis and have rated them in a range from highly to not recommended. They relate the value of using trade books to encourage math abilities and positive attitudes to math, and to the newly developed standards of the National Council of Teachers of Mathematics. The books are grouped into four categories: early concepts (counting), numbers, measurement and geometry. Bibliographic information is given for each title, as is rating, concepts emphasized, grade level and an annotation. There are separate author and title indexes. A new edition is in preparation. Highly recommended for elementary school collections. [R: ARBA 94]

1009 Thomas, Rebecca L. **Connecting**
E **Cultures: A Guide to Multicultural Literature for Children**. New Providence, N.J.: Bowker, 1996. 676p. $40.00. ISBN 0-8352-3760-5.

This bibliography contains 1,637 titles of fiction, folk tales, poetry and songs for preschool and elementary grades that reflect aspects of world cultures and ethnic cultures within the United States. Listed alphabetically by author, each entry includes bibliographic information, suggested grade level, cultural setting, a brief summary and up to six subject headings. The indexes make the volume especially helpful for curriculum planning as the detailed subject indexing is reflected in an extensive subject index. There are also cultural and grade level indexes in addition to title and illustrator indexes. Highly recommended for elementary collections.

1010 VanMeter, Vandelia. **American History for Children and Young Adults: An Annotated Bibliography**. Englewood, Colo.: Libraries Unlimited, 1997. 325p. $38.50. ISBN 0-56308-496-1.

A comprehensive bibliography of American history fiction and nonfiction titles for elementary and secondary students, is useful as both a collection management tool and as a guide to instruction.

The arrangement is chronological with subject arrangement within historical periods. Each item has bibliographic information, grade level, and a brief annotation. There is a grade level index.

1011 **What Do Children Read Next?: A**
E+   **Reader's Guide to Fiction for Children**. 2d ed. Detroit, Mich.: Gale Research, 1997. 1135p. $55.00. ISBN 0-8103-6448-4.

1012 **What Do Young Adults Read Next?: A Reader's Guide to Fiction for Young Adults**. 2d ed. Detroit, Mich.: Gale Research, 1997. 816p. $55.00. ISBN 0-8103-6449-2.

In *What Do Children Read Next?* almost 2,000 annotations of children's book titles each suggest five other related titles that might be enjoyed. The primary entries give author, title, publishing data, age range, subject, major characters' names, setting, a summary, awards or other books by the author and review sources. The other suggested titles are briefly described. Books are for students grades 1-8. Nine indexes provide access for both reading guidance and curricular planning. Highly recommended for elementary and middle schools.

What Do Young Adults Read Next?, a companion to *What Do Children Read Next?*, contains more than 1,500 full entries, each with three to five other suggested titles. Each main entry gives bibliographic data, age range, subject, setting, summary, review sources, and awards. Ten indexes provide many access points for reading guidance and development of bibliographies to support units. As in the companion volume, the author's introduction gives a good perspective of the status of writing for young adults in the 1990s. This source covers grades 6–12, so middle schools need both volumes; high schools need only this one.

1013 Wilson, George, and Joyce Moss.
E   **Books for Children to Read Alone: A Guide for Parents and Librarians**. New Providence, N.J.: Bowker, 1988. 184p. $41.00. ISBN 0-8352-2346-9.

This important bibliography identifies books that primary children can read on their own. Two readability scales, Spache and Fry, were used, but more prominence was given to books that interested readers in this age group. The authors believe, and their own work with children has confirmed, that children read what they want to read. Beginning with wordless or nearly wordless books for pre-readers and beginning readers, the books are listed by each half of the first three grades. Each title is annotated and given a subject heading and a genre category. An appendix lists books in series, and there are subject, readability, author and title indexes. Highly recommended for elementary schools, and useful for middle schools with students still reading on primary levels.

BIOGRAPHY AND CRITICISM

1014 Berger, Laura Standley, ed.
E+   **Twentieth-Century Children's Writers**. 4th ed. Detroit, Mich.: St. James Press, 1995. 1,272p. $140.00. ISBN 1-55862-177-6.

Seven hundred twentieth-century writers of children's books in English—fiction, nonfiction, poetry and drama—are covered in this source with brief personal and career information and lists of awards. Their works are listed in chronological order of their publishing, and there is a long summary and analysis of the body of their work. These signed essays often focus on important titles and show the development of the writer. An appendix lists and describes notable authors from the 19th century as well as foreign language authors whose works have been translated into English. A list of titles with authors and copyright dates acts as an index. The earlier editions included young adult writers, but they have been moved to a separate volume. Recommended for professional collections and for student collections in middle schools.

1015 Berger, Laura Standley. **Twentieth-Century Young Adult Writers**. Detroit, Mich.: St. James Press, 1994. 830p. $140.00. ISBN 1-55862-202-0.

Biographies of 400 young adult authors, bibliographies of their works and signed critical essays about their writing make this reference a useful tool for middle and high school collections. From Edgar Rice Burroughs to Francesca Block, adult authors who are read by teenagers and authors who are often studied in high school classes, this source will have most of the authors and titles young people read. A title list acts as an index.

1016 **Children's Literature Review**. 46v- . Detroit, Mich.: Gale Research, 1987– . $125.00/vol. ISSN 0362-4145.

Each volume in this series contains biographical/critical information about 10-14 children's authors, commentaries excerpted from reviews and other articles, comments by the authors, their portraits, and illustrations from their books. Selected volumes feature essays written especially for the series by such noted critics and authors as Zena Sutherland, John Rowe Townsend, Sheila A. Egoff, and Rudine Sims. Cumulative indexes to authors and titles appear in each volume. Appendixes identify the sources from which material has been drawn. [R: ARBA 90; BL, 1 Feb 89]

1017 Day, Frances Ann. **Latina and Latino Voices in Literature for Children and Teenagers**. Portsmouth, N.H.: Heinemann, 1997. 229p. $28.00pa. ISBN 0-435-07202-1.

This is a comprehensive source of information about Latina and Latino authors and their works. A useful introduction discusses evaluating books for bias, based on a similar list from the Council on Interracial Books for Children. Twenty-three authors receive full biographical and critical treatment, with individual analysis of their works. These entries include a photograph and author's comments, full description of the

works and ideas for using them with children, related titles, grade levels and subject analysis. Fifteen additional authors receive shorter treatment, highlighting one title, and a long list of other authors' names appear in an appendix. Other appendices list literature activities, the authors arranged by birthday, Latina and Latino holidays and valuable lists of resources, one for young people and one for the adults who work with them. There are separate title, illustrator, awards and subject indexes. Recommended for all grade levels.

1018 Drew, Bernard A. **The 100 Most Popular Young Adult Authors: Biographical Sketches and Bibliographies**. rev. ed. Englewood, Colo.: Libraries Unlimited, 1997. 531p. $55.00. ISBN 1-56308-615-8.

This is a useful supplementary tool for brief biographical information about authors writing books from upper elementary to adult levels which are of interest to young adults. Coverage is of mostly contemporary American authors, but other nationalities and classic writers are included as well. Arranged alphabetically, each entry gives biographical data, the types of books written and some critical analysis. Lists for further reading are appended. Middle and high school collections may want this as an additional source.

1019 Hopkins, Lee Bennett. **Pauses:**
E+ **Autobiographical Reflections of 101 Creators of Children's Books**. New York: HarperCollins, 1995. 233p. $23.00. ISBN 0-06-024748-7.

Hopkins has interviewed many children's authors and has selected 101 of them to include in this work. The individuals are divided into four categories: authors, author/illustrators, illustrators and poets. Each entry has a brief biographical sketch and four to ten paragraphs of the person's reflections about writing or illustrating in general and about individual books. These vignettes will provide touches of realism to author units. Recommended for elementary and middle school collections.

1020 **Junior Book of Authors**. 2d ed.
E+ Bronx, N.Y.: H. W. Wilson, 1951. 309p. $40.00. ISBN 0-8242-0028-4.

1021 **More Junior Authors**. Bronx, N.Y.:
E+   H. W. Wilson, 1963. 235p. $35.00.
      ISBN 0-8242-0036-5.

1022 **Third Book of Junior Authors**.
E+   Bronx, N.Y.: H. W. Wilson, 1972.
      320p. $45.00. ISBN 0-8242-0408-5.

1023 **Fourth Book of Junior Authors &**
E+   **Illustrators**. Bronx, N.Y.: H. W.
      Wilson, 1978. 370p. $45.00. ISBN
      0-8242-0568-5.

1024 **Fifth Book of Junior Authors &**
E+   **Illustrators**. Bronx, N.Y.: H. W.
      Wilson, 1983. 357p. $48.00. ISBN
      0-8242-0694-0.

1025 **Sixth Book of Junior Authors &**
E+   **Illustrators**. Bronx, N.Y.: H. W.
      Wilson, 1989. 345p. $48.00. ISBN
      0-8242-0777-7.

1026 **Seventh Book of Junior Authors &**
E+   **Illustrators**. Bronx, N.Y.: H. W.
      Wilson, 1996. 370p. $50.00. ISBN
      0-8242-0873-0.

Those seeking information on the most important creators of juvenile and young adult literature can rely on this ongoing set, which began in 1934. With the addition of the 235 biographical and autobiographical profiles of prominent authors and illustrators contained in the *Seventh Book*, the set now contains over 1,700 entries. It should be noted that the first three books treat authors only; beginning with the *Fourth Book*, illustrators receive attention.

Essays focus on the lives and careers of notables from Hans Christian Andersen, Randolph Caldecott, Kate Greenaway, and A. A. Milne to those who have recently achieved prominence. Entries have author/illustrator pictures and autographs, biographical sketches, lists of works and other sources. Each volume contains an index to all previous works in the series. Highly recommended.

1027 **Something about the Author Auto-**
E+   **biography Series**. Detroit, Mich.:
      Gale Research, 1986– . semiannual.
      $85.00/volume. ISSN 0085-6842.

This companion set to *Something about the Author*, which began in 1986, is the only ongoing

series in which juvenile authors discuss their lives, careers, and published works. Each volume contains essays by 20 established writers or illustrators (e.g., Evaline Ness, Nonny Hogrogian, Betsy Byars, Jean Fritz) who represent all types of literature, preschool to young adult.

The authors/illustrators are given the freedom to express what they want to say, without a set format for the essay. Some articles focus on biographical information, while others emphasize the writing career. Most, however, address young readers and provide family background, discuss the writing experience, and cite some factors that influenced it. Illustrations include portraits of the authors as children and more recent action pictures and portraits. There are cumulative indexes by authors, important published works, and geographical locations mentioned in the essays. [R: ARBA 91]

1028 **Something about the Author: Facts**
E+   **and Pictures about Contemporary**
      Authors and Illustrators of Books for
      Young People. 96v- . Detroit, Mich.:
      Gale Research, 1971– . $96.00/vol.
      ISSN 0267-816X.

This important series gives comprehensive coverage of the individuals who write and illustrate books for children. Each new volume adds about 100 profiles. Entries include career and personal data, a bibliography of the author's works, information on works in progress and references to further information. A section called "Sidelights" provides items about the personal life of the individual. Published entries are often updated in later volumes. Volume 54 indexed volumes 1-54 and included a character index. This is an expensive set, but one that will be used extensively in elementary and middle schools.

BOOKTALKING

1029 Bodart, Joni Richards, ed. **The Book-**
E+   **talkers' Companion**. Worthington,
      Ohio: Linworth Publishing, 1994– .
      semiannual. $19.95. ISSN 1077-3029.

Bodart, who is the author of many titles about booktalking (the Booktalk! and Awards series, Wilson, 1980–1997; *New Booktalker*, Libraries Unlimited, 1992, 1993, and columns in *Library Talk* and *Book Report*), edits this companion which has articles and approximately 125 booktalks written by librarians. The five-minute talks are arranged by genre and books for all grade levels are included, as are adult titles. Entries contain bibliographic citations, grade levels, a rating system based on the VOYA system of popularity and quality rankings, lists of reviews and the actual talk. There are separate author, title, subject and grade level indexes. Recommended for all libraries.

1030 Bodart, Joni Richards. **Booktalking the Award Winners 3**. Bronx, N.Y.: H. W. Wilson, 1997. 192p. $32.00. ISBN 0-8242-0898-6.

1031 Bodart, Joni Richards. **Booktalking the Award Winners: Children's Retrospective Volume**. Bronx, N.Y.: H. W. Wilson, 1997. 350p. $32.00. ISBN 0-8242-0901-X.

These are the latest in the Award Winners booktalking series. *Award Winners 3* includes titles from a wide variety of awards presented during 1994 and 1995 such as the John Newbery Medal, the Margaret A. Edwards Award, the Coretta Scott King Award, Best Books for Young Adults and Notable Children's Books. Bibliographies and indexes help identify books on themes and interests to target specific audiences.

The retrospective volume contains booktalks for titles published before 1992 when the Award Winners series was begun. More than 375 titles which won the Newbery, Caldecott, Hans Christian Andersen Awards and others are included. In preparation is an index to the entire Wilson Booktalking Series, both the Awards and Booktalk! series.

1032 Gillespie, John T., and Corinne J. Naden. **Juniorplots 4: A Book Talk Guide for Use with Readers Ages 12–16**. New Providence, N.J.: Bowker, 1993. 450p. $42.00. ISBN 0-8352-3167-4.

1033 Gillespie, John T., and Corinne J. Naden. **Middleplots 4: A Book Talk Guide for Use with Readers Ages 8-12**. New Providence, N.J.: Bowker, 1994. 434p. $45.00. ISBN 0-8352-3446-0.

1034 Gillespie, John T., and Corinne J. Naden. **Seniorplots: A Book Talk Guide for Use with Readers Ages**

15–18. New Providence, N.J.: Bowker, 1989. 386p. $43.00. ISBN 0-8352-2513-5.

Specifically designed as book talk aids, these titles from the Bowker Book Talk Series list appropriate books for each age group. Each guide lists about 80 books, and the entries give a thorough summary, an idea of thematic material, suggestions for book talks and activities, and a series of related titles with short descriptions. Books are listed in broad subject areas of interest to the audience. There are separate author, title and subject indexes; separate cumulative indexes are included in continuing titles in the series.

1035 Gillespie, John T., and Corinne J.
E+ Naden. **The Newbery Companion: Booktalk and Related Materials for Newbery Medal and Honor Books**. Englewood, Colo.: Libraries Unlimited, 1996. 406p. $48.00. ISBN 1-56308-356-6.

Information about John Newbery and the Award is combined with booktalk suggestions in this useful book for all collections. The award-winning books and the honor books are presented in chronological order with full treatment for the winners: an introduction, plot summaries, themes and subjects, suggested sequences to use for booktalking, other titles related by theme or subject and a bibliography of information about the book and author. Entries for the honor books are limited to substantial annotations. A general bibliography, author, title, and winner subject indexes are helpful. Highly recommended for elementary and middle schools; some high schools will want this as well.

1036 Thomas, Rebecca L. **Primaryplots 2:
E A Book Talk Guide for Use with Readers Ages 4-8**. New Providence, N.J.: Bowker, 1993. 431p. $42.00. ISBN 0-8352-3411-8.

This book in the Bowker Book Talk Series follows the same format as the titles for older students, but lists 150 picture books for the age group. The indexes include current edition author, illustrator, title and subject indexes as well as cumulative indexes which cover both *Primaryplots 1* (Bowker, 1989) and *Primaryplots 2*. Highly recommended for primary collections.

DICTIONARIES AND ENCYCLOPEDIAS

1037 Carpenter, Humphrey, and Mari
E+   Prichard. **Oxford Companion to
       Children's Literature**. New York:
       Oxford University Press, 1984. 586p.
       $55.00. ISBN 0-19-211582-0.

This work, though designed for those who work
with children from grade 5 through middle school
and above, also has reference value for the children themselves. The 2,000 entries, written in a
lively style, cover authors, illustrators, fictitious
characters, children's magazines, films and comic
strips. Moreover, the volume provides plot summaries, discusses genres, and includes other topics relevant to nineteenth- and twentieth-century
children's books (primarily from the English-
speaking world). [R: ARBA 85; BL, 15 Apr 84;
LJ, 15 Apr 85; SLJ, Aug 84; WLB, Oct 84]

1038 Carruth, Gorton. **The Young
E+   Reader's Companion**. New Provi-
       dence, N.J.: Bowker, 1993. 681p.
       $49.95. ISBN 0-8352-2765-0.

This reference tool for young people is an easier
to use format than the *Young Adult Reader's
Adviser*. It is an alphabetically arranged encyclopedia of the best classic and contemporary titles
and authors for students, K–12. Some 800 titles,
750 authors and about 300 historical people and
events are listed. Entries range in length from a
quarter column to a whole column. There is a
subject index. Highly recommended for all levels.

PLOT OUTLINES

1039 **Beacham's Guide to Literature for
E+   Young Adults**. Washington, D.C.:
       Beacham, 1990–1994. v.1-3: $189.00/
       set, ISBN 0-933833-11-3; v.4: $63.00,
       ISBN 0-933833-16-4; v.5: $63.00,
       ISBN 0-933833-25-3; v.6-8: $195.00/
       set, ISBN 0-933833-32-6.

Students, teachers, and librarians will welcome
this excellent set, which surveys and analyzes outstanding books for young adult readers. Among
the more than 600 titles (novels, short story collections, nonfiction works, and biographies) the
reader will find many that tell of earlier times and
places and others that examine the age-old problem of growing up. Some portray a stable and
secure world, while others treat issues that challenge today's young people. School reading lists
frequently cite titles examined in the set.

For each book, the guide provides biographical information about the author and a
description of the book's setting, an analysis of
its theme and characters, an assessment of its literary quality, its relevance to today's society, suggested topics for assignments and discussions,
and a bibliography of critical reviews. A thematic
index supports the alphabetical arrangement.
Appropriate for upper elementary through high
school levels. [R: BL, July 90; VOYA, Apr 91;
WLB, June 90]

1040 Magill, Frank N., ed. **Masterplots II
E+   Juvenile and Young Adult Fiction
       Series**. 4v. Pasadena, Calif.: Salem
       Press, 1991. $365.00/set. ISBN
       0-89356-579-2.

1041 Magill, Frank N., ed. **Masterplots II
       Juvenile and Young Adult Biography
       Series**. 4v. Pasadena, Calif.: Salem
       Press, 1997. $365.00/set. ISBN
       0-89356-700-0.

1042 Magill, Frank N., ed. **Masterplots II
       Juvenile and Young Adult Literature
       Series: Supplement**. 3v. Pasadena,
       Calif.: Salem Press, 1997. $275.00/set.
       ISBN 0-89356-916-X.

The *Fiction Series* analyzes 480 novels while the
Biography Series analyzes 521 biographies and
autobiographies. The supplementary *Literature
Series* includes 207 more novels, 21 more biographies and short stories, poetry collections, plays,
and nonfiction. Each set, which covers works for
students from intermediate grades through high
school, including some adult works, is arranged
by title. The index in the *Literature Series* is
cumulative for the other two sets.

As with other *Masterplots* volumes, these
works are useful for preparing booktalks,
answering reference questions and as a baseline
for beginning analysis. Highly recommended for
all middle and high school collections; many elementary schools will find the sets useful as well.

POETRY

1043 Hall, Donald, ed. **Oxford Book of
E+   Children's Verse in America**. New
       York: Oxford University Press, 1985.
       319p. $35.00; $14.95pa. ISBN 0-19-
       503539-9; 0-19-506761-4pa.

If poetry anthologies are to be duplicated in the reference collection, the *Oxford Book* is a good choice. It consists of some 250 popular American poems for children, some well-known and some not, from all periods of history. Along with poets of the past (e.g., Clement Clark Moore, Mary Mapes Dodge, James Whitcomb Riley) are some who are modern (e.g., Langston Hughes, John Ciardi, David McCord). [R: SLJ, May 86]

1044   Harrison, Michael, and Christopher
E+   Stuart-Clark, eds. **The Oxford Trea-
      sury of Children's Poems**. New York:
      Oxford University Press, 1994. 174p.
      $14.95pa. ISBN 0-19-276134-X.

Some 150 poems by English-speaking poets from William Butler Yeats to Shel Silverstein make up this collection. Poems are loosely grouped by subject (e.g., cars, night, shadows). Illustrations by a number of artists add little to the work, which otherwise is excellent. [R: BW5 Mr 95]

1045   **Index to Children's Poetry**. Bronx,
E+   N.Y.: H. W. Wilson, 1942. 966p.
      $63.00. ISBN 0-8242-0021-7.
      First Supplement. 1954. 405p. $40.00.
      ISBN 0-8242-0022-5. *Second
      Supplement*. 1965. 453p. $40.00.
      ISBN 0-8242-0023-3.

1046   **Index to Poetry for Children and
E+   Young People: 1964–1969**. Bronx,
      N.Y.: H. W. Wilson, 1972. 574p.
      $53.00. ISBN 0-8242-0435-2.

1047   **Index to Poetry for Children and
E+   Young People: 1970–1975**. Bronx,
      N.Y.: H. W. Wilson, 1978. 471p.
      $53.00. ISBN 0-8242-0621-5.

1048   **Index to Poetry for Children and
E+   Young People: 1976–1981**. Bronx,
      N.Y.: H. W. Wilson, 1983. 350p.
      $53.00. ISBN 0-8242-0681-9.

1049   **Index to Poetry for Children and
E+   Young People: 1982–1987: A Title,
      Subject, Authors, and First Line
      Index**. Bronx, N.Y.: H. W. Wilson,
      1989. 574p. $58.00. ISBN 0-8242-
      0773-4.

1050   **Index to Poetry for Children and
E+   Young People: 1988–1992: A Title,
      Subject, Authors, and First Line
      Index**. Bronx, N.Y.: H. W. Wilson,
      1994. 358p. $58.00. ISBN 0-8242-
      0861-7.

This series is the key to poetry in any youth collection. It indexes anthologies by author, title, subject and first line and is essential both for identifying the elusive poem and for adding poetry on specific subjects to whole-language units, booktalks, bibliographies and thematic celebrations. The anthologies indexed are important for collection analysis and collection management. The indexes and the volumes analyzed are not candidates for weeding. Essential for every collection at every level.

1051   Opie, Ione, and Peter Opie, eds. **The
E   Oxford Dictionary of Nursey
      Rhymes**. New York: Oxford
      University Press, 1997. 559p. $45.00.
      ISBN 0-19-860088-7.

Nursery rhymes, songs, and riddles comprise this comprehensive and authoritative work. The 550 entries, arranged alphabetically by keyword, give the standard version of each rhyme followed by other known versions. Indexing is by notables associated with the rhymes and first lines.

PROGRAMS AND ACTIVITIES

1052   Briggs, Diane. **52 Programs for
E   Preschoolers: The Librarian's Year-
      Round Planner**. Chicago: American
      Library Association, 1997. 217p.
      $28.00. ISBN 0-8389-0705-9.

An experienced children's public librarian suggests books, music, games, poems, activities, flannel board, finger plays, video and crafts that can be assembled for a storytime. Themes include holidays, cultures, animals and a variety of others. School librarians can easily adapt these suggestions to their own preschool and primary plans.

1053   Cooper, Kay. **The Neal-Schuman
E+   Index to Fingerplays**. New York:
      Neal-Schuman, 1993. 319p. $29.95.
      ISBN 1-55570-149-3.

This source indexes 60 books that contain fingerplays. The bibliography of these titles and the keys used to indicate them are in the middle of the volume. The first part of the book is an alphabetical list of first (or only) lines referenced to the source(s) and with subjects assigned. The most useful part of the book is the index by subject which identifies fingerplays by typical units used in K–3 curricula. There is a special index by days of the year, and an index of key words so that teachers can use fingerplays as an alphabet letter teaching device. Recommended for all preschool and primary collections.

1054 Defty, Jeff. **Creative Fingerplays and**
E   **Action Rhymes: An Index and Guide**
     to Their Use. Phoenix, Ariz.: Oryx
     Press, 1992. 255p. $29.50. ISBN
     0-89772-709-7.

Intended for adults who work with young children, this collection of verses appropriate for lessons, programs, and enjoyment will be useful for parents, students working with young children, teachers, and librarians. The verses are selected because they provide active learning possibilities, and are developmentally appropriate. The first part of the work discusses evaluating, selecting, and teaching fingerplays, and there are several chapters of examples to use with infants along with techniques to use. One chapter is devoted to children learning English as a second language and others with special needs. A useful chapter describes a core repertoire. Part two contains a subject and first-line index to 3,000 fingerplays and other action rhymes found in 95 sources. There is also a general index. Recommended for professional and parent collections in elementary schools and for reference and circulating collections in high schools with child care programs. [R: ARBA 93]

1055 Delamar, Gloria T. **Children's**
     Counting-Out Rhymes, Fingerplays,
     Jump-Rope and Bounce-Ball
     Chants and Other Rhythms: A
     Comprehensive English-Language
     Reference. Jefferson, N.C.:
     McFarland, 1983. 224p. $27.50.
     ISBN 0-89950-064-1.

Teachers, librarians, parents and child care providers will discover hundreds of ways to entertain and educate children in this collection of rhythmic and dramatic activities for young children. Fingerplays, tongue twisters, and narrative verses are just a few of the kinds of folk entertainments provided in this anthology. Each rhyme or narrative is accompanied by directions where appropriate. There is an index of first lines, authors, and selected subjects. This is a must purchase for elementary school collections and for high schools with teen parents and child care units.

1056 DeSalvo, Nancy. **Beginning with**
E   **Books: Library Programming for**
      Infants, Toddlers, and Preschoolers.
      Hamden, Conn.: Library Professional Publications, 1993. 186p.
      $27.50pa. ISBN 0-208-02318-6.

Program ideas for infants and toddlers, as well as three to five year olds are presented in this work intended for public librarians, but useful as well to school librarians who are involved with preschools and kindergartens. Introductory chapters discuss the importance of library services to young children and their parents. Sample session plans are given for each age group and include book, film, record and activity suggestions. Appendices list standard works for children in the various media, and multiple indexes provide access to materials used in the text. Recommended for parent collections and for schools with early childhood programs.

1057 Jenkins, Christine, and Sally Free
E   man. **Novel Experiences: Literature**
      Units for Book Discussion Groups in
      the Elementary Grades. Englewood,
      Colo.: Teacher Ideas Press/Libraries
      Unlimited, 1991. 231p. $23.00pa.
      ISBN 0-87287-730-2.

Designed as a guide to literature discussion groups, such as Junior Great Books, this work includes 35 literature units for new titles (e.g., *The Beast in Ms. Rooney's Room*) and classics (e.g., *Homer Price*) for grades 2 through 6. Related titles accompany each unit. Despite some criticisms, such as the repetition of activities in different units, the work is clearly written and will be helpful to libraries and teachers planning book discussion programs. [R: SLJ, June 91]

1058 Kelly, Joanne. **The Battle of Books:**
E+   **K–8**. Englewood, Colo.: Libraries
      Unlimited, 1990. 199p. $23.50pa.
      ISBN 0-87287-779-5.

Detailed instructions for the popular reading game, "The Battle of Books," created in 1938, make up this work. The contest requires teams to answer questions based on the plots, settings, and characters of books. Over 850 questions on popular contemporary novels, award books, and classics are included in Kelly's work. The questions on index cards are arranged by grade level, then by difficulty. Kelly suggests skits for a number of the books and provides reproducible publicity ideas, scorecards, bookmarks, and certificates.

Disk versions allow teachers or librarians to add questions, to tailor the game to groups of various sizes or to different age levels, and to record dates and groups with whom specific questions were used. The written skits are contained in a word-processing program.

The computer disk alone may be purchased in AppleWorks, Microsoft Works or ASCII command delimited file formats for around $26.00 each. A book and disk is $40.00.

READING ALOUD

1059 Freeman, Judy. **More Books Kids**
E   **Will Sit Still For: A Read-Aloud**
       Guide. New Providence, N.J.:
       Bowker, 1995. 869p. $49.95. ISBN 0-8352-3520-3.

This update of *Books Kids Will Sit Still For* (1990) adds 1,400 new titles, most published between 1990 and 1995. It highlights books that are good to read aloud to children from preschool through grade six. Fiction titles are listed by grade level, with separate sections on folk tales, fairy tales, myths and legends, nonfiction and biography and poetry and other literature. Each entry gives bibliographic information, a good annotation and subject headings for the item. Often other titles are included in annotations. At least as important as the book lists are the introductory chapters which convey Freeman's strongly held opinions (all on target) about book publishing, reading aloud, and the importance of school libraries. The book concludes with an excellent professional bibliography, and separate author, illustrator, title and detailed subject indexes. This is a first purchase for every elementary collection.

1060 Trelease, Jim. **The Read-Aloud**
E+   **Handbook**. 4th ed. New York: Penguin Books, 1995. 387p. $12.95pa. ISBN 0-14-046971-0.

Trelease's book has become a classic, well known by teachers, librarians and parents. Now in its

fourth edition, the text is still inspirational and the read-aloud program and title suggestions are as valid as ever. The bibliography of notes to the text chapters is especially useful to librarians as it pulls evidence of the value of reading aloud from non-library sources. The annotated list of suggested titles to read aloud is keyed to grade levels and is also valuable. This source should be in parent and professional collections in every school, including high schools with parenting classes.

STORYTELLING

1061 Bauer, Caroline Feller. **Caroline**
E+   **Feller Bauer's New Handbook for**
       Storytellers: With Stories, Poems,
       Magic, and More. Chicago: American Library Association, 1993. 550p.
       $30.00pa. ISBN 0-8389-0613-3.

Bauer is a well-known cheerleader for presenting books, poetry and stories to young people. This title updates the original *Handbook* (1977) with new material, including a new section on family storytelling, and revised lists of stories, books and poems. The first part of the book is an introduction to storytelling. Part two tells where to find stories and poems and jokes and riddles to tell. The third section of the book is called "multimedia" storytelling and includes suggestions for working with pictures, chalk and flannel boards, puppets, magic and music as well as slides and videos. The final part discusses programming for all ages and covers booktalking, book parties and creative dramatics. The volume is filled with short pieces to tell and illustrations of props to make. Many booklists of source material are included. Highly recommended for new and experienced storytellers.

Bauer has also published books for ALA in the Mighty Easy Motivators series, each of which addresses in depth one of her topics in the *Handbook*. Titles include *Leading Kids to Books through Magic* (1996) and *Leading Kids to Books through Puppets* (1997).

1062 Greene, Ellin. **Storytelling: Art and**
E+   **Technique**. 3d ed. New Providence,
       N.J.: Bowker, 1996. 333p. $39.00.
       ISBN 0-8352-3458-4.

This source is from the perspective of public libraries, but the ideas and practices suggested are relevant for school libraries as well. The work covers all aspects of storytelling from the history and biographies of the great American librarian/ storytellers to selecting and preparing stories to adjusting for different age audiences. An especially useful chapter describes storytelling techniques to use for children with special needs and in non-library settings. Another chapter describes children and young adults as storytellers. Suggestions for stories are given throughout the text and an appendix lists many resources for finding stories. The book is illustrated with photographs and has a glossary and a general index. Highly recommended.

1063 **National Storytelling Directory**.
E   Jonesborough, Tenn.: NAPPS, 1994– . annual. $7.95pa. ISSN 1079-3607.

This directory, published by the National Association for the Preservation and Perpetuation of Storytelling, lists U.S. persons, places, and events connected with storytelling. Among those cited are storytellers, organizations, conferences, festivals, centers, institutes/educational opportunities, and books about the art. For storytellers listed (they paid a fee to be included), the slim volume gives addresses, telephone numbers, and information about their repertoires. Advertisements

that publicize workshops, programs, and publications keep the cost of the directory low. Recommended for schools with an interest in the art. [R: ARBA 91]

1064 Pellowski, Anne. **The World of Story-**
E   **telling: A Practical Guide to the Origins, Development, and Applications of Storytelling**. enlarged rev. Bronx, N.Y.: H. W. Wilson, 1990. 311p. $40.00. ISBN 0-8242-0788-2.

Anyone interested in the background of storytelling will welcome this guide, an update of a 1977 work. Pellowski reviews the oral tradition from which literature for children grew; addresses the controversy between storytellers and folklorists; discusses the types, formats, and styles of storytelling; and covers the training of storytellers. The new edition incorporates recent research and offers the author's own insights gained from teaching and practicing the art. An index and a bibliography of training manuals and story collections conclude the volume. This excellent guide is highly recommended. [R: SLJ, Oct 90; SLJ, May 91]

Communication

GENERAL WORKS

1065 Newton, David. **Violence and the Media: A Reference Handbook**. Santa Barbara, Calif.: ABC-CLIO, 1996. 254p. $39.50. ISBN 0-87436-843-X.

The focus of this reference and resource guide is how violence in mass media affects viewers. An overview discusses the varieties of media with which the researcher may be concerned, not only motion pictures and television, but also specifically cartoons, pop music and video games. The work provides a chronology, biographical sketches and a good documents section which includes laws, policy statements, research reports and opinions. There is a directory of concerned organizations and a selected list of both print

and nonprint resources. A glossary and index are included. Useful for both middle and high school collections. [R: ARBA 97]

1066 Weiner, Richard. **Webster's New World Dictionary of Media and Communications**. 2d ed. New York: Macmillan, 1996. 676p. $39.95. ISBN 0-02-860611-6.

This comprehensive and well-designed dictionary defines 30,000 terms, including jargon and slang, covering a wide range of areas (e.g., communications, technology, marketing, journalism), 27 fields in all. High school students who need such material will find this a useful dictionary. [R: ARBA 98]

FORENSICS

1067 Sutton, Roberta Briggs. **Speech Index: An Index to 259 Collections of World Famous Orations and Speeches for Various Occasions**. 4th ed. Lanham, Md.: Scarecrow Press, 1966. 947p. $72.50. ISBN 0-8103-0138-8.

1068 Mitchell, Charity. **Speech Index: An Index to Collections of World Famous Orations and Speeches for Various Occasions: Fourth Edition Supplement, 1966–1980**. Lanham, Md.: Scarecrow Press, 1982. 466p. $65.00. ISBN 0-8108-1518-4.

Speech Index provides access to collections of published orations by author, subject, and type of speech. The main volume includes all material in three previous volumes (1935–1962), with added indexing for 1962–1965. Mitchell's update cumulates the 1966–1970 and 1971–1975 supplements to the 4th edition.

1069 **Vital Speeches of the Day**. Mount Pleasant, S.C.: City News Publishing, 1934– . semimonthly. $30.00/yr. ISSN 0042-742X.

Each semimonthly issue contains the full text of some 12 to 15 addresses on public issues delivered by important figures. The editors attempt to select speeches pertaining to all sides of controversial issues. An annual index is published in November; the serial is also indexed in *Readers' Guide to Periodical Literature*. Recommended for high schools.

JOURNALISM

1070 **Editorials on File**. New York: Facts on File, 1969– . semimonthly. $380.00/yr. ISBN 0-685-42114-7.

This subscription service consists of editorial and editorial cartoons on various topics in the news. The compilers attempt to balance liberal, conservative, and moderate positions drawn from 150 newspapers in all 50 states, the District of Columbia, and Canada. Each issue contains some 200 editorials plus cartoons on 10 to 12 important issues. Subjects are introduced by brief factual surveys. Indexed once each month and cumulated on a quarterly, six-month, nine-month, and annual basis. Subscription cost includes a binder.

1071 **Gale Directory of Publications and Broadcast Media**. Detroit, Mich.: Gale Research, 1990– . annual. $265.00/yr. ISSN 0892-1636.

Long known as the *Ayer Directory of Publications* and later the *ISM Directory of Publications*, this annual has had a variety of publishers. When Gale became its publisher, the name was changed to the current title and broadcast media was added. The aim is to supply directory information for magazines, newspapers, radio and television stations and cable companies in Canada and the United States and its territories and possessions.

Entries, arranged by state and province and then city, begin with brief demographics. For periodicals, the listings give title, publisher, address, telephone and fax numbers, content, date established, frequency, contact persons, subscription price, advertising rates, circulation and special notes. Broadcast media entries give complete contact information and other data useful to marketing and advertising professionals: station call letters and channel, Area of Dominant (AOD) influence, mailing address, telephone and fax numbers, network affiliation, top three local programs with air time, and more. A master alphabetical/keyword index provides access.

1072 McKerns, Joseph P., ed. **Biographical Dictionary of American Journalism**. New York: Greenwood Press, 1989. 820p. $59.95. ISBN 0-313-23818-9.

Using the format of *Dictionary of American Biography*, this source provides biographical essays, contributed by 133 subject specialists, on some 500 deceased or retired American journalists. Readable profiles give dates, a summary of achievements, a chronological narrative of the person's life, and a bibliography of works by and about the subject. Indexing includes names of publications or broadcast companies and other topics related to the biographees. The appendix lists the subjects by media, professional field, and Pulitzer prizes won. [R: ARBA 90; BL, 1 Sept 89; LJ, 15 June 89; WLB, Nov 89]

RADIO

1073 **The ARRL Handbook for the Radio Amateur**. Newington, Conn.: American Radio Relay League, 1985– . annual. $30.00. ISSN 0890-3565.

Formerly the *Radio Amateur's Handbook*, this comprehensive and authoritative handbook offers instructions and information needed to participate in ham-radio activities. Its contents cover fundamental principles, rules and regulations and other technical data, as well as instructions for building receivers, transmitters and other equipment. Those holding editions prior to 1995 will want to update because of changes in format; new editions also include software (DOS format). [R: ARBA 93]

1074 Lackmann, Ronald W. **Same Time, Same Station: An A-Z Guide to Radio from Jack Benny to Howard Stern**. New York: Facts on File, 1996. 370p. $45.00. ISBN 0-8160-2862-1.

Performers, writers, directors and radio shows are listed alphabetically in this one-volume encyclopedia that covers North American national radio broadcasting from the 1920s to the present. The brief biographies of individuals are supported by descriptions of programs which include cast lists, theme songs, histories, air times and networks. Seven appendices include chronologies, sponsors, other personalities and lists of organizations such as museums and fan clubs. There is a selected bibliography and an index. There is a list of stations that replay old programming; one wishes there were an audiography of available recorded shows. This is a good source of information for American history, sociology and communications classes, and for the interdisciplinary decade units. Recommended for high schools. [R: ARBA 97]

TELEVISION AND VIDEO

1075 Bianculli, David. **Dictionary of Teleliteracy: Television's 500 Biggest Hits, Misses, and Events**. New York: Continuum, 1996. 416p. $29.95. ISBN 0-8264-0577-0.

Despite the nagging thought that teleliteracy might be an oxymoron, Bianculli makes an important case for the need to supplement standard sources which ignore television (Bartlett and Hirsch, e.g.) with a comprehensive guide to the major events of American television in its first 50 years, from 1945–1995. He annotates and analyzes 500 such program events, including programs still running. He excludes commercials and most sports, limiting himself to the World Series and the Super Bowl. Included are regular programming and specials such as annual awards programs, news, special news features, children's shows, talk shows and soap operas. Entries are arranged alphabetically, and give the name of the show, its dates and its network; annotations are of various length, the Smothers Brothers/CBS censorship feud is one example of extended coverage. Many photographs add interest to an already interesting narrative. There is a bibliography and both name and title indexes. This is a popular culture resource that will become more valuable with the passage of time. Highly recommended wherever it can fit into the high school curriculum and for browsing as well. [R: ARBA 97]

1076 Brooks, Tim. **The Complete Directory to Prime Time Network TV Shows, 1946–Present**. 6th ed. New York: Ballantine Books, 1995. 1440p. $23.00. ISBN 0-345-39736-3.

This volume provides a historical survey of network television, including technical changes and trends in programming, beginning with "Vaudeo" (1946–1957) to the "soaps" of the 1980s. The main body of the work lists all prime-time, regular and network series, and top syndicated programs aired primarily in the evenings.

Each entry includes dates for the first and last broadcasts, days, times, and networks, names of regular casts and guests, and a description of the series. The 6th edition covers original cable, syndicated and new networks' productions.

1077 Davis, Jeffery. **Children's Television, 1947–1990**. Jefferson, N.C.: McFarland, 1995. 285p. $42.50. ISBN 0-8995-0911-8.

This is a basic reference source that describes programs children watched in the first forty years of television. It covers all types of programming such as action, cartoons, comedy, informative, puppets, westerns and specials. Programs included were not necessarily intended for young audiences, for example, the Brady Bunch and Gilligan's Island. Each show is described with a narrative that gives the number of episodes, actors, plots, network, time, dates and syndication details. Four appendices list awards, landmarks, series in prime time and programs that originated in radio or movies. There is an index. This source provides a convenient source of raw material for analysis by sociology, American culture, history and child study classes.

1078 Erickson, Hal. **Syndicated Television: The First Forty Years, 1947–1987**. Jefferson City, N.C.: McFarland, 1989. 418p. $55.00. ISBN 0-89950-410-8.

Within each chronologically arranged decade, *Syndicated Television* is organized by genre from adventure/mystery to women's programs. Each entry is described in three lines to a page, written in an informal, readable style. A comprehensive index accesses the information by title, cast (including minor personalities), producers, writers, and other such factors. This work complements *The Complete Directory to Prime Time Network TV Shows*. [R: ARBA 90; BL, 15 Dec 89; LJ, Aug 89; WLB, Nov 89]

1079 Erickson, Hal. **Television Cartoon Shows: An Illustrated Encyclopedia, 1949 through 1993**. Jefferson City, N.C.: McFarland, 1995. 659p. $75.00. ISBN 0-7864-0029-3.

This source includes only made-for-television animated cartoons that were broadcast between January 1, 1949 and December 31, 1993. There is an extended history of such cartoons followed by an alphabetical listing by official title of program. Each entry lists the cartoon's network, cable or syndicate, the dates of its broadcast, production and voice credits and a synopsis and critique. Spin-offs and sequels are listed under the heading for the original show. Entries vary in length, depending on the relative importance of the cartoon; the Flintstones entry is about 10 pages, that for the Simpsons is 6 pages. An additional section is a narrative about cartoon voices. There is a selected bibliography and an excellent index. Recommended for high school film and video studies. (R: ARBA 96]

1080 Shapiro, Mitchell E. **Television Network Prime-Time Programming, 1948–1988**. Jefferson, N.C.: McFarland, 1989. 743p. $58.50. ISBN 0-89950-412-4.

Tables and timelines cover prime-time programming (7 p.m. to 11 p.m., Eastern Standard Time) of commercial networks, 1948 to 1988. The work is divided into seven chapters, one for each day of the week, that provide the program's name and type, episode running time, and previous/new times for every month of the 40-year span. This work complements *Syndicated Television: The First Forty Years: 1947–1987*. [R: ARBA 90; WLB, Nov 89]

WRITING AND REPORTS

1081 **The Chicago Manual of Style**. 14th ed. Chicago: Chicago University Press, 1993. 921p. $40.00. ISBN 0-226-10389-7.

This style manual, widely accepted by publishers, writers, colleges, and universities, is a required holding for most high school libraries. The book provides extensive coverage of footnote/bibliographic form, organization, and manuscript preparation. It recommends the author-date method of documentation as the most practical, with endnotes as the preferred form. The 14th edition added information about computer word processing and desktop publishing, and revised documentation, copyright, and foreign language sections. *A Manual for Writers of Term Papers, Theses and Dissertations* abridges this work. [R: ARBA 93]

1082 Gibaldi, Joseph. **MLA Handbook for Writers of Research Papers**. 4th ed. New York: Modern Language Association of America, 1995. 293p. $13.50pa. ISBN 0-87352-565-5.

This update of a standard work, first published in 1977, has high school and college students as its primary audience. It now includes citations for electronic and some Internet sources as well as an expanded section on punctuation. The manual is divided into six chapters: research and writing, the mechanics of writing, the format of the research paper, preparing the list of works cited, documenting sources, and abbreviations and reference works. It gives rules on abbreviations, footnotes, bibliographies, and other matters of style, and it recommends parenthetical documentation and the use of a works-cited page rather than a bibliography. Also provided are examples that illustrate rules, sample pages, and an index.

1083 Henderson, Kathy. **Market Guide for**
E+   **Young Writers**. 5th ed. Cincinnati,
      Ohio: Writer's Digest Books, 1996.
      309p. $16.99pa. ISBN 0-89879-721-7.

This handbook presents information about markets for writing by children and young adults in the same way as traditional writer's market guides for adults. The new edition has not only revised and updated the markets and contests, but has also included electronic publishing information. One section discusses things to avoid such as markets and contests that require large pre-payments or the purchase of publications. Narrative chapters on writing, marketing, getting published, manuscript preparation and commonly asked questions and a section profiling young authors and professional editors precede the market and contest lists which make this a reference source. Symbols designate those entries which require fees, are for Canadian young people, or are for serious older young writers. Each entry gives directory information, submission information, editor's remarks, and subscription rates. An appendix deals specifically with writing plays and there is an index. This source should be in all collections at every level, and it should be introduced to both teachers and students. [R: ARBA 97]

1084 Hodges, John C. **Harbrace College**
      Handbook. 13th ed. San Diego,
      Calif.: Harcourt Brace Jovanovich,
      1997. 768p. $30.75. ISBN 0-15-
      503948-2.

1085 Kramer, Melinda G. **Prentice Hall**
      Handbook for Writers. 12th ed.
      Englewood Cliffs, N.J.: Prentice-
      Hall, 1995. 725p. $25.60. ISBN 0-13-
      037425-3.

Intended for high school and college students, each of these guides to English usage contains substantial sections on writing research papers. Both Harbrace and Prentice-Hall cover the Modern Language Association and American Psychological Association documentation styles and provide excellent examples. Recommended for high schools. [R: BL, 1 Apr 91]

1086 Markman, Roberta H., Peter T.
      Markman, and Marie L. Waddell. **10**
      Steps in Writing the Research Paper.

5th ed. New York: Barron's Educational Series, 1994. 160p. $9.95. ISBN 0-8120-1868-0.

This detailed guide may overwhelm some students; nonetheless, it is a cogent work, covering the research paper in depth. Since this manual appeared in 1965, it has been considered a standard of its genre. New information in this edition includes the use of online computer searching; the citation of material from software, videotape, television, and radio; and documentation through parenthetical referencing. One perceptive chapter addresses plagiarism. Sample papers demonstrate two popular styles of documentation, one using traditional footnotes, and the other using parenthetical referencing. Recommended for high schools.

1087 McInerney, Claire. **Tracking the**
      Fact: How to Develop Research
      Skills. Minneapolis, Minn.:
      Lerner, 1990. 64p. $14.95. ISBN
      0-8225-2426-0.

Designed for students in grades 4 through 7, this small volume covers the major steps in researching and writing papers and executing research projects. With emphasis on the importance of planning and preliminary research, the book treats primary sources, interviews, and secondary accounts. It also covers basic library skills, traditional works such as *Readers' Guide*, and the new technologies. The manual has sections on note cards, preparing the final draft, and making bibliographies. Excellent examples, numerous charts, and outlines are provided. A bibliography and index complete the guide. Recommended for elementary and middle school levels. [R: BR, Mar/Apr 91; SLJ, Jan 91]

1088 Miller, Joan I., and Bruce Taylor. **The**
      Punctuation Handbook. West Linn,
      Oreg.: Alcove Publishing, 1989. 89p.
      $4.95. ISBN 0-937473-14-6.

This small volume explains the rules of punctuation in lucid language, illustrated with simple examples. Guidelines for using the "17 marks" (apostrophe through vigule) are followed by a section on capitalization, examples of proofreaders' marks, and a glossary of terms used in the text. Recommended for secondary schools. [R: ARBA 90]

1089 **Poet's Market**. Cincinnati, Ohio; Writer's Digest Books, 1986– . annual. $19.95. ISSN 0883-5470.

This annual lists 1,800 places where writers can place their poetry for publication. It also has articles and interviews which advise how to go about publishing poetry and lists relevant resources. A separate section lists grants, contests and awards. There are geographical, subject and general indexes.

1090 **Publication Manual of the American Psychological Association**. 4th ed. Washington, D.C.: American Psychological Association, 1994. 368p. $29.95. ISBN 1-55798-243-0.

This style manual is used by many disciplines in addition to psychology. It is divided into chapters that deal with the content and organization of a manuscript, writing style and grammar, editorial style for punctuation, spelling, capitalization, notes, reference lists, manuscript preparation and manuscript production. Additional sections contain an explanation of A. P. A. Journals and a bibliography. Appendices include information on theses, dissertations and student papers. While this manual is most often used at the college level, it should be available in high schools where students are taking Advance Placement courses or distance courses from colleges and universities.

1091 Slade, Carol. **Form and Style: Theses, Reports, Term Papers**. 10th ed. Boston: Houghton Mifflin, 1997. 250p. $24.76. ISBN 0-395-79655-5.

Known until the 9th edition as *Campbell's Form and Style*, this handbook incorporates the bibliographic style of the *MLA Handbook* and the *Chicago Manual of Style*. It describes formats for all materials including computer software, the Internet and the World Wide Web. This is an appropriate style manual for high school students.

1092 Strunk, William, Jr., with E. B. White. **The Elements of Style**. 3d ed. Old Tappan, N.J.: Allyn & Bacon, 1979. 85p. $11.95; $5.95pa. ISBN 0-02-418190-0; 0-205-19158-4pa.

"Will Strunk loved the clear, the brief, the bold, and his book is clear, brief, and bold." This small volume, revised by award-winning children's writer and essayist White, is a valuable addition to any library. It is prescriptive, conservative, and humorous; in sum, it is the best book available on how to write English prose. Rules of good usage are stated, followed by incorrect and correct examples. [R: ARBA 80; LJ, 15 May 79]

1093 Sutcliffe, Andrea J., ed. **The New York Public Library Writer's Guide to Style and Usage**. New York: HarperCollins, 1994. 838p. $35.00. ISBN 0-06-270064-2.

The title to this source should read ...Writer's and Publishing Guide, as the combination of writing and publishing makes the guide especially useful. The first three sections are a writing guide in the descriptive manner emphasizing contemporary usage for informal writing and speaking. Also included are discussions about avoiding bias and sexist language, 1,000 frequently misused words, grammatical controversies and the importance of consistency within a document. The final two sections treat preparing manuscripts and designing, producing and printing publications. Computer applications for both writing and publishing are treated throughout the work. More than 50 illustrations, charts and tables and 145 sidebars on the history and traditions of writing and publishing add interest. While some may wish for a more traditional viewpoint on usage, this guide will be one of the most used in any secondary library. Highly recommended. [R: ARBA 95]

1094 Turabian, Kate L. **A Manual for Writers of Term Papers, Theses, and Dissertations**. 6th ed. Chicago: University of Chicago Press, 1996. 308p. $12.95. ISBN 0-226-81627-3.

This well-known and widely used handbook abridges *The Chicago Manual of Style*. The chapters treat such topics as parts of the paper; abbreviations and numbers' spelling and punctuation; capitalization, quotations, and underlining; illustrations; and footnotes and bibliographies.

This new edition reflects the changes in the *Chicago Manual of Style* including word processing and citations of electronic sources, including Web sites. Sample pages serve as models for the title page, table of contents, and other sections of the paper. This volume continues to be a standard guide for writing term papers. Recommended for high schools. [R: BL 1 July 95]

1095 The Writer's Handbook. Boston, Mass.: Writer, Inc., 1936– . $32.70. annual. ISSN 0084-2710.

Those seeking suggestions on how to write fiction and nonfiction in various formats and how to market the finished product will welcome this standard handbook. Articles on writing and manuscript preparation make up much of each annual. The main part of the book is a market guide, mainly to the periodical field but including radio, television, and book publishing as well. For each publisher the entry provides name, address, editor, editorial requirements, type of material sought, payment rate, and other useful information. A list of literary agents and organizations for writers is also included. This work is far more than a directory of publishers. Its articles on how to write for specific markets make it a first choice of publications of its kind. [R: ARBA 91]

1096 Writer's Market. Cincinnati, Ohio: Writer's Digest Books, 1922– . annual. $24.95. ISSN 0084-2729.

Published annually since 1922, this guide to markets for prospective writers covers over 4,000 outlets from book and magazine publishers to script producers and greeting card companies. Each entry offers name and address, type of material sought, editorial needs, submission requirements, payment rates, and other useful data. Essays offer advice on pricing, researching the market, establishing copyright, and self-promotion. [R: ARBA 91]

Decorative Arts

ARTS AND CRAFTS

1097 Fleming, John, and Hugh Honour. **The Penguin Dictionary of the Decorative Arts**. New York: Harper & Row, 1990. 896p. $65.00pa. ISBN 0-670-82047-4.

A revision of the 1974 work, this dictionary emphasizes the decorative arts of Europe and North America since the Middle Ages, discussing all styles and the artists who created them. Some 5,000 entries, 600 new to this edition, are illustrated with over 1,000 black-and-white photographs and 67 color plates. Styles, techniques, and individual pieces (e.g., furniture, costume, china, glass) are well covered.

1098 Pile, John F. **Dictionary of 20th-Century Design**. New York: Facts on File, 1990. 312p. $35.00. ISBN 0-8160-1811-1.

Design is defined in this work as "useful artifacts" rather than the older terms of craft or applied art; further, the term *design* implies a designer. Included in the source, therefore, are some individuals such as architects, engineers, potters, weavers, metal workers and photographers. Integrated within an alphabetical arrangement are entries about design as it relates to products, graphics, interiors, typography and advertising. Also included are styles, firms, critics, places, technical terms, materials and techniques and magazines and journals. It does not include town planning or landscape design. Most articles refer to the 20th century, with a few late and important 19th century entries.

The range of entries is wide from Airstream trailers and Laura Ashley to the Corvette, Eames chairs and Earl Tupper. Two hundred drawings and photographs accompany the articles. There is an index. Highly recommended to support secondary art and design courses. [R: ARBA 92]

FASHION AND COSTUME

1099 Baclawski, Karen. **The Guide to Historic Costume**. New York: Drama Book Publishers, 1995. 239p. $28.00pa. ISBN 0-8967-6213-0.

This guide is most useful as a reader's advisor for British novels, but also serves as a resource for drama productions and fashion classes. Despite its purpose as a historic guide, unlike most costume books it is arranged alphabetically from Aprons to Wellingtons. The juxtapositions of modern and historic garments due to the volume's arrangement can be disconcerting. The items included are taken from fashionable and everyday dress that have survived and are in the collections of British museums. Each entry gives the history and development of the garment; more than 250 splendid illustrations accompany the text. A glossary, a list of the British museums and a bibliography complete the work.

1100 Calasibetta, Charlotte Mankey. **Fairchild's Dictionary of Fashion**. 2d ed. New York: Fairchild Publications, 1988. 749p. $60.00. ISBN 0-87005-635-2.

An update of a 1982 dictionary, this work defines over 15,000 cultural and artistic terms related to fashion from classical to modern times. Over 500 black-and-white drawings, 16 pages of full-color illustrations, and a biographical index of designers support the concise definitions. Recommended for high school libraries requiring a reference tool on fashion. [R: ARBA 89; BL, 15 Dec 88]

1101 Martin, Richard H. **The St. James Fashion Encyclopedia: A Survey of Style from 1945 to the Present**. Detroit, Mich.: Visible Ink, 1997. 438p. $29.95. ISBN 0-7876-1036-4.

This attractively designed biographical and historical source which is a revised edition of *Contemporary Fashion* (St. James Press, 1995), has 200 essays on designers since 1945. Most individuals are western, although a few Japanese designers are included. The fashion areas covered are mens' and womens' clothing and accessories such as hats, shoes and jewelry. Each entry contains the name, an identifier (such as American designer), brief biographical facts and an essay that emphasizes the career and its importance. Photographs accompany many entries. A separate list of additional designers is attached with very brief entries. There is a nationality index.

1102 Racinet, Albert. **The Historical Encyclopedia of Costumes**. New York: Facts on File, 1988. 320p. $45.00. ISBN 0-8160-1976-2.

This work condenses Racinet's classic six-volume set, *History of World Costume (1876–1888)*, and translates it into English for the first time. Its text and 2,000 illustrations, most in full color,

cover worldwide costumes from ancient Egypt to nineteenth-century Europe—royalty, the working class, soldiers, and the poor. High school libraries should consider acquiring this volume. [R: ARBA 89; BL, 15 Feb 89; LJ, Dec 88]

1103 Stegemeyer, Anne. **Who's Who in Fashion**. 3d ed. New York: Fairchild Publications, 1996. 300p. $43.00pa. ISBN 1-56367-040-2.

Some 250 established international fashion designers, promising newcomers, and influential persons in related fields are the focus of this work. All articles are short; only the famous receive a page or more of space and several illustrations. There is a bibliography. Black-and-white photographs and 16 pages of full-color plates illustrate the volume, which is appropriate for high school libraries. [R: ARBA 90]

1104 Wilcox, Ruth Turner. **The Dictionary of Costume**. New York: Scribner, 1977. 406p. $60.00. ISBN 0-684-15150-2.

1105 Wilcox, Ruth Turner. **Five Centuries of American Costume**. New York: Scribner, 1977. 224p. $40.00. ISBN 0-684-15161-8.

1106 Wilcox, Ruth Turner. **Folk and Festival Costumes of the World**. New York: Scribner, 1977. 240p. $55.00. ISBN 0-684-15379-3.

1107 Wilcox, Ruth Turner. **Mode in Costume**. New York: Scribner, 1974. 480p. $18.00. ISBN 0-684-13913-8.

Wilcox, an authority on costume, has written several standard works on the subject. *The Dictionary of Costume* contains 3,200 entries on articles of clothing worldwide and from all periods—jewelry, underclothing, fabrics, lace, folk costume, high fashion, academic and military dress, tailoring, and dressmaking tools and terms. There are also 60 brief biographies of notables.

Five Centuries of American Costume, which focuses on the people of North and South America, present costumes from the sixteenth to the twentieth century and includes clothing of Native Americans, the military, and children.

Folk and Festival Costumes of the World describes and illustrates traditional costumes from 150 countries. The arrangement is alphabetical by country, with one page of text accompanying a facing plate of six or more black-and-white drawings. *Mode in Costume* surveys the history of fashion from 3000 B.C. (ancient Egypt) to 1958. Drawings illustrate the text.

FURNITURE AND INTERIOR DESIGN

1108 Banham, Joanna. **Encyclopedia of Interior Design**. 2v. Chicago: Fitzroy Dearborn Publishers, 1997. $250.00/set. ISBN 1-884964-19-2.

This two-volume set offers introductory information about a comprehensive list of subjects related to secular interior design. Architects,. designers, room types, decoration, items of furniture, periods and styles are arranged alphabetically. The signed critical articles are broad historical surveys and have additional readings; many are illustrated with black and white photographs. Despite country articles with an international scope and entries for ancient history, the scope is largely European and North American from the 19th and 20th centuries. Entries include such topics as Art Deco, bathrooms, cabinets, chintz, doors, Thomas Jefferson, rococo, stoves and wallpaper. This set would be of use to many curricular areas in high schools.

1109 Byars, Mel. **The Design Encyclopedia**. New York: Wiley, 1994. 612p. $60.00. ISBN 0-471-02455-4.

The decorative and applied arts from the last 125 years are the subjects of this work which emphasizes people, organizations and materials. Furniture, textiles, glass, metalware, wallpaper, interiors and ceramics are among the objects covered. The work is multinational in scope, emphasizing Eastern and Western Europe, North and South America, Australia and Japan. Entries are alphabetical with the biographies including general biographical information, career and exhibitions and awards. There is a chronology of international exhibitions from 1851–1992 and a list of specialized exhibitions from roughly the same time period. The section of plates shows 118 classic design items. Recommended for art and design classes in high schools. [R: ARBA 95]

TEXTILES

1110 Jerde, Judith. **Encyclopedia of Textiles**. New York: Facts on File, 1992. 260p. $45.00. ISBN 0-8160-2105-8.

Excellent illustrations, many in color, enhance this dictionary. Color plates show fabrics and designs, drawings are used to help explain processes and black and white photographs accompany entries on equipment. Tables categorize fabrics by generic name, trade name, manufacturer and characteristics. The brief entries describe the history, production and care of fabrics in three concise paragraphs. Other types of entries cover people, finishes, dyes, printing, weaving and legal issues. There is a bibliography and a classified subject index that complements the alphabetical arrangement. This source would be useful for both art design and sewing classes in middle and high schools.

1111 **Textile Terms and Definitions**. 10th ed. Manchester, England: Textile Institute, 1995. 401p. $90.00. ISBN 1-870812-77-8.

Published since 1954 this dictionary is the established authority of standard definitions for all aspects of textiles and textile manufacturing. Coverage includes terms relating to the design, science, technology, manufacture, management, testing, use and marketing of textiles. Entries are for fibers, fabrics, processes, equipment, floorcoverings and clothing. There is a British emphasis, but American terms are also included. Entries are arranged alphabetically and although brief, consist of definitions and explanations. Drawings are used where appropriate. This source is recommended for high schools with design and textile or clothing production courses.

Film Study

DICTIONARIES AND ENCYCLOPEDIAS

1112 Bogle, Donald. **Blacks in American Film and Television: An Encyclopedia**. New York: Garland, 1988. 510p. $85.00. ISBN 0-8240-8715-1.

This reference work, filled with facts and strong opinions, provides highly critical evaluations of over 260 films (Hollywood and independent) and over 100 television series, specials and programs featuring Black performers. A profile section traces the careers of some 100 Black actors and a few directors. Excellent illustrations, a bibliography and a substantial index support the text. Although this work is now outdated, it presents a comprehensive historical background of African American entertainers and is recommended for high schools.

1113 Halliwell, Leslie. **Halliwell's Film and Video Guide**. New York: HarperCollins, 1977. annual. 1312p. $22.50pa. ISBN 0-06-273505-5.

This annual publication covers the history of film. It lists thousands of films and television movies from the United States and the United Kingdom. Each film listing gives actors, writers, directors, producers and a plot summary and critical evaluation. A rating system and symbol of availability on videotape are attached. This is a standard source for film information.

1114 **International Dictionary of Films and Filmmakers**. 3d ed. 4v. Detroit, Mich: St. James Press, 1997. $500.00. ISBN 1-55862-199-7.

Each volume of this set covers a different aspect of film and filmmaking. Volume 1 contains 680 entries of selected films. The format for entries gives cast lists with roles played, major awards, crew members and location data. The 3rd edition adds a geographic index. Volume 2 has 500 entries for directors with brief biographies, complete filmographies, and a signed essay. Volume 3 lists 500 actors and actresses with similar information. The entries in Volume 4 include writers and production artists such as animators. All volumes have many

photographs. This set is recommended for high schools that offer film studies courses.

1115 Katz, Ephraim. **The Film Encyclopedia**. 2d ed. New York: HarperCollins, 1994. 1496p. $25.00pa. ISBN 0-06-273089-4.

More than 7,000 entries of individuals, studios, styles, film genres, organizations, events, jargon and technical terms are covered in this one-volume comprehensive dictionary of film. No specific film titles are included. The coverage is international, but the emphasis is on the United States and the U.K. Biographical entries for directors, producers, stars, screenwriters and cinematographers have film credits. Entries vary in length from one sentence definitions to two or more columns. Tables give such information as Academy Award Winners. This is an indispensable source for film collections. [R: ARBA 95]

1116 Konigsberg, Ira. **The Complete Film Dictionary**. New York: New American Library, 1989, c1987. 512p. $18.95pa. ISBN 0-452-00980-4.

This dictionary covers all aspects of the film industry—technology, production, distribution, economics, history and criticism. Over 3,500 clear, easy-to-understand entries also address the artistic approach to film making by genre: fictional, documentary and experimental. Line drawings and motion-picture stills complement the text. This dictionary is an excellent choice for high schools.

1117 Siegel, Scott, and Barbara Siegel. **The Encyclopedia of Hollywood**. New York: Facts on File, 1990. 499p. $45.00. ISBN 0-0160-1792-1.

This who's who of stars, producers, directors, cinematographers and other filmmakers offers a survey of the American industry in some 700 brief entries, many with black-and-white photographs. The work also offers succinct summaries of famous movies and discusses the various film genres, technical advances and behind-the-scenes activities involved in producing movies.

Not so comprehensive as the *International Directory of Film and Filmmakers*, but more appropriate when an inexpensive film resource is needed for general reference.

1118 Stanley, John. **Creature Features Movie Guide Strikes Again: An A to Z Encyclopedia to the Cinema of the Fantastic**. 4th rev. ed. Pacifica, Calif.: Creatures at Large Press, 1995. 454p. $20.00pa. ISBN 0-940064-09-X.

John Stanley is the host of "Creature Features" which is a popular San Francisco show, and in his series of guides reviews with critical humor thousands of films in which extrahuman forces play a major role. Included are feature films, and films made for direct video distribution or for television—network, syndicated and cable. Entries contain major cast credits, director, and a synopsis supported by movie stills and photographs. Standard film guides do not list many of the films reviewed in the Stanley guides.

A mass market paperback (Berkley, 1997, 582p. $7.99) is also available with the title *Creature Features: The Science Fiction, Fantasy, and Horror Movie Guide*.

FILMOGRAPHIES

1119 Hicken, Mandy, and Ellen Baskin. **Enser's Filmed Books & Plays, 1928–1991**. 5th ed. Brookfield, Vt.: Ashgate, 1993. 750p. $84.95. ISBN 1-8574-026-8.

This useful source lists films alphabetically and gives the production company and the author, title and publisher of the book or play from which the film was adapted. An author index lists the books with original title and publisher matched with the film title and date. A final index lists original titles of books with authors and the new name given to the film. Highly recommended for high school collections to support both film and literature courses.

HANDBOOKS

1120 Gehring, Wes D., ed. **Handbook of American Film Genres**. New York: Greenwood Press, 1988. 405p. $69.50. ISBN 0-313-24715-3.

Students who require an introduction to the concept and classification of film genres and critical and historical literature on filmmaking will find this volume of use. Nineteen chapters group types into five broad categories: action/adventure, comedy, fantasy, songs and soaps, and nontraditional. Each chapter consists of essays that define and analyze the genre, a bibliographic essay on secondary literature, and a selective filmography that lists significant examples of the genre. Indexed by name and title. High schools that support strong film-study programs may wish to consider this scholarly work. [R: BL, 1 Nov 88]

Fine Arts

BIOGRAPHY

1121 Ergas, G. Aimee. **Artists: From**
E+   **Michelangelo to Maya Lin**. 2v. Detroit, Mich.: U*X*L, 1995. $38.00/ set. ISBN 0-8103-9862-1.

Biographies of 62 sculptors, painters, architects, photographers, illustrators and designers from Europe and North America are presented in this attractive two-volume set. Coverage includes artists from the Renaissance to the present. Each volume has a contents list of entries of both volumes, a classified list of the artists by field and medium, a glossary, and a chronology (1501–1995) with a timeline at the bottom of the pages. The alphabetically arranged entries vary in length from 5 to 10 pages and have a portrait, dates, quotations, and subheadings which organize the narrative. Boxed sidebars highlight important works, events and art styles. There are 140 illustrations of the artists and their works. The selection of artists includes the most important masters, but the modern artists include many women and minorities. The coverage of women artists is especially strong and includes such individuals as Berenice Abbott, Judy Chicago, Frieda Kahlo, Kathe Kollwitz, Faith Ringgold, and

August Savage in addition to Maya Lin. There is a list of further reading. The index in each volume includes entries in both volumes. This outstanding set should be in every middle school; it is also appropriate for many upper elementary and high school collections. [R: ARBA 96]

1122 Goulart, Ron. **The Great Comic Book Artists**. New York: St. Martin's Press, 1989. 128p. $12.95. ISBN 0-312-34557-7.

1123 Goulart, Ron. **The Great Comic Book Artists. Volume 2**. New York: St. Martin's Press, 1986. 122p. $12.95. ISBN 0-312-01768-5.

Summaries of the careers of comic-book artists, historical and contemporary, comprise these volumes (60 in volume 1 and 56 in volume 2). Each one-page essay contains biographical, critical, and career information, supported by a black-and-white illustration of the artist's work on the opposite page. Students interested in a career in the field will enjoy this brief introduction to the world of comic-book artists. [R: ARBA 87; ARBA 91; LJ, 15 June 86; VOYA, Dec 89]

1124 Gowing, Lawrence, ed. **A Biographical Dictionary of Artists**. rev. ed. New York: Facts on File, 1995. 784p. $50.00. ISBN 0-8160-3252-1.

No major Western artist is missing from this lavishly illustrated work. Architects, painters, sculptors, stage designers, landscape designers and book illuminators are all represented. An extensive chronology divided into three major periods: Romanesque to Baroque, Baroque to Realism and Impressionism to the present, is further classified by country. The artists are then listed in alphabetical order with articles varying from about one paragraph to two pages for Picasso. A glossary and an index complete this beautiful book. Highly recommended for middle school and high school. [R: ARBA 96]

1125 Marks, Claude. **World Artists, 1950–1980: An H. W. Wilson Biographical Dictionary**. Bronx, N.Y.: H. W. Wilson, 1984. 912p. $83.00. ISBN 0-8242-0707-6.

1126 Marks, Claude. **World Artists, 1980–1990: An H. W. Wilson Biographical Dictionary**. Bronx, N.Y.: H. W. Wilson, 1991. 413p. $58.00. ISBN 0-8242-0827-7.

Marks provides profiles and critical commentaries for world-renowned artists (312 in the foundation volume and 120 in the second) who represent a variety of styles and movements in painting, sculpture, and the graphic media. The evaluations cite statements by critics and reviewers and often quote the artists. Each essay is followed by lists of the artist's works, major exhibits, and a bibliography of reviews. These authoritative and readable volumes are recommended for middle schools and high schools. [R: ARBA 92; WLB, Oct 91]

DICTIONARIES AND ENCYCLOPEDIAS

1127 Apostolos-Cappadona, Diane. **Dictionary of Christian Art**. New York: Continuum, 1994. 376p. $39.50. ISBN 0-8264-0779-X.

All aspects of Christian art are included in this basic reference. Alphabetically arranged entries cover terms from art history, biblical studies, church history, Christian theology, signs and symbols, objects, events, places, and some individual theologians, artists and art works. There are 162 black and white illustrations, a bibliography and an index. Useful for art history and religious study courses. [R: ARBA 96]

1128 Brownstone, David, and Irene
E+ Franck. **Timelines of the Arts and Literature**. New York: Harper-Collins, 1994. 711p. $30.00. ISBN 0-06-270069-3.

A detailed chronology of cultural history from cave paintings to the Beatles is presented in this large volume which complements general timelines that cannot cover the arts so specifically. The scope is wide and includes painting, sculpture, photography, architecture, popular and classical music, film, theater, television, dance and opera, fiction and poetry and even circuses and other minor arts. World events are noted for perspective. Arrangement is chronological and then by broad art categories. The first section is for the time period before 1499, then sections are by century, then decade, and finally, year-by-year. Headings of key words are at the top of pages and there is an index. This source belongs in every high school reference collection for both art and history classes. [R: ARBA 95]

1129 Carr-Gomm, Sarah. **The Dictionary of Symbols in Western Art**. New York: Facts on File, 1995. 240p. $22.95. ISBN 0-8160-3301-3.

Allusions in pictures are the topic of this book which is intended to be a guide to the meanings of works of art. Symbols based on the saints and martyrs, on myth and the Bible and on characters and episodes from the Middle Ages to the 19th century are listed, defined and explained. There are special highlighted features on the treatment of major themes or topics such as "Adam and Eve," "Birds," "Landscapes" and "Still Lifes." Arrangement is alphabetical with cross-references and there are indexes by artist and supplementary words for which there are no main entries. Appropriate for both middle and high schools. [R: ARBA 96]

1130 **Dictionary of the Arts**. New York: Facts on File, 1994. 564p. $29.95. ISBN 0-8160-3205-X.

This comprehensive handbook covers terms from a long list of the fine, applied and practical arts such as painting, photography, cinema, theater, music, dance, world and classical literature (including fairy tales), fashion and design. A sampling of entries includes "Invisible Man," "Ionic," "Irons, Jeremy," "Irving, John," "Irving, Washington," "Islamic Architecture" and "Ives, Charles." It attempts to put all articles within a cultural/historical context. Broader topics are treated in longer entries. The text is interspersed with chronologies, quotations and tables in boxes between entries. Arrangement is alphabetical. Unfortunately there are no illustrations; nonetheless this is an excellent and affordable dictionary and is recommended for both middle and high school collections. [R: ARBA 95]

1131 **International Encyclopedia of Art**.
E+   8v. New York: Facts on File, 1996–1997. $136.00. ISBN 0-8160-3327-7.

This set introduces world art, including both folk and fine art. Ancient Mediterranean, African, Far Eastern and Latin art are covered in one volume,

while European and North American (including Native American) art are covered in two volumes each. Arrangement is roughly chronological with 40 color and 60 black and white photographs in each volume. Sidebars and boxes are used for biographical and background information. Each volume contains a table of contents, a timeline, a bibliography and an index. The easy reading level and attractive layout make this set useful as a basic guide to world art for all collections. Volumes are available separately as well.

1132 Janson, Horst W., and Anthony F. Janson. **History of Art**. 5th ed. New York: Abrams, 1995. 856p. $60.00. ISBN 0-8109-3421-3.

A standard art history, this work surveys Western painting, sculpture, and architecture from the earliest times to the present. Although it is a textbook, this handsomely illustrated volume is also an excellent reference source for high schools. *History of Art for Young People* is more suitable for younger students.

1133 Janson, Horst W., and Anthony F.
E+   Janson. **History of Art for Young People**. 5th ed. New York: Harry Abrams, 1997. 632p. $49.50. ISBN 0-8109-4150-3.

This work is a rewritten version of *History of Art* for young readers, grades 5 to 9. In addition to a lucid text, the work includes 434 outstanding plates; maps; a glossary; a synoptic table that lists events in political history, religion, literature, science, architecture, and painting; and an index. This book was also published by Prentice Hall in 1997 under the title *A Basic History of Art*. Recommended for elementary and middle schools.

1134 Norwich, John Julius, ed. **Oxford Illustrated Encyclopedia, Vol. 5: The Arts**. New York: Oxford University Press, 1990. 502p. $49.95. ISBN 0-19-869137-8.

This work, the fifth of a projected eight-volume set, can stand alone as a general study of the fine arts. It covers music, literature, drama, painting, sculpture, architecture, cinema, and decorative and applied arts. Entries of one to three paragraphs survey the major works, performances, and so forth, of architects, writers, composers, performers, and other artists. Technique or style and country or period are provided. The volume includes modern individuals in the arts (e.g., Margaret Atwood, Steven Spielberg, Luciano Pavorotti) as well as famous artists of the past.

The work has internal cross-referencing and see references and beautiful, well-chosen illustrations in black-and-white and color (e.g., photographs, charts, diagrams). There are no references to other volumes in the set. This survey of the fine arts is highly recommended for high schools. [R: ARBA 92]

DIRECTORIES

1135 **Artist's & Graphic Designer's Market**. Cincinnati, Ohio: Writer's Digest Books, 1995– . annual. $24.99. ISSN 1075-0894.

Published since 1975 and originally titled *Artist's Market*, this source is for finding places to sell fine art, illustrations, graphic design, animation and cartoons. More than 2,500 buyers are listed from card and poster companies to books and magazines and galleries and ad agencies. Entries give pay rates, royalties, submission guidelines, and complete directory information including Web sites and e-mail addresses. Introductory chapters give hints and tips for selling art. There is a list of further resources in both paper and Internet publications. A brief guide to other special markets (medical illustration, religious art, t-shirts), a glossary, and an index complete the volume. As important to artists as writer's guides are to authors, this annual should be in all high school collections.

HANDBOOKS

1136 Mayer, Ralph. **The Artist's Handbook of Materials and Techniques**. 5th ed. New York: Viking, 1991. 761p. $45.00. ISBN 0-670-83701-6.

Designed to present a wide range of artists' materials and techniques, Mayer's handbook includes chapters that explain painting with oil, tempera, watercolor, and gouache. Other chapters deal with specific kinds of paintings, such as murals, and the chemistry of materials, solvents, and thinners. Appendixes provide technical data, such as oil absorption and conversion factors. There is a detailed index. This is a standard source for studio art classes in secondary schools. [R: ARBA 92]

INDEXES

1137 Havlice, Patricia P. **World Painting Index**. 2v. Metuchen, N.J.: Scarecrow Press, 1977. $125.00. ISBN 0-8108-1016-6.

1138 Havlice, Patricia P. **World Painting Index: First Supplement, 1973– 1980**. 2v. Metuchen, N.J.: Scarecrow Press, 1982. $99.50. ISBN 0-8108-1531-1.

1139 Havlice, Patricia P. **World Painting Index: Second Supplement, 1980– 1989**. 2v. Metuchen, N.J.: Scarecrow Press, 1995. $140.50. ISBN 0-8108-3020-5.

These volumes continue and supplement the older standard works by Isabel Monro and Kate Monro, *Index to Reproductions of American Paintings* (Wilson, 1948), its supplement, *Index to Reproductions of American Paintings* (Wilson, 1964) and *Index to Reproductions of European Paintings* (Wilson, 1956) as well as Smith and Moure's *Index to Reproductions of American Paintings* (Scarecrow, 1977). The 1977 volume indexes paintings reproduced in books published from 1940 to 1975; the supplements together extend coverage to 1989.

Each of the Havlice volumes contains a numbered bibliography of sources arranged by main entry. The main section lists painters and their works with codes that refer to the bibliographies. The second volume consists of a list of the paintings, arranged alphabetically by title, with references to the artist list in the first volume. These tools are useful for both teachers and students in identifying paintings to accompany lessons and reports; the possiblities of color scanning for computer generated presentations only increases the value of such resources.

ARCHITECTURE

1140 Maddex, Diane, ed. **Built in the U.S.A.: American Buildings from Airports to Zoos**. Washington, D.C.: Preservation Press, 1985. 189p. $8.95. ISBN 0-471-14500-9.

Forty-two types of buildings, arranged alphabetically from airports to zoos, are described and illustrated with black-and-white photographs.

Structures range from common ones (e.g., banks, libraries) to the more unusual (e.g., decorated sheds). Articles provide historical background, importance, and function for each. There are a selective bibliography and a directory of organizations concerned with specific types of structures. This work is a companion volume to *What Style Is It?* (Preservation Press, 1984). [R: ARBA 86; BL, 15 June 85; LJ, 15 May 86]

1141 Phillips, Steven J. **Old-House Dictionary: An Illustrated Guide to American Domestic Architecture**

(1600–1940). Lakewood, Colo.: American Source Books, 1989. 239p. $12.95pa. ISBN 0-471-14407-X.

This work has 450 line drawings and clear, precise definitions of 1,500 terms. Definitions note synonyms, but there is no cross-referencing; the topic index is entitled "Cross-references." The emphasis on illustration is an asset; it makes the volume useful as a reverse dictionary for those who know what something looks like but do not know its name. Recommended for secondary collections as a supplement to American history references.

Language

GENERAL WORKS

1142 Crystal, David, ed. **The Cambridge Encyclopedia of Language**. 2d ed. New York: Cambridge University Press, 1997. 496p. $69.95. ISBN 0-521-55050-5.

This work, the first encyclopedic survey of its kind, covers language and the many branches of linguistic science. More than 60 essays, all generously cross-referenced, discuss the major areas of language study. Hundreds of tables, charts, maps and other illustrations support the text. Appendices include a glossary of over 1,000 linguistic terms, a table of the world's languages and an extensive bibliography. Indexed by language, author and subject. This outstanding work is recommended for high school libraries.

1143 Crystal, David. **The Cambridge Encyclopedia of the English Language**. New York: Cambridge University Press, 1995. 489p. $49.95. ISBN 0-521-40179-8.

Following the pattern of his *Encyclopedia of Language*, the author describes the English language in a comprehensive and absorbing work. Presented in text and illustration on double-page spreads, explanations and examples of each topic are clear and engaging. General topics covered are the history of English, vocabulary (including etymology), grammar, spoken and written

English, using English and learning English. Cross-references link information among sections. Subsections include such essays as the effects of Shakespeare and Dickens on the language and "grammar mythology." Wonderful illustrations such as newspaper headlines, charts, diagrams, maps and even the *Cat in the Hat* are used, along with written examples to demonstrate and explain. Seven appendices and three indexes complete the volume. Highly recommended for teachers and students in secondary schools.

1144 Purves, Alan C. and others. **Encyclopedia of English Studies and Language Arts**. 2v. New York: Scholastic, 1994. $150.00. ISBN 0-590-49268-3.

This set explains the teaching of English language, literature and composition. One of its audiences is administrators; it is also useful for teachers of other disciplines who are team teaching with English teachers. Coverage is teaching from kindergarten through graduate students. Areas discussed are reading, media, drama, technology, curriculum teaching and learning, assessment and pedagogy. Entries range from 300 to 3,000 words with extended definitions, description and historical context. Issues of controversy are addressed from multiple viewpoints. There is a list of further reading and a topical index. Recommended for professional collections in school and district libraries. [R: ARBA 95]

ENGLISH AS A SECOND LANGUAGE

1145 **English Language and Orientation Programs in the United States**. 12th ed. New York: Institute of International Education, 1997. 359p. $42.95. ISBN 0-87206-238-4.

This directory identifies English-language programs for foreign students who hope to study in the United States. The listings are divided into Intensive English programs and English as a Second Language programs, and arranged by state under each category. Each of the 800 courses and programs are listed with directory information, dates, descriptions, cost, housing, credits and details about classes. Appendices list such things as TESOL standards by program. Indexes are by institution, beginning dates and English programs for specific purposes. For professional and guidance collections.

UNABRIDGED DICTIONARIES

1146 **The Oxford English Dictionary: CD-ROM for Windows**. (20 vol. unabridged edition). New York: Oxford University Press, 1994. CD-ROM (Windows ISBN 0-1986-1260-5, Macintosh ISBN 0-1996-1727-9). $395.00 or network.

1147 Simpson, J. A., and E. S. C. Weiner, eds. **The Oxford English Dictionary**. 2d ed. 20v. New York: Oxford University Press, 1989. $3,000.00/set. ISBN 0-19-861186-2.

1148 Simpson, J. A., Edmund Weiner, and John Weiner, eds. **Oxford English Dictionary Additions Series**. 2v. New York: Clarendon, 1994. $45.00/vol. ISBN 0-19-861292-3 (v.1); 0-19-861299-0 (v.2).

The CD-ROM version of the second edition of the *Oxford English Dictionary* (Oxford University Press, 1989) makes it more accessible to school libraries.

OED 2 treats over 500,000 words, providing spellings, pronunciations (using the International Phonetic Alphabet instead of the original pronunciation system), parts of speech, kinds of terms, statuses and morphologies, and meanings. The latter are chronologically arranged from the word's recorded appearance to contemporary times. Illustrative quotations, 2.4 million of them, reflect usage and changes in meaning throughout the word's history. The revision merges all words contained in the original work and its supplements, with the addition of some 5,000 new words that have entered the language during the last decade.

The additions series supplements the second edition with new words or new information about words in the main set. An abridged version of the dictionary is also available as *The New Shorter Oxford English Dictionary* [CD-ROM].

1149 Flexner, Stuart Berg, ed. **Random**
E+ **House Dictionary of the English Language**. 2d revised and reprinted ed. New York: Random House, 1993. 2478p. $89.95. ISBN 0-679-42917-4.

1150 **Random House Unabridged Electronic Dictionary on CD-ROM**. Version 1.7. Random House, 1994. CD-ROM (Windows, Macintosh). $79.00. ISBN 0-679-44045-3.

This comprehensive dictionary, first published in 1966, emphasizes current language. The 2d edition indicates changes in pronunciation, usage, and definitions. Some 50,000 new words coined over the last 2 decades and 75,000 new definitions are included in the more than 300,000 entries. The revision also contains more sample sentences, usage notes, synonyms and antonyms, and illustrations. Coverage of regional English has been expanded, and dates when words entered the language have been added.

The work opens with essays on the history of the English language, changes in usage, U.S. dialects, and pronunciation, followed by an extensive exposition on how to use the dictionary. Definitions are arranged according to their frequency of use. On the whole, definitions are clear and accurate; examples of usage are helpful; and the dictionary's efforts to include very current terminology, gender-neutral definitions, and modern tendencies in spelling have been achieved. Biographical and geographical entries, listed in the main alphabet, reflect updating in information and population figures. The appendix contains such material as lists of signs and symbols; a directory of colleges and universities; copies of the Declaration of Independence and the U.S. Constitution; basic foreign language dictionaries for French, Spanish, Italian, and German; a style manual with sections on writing term papers and resumes; and an atlas.

Despite this work's extensive coverage of the language, it does not compare in comprehensive or authority with *Webster's Third*. Nonetheless, it is recommended for all levels of school libraries.

The strength of this CD-ROM is that there are 115,000 spoken pronunciations. Two thousand line drawings have been added since version one and there is now some documentation. Access to the CD-ROM is either by icon or hot key from a word processor. Search methods allow both word spelling or browse as well as definition searches. There are Boolean capabilities and phrases and idioms can be searched. This is an excellent CD-ROM dictionary for secondary schools. [R: ARBA 88; BL, 15 Feb 88; LJ, 15 Nov 87; WLB, Dec 87; WLB, Feb 88]

1151 **Webster's Third New International Dictionary of the English Language**. 3d unabridged ed. Springfield, Mass.: Merriam-Webster, 1993. 2662p. + addenda. $119.00. ISBN 0-87779-201-1.

The current edition of this prestigious work, first published in 1828, appeared in 1961. Due to periodic revision, a new copyright is issued about every five years.

The 3rd edition is different from previous ones by being descriptive rather than prescriptive: the new objective is to record the language, not to limit coverage to what linguists consider correct usage. Labels such as "slang" are used sparingly, and the description "colloquial" has been replaced by "substandard" or "nonstandard." There are many deletions: gazetteer and biographical entries, foreign words and phrases, literary allusions and words that became obsolete before 1755.

The 464,000 entries include 50,000 new words and 50,000 new meanings for old words. The 1993 printing includes an addenda with about 14,000 new words and meanings that have entered the language since 1961. Illustrative quotations are taken from contemporary sources, but citations are incomplete. Definitions, listed in historical order, are usually clear and easily understood. Etymologies and pronunciations are included. *Webster's Tenth Collegiate Dictionary* is

an abridged version of this work. *Webster's Third* is updated every five years; an occasional supplement of new words is issued.

DESK DICTIONARIES

1152 **American Heritage Dictionary of the English Language**. 3d ed. Boston: Houghton Mifflin, 1992. 2184p. $45.00. ISBN 0-395-44895-6.

The major revision of this dictionary, represented as the third edition, added 16,000 new words and meanings to a distinguished major dictionary. Now containing over 200,000 words and 4,000 illustrations, this must be considered one of the first dictionaries for a school to purchase. It includes people. The number of synonyms has increased and regionalisms are included with notes. Illustrations are in the margins near the relevant word and definition. An essay about Indo-European language, a table of sound correspondences and a dictionary of root words are appendices. Available on *Microsoft Bookshelf*.

1153 Barnhart, Robert K., and Sol
E+ Steinmetz with Clarence L. Barnhart, eds. **Third Barnhart Dictionary of New English**. Bronx, N.Y.: H. W. Wilson, 1990. 565p. $52.00. ISBN 0-8242-0796-3.

The present volume—an update of the *First* and *Second Barnhart Dictionary of New English*, now out of print—covers 12,000 new terms that have come into use during the last 30 years. Some entries update information contained in earlier editions. Each entry includes at least one quotation that helps the reader understand the meaning of the term. Pronunciation, etymology, and usage notes are provided where necessary. The editors, themselves distinguished lexicographers, have called upon scholars throughout the world to assist them in making this the most authoritative dictionary of new words to date. Highly recommended for all levels as a supplement to other dictionaries. [R: ARBA 91; BL, 1 Dec 90; LJ, 1 Oct 90; WLB, Oct 90]

1154 **The Oxford Dictionary and Thesaurus**. American ed. New York: Oxford University Press, 1996. 1828p. $30.00. ISBN 0-19-509949-4.

This convenient work combines *The Concise Oxford Dictionary of Current English* and *The Oxford Thesaurus*. Definitions with synonyms are listed in one convenient alphabetical order. Standard dictionary information is given for each of the 100,000 main entries. This is a useful dictionary for secondary collections.

1155 Webster's Tenth New Collegiate
E+   Dictionary. Springfield, Mass.: Merriam-Webster, 1993. 1564p. $19.95. ISBN 0-87779-708-0.

1156 Merriam-Webster's Collegiate Dictionary. Springfield, Mass.: Merriam-Webster, 1996. CD-ROM (Windows, Macintosh). $39.95. ISBN 0-87779-713-7.

Based on *Webster's Third International Dictionary*, this desk dictionary reflects the descriptive philosophy of the parent volume. The dictionary lists upwards of 150,000 entries and emphasizes contemporary pronunciation, meaning and use. This is one of the finest mid-sized dictionaries available and should be in every collection at every level.

The CD-ROM version contains all of the entries in the 10th edition and searching strategies make it possible to use language in many new ways. The many features of this product show the remarkable advantages of electronic dictionaries such as finding words when one is unsure of the spelling and the ability to search words by language derivation, by date they entered the language and by combination of these factors. The use of this tool in an interdisciplinary class of history or culture and language is alone worth the price. Highly recommended for all middle and high school collections.

1157 Webster's New World Dictionary of American English. 3d ed. college edition. New York: Prentice Hall, 1994. 1574p. $17.95. ISBN 0-671-88243-0.

This highly regarded dictionary, first published in 1953 and frequently revised, emphasizes the English language as used in the United States. It is an authoritative work noted for its clarity and currency.

This edition's 150,000 entries arrange definitions in historical order and provide etymologies, pronunciation, irregularly formed plurals, spelling variations, and capitalization. More than 11,000 words or meanings of U.S. origin are identified by a star preceding the word. Usage labels (e.g., slang, vulgar) or comments (e.g., nonstandard) are added where appropriate, and short phrases illustrate meaning. Synonyms indicating shades of meaning, antonyms, and frequent usage notes are among other useful features.

JUVENILE DICTIONARIES

1158 The American Heritage First
E   Dictionary. Boston: Houghton Mifflin, 1994. 362p. $13.95. ISBN 0-395-67289-9.

1159 The American Heritage Children's
E+   Dictionary. Boston: Houghton Mifflin, 1994. 842p. $15.95. ISBN 0-395-69191-5.

1160 The American Heritage Student
E+   Dictionary. Boston: Houghton Mifflin, 1994. 1094p. $16.95. ISBN 0-395-55857-3.

The *First Dictionary* contains entries chosen from first primers, reading textbooks, and common vocabulary. The six or seven words defined on each page are used in sample sentences; only a few word games and homonyms. Recommended for preschool and primary grades.

Children's Dictionary, for elementary grades, features a large, easy-to-read typeface and clearly written definitions. Each word is followed by the part of speech, synonyms, antonyms, and historical notes set off by color blocks. Each different sense of the word is followed by an illustrative sentence. Some 1,500 color illustrations, drawings, and photographs help to clarify word meanings. *Children's Dictionary* is more comprehensive than the *Macmillan Dictionary for Children*. Highly recommended.

Student Dictionary, intended for students in grades 6 through 9, contains concise, readable definitions enhanced by frequent sentence or phrase illustrations. Margin notes, which include related matter such as word histories, are a special feature. Slang is clearly labeled as such, and many notes explain correct word usage. Line drawings that illustrate words and notes are located in a wide column on each page. There are a number of appendixes, including a style manual and a guide to the metric system. *Student Dictionary* is recommended, but it falls behind the *Macmillan Dictionary for Students* in overall quality. [R: ARBA 97; RBB 94-95]

1161 Eastman, Philip D. **The Cat in the**
E   **Hat Beginner Book Dictionary**.
      Random House, 1980. 144p. $14.00.
      ISBN 0-394-81009-0.

The Cat in the Hat...Dictionary provides a sense of fun with words and serves as both a wordbook (words identified visually and usually grouped thematically) and a dictionary. It defines more than 1,000 words with humorously captioned pictures. The background color changes with each letter of the alphabet. Pages, in two columns with two to four entries each, are relatively uncluttered. Both Spanish and French versions are available.

1162 Grisewood, John and others. **The**
      Kingfisher First Dictionary. New
      York: Kingfisher, 1995. 180p. $14.95.
      ISBN 1-85697-645-9.

More than 1,500 words and 1,000 color illustrations make this attractive dictionary appealing to primary grade children. Words are in bold face with definition, sample sentence and picture. There are spelling tips and word game boxes. Days of the week, months of the year and other useful categories of words are appended.

1163 Hayward, Linda. **The Sesame Street**
E   **Dictionary: Featuring Jim Henson's**
      Sesame Street Muppets. New York:
      Random House/Children's Televi-
      sion Workshop, 1980. 253p. $18.00.
      ISBN 0-394-84007-0.

The Sesame Street Dictionary is as much a mainstay to librarians as the television program has been to children. Designed for preschool through grade 3, it briefly defines 1,300 words and illustrates them in amusing sentences and pictures, often in balloons coming out of character's mouths. The dictionary builds vocabulary and reading readiness for the very young and serves as a beginning dictionary for children in the primary grades. Highly recommended. [R: ARBA 81]

1164 Hillerich, Robert L. **The American**
E   **Heritage Picture Dictionary**. Bos-
      ton: Houghton Mifflin, 1986. 138p.
      $11.95. ISBN 0-395-69585-6.

Preschool children will enjoy this workbook/ dictionary containing some 900 entries. The work is intended to be enjoyed as a picture book while promoting reading and writing. In each of the columns (two per page), there are two or three entries with a brief, simple definition or a picture illustrating the word. Many of the illustrations are of scenes (rather than objects) that depict multiracial and multiage characters. A group of topical pictures (e.g., supermarkets, zoos) conclude the volume. Recommended. [R: BL, 15 Feb 87; BL, 15 Jan 90]

1165 **Macmillan Dictionary for Children**.
E   New York: Macmillan, 1989. 864p.
      $15.00. ISBN 0-02-761561-8.

1166 **Macmillan Dictionary for Children**
      CD-ROM. New York: Macmillan,
      1995. CD-ROM (Windows). $59.99.
      ISBN 0-671-51745-7.

This excellent dictionary, almost identical in content to the *Macmillan School Dictionary*, is designed for grades 3 through 6 and is a good choice for elementary school libraries.

Clear definitions for 35,000 words include frequent color pictures to assist in clarifying meaning. Syllabication, pronunciation, parts of speech, and different word forms are provided. Pronunciation guides are clear and well placed, and highlighted guide words assist the reader in finding the proper page. There are also a 10-page section on how to use a dictionary and a reference section that consists of U.S. and world history timelines, pictures of the presidents, national flags, world maps, and tables of weights and measures. [R: ARBA 90; SLJ, May 90]

The CD-ROM version is based on the print version and has over 12,000 entries, 1,000 pictures and 400 sound effects. Each word is both printed and pronounced. An audio tour leads users through the simple search directions. Options are "find," "games," "notes," and "help." Students can type in words or browse through a word list. Words are defined, pronounced and hot linked to related words. There are word histories and language notes as well. Unlike most other CD-ROM dictionaries, it is possible to both download and print without using a word processing program. Highly recommended for first purchase CD-ROM dictionary for elementary collections.

1167 **My First Dictionary.** San Francisco: Harper, 1997. $15.50. ISBN 0-673-28509-X.

This work defines words that primary grade children encounter while reading books. Definitions have sample sentences or illustrations or both. Multiple forms of a word (e.g., noun, verb) are numbered in one entry; homonyms are treated in separate entries. Alternative word forms—plurals, past tense, comparatives, and superlatives—conclude many definitions. Large type and boldfaced lettering are featured throughout this dictionary, which is intended for the primary grades. Highly recommended.

1168 **My First Incredible, Amazing**
E **Dictionary.** New York: DK Multimedia, 1994. CD-ROM (Windows, Macintosh). $29.95.

Both pre-readers and early readers can use this interactive dictionary which is limited to 1,000 words. Words can be found in a list, typed in or identified by picture. Each word is pronounced and has a picture. A click on the picture results in some sound and/or motion. Words used in the definitions are linked to their own meanings and linked to broader and related words. Games help practice reading, spelling and defining. Moving around in the dictionary is simple with a little practice. Screens can be printed or copied to clipboards. Primary children will enjoy and learn from this CD-ROM, if older children, teachers and librarians will let them have a turn. Also available as *My First Amazing Words and Pictures Activity Pack* with CD-ROM, stickers, flash cards, a board book and an activity book. Highly recommended for preschool and primary collections.

1169 Root, Betty. **My First Dictionary.**
E New York: Dorling Kindersley, 1993. 96p. $14.95. ISBN 1-56458-277-9.

Each of the 1,000 words in this colorful dictionary is accompanied by an illustration. Within the definitions, other related words appear in bold face. Although produced by a British publisher, the dictionary has been adapted for American children and their parents and teachers; word games are at the end. Recommended for preschool and primary grades.

1170 Scarry, Richard. **Richard Scarry's**
E **Best Word Book Ever.** New York:

Western/Golden Press, 1963. 91p. $6.95. ISBN 0-307-15510-2.

Challenging and often humorous story-pictures in color have made this word book for preschool children a popular choice for three decades. Each object in the illustration is labeled.

1171 **Scholastic Children's Dictionary.**
E New York: Scholastic Reference, 1996. 648p. $16.95. ISBN 0-590-25271-2.

This colorful and attractive dictionary features simple definitions and clear pronunciations. Words are bold face and set out from definitions, so they are easy to find on the page. Information boxes give word histories, prefixes, suffixes and synonyms where appropriate. Related words and homophones are listed near the end of entries. Illustrations are placed adjacent to the word, and some illustrations give names of parts of words or phrases as in a visual dictionary; examples are the entries for horse, oil rig and escalator. Several useful features at the end of the dictionary include the Braille alphabet, the American Sign Language alphabet, a world map and world flags, a U.S. map and fact table and a list of the presidents. Highly recommended for grades 3–6.

1172 **Webster's Elementary Dictionary.**
E Springfield, Mass.: Merriam-Webster, 1990. 600p. $18.95. ISBN 0-8123-6247-0.

1173 **Webster's School Dictionary.** reprint ed. Springfield, Mass.: Merriam-Webster, 1994. 1184p. $12.95. ISBN 0-87779-280-1.

The *Elementary Dictionary,* which contains over 32,000 entries, 600 illustrations in full color, and thousands of usage examples, is designed for children in grades 4 through 6. The *School Dictionary,* designed for grades 9 through 12, includes 85,000 entries and 91,000 definitions. An appendix includes sections on biography, geography, signs and symbols, chemical elements, and writing. *Webster's Intermediate Dictionary* (Merriam-Webster, 1977) for grades 6 through 8, is available in a large-type edition only. It includes 65,000 words.

The dictionaries are attractively formatted, and definitions can be easily understood by the intended audience. Recommended.

PICTURE DICTIONARIES

1174 Clark, M., and Bernadette Mohan, eds. **The Oxford-Duden Pictorial English Dictionary**. 2d ed. New York: Oxford University Press, 1995. 811p. $18.95. ISBN 0-19-861311-3.

The purpose of this work, based on the German *Duden Bildworterbuch*, is to enable readers to determine the English-language term for objects they can identify visually. The illustrations are grouped in broad categories (e.g., the Earth, man and his social environment). Objects are labeled with the English-language term (British spellings and American equivalent for most). French and German versions are also available. The new edition updates objects in computing and other technologies.

1175 Corbeil, Jean Claude, and Ariane
E+   Archambault. **The Facts on File Junior Visual Dictionary**. New York: Facts on File, 1989. 159p. $18.95. ISBN 0-8160-2222-4.

In the style of the author's *Facts on File Visual Dictionary* for adults, this juvenile work pictures well-known objects in color and identifies their parts. For example, 15 parts of an electric guitar are labeled. The table of contents lists the themes under which items are arranged (e.g., clothing, farms, food, the human body). Pictures, captioned at the top, are of good quality, making the work attractive. Recommended. [R: ARBA 90; BL, 15 Jan 90; SLJ, Apr 90; SLJ, May 90; SLJ, June 90]

1176 Corbeil, Jean Claude. **The Facts on**
E+   **File Visual Dictionary**. New York: Facts on File, 1986. 797p. $29.95. ISBN 0-8160-1544-9.

Thousands of objects and their parts are labeled in this graphic presentation. The aims are to indicate "the specialized vocabulary currently used in every field," and to "look up the word from the picture" and "find the picture from the word." Under measuring devices, for example, there are drawings for devices that measure time (e.g., hourglass, sundial, grandfather clock), pedometers, horizontal seismographs, and others. Each page is captioned, and each item and its parts is clearly labeled. The table of contents lists over 40 topical sections with their subsections. There are general, topical, and specialized (e.g., athletics, automobile, baseball, bicycle, camping) indexes. [R: ARBA 87]

1177 Evans, Jo, ed. **Ultimate Visual Dictionary**. New York: Dorling-Kindersley, 1994. 637p. $39.95. ISBN 1-56458-648-0.

This dictionary covers the natural world, physical science, technology, transportation, the fine arts, music and sports. More than 30,000 words identify 270 items and parts of items. Thousands of photographs, charts and other illustrations help identify the terms. Having this in the reference collection might allow regular circulation of the single subject books in the publisher's Visual Dictionary series.

1178 **Macmillan Visual Dictionary**. New York: Macmillan, 1992. 862p. $45.00. ISBN 0-02-528160-7.

1179 **Macmillan Visual Dictionary: Multilingual Edition**. New York: Macmillan, 1994. 959p. $60.00. ISBN 0-02-578115-4.

Color pictures identify and analyze objects from everyday life. Subjects covered are from the environment, arts, communication and transportation. Pictures of the objects are accompanied by words that name the objects and their parts. The section on architecture has blueprints, landscape designs, architectural symbols and construction details. Other sections include astronomy, geography, plants and gardening, animals, human anatomy, farming, furnishing, repairs, clothing and accessories, and office equipment. There are also sections for measuring devices and instruments, health and safety items, energy, machinery and weapons. The user looks in the table of contents if the description can be identified and in the index if the term is known and a picture of the item desired.

The multilingual edition is the same as the *Visual Dictionary*, but the terms are given in English, French, Spanish and German.

AMERICANISMS AND SLANG

1180 Ammer, Christine. **The American Heritage Dictionary of Idioms**. New York: Houghton Mifflin, 1997. 729p. $30.00. ISBN 0-395-72774-X.

This work is one of the largest of the dictionaries intended to explain the peculiarities of American expression. Entries are defined with examples of use and historical derivation is included when known. This is an excellent source for secondary collections.

1181 Cassidy, Frederic G., ed. **Dictionary of American Regional English**. 3v. Cambridge, Mass.: Harvard University Press, 1985. 903p. $75.00/vol. ISBN: 0-674-20511-1 (v.1); 0-674-20512-X (v.2); 0-674-20519-7 (v.3).

The first of a projected 5-volume set and the only work of its kind, this dictionary represents an effort to systematically record the variations in English spoken in different sections of the United States. It includes unusual meanings for common terms, regional colloquialisms, and words found only among particular social or ethnic groups. None are found in standard dictionaries.

Each entry gives definition, part of speech, variant spellings, pronunciation, alternative forms, usage labels and cross-references. The work has dated quotations that illustrate the word's evolution and computer-generated maps that show geographical distribution of the word's usage. This work, no doubt, will become a classic. [R: ARBA 86; BL, 1 Apr 86; LJ, 1 Nov 85; LJ, 5 Apr 86; WLB, Nov 85]

1182 Chapman, Robert L., ed. **New Dictionary of American Slang**. New York: HarperCollins, 1986. 485p. $35.00. ISBN 0-06-181157-2.

Chapman's work provides slang from all periods, plus hundreds of new terms coined during the past two decades that reflect the drug scene, the computer age, the yuppie generation, and many other facets of society. Other entries update information contained in earlier work.

Entries provide pronunciation, word-class and dating labels, definitions, illustrative phrases, and cross-references. Like others of its kind, this dictionary contains taboo or vulgar words and similar nonstandard terms that are not found in general dictionaries of English. [R: ARBA 88; BL, 15 Dec 86]

1183 Dickson, Paul. **Slang! The Topic-by-Topic Dictionary for Contemporary American Lingoes**. New York: Simon & Schuster, 1990. 295p. $9.95pa. ISBN 0-671-67251-7.

This inexpensive dictionary of current American slang classifies 3,900 terms under 24 subject categories, from auctioneering to yuppie slang. In compiling the work, Dickson used the Tamony Collection of Slang and the University of Missouri and drew upon the expertise of over 200 consultants.

Emphasis of the book is on definitions, with little attention given to etymologies. Some entries offer illustrative examples of use from the media. Sources are listed at the end of each chapter and in a comprehensive bibliography at the end of the volume. There is a detailed index.

Slang! is recommended as a supplement to other current works, such as Chapman's *New Dictionary of American Slang*, a basic source for high school libraries. [R: ARBA 91; BL, 1 June 90; Kliatt, Apr 90; LJ, 1 Apr 90]

1184 Hendrickson, Robert. **Whistlin' Dixie: A Dictionary of Southern Expressions**. New York: Facts on File, 1993. $24.95. 288p. ISBN 0-8160-2110-4.

This is the first of the publisher's Dictionary of American Regional Expressions series. An introduction discusses diversity, dialects and pronunciations. Words and phrases are listed in bold face in alphabetical order. Entries give the use and meaning, some with derivations and most with examples and the source if it is literary. Such entries as "since the hogs et grandma" will enchant readers and motivate writers. Other titles in the series are *Happy Trails*, *Yankee Talk* and *Mountain Range*, with others planned. An alternative to *Happy Trails: A Dictionary of Western Expressions*, is Facts on File's outstanding *Dictionary of the American West* (1993).

1185 Lewin, Ester and Albert E. Lewin. **The Thesaurus of Slang**. revised and expanded ed. New York: Facts on File, 1997. $50.00. 464p. ISBN 0-8160-2898-2.

The unique feature of this slang dictionary (and thus its designation as a thesaurus) is that it lists the formal English word followed by all of the slang words or phrases that substitute for it. The new edition brings the total to about 165,000 expressions. There are 52 new terms for "drunk" and more than 800 total. Other new terms deal with drugs; there are also 85 new derogatory words for "stupid." This is a useful work and may serve as a tool of special interest to teachers.

1186 Lighter, J. E. **Random House Historical Dictionary of American Slang**. Vol. 1. New York: Random House, 1994. 1006p. $55.00. ISBN 0-394-54427-7.

1187 Lighter, J. E. **Random House Historical Dictionary of American Slang**. Vol. 2. New York: Random House, 1997. 984p. $65.00. ISBN 0-679-43464-X.

Lighter treats American slang as seriously as the *O.E.D.* treats the rest of the English language. This comprehensive source now covers A-R; volume three, which will complete the project, is in progress. Volume one has an introduction which includes the history of the use of slang in America and a selective annotated bibliography. Each word or phrase entry includes the part of speech, the etymology, a field label describing the likely user, a definition, variant forms, cross-references and quotations, sources and dates. A simple slang word such as "ace" has 17 meanings as a noun, 4 as an adjective and 6 as a verb in addition to its use as the first word in 17 phrases! This is the definitive dictionary of American slang.

1188 Makkai, Adam, and others. **Dictionary of American Idioms**. 3d ed.
E+ Hauppauge, N.Y.: Barron's Educational Series, 1995. 455p. $12.95. ISBN 0-8120-1248-8.

Similar to *NTC's American Idioms Dictionary*, this work would be especially useful to students who speak English as a second language; its 5,000 words and phrases duplicate as well as supplement the competition. Expressions are defined in clear, formal language, and cross-references are generously used. Since neither work is expensive, secondary school libraries should have both. [R: ARBA 96]

1189 Smitherman, Geneva. **Black Talk: Words and Phrases from the Hood to the Amen Corner**. Boston: Houghton Mifflin, 1994. 243p. $17.95; $10.95pa. ISBN 0-395-67410-7; 0-395-69992-4pa.

A good introduction about African American language is followed by a dictionary of words and phrases used by young urban Blacks. Both meanings and explanatory comments are given. Cross-references lead to related or synonymous terms, and note is made of terms that have crossed over to general use. The glossary serves not only as a translation device, but charts the development of word use in the culture. The approach is not scholarly but descriptive, and terms include all types of slang from rap to sex to drugs to daily life. The book is illustrated with cartoons. This source will make language study seem relevant to many students. Recommended for high school collections as a supplement to standard dictionaries and word books.

1190 Spears, Richard A. **NTC's American Idioms Dictionary**. 2d ed. Lincolnwood, Ill.: National Textbook, 1993. 532p. $16.95. ISBN 0-8442-0825-6.

This work, which opens with a long exposition on how to use the dictionary, provides extensive coverage of American idioms. The main entry gives the full form of the idiom, followed by variant and shorter versions. Additional access is provided by the 100-page phrase finder index. Special types of phrases (e.g., slang, folksy, informal) are so labeled, but Spears makes "no attempt to instruct the user in English grammar." Entries include one or more definitions and examples of usage. Recommended for secondary schools. [R: ARBA 95]

1191 Terban, Marvin. **Scholastic Dictionary of Idioms**. New York: Scho-
E+ lastic Reference, 1996. 245p. $15.95. ISBN 0-590-27549-6.

Idioms are defined and their origins briefly traced in an introduction and then arranged alphabetically by the first word. Entries have the phrase, use it in a sentence with the idiom highlighted in yellow, meaning and origin. Humorous drawings are interspersed throughout the text. An alphabetical index by first word with cross-references and a key word index complete the volume. Highly recommended for intermediate grades; appropriate for middle schools as well.

ETYMOLOGY

1192 Barnhart, Robert K., ed. **The Barnhart Dictionary of Etymology**. Bronx, N.Y.: H. W. Wilson, 1988. 1284p. $64.00. ISBN 0-8242-0745-9.

This work, the first scholarly etymological dictionary to appear in almost 25 years, is edited by Robert K. Barnhart, who coedited several well-known works with Clarence Barnhart, his father.

These include *The World Book Dictionary* and *Third Barnhart Dictionary of New English*. Several eminent U.S. language scholars have ably assisted him.

The 30,000 entries focus on current U.S. English and provide spelling variations, pronunciation, part of speech, a short definition, date of first recorded use in English, information about the language from which the word evolved, and (in some cases) comments on the word's history. Words of U.S. origin are so indicated. The work includes scientific and technical words, regional English, slang, product names, and recent words. Recommended for high schools. [R: ARBA 89; BL, 15 Dec 88; LJ, 15 Apr 89]

1193 Morris, William, and Mary Morris. **Morris Dictionary of Word and Phrase Origins**. 2d ed. New York: Harper & Row, 1988. 669p. $35.00. ISBN 0-06-015862-X.

The Morrises, well-known lexicographers, published a dictionary of the same title in 1977, a revision of a three-volume work published between 1962 and 1971. This new revision, which provides histories of interesting words and phrases in the English language, is similar in concept to several books by John Ciardi. Like Ciardi's works, the etymologies and phrase origins are presented in a readable style, making them a joy to browse. [R: ARBA 89; BL, 1 Oct 88]

FOREIGN PHRASES

1194 Guinagh, Kevin. **Dictionary of Foreign Phrases and Abbreviations**. 3d ed. Bronx, N.Y.: H. W. Wilson, 1983. 261p. $44.00. ISBN 0-8242-0675-4.

This work represents a substantial revision of the 2d edition, which appeared in 1972. Foreign expressions, proverbs, mottoes, maxims, abbreviations, and more are listed in a single alphabet. Languages covered include French, German, Greek, Hebrew, Irish, Italian, Latin, Portuguese, Russian, and Spanish. Entries for the over 5,000 phrases and abbreviations commonly used in English often give brief explanations of obscure meaning or items of particular historical interest. [R: ARBA 84; BL, 1 Dec 83; WLB, Apr 83]

RHYMES

1195 Espy, Willard R. **Words to Rhyme With: For Poets and Song Writers**.

New York: Facts on File, 1986. 656p. $55.00. ISBN 0-8160-1237-7.

The 80,000 rhyming words in this book are divided by sound into single, double, and triple rhyme lists, arranged in each section by initial vowels. Syllables are spelled phonetically. This reference tool is so complex that its use is restricted to high school students. It is the most comprehensive rhyming dictionary available. [R: ARBA 87; LJ, 15 Sept 86; WLB, Nov 86]

1196 Young, Sue. **The New Comprehensive American Rhyming Dictionary**. New York: William Morrow, 1991. 622p. $14.00. ISBN 0-380-71392-6.

Organized by vowel sounds and final syllables expressing those sounds, this work uses its own easy-to-use pronunciation system. Young's dictionary, which deserves a place beside more standard works, offers many more phrases and slang terms and does not emphasize matching the consonant sound preceding an accented vowel, as other dictionaries do. This is an imaginative, practical work. Recommended for high schools. [R: BL, 15 June 91; WLB, June 91]

1197 Young, Sue K. **The Scholastic**
E **Rhyming Dictionary**. New York: Scholastic Reference, 1994. 213p. $14.95; $6.95pa. ISBN 0-590-49460-0; 0-590-96393-7pa.

This simple rhyming dictionary discusses rhymes in a brief introduction and then lists rhyming sounds beginning with each vowel sound. Blue and black letters on gray, blue and white backgrounds which create a boxed effect and drawings all make this a graphically pleasing work. An index of words and their rhyming sounds complete the dictionary. Recommended for elementary school collections.

SYNONYMS

1198 Chapman, Robert L., ed. **Roget's International Thesaurus**. 5th ed. New York: HarperCollins, 1992. 1141p. $19.95; $13.95pa. ISBN 0-06-270014-6; 0-06-272037-6pa.

Like its ancestor, the pioneering work of Peter Mark Roget (1852), this volume classifies thought under 1,073 categories, thereby offering the user a variety of ways to express an idea. Boldface type indicates the most commonly used terms. The index of over 325,000 entries is essential for the use of the thesaurus. Available on *Microsoft Bookshelf*. [R: ARBA 78; WLB, Jan 78]

1199 Hellweg, Paul, ed. **Facts on File Student's Thesaurus**. New York: Facts on File, 1991. 287p. $27.95. ISBN 0-8160-1634-8.

Designed for students in middle school and junior high, this thesaurus incorporates entries for more than 5,000 of the most commonly used words in English, with synonyms, antonyms and sample sentences for each meaning. For ordinary words that may have 25 or more synonyms, this work lists only the most obvious. This clear and easy-to-use work is recommended. [R: ARBA 92; RBB, 90-91]

1200 Kahn, John Ellison, ed. **Illustrated Reverse Dictionary: Find the Words on the Tip of Your Tongue**. Pleasantville, N.Y.: Reader's Digest, 1990. 608p. $25.00. ISBN 0-89577-352-X.

Although akin to a thesaurus, this attractive book is not a dictionary in the true sense, rather it is a combination thesaurus and visual dictionary. Its purpose is to jog users' memories and help them find the right words through synonyms, common phrases, antonyms and word association. It groups associated words and phrases under a single access point. Each of the 70,000 words included is defined and related to its access word. Quick reference charts define words for a subject (e.g., deciduous trees, embroidery stitches). Over 400 color illustrations, diagrams, charts and photographs help to clarify the text.

Students and other users must be encouraged to try this new work, since it is unlike traditional thesauri or synonym dictionaries. The *Reverse Dictionary* has enough to offer through its new format to deserve a recommendation for secondary schools. [R: BL, 15 Apr 91]

1201 Landau, Sidney I., and Ronald J. Bogus, eds. **The Doubleday Roget's Thesaurus in Dictionary Form**. Garden City, N.J.: Doubleday, 1987. 804p. $14.95. ISBN 0-385-23997-1.

Despite the words "Roget" and "thesaurus" in the title, which may imply a classified arrangement, the entry words in this volume are listed in

alphabetical order. Some 250,000 synonyms and antonyms, including slang, are provided, but with little guidance in word selection. This work's arrangement will appeal to those who find *Roget's International Thesaurus* awkward to use.

1202 Morris, Christopher G., ed. **Harcourt**
E+ **Brace Student Thesaurus**. New York: Harcourt Brace, 1994. 312p. $18.00. ISBN 0-15-200186-7.

While not visually appealing, this excellent thesaurus has 800 entries and 150 color pictures which include portrayals of individuals from many cultures. From the main entries, 3,500 synonyms, and 500 antonyms are covered. Highly recommended for intermediate grades and as an easy thesaurus for the middle grades.

1203 **Roget's II: The New Thesaurus**. 3d ed. Boston: Houghton Mifflin, 1995. 1,280p. $20.00. ISBN 0-395-68722-5.

Unlike the traditional Roget thesauri, *Roget's II* is alphabetically arranged to provide "rapid access to synonyms, which are grouped by precise meaning." This work, which can stand alone without the support of a general dictionary, offers brief definitions of words, parts of speech, synonyms, near-synonyms, antonyms, near-antonyms, and idioms, with a category index. A system of secondary entries cross-references words to main entries. This edition removed illustrative quotes, but added slang, regionalisms and idioms.

Whether this revamped method of organizing a synonym dictionary is more useful than the conventional system of *Roget's International Thesaurus* or the alphabetically arranged *Webster's Collegiate Thesaurus* remains moot; *Roget's II* is worth a try. Recommended for high school libraries. [R: ARBA 96; RBB, 95-96]

USAGE AND GRAMMAR

1204 Chalker, Sylvia and Edmund Weiner. **The Oxford Dictionary of English Grammar**. New York: Oxford University Press, 1994. 448p. $25.00. ISBN 0-19-861242-7.

This is not a how-to-use-the-language grammar book. It is a source that defines the words we use when we talk about grammar, linguistics and phonetics. More than 1,000 terms from both British and American English are defined and illustrated with examples. Both teachers and students in secondary schools will find this work useful.

1205 Fowler, H. W., ed. revised by R. W. Burchfield. **The New Fowler's Modern English Usage**. 3d ed. New York: Oxford University Press, 1996. 864p. $25.00. ISBN 0-19-869126-2.

Fowler has been the prescriptive guide to the use of the English language since the first edition in 1926. Now R. W. Burchfield, the editor of the 1972 supplement to the *Oxford English Dictionary* has moved the work toward a more descriptive nature and the results will anger many and please many more. This new edition is a pleasure to use and discusses both historical usage and style with a completely re-edited view of 20th century language developments, including American English. The 3,500 entries are written clearly and often quote Fowler. Arrangement is alphabetical. Many libraries will choose to keep the 1965 edition of *Fowler* as well as to buy the new edition. Highly recommended for all secondary school libraries and for professional collections. [R: ARBA 97]

1206 Freeman, Morton S. **Handbook of Problem Words & Phrases/Word-watcher's Guide to Good Writing & Grammar**. Cincinnati, Ohio: Writer's Digest Books, 1990. 296p. $16.99pa. ISBN 0-89879-436-6.

In a conversational style, this volume addresses common problems such as usage, pronunciation, and spelling, but it does not answer all questions. However, its well-organized format and readability make it a good choice for middle and high school libraries. [R: ARBA 91; BL, 15 Oct 90]

1207 Hale, Constance, ed. **Wired Style: Principles of English Usage in the Digital Age**. San Francisco, Calif.: Hard Wired, 1996. 158p. $15.95. ISBN 1-888869-01-1.

This guide to the evolving use of language in the cyber age is intended to describe the way people talk on the Internet. The underlying principles are based on use rather than rules. Separate chapters discuss style and language; there is a glossary, a chapter each on jargon and colloquialisms, and a section on the future. An appendix has guidelines for citing URLs, including form, punctuation and capitalization. There is an index, but access to specific information is limited. Various versions of the text can be found at www.hardwired.com. This spiral-bound dictionary of the "post-Gutenberg era" is guaranteed to offend as many as it cheers. [R: ARBA 97]

1208 Phythian, B. A. **A Concise Dictionary of Confusables: All Those Impossible Words You Never Get Right**. New York: Wiley, 1990. 198p. $10.95pa. ISBN 0-471-52880-3.

Phythian, a British headmaster, has produced a commendable work that attempts to clarify differences in meaning between words that are often confused with one another. Some 2,000 words have been selected for inclusion. Alphabetically arranged entries are clear and informative. This work will not replace other standard usage dictionaries, but it is a useful supplement to them. Recommended for secondary schools. [R: BL, 1 Jan 91]

1209 Urdang, Laurence. **Dictionary of Confusable Words**. New York: Facts on File, 1988. 391p. $35.00. ISBN 0-8160-1650-X.

Of British imprint, with some changes for American readers, this dictionary defines everyday terms often confused with each other (e.g., atomic and nuclear, motor and engine). They are drawn from science, art, business, and specialized areas. The major shortcoming is Urdang's occasional use of technical language, but overall this is a worthwhile addition to high school libraries. [R: ARBA 89; BL, 15 Nov 88]

CHINESE DICTIONARIES

1210 **A Modern Chinese-English Dictionary**. New York: Oxford University Press, 1990. 1,260p. $29.95. ISBN 0-19-585189-7.

This is a general dictionary for students and travelers that includes new words and phrases and new meanings for old words and phrases. Language derived from political, economic, legal, scientific cultural and artistic use is incorporated. More than 4,000 single-character and 50,000 multiple-character entries are included. Arrangement is alphabetical by Pinyan system. Recommended for high school collections.

1211 **The Oxford-Duden Pictorial Chinese and English Dictionary**. New York: Oxford University Press, 1989. 856p. $45.00. ISBN 0-19-584203-0.

Topics are displayed on double-page spreads with both English and Chinese terms listed under boxed illustrations. Details of the pictures are numbered and the numbers act as keys for the terms, thus permitting many details to be identified. Almost 400 topics are included. Comprehensive indexes in each language are included. Highly recommended.

FRENCH DICTIONARIES

1212 **Collins Robert French-English, English-French Dictionary**. 4th ed. New York: HarperCollins, 1995. 2,016p. $50.00. ISBN 0-06-275519-6.

Thousands of contemporary references have been added to this edition to make it more useful for students, tourists and business travelers. A center section titled "Language in Use" has examples of idioms and colloquialisms. Useful appendices include specifics of grammar and usage of both French and English verbs, and convenient charts of numbers and dates, weights, measures and temperatures. Recommended for secondary collections.

1213 Eastman, Philip D. *Cat in the Hat*
E   **Beginner Book Dictionary in French and English**. New York: Random House, 1965. 144p. $15.95. ISBN 0-394-81063-5.

This French-language version of *Cat in the Hat Beginner Book Dictionary* is the same work with added translations of each caption printed in a different color. It also provides a guide to pronunciation.

1214 **Harrap's French Dictionary**. rev. ed. New York: Macmillan, 1991. 1,844p. $27.95. ISBN 0-1338786-19.

Various editions abridge the four-volume *Harrap's Standard French and English Dictionary* which was published in 1980. This revision of an original abridgment is for students, travelers and general readers and emphasizes American usage and includes colloquialisms and slang. Examples of sentences are given in both languages.

1215 **Larousse Standard French-English, English-French Dictionary**. New York: Larousse Kingfisher Chambers, 1995. 1,968p. $29.95. ISBN 2-03-420260-0.

This edition is newly revised to include new words from business and technology and to increase the international scope of the language. The Larousse dictionaries have always attempted to place definitions in a cultural and historical context. It contains about 220,000 references and 400,000 translations and has special sections on grammar, letter writing, and idiomatic expressions used in specific situations. Also available in compact and concise editions. Highly recommended.

1216 Lipton, Gladys C. **Beginning French**
E   **Bilingual Dictionary: A Beginner's Guide in Words and Pictures**. 2d ed. Hauppauge, N.Y.: Barron's Educational Series, 1989. 385p. $6.95. ISBN 0-8120-4273-5.

This dictionary is designed for elementary school students who have just begun to learn French. It provides short, simple definitions; masculine and feminine articles; an example sentence that uses the word (with translation); and one or two small drawings on every page. Pronunciation is given in the phonemic alphabet, an easier system to use than the International Phonetic Alphabet. The appendix contains lists of days, months, personal names, classroom expressions, numbers, conversion tables, grammar terms, and a brief French verb supplement. The print and drawings are very small, and the drawings do not add much to the text. Both illustrations and sample sentences sometime convey sex-role stereotypes.

1217 **The Oxford-Duden Pictorial French and English Dictionary**. New York: Oxford University Press, 1989. 880p. $17.95pa. ISBN 0-19-869154-8.

Three hundred and eighty-four topics are pictorially displayed on double-page spreads with both English and French terms keyed to the illustrations printed below. Subjects include such things as astronomy, automobiles, swimming and supermarkets. Comprehensive indexes in each language are included. Highly recommended.

1218 **The Oxford-Hachette French Dictionary: French-English, English-French**. 2d ed. New York: Oxford University Press, 1994. 2,016p. $39.95. ISBN 0-19-860068-2.

1219 **Oxford-Hachette French Dictionary**. New York: Oxford University Press, 1996. CD-ROM (Macintosh and Windows). $49.95. ISBN 1-1926-8306-3 (Macintosh); 1-1926-8307-1 (Windows).

1220 **Concise Oxford-Hachette French Dictionary**. New York: Oxford University Press, 1995. 1,504p. $25.00. ISBN 0-19-864329-2.

Built from two ten-million word databases from current writing examples in literature and journalism in French and English, this dictionary is current and comprehensive. It contains more than 355,000 entries as well as an extensive center section that deals with colloquial speech, correspondence, advertisements, telephone and e-mail use. Available in CD-ROM and concise editions. All of these versions are recommended for first purchase.

GERMAN DICTIONARIES

1221 **Cassell's German-English, English-German Dictionary**. rev. ed. New York: Macmillan, 1986. 1,580p. $25.00. ISBN 0-02-522920-6.

This dictionary has been published since 1888 by various publishers; formerly titled the *New Cassell's German Dictionary* (Funk & Wagnalls). This is a standard and reliable source and is especially noted for its useful phonetic pronunciations. It is also available in a concise version.

1222 **Collins German-English, English-German Dictionary**. 3d ed. New York: HarperCollins, 1997. 1,728p. $55.00. ISBN 0-06-270199-1.

There is extended coverage of new terms from computers, business, medicine and politics in this edition. The "Language in Use" section gives appropriate examples in speaking and writing. This is a good dictionary for secondary collections.

1223 **The Oxford-Duden German Dictionary: German-English, English-German**. New York: Oxford University Press, 1990. 1,696p. $39.95. ISBN 0-19-864171-0.

1224 **Concise Oxford-Duden German Dictionary**. New York: Oxford University Press, 1992. 1,408p. $18.95. ISBN 0-19-864180-X.

1225 **Oxford-Duden German Dictionary**. New York: Oxford University Press, 1996. CD-ROM (Macintosh and Windows). $49.95. ISBN 1-1926-8311-X (Macintosh); 1-1926-8310-1 (Windows).

The editors of this new German dictionary, which took more than a decade to compile, have made a concerted effort to overcome some of the shortcomings of bilingual dictionaries. "Sense indicators" are used to clarify variant meanings and to make the transition from one language to the other easier and more accurate. Sentences and phrases are frequently used, and subject labels indicate special vocabulary for a field. The publisher's claim that this work contains the "fullest and most up-to-date coverage" of any one-volume dictionary is most likely justified. Also available in concise and CD-ROM versions. [R: ARBA 91]

1226 **The Oxford-Duden Pictorial German and English Dictionary**. 2d ed. New York: Oxford University Press, 1995. 872p. $19.95. ISBN 0-19-864502-3.

This edition brings the German dictionary into comparable format with those of the other languages. It includes illustrations for objects with German and English terms keyed to the pictures. Some 28,000 items are arranged by 384 categories (e.g. playgrounds, department stores, various manufacturing processes). All terms are indexed in both German and English.

HEBREW DICTIONARIES

1227 Ben-Abba, Dov, ed. **The Meridian Hebrew-English, English-Hebrew Dictionary**. New York: Meridian, 1994. 720p. $17.95. ISBN 0-452-01121-3.

The purpose of this dictionary is to provide Hebrew and English equivalents for everyday language needs, with areas in the sciences, the arts, sports and slang covered. The 35,000 entries are in English and Hebrew characters. Basic Hebrew and English grammar is also covered.

1228 Burstein, Chaya M. **The Jewish Kids' Hebrew-English Wordbook**. Philadelphia: Jewish Publications Society, 1993. 39p. $16.95. ISBN 0-827-60381-9.

E

About 500 Hebrew words with the English equivalent are listed by topics that children use such as family, holidays, animals and play.

1229 Doniach, N. S. and A. Kahane. **The Oxford English-Hebrew Dictionary**. New York: Oxford University Press, 1995. 1,024p. $65.00. ISBN 0-19-864322-5.

More than 75,000 entries make this the most comprehensive dictionary appropriate for schools. Created to reflect new language scholarship and contemporary usage, the dictionary includes current idioms and phrases, slang, colloquialisms and American terms.

ITALIAN DICTIONARIES

1230 **Cassell's Italian Dictionary: Italian-English, English-Italian**. New York: Macmillan, 1982. 1,150p. $24.95. ISBN 0-02-522540-5.

Previous editions were published by Funk & Wagnalls. This is a standard general dictionary with contemporary vocabulary and usage. It is periodically revised and reprinted.

1231 **Collins English-Italian, Italian-English Dictionary**. New York: HarperCollins, 1995. 666p. $25.00. ISBN 0-06-2775517-X.

This is a reasonably priced Italian-English dictionary suitable for secondary schools. The vocabulary is contemporary and practical and examples of translations are excellent.

1232 **The Oxford-Duden Pictorial Italian and English Dictionary**. New York: Oxford University Press, 1995. 880p. $19.95. ISBN 0-19-864517-1.

This source follows the same pattern as the others in the series. Arrangement is by topic with terms in both languages keyed to numbers from the two pages of related illustrations. Full indexes in each language are provided.

JAPANESE DICTIONARIES

1233 Nakao, Seigo. **Random House Japanese-English, English-Japanese Dictionary**. New York: Random House, 1995. 688p. $22.00. ISBN 0-679-44149-2.

This contemporary dictionary used sources such as newspapers and magazines to identify the terms to be included in its 60,000 entries. Coverage is good for cultural terms and technology is well represented with such terms as *fakkusu* (fax). The work is for both spoken and written Japanese, so entries are in both Roman letters and in the Japanese characters. Recommended for secondary schools.

1234 **The Oxford-Duden Pictorial Japanese and English Dictionary**. New York: Oxford University Press, 1989. 832p. $21.95. ISBN 0-19-864327-6.

Pictorial dictionaries are useful for students to increase vocabulary and for travelers to carry with them. Pictures of hospitals and doctor's and dentist's offices, clothing, houses and furniture, supermarkets, airports and libraries (and about 380 more items) are labeled with numbers which are keys for the terms printed below in each language. Complete indexes in each language provide quick access. Highly recommended.

LATIN DICTIONARIES

1235 **Cassell's Latin Dictionary: Latin-English, English-Latin**. New York: Macmillan, 1977. 883p. $24.95. ISBN 0-02-522580-4.

This remains a standard work and the best choice of an inexpensive, one-volume Latin dictionary. The 30,000 entries include geographical and proper names, etymological notes, and illustrative quotations.

RUSSIAN DICTIONARIES

1236 Howlett, Colin. **The Oxford Russian Dictionary: Russian-English, English-Russian**. New York: Oxford University Press, 1994. 1,360p. $49.95. ISBN 0-19-864189-3.

This is an updated and combined edition of two previously separate volumes published by Oxford Press in 1984. There are 5,000 new words and phrases added and the work now includes more than 180,000 entries and 290,000 translations. The Russian section has examples drawn from literature and newspapers and the dictionary has excellent coverage of science and technology as well as idiomatic and everyday language. A pocket version is also available. Highly recommended.

SPANISH DICTIONARIES

1237 Castillo, Carlos, and Otto F. Bond, comps. **The University of Chicago Spanish Dictionary: A New Concise Spanish-English of Words and Phrases Basic to the Written and Spoken Languages of Today, Plus a List of 500 Spanish Idioms and Sayings, with Variants and English Equivalents**. 4th ed. Chicago: University of Chicago, 1987. 475p. $23.95; $8.95pa. ISBN 0-226-10400-1; 0-226-10402-8pa.

Compiled for the use of American learners of Spanish and Spanish-speaking learners of English, this work makes a special effort to include references to usage in the United States and Spanish America. It provides a short history of the language, a list of 500 common Spanish-English idioms and proverbs, and a similar English-Spanish section. More than 32,000 entries give pronunciation, part of speech, definitions, and occasional examples of usage. This excellent work is recommended for secondary schools. [R: ARBA 90]

1238 **Collins Spanish-English, English-Spanish Dictionary: Unabridged**. 5th ed. New York: HarperCollins, 1997. 1,679p. $55.00. ISBN 0-06-270207-6.

Older editions emphasized British English and Latin American Spanish, but this new edition is comprehensive in its treatment of the language internationally. It has also completely updated the computer and medical vocabulary. There are now 230,000 references and 444,000 translations, and 1,000 sidebars provide contextual understanding in relation to life in Spanish-speaking countries. This attractive dictionary is recommended for first purchase. HarperCollins publishes Spanish and English bilingual dictionaries in a number of smaller versions as well.

1239 Eastman, P. D. *Cat in the Hat* **Begin-**
E **ner Book Dictionary in Spanish and English**. New York: Random House, 1966. 133p. $16.00. ISBN 0-394-81542-4.

This book, the Spanish-language version of *Cat in the Hat Beginner Book Dictionary*, reprints the original work, adds Spanish translations of the captions (printed in a different color), and provides a guide to pronunciation.

1240 **Facts on File English/Spanish Visual**
E+ **Dictionary**. New York: Facts on File, 1992. 928p. $39.95. ISBN 0-8160-1546-5.

Thousands of words about astronomy, geography, animals, architecture, transportation, music, sports, food and clothing are identified by topical drawings. The handsome illustrations contain the words within the illustration blocks with the English word in black and the Spanish word in blue type. Indexed in both Spanish and English. Recommended for all levels.

1241 **Larousse English-Spanish, Spanish-English Dictionary**. New York: Larousse, Kingfisher Chambers, 1996. 1,505p. $29.95. ISBN 2-03-420280-5.

This new dictionary contains 180,000 references and 350,000 translations which cover each language from its international perspectives. In addition to the standard vocabulary, it includes extended coverage of professional, technical and literary terms as well as many cultural entries. Recommended as an excellent mid-sized dictionary for secondary schools.

1242 Lipton, Gladys C. **Beginning Spanish**
E   **Bilingual Dictionary: A Beginner's**
     Guide in Words and Pictures. 2d ed.
     Hauppauge, N.Y.: Barron's Educa-
     tional Series, 1989. 400p. $6.95pa.
     ISBN 0-8120-4274-3.

There are about 2,600 entries in this dictionary
and they include definitions, phonetic transcrip-
tions and a sentence using the word. Many
entries include pictures. This is a good dictionary
for elementary collections in schools with a
Spanish language curriculum.

1243 **The Oxford-Duden Pictorial Spanish**
     and English Dictionary. 2d ed. New
     York: Oxford University Press, 1995.
     880p. $19.95pa. ISBN 0-19-864515-5.

Parallel word lists appear below 384 topical pictures keyed to the words with numbers. Most are
drawings, but there are 6 color entries. Useful
subjects from anatomy to nature to business to
public buildings to clothing and hair styles are
covered. The volumes in this series are good for
vocabulary building.

1244 **The Oxford Spanish Dictionary:**
     Spanish-English, English-Spanish.
     New York: Oxford University Press,
     1994. 1,888p. $39.95. ISBN 0-19-
     864510-4.

1245 **Oxford Spanish Dictionary**. New
     York: Oxford University Press, 1996.
     CD-ROM (Macintosh and Win-
     dows). $49.95. ISBN 0-1926-8309-8
     (Macintosh); 0-1926-8308-X
     (Windows).

This is an authoritative and comprehensive dictionary, covering Spanish wherever it is spoken,
even Hispanic American vocabulary is included.
Entries have extensive illustrative sentences and
grammar and usage issues are addressed. More
than 250,000 words and phrases are defined and
many useful appendices provide additional
information. Also available in CD-ROM. Highly
recommended.

1246 Raventos, Margaret H. and David L.
     Gold. **Random House New Spanish-**
     English, English-Spanish Dictio-
     nary. New York: Random House,
     1995. 650p. $18.00. ISBN 0-679-
     43897-1.

This popular dictionary includes more than
60,000 entries of the most typically used vocabulary for students and travelers. It uses new alphabetization rules and most current spellings.
Coverage is for both European and Latin American Spanish. Useful appendices include dates,
numbers and road and street signs. Recommended for secondary schools.

Literature

BIOGRAPHY

1247 Brown, Susan W., ed. **Contemporary**
     Novelists. 6th ed. Chicago: St. James
     Press, 1996. 1,173p. $160.00. ISBN 1-
     55862-189-X.

Published since 1972, this edition reflects major
revisions since the previous volume (1991).
Arranged alphabetically by author, the entries
give brief biographical facts, a list of their publications separated by genre, a bibliography of
critical studies and signed historical and critical
essays. More than 650 writers, based on recommendations of a group of advisors, were selected
for this edition. A list of titles with dates and
authors serves as an index. Recommended for

schools that cannot afford the standard, ongoing
resources.

1248 **Contemporary Authors**. 158v- .
     Detroit, Mich.: Gale Research,
     1962– . $134.00/volume. ISBN varies.

1249 **Contemporary Authors New Revi-**
     sion Series. 60v- . Detroit, Mich.:
     Gale Research, 1981– . $140.00/
     volume. ISBN varies.

An ongoing series, this work provides basic personal, career, and publication information for
some 91,000 authors to date, many of whom are
not profiled elsewhere. Each new volume adds

about 900 new entries. All types of writers receive attention, except those in highly technical fields. Also included are persons prominent in communications: newspaper and television reporters and correspondents, columnists, editors, photojournalists, screenwriters, and scriptwriters. In addition, *Contemporary Authors* covers those deceased since 1900 whose works still attract interest. Cumulative indexes appear in alternate volumes and refer to the volumes in the set and to authors included in Dictionary of Literary Biography or any of the other Gale Literary Criticism series.

The *Contemporary Authors New Revision Series* is a separate set that contains updated profiles of authors who have been highly productive since they appeared in *Contemporary Authors*. Gale is in the process of loading the *Contemporary Authors* databases onto their online information system, GaleNet. The schedule for additions is available on their website, www.gale.com. Both series are recommended as basic sources for high schools. [R: ARBA 92]

1250 **Contemporary Authors Cumulative Index**. Detroit, Mich.: Gale Research, 1976– . $10.00pa. ISSN 0196-0245.

Published with every second volume of *Contemporary Authors*, each issue of this index is cumulative from its first volume. It includes entries in *Contemporary Authors*, *Contemporary Authors New Revision Series* and *Something About the Author*.

1251 **Cyclopedia of Literary Characters II**. 4v. Pasadena, Calif.: Salem Press, 1990. $300.00. ISBN 0-89356-517-2.

Similar to the original work published in 1963 to accompany *Masterplots*, this set covers some 5,000 characters in 1,437 works from the following volumes of *Masterplots II: American Fiction, British and Commonwealth Fiction, World Fiction, Drama*, plus 20 works selected from the *Short Story* volumes. Arranged alphabetically by title, characters for each work are listed in order of importance. Central characters are described more fully, and pronunciations for names are provided when necessary. Indexed by title, author, and character.

The set enables the reader to become familiar with personalities from important works or to identify the books in which specific characters

appear. A new five volume edition is in preparation. Recommended for high schools. [R: ARBA 91; BL, 1 Jan 91; LJ, Dec 90; WLB, Dec 90]

1252 **Cyclopedia of World Authors**. 3d rev. ed. 5v. Pasadena, Calif.: Salem Press, 1997. $350.00. ISBN 0-89356-434-6.

This new edition replaces *Cyclopedia of World Authors II*. Biographies of authors is accompanied by critical information. Recommended for high schools.

1253 **Dictionary of Literary Biography**. 184v– . Detroit, Mich.: Gale Research, 1978– . $140.00/vol. ISBN varies.

1254 **Dictionary of Literary Biography Yearbooks**. 17v– . Detroit, Mich.: Gale Research, 1981– . $140.00/vol. ISBN varies.

1255 **Dictionary of Literary Biography Documentary Series**. 16v– . Detroit, Mich.: Gale Research, 1982– . $140.00/vol. ISBN varies.

The intent of this series is to show the importance of literature in the culture of a nation. The volumes are organized by topic, period or genre. For example, volume 61 of the *DLB* focuses on American children's authors and illustrators since 1960. The series began by describing writing themes in the United States, but broadened its focus to include western Europe, eastern Europe, Latin America, and so on. Individual author entries trace the development of each writer's career within these frameworks.

The *Yearbooks* update the previously published entries, while the *Documentary Series* is focused on narrower topics such as the three classic "hardboiled" mystery writers; one volume is limited only to Tennessee Williams. Two concise *DLB* sets were published: *American Literary Biography* in six volumes (1988–1989) and *British Literary Biography* in eight volumes (1991–1992). These volumes were arranged chronologically to cover the major eras in the respective national literatures.

Each volume has a cumulative index, and the titles of all of the series are repeated in the front of each volume. These sets are illustrated with drawings, paintings and photographs. Gale Research is adding the information in the *DLB* volumes to its online database, GaleNet. The first items to be loaded are the essays on 20th century American authors. The online system will allow searchers to sort by genre, nationality, ethnicity, years of birth or death, subject, theme and key word.

1256 Flores, Angel. **Spanish American Authors: The Twentieth Century**. Bronx, N.Y.: H. W. Wilson, 1992. 915p. $100.00. ISBN 0-8242-0806-4.

Biographies of more than 330 important Latin American novelists and poets are included in this excellent source. Bibliographies attached to the articles include works by and criticism of the authors. Recommended for high school collections.

1257 Hedgepeth, Chester. **Twentieth-Century African American Writers and Artists**. Chicago: American Library Association, 1991. 323p. $50.00. ISBN 0-8389-0534-X.

This source gives biographical and critical information about "contemporary" (work accomplished in the 20th century) writers, painters, sculptors and musicians. Specific criteria were established for inclusion, depending upon the art form. Poets must have been published in 10 journals; novelists had to have 2 books published; composers must have had 7 public performances; and artists must have exhibited in major museums. The essays were submitted to all living individuals for their comments. Entries are alphabetical with a category classification in an appendix. The entries include name and dates, a descriptive identification, a brief biography and an extended criticism of the place of their works. Bibliographies of works by and about are appended. This is an excellent resource about the most important African Americans in the arts during the century. Highly recommended for secondary schools. [R: ARBA 92]

1258 Pringle, David. **Imaginary People: A Who's Who of Fictional Characters from the Eighteenth Century to the Present Day**. 2d ed. Brookfield, Vt.: Ashgate Publishing, 1996. 296p. $49.95. ISBN 1-85928-162-1.

Pringle identifies and describes fictional characters from novels (since Defoe), comic books,

films and TV series. Characters are traced through series, their appearances in other media, or in books by other authors. From Conan the Barbarian to Huckleberry Finn to Hannibal Lecter to Winnie the Pooh, the selection of characters and their interesting descriptions make this both a reference and a browsing resource. Highly recommended for secondary collections.

1259 **The Scribner Writers Series on CD-ROM**. New York: Scribner, 1997. Windows. $595.00. ISBN 0-684-19584-4.

Essays on 510 writers and works from nine Scribner sets, including *Ancient Writers*, *American Writers*, *British Writers*, *European Writers* and *Latin American Writers*. Entries are both biographical and critical and are browsable by writer's names, by genre, by time period or by nationality. Other search categories include language, race and sex. Key words may be searched and hotlinks allow users to jump between related essays. There is a printing option and icons for displays such as bibliographies.

The CD-ROM is more affordable than the original sets; however, those libraries needing more comprehensive coverage may want to consider one or more of them: *African Writers* (1997, 2v.); *African American Writers* (1991); *Ancient Writers, Greece and Rome* (1982, 2v.); *American Writers* (1974– , 12v. including *Essential American Writers: A Retrospective Supplement*, 1997); *British Writers* (1979, 7v.); *European Writers* (1983–1991, 14v.); *Latin American Writers* (1989, 3v.); *Modern American Women Writers* (1991); *Science Fiction Writers* (1982); and *Supernatural Fiction Writers*, (1985, 2v.).

1260 Watson, Noelle, ed. **Reference Guide to Short Fiction**. Detroit: St. James Press, 1994. 1052p. $130.00. ISBN 1-555862-334-5.

Part one of this source lists significant writers of short fiction from the 19th and 20th centuries; some living authors are included. The scope is international, but the focus is on writers in the English language. Coverage is from Scott and Irving to Oates and Walker. Entries include a biography, a complete list of published books, a bibliography of critical studies and a signed critical essay. [R: ARBA 95]

The second part of the work contains signed essays about the works themselves. The two sections are each arranged alphabetically Lists of both writers and works precede the introduction and there is a title index. Highly recommended for high schools.

1261 **American Authors, 1600–1900: A Biographical Dictionary of American Literature**. Bronx, N.Y.: H. W. Wilson, 1938. 846p. $76.00. ISBN 0-8242-0007-1.

One of the well-known Wilson Author series, this volume contains biographies of 1,300 authors who contributed to the development of American literature, from the founding of Jamestown (1607) to the end of the nineteenth century. Each essay describes the author's life, discusses past and present significance, and evaluates principal works. Some 400 portraits illustrate the volume. These biographies are incorporated in the CD-ROM *World Authors 800 B.C.–Present*.

1262 **British Authors Before 1800: A Biographical Dictionary**. Bronx, N.Y.: H. W. Wilson, 1952. 584p. $64.00. ISBN 0-8242-0006-3.

1263 **British Authors of the Nineteenth Century**. Bronx, N.Y.: H. W. Wilson, 1936. 677p. $64.00. ISBN 0-8242-0007-1.

These works contain more than 1,650 biographical profiles (650 before 1800 and 1,000 during the nineteenth century) of writers, philosophers, theologians, critics, and others who achieved eminence in British literature before the twentieth century. Articles focus on their lives and most influential writings. Portraits accompany many of the entries. These biographies are incorporated in the CD-ROM *World Authors 800 B.C.–Present*. Recommended for secondary schools.

1264 **European Authors 1000–1900: A Biographical Dictionary of European Literature**. Bronx, N.Y.: H. W. Wilson, 1967. 1,016p. $77.00. ISBN 0-8242-0013-6.

As do other volumes in the Wilson Author series, this one focuses on a wide range of influential writers: historians, theologians, philosophers, educators, critics, and literary figures. Profiles of 967 authors summarize each person's life and

examine the principal works translated into English. All authors were born after A.D. 1000 and were deceased prior to 1925. French and German writers dominate, followed by Russian authors. Portraits accompany about one-third of the sketches. These biographies are incorporated in the CD-ROM *World Authors 800 B.C.–Present*.

1265 **Greek and Latin Authors, 800 B.C.–A.D. 1000: A Biographical Dictionary**. Bronx, N.Y.: H. W. Wilson, 1980. 490p. $68.00. ISBN 0-8242-0640-1.

This excellent biographical dictionary, one of the Wilson Authors series, contains brief profiles of 376 writers who contributed to the rich and varied literature of the classical world. Each essay contains critical comments and a bibliography of the best editions and translations. The appendix lists authors chronologically by century. These biographies are incorporated in the CD-ROM *World Authors 800 B.C.-Present*. [R: ARBA 81]

1266 **Index to the Wilson Author Series**. Bronx, N.Y.: H. W. Wilson, 1997. 136p. $27.00. ISBN 0-8242-0900-1.

An alphabetical index to the 10,000 authors in the Wilson Author Series as well as almost 2,000 biographies from the Junior Authors and Illustrators series. Covers a total of 19 author biography titles. Recommended for schools holding the print versions of the series.

1267 **World Authors: 1900–1950**. 4v. Bronx, N.Y.: H. W. Wilson, 1996. $395.00. ISBN 0-8242-0899-4.

1268 **World Authors: 1950–1970**. Bronx, N.Y.: H. W. Wilson, 1975. 1,593p. $95.00. ISBN 0-8242-0419-9.

1269 **World Authors: 1970–1975**. Bronx, N.Y.: H. W. Wilson, 1980. 893p. $85.00. ISBN 0-8242-0641-X.

1270 **World Authors: 1975–1980**. Bronx, N.Y.: H. W. Wilson, 1985. 829p. $85.00. ISBN 0-8242-0715-7.

1271 **World Authors: 1980–1985**. Bronx, N.Y.: H. W. Wilson, 1991. 938p. $85.00. ISBN 0-8242-0797-1.

1272 **World Authors: 1985–1990**. Bronx,
N.Y.: H. W. Wilson, 1995. 970p.
$85.00. ISBN 0-8242-0875-7.

1273 **World Authors: 800 B.C.–Present**.
Bronx, N.Y.: H. W. Wilson, 1997.
CD-ROM (DOS, Windows and
Macintosh). $595.00 with annual
updates at $95.00; pricing varies for
network licenses.

1274 **World Authors: 1900–Present**.
Bronx, N.Y.: H. W. Wilson, 1997.
CD-ROM (DOS, Windows and
Macintosh). $495.00 with annual
updates at $95.00; pricing varies for
network licenses.

1275 **World Authors: 1950–Present**.
Bronx, N.Y.: H. W. Wilson, 1997.
CD-ROM (DOS, Windows and
Macintosh). $295.00 with annual
updates at $95.00; pricing varies for
network licenses.

The print World Authors series covers some
4,742 authors from all over the world who wrote
in English or whose works have been widely
translated into English. The 1900–1950 set
replaces *Twentieth Century Authors* and its supplement. There was a complete revision of those
works which resulted in new biographical information and the newest criticism. The other titles
bring coverage up to 1990. The biographies are
clearly written, often with comments by the
author, accompanied by photographs and references about the author's life and of criticism of
the works.

The CD-ROM versions include various sections of the total Wilson database. *World Authors,
1900–Present* contains information on 10,000
authors from the print titles *Greek and Latin
Authors 800 B.C.–A.D. 1000, European Authors
1000–1900, British Authors Before 1800, British
Authors of the Nineteenth Century, American
Authors 1600–1900* and *World Authors 1900–
Present*. Entries include biographical information, critical information, bibliographies and
photographs. *World Authors 1900–Present* covers
5,300 authors while *World Authors 1950–Present*
covers 2,700 authors. *World Authors: 800 B.C.–
Present* is also available via OCLC FirstSearch,
UMI ProQuest Direct and SilverPlatter Information Systems.

DICTIONARIES AND ENCYCLOPEDIAS

1276 Baldick, Chris. **The Concise Oxford
Dictionary of Literary Terms**. New
York: Oxford University Press, 1990.
246p. $10.95pa. ISBN 0-19-282893-2.

This work defines more than 1,000 literary
terms—"hard words alphabetically arranged and
briefly explained." The explanations are clear
and tell how the term is used with an example or
clarification that identifies the meaning in the
context of literary criticism. Some entries are
longer, especially for major critical theories such
as deconstruction. There is a list of further references as well as some entry bibliographies. This
is a literary dictionary appropriate for high
school students and teachers.

1277 Benet, William Rose, and Bruce
E+ Murphy, eds. **Benet's Reader's Encyclopedia**. 4th ed. New York: Harper-
Collins, 1996. 1144p. $50.00. ISBN
0-06-270110-X.

Any reader encountering an unfamiliar reference should be able to find a quick and satisfactory response from the *Reader's Encyclopedia*.
There are thousands of entries that encompass
author's biographies, identification of characters,
references to mythology, literary terms and a
myriad of other topics about which one might
want an explanation. This new edition strength-
ens the international approach as it includes
more references from Africa and the Middle
East and the newly independent Eastern European countries. More women writers have also
been added. This is a necessary holding in almost
any library.

1278 **Brewer's Dictionary of Phrase &**
E+ **Fable**. 15th ed. revised by Adrian
Room. New York: HarperCollins,
1995. 1182p. $45.00. ISBN 0-06-
270133-9.

First published in 1870, this update of the 1989
fourteenth edition has been revised extensively.
Entries have been reworded, restyled and rewritten. Old entries have been weeded and replaced
and facts, figures and dates have been updated.
There are more etymologies, more names of fictional characters and more entries of American
origin. Material ranges from Greek mythology
and the Bible to the 1990s.

Expressions are listed by key word with extensive indexing complete with cross-references. Numerous lists provide such things as the dying words of famous people, symbols of saints and the symbolic uses of flowers and trees. This classic work belongs in all libraries at all levels.

1279 Encyclopedia of World Literature in the 20th Century. 2d ed. 4v. + index. New York: Ungar, 1981–1989. $600.00. ISBN 0-8103-9619-X.

1280 Encyclopedia of World Literature in the 20th Century: Supplement and Index. New York: Ungar, 1993. $150.00. ISBN 0-8264-0571-1.

The original set is a definitive work on world literature in the twentieth century and includes biographical and critical information on national literatures (American, European, Asian and African), literary movements and authors. Arrangement is alphabetical; the author entries include photographs and bibliographies.

The supplement includes a complete index to the whole set and updates the national articles, contains entries on 400 authors not previously covered, addresses new literary critical approaches, and adds new articles that bring the coverage up to the 1990s. This set is highly recommended for high schools.

1281 Harmon, William, and others. **A Handbook to Literature**. 7th ed. New York: Prentice Hall, 1995. 647p. $46.50. ISBN 0-13-234782-2.

This standard work, sometimes referred to as "Thrall and Hibbard," (the original compilers), and recently edited by Hugh C. Holman and William Harmon, contains entries on literary terms, concepts, schools, movements and critical theories. This excellent source has become a standard for high schools, both as a reference tool for literature classes and as a reader's advisor.

1282 Manguel, Alberto, and Gianni Guadalupi. **The Dictionary of Imaginary Places**. San Diego, Calif.: Harcort Brace Jovanovich, 1987. 454p. $19.00pa. ISBN 0-15-626054-9.

The Dictionary of Imaginary Places, an update of a 1981 work, provides descriptions, illustrations, and maps of fanciful worlds (e.g., Middle Earth,

Lilliput, Narnia). Excluded are heavens and hells, future places, worlds that mimic real places, and other planets. This work is a good reference source and fun to browse. [R: ARBA 88]

1283 Merriam-Webster's Encyclopedia of
E+ Literature. Springfield, Mass.: Merriam-Webster, 1995. 1236p. $39.95. ISBN 0-87779-042-6.

This excellent desk reference is a combined project of Britannica and Merriam-Webster. The scope is international and covers authors, plots, characters, terms, styles and criticism of serious and popular literature, science fiction, mystery and folklore. Each entry includes definitions, pronunciation and etymologies. This is a quick reference source, a reader's advisor and a teacher's resource. Highly recommended for collections at all levels. [R: ARBA 96]

1284 Ousby, Ian, ed. **The Cambridge Guide to Literature in English**. 2d ed. New York: Cambridge University Press, 1994. 1061p. $49.95. ISBN 0-521-44086-6.

This guide covers English literature produced anywhere in the world. It lists authors and titles, characters and terms. The brief entries include some analysis. This is a useful dictionary and bibliography source for high schools requiring this kind of coverage.

1285 Seymour-Smith, Martin. **Dictionary of Fictional Characters**. rev. ed. Boston: The Writer, 1992. 579p. $18.95pa. ISBN 0-87116-166-4.

Seymour-Smith has revised and updated this title, previously edited by Freeman and Urquhart. This edition lists some 50,000 characters from novels, short stories, poems, plays and opera. Most entries are from British and American literature, but works translated into English are also included. Each character is identified within the context of the work in which it appears and the relationship of each to other characters. Separate author and title indexes enable the reader to find the characters of a particular work. Recommended for secondary schools.

1286 Snodgrass, Mary Ellen. **Encyclopedia of Satirical Literature**. Santa Barbara, Calif.: ABC-CLIO, 1996. 559p. $65.00. ISBN 0-87436-856-1.

This one-volume work has alphabetically arranged essays about devices, modes, literary periods, writers, titles and characters of works the author has identified as representing satirical writing. Entries include such items as *Animal Farm* and *Handmaid's Tale*, camp, invective, irony and H. L. Mencken, and give pronunciation, definitions, commentary and examples. Cross-references lead to related items and sources are given. Length of entries vary. A chronology lists entries from the 18th century B.C. to 1995. A list of primary sources, a bibliography and an index conclude the volume. This work will be useful to high school literature teachers and students. Other titles in the series such as *Encyclopedia of Allegorical Literature, Encyclopedia of Apocalyptic Literature, Encyclopedia of Utopian Literature*, and *Encyclopedia of Traditional Epics* should also be considered. [R: ARBA 97]

1287 Stephens, Meic, comp. **A Dictionary of Literary Quotations**. New York: Routledge, 1990. 193p. $25.00. ISBN 0-415-04129-5.

The more than 3,000 quotations collected are "literary" in the sense that they refer to reading, writing, journalism and other topics related to books. Most of those quoted are English-language writers, but a few are foreign authors widely translated into English such as Camus and Pasternak. Sources include speeches, diaries, interviews and the subject's own writings.

The arrangement is under 180 topics; e.g., censorship, joys of reading, and are also accessed by many cross-references and a detailed subject index. Since there is little duplication with other standard quotation books, this compilation is a useful supplement to them.

PLOT OUTLINES

1288 **Masterplots Complete**. Englewood Cliffs, N.J.: Salem Press, 1997. $750.00. CD-ROM (Windows and Macintosh). ISBN 0-89356-263-7.

1289 **Masterplots II: African American Literature Series**. 3v. Englewood Cliffs, N.J.: Salem Press, 1994. $275.00. ISBN 0-89356-574-6.

1290 **Masterplots II: American Fiction Series**. 6v. Englewood Cliffs, N.J.:

Salem Press, 1986–1994. v.1–4, $325.00; v.5–6, $185.00. ISBN 0-89536-456-7 (v.1–4); 0-89356-719-1 (v.5–6).

1291 **Masterplots II: British and Commonwealth Fiction Series**. 4v. Englewood Cliffs, N.J.: Salem Press, 1987. $365.00. ISBN 0-89356-468-0.

1292 **Masterplots II: Drama Series**. 4v. Englewood Cliffs, N.J.: Salem Press, 1990. $365.00. ISBN 0-89356-491-5.

1293 **Masterplots II: Nonfiction Series**. 4v. Englewood Cliffs, N.J.: Salem Press, 1989. $365.00. ISBN 0-89356-478-8.

1294 **Masterplots II: Short Story Series; Short Story Series Supplement**. 10v. Englewood Cliffs, N.J.: Salem Press, 1986; 1996. v.1–6, $425.00; v.7–10, $325.00. ISBN 0-89356-461-3 (v.1–6); 0-89356-769-8 (v.7–10).

1295 **Masterplots II: Women's Literature Series**. 6v. Pasadena, Calif.: Salem Press, 1995. $500.00. ISBN 0-89356-898-8.

Masterplots is the best known of the plot summary sources. Each entry lists characters, setting and theme as well as a long synopsis of plot and some critical analysis. Print sets have been updated with annual volumes and revised sets. The print volumes are still available for those libraries needing only some sets.

The CD-ROM combines the entries from 80 volumes of *Masterplots* (12v. 1976 rev. ed.) and the *Masterplots II* series (1986–1996). It also includes related entries from *Cyclopedia of Literary Characters, Cyclopedia of Literary Characters II* and *World Authors II*. It provides the plot summaries and analyses of the print versions, and makes them searchable by author, themes, setting, title, character names and combinations. Hypertext allows links from book summary to author profile or character description. There are variable printing options.

1296 **Monarch Notes**. Princeton, N.J.: Thynx, 1992– . CD-ROM (Windows and Macintosh). $79.95. ISBN 1-8788-0519-3.

All of the *Monarch Notes Study Guides* are included on this disc. The story summaries, character descriptions, criticism and bibliographies are present in full text. In addition there are music clips, photographs, spoken excerpts, videos and animations. There is also a glossary of literary terms. Searching is by title, author, keyword and phrase. Some find the multimedia distracting, but students will appreciate the comprehensiveness and ease of use of this CD-ROM. Recommended as a study guide for secondary school collections.

CRITICISM

1297 **Black Literature Criticism**. 3v.
Detroit, Mich.: Gale Research, 1991.
$275.00. ISBN 0-8103-7929-5.

This set provides excerpts of critical works on the writing of 125 prominent international Black authors from the past 200 years. Authors from the United States, South Africa, Nigeria and other countries are represented. Each entry consists of an author profile, the excerpts from critical studies and sources for further reading by and about the author. Some entries were pulled from other Gale databases; some were written especially for this source. Indexes provide access. Recommended for high school collections.

1298 **Contemporary Literary Criticism**.
102v–. Detroit, Mich.: Gale
Research, 1984– . $134.00/vol. ISBN
varies.

1299 **Twentieth-Century Literary Criticism**. 70v– . Detroit, Mich.: Gale
Research, 1981– . $134.00/vol.
ISBN varies.

1300 **Nineteenth-Century Literature Criticism**. 61v– . Detroit, Mich.: Gale
Research, 1981– . $134.00/vol.
ISBN varies.

These series, each of which focuses on a specific period, provide critical excerpts from a variety of sources that offer contrasting evaluations of an author or a given work. In addition to the critiques, the following are included for each author: a portrait, a biographical/critical introduction written by Gale editors, a list of principal

works, and citations of critical books and articles. In each volume, an appendix lists works from which critical comments have been drawn.

Authors included in *Contemporary Literary Criticism* are still living or died after December 31, 1959. Those included in *Twentieth-Century Literary Criticism* died between 1900 and 1959; those in *Nineteenth-Century Literature Criticism* had died before 1900.

Other chronological Gale Literary Criticism series include *Literature Criticism from 1400-1800* (33 vol.; ongoing) and *Classical and Medieval Literature Criticism* (22 vol.; ongoing). There is a separate series *Shakespearean Criticism* (32 vol.; ongoing). A selection of major authors from the other series was published in 1992 as *World Literature Criticism, 1500 to the Present* in six volumes.

Contemporary Literary Criticism is being added to the Gale online information system as *CLC Select*. All of these items are appropriate for high school collections.

1301 **Hispanic Literature Criticism**. 2v.
Detroit, Mich.: Gale Research, 1994.
$190.00. ISBN 0-81039-145-7.

Seventy-one writers from the United States, Mexico, Cuba, Spain, Chile, Argentina, Guatemala, and other South American countries as well as Portugal and Spain are included in this guide to criticism. The authors are from about the last 100 years. Arrangement is alphabetical by author with author profiles, a chronology of major works and excerpts from critical articles. There are author, title and nationality indexes. Useful for high school collections, as these authors are among those most often studied.

1302 Kirkpatrick, D. L., ed. **Reference Guide to English Literature**. 2d ed.
3v. Detroit, Mich.: St. James Press, 1991. $295.00. ISBN 1-55862-078-8.

Earlier versions of most of the entries in this set, which covers British writers and writing, were published in *Great Writers of the English Language* (1978) and in the first edition of this title (1984). Biographies and critical essays on writers comprise the first two volumes, while the third volume has essays about works. There is a title index. The signed articles on both the writers and the works are appropriate for high school students.

DRAMA

1303 Berney, Kate, ed. **Contemporary Dramatists**. 5th ed. Chicago: St. James Press, 1993. 843p. $140.00. ISBN 1-55862-185-7.

The 450 living playwrights writing in English were selected for this volume by an international group of critics, scholars and writers. The clearly defined entries include biographical, bibliographic and critical information. These playwrights include those most likely to be studied in high schools.

1304 **Drama Criticism**. 6v. Detroit, Mich.: Gale Research, 1991. $87.00/vol. ISBN varies.

This set includes dramatists from all time periods and all countries. Each volume identifies about 15 dramatists, gives biographical and bibliographic information and selected excerpts from critical studies which focus on both literary and performance standards. Each volume's index is cumulative. This set is appropriate for high schools.

GENRE

1305 Clute, John and John Grant. **The Encyclopedia of Fantasy**. New York: St. Martin's, 1997. 1049p. $75.00. ISBN 0-312-15897-1.

This is a comprehensive guide to all aspects of fantasy including authors, titles, films, motifs, recurring themes, conventions and fantasy related horror and the supernatural. Coverage is from the 1850s with some references to earlier folktales, fairy tales and epics that have influenced modern fantasy. Examples of entries show the breadth of the resource: Lloyd Alexander is just one of the children's authors included; Northrop Frye is one of the literary theorists whose work can be used to analyze the genre; heroic fantasy is one type of fantasy defined; portals is but one of the conventions included. Articles range in length from brief descriptions to longer entries for major topics such as "children's fantasy." This is a companion to the *Encyclopedia of Science Fiction* and contains cross-references to that work. Highly recommended for collections where fantasy is taught or popular.

1306 Clute, John, and Peter Nicholls. **The Encyclopedia of Science Fiction**. 2d ed. New York: St. Martin's, 1993. 1408p. $75.00. ISBN 0-312-09618-6.

Biographies, themes, conventions and inventions are all included in one of the most comprehensive works ever published about science fiction. Historical, bibliographical and critical information is presented in more than 4,000 entries. This is an outstanding work most high schools will want.

1307 Herald, Diana Tixier. **Genreflecting: A Guide to Reading Interests in Genre Fiction**. 4th ed. Englewood, Colo.: Libraries Unlimited, 1995. $38.00. ISBN 1-56308-354-X.

The purpose of *Genreflecting*, which has been expanded to reflect the newest popular fiction, is to assist the librarian and the reader in identifying books of interest to a wide audience. The work is divided into seven chapters: westerns, crime, adventure, romances, science fiction, fantasy and horror. Each chapter discusses themes and types and then describes a variety of topics appropriate to the category: best authors, anthologies, bibliographies, criticism, films, magazines, publishers, reviews, associations, and awards. Indexes include author-title, subject, and series characters.

1308 Mote, Dave, ed. **Contemporary Popular Writers**. Chicago: St. James Press, 1997. 528p. $130.00. ISBN 1-55862-216-0.

This first edition makes it easy to locate information about the most widely read of the 20th century writers in English. Included are novelists, short story authors, nonfiction writers, poets and playwrights. Elmore Leonard, Jackie Collins, Danielle Steel, Stephen King, Piers Anthony and Dave Barry can all be found here. Biographic, bibliographic, and critical information is given for each. There are indexes by author, nationality, genre and title. Recommended for high schools where popular authors are included in the literature curriculum.

1309 Pederson, Jay P., and Robert Reginald, eds. **St. James Guide to Science Fiction Writers**. 4th ed. Chicago: St. James Press, 1996. 1,175 p. $140.00. ISBN 1-55862-179-2.

Formerly *Twentieth-Century Science-Fiction Writers*, this new edition adds 50 entries. More than 600 of the most important and influential authors are included such as Asimov, Herbert and Zelazny as well as William Golding, Michael Crichton and Madeleine L'Engle. Entries are arranged alphabetically by author and contain biographies, lists of works and critical essays. Foreign and 19th century writers are in an appendix. A series and title list give the author's name and serves as an index. This is a useful guide to science fiction for high school students and teachers.

1310 Pederson, Jay P., and Taryn Benbow-Pfalzgraf, eds. **St. James Guide to Crime and Mystery Writers**. 4th ed. Chicago: St. James Press, 1996. 1,264p. $140.00. ISBN 1-55862-178-4.

Formerly published as *Twentieth-Century Crime and Mystery Writers* (St. Martin's, 1991), this is a biographical and critical study of 650 English-language writers. Entries give biographies, titles of all works, critical studies, often writer's comments about their own work and a signed critical essay. There is a series/title list that gives the author's name and thus acts as an index. High schools with genre literature courses or mystery fans will find this useful.

1311 Pringle, David, ed. **St. James Guide to Fantasy Writers**. Chicago: St. James Press, 1996. 711p. $140.00. ISBN 1-55862-205-5.

Pringle, the author of *Modern Fantasy* (Harper-Collins, 1989), has compiled a new reference to more than 400 authors of heroic fantasy, sword and sorcery, adult fairy tales and fables. Intended for high school and college students and all adult fantasy readers, the entries follow the pattern of other *St. James Guides*. Biographical and bibliographical information is accompanied by 1,000 word signed critical essays which place the authors and their works in the world of 20th century fantasy writing. Some important originators of the genre, dating back to the 17th century are also included. There is a title index, a list of foreign-language fantasy writers and a comprehensive reading list about the genre.

1312 **St. James Guide to Horror, Ghost and Gothic Writers**. Detroit, Mich.: St. James Press, 1997. 600p. $140.00. ISBN 1-55862-206-3.

Clive Barker, Marry Higgins Clark, Anne Rice and Edgar Allan Poe are among the 450 authors selected for inclusion in this critical and biographical guide. Arranged alphabetically by author the signed entries give biographical information and critical essays that help the reader understand the place of the author within the genre. There is a title index and a reading list about the genre.

1313 **Twentieth-Century Western Writers**. 2d ed. Detroit, Mich.: St. James Press, 1991. 848p. $140.00. ISBN 0-91228-998-8.

Almost 500 modern writers of novels and stories which are set in the American frontier are included in this guide. Biographical and critical information is provided for each author. The writer's own comments are included when available. Such authors as Michael Dorris, Louise Erdrich, Tony Hillerman and Laura Ingalls Wilder can be found here. There is a series/title index. Recommended for high schools with western genre studies.

1314 Vasudevan, Aruna, and Lesley Henderson, eds. **Twentieth-Century Romance and Historical Writers**. 3d ed. Chicago: St. James Press, 1994. 890p. $140.00. ISBN 1-55862-180-6.

Includes more than 500 writers of romance and historical literature, giving biographical data, a list of their works, comments by the author and a signed critical essay, emphasizing the writer's style and contribution to the genre. The selected authors range from popular writers such as Danielle Steel and Barbara Cartland to James Michner and Pearl Buck. This is the most comprehensive work available on historical and romance novels. For high schools with genre studies.

POETRY

1315 **The Columbia Granger's Guide to Poetry Anthologies**. 2d ed. New York: Columbia University Press, 1994. 440p. $75.00. ISBN 0-231-10104-X.

1316 **The Columbia Granger's Index to Poetry in Anthologies**. 11th ed. New York: Columbia University Press, 1997. 2229p. $275.00. ISBN 0-231-10130-9.

1317 **The Columbia Granger's Index to Poetry in Collected and Selected Works**. New York: Columbia University Press, 1996. 1913p. $225.00. ISBN 0-231-10762-5.

1318 **The Columbia Granger's World of Poetry on CD-ROM**. New York: Columbia University Press, 1995. CD-ROM (Windows and Macintosh). $695.00. ISBN 0-231-10158-9.

Granger's Index to Poetry in Anthologies has been a standard reference tool since its introduction in 1904. The latest edition indexes 75,000 poems from 379 anthologies representing 11,000 poets by title, author, subject and first line. The most recent editions have added last lines; there are 10,000 in the eleventh edition. Recommended anthologies for first purchase are highlighted. The source now indexes old anthologies that may still be held as well as new anthologies; nonetheless, older copies should be kept for complete access to established poetry collections.

The *Guide to Poetry Anthologies* provides a capsule review of each of the anthologies indexed in the seventh, eighth, ninth and tenth editions of the *Index to Poetry in Anthologies*. Reviews describe the scope and organization of each anthology and judge its value in terms of originality and poetic quality. The guide is arranged by category and there are recommendations for first and additional purchases.

In effect, there are now two volumes of *Granger's*, a companion that indexes collected works of individual poets has now been published as the *Index to Poetry in Collected and Selected Works*. More than 50,000 poems from 275 volumes representing 251 individual poets (including children's poets) are indexed in the first edition. This complementary work significantly adds to the possibilities access of any particular poem.

The CD-ROM version includes the indexes as well as full-text of 10,000 poems no longer under copyright protection and quotations from 7,500 other poems.

1319 **The New Princeton Encyclopedia of Poetry and Poetics**. rev. ed. Alex Preminger and others. Princeton, N.J.: Princeton University Press, 1993. 1383p. $150.00. ISBN 0-691-03271-8.

Published previously in 1965 and 1974 as *The Princeton Encyclopedia of Poetry and Poetics*, this work combines the functions of a poetry dictionary with history and criticism of the world's poetry. Expanded coverage of non-Western poetry and of literary criticism mark this new revision. Recommended for advanced poetry programs in high schools.

1320 **Poetry Criticism**. 17v– . Detroit, Mich.: Gale Research, 1990– . $98.00/vol. ISBN varies.

Poets from all countries and time periods are included in this source. Each poet entry includes biographical and critical introductions and a bibliography of their works. Selected excerpts from critical articles give a notion of the poet's development. Often photographs of the poets accompany the articles and there is always a list of further reading. Indexes are cumulative.

1321 Riggs, Thomas, ed. **Contemporary Poets**. 6th ed. Chicago: St. James Press, 1996. 1,336p. $160.00. ISBN 1-55862-191-1.

An attempt has been made in this new edition to include the international body of poets who write in English. About 120 new poets have been added so that there are now almost 800 entries. The arrangement is alphabetical with information provided on each poet's background and writing. The signed critical essays are appropriate for the needs of high school students. There is a nationality index.

1322 Williams, Miller. **Patterns of Poetry: An Encyclopedia of Forms**. Baton Rouge, La.: Lousiana State University Press, 1986. 203p. $14.95. ISBN 0-8071-1330-1pa.

Despite its subtitle, *Patterns of Poetry* is not an encyclopedia; moreover, it is arranged in chapters instead of alphabetically. The main sections cover fully and loosely defined traditional stanza patterns, traditional poems of set and indefinite length, nonspecific forms and formal elements and variations in the stanzas and poems.

A detailed index gives easy access to poetic terms, which are clearly defined and illustrated. Because the content is excellent, this work is suggested for high school libraries.

SHORT STORIES

1323 **Short Story Criticism**. 26v- . Detroit, Mich.: Gale Research, 1987– . $99.00/vol. ISBN varies.

Much like *Contemporary Literary Criticism* and the other Gale critical literature series, each volume of *Short Story Criticism* contains excerpts of critical writings on a selected group (usually 8–10) of short story writers. Occasionally, one important short story of a major writer will be featured. Appropriate for high school collections.

1324 Yaakov, Juliette. **Short Story Index: An Index to Stories in Collections and Periodicals**. New York, H. W. Wilson, 1974– . annual. $90.00. ISSN 0360-9774.

The annual *Short Story Index*, published each September, indexes stories published in collections and magazines during the year and lists them in a single alphabet by author, title and subject. The list of collections indexed, which also serves as a selection aid, provides full bibliographic information needed to locate any cited story.

Five year cumulations replace annual volumes and are available starting from the 1950–1954 period; a single volume indexes short stories published in collections from 1900 to 1949.

AMERICAN LITERATURE
Dictionaries and Encyclopedias

1325 Andrews, William L, Frances Smith Foster, and Trudier Harris, eds. **The Oxford Companion to African American Literature**. New York: Oxford University Press, 1997. 866p. $55.00. ISBN 0-19-506510-7.

Articles in this work include 400 biographical articles as well as entries on cultural movements, genres, works, characters, slave narratives and preaching. Coverage is from the colonial period to the present. A long five-part essay on African

American literary history is essential reading. Children's and young adult literature is well represented with a long article and entries for many children's writers from Lucille Clifton to Virginia Hamilton. The work is indexed. This source should be in every secondary collection.

1326 Davidson, Cathy N., and Linda Wagner-Martin, eds. **The Oxford Companion to Women's Writing in the United States**. New York: Oxford University Press, 1995. 1021p. $60.00. ISBN 0-19-506608-1.

This comprehensive guide lists authors and women's writing issues and the styles, genre and topics with which they are associated. Minority writers, lesbian writers, diarists and nonfiction writers are all included. Articles on theory and criticism and genres are generally longer; the article on children's literature, for example, is five pages. The almost 800 entries are in alphabetical order with timelines and an index. This source is recommended for a wide variety of curricular applications.

1327 Hart, James D. **The Oxford Companion to American Literature**. 6th ed. revised by Phillip W. Leininger. New York: Oxford University Press, 1995. 779p. $60.00. ISBN 0-19-506548-4.

This guide has been a standard since its first publication in 1941. The newest edition adds 181 entries and the expected revisions and updates. Space has been made by removing most entries on presidents and colleges. The focus is on authors and their writings, past and present. Other entries deal with events, awards, societies, magazines, literary terms and characters. There are summaries of novels, stories, essays, poems, plays, histories and other narratives as well as brief biographies. The source is not just a guide to literature, but a reader's handbook as well. Recommended for first purchase in every secondary school library.

1328 Ruoff, A. LaVonne Brown. **American Indian Literatures: An Introduction, Bibliographic Review, and Selected Bibliography**. New York: Modern Language Association of America, 1990. 200p. $45.00. ISBN 0-87352-191-9.

Covering the period 1500 to the present, this scholarly, comprehensive work surveys the Native American oral tradition and written literature, a long-neglected area. The work opens with an introduction to the literature, followed by a section containing essays on bibliographies and research guides; anthologies, collections, and re-creations; and scholarship and criticism. An extensive classified bibliography cites all works mentioned in the essays and additional titles. When a Native American author is named in the text, the tribal affiliation is given in parentheses. High schools with Native American enrollment or programs which emphasize Native American studies should consider this work. [R: ARBA 92; BL, 1 Mar 91]

1329 Salzman, Jack, ed. **The Cambridge Handbook of American Literature**. New York: Cambridge University Press, 1986. 286p. $35.95. ISBN 0-521-30703-1.

The Cambridge Handbook focuses on 750 of the most significant writers, literary movements and journals. It also provides plot summaries of major works and side-by-side chronologies of American history and literature. Its publication date is recent enough that minorities and women are adequately covered. The work is a less expensive alternative to *The Oxford Companion to American Literature* which is more comprehensive. High schools will need one of these volumes.

1330 Salzman, Jack. **Major Characters in American Fiction**. New York: Holt, 1996. 960p. $25.00. ISBN 0-8050-3060-3.

More than 1,500 characters from novels and short stories written in America from 1970 to 1992 are listed in alphabetical order. A "biography" is given for each. The broad scope means that there are entries for characters as diverse as Dorothy, Beloved, Scarlett O'Hara, Lew Archer and Jin-Mei Woo. There is a list of authors with characters and titles and a list of titles with characters' alternate names. Highly recommended for American literature collections in secondary schools.

1331 Western Literature Association. **A Literary History of the American West**. Fort Worth, Tex.: Texas Christian University Press, 1987. 1353p. $79.50. ISBN 0-87565-021-X.

This monumental work provides extensive coverage of the movements, trends, and genre of western literature, including biographies of several hundred authors and a critical analysis of the works of each. Major divisions include such subjects as "Encountering the West" and "Precursors of the Western Novel." An analytical section, divided geographically, contains biographies and critical reviews of over 40 major authors (e.g., Mark Twain, Paul Horgan, Bernard De Voto). "Rediscovering the West" includes essays on Native American poetry, western movies, television, and film.

Written by subject specialists, each of the 80 authoritative essays concludes with a bibliography of primary sources and secondary accounts. A list of 126 major reference works and an index conclude the volume. Recommended for high schools with an interest in western literature. [R: ARBA 89; BL, Aug 89; LJ, 15 Apr 88]

Biography

1332 Kanellos, Nicolas, ed. **Biographical Dictionary of Hispanic Literature in the United States: The Literature of Puerto Ricans, Cuban Americans, and Other Hispanic Writers**. Westport, Conn.: Greenwood Press, 1989. 357p. $75.00. ISBN 0-313-24465-0.

This work focuses on 50 important contemporary Hispanic literary figures. Cuban American writers predominate. Mexican American authors are excluded as they are covered in *Chicano Literature*. The introduction is a survey of Hispanic literature and is followed by two- to three-page profiles of the authors. Each signed biography has an analysis of the author's major themes, a brief critical review and a bibliography of works by and about the writer. A general bibliography, an author-title index and a list of contributors conclude the volume. Despite the limited number of entries, this reference tool covers the authors comprehensively and would support Hispanic studies programs.

1333 Mainiero, Lina, ed. **American Women Writers: A Critical Reference Guide from Colonial Times to the Present**. 4v. New York: Ungar, 1979–1982. $380.00. ISBN 0-8044-3150-7.

1334 Green, Carol H, and Mary G. Mason, eds. **American Women Writers: A Critical Reference Guide from Colonial Times to the Present**. Vol. 5. New York, Ungar, 1994. $95.00. ISBN 0-826406033.

The original set contains biographical essays on over 1,000 American women authors of literary, popular and juvenile fiction and nonfiction. Entries consist of brief biographical data, an essay on the author's significance, and a list of works by and about her.

The supplementary fifth volume adds information about women who are still writing since the publication of the basic set and new entries for 145 women who are new writers or who were overlooked in the first four volumes, including minorities and newly discovered writers of diaries and journals. This comprehensive source supplements the coverage of standard references and is highly recommended for high school collections.

1335 Martinex, Julio A. and Francisco A. Loeli, eds. **Chicano Literature: A Reference Guide**. Westport, Conn.: Greenwood Press, 1985. 492p. $79.50. ISBN 0-313-23691-7.

The editors have defined Chicano literatue as that which has been "written since 1848 by Americans of Mexican descent or by Mexicans in the United States who write about the Chicano experience." Thirty entries consist of biographical/critical articles about literary figures and the remaining ten entries treat literary genres and topics such as Chicano philosophy. Entries include selective bibliographies. High schools with Chicano populations and Hispanic programs should consider this work.

ENGLISH LITERATURE
Dictionaries and Encyclopedias

1336 Drabble, Margaret. **The Oxford Companion to English Literature**. 5th ed. rev. New York: Oxford University Press, 1995. 1171p. $60.00. ISBN 0-19-866221-1.

1337 Drabble, Margaret, and Jenny Stringer, eds. **The Concise Oxford Companion to English Literature**. New York: Oxford University Press, 1996. 672p. $14.95pa. ISBN 0-19-280039-6.

Drabble continues her revision of this standard source. This edition has dropped allusion entries in order to add major authors from all countries. Old authors newly discovered and new authors have been added. Classical author articles have been rewritten to strengthen the emphasis on influences to English literature. Entries include authors of all genres, works, societies, prizes, publishers, some artists and composers. The selection of American authors is from an unapologetic British point of view; one will find Updike, Mailer, Bellows and Morrison, but neither Stegner nor Smiley. Individuals and their works are described, not criticized, in this work which intends to satisfy immediate curiosity and to direct the reader to further materials. Other features include an extensive chronology of English literature from about 1000 to 1994, and a list of prize winners, including the Carnegie Medal. Highly recommended for secondary libraries.

Biography

1338 Shattock, Joanne. **The Oxford Guide to British Women Writers**. New York: Oxford University Press, 1993. 492p. $35.00. ISBN 0-19-214176-7.

A broad definition of British means that Anne Bradstreet (born in Britain) and Sylvia Plath (worked in Britain) are among the 400 women from medieval times to the present who are included in this dictionary. Authors of all genres, even travel, film and children's books are represented. One can find a range of writers from Austin and the Brontes to Agatha Christie, Mary Norton and Mrs. Sherwood. Each one to two page entry gives the life and career, major publications, significant contributions and a context of her contemporaries. This is an excellent quick reference source and its extensive bibliography leads to more in-depth material. Recommended for high schools.

Shakespeare

1339 Andrews, John F., ed. **William Shakespeare: His World, His Work, His Influence**. 3v. New York: Scribner, 1985. $285.00/set. ISBN 0-684-17851-6.

This beautiful set, produced under the supervision of the editor of *Shakespeare Quarterly*, will interest many high school students, teachers and librarians. Volume 1, "His World," presents articles on life in Elizabethan England; volume 2, "His Work," focuses on comedies, tragedies, sonnets, and other poems; and volume 3, "His Influence," deals with Shakespeare's influence on drama and the modern theater. Articles also cover his treatment in history, the teaching of Shakespeare, and Shakespeare-related institutions.

All essays, contributed and signed by American and British scholars, conclude with a bibliography. Most articles are illustrated with black-and-white drawings and photographs. The last volume contains an index to the set. This is an important source that could become a classic. High school libraries able to afford its high cost should consider it as a first purchase. [R: ARBA 86; BL, 1 Mar 86]

1340 Cahn, Victor L. **Shakespeare the Playwright: A Companion to the Complete Tragedies, Histories, Comedies, and Romances**. Westport, Conn.: Greenwood Press, 1991. 865p. $75.00. ISBN 0-313-27493-2.

This work is a study guide to Shakespeare's 37 plays and includes quotes, paraphrases and critical comments. Cahn's straightforward approach makes this volume an excellent source for high school students. Bibliographies conclude each chapter and the book. Indexes lead to connections between plays.

1341 DeLoach, Charles, comp. **The Quotable Shakespeare: A Topical Dictionary**. Jefferson, N.C.: McFarland, 1988. 544p. $43.50. ISBN 0-89950-303-9.

This work identified Shakespearean quotations that "Contain...a philosophical axiom, a general truth or a fundamental principle"; also included are some that will inspire and delight readers. The volume contains 6,516 numbered quotations arranged alphabetically under 1,000 topics. Each entry from a play cites character's name, quotation and title of the play, act and scene as it appears in the *Riverside Shakespeare* (Houghton Mifflin, 1974). Poetry quotations are identified by line or sonnet number. The indexes provide approaches to the content by play title, sonnet, character and topic (which serves as a partial keyword index). This unique source is an appropriate addition to high school libraries.

1342 Onions, C. T. **A Shakespeare Glossary**. New York: Clarendon Press, 1986. 326p. $17.95pa. ISBN 0-19-812521-6.

Most students require assistance with the language of the seventeenth century, for many words today mean something quite different from what they meant back then. Relying on textual studies and computer-generated concordances of Shakespeare, the current edition has updated Onion's glossary and added many new entries. After a word is defined, one or more examples of Shakespeare's use of it are cited; they are taken from the *Riverside Shakespeare* (Houghton Mifflin, 1974). Recommended for high schools. [R: ARBA 88]

1343 Scott, Mark W., ed. **Shakespeare for Students: Critical Interpretations of As You Like It, Hamlet, Julius Caesar, MacBeth, The Merchant of Venice, A Midsummer Night's Dream, Othello, and Romeo & Juliet**. Detroit, Mich.: Gale Research, 1992. 529p. $86.00. ISBN 0-8103-8247-4.

1344 Dominic, Catherine C., ed. **Shakespeare for Students: Critical Interpretations of Henry IV, Part One, Henry V, King Lear, Much Ado About Nothing, Richard III, The Taming of the Shrew**. Detroit, Mich.: Gale Research, 1996. 550p. $86.00. ISBN 0-7876-0157-8.

Entries for each of the plays, often read in high school, give an introduction and overview, list of the major characters, a plot summary and critical discussions about themes, topics and style. About 20% of the material is from Gale's *Shakespearean Criticism*. There are bibliographic citations for the entries as well as sources for further study, including media adaptations. An index covers major themes and characters. Beginning students of Shakespeare will find these sources indispensable.

AUSTRALIAN LITERATURE

1345 Wilde, William H., and others. **The Oxford Companion to Australian Literature**. 2d ed. New York: Oxford University Press, 1994. 833p. $85.00. ISBN 0-19-553381-X.

First published in 1985, this comprehensive guide to the literature and culture of Australia is an outstanding reference work. Over 3,000 entries provide an overview of the country's literary life from the first English settlement in 1788. Authors, important literary works, characters and topics related to literature, art and history are included. The alphabetically arranged essays, most of which are brief, are well written and interesting. This is not an essential holding for most high schools, but it is a lively volume for those that require material on Australia.

CLASSICAL LITERATURE

1346   Howatson, M. C., ed. **The Oxford Companion to Classical Literature**. 2d ed. New York: Oxford University Press, 1989. 615p. $55.00. ISBN 0-19-866121-5.

Updating the 1937 work edited by the distinguished Paul Harvey, this revision is a worthy successor. It covers classical literature from the appearance of the Greeks, around 2200 B.C., to the close of the Athenian philosophy schools in A.D. 529. It includes articles on authors, major works, historical notables, mythological figures, and topics of literary significance. Short summaries of major works, chronologies, charts, and maps are special features. [R: ARBA 90; BL, 1 Nov 89; WLB, Sept 89]

FRENCH LITERATURE

1347   Dolbow, Sandra W. **Dictionary of Modern French Literature: From the Age of Reason through Realism**. New York: Greenwood Press, 1986. 365p. $65.00. ISBN 0-313-23784-0.

Articles cover all major authors of the Regency period (which began in 1715) to 1980, including historians, dramatists, poets, and philosophers. Essays that cover significant authors (e.g., Rousseau, Voltaire) are six or more pages in length, but most are only one or two pages long. All have appended bibliographies that cite English-language items published between 1980 and 1985. Appendixes provide a chronology of important literary and historical events and a list of entries, grouped by subject. [R: ARBA 87; BL, 15 Oct 86; LJ, 1 Oct 86]

GERMAN LITERATURE

1348   Garland, Henry and Mary Garland. **The Oxford Companion to German Literature**. 3d ed. New York: Oxford University Press, 1997. 951p. $75.00. ISBN 0-19-815896-3.

This newest edition, the last to be revised by Mary Garland, reflects the reunification of Germany, and the new appreciation of women writers. These changes are within the character of this title which has always placed German literature in the context of its political and cultural background. Entries cover a broad range of writers, works with plot summaries, genres, literary movements, characters, historical figures and events and literary devices. This is an essential work for advanced German language programs.

HISPANIC LITERATURE

1349   Foster, David William, comp. **Handbook of Latin American Literature**. 2d ed. New York: Garland, 1992. 799p. $95.00; $24.95pa. ISBN 0-8153-0343-2; 0-8153-1143-5pa.

The approach of this work is to present long signed essays about the literature of the Latin American countries, emphasizing the important issues, events and writers in a social context. Coverage is from the first European settlements to the present. The new edition updates the articles and adds sections on Peru, Latino writing in the U.S., popular literature and film. There is a name index. Recommended for advanced high school students.

1350   Smith, Verity, ed. **Encyclopedia of Latin American Literature**. Chicago: Fitzroy Dearborn, 1996. 1000p. $125.00. ISBN 1-884964-18-4.

There are several new guides to Latin American literature, and this is one of the most comprehensive and useful. In addition to writers, works, styles and literary and publishing terms, there are survey articles on the literary production of each country. The writers' profiles average about two pages and include biographical and critical information in signed essays with bibliographies. This is one of the few places one can find an article on Caribbean women writers, past and present. Recommended for those high schools with extensive Latin American literary or culture studies.

1351 Sole, Carlos A, and Maria Isabel Abreu, eds. **Latin American Writers**. 3v. New York: Scribner, 1989. $285.00/set. ISBN 0-684-18463-X.

Latin American writers who represent many literary genres are included in this set. The essays cover 176 authors from the colonial period to the present, and each entry contains a short biography, an evaluation of the writer's works and style, and a bibliography of the author's writings. The arrangement is chronological with indexing by name and country. Recommended for high school libraries. [R: ARBA 90; BR, Mar 90; SLJ, May 90]

RUSSIAN LITERATURE

1352 Kasack, Wolfgang. **Dictionary of Russian Literature since 1917**. New York: Columbia University Press, 1988. 502p. $69.50. ISBN 0-231-05242-1.

A translation of Kasack's *Lexikon der russischen Literatur ab 1917* (1976) and its supplement (1986), this major work contains entries for Russian (not Soviet) literature, including 619 authors, literary scholars, and translators to belles-lettres. The biographical section provides the usual data, plus membership in the Communist Party, date of emigration (if applicable), pseudonyms, and position in the writer's union. Journals, movements, and other literary topics also receive attention. A separate section lists the author's works. Indexed by name and subject.

More authors are included in this work than in Victor Terras's *Handbook of Russian Literature*. High schools that teach the Russian language and culture will find this authoritative work useful.

1353 Terras, Victor, ed. **Handbook of Russian Literature**. New Haven, Conn.: Yale University Press, 1985. 558p. $26.00pa. ISBN 0-300-04868-8.

This alphabetically arranged handbook, containing almost 1,000 signed articles, was prepared by American scholars. It treats the authors, critics, theorists, history, terminology, literary movements, journals, publishers, societies, and organizations of Russian literature. Essays on authors cite their principal works and their most important translations. Most entries end with a bibliography; a general bibliography and an index conclude the volume. [R: ARBA 86; BL, 15 May 85; LJ, 1 June 85]

SCANDINAVIAN LITERATURE

1354 Zuck, Virpi, ed. **Dictionary of Scandinavian Literature**. New York: Greenwood Press, 1990. 792p. $105.00. ISBN 0-313-21450-6.

This dictionary represents the first attempt to compile (in English) a comprehensive work of the literature of five Nordic languages plus Faroese, Inuit, and Sami. The volume consists of 400 articles that cover authors and other topics. Entries for writers list their major works, English translations, and literary criticism. A bibliography arranged by subject and an index conclude the work. This resource adds a new dimension to literature collections. [R: ARBA 92; LJ, 1 May 90; LJ, 15 Apr 91]

Music

BIOGRAPHY

1355 **Baker's Biographical Dictionary of Musicians**. 8th ed. revised by Nicolas Slonimsky. New York: Schirmer Books, 1992. 2115p. $125.00. ISBN 0-02-872415-1.

Since this work appeared in 1900, it has become a classic. More than 13,000 entries cover musicians both living and deceased, classical and popular, worldwide and historical: composers, singers and other performers, instrumentalists, conductors, critics librettists, impresarios, instrument makers, scholars and patrons. Those included range from Bach, Pavarotti and Handel to Loretta Lynn and Elvis Presley. The profiles, from a few lines to multi-page accounts, are enlightening and entertaining. This important work is recommended for secondary schools. *Baker's Biographical Dictionary of 20th Century Classical Musicians* (Schirmer, 1997) is the first of a planned series of specialized Baker's titles.

1356 Ewen, David. **American Songwriters: An H. W. Wilson Biographical Dictionary**. Bronx, N.Y.: H. W. Wilson, 1987. 489p. $68.00. ISBN 0-8242-0744-0.

This work is filled with 146 composers and lyricists who created the best-known American popular songs (e.g., Irving Berlin, George M. Cohan, Bob Dylan, Stephen Foster, George Gershwin, Oscar Hammerstein II). The text narrates the performance history of more than 5,500 of their songs, providing the background, movie or Broadway shows in which they were performed, and who recorded them. A great deal of attention is given to the critical reception of specific songs and statistics, such as appearances on "Your Hit Parade" and successive Broadway performances. Indexing is by song only.

This work supersedes Ewen's *Popular American Composers* (1962) and its first supplement (1973). Recommended for secondary schools. [R: ARBA 88]

1357 Ewen, David. **Great Composers, 1300–1900: A Biographical and Critical Guide**. Bronx, N.Y.: H. W. Wilson, 1966. 429p. $62.00. ISBN 0-8242-0018-7.

1358 Ewen, David. **Composers Since 1900: A Biographical and Critical Guide**. Bronx, N.Y.: H. W. Wilson, 1969. 639p. $69.00. ISBN 0-8242-0400-X.

1359 Ewen, David. **Composers Since 1900: First Supplement: A Biographical and Critical Guide**. Bronx, N.Y.: H. W. Wilson, 1981. 328p. $49.00. ISBN 0-8242-0664-9.

This series profiles major and less well known composers who have shaped the international development of music over the last seven centuries. The foundation volume covers 200 composers for the period 1300–1900; *Composers Since*

1900 and the supplement add 267 biographical sketches. The latter also contains new material on some composers included in the first volume. For the two volumes on the twentieth century, Ewen interviewed many of the subjects. Each entry provides biographical and critical information, a list of major works, recommended sources about the composer, and (usually) a portrait.

1360 **International Who's Who in Music and Musician's Directory**. 15th ed. Volume 1: Classical and Light-Classical Fields. Cambridge, Eng.: Melrose Press, 1996. 1357p. $175.00. ISBN 0-948875-22-4.

1361 **International Who's Who in Music and Musician's Directory**. 1st ed. Volume 2: Popular Music. Cambridge, Eng.: Melrose Press, 1996. 950p. $175.00. ISBN 0-948875-07-0.

The standard *International Who's Who* of classical figures now has a second volume which covers popular musicians. Together they cover 13,000 living individuals. The emphasis is on western music, but there is international representation. The popular music volume includes musicians from pop, rock, folk, jazz, blues and country music. Entries are alphabetical within the respective volumes and give performing and birth names, an identification statement, some information about personal lives and information about study and careers including recordings and performances. Current management and addresses are given. Useful appendices list such things as orchestras, music libraries, music conservatories, recording companies, management companies, booking agents, musical publishers, festivals and organizations. Recommended for high school collections.

1362 Randel, Don Michael, ed. **The Harvard Biographical Dictionary of Music**. Cambridge, Mass.: Belknap Press/Harvard University Press, 1996. 1013p. $39.95. ISBN 0-674-37299-9.

This companion to the *New Harvard Dictionary of Music* lists composers, performers and conductors associated with western concert music from the earliest times to the present. Basic information about each entry gives name and dates, an identification, and a brief biography emphasizing career contributions. Bibliographies accompany the entries. Articles range from the Bachs to Bing Crosby and Billy Joel and from Karajan and Poulenc to Cole Porter. This is an excellent quick reference tool for both middle and high school music collections. [R: ARBA 97]

CHRONOLOGIES

1363 Burbank, Richard. **Twentieth Century Music: Orchestral, Chamber, Operatic, & Dance Music, 1900–1980**. New York: Facts on File, 1984. 485p. $50.00. ISBN 0-87196-464-3.

This attractive work, a chronology of musical events of the first 80 years of this century, is arranged by year and then by 5 headings: opera; dance; instrumental and vocal music; births, deaths, and debuts; and related events. The sections that cover compositions cite their premieres with conductors, casts, dancers, choreographers, orchestras, and performance locations. The fourth section, among other things, summarizes the contributions of deceased dancers and musicians. Related events include developments in the film and recording industries. Many illustrations and a detailed index are provided. [R: ARBA 85; BL, 1 Nov 85; WLB, Sept 84]

DICTIONARIES AND ENCYCLOPEDIAS

1364 Ardley, Neil. **Music: An Illustrated**
E+ **Encyclopedia**. New York: Facts on File, 1986. 192p. $18.95. ISBN 0-8160-1543-0.

A comprehensive introduction to all aspects (technical, historical, geographical, and biographical) of classical and popular music, this work is an excellent addition to any collection serving children in grades 5 through 8. It provides chapters on such varied topics as musical instruments, folk and ethnic music, opera and ballet, theory and notation, and music making.

Numerous illustrations, three or four to a page, include black-and-white and color photographs of musicians and musical events, detailed drawings of instruments, and diagrams of theory and sound systems. This handsome work is highly recommended. [R: ARBA 87; BL, 15 Dec 86; SLJ, May 87]

1365 Arnold, Denis, ed. **The New Oxford Companion to Music**. 2v. New York: Oxford University Press, 1983. $150.00/set. ISBN 0-19-311316-3.

This work is based on the standard *Oxford Companion to Music* (10 editions, 1938–1970); nonetheless, the text has been extensively rewritten. Some 6,600 articles, ranging from 50 words to several pages, provide international coverage. Entries for composers predominate, but those for individual works are numerous. Other essays cover musical theory, instruments, styles, forms, and terms. Illustrations, which consist of black-and-white photographs, line drawings, and musical examples, are scattered throughout the set. Recommended for high schools. [R: ARBA 84]

1366 Hitchcock, H. Wiley, and Stanley Sadie, eds. **The New Grove Dictionary of American Music**. 4v. New York: Grove's Dictionaries of Music, 1986. $725.00/set. ISBN 0-943818-36-2.

A spin-off of *The New Grove Dictionary of Music and Musicians*, this set contains 5,000 articles on all aspects of American music, popular and classical. Some entries revise and expand those in the original set, but others were written especially for this work. This significant publication is the definitive work on American music. [R: ARBA 88]

1367 Kennedy, Michael, and Joyce Bourne, eds. **The Oxford Dictionary of Music**. 2d ed. New York: Oxford University Press, 1994. 985p. $35.00. ISBN 0-19-869162-9.

More than one thousand new entries have been added to the dictionary since its first edition in 1985, and 80% of the others have been revised. The scope is classical music and jazz. American nomenclature is used. People, terms, groups, instruments and works are included in alphabetical order. Definitions and descriptions for terms and biographies for individuals are treated briefly. Entries for individuals include Dorsey, Foster, Gershwin, Gottschalk and (Scott) Joplin. Some general topics receive longer entries. This is a useful, general purpose music dictionary. Recommended for secondary collections. [R: ARBA 96]

1368 Raeburn, Michael, and Alan Kendall, eds. **Heritage of Music**. 4v. New York: Oxford University Press, 1989. $225.00/set. ISBN 0-19-520493-X.

This history of western music consists of broad chapters that usually focus on one or more major composers of a particular period and the times in which they lived. Each of the four volumes, chronologically arranged within, cover an era: classical music and its origin, the Romantic period, the nineteenth-century legacy, and music of the twentieth century. Profiles of relevant composers are appended to the end of each volume, the last of which contains an index to this handsome set. This excellent survey of musicology shows how music reflects the times and events of composers' lives. [R: ARBA 90; LJ, 15 Oct 89; RBB, 15 Dec 89]

1369 Randel, Don Michael. **The New Harvard Dictionary of Music**. Cambridge, Mass.: Belknap Press/ Harvard University Press, 1986. 942p. $39.95. ISBN 0-674-61525-5.

A standard source for more than 50 years, this work contains some 6,000 terms, concepts, and histories for many kinds of music, including jazz and rock, and the music of Africa, Asia, Latin America, and the Near East. Descriptions of musical instruments, 250 musical examples, and black-and-white drawings are provided. Biographical entries are omitted. Longer articles have bibliographies. Recommended for secondary schools. [R: ARBA 87; BL, 1 Mar 87; LJ, Jan 87; LJ, 15 Apr 87]

1370 Sadie, Stanley, ed. **The New Grove Dictionary of Music and Musicians**. 6th ed. 20v. New York: Grove's Dictionaries, 1980. $2,300.00/set; $550.00pa/set. ISBN 0-333-23111-2; 1-56159-174-2pa.

The latest edition of this standard, comprehensive work contains 22,500 articles that include biographies of composers, writers, publishers, and instrument makers; terms; instruments; musical works; and music history. The emphasis, however, is on biographical entries, of which there are 16,500. The set covers popular, folk, and classical music from earliest times to the present. Over 3,000 illustrations (tables, technical diagrams, family trees, musical autographs, and portraits), 500 pages of bibliographies, and a detailed index support the work. This is the best work available on music and musicians, but most high schools will find it difficult to afford unless justified by a serious music history and appreciation curriculum. *The Norton/Grove Concise Encyclopedia* is an alternative.

1371 Sadie, Stanley, and Alison Latham, eds. **The Norton/Grove Concise Encyclopedia of Music**. New York: W. W. Norton, 1994. 850p. $42.50. ISBN 0-393-03753-3.

High schools that do not need (or are unable to afford) the 10-volume *New Grove Dictionary of Music and Musicians*, on which this volume is based, will find this authoritative (and in some cases, updated) work useful. The 10,000 alphabetically arranged entries, written by subject specialists, cover all areas of music (e.g., composers, instrumentalists, performers, terminology). There are 1,000 entries under names of individual works. The emphasis is on classical music, but some attention is given to rock and popular music. Illustrations include pictures of instruments, diagrams for the symphony orchestra, and music examples. [R: ARBA 90; LJ, Jan 89; RBB, 1 Apr 89]

BANDS

1372 Holston, Kim R. **The Marching Band Handbook**. 2d ed. Jefferson, N.C.: McFarland, 1994. 172p. $28.50. ISBN 0-89950-922-3.

First published in 1984, this directory consolidates information found elsewhere and adds interviews with band directors and members. Divided into sections such as marching competitions, military bands, parades, twirling, clinics and fund raising, each chapter has interviews, directories, associations and bibliographies. The book is illustrated with photographs. There is a general bibliography of books and periodicals and an index. Any band director or group sponsor looking for events to enter and information about the various topics will appreciate this source. [R: ARBA 96]

CHORAL

1373 White, J. Perry. **Twentieth-Century Choral Music: An Annotated Bibliography of Music Suitable for Use by High School Choirs**. 2d ed. Metuchen, N.J.: Scarecrow Press, 1991. 226p. $26.50. ISBN 0-8108-2394-2.

White's bibliography, a revision of his 1983 work, focuses on twentieth-century choral music of high quality and lasting value. The 2d edition added 120 pieces, most of which were published after 1980. Each of the 360 entries evaluates the piece's appropriateness for performance by junior and senior high school ensembles of varying size, skill and maturity. The entries also provide composer, title, voicing, accompaniment, text, range, difficulty, style, comments, publisher, date and level (junior high through college). A directory of musical publishers and composer and title indexes complete the volume. Recommended for secondary collections.

CLASSICAL

1374 Cummings, David, ed. **Random House Encyclopedic Dictionary of Classical Music**. New York: Random House, 1997. 788p. $45.00. ISBN 0-679-45851-4.

First published in 1947 as the *Everyman's Dictionary of Music* and revised often under various titles, this major revision includes 1,500 new entries. Opera plot summaries have been added as display boxes and feature boxes have been added for major figures. Two hundred illustrations and 400 quotations add both graphics and interest. Entries include people, theory, terms, forms, orchestras and operas. Despite the additions and the title, this is a dictionary with brief entries. The appendices add a chart of opera roles, a chronology from 1594 and a list of recommended recordings. Useful for all secondary libraries.

INSTRUMENTS

1375 Baines, Anthony. **The Oxford Companion to Musical Instruments**. New York: Oxford University Press, 1992. 404p. $49.95. ISBN 0-19-311334-1.

This convenient and attractive guide lists ancient to contemporary musical instruments and gives both history and technical information. Many illustrations, both drawings and photographs help to clarify the text. Coverage is international; it includes not only instruments limited to one region, but also has longer articles for countries/continents which discuss the kind of instruments developed there. Instrument makers appear in an appendix. Highly recommended for secondary collections.

OPERA

1376 Lazarus, John. **The Opera Handbook**. Boston, Mass.: G. K. Hall, 1987. 242p. $30.00. ISBN 0-8161-9094-1.

This attractive book, a volume in the G. K. Hall Performing Arts Handbook Series, treats opera for each country in a separate chapter—Italy, France, Great Britain, Russia, and the United States. There is also a general chapter for other countries in Europe. Each entry, selected from operas most frequently performed in the 1980s, gives a plot summary, factual data, critiques, and guidance for listeners. A "Databank" section provides brief biographies of contemporary opera singers. Indexed. This volume is suggested for high school level.

Other volumes in the series include *The Film Handbook*, *The Jazz Handbook*, and *The Dance Handbook*. [R: ARBA 91; BR, Jan/Feb 91; BL, 1 Sept 90; LJ, July 90]

POPULAR
General

1377 Gammond, Peter. **The Oxford Companion to Popular Music**. New York: Oxford University Press, 1991. 739p. $49.95. ISBN 0-19-311323-6.

The emphasis of this companion is on the history of popular music as a whole from about 1850 to about 1985, and from the English-speaking world. The author, who has written widely on popular music, defines it as that music which would not be found in a reference on classical music. Coverage is of the elements, personalities, periods, styles, titles and instruments used in popular music. Because it includes such a wide range of folk, country, jazz, blues, soul, rock and roll and musical theater the entries are necessarily selective. Entries are usually brief: songwriter Sammy Fain has 1 column, the Beatles have 2 columns, Willie

Nelson and Lotte Lenya each get 1 paragraph. Arrangement is alphabetical and there are indexes by names of people and groups, by shows and films and by songs and albums. This is an excellent resource for secondary collections.

1378 Larkin, Colin, ed. **The Guinness Encyclopedia of Popular Music**. 2d ed. 6v. New York: Stockton Press, 1995. $495.00/set. ISBN 1-56159-176-9.

A broad range of popular music is covered in this encyclopedia. It covers film and Broadway musicals, every sort of jazz, blues and soul, African pop, reggae, rock "n' roll and heavy metal, Latin and folk. It is not international in the sense that popular music from India, the Far East and Arabia receive little attention. Entries include the types of music and the groups and individuals who write and perform it, organizations and recording labels. Arrangement is alphabetical throughout the volumes. There are extensive bibliographies both by artist and by subject. A general index and a quick reference guide to all entries provide additional access. This is an excellent set and would support culture and music programs in both high school and middle school. [R: ARBA 96]

1379 Lissauer, Robert. **Lissauer's Encyclopedia of Popular Music in America: 1888 to the Present**. 2d ed. 3v. New York: Facts on File, 1996. $185.00/set. ISBN 0-8160-3238-6.

This guide covers a wide scope of popular music from theater and operetta, movie songs, jazz, ragtime, folk, pop, gospel, novelty songs, minstrels, ethnic songs, war songs and gospel songs. It includes songs that would not be acceptable today; these are often particularly enlightening. The songs are listed alphabetically by title with subsections listing them chronologically and by writers/composers/lyricists. There is a selected bibliography.

Each entry gives the title, writer(s), year, performer, publisher, awards, and comments. Song lyrics are not included. This is a comprehensive source of song titles, and is recommended for high schools with advanced American culture and music history programs.

Country

1380 **The Comprehensive Country Music Encyclopedia**. New York: Times Books, 1994. 449p. $25.00. ISBN 0-8129-2247-6.

Garth Brooks was 12 when the *Country Music Encyclopedia* was published in 1974. This completely new work, also by *Country Music Magazine* editors, replaces that volume. Almost 700 entries, most biographical, and 600 excellent photographs cover both national and regional country music. This honest and comprehensive work is highly recommended for secondary collections with an interest or curricular need for information about this branch of music.

Jazz

1381 Case, Brian, and Stan Britt. **The Harmony Illustrated Encyclopedia of Jazz**. 3d ed. revised and updated by Chrissi Murray. New York: Harmony Books, 1987. 208p. $13.95pa. ISBN 0-517-56443-2.

The 3rd edition of this informative work covers 450 jazz musicians and a few topics. The biographical entries provide compact career information, assess the subject's contribution, often list significant recordings, and conclude with discographies of recordings. The appendix provides briefer entries for 100 less-prominent jazz musicians. Indexed. [R: ARBA 88]

1382 Kernfeld, Barry, ed. **The New Grove Dictionary of Jazz**. 2v. New York: Grove's Dictionaries of Music, 1988. $50.00. ISBN 0-312-11357-9.

This work is a spin-off from the monumental *New Grove Dictionary of Music and Musicians*, but few of its articles have been drawn from the parent set. Most of the 4,500 signed essays, which explore all aspects of jazz, were specially prepared for this work.

The 250 contributors from 25 nations provide encyclopedic coverage for mainstream and progressive jazz, theory, instrumentation, performers, composers, bands, and film. More than 3,000 biographies predominate. Entries for broad topics are extensive, while others are little more than definitions or identifications. This excellent work, which is likely to become the standard source for the field, is recommended for high schools. [R: ARBA 90; LJ, 15 Apr 89; RBB, 15 Apr 89; WLB, Feb 89]

Musicals

1383　Bloom, Ken. **American Song: The Complete Musical Theatre Companion**. 2d ed. 2v. New York: Schirmer, 1996. $175.00/set. ISBN 0-02-870484-3.

This encyclopedic treatment of American musicals provides data on more than 4,800 musical productions from 1877 to 1995, including 1,600 additional shows since the first edition. The scope is comprehensive, covering New York shows on and off Broadway, resident theater productions, shows that never made it to New York, tours that missed New York, selected nightclub shows, vaudeville, burlesque, and original television musicals. Plays with original songs and English and French productions of American shows are also included. All information is verified by primary source materials such as programs and playbills. Each numbered entry gives the date opened, type of musical, theater, production personnel, cast, songs, and notes. Shows are listed alphabetically and there are name, song, and chronological indexes; with no table of contents and no clear labeling, the indexes are not easy to identify. This is a good ready reference tool for theater, music and history classes. [R: ARBA 97]

1384　Gänzl, Kurt. **The Encyclopedia of the Musical Theatre**. 2v. New York: Schirmer, 1994. $175.00. ISBN 0-02-871445-8.

This compilation includes about 3,000 of the most important people and plays of the musical stage in the 19th and 20th century. The scope is western musical theater and coverage is of France, Austria, Britain, the United States, Hungary, Germany and Australia. Entries are for writers and composers, performers and works. Arrangement is alphabetical and some entries have bibliographic references. This is an excellent source and should be in every high school with a music history or drama curriculum. [R: ARBA 95]

Rap

1385　Stancell, Steven. **Rap Whoz Who: The World of Rap Music**. New York: Simon & Schuster Macmillan, 1996. 339p. $22.95pa. ISBN 0-02-864520-0.

This guide provides information about individual performers and groups, record labels and producers of rap music. Entries vary in length, but each gives background, a discography and critical comments. Boxed terms and interviews, photographs and an index all add to the usefulness of the volume. Recommended for secondary collections.

Rock

1386　Helander, Brock. **The Rock Who's Who**. 2d ed. New York: Schirmer Books, 1996. 849p. $75.00. ISBN 0-02-871031-2.

This source is not so comprehensive in coverage as *The New Rolling Stone Encyclopedia of Rock and Roll.* Helander covers just under 400 individuals and groups; however, entries are not only narrative, but contain a historical discography for each entry. Charts list album title, label, catalog number, year of release and format, making the source useful not only for history and criticism, but also for collection building. There is an extensive bibliography and a good general index. Recommended to complement *The New Rolling Stone Encyclopedia.*

1387　Romanowski, Patricia, and Holly George-Warren, eds. **The New Rolling Stone Encyclopedia of Rock and Roll**. New York: Fireside, 1995. 1120p. $25.00. ISBN 0-684-81044-1.

Rock music has changed since the first edition of this work in 1983. Music videos have replaced disc jockeys as the primary marketing tool, cassettes and compact discs have replaced LPs, synthesizers have replaced real instruments, hip hop, punk and alternative styles have branched out, and rock has entered/become mainstream music. This revised edition accounts for all of those changes, and even Madonna, as it documents rock from its beginnings through its changes and on to its current status. More than 1,800 artists and groups are included in alphabetical order; coverage is comprehensive from the Meat Puppets to the Grateful Dead. Highly recommended.

SONGS

1388 Bianco, David. **Heat Wave: The Motown Fact Book**. Ann Arbor, Mich.: Pierian Press, 1988. 524p. $55.00. ISBN 1-56075-011-1.

This work provides comprehensive coverage for 5,500 Motown recordings released in the United States and the United Kingdom from 1959 through 1986, 6,700 artists who performed on the recordings, and 8,599 references to songs and record titles. The short biographical entries for stars who made their reputations on Motown records include complete Motown discographies, selected discographies for non-Motown recordings, and short bibliographies of books and articles for some artists.

Separate chronologies for U.S. and U.K. recordings include label and record number, date of release, title and artist, and availability on compact disc or cassette. The chronologies are indexed by name (individual and group), song and record titles, date, and record number. The appendix lists five labels related to Motown and records produced under these labels. [R: ARBA 89; BL, 1 Jan 89; WLB, Oct 88]

1389 Bronson, Fred. **The Billboard Book of Number One Hits**. 4th ed. New York: Watson-Guptill, 1997. 912p. $24.95pa. ISBN 0-8230-7641-5.

The Billboard popularity charts began in 1940, but Bronson did not begin his coverage until 1955. This source lists every song that reached the number one position every week since that time. Each week's summary lists the top five songs and for the top hit the entry lists the artist or group, label, songwriter, producer, date it became number one, length of time on the chart and some notes about each song from the artist. There are many illustrations of performers. This work has become a history of one aspect of modern culture.

1390 Lax, Roger, and Frederick Smith. **The Great Song Thesaurus**. 2d ed. New York: Oxford University Press, 1989. 774p. $85.00. ISBN 0-19-505408-3.

Over 11,000 of the best-known songs of the English-speaking world are identified in this work. The main section consists of song titles arranged alphabetically; for each are provided lyricist, composer, year of composition, musical or film in which the song was featured,

performer associated with it, and other facts of interest.

Eight other sections include "Lyric Key Lines," new to this edition, which indexes songs by their best-known lines; British song titles; "The Greatest Hits," a chronological list of notable hits from 1958 through 1986, in which many songs are placed in historical context; a chronological list of award-winning songs; "Themes, Trademarks, and Signatures"; a thematic index arranged by over 2,000 headings; "American and British Theatre, Film, Radio, and Television," which associates songs with their source of popularity; and notes on significant lyricists and composers. This work stands alone as the only reference source of its kind. [R: ARBA 90]

1391 Reed, W. L., and M. J. Bristow, eds.
E+   **National Anthems of the World**. 9th ed. New York: Cassell Academic, 1997. 608p. $90.00. ISBN 0-304-34925-9.

The various editions of this title reflect changes in world politics. The anthems are presented in alphabetical order by nation and entries include a piano score, lyrics in the native language, a transliterated phonetic version for singers, and an English translation. Verses that are additional to those normally sung are also included. Schools with world culture programs, student exchange programs and foreign student populations will find this comprehensive and unique reference source useful.

1392 Whitburn, Joel. **The Billboard Book of Top 40 Hits**. 6th ed. New York: Billboard Publications, 1996. 831p. $21.95pa. ISBN 0-8230-7632-6.

Whitburn is a long-time author of recording statistics for the industry; this volume is one of his references intended for the public. The work lists the titles that were among the top 40 hits, based on information from the weekly issues of *Billboard* from 1955 to the present. The charts are arranged alphabetically by artist, giving the recording titles, dates they made the list, how high they ranked and for how many weeks. Labels and recording numbers are also supplied. An alphabetical list of song titles follows and provides another means of access. A final section lists record holders for the time period and by decade. Illustrations of album covers add interest. This will be of use to music and American culture classes. [R: ARBA 97]

Mythology and Folklore

GENERAL WORKS

1393 Thompson, Stith. **The Folktale**. Berkeley, Calif.: University of California Press, 1977. $69.50; $14.95pa. ISBN 0-404-15373-9; 0-520-03539-2pa.

Thompson summarizes in this guide his life-long study of world folklore which resulted in the *Motif-Index of Folk Literature* (Indiana University Press, 1955–1958). Two introductory chapters discuss the universal nature of oral tales and the structures and forms they follow. The second part of the book treats western folktales, and the final part uses the Native American as a prototype of primitive cultural folklore. Recommended for professional collections.

DICTIONARIES AND ENCYCLOPEDIAS

1394 Bell, Robert E. **Dictionary of Classical Mythology, Symbols, Attributes, & Associations**. Santa Barbara, Calif.: ABC-CLIO, 1982. 390p. $60.00. ISBN 0-87436-305-5.

This excellent work consists of over 1,000 entries that name mythological characters, summarize each myth, and explain the meaning of the symbol. Bell often cites *Loeb Classical Library*. A "Guide to Persona," which identifies all topical entries associated with a given character, concludes the volume. Highly recommended. [R: ARBA 83]

1395 Briggs, Katharine Mary. **An Encyclopedia of Fairies: Hobgoblins, Brownies, Bogies, and Other Supernatural Creatures**. New York: Pantheon Books, 1976. 481p. $12.95. ISBN 0-394-40918-3.

Folk creatures, such as those named in the book's subtitle, and the authors who wrote about them are found in this British work. The type and motif indexes are based on Stith Thompson's *Motif-Index of Folk Literature* (Indiana University Press, 1955–1958). Appropriate for professional collections. [R: ARBA 78]

1396 Cavendish, Richard, and Brian Innes, comps. and eds. **Man, Myth and Magic: The Illustrated Encyclopedia of Mythology, Religion and the Unknown**. 21v. New York: Marshall Cavendish, 1995. $549.00/set. ISBN 1-85435-731-X.

The new edition of this standard encyclopedia of belief and behavior has added articles on near-death experiences, urban legends, Ley Lines, and several New Age topics and alternative therapies. Other articles and bibliographies have been updated and revised. The source retains its purpose of relating speculative information with "sympathetic neutrality." The variety of entries is impressive and includes such things as superstitions, legends, myths, magic, witchcraft, astrology, plant lore, unexplained phenomena, and symbols used in art, drama and poetry. Brief articles on such topics as acupuncture, the Mennonites, Odysseus, and wishing wells are listed alphabetically with longer overview articles on such things as Arthur, the Dead Sea Scrolls, and death. Coverage is world wide and from prehistory to the 20th century. Volume one lists the contributors and editorial board, a contents list for all volumes and a 21 section classified bibliography. The same 21 general topics are classified in the study index in volume 21 which also contains the extensive general index. This set is useful for many subject areas including math, science, literature, art and psychology as well as providing motivation in selecting topics for research papers, especially in the grade 8–10 range. Highly recommended for secondary collections. [R: ARBA 96]

1397 Grimal, Pierre. **A Concise Dictionary of Classical Mythology**. Cambridge, Mass.: Blackwell, 1990. 456p. $135.00. ISBN 0-8288-2616-1.

First published in French (1951), this excellent English translation by A. R. Maxwell-Hyslop is an interesting and attractive volume. Intended for college students studying the humanities, the dictionary is appropriate as a reference source at all levels. The work indicates variant spellings, gives alternative versions of many myths, provides genealogical charts, cites classical authors, and lists relevant editions of myths. The volume is handsomely illustrated and indexed. This competent and authoritative dictionary is a worthwhile addition to library reference shelves.

The condensed version of this work may be adequate for some libraries. The author has shortened the entries by excluding minor variants of the myths and concentrating on the major versions of others. [R: ARBA 87; BL, 15 Jan 91; LJ, 15 Sept 90]

1398 Leach, Maria. **Funk & Wagnalls Standard Dictionary of Folklore, Mythology and Legend**. New York: HarperCollins, 1984. 1236p. $40.00. ISBN 0-06-250511-4.

This paperback reissue of a work published in 1949–1950, is a standard reference work. Survey articles discuss regions and special topics—fairy tales, ballads, and dances—and concise essays treat gods, heroes, folk tales, customs, beliefs, superstitions, motifs, and other topics related to world culture.

1399 Mercatante, Anthony S. **The Facts on File Encyclopedia of World Mythology and Legend**. New York: Facts on File, 1988. 807p. $95.00. ISBN 0-8160-1049-8.

This outstanding work encompasses myths, legends, folklore, and fables around the world and throughout the ages. Over 3,000 entries, enhanced by over 400 black-and-white illustrations, comprise the encyclopedia. Concise and well-written articles describe the subject (e.g., historical characters, saints, rulers, sacred relics, animals), provide historical notes, and indicate works in which the subject appears. Brief plot summaries and cross-references are numerous.

The extensive annotated bibliography is arranged by culture and nation, subject, and type of collection. A key to variant spellings and general, cultural, and ethnic indexes conclude the volume, which is recommended for middle schools and high schools. [R: ARBA 89; BR, Nov/Dec 88]

1400 Rovin, Jeff. **The Encyclopedia of**
E+ **Monsters**. New York: Facts on File, 1989. 390p. $35.00; $19.95pa. ISBN 0-8160-1824-3; 0-8160-2303-4pa.

Beasts, fiends, specters, werewolves, mummies, and monsters of all types and times come to life and haunt the pages of this excellent work. The information gives a short history of monsters since 4000 B.C. and identifies them as characters unknown to science who arise to frighten human beings. They may appear in motion pictures, television, literature, comic books, mythology, folklore, religion, toys, computer games, or even bubble-gum trading cards.

Each entry gives the monster's name, nickname, species, gender, and size. It also provides a life story (which includes a description of its features and powers), a picture, and comments by the author. The appendix contains brief information about the monster's first appearance and location, pictures of some characters, and reproductions of comic-book covers. There is a detailed index.

Librarians may wish to purchase a second copy for the circulating collection, since this work is likely to be a popular holding at all levels. [R: ARBA 90; LJ, 1 Sept 89; RBB, 15 Nov 89]

HANDBOOKS

1401 Bierhorst, John. **The Mythology of North America**. New York: Morrow, 1985. 259p. $10.00pa. ISBN 0-688-06666-6.

This work, which provides a survey of Native American mythology, identifies 11 mythological regions and their tales. Bierhorst examines recurring patterns and themes, describes the unique characteristics of the myths, and compares their themes and elements to mythologies of other cultures. Illustrations, maps, and an index are included. [R: BL, 15 June 85; SLJ, Aug 85]

1402 Cohen, Hennig, and Tristram Potter Coffin, eds. **The Folklore of American Holidays**. 2d ed. Detroit, Mich.: Gale Research, 1991. 461p. $99.00. ISBN 0-8103-7602-4.

This is a massive compilation of beliefs, legends, superstitions, proverbs, riddles, poems, songs, dances, plays, pageants, fairs, foods, and processions associated with 133 American calendar customs and festivals. The entries, in calendar arrangement, range from less than one-half page to 30 (Christmas) and include ideas for holiday programs. The second edition improves coverage of ethnic celebrations. A five-part index provides access by subject; ethnic and geographical area; collectors, informants, and translators; song titles and first lines; and motifs and tale types.

1403 South, Malcolm, ed. **Mythical and Fabulous Creatures: A Source Book and Research Guide**. Westport, Conn.: Greenwood Press, 1987. 393p. $49.95. ISBN 0-313-24338-7.

Mythical and fantastic creatures are discussed in this outstanding work. The introduction surveys the place of imaginary creatures in literature and art, illustrates several such places, and provides a glossary.

Part 1 examines birds and beasts (e.g., the phoenix, dragons, unicorns, girffins), human-animal composites (e.g., centaurs, manticores, mermaids, harpies, gorgons, sphinxes), creatures of darkness (e.g., vampires, werewolves), and giants and fairies. Each 20- to 30-page essay provides extensive information about the origin of the creatures and their treatment in myths, folklore, literature, film, sculpture, and art from classical to modern times. Each essay concludes with a bibliography.

Part 2 contains a general bibliography and covers a miscellany of other beings that do not fit into the categories in part 1 (e.g., Cerberus, the three-headed dog that guards the gates of Hades; Pegasus, the flying horse). This outstanding work is highly recommended for high schools where it will provide background for literature classes. [R: ARBA 88; BR, May/June 89; LJ, 15 June 87; RBB, July 87]

INDEXES

1404 Ireland, Norma Olin. **Index to**
E+   **Fairy Tales, 1949–1972; Including**

Folklore, Legends, & Myths, in Collections. Westwood, Mass.: F. W. Faxon, 1973. 741p. $52.50. ISBN 0-8108-2011-0.

1405 Ireland, Norma Olin. **Index to Fairy Tales, 1973–1977; Including Folklore, Legends, & Myths, in Collections, Fourth Supplement**. Westwood, Mass.: F. W. Faxon, 1979. 259p. $35.00. ISBN 0-8108-1855-8.

1406 Ireland, Norma Olin. **Index to Fairy Tales, 1978–1986; Including Folklore, Legends, & Myths, in Collections, Fifth Supplement**. Metuchen, N.J.: Scarecrow, 1989. 575p. $55.00. ISBN 0-8108-2194-X.

1407 Sprug, Joseph W., comp. **Index to Fairy Tales, 1987–1992; Including 310 Collections of Fairy Tales, Folktales, Myths and Legends**. Metuchen, N.J.: Scarecrow, 1994. 587p. $59.50. ISBN 0-8108-2750-6.

The basic *Index to Fairy Tales, Myths and Legends*, compiled by Mary H. Eastman (Boston: F. W. Faxon, 1926), and its first supplement (1937) and second supplement (1952) are now out of print. The third supplement (1973) indexes 406 collections under 3,000 headings; the fourth supplement (1979) indexes 130 collections.

The fifth supplement indexes 262 collections published between 1978 and 1986 under 2,000 subject headings. It has added a number of headings that reflect current times and the changing interests of children. All volumes begin with a list of collections analyzed, followed by a subject-title index.

Index to Fairy Tales, 1987–1992 includes locations with all entries (author, title, and subject) and makes some related changes in format. It also includes some pre-1987 titles that had not been indexed in previous volumes.

Philosophy

1408 Edwards, Paul, ed. **Encyclopedia of Philosophy**. 4v. New York: Macmillan, 1973. $450.00. ISBN 0-02-894950-1.

1409 Borchert, Donald M., ed. **Encyclopedia of Philosophy: Supplement**. New York: Macmillan, 1996. 775p. $160.75. ISBN 0-02-8646290.

Originally published in 8 volumes in 1967, this work is international in scope and authority, covering Eastern and Western philosophy for all periods of time. It is highly recommended for advanced high school students of many subjects. The set analyzes relevant themes in history, psychology, religion, the sciences and other disciplines. The signed articles range in length from brief to 65,000 words. There is an analytical index.

The supplement adds 357 entries addressing issues that were omitted from the original set or which have become important since that time. Entries are clear and provide a balanced approach to controversial topics. There are bibliographies and an index.

1410 Well, Donald A., ed. **An Encyclopedia of War and Ethics**. Westport, Conn.: Greenwood Press, 1996. 539p. $95.00. ISBN 0-313-29116-0.

The articles in this encyclopedic source raise ethical and moral issues related to war. Covered are concepts, people, laws, events and incidents, types of warfare and weapons, terms, religious perspectives, specific wars, war trials and pacifism. There are specific articles on Gandhi, the Holocaust and "children and war." The signed articles are arranged alphabetically with related cross-references and bibliographies. There is an index. This is an essential source for any study of war and peace; highly recommended for high school collections. [R: ARBA 97]

Quotations

See also specific groups and subjects for quotations by and about limited areas.

1411 Augarde, Tony, ed. **The Oxford Dictionary of Modern Quotations**. New York: Oxford University Press, 1991. 371p. $45.00. ISBN 0-19-866141-X.

This collection of quotations focuses on persons of the twentieth century. The 5,000 quotations are arranged alphabetically by personal name, from Abbott and Costello (their "Who's on First" routine) to Frank Zappa. Some quotations were uttered by persons from popular culture, such as Sonny Bono, and others come from writers, such as James Baldwin. It should be noted, however, that about half the people quoted are from Great Britain and are not widely known in this country. Exact sources are provided, and there is an extensive keyword index. This dictionary will supplement *Bartlett's Familiar Quotations* and other standard sources. [R: ARBA 92; BL, 1 May 91; SLJ, Nov 91; WLB, Sept 91]

1412 Bartlett, John. **Familiar Quotations**. 16th ed. Justin Kaplan, ed. Boston, Mass.: Little, Brown, 1992. 1405p. $45.00. ISBN 0-316-08277-5.

1413 Bartlett, John. **Bartlett's Familiar Quotations**. New York: Time Warner Electronic Publishing, 1995. CD-ROM ISBN 1-5730-4901-8 (Windows); 1-5730-4951-4 (Macintosh). $29.95.

The epitome of quotation books, Bartlett's began in 1855. More than 22,000 quotations are arranged chronologically by the birth date of the person quoted and there are extensive indexes by author, subject and keyword. Emphasis is on British and American quotations, with the Bible and Shakespeare amply represented. Exact references to original sources and helpful historical footnotes are provided. Each edition deletes and adds quotations, so it is wise to retain earlier copies.

The multimedia CD-ROM edition includes all of the quotations in the paper copy as well as pictures, sound and video quotations. The version retains the flavor of a book, but allows hyperlinks via icons to multimedia renditions. Schools at all levels will want both versions of this classic work.

1414   Fergusson, Rosalind, comp. **The Facts on File Dictionary of Proverbs**. New York: Facts on File, 1983. 331p. $27.95. ISBN 0-87196-298-5.

More than 7,000 proverbs, drawn from all nations and all time periods, are listed in this collection. The arrangement is by 188 general categories subdivided by specific topics. Unlike *The Concise Oxford Dictionary of Proverbs*, this work does not trace the saying's history, but notes often clarify its meaning. Frequent cross-references and indexing by keyword provide access. [R: ARBA 84; BL, 1 June 84; WLB, Nov 83]

1415   Gross, John, comp. **The Oxford Book of Aphorisms**. New York: Oxford University Press, 1983. 383p. $35.00; $12.95pa. ISBN 0-19-214111-2; 0-19-282015-X.

Aphorisms, maxims, quotations, and pensees from ancient times to the present comprise this volume. Entries, arranged under subjects such as good and evil, provide the originator, source, and date for the sayings (if known). [R: ARBA 84; BL, 1 Apr 83; LJ, 15 Mar 83; WLB, Sept 83]

1416   Partington, Angela, ed. **The Oxford Dictionary of Quotations**. rev. 4th ed. New York: Oxford University Press, 1996. 1075p. $39.95. ISBN 0-19-860058-5.

Published since 1941, this has become one of the standard quotation books. This revision of the 1992 fourth edition has expanded the selection of American and non-English entries, non-literary

field entries, and entries from women poets. Hymns and songs which had been removed in an earlier edition have been restored. Arrangement is alphabetical by the author quoted, with separate sections for anonymous sayings, ballads and biblical quotations. The appendices include a section of sayings of the 90s, popular misquotations and slogans. A comprehensive 300 page keyword index provides access. Recommended as an easy-to-use quotation source for all secondary collections.

1417   Simpson, J. A., ed. **The Concise Oxford Dictionary of Proverbs**. New York: Oxford University Press, 1982. 256p. $24.95; $8.95pa. ISBN 0-19-866131-2; 0-19-280002-7pa.

Over 1,000 proverbs commonly used in Great Britain during the twentieth century, and some that originated elsewhere, appear in this work. Each is entered under the first significant word, with cross-references from other key words in the saying. Chronologically arranged illustrations show its first and notable usages and current examples. Since proverbs are excluded from quotations books, this dictionary and others, such as *Facts on File Dictionary of Proverbs*, are useful supplements to them. [R: ARBA 84]

1418   Simpson, James B., comp. **Simpson's Contemporary Quotations: The Most Notable Quotes from 1950 to the Present**. New York: Harper-Collins, 1997. 657p. $30.00. ISBN 0-06-270137-1.

This serves as an update to Simpson's earlier *Contemporary Quotations* titles (Crowell, 1964 and Houghton Mifflin, 1988) and contains 11,300 quotations with a special emphasis on quotations since 1988. Entries are arranged under three major headings—the world, humankind and communications and the arts—and subdivided by topics such as family life, love, religion, humor and wit, law and sports. Each quotation is followed by the source and date. There is an index by sources, by subjects and keywords and a brief key line index of the "most quotables." This tool supplements all other quotation books and will provide students with quotations from people they will recognize.

Religion

See also **Ethnic Minorities (Social Sciences)**.

ATLASES

1419 Pritchard, James B., ed. **The Harper-Collins Concise Atlas of the Bible**. San Francisco: Harper, 1997. 152p. $25.00pa. ISBN 0-06-251499-7.

The new paperbound *Concise Atlas* is based on the 1987 original Atlas and is about half the size and price. It relates land features and location to the literary and historical contexts of the Bible from the earliest evidence of humankind in Palestine during the Paleolithic Era to about 150 A.D. The maps are supplemented with site reconstructions and color photographs. This is a good complement to *Harper's Bible Commentary* and the *HarperCollins Bible Dictionary* and is highly recommended for all secondary collections.

BIOGRAPHY

1420 Bowden, Henry W. **Dictionary of American Religious Biography**. 2d ed. Westport, Conn.: Greenwood Press, 1993. 572p. $70.50. ISBN 0-313-27825-3.

Now containing 550 biographical profiles, this record of individuals from all denominations is a useful tool. Each entry gives a summary of the person's life followed by an essay discussing the context of the contribution, and a bibliography of works by and about the individual. Included are ministers, missionaries, cult leaders, freethinkers and lay persons. This source is appropriate for American history and culture classes as well as religious studies.

1421 Kelly, John N. D. **The Oxford Dictionary of Popes**. New York: Oxford University Press, 1986. 347p. $12.95pa. ISBN 0-19-282085-0.

This scholarly and objective work, arranged chronologically, covers the 264 Popes who followed Peter. Entries include each Pope's family, educational background, prepapal career and activities in office, followed by a selective bibliography. An appendix refutes the fable that an Englishwoman named Joan was elected Pope in 855. An extensive index provides excellent topical access.

1422 Lippy, Charles, ed. **Twentieth Century Shapers of American Popular Religion**. Westport, Conn.: Greenwood Press, 1989. 494p. $89.50. ISBN 0-313-25356-0.

This excellent volume provides biographies and bibliographic information about 64 important individuals in popular religion. Signed articles address both positive and negative aspects of each person's life, analyze his or her contribution and importance and give a critical summary. Entries are alphabetical and balanced between earlier figures such as Billy Sunday and Marcus Garvey and later ones including Jim Bakker and Jimmy Swaggert. This source is appropriate for high school collections to support religious studies, American culture, American history and sociology courses.

DICTIONARIES AND ENCYCLOPEDIAS

1423 Breuilly, Elizabeth, Joanne O'Brien, and Martin Palmer. **Religions of the World: The Illustrated Guide to Origins, Beliefs, Traditions & Festivals**. New York: Facts on File, 1997. 160p. $29.95. ISBN 0-8160-3723-X.

This clear illustrated introduction to the world's religions gives an overview of the major groups. It covers Judaism, Christianity, Islam, Hinduism, Buddhism, Jainism, Shinto, Taoism, Skhism and Bahai. Each chapter gives beliefs and practices as well as describing major festivals. Religious calendars and population distributions are helpful features. The photographs, maps and charts extend the text of this attractive guide. Recommended for all secondary collections.

1424 Catholic University of America editorial staff. **New Catholic Encyclopedia**. 18v. New York: McGraw-Hill, 1967–1989. $940.00/set. ISBN 0-07-010235-X.

The emphasis of this set is on the church in the United States and the English-speaking world. The main set provides coverage through the close of Vatican II; the supplements include articles on more current issues and biographies of notables who died after 1965. Volume 18, the latest supplement, covers the years 1978–1988.

Most of the 17,000 entries are long and scholarly. With both Catholic and non-Catholic scholars contributing, this work is objective, ecumenical, and readable. Scholarly bibliographies support each article, and the analytical index contains some 250,000 entries. [R: ARBA 80]

1425 McBrien, Richard P. **The HarperCollins Encyclopedia of Catholicism**. New York: HarperCollins, 1995. 1349p. $45.00. ISBN 0-06-65338-8.

This comprehensive dictionary has 4,200 entries and 29 longer feature articles. It covers all aspects of Catholicism such as theology, doctrine, canon law, biblical scholarship, history, governing structures, worship, art, and literature. Maps, illustrations, tables and a timeline add information and interest. Many of the 280 contributors are from Notre Dame University and that influence is acknowledged in the foreword. This is a good choice for schools that cannot afford the *New Catholic Encyclopedia*, but even those that hold that work will want this as well.

1426 Melton, J. Gordon. **Encyclopedia of American Religions**. 5th ed. Detroit, Mich.: Gale, 1996. 1150p. $195.00. ISSN 1066-1212.

The fifth edition marks a complete revision, rewriting and expansion of this standard work. There is a new historical essay chapter on interfaith groups. The master name and keyword index have been consolidated while the subject index has been enhanced. Part 1 includes two introductory essays, Part 2 contains 23 historical essays about 20 major religious families which identify key figures, events and doctrinal characteristics, and Part 3 is directory information for individual denominational bodies as well as umbrella and interfaith organizations with cross-references to the proper historical essay. In addition to the subject and keyword indexes, there is a geographical index. A supplement is published between editions.

1427 Melton, J. Gordon, and others. **New Age Encyclopedia: A Guide to Beliefs, Concepts, Terms, People and Organizations**. Detroit, Mich.: Gale, 1990. 586p. $67.00. ISBN 0-8103-7159-6.

An introductory essay traces the historical development of the New Age movement and its current patterns and trends. The main part provides 325 alphabetically arranged entries on a broad range of topics, such as persons, organizations, concepts, beliefs and opposition to New Age beliefs. Among the entries included are New Age music, Shirley MacLaine, yoga, crystals, channeling, rolfing, aroma-therapy and Feldenkrais. A chronology of the movement and a name and keyword index complete the volume. Melton provides an impartial approach to a controversial area. A second edition is in preparation.

1428 Queen, Edward L., II, Stephen R. Prothero, and Gardiner H. Shattuck, Jr. **The Encyclopedia of American Religious History**. 2v. New York: Facts on File, 1996. $99.00/set. ISBN 0-8160-2406-5.

The encyclopedia presents a broad picture of the role and influence of religion in America. People, movements, social issues, ethical issues and multi-cultural and feminist perspectives are all included as are entries on churches and denominations. The signed articles vary in length from about one and a half columns to several pages. There are both subject classified and general indexes. This is a good choice for both middle and high schools to support religious, historical, sociological and cultural information requests. Recommended. [R: ARBA 97]

1429 Wigoder, Geoffrey, ed. **The Encyclopedia of Judaism**. New York: Macmillan, 1989. 768p. $75.00. ISBN 0-02-628410-3.

Judaism focuses on the most important terms, traditions, institutions, and individuals associated with the religion. More than 1,000 current, well-written articles contributed by scholars are enhanced by superb pictures and illustrations, extensive cross-referencing and indexing, and boxes that highlight important data. Articles vary in length according to their importance and range from a few paragraphs to several pages.

This attractive, carefully prepared work provides a concise introduction to many topics related to Judaism. It is highly recommended for secondary schools requiring a reference source on the topic. [R: ARBA 91; LJ, 1 Feb 90; RBB, 1 Mar 90]

HANDBOOKS

1430 Himelstein, Shmuel. **The Jewish Primer: Questions and Answers on Jewish Faith and Culture**. New York: Facts on File, 1990. 254p. $24.95; $13.95pa. ISBN 0-8160-2322-0; 0-8160-2849-4pa.

The Jewish Primer provides simple, forceful explanations of the faith and practices of Judaism. Reform and Conservative forms are briefly covered, but the work's emphasis is on traditional Orthodox beliefs. Himelstein offers succinct discussions of dietary laws, marriage and divorce, holy days, the sabbath, sacred writings, Jewish life, and many other topics, all in question-and-answer format and supported by a subject index. This is an excellent introduction to the tenets of traditional Judaism. [R: BL, 15 May 90; LJ, 15 Apr 90]

1431 Hubbard, Benjamin J., John t. Hatfield, and James A. Santucci. **America's Religions: An Educator's Guide to Beliefs and Practices**. Englewood, Colo.: Teacher Ideas Press, 1997. 162p. $25.00pa. ISBN 1-56308-469-4.

This volume is intended to inform teachers and administrators about the diverse religious beliefs they will encounter in their classrooms, schools and communities. It combines the need for respect for this diversity with the concept of separation of church and state. Major religious groups and their beliefs are covered, along with Native American religions, New Age religion, atheism, Christian Science, Jehovah's Witnesses, Mormonism, Adventism and fundamentalism. Included for each group is background information, practices and classroom concerns. The guide belongs in every professional collection.

1432 Mead, Frank Spencer. **Handbook of Denominations in the United States**. 10th ed. Nashville, Tenn.: Abingdon Press, 1995. 316p. $15.95. ISBN 0-687-01478-6.

The history, doctrines, governance, statistics, and auxiliary institutions of some 200 religious groups in the United States make up the latest edition of this standard handbook, which was last revised in 1990. Many of the essays on individual denominations have been updated to reflect changes, with more attention given to evangelicalism and fundamentalism.

The new edition has been revised so that complex denominational families, in part reflecting new mergers, are identified. Other features include a list of denomination headquarters, a glossary, and a bibliography. Indexed. [R: ARBA 91]

1433 Melton, J. Gordon. **Encyclopedic Handbook of Cults in America**. New York: Garland, 1992. 407p. $65.00; $21.95pa. ISBN 0-8153-0502-8; 0-8153-1140-0pa.

Following an essay on the definition and history of cults in the United States, this work treats 28 groups: older cults, such as the Rosicrucians and Theosophy; the New Age movement; and newer cults, such as the Unification Church and the Rajneesh Foundation. For each group, the text covers its major figures, beliefs, organizational structure, and controversies. A bibliography of books about the cult by both members and nonmembers concludes each entry. Indexed. These unbiased essays about a popular topic make this a worthwhile source on the subject. [R: ARBA 87; RBB, 15 Dec 86]

1434 Weber, Paul J., and W. Landis Jones. **U.S. Religious Interest Groups: Institutional Profiles**. Westport, Conn.: Greenwood Press, 1994. 207p. $69.50. ISBN 0-313-26695-6.

This source analyzes religious groups which actively attempt to influence public policy. An introduction discusses the issue throughout the country's history and the 188 profiles follow in alphabetical order. Each group's entry includes directory information, its origins and development, mission statement, organization and funding, policy concerns and tactics, affiliations and publications. Special comments accompany some entries. The groups represented come from all religious and political perspectives such as the National Right-to-Life, Catholics for a Free Choice, Focus on Family, and the American Jewish Congress. There are also entries for non-religious groups which often deal with religious issues; the A.C.L.U., for example. Appendices list groups by policy area, religious affiliation, political identification, single-issue groups, type of membership, litigants and size of budget. There is a bibliographic essay and an index. This topic is important in many curricular areas and the work is highly recommended.

1435 **Yearbook of American and Canadian Churches**. Nashville, Tenn.: Abingdon Press, 1973– . annual. $29.95. ISSN 0195-9034.

Published over a period of 70 years, this valuable reference yearbook provides accurate statistics and other timely data on over 250 religious groups in North America. For each group, the work gives the names, addresses, and leadership personnel for its headquarters and divisions, as well as a brief history of the denomination. Also provided are directory data for theological seminaries, national and international cooperative organizations, service agencies, colleges and universities, and periodicals published by each church. A calendar for church use covers the next four years. Organization and individual name indexes. E-mail and World Wide Web addresses as well as information about congregations can be found at http://www.ncccusa.org.

BIBLE STUDIES

1436 Achtemeir, Paul J. and others, eds. **The HarperCollins Bible Dictionary**. rev. ed. San Francisco: Harper, 1996. $45.00. 1250p. ISBN 0-06-060037-3.

The highly regarded dictionary has been revised and expanded. It is produced under the auspices of the Society of Biblical Literature. Almost 200 editors and contributors, representing Protestant, Catholic and Jewish scholars, cover all important persons and places in all books of the Bible, including the apocrypha. Also included are theological terms, archaeological sites and words used in the Bible in important or unusual ways. Most entries are concise, but articles on major topics are several pages in length. There are many black and white and color photographs and line drawings, charts and maps. The major essays contain bibliographies. Complemented by

Harper's Bible Commentary and *The HarperCollins Concise Atlas of the Bible* and recommended for all secondary collections.

1437 Anderson, Bernhard W. **Books of the Bible**. 2v. New York: Scribner's, 1989. $179.00. ISBN 0-684-18487-7.

Descriptive and interpretive essays on the books of the Bible appear in this excellent and attractive set. Volume 1 covers the 39 books of the Old Testament/Hebrew Bible; volume 2 contains essays on the Apocrypha and the 27 books of the New Testament. Several general articles provide broad historical insights.

Each essay, written and signed by a renowned scholar, addresses the Bible as literature, with some attention to the oral traditions from which it evolved. References cite numerous standard translations of Biblical texts and a bibliography for further study supports each essay. Each volume includes a chronology and index, but the set lacks maps and illustrations. This is a scholarly but readable work and not intended as a theological treatise. Recommended to high schools as a background source for many disciplines.

1438 Levine, Mark L. and Eugene Rachlis, eds. **The Complete Book of Bible Quotations from the Old Testament**. New York: Pocket Books, 1996. 375p. $16.00pa. ISBN 0-671-53796-2.

1439 Levine, Mark L. and Eugene Rachlis, eds. **The Complete Book of Bible Quotations from the New Testament**. New York: Pocket Books, 1996. 264p. $16.00pa. ISBN 0-671-53797-0.

Formerly published in one volume, *The Complete Book of Bible Quotations,* each volume now contains about 4,000 quotations selected from the King James version of the Bible. Arranged by subject headings, the quotations were selected for their beauty, significance and suitability for illustrating concepts. There are keyword indexes.

1440 Mays, James L. and others, eds. **Harper's Bible Commentary**. San Francisco: Harper, 1988. 1326p. $45.00. ISBN 0-06-065541-0.

The *Commentary* is a companion to the *HarperCollins Bible Dictionary* and frequently refers to it. The eight main sections contain long essays that focus primarily on Biblical meaning and interpretation. Shorter articles treat special topics, such as women in Genesis and Jeremiah's symbolic action. Numerous black-and-white illustrations and color maps support the text.

1441 Metzger, Bruce M., and Michael D. Coogan, eds. **The Oxford Companion to the Bible**. New York: Oxford University Press, 1993. 874p. $55.00. ISBN 0-19-504645-5.

The unique focus of this handbook is that it is about the Bible as an object, a work of literature. The 700 articles are about its writing and organization, translations and publication and its distribution, and are written by more than 250 scholars from around the world. Entries include individuals, events, institutions, ancient life, chronologies, interpretation, use and the influence of the Bible on law, literature, art and music. There are tables, maps, an annotated bibliography and an index. Highly recommended for collections with other Bible reference materials.

1442 Myers, Allen C., ed. **The Eerdmans Bible Dictionary**. Grand Rapids, Mich.: William B. Eerdmans, 1987. 1094p. $25.00pa. ISBN 0-8028-4250-X.

Eerdmans, an expanded and updated translation of a Dutch Bible dictionary (1975), contains almost 5,000 entries. Articles cover all persons and places mentioned in the Bible, explain important Biblical concepts and examine the background and contents of each book of the Bible.

Coverage, which includes canonical and apocryphal books, reflects recent archaeological discoveries and literary, historical and sociological studies. Forty-eight persons from a variety of evangelical denominations contributed the unsigned articles. Bibliographies support major articles; there are a limited number of illustrations, but there are tables, charts, and a 12-page collection of colored maps from Hammond.

This work is not as scholarly as *Harper's Bible Dictionary*, but it is a good source for those who desire a Protestant perspective.

1443 Waller, Lynn. **International**
E+ **Children's Bible Dictionary**. Dallas, Tex.: World Publishing, 1997. 128p. $12.99pa. ISBN 0-8499-4013-3.

This useful dictionary contains about 1,200 definitions, some with illustrations to aid understanding. Entries include Biblical references; some have pronunciation keys. Recommended for upper elementary and middle school collections.

SAINTS

1444 Farmer, David H. **The Oxford Dictionary of Saints**. 4th ed. New York: Oxford University Press, 1997. 592p. $15.95pa. ISBN 0-19-280058-2.

Entries cover more than 1,300 saints with brief entries for the obscure and long entries for the famous. In addition to the biographies, there is information on the cults, mysteries and bizarre associations some of the saints have attracted. This is a readable and useful reference.

Theater and Dance

THEATER
Biography

1445 **Contemporary Theatre, Film and Television**. 19v– . Detroit: Gale, 1984– . annual. $140.00/v. ISSN 0749-064X.

This series, which now approaches 20 volumes, began as a continuation of *Who's Who in the*

Theatre. It provides biographical and career information on currently popular theater, film and television performers, directors, producers, writers, designers, managers, choreographers, technicians, composers, executives, dancers and critics. Each volume covers some 700 individuals, many sketches have photographs.

Entries are similar in format to *Contemporary Authors* and give complete career credits for work in the three media, as well as information on recordings, awards and memberships. Personal information includes birthdate, original name, parents and spouses, education, political and religious affiliations and address. Each volume contains a cumulative index for all previous annuals.

Dictionaries and Encyclopedias

1446 Banham, Martin, ed. **The Cambridge Guide to Theatre**. rev. ed. New York: Cambridge University Press, 1995. 1233p. $49.95. ISBN 0-521-43437-8.

The Cambridge Guide presents a broad view of theater and is a comprehensive guide to both history and current practice. This revised edition of the 1988 work adds 200 entries and reworks many of the old. It is international in scope and has contributors from 25 countries. Its definition of theater encompasses a broad range of activities and there is a contents list of the "less obvious" entries such as magic, animals as performers and stage food. Other articles are about practitioners, national traditions, theory, criticism, censorship, lighting and sound, design, buildings, puppets and cabaret. Entries are alphabetical with cross-references. This excellent guide is highly recommended for high schools.

1447 Bordman, Gerald M. **The Oxford Companion to American Theatre**. 2d ed. New York: Oxford University Press, 1992. 735p. $60.00; $13.95pa. ISBN 0-19-507246-4; 0-19-506327-9pa.

More than 3,000 alphabetically arranged entries, including new articles on individuals, groups and plays from the eight years since the first edition, appear in this thoughtful work. Many entries provide information on playwrights, performers, producers, composers, librettists, choreographers and designers from the legitimate state. Performers from vaudeville, minstrel shows and other forms of popular theater are included as well. Entries for individual plays and musicals give plot summaries and brief commentaries. Others cover theater buildings, organizations and theater terminology. This is a worthwhile supplement to the *Oxford Companion to the Theatre* (1983), a standard reference tool on western theater.

1448 Hodgson, Terry. **The Drama Dictionary**. New York: New Amsterdam, 1989. 432p. $35.00. ISBN 0-941533-40-9.

Entries in this work vary in length from a few lines to several pages; they define 1,300 critical and technical terms commonly heard in the theater. Some 30 line drawings add interest. Many entries contain suggestions for further reading. The work's purpose is to provide a useful source on dramatic practice, theory and criticism rather than exhaustive coverage of terminology. High school students can acquire a working vocabulary of the theater from this useful source.

Handbooks

1449 Eaker, Sherry, ed. **The Back Stage Handbook for Performing Artists**. 3d ed. New York: Back Stage Books, 1995. 239p. $18.95. ISBN 0-8230-7599-0.

This work discusses the business side of the performing arts and gives practical advice for beginning and veteran actors, singers, dancers and models. Its "how-to" and "who-to-contact" articles are arranged by categories such as basic tools, training, finding work and working in the theater. Among the topics addressed are agents, photographers, resumes, and auditions. Several essays alert the reader to exploitation schemes.

1450 Guernsey, Otis L., and Jeffrey Sweet, eds. **The Best Plays**. New York: Limelight Editions, 1992– . annual. $47.50. ISSN 1071-6971.

This series, also know as the *Theater Yearbook*, has been published since 1926. Currently the annuals include script excerpts and digests as well as production information for New York plays, plays produced outside New York and for theater festivals. Entries give cast listings, directors, dates and summaries. Sections also list awards and actors.

1451 Willis, John. **Theatre World**. New York: Applause Theatre Book Publishers. annual. $49.95.

This annual survey of the American theater emphasizes Broadway productions, with some attention given to off-Broadway plays, regional theater and touring companies. Casts, dates of opening and closing and other descriptive data are given, but there are no critical comments. Photographs accompany most entries. Biographical sketches of outstanding performers, producers and other theatrical notables are included.

Indexes

1452 **Play Index**. Bronx, N.Y.: H. W. Wilson, 1949– . irregular. $80.00. ISSN 0554-3037.

Eight cumulative editions provide comprehensive coverage of thousands of plays contained in collections or published separately. Included are all types of works from puppet plays to classical drama. Author, title, subject and dramatic style entries are arranged in a single alphabet with additional sections for cast analysis (number and gender of characters), a list of collections analyzed and a directory of publishers. The author entry contains a descriptive note and indicates size of cast and number of sets required. Symbols note which plays are suitable for children and young people. This index is an excellent source for locating published plays.

DANCE

1453 Warren, Gretchen Ward. **Classical Ballet Technique**. Tampa, Fla.: University of South Florida Press, 1989. 395p. $85.00; $39.95pa. ISBN 0-8130-0895-6; 0-8130-0945-6pa.

This volume covers the theory, tradition, and movements of classical ballet; defines the vocabulary of the field; and suggests ways in which ballet should be taught. Over 2,600 black-and-white photographs illustrate correct and incorrect movements, poses, and exercises. Other features include a glossary, a pronunciation guide, a selective bibliography, and an essay on classroom etiquette. Indexed. [R: ARBA 91; LJ, Jan 90; RBB, 1 Nov 90]

PART FIVE

Astronomy

GENERAL WORKS

1454 Ronan, Colin A. **The Universe Explained: The Earth Dweller's Guide to the Mysteries of Space.** New York: Holt, 1994. 192p. $35.00. ISBN 0-8050-3488-9.

Ronan is an astronomer, an author and a teacher and this excellent source combines narrative with many colored photographs and diagrams to discuss the planets, the stars, the sun and the galaxies. The focus of the work is a knowledge of the universe, the theories of evolution, and how it all works. Each issue is posed as answers to questions with supporting evidence in a two-page spread. Cross-references are ranged along the right side of the spread to other sections of the text so that the reader can build up relationships among the topics. Articles discuss equipment and there are many sky maps. A brief bibliography and an index complete the work. Secondary libraries may need both reference and circulating copies; highly recommended. [R: ARBA 96]

ATLASES

1455 Audouze, Jean and Guy Israel, eds. **The Cambridge Atlas of Astronomy**. 3d ed. New York: Cambridge University Press, 1994. 470p. $90.00. ISBN 0-521-43438-6.

The signed chapters in this encyclopedia atlas include introductory information and an essay about what contemporary astronomy is all about. Separate chapters discuss the sun, the solar system, stars and galaxies. Standard topics such as white dwarves and radio galaxies are well covered. A final section looks at cosmology, the extraterrestial life debate, and the history of astronomy. The narratives are complemented with a rich variety of illustration: photographs, charts, graphs and maps. Supplemental material includes a sky map, a bibliography of further reading, and a combination glossary/index. This is an excellent source for high school collections.

1456 Vehrenberg, Hans. **Atlas of Deep-Sky Splendors**. 4th ed. New York: Cambridge University Press, 1983. 242p. $39.95. ISBN 0-521-24834-0.

High-quality photographs of deep-space objects—galaxies, star clusters, and nebulas—are the hallmark of this excellent atlas designed for the amateur astronomer. The 113 charts of star fields show more than 400 nonstellar objects. Star charts, small finder charts, and a list of the objects in the photographs appear on the right-hand page; the left-hand page contains commentary and photographs of selected objects in the chart. The text of this edition has been updated with the addition of lesser-known objects and many photographs. For secondary schools. [R: ARBA 85; SBF, May/June 85]

DICTIONARIES AND ENCYCLOPEDIAS

1457 Angelo, Joseph A., Jr. **The Extraterrestrial Encyclopedia: Our Search for Life in Outer Space**. New York: Facts on File, 1991. 254p. $40.00. ISBN 0-8160-2276-3.

This work covers the attempts to search for and signal life forms in space. The scope is broad and includes planets and galaxies, discussions of "life" based on chemical evidence and other considerations, ethical questions, scientific speculation and science fiction, and places which carry out research. Arrangement is alphabetical and entries vary from brief definitions with explanations to about three pages. The 100 illustrations include some in color, and there are tables and charts. Reference and reading lists and a complete index complete the volume. Generally, the language is non-technical and the encyclopedia is recommended for middle and high schools.

1458 **Cambridge Astronomy Dictionary**. New York: Cambridge University Press, 1996. 238p. $29.95; $14.95pa. ISBN 0-521-58007-2; 0-521-58991-6pa.

Concise entries about the science of astronomy make up this dictionary. It does not include space exploration; "satellite" means "moons" in this source, with artificial satellites relegated to a two-sentence historical entry. Major planets and a few other topics have longer articles; all entries are clearly explained and show the development of knowledge with people and dates for relevant discoveries. Included are 100 biographies of people from ancient to modern times, equipment and observatories, theories, planets and other bodies in space, and relevant physics. This is a useful source and is recommended for secondary schools. [R: ARBA 97]

1459 Illingworth, Valerie, ed. **The Facts on File Dictionary of Astronomy**. 3d ed. New York: Facts on File, 1994. 520p. $29.95. ISBN 0-8160-3184-3.

More than 3,500 entries describe objects, equipment, elements, time, observatories, astronomy and space science. The third edition includes substantial updating with more than 1,000 new entries. Arranged alphabetically the entries vary from one sentence to two pages. Drawings and 12 tables enhance the text; vocabulary is fairly technical but is appropriate for high school students. [R: ARBA 95]

1460 Room, Adrian. **Dictionary of Astro-**
E+   **nomical Names**. New York: Routledge, 1988. 282p. $27.50. ISBN 0-415-01298-8.

The origins of the names of stars, planets, and other celestial bodies comprise the focus of this readable work. A glossary and a lengthy history of astronomical names (ancient terms from Greek, Latin, and Arabic, and others derived from personal names since the sixteenth century) introduce the volume. Entries in the main body, arranged by popular name, give the origin of

each name; the person who gave it its name, if known; cross-references to related terms, and any alternative names. Appendixes provide lunar crater and asteroid names. Recommended for all levels. [R: ARBA 90]

HANDBOOKS

1461 Bakich, Michael Eli. **The Cambridge Guide to the Constellations**. New York: Cambridge University Press, 1995. 320p. $49.95; $19.95pa. ISBN 0-521-46520-6; 0-521-44921-9pa.

This manual begins with more than 30 lists and tables such as biblical references to constellations, the 200 brightest stars, star names and an alphabetical list of constellations. The main part of the work is an alphabetical encyclopedia of 120 constellations. Each long entry gives the name, its meaning and pronunciation, bordering constellations, brightness, size, visible stars and interesting facts. There are illustrations and a sky map for each constellation. A glossary and list of references and sources complete the work. Recommended for secondary schools with good astronomy programs. [R: ARBA 96]

1462 Pasachoff, Jay M. **A Field Guide to the Stars and Planets**. 3d ed. Boston: Houghton Mifflin, 1992. 502p. $24.95; $15.95pa. ISBN 0395-53764-9; 0-395-53759-2pa.

This working field guide is also a good, standard reference book. The narrative chapters provide general information about the skies and the objects found there and specific information about constellations, stars, nebulae, galaxies, planets, comets, asteroids, meteors, and the sun and moon. One chapter deals with the constellations and the ancient myths associated with them. The chapters are profusely illustrated with sky maps, charts, tables and photographs. Fourteen appendices include convenient charts and tables about such topics as the properties of the planets. There is a glossary, information about telescopes, and a classified bibliography which includes magazines and associations as well as books. There is a sky map which acts as an index to the atlas charts as well as a general index. Highly recommended for secondary collections. [R: ARBA 94]

Biology

☐ ―― ☐

See also **Pets, Zoology.**

1463 The Diagram Group. **Life Sciences on File.** New York: Facts on File, 1985. 304p. $155.00. ISBN 0-8160-1284-9.

This set of reproducible charts and diagrams contains more than 300 drawings keyed to the study of biology, zoology, and botany. The contents, arranged by broad areas, include such topics as reproduction, evolution, nutrition, respiration, and plant and animal growth. Drawings are clear and well captioned. A detailed table of contents and an index provide access to the subject matter. Designed primarily for college level, the collection contains enough basic material to warrant selection for high school libraries.

1464 **Encyclopedia of Nature: The Essen-**
E+   **tial Multimedia Reference Guide to the Natural World.** New York: Dorling Kindersley, 1995. CD-ROM (Macintosh). $39.95. ISBN 07-894-0041-3.

Both an exploratory multimedia program and a reference tool, the encyclopedia is rich with access points to the basic database. From the contents "console" it is possible to choose among mammals, fish, amphibians, reptiles, insects, invertebrates, birds and plants and fungi. From the same screen one may also search prehistoric life, evolutionary theory, habitats, the microworld, climate and conservation. A browse search can be done from an index screen/alphabetical menu. There are *see also* hyperlinks and various other approaches. The entries consist of narrative (both text and spoken), fact boxes, timelines and are often accompanied by video clips. Entries from some topics are presented as pages in books. The information in the database has been carefully selected and designed for the multiple approaches. Highly recommended for elementary and middle schools. [R: ARBA 97; BL, 1 Nov 95]

1465 Margulis, Lynn and Karlene V. Schwartz. **Five Kingdoms: An Illustrated Guide to the Phyla of Life on**
Earth. 3d ed. New York: W. H. Freeman, 1998. 448p. $39.95. ISBN 0-7167-3026-X.

This work describes and illustrates all major groups of organisms in the five kingdoms now accepted by most biologists: bacteria, algae and related forms, fungi, animals, and plants. Within each kingdom, the phyla are presented from the simplest to the more complex. Text, photographs, and drawings with "family tree" charts, a glossary, bibliographies, and an index make this a useful reference source. The language is somewhat technical, limiting the work to high school collections where it will be helpful to both teachers and students; the taxonomic approach will be a complement to programs with an ecological base.

1466 Milner, Richard. **The Encyclopedia of Evolution: Humanity's Search for its Origins.** New York: Facts on File, 1990. 481p. $45.00. ISBN 0-8160-1472-8.

The informal writing in this source should not disguise its usefulness. People, animals, ideas, places, fossil evidence, popular culture, and events are all included. Articles cover Adam and Eve, Creationism, Gertie the Dinosaur and all sorts of related issues. Several pages and subsections cover Darwin and Darwinian theories; Stephen Jay Gould (who wrote the foreword) and his ideas are present, but not those of Dawkins or Dennett. Each entry follows the pattern of topic title, entry, cross-references and further reading sources. Maps and photographs are included. Arrangement is alphabetical, but because the articles range from one paragraph to multiple pages, the index is necessary. Highly recommended for both middle and high schools. [R: ARBA 92; SLJ, June 91]

1467 Reich, Warren Thomas, ed. **Encyclopedia of Bioethics.** 5v. New York: Macmillan, 1995. $425.00/set. ISBN 0-02-897355-0.

The revised edition reflects the new challenges in the life sciences and health care brought about by advancing technology. The work covers bioethics in terms of science, social, environmental and global aspects. Such topics as population, animal rights, sexism, abuse, adoption, gender, genetics, death and dying and mental health are covered. There is a list of topics in the beginning of the first volume that reads like a list of typical high school reports. Alphabetical arrangement, overviews, subheadings, and bibliographies serve to make the text of the long articles approachable. There is also an index. Articles tend to discuss sociocultural and legal issues along with ethics. As the introduction points out, the discipline has expanded, become more specialized and more controversy within the field has developed. Topics, therefore, may have multiple articles; articles are signed. Extensive appendices give texts of codes, oaths and directives. Highly recommended for high school collections. [R: ARBA 96]

1468 Rudin, Norah. **Dictionary of Modern Biology**. Hauppauge, N.Y.: Barron's Educational Series, 1997. 504p. $15.95pa. ISBN 0-8120-9516-2.

This comprehensive dictionary has clear definitions and excellent illustrations. Arranged alphabetically with cross-references (including those from common to scientific names), the work also has useful appendices with time scales, taxonomic classes, endangered species, and so on. Both teachers and students in secondary schools will find this an outstanding reference; some schools may consider a classroom set appropriate.

1469 Tootill, Elizabeth. **The Facts on File Dictionary of Biology**. New York: Facts on File, 1988. 326p. $12.95. ISBN 0-8160-1865-0.

Concepts and terms from basic biology are covered in this useful dictionary. Some 40 drawings add to the clear definitions. The A–Z arrangement with cross-references makes it easily used by middle school and high school students. Recommended.

Botany

FLOWERING PLANTS

1470 Niering, William A. and Nancy C.
E+ Olmstead. **The Audubon Society Field Guide to North American Wildflowers, Eastern Region**. New York: Knopf, 1979. 863p. $19.00. ISBN 0-394-50432-1.

1471 Spellenberg, Richard. **The Audubon Society Field Guide to North American Wildflowers, Western Region**. New York: Knopf, 1979. 863p. $19.00. ISBN 0-394-50431-3.

These field guides describe 600 wildflower species arranged by color, with notes on some 400 others. The 700-plus color photographs in part 1 are keyed to their identification and descriptions in part 2. These excellent, beautiful volumes are highly recommended for all levels. [R: ARBA 80; BL, 1 Dec 80]

1472 Peterson, Roger Tory. **Peterson First**
E+ **Guide to Wildflowers of Northeastern and Northcentral North America**. Boston: Houghton Mifflin, 1986. 126p. $4.95. ISBN 0-395-40777-X.

This was one of the first titles in the First Guide series and is a good example of the thought behind this version of the Peterson field guides. Wildflowers selected for the first guide are those most likely to be encountered by a beginning naturalist. Pictures have arrows identifying unique features of a wildflower and the text description of that feature is italicized in the accompanying narrative. Rather than a table of contents, the wildflowers are organized by the color and the color is reproduced in triangles at the top of the appropriate pages. There is an index. Recommended for all levels.

NONFLOWERING PLANTS

1473 Huffman, D. M., and others. **Mushrooms and Other Fungi of the Midcontinental United States**. Ames, Iowa: Iowa State University Press, 1988. 326p. $24.95. ISBN 0-8138-1168-6.

The midwest prairie, a mushroom hunter's paradise, receives the attention of this excellent guide to edible and inedible fungi. The introduction describes mushroom biology, explains how to identify the fungi, and lists the different kinds found in each season. The text covers 250 of the most common, showy species; describes each mushroom in nontechnical language; and illustrates them with excellent color photographs. The number treated is only a fraction of the species that grow in the area, but the volume is a good guide for the beginner. [R: ARBA 90]

1474 Phillips, Roger. **Mushrooms of North America**. Boston: Little, Brown, 1991. 319p. $29.95pa. ISBN 0-316-70613-2.

Amateur and professional mycologists will welcome this beautifully illustrated and informative volume. The more than 1,000 photographs were shot in a studio rather than in the field so as to capture external and internal detail. Specimens representing various stages of growth are included. Each mushroom is described in detail (cap, gills, stem, and spores), and explanations are given about where and when it can be found and whether it is edible. Highly recommended for high schools. [R: ARBA 92; LJ, 15 June 91]

TREES AND SHRUBS

1475 Brockman, C. Frank. **Trees of North America: A Field Guide to the Major Native and Introduced Species North of Mexico**. New York: Golden Press, 1968. 280p. $11.95. ISBN 0-307-13658-2.
E+

Almost 600 species of North American trees are described and illustrated in this excellent guide, one of the Golden Field Guides. Distribution maps are also provided. Suggested for grades 6 and up.

1476 Burnie, David. **Tree**. New York: Knopf, 1988. 63p. $19.00. ISBN 0-394-89617-3.
E+

The introduction to this excellent work explains the role of trees in history and culture and describes the three categories of trees (needle-leaved, broad-leaved, and palm). Two-page, poster-format chapters cover all phases of a tree's life from birth to death: anatomy, physiology, growth and development, and reproduction. Other chapters treat ecosystems, lumber production, uses of wood, tree diseases, and pollution. Superb photographs illustrate this small volume. Recommended for upper elementary grades through high school. [R: BL, 1 Dec 88; SLJ, Dec 88]

1477 Jorgenson, Lisa. **Grand Trees of America: Our State and Champion Trees**. Niwot, Colo.: Roberts Rinehart Publishers, 1992. 120p. $8.95pa. ISBN 1-879373-15-7.
E

This simple book describes both state trees and champion trees—those recorded as largest of their species by the National Register of Big Trees. Introductory material is followed by the state trees arranged alphabetically by state. Each entry gives the common and scientific names, height, diameter, leaves, flowers, bark, shape and year designated. There are narrative paragraphs about that tree and/or its species. Black and white drawings of the tree and leaves are included. A sentence tells how many champion trees are found in the state and a cross-reference leads from the state tree species to its champion if found in another state. The state trees are followed by a list of species without a designated champion, directions for nominating trees for that status, and a form to complete for the nomination. Although this book will be useful, there is no clear definition of a "champion tree" and no champion trees are described if they are not also a state tree. In addition there is no index. Recommended for elementary schools, nonetheless, because of its unique features. [R: ARBA 94]

1478 Kricher, John C. **A Field Guide to Eastern Forests, North America**. Boston: Houghton Mifflin, 1988. 368p. $17.95. ISBN 0-395-47953-3pa.
E+

Unlike some earlier Peterson Field Guides that deal with one species (e.g., birds, flowers, trees), Kricher's guide considers all species, from insects to trees, in a particular habitat and the interaction among them. The attempt is to interpret nature, not to identify species.

The arrangement, by observable patterns (e.g., disturbance and pioneer plants, patterns of spring), suggests how to identify the patterns. Species included are indigenous to the area or groups studied. Chapters end with an ecological questionnaire; drawings illustrate each section. *The Audubon Society's Eastern Forest* (Alfred A. Knopf, 1985), a similar work, is illustrated with photographs instead of drawings. [R: ARBA 89; LJ, Dec 88; WLB, Dec 86]

1479 Phillips, Roger and Martyn Rix. **Shrubs**. New York: Random House, 1989. 288p. $27.50pa. ISBN 0-679-72345-5.

Over 1,900 shrubs are identified in this quick-reference source. The brief information gives genus and species, common and family names, hybridization, parentage, place of origin, a brief description, and where the plant thrives. Excellent pictures of leaves, flowers, and stem conformations make this volume useful for identification. Indexed by scientific and common name. [R: ARBA 90; BL, 15 Mar 89; LJ, 15 Apr 89]

Chemistry

1480 Bennett, H., ed. **Concise Chemical and Technical Dictionary**. 4th ed. New York: Chemical Publishing, 1986. 1271p. $160.00. ISBN 0-8206-0310-4.

Some 100,000 terms, including chemicals, drugs, trade names, and property products, that cover all fields of scientific and technical development are briefly described in this handbook. It is intended for the beginning student, but some knowledge of chemistry is required to understand several definitions. Useful features include pronunciation of chemical words and vitamin values for important food stuffs. Recommended for high schools. [R: ARBA 87]

1481 **CRC Handbook of Chemistry and Physics**. Cleveland, Ohio: CRC Press, 1922– . annual. $110.00. ISSN 0147-6262.

Since 1922 this has been the standard handbook for the physical sciences. Tables and charts with narrative definitions (800 terms are defined with cross-references to other parts of the volume) and narrative introductions to each section combine to provide both conceptual and practical information. Sixteen sections cover basic constants, nomenclature, organic and inorganic compounds, elements, properties, biochemistry, analytical chemistry, molecular structure, and atomic physics. Final sections cover quick lab data and health and safety. Although this work may seem incomprehensible to non-scientists, it

is the most used laboratory manual and should be in every high school. Teachers and some students in middle school will also find it useful.

1482 Daintith, John, ed. **The Facts on File Dictionary of Chemistry**. New York: Facts on File, 1988. 249p. $12.95. ISBN 0-8160-2367-0.

More than 2,000 words and terms covering chemical processes, the elements, compounds, formulae and equipment are included in this dictionary. Useful appendices list the elements, physical constants, elementary particles, the Greek alphabet and the periodic table. The A–Z arrangement, the clarity of the non-technical definitions and the accompanying illustrations make this an appropriate source for secondary collections.

1483 Dean, John Aurie. **Lange's Handbook of Chemistry**. 14th ed. New York: McGraw-Hill, 1992. $110.00. ISBN 0-07-016194-1.

This manual contains some of the same material as the *CRC Handbook of Chemistry and Physics*, but is organized differently and may be more appropriate for the high school chemistry teacher and student. The first of 11 sections deals with 4,000 organic compounds with all of the usual properties in tables. Section two gives general information, mathematics, and conversion tables, while section three has data on 1,400 inorganic compounds. Section four covers atoms, bonds and radicals, while sections five to ten include more specific information about such things as thermodynamic properties. The final section gives practical laboratory information. There is a brief general table of contents, and useful detailed tables of contents with each section. An index provides further access. This standard chemistry handbook should be in all high school collections.

1484 Eagleson, Mary, trans. and rev. **Concise Encyclopedia Chemistry**. New York: Walter de Gruyter, 1994. 1201p. $69.95. ISBN 0-89925-457-8.

Twelve thousand brief entries cover inorganic, organic, physical and technical chemistry and chemical engineering. Supplemented with almost 2,000 tables and figures, the work is intended as an overall view of the discipline. Arranged alphabetically with cross-references, the entries range from one or two sentences to two pages in length and include chemical substances (natural and synthetic), pharmaceuticals, formulas, compounds and processes. Comprehensive entries for the elements include abundance, sources, methods of refining, applications, and history. There is a copy of the periodic table as endpapers. While the language is technical, this is a good complement to the *CRC Handbook of Chemistry and Physics* and may be more useful in many high school collections. [R: ARBA 95]

1485 Furr, A. Keith, ed. **CRC Handbook of Laboratory Safety**. 4th ed. Boca Raton, Fla.: CRC Press, 1995. 783p. $125.00. ISBN 0-8493-2518-8.

The handbook covers responsibilities for the safe laboratory, emergency programs, lab facility design and operations, non-chemical labs, and personnel protective equipment. An appendix has a safe laboratory checklist. There is an index. This source should be available in every district professional collection. [R: ARBA 97]

1486 Lewis, Richard J., Sr. **Hawley's Condensed Chemical Dictionary**. 13th ed, rev. New York: Van Nostrand Reinhold, 1996. 2,500p. $99.95. ISBN 0-442-02324-3.

Published since 1919, and extensively revised and reorganized during the last several editions, this work combines the features of dictionary and encyclopedia. There are both technical data and descriptive information. Terms include chemicals and raw materials, chemical processes, equipment, trademarked products, chemists, Nobel prize winners, societies and associations. Entries give historical information, and etymologies of terms. Entries for chemicals and raw materials contain descriptions, occurrence, hazards and use; environmental notations such as "use prohibited" or "use restricted" are given. Arrangement is alphabetical. Some longer articles are signed. This is an excellent source for high school reference collections.

1487 Shugar, Gershon J., and John A. Dean. **The Chemist's Ready Reference Handbook**. 1v. New York: McGraw-Hill, 1990. $89.50. ISBN 0-07-057178-3.

This compendium of data, written by experts, is designed for levels of practicing laboratory chemists. Practical suggestions for conducting safe and successful experiments are emphasized. Indexed. This is an advanced work, but it would be useful to chemistry teachers and students with some background in chemistry. [R: ARBA 91]

Computers and Electronics

1488 Bitter, Gary G., ed. **Macmillan Encyclopedia of Computers**. 2v. New York: Macmillan, 1992. $200.00. ISBN 0-02-897045-4.

The general nature of articles in this set means that the information is not outdated. The 200 entries deal with the role of computers in our world—in business, industry, education, government and personal life. Basics of hardware and software design are covered. Biographies of individuals who have played influential roles in computers are included, both historical in nature, with entries for Babbage and Byron, and recent with articles about Hopper, Gates and Jobs.

Other general topics cover artificial intelligence, careers, hacking, robotics, and viruses. Signed articles are arranged alphabetically and range from the 500 word biographies to 2,000-5,000 words for the topical essays. Tables and diagrams add to the clarity of the text which is intended for students and non-specialists. This is a reasonable purchase for base level computer information for high school libraries. [R: ARBA 93]

1489 Downing, Douglas and Michael Covington. **Dictionary of Computer Terms**. 4th ed. Woodbury, N.Y.: Barron's, 1995. 357p. $9.95pa. ISBN 0-8120-9023-3.

About 1,300 terms are defined and explained in this pocket-sized dictionary. Definitions range from one sentence to three pages and average about 30-50 words. Included are issues, applications, and technological terms. Line drawings, tables and diagrams add meaning. This is a useful small dictionary, consistently brought up to date with new editions. [R: ARBA 96]

1490 Freedman, Alan. **The Computer Glossary: The Complete Illustrated Desk Reference**. 7th ed. New York: AMACOM, 1995. 456p. $36.95; $24.95pa. ISBN 0-8144-0268-2; 0-8144-7872-7pa.

The author has kept this glossary up to date since its first publication in 1981. It is intended to provide meaningful definitions of every important computer term relating to both hardware and software. Its scope ranges from historical entries to current information and covers personal computers, minis, and mainframes. Basic terms, graphics and multimedia, communications, applications, programming and advanced concepts are all defined and explained. Contemporary and historical photographs add interest. Entries vary in length from short definitions to multiple pages for such topics as chips. The alphabetical arrangement, clear text and good design make this an excellent source for all professional collections and for high schools. Highly recommended. [R: ARBA 96]

1491 Gibilisco, Stan and Neil Sclater, eds. **Encyclopedia of Electronics**. 2d ed. Blue Ridge Summit, Pa.: Tab Professional and Reference Books, 1990. 960p. $69.50. ISBN 0-8306-3389-8.

Well written and well designed, this encyclopedia updates the 1985 edition and is directed toward both lay persons and scientists. The work contains over 3,000 long, detailed articles, ranging from a paragraph to over a page, that explain electronic terms. Every page includes one or more simple line drawings that give added support to the clear explanations, which are written in plain English. Only those computer terms that are important to the wide field of electronics are included. This impressive work is recommended for high schools. [R: ARBA 91; BL, 1 Nov 90]

1492 Gibilisco, Stan. **The Illustrated Dictionary of Electronics**. 7th ed. Blue Ridge Summit, Pa.: Tab Books, 1997. 736p. $39.95. ISBN 0-07-024186-4.

This often-updated dictionary is a standard source appropriate for high schools with electronics classes. Each edition lists new terms and updates others and extends and revises the drawings and diagrams that make it so useful. Definitions use little jargon and cover a broad range of subjects, including equipment and relevant mathematics and physics.

Earth Sciences

ATLASES

1493 **Small Blue Planet: The Real Picture World Atlas**. version 2.03. San Francisco: Now What Software, 1993, 1995. CD-ROM (Windows and Macintosh). $39.95.

The new reference feature in this outstanding CD-ROM is the gazetteer of nations with fact boxes and a pronunciation list of phrases in the country's official language. This feature, added to the views of the earth from space satellite photographs obtained from NASA, National Geographic, the U.S. Geologic Survey and the

Defense Department, make this CD-ROM the standard for excellence. Navigating the program is simple, the help screens describe each icon's function, and the photographs are glorious. Features such as applying a political map to a topographic map are elegant. Highly recommended for all secondary reference collections and for inspiring multi-discipline units.

1494 Van Rose, Susanna. **The Earth Atlas**.
E+   New York: Dorling Kindersley, 1994. 63p. $19.95. ISBN 1-56458-626-X.

This visual guide shows the forces that formed and continue to shape the earth today. Some articles are about geologic processes such as the formation of the planet, tectonic plates, volcanoes, earthquakes and erosion, while others deal with specific features such as the ocean floor, rivers and coastlines. A final section shows and compares igneous, sedimentary and metamorphic rocks. The strength of the work is its design and illustrations. The graphics, maps, photographs and their captions provide meaning and explanations to the text. The layouts are both appropriate and dramatic; they are not held to some design formula, but are tailored to each subject. A brief but adequate index gives access to specific information. Highly recommended for elementary and middle schools. [R: ARBA 95]

DICTIONARIES AND ENCYCLOPEDIAS

1495 Allaby, Ailsa, and Michael Allaby. **The Concise Oxford Dictionary of Earth Sciences**. New York: Oxford University Press, 1991. 410p. $12.95. ISBN 0-19-286125-5.

The scope of this dictionary for both specialists and students is the broad range of sciences that are included in the contemporary study of earth sciences: climatology, meteorology, economic geology, engineering geology, geochemistry, geophysics, hydrology, mineralogy, oceanography and petrology. Also covered are the philosophy, history and biography of the science. This is a dictionary of more than 6,000 entries intended to define terms; extended explanations are included for some topics. Some of the information comes from the *Oxford Dictionary of Natural History*. This dictionary is appropriate for high school collections. [R: ARBA 92]

1496 Dasch, E. Julius, ed. **Macmillan Encyclopedia of Earth Sciences**. 2v. New York: Macmillan, 1996. $190.00/ set. ISBN 0-02-883000-8.

This is a broad look at earth sciences, not in any way limited to geology. It brings the scientific backgrounds of physics, chemistry, biology and mathematics to an evolutionary look at earth sciences and environmental studies. Based on the major changes in the discipline within the 20th century, the work focuses on solid earth processes, surficial earth processes, earth resources and stewardship, earth sciences in the public eye and earth in space. Subdisciplines are covered, as well as some individuals. Issues such as "Women in Earth Science" are addressed. The 360 signed entries are of various lengths, are arranged alphabetically and have attached bibliographies. The articles are accompanied by tables and photographs and there are color inserts in each volume. Highly recommended for secondary schools. [R: ARBA 97]

1497 Levinson, David. **Human Environments: A Cross-Cultural Encyclopedia**. Santa Barbara, Calif.: ABC-CLIO, 1995. 284p. $49.50. ISBN 0-87436-784-0.

This is a unique approach to the environment as it describes general adaptive practices in subsistance, beliefs, and nature concepts and illustrates them by the practices of 150 cultural groups from around the world. Broad topics, such as agriculture, the annual cycle, ranching, seasons, time, and wind are arranged in alphabetical order. The long narratives then use examples from the cultural groups to examine good environmental behaviors. Cultures include the Native Americans and Amish from North America, and groups from Africa, Central and South America, Europe and Asia, and Oceania. Tables, maps and photographs are used appropriately throughout. This reference source would be particularly useful for cross-discipline units in science and world cultures. Recommended for high school collections. [R: ARBA 96]

HANDBOOKS

1498 Gregory, K. J., ed. **The Earth's Natural Forces**. New York: Oxford University Press, 1990. 256p. $45.00. ISBN 0-19-520860-9.

A profusely illustrated volume in The Illustrated Encyclopedia of World Geography series, this work surveys the Earth's regions and describes the geographical forces, climate, and natural phenomena (e.g. hurricanes) that created and modified the Earth's surface. Color maps depict the land, showing topographical features, and color photographs display the results of natural forces. Suggested for high schools. [R: ARBA 92; LJ, Jan 91; RBB, 15 Jan 91; WLB, Mar 91]

1499 Lambert, David. **Earth Science on File**. 1 looseleaf v. New York: Facts on File, 1988. $165.00. ISBN 0-8160-1625-9.

This collection of reproducible materials consists of more than 1,000 charts of geomorphic principles and phenomena, such as the Earth's formation, volcanoes, minerals, earthquakes, glaciers, types of rainfall, river formation, and geological ages. The drawings are grouped in several sections: "Earth and Space," "Shaping the Surface," "The Restless Rock," "Earth History," "Air and Ocean," "Resources," and "Maps, Tables and Scales." This is a valuable collection for grades 7 through 12. [R: ARBA 89; BL, June 89; BR, May/June 89; SBF, Sept/Oct 89]

CLIMATE AND WEATHER

1500 Conway, H. McKinley and Linda L. Liston, eds. **The Weather Handbook: A Summary of Weather Statistics for Selected Cities throughout the United States and Around the World**. Atlanta, Ga.: Conway Research, 1990. 548p. $39.95. ISBN 0-910436-290.

This is a convenient source of weather statistics covering 850 cities world wide (250 U.S. cities). Arranged by states or continent and country, the data are arranged in easy to read tables, but give only temperature, humidity, and precipitation. Other features include maps, tracking of weather disasters, and all-time records. There is an index. This is a supplement to almanacs and Internet weather sources. [R: ARBA 92]

1501 Day, John A. **Peterson First Guide to**
E+   **Clouds and Weather**. Boston: Houghton Mifflin, 1991. 128p. $4.95. ISBN 0-395-56268-6.

This is one of the simplified Peterson guides. This volume has more text than the other guides to explain the atmospheric background information necessary in weather observations. Divided into sections dealing with clouds, colors in the sky and precipitation, the photographs accompanying the narrative are excellent. There is an index, but like the others in the series, no table of contents. Highly recommended for all levels.

1502 Schneider, Stephen H., ed. **Encyclopedia of Climate and Weather**. 2v. New York: Oxford University Press, 1996. $195.00/set. ISBN 0-19-509485-9.

This is a multidiscipline encyclopedia set that brings together practical and scientific issues related to the modern study of weather. Scientific principles from physics, chemistry, astronomy, and ecology are applied to agriculture, forestry, recreation, aviation, shipping and human health. Coverage includes biomes, fuels, forests, oceans, glaciers and energy systems. History, political science and literature are also included. The alphabetically arranged articles vary from brief definitions to multiple columns; country and regional weather summaries are comprehensive. Some topics are treated in essays that are subdivided. A few biographies are included. Articles have bibliographies and there is a glossary, a directory of contributors, and an index. This is an excellent source and is highly recommended for middle and high school science collections. [R: ARBA 97]

FOSSILS AND PREHISTORIC LIFE

1503 **Dinosaur Hunter**. New York: DK Multimedia, 1996. CD-ROM (Windows). $29.95. ISBN 0-7894-0901-1.

There are many problems with this CD-ROM including navigation, large memory requirements and sluggishness of response even on a fast computer. The darkness of the pictures can be changed via options; one wonders why the default is so dark as to be unintelligible. Many video segments are disorienting, as they show living animals behaving as some scientists "believe" dinosaurs may have behaved, the only possible way to apply video technology to this topic. The video clips showing how dinosaur bones are recovered are entirely appropriate. If anything redeems the product, it is the clear and concise information about 50 dinosaur species, accessible most easily from an index with special views and good text and with cross-references to related species. Its ready reference capabilities are realized much more fully than its "virtual" museum features. Many elementary and middle school collections will find this a popular addition.

1504 Lambert, David. **The Ultimate**
E+ **Dinosaur Book**. New York: Dorling Kindersley, 1993. 192p. $29.95. ISBN 1-56458-304-X.

This is a narrative encyclopedia with pictures and charts. The chapters begin with an overview of dinosaurs: definition, origins, anatomy, extinction theories, and how the bones are found, retrieved and reconstructed. The introductory information is followed by profiles of 55 dinosaur genera, each with a two-page spread giving the name, a background narrative, its life and behavior, a picture of its skeleton, the fossil record, and restoration details. There is a fact file box showing where and when the dinosaur lived. Finally a 638 name pronouncing dictionary lists alternate and currently acceptable terms. There are both a glossary and an index. This beautiful and balanced work should be at all levels. Highly recommended. [R: ARBA 94]

1505 Lambert, David and the Diagram Group. **The Field Guide to Prehistoric Life**. New York: Facts on File, 1985. 256p. $73.00; $14.95pa. ISBN 0-8357-4250-4; 0-8160-1389-6pa.

Prehistoric animals and plants are included in this work which uses a field-guide structure to discuss prehistoric organisms and their fossil record. The focus is on pictures and descriptions of what organisms lived when. Life-like restorations, reconstructed skeletons, illustrations, diagrams and family trees supplement the text. The work is arranged in chapters each with a brief introduction, covering fossils in general, fossil plants, invertebrates, fish, amphibians, reptiles, birds, and mammals. There is a chronology and a section on fossil hunting. Books for further reading and an index are included. This is recommended for secondary collections. [R: ARBA 96]

1506 Sattler, Helen Roney. **The New Illustrated Dinosaur Dictionary**. New York: Lothrop, Lee & Shepard, 1990. 363p. $24.95. ISBN 0-688-08462-1.

An introduction provides a classification table of dinosaurs, a multipage pictorial chart showing relationships among them, and maps of the world as it may have been during the Mesozoic age. The main body of the work contains alphabetically arranged entries describing each dinosaur's physical appearance, specifying its family and eating habits, and indicating the fossil material found. Line drawings illustrate the dinosaur's distinguishing features. [R: BL, 15 Jan 90; SBF, Mar 91]

MINERALOGY AND GEMSTONES

1507 Pellant, Chris. **Rocks, Minerals & Fossils of the World**. Boston: Little, Brown, 1990. 175p. $19.95. ISBN 0-316-69796-6.

Secondary school students will find this a useful guide. Some 150 rocks are classified by type—igneous, metamorphic, or sedimentary. Identifying characteristics (crystal shape, color, luster, cleavage, and hardness) are provided for over 250 minerals. Fossils, which receive the most attention, are organized by such types as trilobites, corals, and crinoids. The work's strength lies in its beautiful photographs, which are equally useful for identification. [R: ARBA 91; BL, 15 June 90; Kliatt, Sept 90]

1508 Roberts, Willard Lincoln, and others. **Encyclopedia of Minerals**. 2d ed. New York: Chapman & Hall, 1990. 979p. $115.00. ISBN 0-442-27681-8.

This revision of a 1974 work, a basic reference tool on the subject, includes more than 400 new minerals discovered during the interim and expanded knowledge about others. The volume covers 3,200 minerals in all, giving chemical composition, hardness, density, cleavage, description, mode of occurrence, and references to additional sources. Black-and-white photographs and drawings support the text. A section of outstanding color photographs of over 300 minerals is a special feature. This encyclopedia is considered to be the best of its kind in English.

Food and Nutrition

□ _____ □

1509 Darling, Jennifer, ed. **Better Homes and Gardens New Cook Book**. 11th ed. Des Moines, Iowa: Meredith Books, 1997. 576p. $34.95. ISBN 0-69-620644-7.

About half of the 1,200 recipes in this edition are new, revised or updated to reflect new nutritional and lifestyle requirements. Menu planning, suggestions for lowering fat content and new cooking techniques are all featured. Unlike the new edition of *Joy of Cooking*, food preservation chapters have been retained. This standard cookbook is recommended for all collections.

1510 Herbst, Sharon Tyler. **Food Lover's Companion: Comprehensive Definitions of Over 3000 Food, Wine, and Culinary Terms.** New York: Barron's, 1990. 582p. $11.95. ISBN 0-8120-4156-9.

This small inexpensive volume contains a wealth of information on food. Entries, ranging from a sentence to two pages, define over 3,000 terms about dishes and sauces, kitchen equipment, styles of preparation, foreign foods, brand names, and more. Other features include pronunciations for foreign words, an additives directory, substitutes for ingredients, an herb and spice chart, and illustrations of meat cuts. Highly recommended. [R: ARBA 91; BL, 1 June 90]

1511 Montagne, Prosper. **Larousse Gastronomique: The New American Edition of the World's Greatest Culinary Encyclopedia**. Jenifer Harvey Lang, ed. New York: Crown, 1988. 1193p. $60.00. ISBN 0-517-57032-7.

This edition of this classic dictionary is a translation of a completely rewritten French revision, further edited for an American audience. Changes incorporate modern research, social change, improved equipment, and dietary concerns. The work is an integration of nutrition science and the art of cookery. Entries are in alphabetical order and include terms from cooking and food production including ingredients and methods. Recipes are interspersed throughout. This is a standard work recommended for high school collections.

1512 Moore, Carolyn E., and others.
E   **Young Chef's Nutrition Guide and Cookbook**. Hauppauge, N.Y.: Barron's Educational Series, 1990. 281p. $13.95. ISBN 0-8120-5789-9.

The recipes in this cookbook for beginners reflect changes in nutritional awareness and eating habits. In addition to ingredients and food value, each recipe lists utensils and indicates the level of skill required. Recommended for students in grades 4 to 6. [R: BL, 1 Jan 90; Kliatt, Sept 90; SLJ, Aug 90]

1513 Rinzler, Carol Ann. **The Complete Book of Herbs, Spices, and Condiments: From Garden to Kitchen to Medicine Chest**. New York: Henry Holt, 1991. 199p. $12.00. ISBN 0-8050-1618-X.

For each of the 112 entries on herbs, spices, and condiments, this work gives one or two pages of information about food preparation, cooking, nutritional value, chemical properties, medicinal benefits, how it can be grown and used, and possible side effects. A final section covers hazardous herbs. Indexed. Thirty-six line drawings illustrate the book, which is filled with fascinating information. [R: ARBA 91; BL, 1 June 90; LJ, Feb 90]

1514 Rombauer, Irma S. and others. **Joy of Cooking**. New York: Scribner, 1997. 1136p. $30.00. ISBN 0-684-81870-1.

This new version, the first edition in 20 years, and edited by Ethan Becker, the grandson of Irma Rombauer, is intended to bring this American classic cookbook up to date in nutrition, sophistication and cooking techniques. Many of the features of the best-selling standard have been retained, such as listing ingredients within the recipe at the point they are added. All libraries that kept reference copies of the older editions, will want to add this one, but perhaps keep the older editions as well. One looks in vain for several favorites in the new *Joy*; no directions for cooking terrapin, for example.

1515 Spence, Annette. **Nutrition**. New York: Facts on File, 1988. 128p. $18.95. ISBN 0-8160-1670-4.

Nutrition, a volume in the *Encyclopedia of Good Health*, relates eating habits to one's growth and development. The work provides essential, scientifically accurate information about nutrition in an easily understood style for young people ages 10 and up. Pictures, drawings, charts, and diagrams illustrate the text, which also is supported by a glossary, a bibliography, and an index. [R: ARBA 90; BR, Sept/Oct 89; RBB, Aug 89]

1516 Tamborlane, William V., ed. **The Yale Guide to Children's Nutrition**. New Haven, Conn.: Yale University Press, 1997. 415p. $18.00pa. ISBN 0-300-07159-8.

This collection of information from more than 50 physicians, nurses and dietitians covers nutrition from infancy to adolescence. The emphasis is on developmental nutrition. In addition to coverage of normal needs, the work covers specific common concerns such as family eating habits, vegetarianism, feeding sick children, special needs of athletes, and the dangers of alcohol for youth. Further information is given on eating disorders, childhood obesity and food allergies. Some recipes are included. This source will support nutrition and child care classes and is appropriate for both parent and reference collections; an excellent index provides access to specific data. Recommended for high schools.

1517 **The Visual Food Encyclopedia**. New York: Macmillan, 1996. 685p. $45.00. ISBN 0-02-861006-7.

This guide intends to be a summary of "everything known about food." An introduction discusses nutrients and then chapters organized by type of food (such as legumes, meats, fish, nuts and seeds, cereals and grains, crustaceans, poultry, milk and dairy, fruits and vegetables) list individual foods and tell their origin and description and give suggestions for purchasing, preparing, cooking and storing. Specific uses and charts of nutritional value are also included. More than 1,000 foods are described and more than 1,300 illustrations add greatly to the text. The arrangement makes the index indispensable for reference purposes. A glossary and a bibliography are attached. This beautiful book is highly recommended for secondary collections.

Health and Family

CHILD ABUSE

1518 Kinnear, Karen L. **Childhood Sexual Abuse: A Reference Handbook**. Santa Barbara, Calif.: ABC-CLIO, 1995. 333p. $39.50. ISBN 0-87436-691-7.

This volume in the Contemporary World Issues series is primarily concerned with the issue in the United States, and is flawed by awkward phrasing, incorrect grammar, and inappropriate use of slang terms. The purpose of the volume, as with the others in the series, is to survey the literature and other resources on the topic with a narrative that summarizes research findings. For subjects with controversial natures, balance is attempted, often without any indication of the quality of the research behind the disparate views. The introductory essays deal with such issues as the incest taboo, children at most risk, perpetrators, causes, effect, indicators, false allegations, intervention and treatment. Also included are sections on repressed/false memories, child exploitation and prostitution, ritual abuse, and child pornography. The rest of the work includes a chronology, biographical sketches, data and documents, a directory of organizations and a bibliography of print and nonprint resources. This source needs to be used with caution as a reference by high school students. [R: ARBA 96]

DEATH AND DYING

1519 Kastenbaum, Robert, and Beatrice Kastenbaum, eds. **Encyclopedia of Death**. Phoeniz, Ariz.: Oryz Press, 1989. 295p. $74.50. ISBN 0-89774-263-X.

This encyclopedia contains 130 succinct and cogent articles about death and dying. They analyze such issues as attitude toward death, the representation of death in literature and mythology, violent death, bereavement counseling, hospice care, funeral rites, and the meaning of death. Balanced treatment of opposing opinions is provided for controversial issues such as gun control, euthanasia, the death penalty, and prolonging life. Articles of one to several pages end with bibliographies of current material. Frequent cross-references, a 14-category guide to topics, and a subject index all provide outstanding access to the text. This important work is recommended for high schools. [R: ARBA 90; BL, 15 Feb 90; WLB, Jan 90]

DRUGS AND SUBSTANCE ABUSE

1520 **Drug, Alcohol, and Other Addictions: A Directory of Treatment Centers and Prevention Programs Nationwide**. 2d ed. Phoenix, Ariz.: Oryx Press, 1993. 646p. $68.50pa. ISBN 0-89774-623-6.

This directory of more than 12,000 programs and facilities engaged in prevention and treatment of addictions is arranged by state, city, and then alphabetically by name of program. Each entry includes basic directory information, descriptions of the addiction treated, setting, special programs, accommodations, payment methods, and any parent organization. It includes nationally known and sophisticated treatment centers as well as local groups such as high school chapters of SADD. It would have been helpful to include descriptions of staff and ages accepted for treatment, and the lack of an index makes it difficult to identify centers by name. Nonetheless, this source should be in high school collections. [R: ARBA 94]

1521 Jaffe, Jerome H., ed. **Encyclopedia of Drugs and Alcohol**. 4v. New York: Macmillan, 1995. $340.00/set. ISBN 0-02-897185-X.

The scope of this comprehensive encyclopedia is broader than the title indicates; it is an encyclopedia of substance use and abuse, and covers addictions of many types, including eating disorders. It was intended for non-specialists with information presented in non-technical language understandable by anyone who has had a high school biology class—many entries do not even require that background. The encyclopedia covers international issues such as drug trafficking and has articles on regions and countries and their specific drug issues. Included are entries about the effects of drugs on the body as well as many articles about social, political, historical, and legal issues. Prevention and treatment are well covered. There is a list of topics in volume one; articles are listed alphabetically with cross-references and an index in volume four. Topics include those which are often treated in high school sociology, psychology, and health classes such as addicted babies, anabolic steroids, caffeine, prescription drug abuse, and tobacco. Some entries are brief, identifying articles, while others are overview articles of five or more pages. All entries are signed with bibliographies. Photographs, diagrams, tables, and maps add to the narrative. In addition to the index, volume four has five appendices, including directories, statistics, state lists of treatment and prevention programs, and a schedule of controlled substances. Highly recommended for high schools and for middle schools with extensive drug education programs. [R: ARBA 97]

1522 O'Brien, Robert and Morris Chafetz. **The Encyclopedia of Alcoholism**. 2d ed. New York: Facts on File, 1991. 400p. $50.00. ISBN 0-8160-1955-X.

The more than 600 entries in this work, arranged alphabetically, cover a broad spectrum of topics and terms (e.g., alcoholic beverages, legal aspects, effects on the body, psychological and sociological effects, treatment, organizations). Clearly written entries range from a short identification to multipage articles.

Tables and graphs provide data on legal drinking age by state; alcohol use by such factors as age, race, and sex; tax revenues; and demographic correlation with drinking. The appendix includes extensive lists of national and state organizations and agencies. A lengthy bibliography and subject index conclude the volume. Highly recommended for middle and high schools. [R: ARBA 92; RRB, 1 Nov 91; WLB, Nov 91]

1523 O'Brien, Robert and others. **The Encyclopedia of Drug Abuse**. 2d ed. New York: Facts on File, 1990. 500p. $50.00. ISBN 0-8160-1956-8.

First published in 1984, the second edition was acclaimed as an outstanding reference source and highly recommended for students, seventh grade and up, with over 500 entries on all aspects of drug abuse. The text, alphabetically arranged, treats topics and terms related to biological, medical, social, and legal factors regarding drugs and their abuse; organizations and government agencies concerned with drug abuse and related diseases; drugs and pregnancy; abuse among specific social groups; and treatment options.

Appendixes include glossaries of street language and slang, tables of drug laws and patterns of usage, and sources of information. A bibliography and subject index conclude the volume. Highly recommended for middle and high school. A complementary volume is *The Encyclopedia of Alcoholism*.

FAMILY AND PARENTING

1524 Cline, Ruth K. J. **Focus on Families: A Reference Handbook**. Teenage Perspectives series. Santa Barbara, Calif.: ABC-CLIO, 1990. 233p. $39.50. ISBN 0-87436-508-2.

The Teenage Perspectives series, to which *Focus on Families* belongs, provides access to information of interest to adolescents. This work covers adoption, single-parent families, grandparents and other relatives, siblings, stepfamilies, divorce, children of divorce, and child abuse.

Each chapter provides background information; definitions of terms; statistics; and briefly annotated citations of fiction, nonfiction, articles, and nonprint materials. Some chapters describe support organizations, many with telephone numbers for hotlines and treatment centers. Author, subject, and title indexes give access to the text. Despite the inclusion of some dated material, this work is recommended for secondary schools, since no comparable guide is available. [R: ARBA 91; BL, 15 June 90; BR, Sept/Oct 90]

1525 DeFrancis, Beth. **The Parents' Resource Almanac: Where to Write, Who to Call, What to Buy, and How to Find Out Everything You Need to Know**. Holbrook, Mass.: B. Adams, 1994. 779p. $39.95; $15.00pa. ISBN 1-55850-396-X; 1-55850-394-3pa.

This combination directory and bibliography also has interspersed throughout boxed lists of information, tips, and guidelines. It is primarily a list of print and nonprint information sources and a directory of organizations concerned with children and child care. Included are a comprehensive array of sources such as free and inexpensive materials, government publications, books, periodicals, computer software, video tapes and mail order catalogs. Entries are by topic. There is a good general table of contents and detailed tables of contents for each chapter. Chapter headings include such topics as child development, child safety, health, food and nutrition, grooming and clothes, life changes and family options, education, choosing children's books, magazines for kids, kids and computers and family travel. Nine appendices are lists of such things as children's book publishers and zoos and aquariums. There is an index. Recommended for parents' collections and for the child care curriculum. [R: RBSL 96]

1526 Stoppard, Miriam. **Complete Baby and Child Care**. New York: Dorling Kindersley, 1995. 351p. $29.95. ISBN 1-56458-850-5.

This is an attractive and comprehensive book that will be useful for child care units and for parent collections. Its approach includes infants, toddlers, and 3–5 year olds, fathers, single-parent families, special needs children, child care, multiple births, vegetarian babies, baby massage, gender differences and treatments, and baby first aid as well as more traditional topics. Chapters on the newborn, everyday care, play and development, and family life are narrative with sidebars and many color illustrations. There is a useful address directory of 54 organizations concerned with children. An index completes the volume. Highly recommended. [R: ARBA 96]

FIRST AID AND SAFETY

1527 **The American Red Cross First Aid and Safety Handbook**. Boston: Little, Brown, 1992. 321p. $16.95. ISBN 0-316-73645-7.

Intended for the lay person, this is both a first aid guide and a text for preparing to deal with emergencies. It discusses prevention and intervention and how to recognize a life-threatening emergency. It also lists health precautions for the rescuer. Charts include the contents of a basic first aid kit. The main section of the book, which has its own table of contents, is an alphabetical listing of major situations that require first aid. Another section deals with home safety with a room-by-room inventory. It also discusses fire prevention and outdoor safety. Finally a red-banded emergency action guide illustrates the steps to take when giving first aid in a variety of situations. The entire book is illustrated with drawings and there are boxed rules, hints and steps. This is an essential work in all collections at all levels.

1528   Walker, Bonnie L., comp. **Injury Pre-
       vention for Young Children: A
       Research Guide**. Westport, Conn.:
       Greenwood Press, 1996. 182p.
       $69.50. ISBN 0-313-29686-3.

This annotated bibliography gives descriptive summaries about selected materials available in nine categories dealing with injury prevention training for those who work with children from infancy to age four. The first category is a general one which includes curriculum guides for child safety training. Other categories cover such topics as burns, firearms, choking, drowning, falls, diseases, and poisons. Materials are arranged alphabetically within the categories, and there are both author and subject indexes. The subject index would be more helpful if references were to items rather than page numbers. Librarians and teachers planning child safety units will find this source useful. School systems with preschool programs will need it to assist in building professional collections. [R: ARBA 97]

1529   Zydlo, Stanley M., and James A. Hill,
       eds. **The American Medical Associa-
       tion Handbook of First Aid**. New
       York: Random House, 1990. 332p.
       $8.95. ISBN 0-614-19674-4.

Although intended for home use, this first aid and emergency manual deserves a place on the reference shelf of all school library media centers. A general introduction to procedures is followed by an alphabetical section that has entries on diseases and injuries, giving background information, symptoms, a list of what to do, immediate action to take, and continual care. Included are sections on the Heimlich maneuver and sports injuries. [R: LJ, Mar 90]

THE HUMAN BODY

1530   **Atlas of Anatomy**. English ed. Haup-
       pauge, N.Y.: Barron's Educational
       Series, 1997. 104p. $19.95. ISBN 0-
       7641-5000-6.

Color plates of human anatomy are arranged by body system. Plates are labeled and some explanations are attached. An excellent index leads to specific information. This text is intended for the non-specialist and is appropriate for secondary school collections.

1531   Burnie, David. **The Concise Encyclo-
E+   pedia of the Human Body**. New
       York: Dorling Kindersley, 1995.
       160p. $19.95. ISBN 0-7894-0204-1.

Almost 400 illustrations accompany the textual explanations of the major human body systems and their functions. Arranged by system or function, two-page spreads combine text, drawings, tables and photographs which provide clear explanations of words, terms, phrases and concepts about the human body. Cross-reference boxes show interrelationships and encourage further explorations. Three excellent sections show reproduction, inheritance and growth and development. Two additional sections give brief listings of diseases and biographies of physiologists. There is a good general index. Highly recommended for upper elementary through high school.

1532   The Diagram Group. **The Human
       Body on File**. New York: Facts on
       File, 1983. 300p. $145.00 loose-leaf
       w/binder. ISBN 0-87196-706-5.

This collection of anatomical drawings, printed in black and white, is designed for classroom use and is reproducible with no copyright restrictions. The collection begins with a survey of the body and includes drawings of joints, bone structure, muscles, nerves, veins and arteries, and the lymphatic system. Additional sections focus on particular parts of the body (e.g., head, spine, organs). A final section traces human development from birth to age 15 and includes charts and graphs of blood pressure, temperature, menstrual cycles, growth, and weight. Identifying captions on the bottom of each page are keyed to numbers marked on the diagram. An index includes all terms used in the drawings. [R: BL, 15 Apr 84; SLJ, May 85; WLB, Nov 83]

1533 The Diagram Group, **Human Body on File: Physiology**. New York: Facts on File, 1996. 288p. $155.00 looseleaf w/binder. ISBN 0-81603-415-X.

This set of 270 charts supplements the focus on anatomy of the earlier *Human Body on File* set by adding text and illustration about the workings and structures of the body. A thorough table of contents as well as an index leads to the chapter divisions that discuss body components, cells and cell division, genetics and the major body systems. The looseleaf format provides a flexibility of presentation that makes this an essential part of secondary reference and teachers collections.

1534 **Ultimate Human Body**. version 2.0. New York: DK Multimedia, 1994. CD-ROM (Windows and Macintosh). $39.95. ISBN 1-7894-1204-7 (Windows); 1-7894-1208-X (Macintosh).

This easy to use CD-ROM is both a reference and teaching tool. Its visual and alphabetical indexes lead the user to text, illustration and pronunciation of body parts and functions. Hyperlinks to related topics are also useful. Graphics, zoom features and animations all combine to make this a good learning device. Recommended for all levels.

1535 Walker, Richard. **The Visual**
E+   **Dictionary of the Skeleton**. New York: Dorling Kindersley, 1995. 64p. $16.95. ISBN 0-7894-0135-5.

Brief narratives introduce each section of skeletons of various organisms. The pictures consist of wonderfully clear skeletons or parts of skeletons with major bones labeled. Included are both endoskeletons and exoskeletons as well as one double page of plant structures. The pictures can be used for both identification and comparison. The first part of the work shows entire skeletons of arthropods, fish, amphibians, reptiles, birds, sea mammals, land mammals and pre-humans, with double pull-out pages that display a large human skeleton. The last part of the dictionary shows bone structure and function, and detailed illustrations of joints, human and animal skulls, backbones, ribcages, pelvises, forelimbs, hindlimbs and hands and feet. Both the table of contents and an index provide access. This

outstanding source is highly recommended for all libraries. [R: ARBA 96]

1536 Westheimer, Ruth K., ed. **Dr. Ruth's Encyclopedia of Sex**. New York: Continuum Publishing, 1994. 319p. $29.50. ISBN 0-8264-0625-4.

The introduction to this book makes it clear it was intended for adolescents as well as older readers; specifically mentioned is the importance for school libraries as a source of materials to further "sexual literacy." The approaches to sexuality are from biological and medical, psychological, cultural, legal, and ethical and religious perspectives. The article on abortion is complete, illustrated and has subheadings reflecting all points of view. It is followed immediately by an article on abstinence. No human sexual behavior is omitted from this work, and all are treated with dignity, honesty and clarity. Articles vary in length, and all long articles have references to ethics, morals and religious beliefs. There is a glossary, a separate glossary of sexual slang, and a classified bibliography. An index complements the broad topical alphabetical arrangement. More than 50 expert contributors, mostly physicians, helped Dr. Ruth write the text which is graphically illustrated with both diagrams and photographs. Highly recommended for high school collections where it will support health, family living, and personal information needs. [R: ARBA 95]

HEALTH AND MEDICINE

See also **First Aid and Safety, Mental Health**.

1537 Ammer, Christine. **The New A to Z of Women's Health**. 3d ed. New York: Facts on File, 1995. 562p. $40.00. ISBN 0-8160-3121-5.

This work was first published in 1983 and this third edition has been updated and enlarged. Its emphasis is still gender-based medicine, notably obstetrics and gynecology, but more general medical information has been added. Arranged alphabetically with cross-references and an index, the entries range from one paragraph to several pages. Appendix A is a list of subject headings by category. Coverage includes the anatomy of reproduction, issues ranging from puberty through menopause to old age, all aspects of pregnancy, child birth, nursing, and infertility, and diseases and disorders (both mental and physical) of special interest to women. Diagnosis and both standard and alternate treatment are discussed, and basic issues of good health, fitness, and medical care are included. Articles are clear and non-technical and drawings and boxed information add meaning to the text. Appendix B is a list of resources and there is an index. Highly recommended for secondary collections. [R: ARBA 96]

1538 Berkow, Robert, ed. **The Merck Manual of Medical Information**. Home ed. Whitehouse Station, N.J.: Merck Research Laboratories, 1997. 1509p. $29.95. ISBN 0-911910-87-5.

This new home edition is based on the standard medical text, the *Merck Manual of Diagnosis and Therapy* which has been published since 1899, and contains nearly all of the text information except for laboratory work and detailed drug treatments. Information has been added on over-the-counter drugs, as well as overviews of anatomy and physiology. Preliminary information includes medical term prefixes, the fundamentals of anatomy, genetics, the aging body and death. The main part of the guide has descriptions of disorders by system or parts of systems. Each description of disorders begins with an introductory section about the biological function of that system. Separate sections deal with cancer, the immune system, infections, men's, women's and children's health issues, and accidents and injuries. Five appendices include, for example, common tests. The work is illustrated with diagrams, drawings, charts and tables. There is a good index. The information in this source is detailed and clear and based on up-to-date medical research. This is an excellent resource for all secondary collections.

1539 Boston Children's Hospital. **The New Child Health Encyclopedia**. New York: Delacorte, 1987. 768p. $22.95. ISBN 0-440-50646-8.

Parents and professionals responsible for the care of children will welcome this excellent encyclopedia, which is based on the experience and knowledge of the Boston Children's Hospital staff members. The book is arranged in four sections. "Keeping Children Healthy" surveys growth and development; "Finding Health Care

for Children" treats the child's hospitalization and visits to the doctor's office; "Emergencies" explains preparations that should be made for possible emergencies; and "Diseases and Symptoms" covers some 300 health concerns, giving signs and symptoms, diagnosis, cause, treatment, and prevention. [R: ARBA 89; LJ, 15 Nov 87]

1540 **Everything You Need to Know About Diseases**. Springhouse, Pa.: Springhouse Publishing, 1996. 918p. $24.95. ISBN 0-87434-822-6.

More than 500 illnesses and conditions are listed in one or two page entries that include causes, symptoms, diagnosis, treatment and self-care. The diseases are arranged by system in 16 chapters, with additional chapters on cancer, immune disorders, infections, injuries and genetic disorders. Charts, tables and drawings accompany the text and special features cover preventing disease and accident, advice for caregivers, and travel tips. An appendix lists mental and emotional disorders in chart format. There is an index. A companion volume, *Everything You Need to Know About Medical Treatments* (Springhouse, 1996) is arranged in a similar order and gives information about why treatments are given, when they should be done, what happens before and during treatment and possible side effects or complications. Each disorder lists drug, surgical, and other disorder-specific kinds of treatments. In addition to system disorders, there are sections on treatments for cancer, infections, traumatic injuries, pain, mental and emotional disorders and cosmetic treatments. The *Diseases* volume would be useful to support most high school health classes, and the *Treatments* volume is excellent if the curriculum deals with that aspect of health care.

1541 Freudenheim, Ellen. **Healthspeak: A Complete Dictionary of America's Health Care System**. New York: Facts on File, 1996. 310p. $30.00. ISBN 0-8160-3210-6.

The author is a writer with an M.A. in public health and has included more than 2,000 nonclinical terms with the basic vocabulary of the health care system. Terms come from insurance, public health, economics, primary care, medical ethics and consumer information sources and include diseases, treatments, laws, and organizations. Entries are alphabetical with cross-references, and an index. Definitions are brief, but complete and charts and tables add to clarity. There are bibliographic references. This source will be useful for health, government, sociology and family life courses and is highly recommended for high school collections. [R: ARBA 97]

1542 **Macmillan Health Encyclopedia**. 9v. New York: Macmillan, 1993. $360.00/ set. ISBN 0-02-897439-5.

The nine volumes in this encyclopedia are arranged by general topic; within each volume/ topic, arrangement is alphabetical. The volumes cover body systems, causes and treatments of diseases and disorders, nutrition and fitness, emotional and mental health, sexuality, legal and illegal drugs, environmental health and healthcare systems. First aid and general health issues are also covered; the entire work is holistic in approach. The arrangement of the volumes leads to some oddities: endometriosis is in the sexuality volume rather than in the disease volumes, some less important functions are treated in multiple volumes, illustrations are repeated from volume to volume. None of the information is treated in great depth, although the approach is honest and explicit. Each volume has its own glossary and index and there is a cumulative index. Recommended for secondary collections. [R: ARBA 94]

1543 Macpherson, Gordon, ed. **Black's Medical Dictionary**. 37th ed. Totowa, N.J.: Barnes & Noble, 1992. 656p. $95.00. ISBN 0-389-20989-9.

This standard dictionary, published regularly since 1906, includes more than 5,000 terms relating to medicine, anatomy, physiology, pathology and therapeutics. Each new edition adds terms and revises existing entries, and the 37th edition added a brief appendix of first-aid care and extended the treatment of drug categories. The text is concise and understandable and the clear language, comprehensive treatment and useful drawings and diagrams overcome any inconveniences of British spellings and address referrals. Highly recommended as a basic medical dictionary for any secondary health collection. [R: ARBA 93]

1544 **The Marshall Cavendish Encyclopedia of Health**. 14v. North Bellmore, N.Y.: Marshall Cavendish, 1991. $299.95/set. ISBN 1-85435-203-2.

This encyclopedia covers anatomy, systems and functions, diseases, first aid, treatments, and drugs in more than 900 one to six page articles with colorful illustrations. Each entry is accompanied by a yellow title bar with questions and answers. The articles have subheadings, photographs and diagrams, and boxed related facts. The last volume contains a first aid handbook, an illustrated glossary, a classified article title list and an index. Highly recommended for middle school and high school health collections. [R: ARBA 92]

1545 Matthews, John R. **Eating Disorders**. New York: Facts on File, 1991. 168p. $24.95. ISBN 0-8160-1911-8.

Part information source and part research guide, this is a beginning handbook for secondary students. The first half of the book discusses the history and treatment of obesity, anorexia and other eating disorders with a chronology from 1689, a summary of legal issues and a few biographies. The second half is a guide to further research with a glossary, directories of programs, organizations, libraries and special collections and a classified bibliography of articles, books, government publications, pamphlets, brochures, and audiovisual materials. The index refers to both parts of the work. There is no mention of child abuse as a cause of eating disorders, and there are other omissions; nonetheless this is a reasonable starting point for reports on the topic.

1546 **Mayo Clinic Family Health 1996 Edition**. Minneapolis, Minn.: IVI Publishing, 1996. CD-ROM (Windows, Macintosh). $39.99.

1547 Larson, David E., ed. **Mayo Clinic Family Health Book**. 2d ed. New York: William Morrow, 1996. 1,500p. $42.50. ISBN 0-688-14478-0.

More than 400 Mayo Clinic physicians and other professionals contributed to this clearly written and useful guide. The second edition provides updates and revisions and a new emphasis on both wellness and self-help. Current developments in medicines, nutrition, tests, exercise and the health care system have been incorporated. More sections of illustrations have been added to extend understanding of back pain, hypertension, heart disease and breast cancer. The source covers more than 1,000 diseases and illnesses.

Arrangement is by five broad subject areas: a chronological health review by age category, wellness, first aid, diseases by systems, and medical care. Appendices, a glossary, a directory of resources and an excellent index conclude the volume. Highly recommended for secondary health classes.

1548 Micheli, Lyle J. **The Sports Medicine Bible: Prevent, Detect, and Treat Your Sports Injuries Through the Latest Medical Techniques**. New York: HarperPerennial, 1995. 339p. $20.00pa. ISBN 0-06-273143-2.

Very much a '90s book about overuse injuries rather than critical trauma caused by sport accidents, this book emphasizes fitness and prevention as well as discussing specific types of injuries. The first sections are about fitness, prevention, strength and flexibility and about diagnosing, treating and rehabilitating injuries in general. The most significant part of the book deals with specific injuries to every part of the body from foot to head and neck with special chapters devoted to skin, problems especially important to females and the elderly, and nutrition. For each of the special body areas, there are sections on symptoms, causes, risks, concerns, self-help, medication, doctor's input, rehabilitation and recovery time. The narrative is supplemented with boxed discussions, tables and drawings, and there is an index. Secondary schools may want both reference and circulating copies. [R: ARBA 96]

1549 Rinzler, Carol Ann. **Feed a Cold, Starve a Fever: A Dictionary of Medical Folklore**. New York: Facts on File, 1991. 226p. $21.95. ISBN 0-8160-2394-8.

The purpose of this dictionary is to separate fact from legend as compared to the latest medical research findings. The resulting work is a wonderfully entertaining and browsable list of folk beliefs about conditions, cures and prevention. Each of the alphabetically arranged entries describe the belief, offer a quick analysis ("alas, no," "absolutely," "bad idea," "close enough," "caution") and summarize the evidence. Tables and charts, a selected bibliography and an index add to the usefulness of the work. Highly recommended as a source to support all secondary health classes. [R: ARBA 92]

1550 Thorpy, Michael J., and Jan Yager. **The Encyclopedia of Sleep and Sleep Disorders**. New York: Facts on File, 1991. 298p. $50.00. ISBN 0-8160-1870-7.

The first single-volume reference work devoted exclusively to sleep and sleep disorders, this authoritative work, written in clear, nontechnical language, is designed for laypersons and health professionals. Beginning with two general essays on the history of sleep research, the main part of the book is composed of over 800 alphabetically arranged entries that describe technical, common, and slang sleep terminology and that incorporate current information on treatment alternatives.

Many entries include bibliographies that cite professional literature as well as popular magazines, newspapers, and books. Organizations that supply information on sleep disorders, sleep centers and laboratories, and national and international classification of sleep disorders are all listed in the appendix. [R: BL, 1 Jan 91; SLJ, May 91]

1551 **The Wellness Encyclopedia: The Comprehensive Family Resource for Safeguarding Health and Preventing Illness**. By the editors of the University of California, Berkeley, Wellness Letter. Boston: Houghton Mifflin, 1991. 541p. $17.95. ISBN 0-395-53363-5.

The Wellness Letter is a publication of the School of Public Health at Berkeley, and this encyclopedia is an expanded and updated compilation of the information presented in the newsletter. This is one of the first sources to emphasize guidelines for preventative health care and one of its purposes is to clarify the kind of superficial information presented to the public by television and periodical media sources. After an introduction about wellness, chapters discuss longevity, nutrition, exercise, self care, and the environment and safety. Information boxes present detailed essays. There is a glossary and an index. Recommended for secondary health/wellness collections. [R: ARBA 92]

MENTAL HEALTH

1552 Bruno, Frank Joe. **The Family Mental Health Encyclopedia**. New York:

Wiley, 1989. 422p, $32.50. ISBN 0-471-63573-1.

This volume consists of articles on mental health written in clear, concise language for the lay person. Entries include terms and concepts (e.g., anxiety, stress, addiction), drugs, persons in the field (e.g., Carl Jung), important schools of thought, and movements. Over 700 alphabetically arranged subject entries and 130 name entries range from brief identification to short articles. When specialized terms are used within an entry, they are italicized and defined at the point of use. Cross-references are generously used. Suggested for high school level. [R: ARBA 90; BL, 1 Sept 89; LJ, 1 Sept 89; SBF, Jan 90]

Mathematics

DICTIONARIES AND ENCYCLOPEDIAS

1553 Borowski, E. J., and J. M. Borwein. **The HarperCollins Dictionary of Mathematics**. New York: Harper-Collins, 1991. 659p. $18.00. ISBN 0-06-461019-5.

This math dictionary is intended for secondary school to master's degree students and includes about 4,000 entries with diagrams and charts. It includes terms, descriptions, and examples and deals with people, devices, operations and properties. It omits computing and economic terminology. Many general and specific topics of importance to high school students and teachers are included such as set theory, topology and the famous Konigsberg Bridge problem. Appendices include tales, symbols and conventions. This is a useful supplement to other math dictionaries for high school collections. [R: ARBA 93]

1554 Downing, Douglas. **Dictionary of Mathematics Terms**. 2d ed. New York: Barron's, 1995. 393p. $10.95pa. ISBN 0-8120-3097-4.

Intended for high school and college math students and teachers, this pocket-sized dictionary covers algebra, analytic geometry, arithmetic, calculus, computers, geometry, logic, matrices, linear programming, probability and statistics, sets, trigonometry, and vectors. It includes theorems, diagrams, and equations and has a list of mathematical symbols. Appendices include a common logarithm table, a trig function table, standard normal distributions, chi-square, t table, t distribution, and f distribution tables. It is a useful addition to high school math dictionary collections. [R: ARBA 96]

1555 James, Robert C., and Glenn James. **Mathematics Dictionary**. 5th ed. New York: Van Nostrand Reinhold, 1992. 548p. $47.50. ISBN 0-442-00741-8.

First published in 1942 this now-standard math dictionary includes terms high school, undergraduate, and graduate students might encounter in math courses. Arranged alphabetically with cross-references the dictionary includes concepts, theorems, formulae, devices, proper names, and branches of the discipline. Definitions are clear and precise. The fifth edition revises and updates topics and adds multilingual indexing in French, German, Russian and Spanish. Highly recommended for high school libraries and for middle schools with advanced math programs.

1556 Lord, John. **Sizes: The Illustrated**
E+   **Encyclopedia**. New York: HarperPerennial, 1995. 374p. $15.00pa. ISBN 0-06-273228-5.

This unusual source gives units of measure from the 20th century back to ancient times. Items from pillows and rings to sunscreens to time to tires to hurricanes to human organs and chicken eggs are arranged in alphabetical order with charts and illustrations. Conversion appendices and an index complete the text. Highly recommended for all collections. [R: ARBA 96]

1557 Schwartzman, Steven. **The Words of**
E+   **Mathematics: An Etymological Dictionary of Mathematical Terms Used in English**. Washington, D.C.: Mathematical Association of America,

1994. 261p. $27.00pa. ISBN 0-88385-511-9.

This dictionary is unique in that it gives the history and background of math terms that commonly appear in elementary, secondary and college curricula. Each of the alphabetically arranged items gives a glossary-like entry explaining the history of the term as well as its part of speech and the source of information. An appendix gives the roots of the terms. Recommended for all levels; this source will be useful to both math and language arts and to units combining the two courses. [R: ARBA 95]

1558 West, Beverly Henderson, and others. **Prentice-Hall Encyclopedia of Mathematics**. Englewood Cliffs, N.J.: Prentice-Hall, 1982. 683p. $39.50. ISBN 0-13-696013-8.

Intended for students from grade 6 upward, this work contains 80 articles arranged alphabetically, algebra to zero. Clearly written essays provide histories, explanations, formulas, and definitions of terms, supported by annotated bibliographies. Seven hundred photographs, drawings, and diagrams illustrate the text. Appendixes contain tables of measures, cubes, roots, and logarithms, and general and biographical indexes give access to the text. This outstanding work is highly recommended for middle and high school libraries. [R: SLJ, Mar 83; WLB, Feb 83]

HANDBOOKS

1559 **CRC Standard Mathematical Tables and Formulae**. 30th ed. Boca Raton, Fla.: CRC Press, 1996. 812p. $39.95. ISBN 0-8493-2479-3.

Both students and teachers need access to this source which gives constants and conversions, and tables used in algebra, analysis, geometry, trigonometry, calculus, probability and statistics, and other mathematics. The appendix gives a list of math symbols and notations. This 30th edition is rearranged, has expanded sections on logic, and several rewritten sections. There is an index. Recommended for middle schools with advanced math classes and for all high schools. [R: ARBA 97]

1560 Hopkins, Nigel J., John W. Mayne, and John R. Hudson. **The Numbers You Need**. Detroit, Mich.: Gale Research, 1992. 349p. $45.00. ISBN 0-8103-8373-X.

This handbook of practical mathematics covers number facts and processes about money, health and fitness, weather and environment, gambling, sports, hobbies, everyday living and popular science. Intended for the consumer, it is a guide that supports new national math standards for integrating math practices with realistic math experiences. Highly recommended for all secondary collections. [R: ARBA 93]

Natural Resource Sciences/ Environmental Science

CONSERVATION

1561 Sayer, Jeffrey A., and Caroline S. Harcourt, eds. **The Conservation Atlas of Tropical Forests: The Americas**. New York: Macmillan, 1996. $128.50. ISBN 0-13-340886-8.

1562 Sayer, Jeffrey A., N. Mark Collins, and Caroline S. Harcourt, eds. **The Conservation Atlas of Tropical Forests: Africa**. New York: Macmillan,

1992. 288p. $128.50. ISBN 0-13-175332-0.

1563 Sayer, Jeffrey A., N. Mark Collins, and Timothy C. Whitmore, eds. **The Conservation Atlas of Tropical Forests: Asia and the Pacific**. New York: Simon & Schuster, 1991. 256p. $128.50. ISBN 0-13-179227-X.

These three companion volumes cover the world's main tropical rainforests. The arrangement of each work follows the same pattern with an introduction covering the status and issues of the rainforest in the particular region. This overview is followed by alphabetically arranged and signed country studies with boxed fact sections, descriptions, specific country issues and governmental policies, conservation efforts, maps, references and other highlighted and boxed entries where appropriate. Each volume has a glossary, species indexes and a general index. Highly recommended for high school environmental collections because of their comprehensive nature and because of the authority behind this set.

ENERGY

1564 Kruschke, Earl R., and Byron M. Jackson. **Nuclear Energy Policy: A Reference Handbook**. Santa Barbara, Calif.: ABC-CLIO, 1990. 246p. $39.50. ISBN 0-87436-238-5.

This survey of the history and development of foreign and domestic nuclear energy policy is part of the Contemporary World Issues series. The authors have attempted to present a judicious description of pro and con positions. Chapters include a chronology; biographies of individuals on both sides of the issue; excerpts from important documents, treaties, and speeches; and a directory of organizations. An annotated bibliography of print and nonprint materials, a glossary, and an index conclude the volume. This useful introduction to an important public issue is recommended for high schools. [R: ARBA 92; BL, 15 Nov 90; BR, Nov/Dec 90]

ENVIRONMENT
Atlases

1565 Lean, Geoffrey. **Atlas of the Environment**. 3d ed. Santa Barbara, Calif.: ABC-CLIO, 1994. 192p. $39.50. ISBN 0-87436-768-9.

This source gives basic facts about natural and human environments and how people affect nature. Forests, wetlands, deserts, croplands, mountains, rivers and seas are discussed by current status, by threats to them and by solutions to their conservation. Arranged by these major biomes, information about populations, foot and water resources, health and education issues is provided to enable people to have a basis for decision making. Other sections emphasize specific global issues such as ozone and the greenhouse effect. The narrative is supplemented with maps and tables. There is a good table of contents but no index. Appropriate for secondary collections. [R: ARBA 95]

Dictionaries and Encyclopedias

1566 Allaby, Michael, ed. **The Concise Oxford Dictionary of Ecology**. New York: Oxford University Press, 1994. 415p. $35.00; $12.95pa. ISBN 0-19-211689-4; 0-19-286160-3pa.

The more than 5,000 terms in this dictionary are of use to multiple disciplines: geographers, architects, planners and students. The terms come from ecology, environmental pollution, conservation, biogeography, animal behavior, evolutionary theory, earth science, botany, and biography. The source avoids political issues, but explains concepts and describes natural processes. It is arranged in alphabetical order with cross-references, especially to embedded definitions. Entries vary in length from one sentence to half a column. The language is fairly technical and this limits the source to high school collections. [R: ARBA 96]

1567 Allaby, Michael. **Dictionary of the Environment**. 3d ed. New York: New York University Press, 1989. 423p. $80.00. ISBN 0-8147-0591-X.

This dictionary defines technical terms specific to the study of the environment and terms from science in general, making it a useful reference tool for the high school collection. Written in nontechnical language, the entries also cite relevant government agencies, voluntary organizations, important regulations, and significant environmental disasters (for which Allaby provides a table of dates, locations, and details). There are numerous cross-references. [R: ARBA 90; BL, 15 Sept 90; SBF, Sept/Oct 89]

1568 Coffel, Steve. **Encyclopedia of Garbage**. New York: Facts on File, 1996. 311p. $60.00. ISBN 0-8160-3135-5.

This work is broader than its title might at first indicate; it is concerned with pollution and all aspects of waste disposal. Included in its entries are issues about all items for disposal from chemicals to appliances as well as techniques and methods of disposal, organizations, laws, people, and hazards. Arranged alphabetically with cross-references and an index, the articles range from short definitions to long entries. It is illustrated with appropriate drawings which help to explain the topics. There is a good selected bibliography. The writing is clear and non-technical and the source is recommended for middle school and high school collections. [R: ARBA 97]

1569 Franck, Irene M. and David Brownstone. **The Green Encyclopedia**. New York: Prentice Hall, 1992. 486p. $35.00; $20.00pa. ISBN 0-13-365685-3; 0-13-365677-2pa.

Clear and balanced entries outline what is known and what is controversial about environmental issues. Articles are arranged alphabetically and include organizations, agencies, people, terms, chemicals, fields of study, kinds of pollution, disasters, conservation methods, and ecosystems. Sources of information and action guides appear in boxed insets. After the alphabetical entries there is a special information section with lists and tables about animal rights, ecotourism, endangered species, wetlands, toxic chemicals, and Superfund sites. "Environmental ABC" is a list of abbreviations used in environmental sciences, and there is a list of related books. This is a convenient and comprehensive source and is highly recommended for secondary collections. [R: ARBA 94]

1570 Jones, Gareth, and others. **The HarperCollins Dictionary of Environmental Science**. New York: HarperPerennial, 1992. 453p. $13.00. ISBN 0-06-461040-3.

Good clear definitions with examples make this a good dictionary for secondary school students. It covers the physical and biological sciences behind the human-built environment and its agricultural and economic underpinnings. The alphabetically arranged entries result in a balanced approach, from cost-benefit analyses to Greenpeace and including the basic international terminology. Drawings, diagrams and charts supplement the text. This source is not overly attractive, but will be extremely useful to both middle and high school students and teachers. [R: ARBA 93]

1571 **McGraw-Hill Encyclopedia of Environmental Science & Engineering**. New York: McGraw-Hill, 1993. 749p. $85.50. ISBN 0-07-051396-1.

Former editions of this work were titled *Encyclopedia of Environmental Science*. This encyclopedia intends to present the current state of knowledge about the environment as well as prospects for the future. It is concerned with the biosphere and all external influences on it and the effects of human activity on Earth's ecosystem. Arranged alphabetically from acid rain to zooplankton, the articles are multi-paged and subdivided. Photos, graphs, charts, equations, and diagrams accompany the signed articles which include bibliographies. Many articles come from the *McGraw-Hill Encyclopedia of Science and Technology* and libraries who hold that title will not need to duplicate the information. For high schools which find the entire encyclopedia too expensive, this volume is a way to add excellent information on this single topic. [R: ARBA 94]

1572 Paehlke, Robert, ed. **Conservation and Environmentalism: An Encyclopedia**. New York: Garland, 1995. 771p. $95.00. ISBN 0-8240-6101-2.

This source represents a viewpoint that is one of principled concern about the environment; it is a good complement to *The Environmental Almanac* which discusses environmental issues in a cost-benefit ratio perspective. The 500 entries range from one column to four (about two pages) and are signed and have bibliographies. Articles fall into three basic categories: ecology, pollution and sustainability. Included are concepts, issues, practices, places, organizations, government agencies, laws, species, habitats, pollutants, efforts toward sustainability, publications and people. The English-speaking world is emphasized, but global concerns are also covered. Arrangement is alphabetical, but headings are sometimes unhelpful as in "Former Soviet Union." An index aids access. Recommended as a useful reference source for environmental studies programs in high schools. [R: ARBA 97]

1573 Stevenson, L. Harold and Bruce C. Wyman. **The Facts on File Dictionary of Environmental Science**. New York: Facts on File, 1991. 294p. $24.95. ISBN 0-8160-2317-4.

This is a comprehensive collection of terms used in environmental studies from a wide range of disciplines such as chemistry, biology, ecology, geology, physics, forestry, engineering, meteorology and slang. Definitions range from one sentence to long paragraphs and reflect world-wide issues while reflecting an American emphasis. Diagrams, drawings, charts and figures support the definitions. Arrangement is alphabetical and there is an index. Appropriate for both middle and senior high collections. [R: ARBA 92]

Directories

1574 Cichonski, Thomas J., and Karen Hill, eds. **Recycling Sourcebook: A Guide to Recyclable Materials, Case Studies, Organizations, Agencies, and Publications.** Detroit, Mich.: Gale Research, 1993. 563p. $75.00. ISBN 0-8103-8855-3.

This is both a list of resources and a set of descriptions of methods and approaches to the collection and recovery, processing, markets, and products involved with recycling. Twenty-eight articles discuss specific materials from paper and plastics to packaging, batteries and tires and diapers. Articles are signed and do not follow exact patterns. Essays also discuss recycling in communities and institutions. A source list of 4,000 organizations, agencies and publications is included as is an appendix of products and materials and a 200 term glossary. There is a subject index. This is a useful combination of resources and information and is recommended for high school collections. [R: ARBA 94]

1575 Jessup, Deborah Hitchcock. **Guide to State Environmental Programs.** 3d ed. Washington, D.C.: Bureau of National Affairs, 1994. 700p. $75.00. ISBN 0-87179-847-6.

Entries for environmental programs for air pollution, water quality, waste disposal and groundwater protection are arranged alphabetically by state. Each entry gives program descriptions and directory information for the overseeing agency. There are discussions of each state's general approach to environmental regulation as well as the impact of federal guidelines and regulations on the states. Appendices provide directory information for the Environmental Protection Agency, the Army Corps of Engineers, state and local agencies and states that have decentralized programs.

1576 Seredich, John, ed. **Your Resource Guide to Environmental Organizations: Includes the Purposes, Programs, Accomplishments, Volunteer Opportunities, Publications and Membership Benefits of 150 Environmental Organizations.** Irvine, Calif.: Smiling Dolphins Press, 1991. 514p. $15.95. ISBN 1-879072-00-9.

Descriptions of 150 national and international nonprofit environmental organizations comprise this directory. A two- to four-page entry for each gives its purpose, programs, accomplishments, publications, and membership benefits. Addresses and telephone numbers of federal and state agencies are also included. [R: ARBA 92; LJ, 15 June 91]

Handbooks and Almanacs

1577 Altman, Roberta. **The Complete Book of Home Environmental Hazards.** New York: Facts on File, 1990. 290p. $24.95. ISBN 0-8160-2095-7.

The three sections of this work are "Environmental Hazards Inside the House" (the largest part), "Environmental Hazards Outside the House," and "Buying an Environmentally Sound House." The volume includes the latest information on radon, asbestos, lead, water, pesticides, formaldehyde, nuclear power and weapons plants, and hazardous waste sites. Each section describes the problem, effects on people, regulations, testing, and solutions. Maps locate hazardous waste and nuclear power plant sites. Each chapter concludes with a state-by-state list of government agencies and consumer groups to contact for further information. [R: ARBA 92; BL, 1 Sept 90; LJ, 1 June 90]

1578 Chase, Jayni. **Blueprint for a Green School.** New York: Scholastic, 1995. 670p. $59.95. ISBN 0-590-49830-4.
E+

This work leaves no pesticide unchallenged, no empty calorie acceptable, and no recycling opportunity ignored. Covering 40 environmental topics, it explains for administrators, teachers, parents, students and maintenance staff how to make a school and its grounds environmentally safe. While warning against pollutants and toxic substances, the book gives positive suggestions for student activities and activism. Charts and drawings accompany the text. Resources include specific materials for children. There is an index. Recommended for all levels, but appropriate especially for elementary and middle schools. [R: ARBA 96]

1579 Gorman, Martha. **Environmental Hazards: Marine Pollution; A Reference Handbook**. Santa Barbara, Calif.: ABC-CLIO, 1993. 252p. $39.50. ISBN 0-87436-641-0.

Following the format of other titles in the Contemporary Word Issues series, this work focuses on pollution of salt waters and estuaries, often ignored or treated within larger water pollution issues. The marine pollution discussed is largely concerned with waters surrounding the United States. After an introduction which gives definitions and describes major pollutants there is a chronology which traces the issue from 300 to 1993. Statistics and legal issues and other data form a valuable section of the book, while the series proscribed biographical sketches are of limited use. The directory of organizations includes some international institutions. The bibliography of print and nonprint sources includes videos and television and radio series. There is a good glossary and an index. Recommended for secondary schools. [R: ARBA 95]

1580 Hoyle, Russ, ed. **Gale Environmental Almanac**. Detroit, Mich.: Gale Research, 1993. 684p. $79.95. ISBN 0-8103-8877-4.

Signed narrative chapters with references attempt to discuss the complexity of environmental issues. The work specifically does not advocate any single viewpoint; of course that in itself is a viewpoint. The almanac examines the links between environmental protection and economic growth, states that scientific certainty in environmental issues is an illusion, promotes the need for legal reform and better technology, and believes that development will continue to make environmental issues a global concern. The purpose of the source is to create environmental literacy by discussing science, law, federal governance, and diplomacy in the context of major developments and issues. The narratives begin with background and historical information, including a chronology from 1841 to 1992 which acts as a framework for the early chapters. Sections are included on science, business, law and government, and international aspects. A final section groups chapters related to the current environmental crises such as climate change and pollution's effects on health. Tables, maps, charts and diagrams add to the narrative; many of the tables provide ready reference information: lists of laws, pesticides, federal agencies and national parks are interspersed throughout. There is a glossary and an index. This work reflects the risk assessment-cost management perspective of environmental studies and thus provides a balance to the many sources which treat the subject from an ideological approach. For this reason it is highly recommended for high school collections. [R: ARBA 95]

1581 Kimball, Debi. **Recycling in America: A Reference Handbook**. Santa Barbara, Calif.: ABC-CLIO, 1992. 254p. $39.50. ISBN 0-87436-663-1.

This guide to both information and resources provides a comprehensive background to the issues involved in waste disposal. It covers environmental impacts of current practice, processes, legislation and long-term principles of recycling. A chronology of waste disposal from 10,000 B.C. to 1990 indicates the scope of the issues and there are sections of biographies, facts, data, and laws and regulations. Reference materials include print resources, videos, databases and networks. There is a glossary as well as a list of acronyms, and an index. Useful for both middle school and high school collections. [R: ARBA 94]

1582 Miller, E. Willard and Ruby M. Miller. **Environmental Hazards: Radioactive Materials and Wastes: A Reference Handbook**. Santa Barbara, Calif.: ABC-CLIO, 1990. 298p. $39.50. ISBN 0-87436-234-2.

The use of radioactive materials by our society has both positive and negative consequences. Radiation is used in medicine for diagnosis and treatment, and nuclear power is a less expensive source of energy. But the dangers of atomic weapons, fear of another Chernobyl, and the safe handling and disposal of radioactive waste all present problems.

This work offers a comprehensive and unbiased treatment of the nature of radiation: its natural and manmade sources, emergency planning and preparedness, effects on health, exposure standards, a history of nuclear development, disposal, and international control of radioactive waste. The volume also contains an extensive bibliography that includes a list of audiovisual materials. [R: ARBA 91; BL, 15 Sept 90; LJ, 15 Apr 90; SLJ, May 91]

1583 Rosenberg, Kenneth A. **Wilderness Preservation: A Reference Handbook**. Santa Barbara, Calif.: ABC-CLIO, 1994. 292p. $39.50. ISBN 0-87436-731-X.

Issues and history of wilderness preservation and conservation in the United States are the focus of this guide which also provides sources for further study. The introduction defines preservation in terms of public lands and both state and private preserves. Issues are divided by kind of wilderness area—forests, rivers and lakes, prairies, deserts and wetlands with a separate section on Alaska. A chronology covers 30,000–2,000 B.C. to the present. Biographical sketches, statistics, quotations and legislation are additional features. A list of protected federal lands are arranged by type—parks, seashores, and so on. There is a directory of concerned organizations and agencies, a classified list of print resources and a list of films, videos and databases. Maps, figures and tables appear throughout the text. There is a glossary and an index. This is a useful source and would be appropriate for all secondary collections. [R: SLJ, May 1995]

NATURAL HISTORY
See also **Biology, Botany, Conservation (Environmental Science), Earth Science, Zoology**.

1584 Allaby, Michael, ed. **The Oxford Dictionary of Natural History**. New York: Oxford University Press, 1985. 688p. $55.00. ISBN 0-19-217720-6.

Intended for students and amateur naturalists, this dictionary defines over 12,000 terms, with emphasis on the scientific names of plants and animals worldwide. It also includes terms from botany, zoology and related areas such as ecology, statistics, earth sciences, atmospheric sciences, biochemistry, and genetics. Cross-references connect common and scientific names. This dictionary is the basis for many of the *Oxford Concise Dictionary* titles. It is suitable for high school students and teachers. [R: ARBA 87; RBB, 15 Oct 86]

1585 Durrell, Gerald, and Lee Durrell. **The Amateur Naturalist**. New York: Knopf, 1982. 320p. $25.00. ISBN 0-679-72837-6.

This guide to observing nature is designed for young adults. The lavishly illustrated work describes 17 nature walks in the woods, along the shore, in marshlands, and even in one's own backyard. Projects, techniques, and equipment are carefully explained. Indexed. Recommended for middle and high school collections. [R: BL, 1 Dec 83]

1586 Emanoil, Mary, ed. **Encyclopedia of Endangered Species**. Detroit, Mich.: Gale Research, 1994. 1230p. $95.00. ISBN 0-8103-8857-X.

This comprehensive guide to 700 plants and animals threatened world wide also lists other endangered species, organizations that are involved and materials for further information. Criteria for inclusion include rankings by the U.S. Fish and Wildlife Service, The World Conservation Union, and the Convention on International Trade in Endangered Species of Wild Fauna & Flora. Distinctions are made between categories such as vulnerable, rare, endangered and threatened. Arranged by class—mammals, birds, reptiles and so on with a separate section for plants—each species is described in one or two pages, sometimes accompanied by a black and white photograph. Boxed information gives the common and scientific name and classification, status and range. Narratives give descriptions and biology, habitat and current distributions and history of conservation measures. There are maps and two indexes: geographic and species which gives both common and scientific names. The text is simple to access and understand. Recommended for upper elementary and secondary collections. [R: ARBA 95]

1587 Lincoln, R. J., and G. A. Boxshall. **The Cambridge Illustrated Dictionary of Natural History**. New York: Cambridge University Press, 1987. 413p. $49.95. ISBN 0-521-30551-9.

Cambridge successfully addresses the needs of a nonscholarly audience for the meaning of terminology related to "the rich diversity of living organisms and their habitats." The clear and concise definitions of technical terms in natural history, illustrated by 700 line drawings, are appropriate for advanced high school students. This work is more selective in its coverage of terminology than *The Oxford Dictionary of Natural History*, but it contains illustrations, which the Oxford dictionary does not. [R: ARBA 88; BL, 1 Mar 88; WLB, Nov 87]

1588   Lowe, David W., and others, eds. **The Official World Wildlife Fund Guide to Endangered Species of North America**. 2v. Osprey, Fla.: Beacham, 1990. $95.00. ISBN 0-933833-17-2.

Volume one of this guide lists endangered plants and mammals while volume two includes birds, reptiles, amphibians, fishes, insects and other invertebrates. Information is authoritative and presented clearly. Many illustrations, some in color, make this an attractive set. New editions adding species newly endangered have been given sequential volume numbers. Now in preparation are new volumes one and two, which are international in scope. These excellent sources are highly recommended for secondary collections.

1589   **The Way Nature Works**. New York: Macmillan, 1992. 359p. $35.00. ISBN 0-02-508110-1.

This one-volume nature encyclopedia has two sections on earth science and seven sections on life science. The earth science sections emphasize how the planet was formed and is changed, and how its soils, oceans, deserts, rivers and lakes and atmosphere are structured. The life science sections deal with evolution, behavior and ecology rather than descriptions of individual organisms. The sections are divided into subsections with explanatory titles; for example, the section "Movement and Shelter" contains a subsection "On the Wing: How Birds and Bats Fly." Each section contains its own table of contents, and each subsection consists of a double-page spread with narrative, illustrations with captions, and a list of cross-references ("connections"). There is a glossary, and an index aids in access. This source is a good supplement to the current approaches to science and is highly recommended for middle school collections. [R: ARBA 94]

Pets

See also **Mammals (Zoology)**.

GENERAL

1590   Fox, Michael W. **The New Animal
E+   Doctor's Answer Book**. New York: Newmarket Press, 1989. 299p. $14.95. ISBN 1-55704-035-4.

Questions collected from the author's practice as a veterinarian and columnist for *McCall's* magazine are answered with sound and sympathetic advice. Many of the inquiries focus on common health problems of animals, but some indicate unusual concerns. Fox also discusses the physical needs of pets and provides insights into the psychology of animal behavior. The volume covers birds, cats, dogs, fishes, gerbils, guinea pigs, and some less common pets. Recommended for elementary and middle schools.

CAGE BIRDS

1591   Vriends, Matthew M. **Simon &
E+   Schuster's Guide to Pet Birds**. New York: Simon & Schuster, 1984. 319p. $15.00. ISBN 0-671-50696-X.

Vriends' guide describes 206 kinds of birds; makes suggestions on choosing one as a pet; and discusses their care, diet and nutrition, housing needs, and diseases. Data on each bird includes classification, characteristics, habitat and distribution in the wild, and behavior patterns, plus other information such as color, whether they sing or talk, food preferences, and whether they should be housed singly or in pairs. The text is illustrated with excellent photographs.

CATS

1592   Taylor, David, with Daphne Negus.
E+   **The Ultimate Cat Book**. New York: Simon & Schuster, 1989. 192p. $29.95. ISBN 0-671-68649-6.

This Dorling Kindersley guide to 100 varieties of domesticated cats covers basic subjects, such as behavior, origins, grooming, health, first aid, and diet, and gives tips on showing cats, reproduction, and other subjects. Each breed, divided into two alphabetical sections (longhair and shorthair), is concisely described and illustrated by 750 superb full-color photographs. Extensive diagrams, charts, and tables provide information on birthing, maternal behavior, and kitten development. Taylor is a British veterinarian, and Negus is an editor of *Cat World International* magazine. A circulating copy is recommended along with one for reference.

DOGS

1593 American Kennel Club. **AKC Complete Dog Book**. 19th ed. New York: Macmillan, 1997. 724p. $32.95. ISBN 0-87605-047-X.

The official American Kennel Club guide describes the standards for the 134 breeds recognized by the A.K.C. More than two-thirds of the breeds have seen changes in standards since the seventeenth edition. Arrangement is by groups, and each breed is described by history and standards. Separate sections discuss the history of the dog and issues of owning, caring for, and training dogs. Black and white photographs accompany breed descriptions and color inserts illustrate many breeds. There is a glossary, sample A.K.C. registration forms and an index. This is a basic, if not beautiful, dog guide and should be in all libraries. [R: ARBA 93]

1594 Bulanda, Susan. **Everything You**
E+ **Always Wanted to Know About Dogs: The Canine Source Book**. 4th ed. Wilsonville, Oreg.: Doral Publishing, 1994. $24.95pa. ISBN 0-944875-35-1.

This is a directory, so it tells only where to find out everything you always wanted to know about dogs. The kinds of addresses found here include organizations, companies and agencies that deal with training, breeding, showing, and using dogs. There is a list of associations that provide support dogs for the disabled. Periodicals about dogs and even catalogs which carry supplies for dogs are also included. Both librarians and students will find this useful.

1595 **The Complete Dog Book for Kids:**
E+ **Official Publication of the American Kennel Club**. New York: Howell, 1996. 274p. $29.95. ISBN 0-87605-458-0.

This is an attractive alternate to the full *AKC Dog Book* for elementary collections. There are full-color portraits of all AKC recognized breeds and limited breed information of interest to young readers.

1596 Fogle, Bruce. **The Encyclopedia of**
E+ **the Dog**. New York: Dorling Kindersley, 1995. 312p. $39.95. ISBN 0-7894-0149-5.

This attractive guide provides coverage of dogs from an international rather than U.S. viewpoint, so the organization of the work is unlike that used by the American Kennel Club. After an introduction, chapters discuss the development and evolution of the dog, dogs and their relationships with humans in folklore, art, religion, literature, film and sport, the anatomy and physiology of the dog, dog behavior and care. A large section is devoted to breeds; most entries are half a page and give boxed key facts such as country and date of origin, use, life expectancy, and weight and height ranges. Lavish color pictures illustrate each breed entry. A glossary and an index complete the volume. Highly recommended for all levels. [R: ARBA 96]

1597 Sylvester, Patricia. **The Reader's Digest Illustrated Book of Dogs**. 2d ed. Pleasantville, N.Y.: Reader's Digest Association, 1994. 384p. $27.00. ISBN 0-88850-205-2.

This highly recommended book for students in grades 7 through 12 includes a general history of dogs, clues to identifying different breeds, and two page descriptions of 145 breeds. For each one the work gives origin, countries where it is registered, nicknames, characteristics (e.g., temperament, general suitability), and appearance. Each breed is illustrated by a full-color photograph. Charts provide information on requirements such as exercise, grooming, and feeding. [R: BL, 1 Jan 90; BR, Mar/Apr 90]

Physics

☐ ── ☐

1598 Lerner, Rita G., and George L. Trigg. **Encyclopedia of Physics**. 2d ed. New York: VCH, 1991. 1408p. $95.00. ISBN 0-89573-752-3.

This edition updates information from the 1980 first edition and incorporates changes in such topics as superconductivity, fractal geometry, chaos theory, solid states, astronomy and artificial intelligence. More than 500 signed entries are arranged alphabetically and are labeled as elementary, intermediate or advanced in difficulty. Generally the articles are more technical than those in the *Macmillan Encyclopedia of Physics*. Tables, photographs and diagrams aid understanding. Both a list of main entries and an index help in access. This is a good additional source for high schools. [R: ARBA 92]

1599 Rigden, John S., ed. **Macmillan Encyclopedia of Physics**. 4v. New York: Simon & Schuster Macmillan, 1996. $400.00/set. ISBN 0-02-897359-3.

This is at once the most comprehensive and most approachable set about physics. It covers basic concepts and phenomena, devices and equipment, concepts, theories and principles, effects, fundamental constants, laws, and includes electricity, particles, space, states of matter as well as subdisciplines. Historical and present insights are presented; there are 50 biographies of deceased physicists. There is a list of categories, a list of articles, common abbreviations and math symbols, and a list of abbreviations to the journals which appear in the bibliographies attached to the signed two to three page articles. Arrangement is alphabetical and there is a glossary and an index. The writing is clear and the volume design leads to understanding; good black and white photographs and diagrams accompany many articles. High school teachers and students will find this work most helpful. Recommended. [R: ARBA 97]

☐ Science and Technology in General ☐

See also **Retrospective Bibliographies (Collection Management)**.

BIOGRAPHY

1600 Bailey, Martha J. **American Women of Science: A Biographical Dictionary**. Santa Barbara, Calif.: ABC-CLIO, 1994. 463p. $60.00. ISBN 0-87436-740-9.

The focus of this source is American women scientists from the 19th and early 20th centuries; women who began their careers after 1950 are not covered. Inclusion is based on such things as entries in *Men and Women of Science*, election to the National Academy of Science or employment by federal or state agencies. An introduction discusses the difficulties American women have had in becoming scientists, and identifies

areas in which they have been employed from universities to museums to business and industry. Each entry lists basic information such as education, career, accomplishments followed by about one page of narrative and a bibliography. Arrangement is alphabetical with a table of contents for each letter. There is a volume bibliography and an index. This is a useful source for both women's studies and science. [R: SLJ, Nov 1994]

1601 Daintith, John. **A Biographical Encyclopedia of Scientists**. 2d ed. 2v. Philadelphia, Pa.: Institute of Physics, 1994. $190.00/set. ISBN 0-75033-0287-9.

This is a revision and expansion of the 1981 edition and includes biographies of 2,000 scientists from earliest times to the present; entries are overwhelmingly male and western. The scope of disciplines is quite broad, including the basic sciences as well as some names from medicine, mathematics, engineering, technology, anthropology, and psychology. Each entry gives basic biographical data (though not many personal details) and emphasizes the main scientific achievements and the nature and importance of those achievements. Length varies from one column to Heisenberg's four columns, Faraday's six columns and Einstein's nine columns. The appendices include a chronology, a list of scientific institutions and a booklist. There are separate name and subject indexes. The language is non-technical and there are occasional drawings, sketches and diagrams to aid in understanding. For secondary schools where scientific biography is needed. [R: ARBA 95]

1602 **Dictionary of Scientific Biography**. 18v. New York, Scribner, 1970–1980, 1990. $1,500.00. ISBNs vary by volume.

The first 14 volumes form the base set of biographies of famous scientists from all times and places. Limited to the pure sciences and math, individuals from technology, medicine, philosophy and behavioral or social sciences are generally excluded. All entries are of those who died before 1970. The first supplement (volume 15) included names omitted from the original set as well as topical essays about science and scientists in India, Mesopotamia, Ancient Egypt, Japan, and the Mayan culture. Volume 16 is an index and a list of scientists by field. The second supplement (volumes 17 and 18, 1990) has some names omitted from the original, but primarily consists of scientists who died between 1970 and 1981. There are relatively few women, even in the supplement, showing the lack of women in science up to 1981 rather than bias on the part of the editors. The format and design of the set and the structure of the essays is similar to the *Dictionary of American Biography*. This set can be used by middle and high school students. Also available is the *Concise Dictionary of Scientific Biography*; a one-volume abridgment which includes only "essential facts" about the entries from the original version.

1603 **The Grolier Library of Science Biographies**. 10v. Danbury, Conn.: Grolier, 1997. $299.00. ISBN 0-7172-7626-0.

This beginning biographical source has world coverage of men and women from all aspects of science. Each of the 2,000 entries includes a portrait, basic biographical information and background data about the era. There is a glossary and a chronology as well as an index. Recommended for secondary collections.

1604 Millar, David, et al. **The Cambridge Dictionary of Scientists**. New York: Cambridge University Press, 1996. 387p. $39.95. ISBN 0-521-56185-X.

This is an updated edition of *Chambers Concise Dictionary of Scientists* (1990). About 1,000 brief biographies of scientists, inventors and mathematicians are arranged alphabetically. Some topical entries are also included. While the biographies are short, there are often interesting personal details that enliven the entries. Recommended for middle and high school collections.

1605 Saari, Peggy and Stephen Allison, eds. **Scientists: The Lives and Works of 150 Scientists**. 3v. Detroit, Mich.: U•X•L, 1996. $99.95. ISBN 0-7876-0959-5.

The strength of this biographical set is that a special effort was made to include women and minorities among the 150 scientists sketched. Both historical and contemporary figures are included. As appropriate for the intended audience, entries feature childhood experiences and motivations for entering the sciences. There is a chronology and an index. Recommended for middle school collections, and some high schools may also find it useful.

1606 Shearer, Benjamin F., and Barbara S. Shearer, eds. **Notable Women in the Life Sciences: A Biographical Dictionary**. Westport, Conn.: Greenwood Press, 1996. 440p. $49.95. ISBN 0-313-29302-3.

1607 Shearer, Benjamin F., and Barbara S. Shearer, eds. **Notable Women in the Physical Sciences: A Biographical Dictionary**. Westport, Conn.: Greenwood Press, 1997. 504p. $49.95. ISBN 0-313-29303-1.

These companion volumes each cover about 100 women scientists from all periods and places, but emphasizing the twentieth century and America. The scope of sciences represented is broad. Entries are arranged alphabetically and average about six pages. Articles are signed by the contributors, some of whom are scientists, some librarians, and some graduate students; entries are somewhat uneven in approach and quality. Each article includes the individual's name and dates, education, contributions and publications. The narrative primarily discusses the women's career with mention of some personal details. Notes and bibliographies are included. An appendix lists the entries by field and by awards won and there is an index. Recommended to support both women's studies and science courses in high schools. [R: SLJ, Nov 96]

1608 Stanley, Autumn. **Mothers and Daughters of Invention: Notes for a Revised History**. Lanham, Md.: Scarecrow Press, 1993. 1116p. $97.50. ISBN 0-8108-2586-4.

The author spent ten years identifying forgotten and neglected women who made creative contributions to agriculture, medicine, mechanics and computer technology. The work points out that the question is not "Why weren't there any women inventors?" but rather, "Why don't we know about the women who were inventors?" The format is uninviting with the 1,100 + pages crammed with information; the subject arrangement and the index help with accessing names, inventions and events. There are 26 supporting appendices with more text. The bibliography is more than 100 pages. Even though this may present more than anyone wants to know about either women or inventors, it is fascinating reading, and despite the author's protestation, comprehensive. Highly recommended for any secondary school with curricular units on inventors or women's studies. [R: ARBA 94]

CHRONOLOGIES

1609 Bruno, Leonard C. **Science & Technology Firsts**. Detroit, Mich.: Gale Research, 1997. 636p. $65.00. ISBN 0-7876-0256-6.

This is a chronology divided into 12 chapters which cover such disciplines as astronomy, biology, chemistry, communications, computers, mathematics and physics. Sometimes the place-

ment of items into only one category was a fine point and cross-referencing is only within chapters; thus the index is essential when looking for a specific event. Coverage is international; science is emphasized more than technology. Most of the brief entries are by year; month and day are given when appropriate. Illustrations are excellent. Entries include such events as the first domesticated animal (dogs in 9,000 B.C.), the first beer brewed (ca. 800 B.C.), and the first cookbook written by a woman (1670). Useful where chronologies and trivia are popular. [R: SLJ, May 97]

1610 Hellemans, Alexander, and Bryan Bunch. **The Timetables of Science: A Chronology of the Most Important People and Events in the History of Science**. New York: Touchstone Books, 1991. 660p. $20.00. ISBN 0-671-73328-1.

The Timetables of Science begins in 2,400,000 B.C. ("Hominids in Africa manufacture stone tools") and ends with events in late May 1988, with 10,000 significant scientific developments, events, and famous scientists in between.

This book is divided into nine major time periods, determined by events important to the evolution of science. Each section is prefaced by a geographical, political, and cultural survey of the era. Entries vary from very brief to some 80 words. About 100 essays scattered throughout the volume focus on special topics (e.g., classic volcanoes). Indexed by name and subject. This is an excellent reference work for high schools.

1611 Malone, John. **Predicting the Future: From Jules Verne to Bill Gates**. New York: M. Evans, 1997. 194p. $19.95. ISBN 0-87131-830-X.

Predictions from many well-known individuals including Jules Verne, Henry Ford and Albert Einstein are arranged chronologically from 1858 to 1996. A one or two page essay explains the reasons for the accuracy or inaccuracy of the prediction. Most deal with science, medicine and technology. There are indexes of predictions and predictors. This complements other scientific chronologies and may suggest activities to science teachers as well as providing ready reference for secondary collections.

DICTIONARIES AND ENCYCLOPEDIAS

1612 Concise Oxford Science Dictionary. 3d ed. New York: Oxford University Press, 1996. 794p. $12.95. ISBN 0-19-280033-7.

More than 8,500 entries are included in this dictionary which covers the basic sciences: chemistry, biology, physics, earth science and paleontology with some terms from astronomy, math and computer science. The entries are alphabetical with extensive cross-referencing. Charts, tables and diagrams are used for additional clarity. While the entries are typically concise and comprehensible, some are more technical and challenging. Recommended for high schools. [R: ARBA 92]

1613 Considine, Douglas M., and Glenn Considine, eds. **Van Nostrand's Scientific Encyclopedia**. 8th ed. 2v. New York: Van Nostrand Reinhold, 1995. $269.95. ISBN 0-442-01864-9.

This now standard general science encyclopedia is comprehensive in its coverage of a broad scope of the basic and applied sciences, including medicine, computer science and engineering. Articles are concise and clear, beginning with summaries and expanding to detailed essays, and accompanied by photographs, diagrams, charts and graphs. Each new edition updates articles and adds new entries for recent discoveries; new in this edition is information about space and genetics. Highly recommended as a first purchase in secondary libraries.

1614 DISCovering Science. Detroit, Mich.: Gale Research, 1996. CD-ROM. $600.00. ISBN 0-8103-7162.

This is a science encyclopedia on a disc. Data pulled from Gale's science databases are searchable via word or person, by a hierarchical search path and with Boolean functions. Links between related entries show relationships as well as providing easy navigation. Coverage is comprehensive with biographies, terms, concepts, theories and discoveries from physical and applied science and mathematics. Directories, career information and experiments are also included. Photographs, maps, drawings, video clips and animation all serve to enhance the textual information. Recommended for high schools.

1615 Eoker, Ronald L. **Dictionary of Science & Creationism**. Buffalo, N.Y.: Prometheus Books, 1990. 263p. $41.95. ISBN 0-87975-549-0.

This dictionary presents the pro-evolution position in the creationist-evolutionist controversy. Concise nontechnical articles provide an "overview of all scientific areas that relate to evolutionary theory." Each entry presents the scientific position and the author's understanding of the creationist interpretations, often referring to works in the extensive bibliography. Not only does the dictionary define terms used by each side but it also cites court cases, such as the Scopes trial, *Edwards vs. Aguillard*, and *McLean vs. Arkansas*. Teachers, administrators, and school board members will welcome this volume. [R: ARBA 91; BL, 1 May 90]

1616 Eyewitness Encyclopedia of Science. New York: DK Multimedia, 1995. CD-ROM (Windows and Macintosh). $39.95. ISBN 0-7894-0092-8.

About 1,700 entries are organized into four categories of science and a biography section. Chemistry, physics, life science and math are further divided into subjects within each discipline. Navigating is easy with clicks on various levers and dials, with hyperlinks and with a good full index. Animation, videos, still photos and audio clips, including read-aloud text are all used to illustrate meaning and not just for effect. Recommended both for browsing and reference in middle schools and high schools.

1617 Graham, Ian and Paul Sterry. **Questions & Answers Book of Science Facts**. New York: Facts on File, 1997. 80p. $19.95. ISBN 0-8160-3655-1.
E+

This attractive book is arranged by broad general topics—space, the world, nature and science/technology. Within each topic, there are several subject areas, and within the subjects are questions and answers. Questions are worthwhile and answers are clear; illustrations accompany each set. The complete index provides access to the work as a reference tool, but it is also useful for browsing and for topic selection. Recommended for upper elementary and middle school collections.

1618 **Great Scientific Achievements**. 10v. Pasadena, Calif.: Salem Press, 1994. $250.00. ISBN 0-89356-860-0.

The time period covered by this set is actually from the mid 1880s to 1994. Arranged chronologically throughout the volumes the 367 articles show the development of scientific theory and application via innovations and inventions. Each entry begins with brief facts and data and an illustration. Clear narratives explain the theory or practice. Twenty-one categories of science are covered, including agriculture, energy, computer science and mathematics. Each volume has a contents page and four indexes to all of the volumes: chronological, alphabetical by key word and title, category and name. Volume ten has a timeline and a general subject index. Recommended for middle schools, and some high schools may find it useful as well.

1619 Jackson, Donald C. **Great American Bridges and Dams**. Washington, D.C.: Preservation Press, 1988. 357p. $19.95pa. ISBN 0-471-14385-5.

Older bridges and dams of technological and historical significance are described in this unusual volume, published by the National Trust of Historical Preservation. The introduction presents a historical survey of each engineering feat (e.g., "Bridges: Spanning the Nation"; "Dams: Controlling a Precious Resource"). The text groups bridges and dams into six geographical regions, which, in turn, are arranged alphabetically by state and site. Basic information is highlighted in the outside margin: name, location, engineer, construction company, year completed, and description of structure. Indexed. Appropriate for secondary schools. [R: ARBA 89; LJ, 1 June 88]

1620 Lafferty, Peter, and Julian Rowe, eds. **The Dictionary of Science**. New York: Simon & Schuster, 1994. 678p. $50.00. ISBN 0-13-304718-0.

This attractive dictionary includes terms from both science and technology. The comprehensive list of topics covered comes from such disciplines as astronomy, biology, mathematics, chemistry and physics as well as medicine, agriculture, food technology, communications, photography, computing and energy. Entries vary in length from one sentence definitions to one column with some whole-page signed entries on special topics. Boxed facts and quotations and puzzles are interspersed throughout the dictionary. Diagrams and tables help add meaning to the text. Published in Great Britain as the *Hutchinson Dictionary of Science,* the narrative is interesting and readable and is intended for both students and the general reader. Appendices include tables of constants, the periodic table, Nobel Prize winners and a list of great scientists. A thematic index complements the alphabetical arrangement. This excellent dictionary is recommended for all secondary collections. [R: SLJ, Nov 94]

1621 **Macmillan Encyclopedia of Science**.
E+   2d ed. 12v. New York: Macmillan, 1997. $325.00. ISBN 0-02-864556-1.

This encyclopedia is organized by subject; each volume deals with a different discipline within science and technology. Progressing from matter and energy to astronomy to earth science to life science to technology, volumes present information in simple terms with colorful illustrations. Each volume contains a glossary and index for that volume, while the final volume contains a combined glossary and general index for the entire set as well as a biographical dictionary of scientists. This is an excellent science encyclopedia for elementary schools, and many middle schools will also find it appropriate.

1622 **McGraw-Hill Encyclopedia of Science and Technology**. 8th ed. 20v. New York: McGraw-Hill, 1997. $1,750.00/set. ISBN 0-07-911504-7.

1623 **McGraw-Hill Multimedia Encyclopedia of Science and Technology**. New York: McGraw-Hill, 1994. CD-ROM (Windows). $1,300.00; $325 (updates).

The standard comprehensive science encyclopedia now contains more than 7,000 entries, including about 1,600 new articles in the latest edition. New findings in biochemistry, paleontology, microbiology and meteorology are also reflected in updates and revisions of older articles. About 13,000 illustrations of all types add to the text. Entries begin with definitions and overviews and then become as complex as is appropriate for the subject matter. All major topics in science and technology are covered including such areas as acoustics, animal anatomy, food engineering, telecommunication and virology. One of the strengths of the set is its indexing: 60,0000 cross-references and a 170,000 entry analytical index provide exceptional access. There is also a topical index by discipline and a section of study guides. This outstanding source is highly recommended for high school collections. The publisher reprints information from this set in a variety of specialized encyclopedias, such as the *Encyclopedia of Environmental Science & Engineering*.

1624 **The New Book of Popular Science**. 6v. Danbury, Conn.: Grolier, 1996. $249.00. ISBN 0-7172-1220-3.

This set is a standard work for all levels from upper elementary through high school. The six volumes are arranged by subject and cover 12 science areas, beginning with astronomy, space science and mathematics. An excellent index in volume six covers the whole set. Articles are long, but written for clarity in a step-by-step format, and each article provides a good general introduction to a topic. Each edition becomes more attractive with more color illustrations and a better layout. Highly recommended.

1625 Parker, Sybil P., ed. **McGraw-Hill Dictionary of Scientific and Technical Terms**. 5th ed. New York: McGraw-Hill, 1994. 2194p. $110.50. ISBN 0-07-042333-4.

More than 100,000 terms with more than 120,000 clear definitions are given in simple language in this dictionary intended for the general population. Words and terms, acronyms and abbreviations are included. Pronunciation and synonyms are given. The typeface and arrangement are also designed for clarity. There are many appendices with such tables as atomic symbols and numbers, math notation, geologic time scale and classification of organisms. Also included here is a biographical listing of 1,500 important scientists. This is a comprehensive and useful dictionary and is appropriate for all secondary collections. The dictionary includes a computer disk version. [R: ARBA 95]

1626 Travers, Bridget, ed. **World of Scientific Discovery**. Detroit, Mich.: Gale Research, 1994. 776p. $69.95. ISBN 0-8103-8492-2.

This encyclopedia treats scientific discovery as a process rather than as a series of separate events. Entries include both topics and biographies integrated into one alphabetical list. Articles tell what and who but also discuss how and why; they cover the knowledge that led to discoveries and discuss the social impact as well. Disciplines covered include the sciences of agriculture, astronomy, biochemistry, biology, chemistry, ecology, geology, mathematics, medicine and health, meteorology, oceanology, pharmacy and physics. The focus is from the late sixteenth century to the present, although some older important discoveries are covered. An attempt to include women and minorities in the 1,083 entries is partly successful. There is both a subject index by the sciences and a general index. Highly recommended for middle and senior high collections. [R: ARBA 95]

1627 Travers, Bridget, and Jeffrey Muhr,
E+ eds. **World of Invention**. Detroit, Mich.: Gale Research, 1994. 770p. $69.95. ISBN 0-8103-8375-6.

This is a comprehensive encyclopedia of both well-known and lesser-known inventors and inventions. Coverage is international and historic, but the emphasis is the period from the beginning of the Industrial Revolution and western, if not American. Attempts have been made to include both women and minority inventors. There are 785 non-biographical entries and 361 biographical entries arranged alphabetically with cross-referencing. The articles average about one column, but there are larger umbrella articles on such broad and complex topics such as aircraft. Invention is defined as a product that owes existence to some person or persons, and is separated from the notion of discovery which is treated in *World of Scientific Discovery*. Coverage is from all fields such as automotive engineering, clothing, everyday items, food, household appliances, musical instruments and weapons, so that one will find inventions as wide-ranging as contact lenses, elevators, false teeth and Teflon. There is a subject index by category and a general index. Written especially for students in non-technical language, this source is appropriate for upper elementary through high school. [R: ARBA 95]

1628 **U·X·L Science CD**. Detroit, Mich.: Gale Research, 1998. CD-ROM (Windows, Macintosh). $400.00/building (30 users). ISBN 0-78761784-9 (Windows); 0-7876-1710-5 (Macintosh).

Broad coverage of physical, social, earth and life sciences as well as mathematics, anthropology, the environment and engineering is available from this database of 2,000 entries with over 1,500 illustrations and 75 video and animation clips. Searching is by using an index, entering terms or browsing a timeline. Students may print or save to disk the information they need. Intended for middle schools, this combination of science dictionary and encyclopedia will be useful as well in upper elementary.

1629 **The World Book Encyclopedia of**
E+   **Science**. 8v. Chicago: World Book, 1997. $149.00. ISBN 0-7166-3394-9.

The eight volumes in the set each cover one aspect of science: astronomy, physics, chemistry, earth science, botany, zoology, physiology and biography. Concepts are discussed in simple language with illustrations and glossaries to explain scientific terms. This set is appropriate for upper elementary and middle school collections, and for high schools needing basic science information.

HANDBOOKS AND YEARBOOKS

1630 Barnes-Svarney, Patricia L. **The New York Public Library Science Desk Reference**. New York: Macmillan, 1995. 668p. $39.95. ISBN 0-02-860403-2.

The basics of major areas of science are described and illustrated in this work that resembles the general *New York Public Library Desk Reference*. Chapters on scientific measurements and symbols as well as a section on time are followed by chapters devoted to the major scientific disciplines as well as meteorology, environmental science, computer science and engineering. Each chapter has a narrative about the discipline and charts, facts and other illustrations. Biographies of famous scientists, historical highlights, terms and a bibliography relevant to each science are included. There is a final chapter with directory information about science resources such as zoos, aquariums and planetariums, parks and caves, and periodicals. An index provides access to ready reference information. Recommended for all secondary collections.

1631 The Carnegie Library of Pittsburgh, Science and Technology Department. **Science and Technology Desk**

Reference: 1,500 Answers to Frequently-Asked or Difficult-to-Answer Questions. Detroit, Mich.: Gale Research, 1993. 741p. $39.95. ISBN 0-8103-8884-7.

This is a non-technical question and answer book about topics dealing in a broad sense with science and technology. There are 1,500 numbered questions with answers and sources. Divided by subject chapters which deal with such topics as animals, house and garage, biology, bridges and buildings, transportation, health, mathematics and space; there is a good subject index which refers to the question number. Both questions and answers are typical of the kinds of information school librarians need. Recommended for all levels. [R: ARBA 94]

1632 Emiliani, Cesare. **The Scientific Companion: Exploring the Physical World with Facts, Figures, and Formulas**. 2d ed. New York: Wiley, 1995. 358p. $19.95. ISBN 0-471-13324-8.

The purpose of this book is to describe how our world originated and evolved, and to provide a quantitative basis for an understanding of the dimensions involved. Chapters cover measurements of time and mass, and the basic chemistry, physics, astronomy, biology and earth science that provide the underpinnings of our world and its development. With 35 tables, 50 new illustrations based on NASA and other aerial photography, nine appendices and an index, the work is a useful desk reference.

1633 Macaulay, David. **The Way Things Work**. Boston: Houghton Mifflin, 1988. 384p. $29.95. ISBN 0-395-42857-2.

1634 Macaulay, David. **The Way Things Work**. version 2.0. New York: DK Multimedia, 1997. CD-ROM (Windows and Macintosh). $59.95. ISBN 0-7894-1253-5.

The Way Things Work (the book) has been popular with all ages since its publication. Attractive and humorous, yet filled with accurate and enlightening text and illustrations, this is a browsing source, an idea source and a reference source. It should be in all collections at all levels.

The Way Things Work (the CD-ROM) is also useful for browsing, for reference and for instruction. The animations actually explain difficult scientific concepts; such devices as the laser are clearly defined and their operation explained and illustrated. Hundreds of mechanical devices are easily found from a picture index and via cross-reference hyperlinks and from an alphabetic list. Highly recommended for all libraries.

Transportation

GENERAL WORKS

1635 Richter, William L. **The ABC-CLIO Companion to Transportation in America**. Santa Barbara, Calif.: ABC-CLIO, 1995. 653p. $55.00. ISBN 0-87436-789-1.

This history of American transportation is comprehensive in that it covers trails, rivers and roads from the colonial period to astronautics in the 1990s. Canals, railroads, airlines and shipping are included as are companies, organizations and associations, laws and individuals associated with transportation. Long articles cover broad topics such as aeronautics and automobiles, while shorter entries cover specifics such as American Airlines or the Lincoln Highway. Illustrations add to the text. There are see also references and bibliographies attached to the entries as well as an index and an extensive final bibliography. A chronology covers the trails and rivers of prehistory and the first bridge at Jamestown up to 1994. Highly recommended for secondary collections. [R: SLJ, May 95]

1636 Wilson, Anthony. **Dorling Kin-**
E **dersley Visual Timeline of Transportation**. New York: Dorling Kindersley, 1995. 48p. $16.95. ISBN 1-56458-880-7.

The publisher's Timeline series is less successful than its Visual Dictionary series because the pages tend to be so cluttered with small illustrations and their randomly placed captions, that accessing information becomes as difficult as in a source that is all compressed text. Because these sources are arranged chronologically, the reader/viewer can gain some sense of the developmental history of the topic, in this case transportation and the technology that has supported it. Transportation here includes everything from wheelchairs to rocket ships. The chronology is divided into four main sections: 10,000 B.C.–A.D. 1799, aptly named "Nature's Pace;" 1780–1879, the steam technology period; 1880–1959, the introduction of both the automobile and aircraft, and 1960–2000. A final page predicts future trends. To further organize the data, a vertical arrangement separates transportation into rows dealing with water, land and air, with a small bottom row highlighting major developments. An index leads to the page, but searching the page for specifics can be complicated. The colorful and sharp reproductions, the use of cutaways and perspectives, and the number and variety of vehicles portrayed make this more suited to browsing than reference; the reference value is pretty much limited to finding the elusive picture. Recommended for this purpose for elementary and middle school collections. [R: ARBA 96]

AUTOMOBILES

1637 **Chilton's Auto Repair Manual**. Radnor, Pa.: Chilton Book Co., 1968– . annual. $26.95/yr. ISSN 0069-3634.

This standard annual covers the most recent five years of the major American automobile repair guides. Arranged by manufacturer and then models/body styles, repairs for systems and components are detailed and illustrated. Separate chapters deal with tools and equipment and basic maintenance. A table of contents and index provide access to specific models and repairs.

Chilton publishes a Total Car Care series that includes a wide range of repair guides for all makes of cars, trucks, vans, and motorcycles, and for specific systems and maintenance operations such as air conditioning, automatic transmissions, brakes, steering, and suspension. There are also manuals for earlier cars of specific manufacturers, such as *Chilton's Chevrolet Mid-Size 1964–88* and model-specific repair manuals, such as *Chevrolet Camaro, 1993–1997*. Spanish-language editions are available for some titles.

High school libraries should have as many of the titles as appropriate; reference copies will be protected by having circulating copies as well.

1638 Edwards, John. **Auto Dictionary**. Los Angeles, Calif.: HP Books, 1993. 194p. $24.95; $16.95pa. ISBN 1-55788-067-0; 1-55788-056-5pa.

This dictionary began as a list of words for ESL students in automotive classes and has developed into a full dictionary that includes racing, hot-rodding, and engineering terms, organizations with addresses, descriptions of components and processes and street slang. Limited to universally accepted language, it does not include regionalisms. Automobile companies are included, but not specific car models. There are no biographies. More than 200 photographs and diagrams add to the clear definitions and examples. Highly recommended for high schools. [R: ARBA 94]

1639 Goodsell, Don. **Dictionary of Automotive Engineering**. 2d ed. Warrendale, Pa.: Society of Automotive Engineers, 1995. 265p. $49.00. ISBN 1-56091-683-4.

About 3,000 terms used in the English-speaking world about automobiles and other vehicles are defined in this dictionary. American terms and spellings are most often the preferred usage, so it is easily accessible. Slang and informal words are included. Areas covered are engineering, driving, automotive parts and tires, mechanics, fuels, testing and electronics. Drawings accompany 100 articles and are useful in clarifying meaning. An appendix lists abbreviations and acronyms. The dictionary arrangement and the simple language used in definitions make this an excellent source for consumers as well as mechanics. Highly recommended for all middle and high schools. Theft protection also recommended. [R: ARBA 97]

1640 Toboldt, William K., and others. **Goodheart-Wilcox Automotive Encyclopedia**. 1995 ed. South Holland, Ill.: Goodheart-Wilcox, 1968– . 782p. $49.28. ISSN 1080-627X.

This handbook has been published in eight earlier versions as a textbook and includes such features as questions at the end of the chapters, but it is also of reference value for the depth and

clarity of its information. It presents the fundamentals of automotive mechanics, including the science behind vehicle functions: electricity, electronics, physics and math. It also covers design, operation, service and repair as well as all of an automobile's parts. The 1995 edition updates chapters on computer controls, anti-lock brakes, air bags and waste disposal. Full-color photographs have been added to the diagrams, charts and black and white photographs. Fifty-four chapters present topical information on tools, functions and parts, including body repair and finishing. A final chapter discusses career opportunities in the automotive industry. Although an occasional female appears in a picture, especially in the career chapter, the effect is overwhelmingly of an area limited to white males. There is a good dictionary of terms and a general index. Highly recommended in both reference and circulating copies for all high schools.

AVIATION AND SPACE FLIGHT

1641 Curtis, Anthony R. **Space Almanac: Facts, Figures, Names, Dates, Places, Lists, Charts, Tables, Maps Covering Space from Earth to the Edge of the Universe**. 2d ed. Houston, Tx.: Gulf Publishing Company, 1992. 746p. $36.95. ISBN 0-88415-039-9.

This compendium of space information—history, exploration, and future developments—is highly recommended for secondary schools. Separate sections (e.g., space shuttles, rockets, astronauts and cosmonauts) provide essays and chronologies, all supported by charts, maps, tables, and photographs. Astronomical data is presented for the Moon, Sun, comets, asteroids, solar system, galaxies, pulsars, quasars, and black holes. The work also includes space news from countries around the world. This is an excellent compilation of facts about moving around in the universe. [R: ARBA 90; BL, 15 Dec 89; LJ, Oct 89]

SHIPS

1642 Pickford, Nigel. **The Atlas of Shipwrecks & Treasure: The History, Location, and Treasures of Ships Lost at Sea**. New York: Dorling Kindersley, 1994. 200p. $29.95. ISBN 1-56458-599-9.

The definition of a treasure ship used for this work is "any ship used to transport high-value cargo of precious metals or artifacts that do not lose their value when immersed for long periods in salt water." This allows a good look at a wide variety of shipwrecks, arranged chronologically in part one. For each era there is a timeline/map followed by specific wrecks. Each entry has descriptions of the ship and its type, details about its sinking and information about recovery or recovery efforts. Fact boxes and wonderful illustrations complete the entries. The second part is a world gazetteer with maps showing locations of ships and salvage attempts. There is a glossary, a bibliography and an index. This is an excellent supplement to world history information sources as well as a browsable book for the curious. Appropriate for both middle and high schools. [R: ARBA 96]

Zoology

ATLASES

1643 Taylor, Barbara. **The Bird Atlas**. New
E   York: Dorling Kindersley, 1993. 64p.
         $19.95. ISBN 1-56458-327-9.

This picture handbook gives a beginning overview of birdlife from each continent. Seven birds from each region within the continents (North American forests and woodlands, for example). All continents and the arctic are covered, with different numbers of regions for each. Each bird illustration is accompanied by a caption that gives its common and scientific names, size, description, and a narrative of behavioral facts. There is also an introduction about birds and their habitats, and there are sections on migration and endangered status. The layout of the table of contents is confusing and misleading as it is unclear that the capitalized continents are sometimes major headings for what follows, and sometimes not. The continent pages have boxed earth science facts that seem unrelated to the book's focus. Some pages are printed vertically and some horizontally. Sizes of birds are given in captions, but no attempt is made to show relative size in the illustrations—a young child may think an owl is as large as an ostrich. This source is recommended for elementary schools only as a source of pictures. [R: ARBA 94]

DICTIONARIES AND ENCYCLOPEDIAS

1644 Allaby, Michael. **The Concise Oxford
         Dictionary of Zoology**. New York:
         Oxford University Press, 1991. 508p.
         $13.95pa. ISBN 0-19-286093-3pa.

Intended for both students and specialists the dictionary lists terms associated with anatomy, behavior, habitats and specific animals. Arrangement is alphabetical with many cross-references; animals are listed by scientific names with cross-references from common names. Many entries are revised from the *Oxford Dictionary of Natural History* although others were created especially for this work. Entries vary from one sentence to 1/3 column and are both descriptive and explanatory. This is a useful additional dictionary for high schools. [R: ARBA 93]

1645 Banister, Keith, and Andrew Camp-
         bell. **The Encyclopedia of Aquatic
         Life**. New York: Facts on File, 1985.
         384p. $45.00. ISBN 0-8160-1257-1.

This colorful work in the Encyclopedia of Animals series treats fish, aquatic invertebrates, and sea mammals, explaining their habitats, physical characteristics, diets, and lives. The volume is extensively illustrated with over 300 underwater photographs, drawings, paintings, and other art work. Students from middle school up should find this book attractive and readable. [R: ARBA 86; BL, 1 Feb 86; LJ, 1 Mar 86; WLB, Feb 86]

1646 McFarland, David, ed. **The Oxford
         Companion to Animal Behavior**.
         New York: Oxford University Press,
         1982. 657p. $49.95. ISBN 0-19-
         866120-7.

Long well-written articles intended for nonspecialists treat all aspects of animal behavior and related disciplines, such as physiology, genetics, and psychology. No individual animals are described. The alphabetically arranged articles are supported by illustrations, maps, and cross-references, but there is no index. Appropriate for advanced high school students.

HANDBOOKS

1647 Porter, Valerie. **Cattle: A Handbook to the Breeds of the World**. New York: Facts on File, 1991. 400p. $45.00. ISBN 0-8160-2640-8.

More than 1,000 breeds and types of cattle from around the world are described in this source. Maps and tables accompany the text and there are color illustrations of some breeds. Arranged geographically, there are chapters on the cattle of Europe, Africa, Asia, America and Australia. There are also sections on evolution, breeding and genetics as well as a separate chapter on the buffaloes. Each breed has a brief physical description followed by a narrative that discusses history, breeding, use, and its current status. Appendices include a glossary, a list of endangered breeds, a directory of organizations. There is a bibliography and an index. Recommended for secondary schools with agriculture programs and for comprehensive animal resource collections. [R: ARBA 93]

BIRDS

1648 Clark, William S. **A Field Guide to Hawks, North America**. Boston: Houghton Mifflin, 1987. 198p. $24.95. ISBN 0-395-36001-3.

While most Peterson Field Guides cover several hundred species, this one focuses on the hawk and its relatives, 39 birds in all. Each account includes a description, similar species, flight patterns, status and distribution, behavior, unusual plumage, and more. The birds, arranged in phylogenetic sequence, are illustrated by color plates and black-and-white photographs. Some species are illustrated in regional variant, male, female, and immature stages. This well-organized guide is highly recommended. [R: ARBA 89; LJ, 15 Apr 88]

1649 Dunne, Pete, David Sibley, and Clay Sutton. **Hawks in Flight: The Flight Identification of North American Migrant Raptors**. Boston: Houghton Mifflin, 1988. 254p. $11.95. ISBN 0-395-51022-8.

This work covers 23 of the most common North American raptors (e.g., falcons, kites, eagles, vultures, ospreys). It identifies them by general body shape when flying (not by specific field marks, which can be seen only through binoculars), the way they move (rhythm and cadence), the places where they are likely to be seen, and when to look for them. Each species, grouped by shared traits of behavior and appearance, is illustrated by pen-and-ink drawings and black-and-white photographs. Recommended for high schools. [R: ARBA 90]

1650 Griggs, Jack L. **American Bird**
E+   **Conservancy's Field Guide to All the Birds of North America**. New York: HarperCollins, 1997. 172p. $19.95pa. ISBN 0-06-273028-2.

Birds in this beautifully designed field guide are arranged by field characteristics such as feeding habits. The four major groupings are by waterbirds, wading and shore birds, landbirds and perching landbirds. The table of contents is on the front and back covers and color coding identifies parts of the guide. Keys and descriptions are on double-page spreads and give range, size, habitat and marks and songs. There is an index with both Latin and common names. As one might expect from this publisher, woven into the text is concern for habitats and environmental effects on bird populations. All libraries will want this new guide to supplement the standard sources.

1651 Perrins, Christopher M., and Alex L.
E+   A. Middleton, eds. **Encyclopedia of Birds**. New York: Facts on File, 1985. 445p. $45.00. ISBN 0-8160-1150-8.

This outstanding work, written by some 90 subject experts, covers 180 families of birds worldwide. For each family, information includes distribution patterns, characteristics, habitat, diet and feeding habits, size, color, calls, and nesting behavior. The text also includes articles on mating rituals, social organization, and other topics, all illustrated by over 400 beautiful color photographs of birds in flight. Highly recommended for grades 5 and up. [R: ARBA 86; BL, Aug 85; LJ, Sept 85; WLB, Oct 85]

1652 Peterson, Roger Tory. **A Field Guide**
E+   **to the Birds: A Completely New Guide to all the Birds of Eastern and Central North America**. 4th ed. Boston: Houghton Mifflin, 1980. 384p. $17.95. ISBN 0-395-26621-1.

1653 Peterson, Roger Tory. **A Field Guide**
E+ **to Western Birds: Field Marks of all Species Found in North America West of the 100th Meridian**. 3d ed. Boston: Houghton Mifflin, 1990. 432p. $22.95. ISBN 0-395-51749-4.

1654 **Peterson Multimedia Guides: North**
E+ **American Birds**. Sommerville, Mass.: Houghton Mifflin Interactive, 1995. CD-ROM (Windows). $69.95. ISBN 0-395-73056-2.

Text and paintings have been completely redone for these editions, flagship books in the Peterson Field Guide series. Bird species are arranged in a modified taxonomic sequence, with some groups (unrelated, but similar in appearance) presented together. Entries emphasize identifying characteristics but cover voice, range, habitat, and similar species. Detailed illustrations show major age, sex, and seasonal differences. Range maps for all species are located in separate sections. Highly recommended for all levels. [R: ARBA 91]

The CD-ROM version combines the full contents of both books and adds 700 bird songs, 15 minutes of video (including Roger Tory Peterson showing how to watch birds), 1 hour of audio commentary, and one-button access to Peterson Online. Searching is by multiple fields: visual characteristics, family, group and Latin names, region, season, habitat, size, color and rarity. This award-winning disc is highly recommended for all levels.

FISH

1655 Page, Lawrence M., and Brooks M. Burr. **A Field Guide to Freshwater Fishes: North America North of Mexico**. Boston: Houghton Mifflin, 1991. 432p. $24.95; $16.95pa. ISBN 0-395-35307-6; 0-395-53933-1pa. [R: ARBA 92]

1656 Eschmeyer, William N., and Earl S. Herald. **A Field Guide to Pacific Coast Fishes of North America: From the Gulf of Alaska to Baja, California**. Boston: Houghton Mifflin, 1983. 336p. $21.95; $14.36pa. ISBN 0-395-33188-9; 0-395-26873-7pa.

1657 Robins, C. Richard, and G. Carleton Ray. **A Field Guide to Atlantic Coast Fishes of North America**. Boston: Houghton Mifflin, 1986. 354p. $24.95; $14.76pa. ISBN 0-395-39198-9; 0-395-31852-1pa.

Together these three field guides cover all known North American fishes. Editions are kept up to date reflecting changes in taxonomy as well as new information on distribution. Notice is made of threatened and endangered species. Descriptions include identification, range, habitat, scientific names and there are references to color plate numbers and to range maps. Glossaries, references and an index are included in each volume. Highly recommended for collections at all levels. (R: ARBA 91]

INSECTS AND SPIDERS

1658 Zim, Herbert Spencer and Clarence
E Cottam. **Insects: A Guide to Familiar American Insects**. rev. ed. New York, Golden Press, 1987. 160p. $6.00. ISBN 0-307-24055-X.

This easy to use identification guide is one of the current Golden Guide series originally edited by Zim and now revised by new editors. The titles in the series all resemble this one with color drawings, range maps and descriptive text on the same pages. These inexpensive guides complement the fuller treatment of the Peterson guides, and are more appropriate for elementary children. This guide lists common insects that children are likely to encounter. A general introduction to insects and their study is followed by individual descriptions. Both table of contents and index provide access.

INVERTEBRATES

1659 Abbott, R. Tucker, and Percy A. Morris. **A Field Guide to Shells: Atlantic and Gulf Coasts and the West Indies**. 4th ed. Boston: Houghton Mifflin, 1995. 350p. $26.95; $16.95pa. ISBN 0-395-69780-8; 0-395-69779-4pa.

This 4th edition of one of the standard Peterson field guides has shifted in emphasis from the previous editions, now focusing on living mollusks rather than dead shells. The descriptions of pelecypods, gastropods, amphineuraus, scaphods and cephalopods are cross-referenced to plates (some in color). The plates are likewise cross-referenced to the descriptions. Appendices include a directory of shell clubs, a diagram of shell parts, a glossary and a bibliography. There is an excellent index. Recommended for all levels where mollusks/shells are studied. [R: ARBA 96]

1660 Preston-Mafham, Rod. **The Encyclopedia of Land Invertebrate Behaviour**. Cambridge, Mass.: MIT Press, 1993. 320p. $45.00. ISBN 0-262-16137-0.

This source fills a need by supplying difficult to find information about invertebrates which spend their adult lives on land, or which walk or fly over land, including ants, bees, beetles, butterflies, crickets, flies and moths. The work is a series of essays describing in straightforward language why invertebrates do the things they do. The emphasis is on behavior rather than biology. Much of the book describes mating, egg-laying and parental care, while other sections are about feeding and defensive behavior. Introductions are general, but then descriptions of specific orders follow. There is an extensive classified bibliography, and indexes by scientific name, by common name, and by general subject. This is a valuable source for high school collections where advanced biology is part of the curriculum. [R: ARBA 95]

MAMMALS

1661 Edwards, Elwyn Hartley. **The Encyclopedia of the Horse**. New York: Dorling Kindersley, 1994. 400p. $39.95. ISBN 1-56458-614-6.

This is a chronologically organized picture encyclopedia which begins with the evolution of the species and intersperses detailed information of 150 modern breeds within the historical narrative. Each breed description includes its origin, development, size, colors, and use. The work concludes with chapters about the working horse, the horse at war, and the sporting horse. Related pieces about saddles, wheeled vehicles, and riding styles are also integrated into the text. The result is an understanding of the "impact of the horse on human history." There is a glossary and a general index. Any school with any interest in horses will want this in the collection. Highly recommended. [R: ARBA 95]

1662 Hendricks, Bonnie L. **International Encyclopedia of Horse Breeds**. Norman, Okla.: University of Oklahoma Press, 1995. 486p. $65.00. ISBN 0-8061-2753-8.

This is the most comprehensive of horse breed books and attempts to document all of the horse and pony breeds on earth in addition to subtypes that are not official breeds. Although the author did not succeed in total coverage (one of the appendices lists breeds not included in this first edition), nonetheless, this is an impressive undertaking with breeds from all over the world unmentioned in other such sources. Breeds are listed in alphabetical order rather than by type and for each the most common names are given followed by origin, aptitudes, average height, and population status. A narrative about the breed's history, description and use complete the entries. In addition to the black and white photographs that accompany most of the entries, there is a color insert. Other appendices include a list of countries of origin, and a horse breeder's association directory. There is a glossary and an index. Horse country middle and high school collections will want this source despite its cost. [R: ARBA 97]

1663 MacDonald, David, ed. **The Encyclopedia of Mammals**. New York: Facts on File, 1984. 895p. $80.00. ISBN 0-87196-871-1.

This beautiful book contains some 700 articles by 180 experts, arranged in 8 categories (e.g., carnivores, sea mammals). Animals covered range from the mouse to the elephant and grizzly bear. Articles, varying in length from 2 to 16 pages, cover physical features, habitat, and range. The 1,150 color plates and 72 color illustrations are an outstanding feature of this award-winning book. It is a first choice for school librarians. [R: ARBA 85; BL, 1 Jan 85; BL, 15 May 85; LJ, Jan 85]

1664 Whitaker, John O. **National Audubon Society Field Guide to North American Mammals**. 2d ed. New York: Knopf, 1996. 937p. $19.00pa. ISBN 0-679-44631-1.

The first edition of this standard guide was published in 1980 and it has now been revised as the result of taxonomic changes and the new information learned about many of the 390 species treated in the work. Intended for field use, the guide includes all of the native land-dwelling or land-breeding species of wild mammals, (including introduced and domesticated animals with wild populations) north of Mexico. Introductory material covers how to use the guide. Tracking guides and color plates form the first part of the guide with references to the species accounts in the second part of the book. The species entries include common and scientific names, description, breeding, habitat, range and similar species. Small maps accompany the entries to delineate range. Appendices include a glossary, a list of endangered and threatened mammals, and range charts. There is an index. This field guide should be in reference collections at all levels, and many schools will want circulating copies as well. [R: ARBA 97]

REPTILES AND AMPHIBIANS

1665 Alderton, David. **Turtles & Tortoises of the World**. New York: Facts on File, 1988. 191p. $25.95. ISBN 0-8160-1733-6.

This excellent worldwide review of turtles and tortoises begins with an introductory exposition of the relationship of these creatures to man, including their role in myths and literature. The chapters that follow examine various aspects of their lives, behavior, evolution, anatomy, reproduction, distribution, diversity, classification, adaptability, and conservation. More than 100 illustrations and photographs, including 60 in full color, illustrate the volume. Recommended for high schools. [R: BR, June 89]

1666 Conant, Roger. **Peterson First Guide**
E+ **to Reptiles and Amphibians**. Boston: Houghton Mifflin, 1992. 128p. $4.95. ISBN 0-395-62232-8.

The Peterson First Guide series are for beginning natural scientists at any level. They are easier than the regular Peterson guides and comparable with the Golden Guides. They attempt to show on one or two pages the most common types of a species and provide both text and picture in one place. This guide lists all of the most common snakes, turtles, lizards, frogs, salamanders and crocodiles that are found in North America. They are shown by type with endangered status, warnings and descriptions

given. An accompanying picture often contains arrows pointing to distinguishing features. The lack of a table of contents in this volume and in the other volumes in the series is a problem. There is an index, but this assumes one knows the name of the observed creature. Recommended for middle schools; other levels may also want this series.

1667 Mattison, Christopher. **The Encyclopedia of Snakes**. New York: Facts on File, 1995. 256p. $35.00. ISBN 0-8160-3072-3.

The subject of this narrative is the generic snake. Intended for amateur herpetologists and general naturalists the work treats the origin, evolution and classification of snakes and then discusses morphology and function, how and where snakes live (habitat, adaptations and world patterns), feeding, defense, and reproduction. A chapter deals with the relationships of snakes and humans, and there are sections on taxonomy and classification with minimum information on individual species. Bibliography notes end each chapter and there is a brief general bibliography and an index. Drawings, color plates, boxed facts, and charts add to the narrative. Recommended for both circulating and reference collections in secondary schools. [R: ARBA 96]

1668 Mehrtens, John M. **Living Snakes of the World in Color**. New York: Sterling Publishing, 1987. 480p. $65.00. ISBN 0-8069-6460-X.

The 540 color photographs of 454 subspecies of snakes provide a good sampling of the more than 3,000 species worldwide. Arranged in three categories—primitive snakes, colubrid snakes (nonpoisonous), and venomous snakes—they are then divided into familiar species, such as vipers, pythons, and rattlesnakes.

Entries provide the common and genus-species names, general habitat and geographical range, and one or two paragraphs on the snake's natural history. At least one photograph accompanies each entry. A small glossary and indexing by common name/subject and by genus/species conclude the volume, which is recommended for secondary schools. [R: ARBA 88; BL, 1 Dec 87; LJ, Dec 87]

1669 Smith, Hobart Muir. **Handbook of Lizards; Lizards of the United States and of Canada**. Ithaca, N.Y.: Comstock Publishing, 1995. 557p. $39.95pa. ISBN 0-8014-8236-4.

1670 Wright, Albert Hazen and Anna Allen Wright. **Handbook of Snakes of the United States and Canada**. 2v. Ithaca, N.Y.: Comstock Publishing, 1994. $59.95pa/set. ISBN 0-8014-8214-3.

1671 Wright, Anna Allen. **Handbook of Frogs and Toads of the United States and Canada**. 3d ed. Ithaca, N.Y.: Comstock Publishing, 1995. 640p. $39.95pa. ISBN 0-8014-8232-1.

Originally published in the 1940s and 1950s these handbooks remain the outstanding sourcebooks for these animals. The current editions are reprints with additional and updated information. Taxonomy has changed, however, and the reprints have charts which compare the current nomenclature with the original. Each volume begins with an introduction which discusses the respective animal in general terms of names, range, size, longevity, characteristics, color, habitat and breeding. Then each species receives the same treatment. Each volume contains illustrations, maps and an index. Recommended for high school collections. [R: ARBA 95, 96]

1672 Stebbins, Robert C. **A Field Guide to Western Reptiles and Amphibians: Field Marks of All Species in Western North America, including Baja California**. 2d ed. Boston: Houghton Mifflin, 1985. 336p. $18.00. ISBN 0-395-38253-X.

In addition to the typical identification elements, this guide includes capture and care information, as these animals are often handled while studied, and not simply observed in the field. The eastern and central guide covers 379 species, while the western guide (including New Mexico, Colorado, Wyoming, Montana, Saskatchewan, the Northwest Territories, and states and provinces to the West) covers 244 species. Each volume contains separate chapters on lizards, salamanders, frogs and toads, turtles and snakes, while the eastern volume also includes crocodiles. A color plate insert complements the descriptions and drawings. Range maps, a glossary, references and an index complete each volume. These guides are standards for collections at all levels.

Author/Title Index

Numbers refer to entry numbers in the text. Alphabetization is word-by-word, with acronyms and numbers interfiled and punctuation disregarded.

Subject Index

Numbers refer to entry numbers.